Fourth Edition

Indigenous Peoples within Canada

A Concise History

Olive Patricia Dickason
William Newbigging

OXFORD
UNIVERSITY PRESS

OXFORD
UNIVERSITY PRESS

Oxford University Press is a department of the University of Oxford.
It furthers the University's objective of excellence in research, scholarship,
and education by publishing worldwide. Oxford is a registered trade mark of
Oxford University Press in the UK and in certain other countries.

Published in Canada by
Oxford University Press
8 Sampson Mews, Suite 204,
Don Mills, Ontario M3C 0H5 Canada

www.oupcanada.com

First Edition published in 2006
Second Edition published in 2010
Third edition published in 2015

Library and Archives Canada Cataloguing in Publication
Dickason, Olive Patricia, 1920-
[Concise history of Canada's First Nations]
Indigenous peoples within Canada : a concise history / Olive Patricia
Dickason and William Newbigging. – Fourth edition.

First edition published under title: Canada's First Nations. Second and
third editions published under title: A concise history of Canada's
First Nations.
Includes bibliographical references and index.
Issued in print and electronic formats.
ISBN 978-0-19-902848-1 (softcover).–ISBN 978-0-19-902851-1 (PDF)

1. Native peoples–Canada–History. I. Newbigging, William, 1963-,
author II. Title. III. Title: Concise history of Canada's First Nations.

E78.C2D536 2018   971.004'97   C2018-901207-2
                                                     C2018-901208-0

Cover design: Laurie McGregor
Interior design: Laurie McGregor

Oxford University Press is committed to our environment.
Wherever possible, our books are printed on paper which comes from
responsible sources.

Printed and bound in the United States of America

7 8 9 — 23 22 21

Brief Contents

Contents

1   Origin Stories

2   At the Beginning

3 First Meetings

4 On the Eastern Edge of the Mainland

5 The Wendat Confederacy, the Haudenosaunee Confederacy, and the European Colonizers

6   Some Indigenous–Colonial Wars

7   The Struggle against British Colonialism

8   Westward and Northward

9   The British Alliance of 1812–14

10   The "Indian Problem": Isolation, Assimilation, and Experimentation

11 Towards Confederation for Canada, Towards Wardship for Indigenous Peoples

12 The First Numbered Treaties, Police, and the Indian Act

13 Time of Troubles

14 Repression and Resistance

15 Tightening the Reins: Resistance Grows and Organizes

16 Development Heads North

17 Canadian Courts and Aboriginal Rights

18 The Road to Self-Government

19 Reconciliation and Revitalization

Maps

Publisher's Preface

As stated in a 2011 headline of *The Globe and Mail*, Olive Dickason wrote the book (quite literally) on Indigenous Peoples' history within Canada. This edition is one of the legacies of that original project.

We have undertaken this edition with Olive's goals in mind: to continue to demonstrate that an Indigenous history is not only possible but is a worthwhile endeavour; to challenge the assumptions about the legitimacy and benevolence of colonization that so often inform the writing of settler-colonizers; and, through concrete historical data, to support and provide evidence for Indigenous land claims and Aboriginal rights in what is now Canada.

With this focus, the early chapters of this text underscore the diverse and complex societies and cultures that existed in North America before European colonizers arrived, and they provide support for the argument that First Nations were, and are, nations, with rights to the land they lived on. This book, then, illustrates the rationale behind Indigenous leaders engaging in trade, military agreements, and, eventually, treaty negotiations with settler-colonial governments. Ensuing chapters provide evidence that Indigenous Peoples retained their autonomous spirit as well as their right to and desire for self-determination throughout all of the interactions between Indigenous and European nations, despite the efforts of the settler-colonial nations. The final chapters summarize and evaluate the most recent efforts of Indigenous Peoples to exercise self-determination, to have land claims respected, and to seek reconciliation for the harms perpetrated by the settler-colonial governments. The goal has been to ensure that readers new to the discipline recognize that these issues are ongoing; at the same time, *Indigenous Peoples within Canada: A Concise History* serves as a straightforward resource of background context for those who are in the process of tackling these issues, whether politically or socially, at the national level or within their own lives.

At the time Olive first wrote, she was under the constraints of the academic world's expectations and biases. While we do not aim to be fully free of the constraints of the discipline of history (and its reliance on documents), the interdisciplinary drive of Indigenous Studies departments, which has been gaining momentum and attention across the country, has allowed for movement and improvement in the study of Indigenous history that has been a long time coming.

With this edition, we are able to do some of the things Olive was unable to do at the time of first publication, such as adding origin stories to the history of "time immemorial," and, as much as possible, using autonyms for all Indigenous groups and individuals throughout the text. We have also benefited from extensive and excellent reviewer feedback that has helped us to improve some of the representations throughout the book, which, while at the time they were written were cutting-edge by virtue of being included at all, we can now identify (with the benefit of new scholarship and the clarity of hindsight) as problematic and in need of change.

We have also revitalized the art program throughout, giving preference to the work of Indigenous artists—including photographers, illustrators, and designers—over historical photos taken by Europeans without clear consent (although a very few historical photos remain, because of their historical importance and power). The inclusion of this art is meant to further incorporate Indigenous perspectives on the history being recounted in these pages. It is also a reminder, throughout the text, that this historical legacy is still being experienced by Indigenous people today.

Unfortunately, this focus on Olive's goals, as well as ongoing evidentiary shortcomings in the discipline of Indigenous history, means that some gaps could not be addressed with this revision, as to do so would require us to write an entirely different book. In particular, we remain aware of the lack of coverage around the lifeways of Indigenous women, and we hope that other books with different mandates will be able to take on this vital project as more material becomes available on this important area of history.

Similarly, the bulk of material covering Inuit and the Métis has remained in the later chapters, despite calls to integrate more coverage of both throughout. Olive's original organization reflects the way in which Inuit and the Métis peoples have had to fight for Aboriginal rights as well as, more generally, any attention, consideration, or respect from the colonizing government bodies across what is now Canada. To change this structure would undermine Olive's organizing principles and would be an undertaking beyond the scope of this new edition.

We hope that you are able to read and enjoy this edition for what it is: a loving treatment of one of the most important books in Canadian history, and a dedicated ethnohistorical account of the Indigenous right to self-determination within what we now call Canada. We also hope that this gives you a solid grounding to better understand the current political climate and the fast-paced changes happening in politics and in the courts, and that it inspires you to keep reading in this increasingly vibrant area of scholarship. As a starting point, OUP Canada publishes a variety of titles in Indigenous Studies; you can find them all at www.oupcanada.com/indigenousstudies.

Acknowledgements

It is a genuine pleasure to thank publicly and profoundly the many people who helped me both with this edition of the text and in a more general way, with the long formation that has given me the background with which to undertake this task. At the National Archives of Canada I was assisted over the years by André Desrosiers, Gilles Durocher, and Marie Lewis. At the Section des cartes et plans of the Bibliothèque Nationale I was helped by Monique Pelletier. At the Art Gallery of Hamilton, the Manager of Collections and Research, Christine Braun, was very helpful.

Historians of the Indigenous Peoples within Canada, however, are required to move beyond the museums and galleries and into the communities. For their insights and wisdom I would like to acknowledge the help generously given to me by Doug Belanger, Joe Tom Sayers, Carol Nadjiwon, and Roland Nadjiwon of Batchewana First Nation; Mike Cachagee of Chapleau Cree First Nation; Judy Syrette and Anne-Marie Jones of Garden River First Nation; Butch Elliott and Germaine Trudeau-Elliott of the Sault Ste Marie Tribe of Chippewa Indians; Elizabeth Angeconeb of Missanabie Cree First Nation; Bob Chiblow and Donnie Mcleod of Mississauga First Nation; Georges Sioui of Wendake and the University of Ottawa; Pipe-carrier Lornie Bob of Atikameksheng Anishnawbek; and Edsel Dodge and Dean Jacobs of Walpole Island First Nation.

A number of colleagues were also helpful and encouraging. Dr Rose Cameron, Dr Cheryl Reed-Elder, and Professor Howard Webkamigad all generously told me of their experiences in residential schools, and Howard was, and is, my patient and helpful source for all Anishinaabe-mowin questions. Cheryl also provided me with many insights into life in the Western Arctic. Dr Harvey Feit, FRSC, of McMaster University, was as always patient and generous. His knowledge of the people of James Bay is extremely valuable. My good friend Dr William Hanley at McMaster University has always been a source of encouragement and insight. Over the years, a number of other scholars took the time to offer me guidance and assistance. Sylvia Van Kirk at the University of Toronto; Jennifer Brown at the University of Winnipeg; Toby Morantz and Allan Greer at McGill University; Donald Smith at the University of Calgary; Patricia Galloway at the University of Texas at Austin; and Trudy Nicks at the Royal Ontario Museum all have my warm thanks.

This edition underwent several reviews that were vital to its preparation. My thanks go to Roland Bohr (University of Winnipeg), Jarvis Brownlea (University of Manitoba), Victoria Freeman (York University), Sarah Nickel (University of Saskatchewan), Jacqueline Romanow (University of Winnipeg), Niigan Sinclair (University of Manitoba), and Gregory Younging (University of British Columbia Okanagan), as well as the reviewers who wished to remain anonymous. Four editors at Oxford University Press were helpful and patient. Caroline Starr, Amy Gordon, Michelle Welsh, and Richard Tallman worked very hard to improve this text.

On a personal note I would like to acknowledge the help and support of my family: my parents Graeme and Barbara Newbigging; my wife Kathryn Kohler; and our children Cameron Newbigging and Janet Newbigging. Finally, I am compelled to note that I drew inspiration from two people who deserve mention here: my old friend W.J. Eccles of the University of Toronto, who first encouraged me to study the history of Indigenous Peoples within Canada, and Karrie Wurmann, a great childhood friend whose adoptive parents took her every week to Tlingit dance classes so that the Tlingit culture of her birth would be able to claim its place alongside their Irish and German backgrounds. As promised, Karrie, I will send you a copy of this edition.

Introduction

Within a generation, First Peoples living within Canada have claimed, or more accurately reclaimed, a place at the centre of the political, economic, and social history of the country. Issues long ignored, or worse, hidden, are now the subjects of editorials, news stories, and investigations on a daily basis. Governments are constantly being called upon to answer hard questions by people across the country. This shift to prominence is one of the central themes of this edition of this text. Only by understanding the reasons both for the long-term neglect and for the recent revitalization can we hope to understand this fascinating history. Only by understanding the past can we hope to learn both from the mistakes that were made and from the courage and resilience of people who have been doing the hard work of building a better future.

We look in vain for a single cause to explain this re-found prominence; history is too complex to allow for simple solutions. We can, however, point to one act of courage that has emerged as a symbol of the determination required to bring change. On 22 June 1990, Elijah Harper held an eagle feather aloft in the Manitoba Legislative Assembly as a powerful protest against a political system that had not been inclusive in its attempts to change the country's constitution. Political actions and protests are important in raising the profile of causes, but actual change requires hard work and constant effort. With that in mind we must look at the contributions of Indigenous people across Canada—such as Professor Cindy Blackstock advocating tirelessly on behalf of children, and Justice Murray Sinclair masterfully leading the Truth and Reconciliation Commission—if we want to find the real reasons for the revitalization. The goal of this text, then, is to put all of this in context.

The challenge confronting the authors of this text is twofold. First, the pace of change has increased exponentially. Even as these lines are being written new developments are unfolding, such as the announcement about the Sixties Scoop payment and the Supreme Court ruling on what is to become of the evidence presented to the Truth and Reconciliation Commission.[1] Similarly, the implications of important recent rulings are not yet fully understood. For example, the 2014 *Tsilhqot'in* **case**, the first legal decision in Canadian history in which a court declared Aboriginal title to lands outside of a reserve, has raised a new set of issues, and historians have not yet had the time to understand and explain the various consequences.[2] These are interesting times indeed.

A second challenge concerns language and perspective. Over the centuries history had become a documents-based discipline. This was not always the case, of course; the ancient Greek writer Herodotus, the "father of history," undertook his researches based on oral traditions. Nevertheless, over time, historians have relied on the written record. This has caused numerous difficulties for historians of the First Peoples living within Canada. The earliest written records, those created by French explorers, traders, missionaries, and officials, employed words and concepts that were not the words and concepts used and understood by the people so described. Problems of interpretation take on a totally different aspect when considering early European accounts of the Americas. For one thing, as one scholar, Ian S. MacLaren, has pointed out, words used in the sixteenth or eighteenth centuries might have different meanings today. For another, what appeared in print could differ markedly from what the author had written. Publishers were sometimes more concerned about sales than about accuracy.[3] Since the printed word should not be taken automatically at face value, the researcher is left with the necessity of cross-checking with whatever other sources are available. These are usually few, and sometimes non-existent.

This text has always embraced the ethnohistorical approach, the attempt to bring the Indigenous perspective to the forefront by moving out of the libraries and archives and into museums, historic sites, and cultural centres. Historians have embraced the possibilities to be found in the study of language and material culture. The ethnohistorical method—the combined use of anthropological, archaeological, linguistic, and historical studies—has offered a generation of Canadian historians important new insights into the history of Indigenous Peoples within what would become Canada. We now know a great deal more about the ways in which they understood their world, and this knowledge is growing constantly.

Language studies offer a particularly exciting possibility for learning in regard to the study of place names, or toponyms. Indigenous place names across the country offer glimpses into how people identified what was significant in their particular environments. They indicate geographical or ecological characteristics, or else recall a historic event that happened on the spot. Unlike Europeans, and with one major exception, Indigenous people do not name places or geographical features after persons or groups. The exception concerns reserves, sometimes named after individuals, such as Ahtahkakoop and Mistawassis. Northern Quebec has switched to Inuktitut for its place names. The study of place names remains one of the most promising means of learning more about the Indigenous perspective on their own history.

Problems of translating concepts and even words from one language to another are notorious for misleading the unwary. The word "father" is a good example of this. For sixteenth- and seventeenth-century Europeans, the connotations of the term included authority and control of the family. In Indigenous languages, the term implied a protector and provider, who could be influential but who lacked authority in the European sense, particularly among matrilineal societies. When the Haudenosaunee, for instance, referred to the French king as "father," they were not placing themselves under his authority. If that had been their intention, they would have used the term "uncle," as the authoritative member in Haudenosaunee families was one's matrilineal uncle—but they never did.[4]

More importantly, the careful use of language allows us to reassert in the text an Indigenous perspective by employing the autonyms—the names by which people referred to themselves—as opposed to the exonyms—the names that others used. To explain this choice, and for the reader to understand its significance, we first must recognize the important connections between language and history. We will do this by means of an example.

When he wrote "Social and Warlike Customs of the Odahwah Indians" in 1858, the Odaawa historian Francis Assikinack discussed a problem that has always bedevilled historians, that of language. He was trying to come to terms with "Manitoulin," a word of great importance to him as it was both the island of his birth and the spiritual homeland of his people. He wrote: "As far as I know, there is no such word in the languages spoken by the Odahwahs, Ojibwas or any of the surrounding tribes. Manitoulin may be a Huron word: but, not being acquainted with the Mohawk, which, I understand nearly resembles the Huron or Iroquois language, I can not say positively."[5]

Assikinack's problem began with the use of the letter "l," a consonant not used in Anishinaabe-mowin, the language of the Odaawa people. He knew that the "l" was used by the Wendat people (he calls them Huron here), so he speculated that "Manitoulin" might be a Wendat word. He was quick to note, however, that he was not acquainted with the Kanienkehaka language (he calls it Mohawk here) and so could not be positive. He decided to call Manitoulin Island "Odaawa-minis," which means simply Odaawa Island, based on the information he had at the time. In fact, we now know that the Wendat word for Manitoulin is "Ekaentoton."[6] The word "Manitoulin" is merely a French transcription of "Mnidoo-mnising," which means the island of the spirit.[7]

The difficulties that Francis Assikinack encountered still confront us today and they are still a great concern to anyone seeking to come to a greater understanding of Canada's Indigenous Peoples. Language is always a powerful tool in the historian's atelier, and to historians of peoples with strong oral traditions language is primordial. Language is a foundational element in this text and it forms the base upon which the history will be constructed. If we hope to create a fair and balanced account of the past, we need to work extra hard to use the linguistic implements available to us. Although it is true that the issue of language creates complexities, as Francis Assikinack demonstrates, it also provides countless opportunities for understanding.

In order to embrace that opportunity, we have decided to represent people in the way they choose to represent themselves. By using examples of descriptive language in general, we are able to gain greater insights into how Canada's First Peoples understood their long and productive relationship with the resources, lands, and waters of this vast country. For some years now historians of Indigenous Peoples within Canada have embraced the use of autonyms, the names by which peoples refer to themselves. This text, in its various editions, has been part of that effort, and in this edition we are taking the attempt to another level. Thus, wherever possible, we will use the correct autonyms.

A number of issues are associated with this effort, but we have taken steps to alleviate the difficulties. In the first place, it is important to note that the old names are still familiar and they exist in the titles of books, in place names, and in the primary documents. Bruce Trigger's magisterial work is called *The Children of Aataentsic: A History of the Huron People to 1660* and not *A History of the Wendat People*. Similarly, we still have Lake Huron, Huron College, Huron County, Huronia, and, of course, the *Jesuit Relations* and all the other French sources use the word "Huron" rather than "Wendat." We also chose to provide people, wherever possible, with their own names as opposed to the translations and corruptions (Joseph Brant, Poundmaker,

xx   Indigenous Peoples within Canada

etc.) that have been used previously. In these cases, the familiar translated name is given in parentheses following the first reference.

A second issue concerns spelling. In his fine study of the community, life, and language of his great-grandfather, Francis Pegahmagabow, the historian Brian D. McInnes lists eight variations in spelling of the Wasauksing place name. Interestingly, they contain shades of meaning: shining rock (twice); white around the shore; something white in the distance; white stakes you can see in the distance; distant outlook; distant view; and shining light.[8] Even when the words are the same, the spellings can differ widely. Many people were contacted to determine the correct spellings of their various autonyms, but they frequently provided different spellings. One said he made it a point of pride to use a different spelling each time he wrote the word. Another said simply that she did not care how the word was spelled; how it was *pronounced* was the important point. Both were making the point that the oral language should take precedence over the written language. The spellings we provide here are thus an inevitable compromise.[9]

Another compromise is to be found in the choice of autonyms themselves. Some people still choose to self-identify with the names they were given by others. For reasons of convenience some choose to retain those names as umbrella terms and refer to themselves by a much more specific autonym. In other cases, the preferred terms remain in dispute, for various reasons. The most difficult word proved to be "Cree." Many people self-identify as Cree or as a group within that umbrella term. We tried to use specific language wherever possible, but we could not always manage this. These kinds of debates are hardly unique to the Indigenous people, but they did present a challenge in the writing of this edition. The chart below, original to this edition, should help readers to learn the autonyms.

We did not take the decision to use autonyms lightly. More and more Indigenous people are using autonyms as a means of reclaiming the past. The opportunity to learn something about the past by understanding the history of the autonyms is something too important to miss.[10] The clash of oral and written cultures brings about many compromises and this one seemed more than justifiable. The promotion of language is a vital component in the promotion of the culture and history of Canada's Indigenous Peoples. On the other hand, timelines—a construct of the written tradition—were retained.

Finally, it is important to note that this edition carries a new title: *Indigenous Peoples within Canada: A Concise History*. In the interests of accuracy and inclusivity, the terms "Indigenous Peoples" and "First Peoples" are the accepted, general, and inclusive terms for the collective of the three groups of Indigenous Peoples within Canada: First Nations, Inuit, and Métis. The term "First Nations" is still to be found in the text where there is a reference to a specific First Nation or group of First Nations. The word "nation" is used in this text because it is used by Indigenous people to describe the members of a distinct community. As mentioned above, "nation" was not originally an Indigenous concept, but it has been embraced over the centuries and is now widely used. It is also a word that the earliest documents used for the same purpose. The United Nations prefers the word "Indigenous" to "Aboriginal," and the government of Canada has recently changed the name of National Aboriginal Day to National Indigenous Peoples Day.

The word "Aboriginal" is still used where it is a legal term or part of a name, as in Aboriginal rights or Aboriginal council. Similarly, "band," as in "band council," is preferred to the word "tribe," which is common in the United States. Of course, older terms—"Indians," "Natives," "Native Americans," and the portmanteau word "Amerindian"—still appear in quotations from documents and in the titles of books and reports. Thus, we have terms like "Indian Act" and "Native Brotherhood." We sincerely hope that Francis Assikinack, Francis Pegahmagabow, and Olive Dickason would approve of these changes and the spirit in which they were made.

Autonym Chart

Umbrella Grouping	Alliance/Confederacy Name (if applicable)	Autonym or Preferred Term of Group/Band	Alternate Spellings (if applicable)	Exonym (name in European History)	Geographic Location (approximate)	Language or Language Group
Inuit ["Eskimo", descendants of Thule and the earlier Dorset people (evolved from the Ancient Inuit or "Paleo Eskimo")]	n/a	Sallirmiut	Sadlermiut	Sadlermiut; Eskimo (likely last of the Dorset people)	Sanikiluaq (northwestern Hudson Bay)	Inuktitut
	n/a	Nunatsiavummiut; Inuit		Eskimo	Nunatsiavut (northern coastal Labrador)	Inuttitut
	n/a	Nunavummiut; Inuit		Eskimo	Nunavut	Inuktitut
	n/a	Nunavimmiut; Inuit		Eskimo	Nunavik (Arctic Quebec)	Inuktitut
	n/a	Kivallirmiut; Inuit		Caribou Eskimo (Inuit)	Nunavut (west and inland of Hudson Bay)	Inuktitut
	n/a	Kitlinermiut	Inuinnait	Copper Eskimo (Inuit)	Nunavut and NWT (Banks and Victoria islands and adjacent central Arctic)	Inuktitut
	n/a	Inuvialuit		Western Arctic Inuit or Mackenzie Delta Inuit; Eskimo	Kuupak (Mackenzie Delta)	Invialuktun
Beothuk	n/a	Beothuk		Beothuk; Red Indians	Island of Newfoundland	Beothukan
	n/a	Innu		Montagnais or Naskapi	Northern Quebec and western Labrador	Innu-aimun (Algonquian)
Cree*		Mushkegowuk	Maskēkowiyiniwak	Western Swampy Cree	Manitoba west through to Saskatchewan	Cree (Algonquian)
	Nishnawbe-Aski	Omushkegowack	Omaškēkowak	Eastern Swampy Cree/ Moose Cree/Lowlands Cree	Western James Bay through to Manitoba	Cree (Algonquian)
	Nishnawbe-Aski	Iynu	Iyyu	James Bay Cree	Eastern James Bay	Cree (Algonquian)
	Nishnawbe-Aski	Oji-Cree		Oji-Cree	Northern Ontario and Manitoba	Oji-Cree (Algonquian)
	Nishnawbe-Aski	Oupeeshepow		East Main Cree; Eastern James Bay Cree	Hudson's Bay	Cree (Algonquian)
	Nishnawbe-Aski	Attikamekw		Attikamegue or Tete de Boules	Nitaskinan (Saint Maurice River Valley, Quebec)	Cree (Atikamekw)

	Nehiyaw-Pwat	Plains Ojibwa		Saulteaux	Historically the Upper Great Lakes and then from Manitoba to Alberta	Anishinaabe-mowin (Algonquian)
	Nehiyaw-Pwat	Plains Cree [or Cree]	Nehiyaw	Plains Cree	Historically northern Ontario and then from Manitoba to Alberta	Cree (Algonquian)
	Nehiyaw-Pwat	Métis		Métis; Metis	Red River Valley and then west into Saskatchewan	Anishinaabe-mowin and French; Michif
Dene [collective name, known in European historical documents as Athapaskans], Dene Confederacy	Dene Confederacy	Tłı̨chǫ		Dogrib	Northwest Territories	Tłı̨chǫ Yatìi (Athabaskan)
	Dene Confederacy	Denésoliné		Chipewyan	Northwest Territories	Denesųłiné (Athabaskan)
	Dene Confederacy	T'atsaot'ine		Yellowknives or Copper People	Northwest Territories	Na-Dené (Athabaskan)
	Dene Confederacy	Dene Dháa	Dane Zaa/Dene Tha	Beaver People	Northwest Territories	Na-Dené (Athabaskan)
	Dene Confederacy	Wet'suwet'en	Dakehl-né	Carrier	Northern British Columbia	Witsuwit'en (Athabaskan)
	Dene Confederacy	Sekani	Tsek'ahne	Sékanis or Interior Carrier	Northern British Columbia	Tsek'ehne (Athabaskan)
	Dene Confederacy	Tsilhqot'in		Chilcotin	Northern British Columbia	Tsilhqot'in (Athabaskan)
	Dene Confederacy	Gwich'in		Kutchin	Yukon	Dinjii Zhu' Ginjik (Athabaskan)
	Dene Confederacy	Tagish		Tagish	Yukon	Tagish, Tlingit (Athabaskan)
	Dene Confederacy	Tutchone			Yukon	Tutchone (Athabaskan)
	n/a	Interior Tlingit		Tlingit	Yukon and northern British Columbia	Lingít, Na-Dené (Athabaskan)
Tr'ondëkHwëch'in	n/a	Tr'ondëkHwëch'in		Han	Yukon	Han-kutchin

Umbrella Grouping	Alliance/Confederacy Name (if applicable)	Autonym or Preferred Term of Group/Band	Alternate Spellings (if applicable)	Exonym (name in European History)	Geographic Location (approximate)	Language or Language Group
Wabanakhik or Wabenaki Confederacy [sometimes referred to in European history as the Dawnland or Atlantic Coast People, or the Abenaki]	Wabanaki Confederacy	Mi'kmaq (singular and as adjective: Mi'kmaw)	Wabenaki	Micmac; Toudamans; Souriquois; Taranteens	Mi'kma'ki (Nova Scotia with fishing and sealing stations on the island of Newfoundland)	Mikmawisimk (Algonquian)
	Wabanaki Confederacy	Wuastukwiuk	Wolastoqiyik or Wulastukw	Maliseet; Etchemin; Eteminquois	New Brunswick and eastern Quebec	Malecite-Passamaquoddy (Algonquian)
	Wabanaki Confederacy	Wabanaki		Abenaki	Quebec, Maine, and New Brunswick	Aroosagunticook (Algonquian)
	Wabanaki Confederacy	Lenni Lenape		Delaware	New Jersey but now southern Ontario	Unami (Algonquian)
	Wabanaki Confederacy	Sokoki		Missiquoi or Western Abenaki	Missiasik in Vermont	Aroosagunticook (Algonquian)
	Omamiwinini	Omamiwinini [group of nations including the Onontchataronon]		Ottawa River Algonquians	Eastern Ontario and western Quebec	Anicinàbemowin (Algonquian)
	n/a	Nipissing		Nipissing	Lake Nipissing	Anicinàbemowin (Algonquian)
	n/a	Amikwa		Amikwa	Northern Georgian Bay	Anicinàbemowin (Algonquian)
Algonquian	n/a	Teme-agama Anishnabay		Temagami	Northeastern Ontario	Anicinàbemowin (Algonquian)
	Niswi-mishkodewin [referred to in European historical record as Three Fires Confederacy, or Council of Three Fires]	Odaawa (pl.: Odaawak) [group of nations]		Ottawa	Northern Lake Huron	Anishinaabe-mowin (Algonquian)

Algonquian (continued)	Niswi-mishkodewin	Ojibwa [group of nations]	Ojibway, Ojibwe	Ojibway; Ojibwe; Chippewa	North of Lakes Huron and Superior	Anishinaabe-mowin (Algonquian)
	Niswi-mishkodewin	Boodwaadmii	Boodawaadomi and sometimes Bodewadomi	Pottawatomi	Between Lakes Huron and Michigan and now in southern Ontario	Anishinaabe-mowin (Algonquian)
	Wabash Confederacy [in what is now the United States of America but were involved in the history of what is now Canada]	Mesquakie (pl.: Meshquakiehaki)		Fox; also Renards and Outagami	West of Lake Michigan and south of Lake Superior	Meskwaki (Algonquian)
	Wabash Confederacy	Osaakii (pl.: Osaakiiwaki)		Sauk; Sac; Osagi	Green Bay	Meskwaki (Algonquian)
	Wabash Confederacy	Giiwigaabaw		Kickapoo	Wabash Valley, south of Lake Michigan	Meskwaki-Myaamia (Algonquian)
	Wabash Confederacy	Piankeshaw		Piankashaw; Pangicheas	Wabash River	Myaamia (Algonquian)
	Wabash Confederacy	Waayaahtanwah		Wea	South of Lake Michigan	Myaamia (Algonquian)
	Wabash Confederacy	Myaamiaki		Miami	South of Lake Michigan	Myaamia (Algonquian)
	Irenweewa [sometimes Illinwek; in European history known as the Illinois Confederacy]	Kaashkaashkia		Kaskaskia	Upper Mississippi Valley	Myaamia-Illini (Algonquian)
	Irenweewa	Kaahokia		Cahokia	Upper Mississippi Valley	Myaamia-Illini (Algonquian)
	Irenweewa	Peewaarehwaa		Peoria	Upper Mississippi Valley	Myaamia-Illini (Algonquian)
	Shaawanwaki			Shawnee	Historically south of Lake Erie and now Oklahoma	Shaawanoki (Algonquian)

Umbrella Grouping	Alliance/ Confederacy Name (if applicable)	Autonym or Preferred Term of Group/Band	Alternate Spellings (if applicable)	Exonym (name in European History)	Geographic Location (approximate)	Language or Language Group
Maskó:ki	Maskó:ki			Muscogee or Creek	Historically Tennesee, now Oklahoma	Muscogee (Muscogean)
Iroquoian-speaking nations; may be referred to in historical record under umbrella term "Iroquois"	n/a	Stadakohnans		St Lawrence Iroquois	Quebec City	Iroquoian
	n/a	Chonnonton		Neutrals	Between Lake Erie and Lake Ontario	Iroquoian
	Haudenosaunee Confederacy (also fall under the term Haudenosaunee) [in European historical record, referred to as Five Nations Iroquois, or Six Nations, or Iroquois League, or Iroquois Confederacy, or Iroquois, or People of the Longhouse]	Kanienkehaka		Mohawk	Historically south of Lake Ontario and east of the Niagara River but now in the Grand River Valley, Ontario, Wahta, Ontario, and in Quebec	Kanienkéha (Iroquoian)
	Haudenosaunee Confederacy	Onyota'aka		Oneida	Historically south of Lake Ontario and east of the Niagara River but now in the Grand River Valley, Ontario	Oneida (Iroquoian)
	Haudenosaunee Confederacy	Onondaga	Onondagega	Onondaga	Historically south of Lake Ontario and rast of the Niagara River but now in the Grand River Valley, Ontario	Onoñda'gegani-gaweño'deñ (Iroquoian)
	Haudenosaunee Confederacy	Onondowaga		Seneca	Historically south of Lake Ontario and east of the Niagara River but now in the Grand River Valley, Ontario, and New York	Seneca (Iroquoian)

	Confederacy			Location	Language
Iroquoian-speaking nations (continued)	Haudenosaunee Confederacy	Guyohkohnyo	Cayuga	Historically south of Lake Ontario and east of the Niagara River but now in the Grand River Valley, Ontario	Cayuga (Iroquoian)
	Haudenosaunee Confederacy	Skarūren	Tuscarora	Moved north to join the Haudenosaunee Confederacy in 1722. Historically in the Carolinas, then south of Lake Ontario and east of the Niagara River but now in the Grand River Valley, Ontario	Skaròrə (Iroquoian)
	Wendat or Wendat Confederacy [in European historical record, referred to as "Huron" or "Huron Confederacy"]	Attignawantan	People of the Bear	Historically Wendake (Penetanguishene Peninsula) but now Quebec City	Wendat (Iroquoian)
	Wendat Confederacy	Attigneenongnahac	People of the Cord	Historically Wendake (Penetanguishene Peninsula) but now Quebec City	Wendat (Iroquoian)
	Wendat Confederacy	Arendarhonon	People of the Rock	Historically Wendake (Penetanguishene Peninsula) but now Quebec City	Wendat (Iroquoian)
	Wendat Confederacy	Tahontaenrat	People of the Deer	Historically Wendake (Penetanguishene Peninsula) but now Quebec City	Wendat (Iroquoian)

Umbrella Grouping	Alliance/ Confederacy Name (if applicable)	Autonym or Preferred Term of Group/Band	Alternate Spellings (if applicable)	Exonym (name in European History)	Geographic Location (approximate)	Language or Language Group
	n/a	Ataronchronon		People of the Marsh	Historically Wendake (Penetanguishene Peninsula) but now Quebec City	Wendat (Iroquoian)
	[Adjacent to Wendat Confederacy]	Tionnontaté		Petun	Southern Georgian Bay	Iroquoian
Niitsitapi [collectively known in in European history as Blackfoot]	Niitsitapiikwan** [known in European historical record as the Blackfoot Confederacy]	Siksika (pl.: Siksikawa)		Blackfoot	Southern Alberta	Siksika (Algonquian)
	Niitsitapiikwan	Piikani	Piikunii; sometimes given as Aapátohsipikáni	Peigan; Northern Peigan	Southern Alberta	Siksika (Algonquian)
	Niitsitapiikwan	Káínaa (pl.: Káínawa)		Blood	Southern Alberta	Siksika (Algonquian)
Tsuu T'ina	Niitsitapiikwan	Tsuu T'ina		Sarcee	Southern Alberta	Tsuut'ina (Athabaskan)
A'ani	Niitsitapiikwan	A'ani	Atsina	GrosVentre	Historically Minnesota and Manitoba but now Montana	Atsina (Algonquian)
Dakota [collective term] Očhéthi Šakówin	Dakhóta Oyápe [Dakota People]	Dakhóta		Eastern Sioux	Southern Manitoba	Dakhótiyapi (Siouan)
	Dakhóta Oyápe	Lakhóta	Lakoda	Teton Sioux or Western Sioux, Assiniboine	Southern and central Saskatchewan	Lakhótiyapi (Siouan)
	Dakhóta Oyápe	Nakoda	Nakota	Stoney and Assiniboine	Central Alberta	Nakodalsga (Siouan)
	Dakhóta Oyápe	Apsáalooke		Crow	Wyoming, Montana, and North Dakota	Dakhótiyapi (Siouan)

Hoocąągra	n/a	Hoocąągra		Winnebago	South of Lake Superior	Hoocąągra (Siouan)
Shoshone	n/a	Shoshone	Shoshoni	Snakes or Gens du Serpent	Wyoming	Shoshone (Numic)
Ktunaxa	n/a	Ktunaxa	Kutenai	Kootenay	Interior of British Columbia	Kutenai (an isolate language)
Tlingit	n/a	Tlingit		Coastal Tlingit	Northern coastal British Columbia	Lingit, Na-Dené (Athabaskan)
Haida	n/a	Haida	Xaayda	Haida	Haida Gwaii (Queen Charlotte Islands)	XaatKil (an isolate language)
Tsimshian	Tsimshian	Tsimshian		Coast Tsimshian	Northern coastal British Columbia	Sm'algyax (Tsimshianic)
	Tsimshian	Nisga'a		Nishga	Northwestern British Columbia	Nisga'a (Tsimshianic)
	Tsimshian	Gitxsan		Gitksan	Northwestern British Columbia	Tsimshianic
Salish	Interior Salish [language affiliation only]	Secwepemc		Shuswap	Interior of British Columbia	Secwepemctsín (Interior Salishan)
	Coast Salish	Songhees		Songish	Vancouver Island	Lekwungen (Coast Salishan)
	Coast Salish	Sḵwx̱wú7mesh	Sḵwx̱wú7mesh-Úxwumixw	Squamish	Southern coastal British Columbia	Sḵwx̱wú7mesh sníchim (Coast Salishan)
	Coast Salish	Nuxalk		Bella Coola	Southern coastal British Columbia	Coast Salishan with some relationship to Interior Salishan
	Coast Salish	Snuneymuxw		Nanaimo	Vancouver Island	Hul'q'umi'num
Wakashan [language group]	n/a	Heiltsuk		Bella Bella	Central coast of British Columbia	Heiltsuk-Oowekyala (Wakashan)
	n/a	Kwakwaka'wakw		Kwakiutl	Central coast of British Columbia	Kwak'wala (Wakashan)
	n/a	Nuu'chah'nulth		Nootka	Central Vancouver Island	Nuu'chah'nulth (Wakashan)

*Nehiyaw, Nehiyawak, Nîhiyawak (Cree). "Cree" is the preferred term by most speakers. The listed groups all identify as Cree. Many of the nations listed here are grouped under the political umbrellas of the Nishnawbe-Aski. Note that the "Plains Cree" (Nehiyaw) also identify as "Cree" and so are listed as "Cree", but are distinct from the Eastern Cree, and so their other preferred term "Plains Cree" is used to retain that distinction in the text.

**Note that the first three were the original members and the last two joined the Confederacy later as affiliates

Dedication

Olive Dickason was proud of the role she played in raising the profile of Indigenous history within Canada. That pride was fully justified. When she entered graduate studies in the 1970s, she found few opportunities for study in her chosen field. Nevertheless, through courage and determination she soon established herself on the leading edge of an emerging movement that hoped to restore Indigenous history to its rightful place at the heart of Canadian history. Others were also part of this effort, but no one did more than Olive to bring Indigenous history back into the mainstream. As I write this dedication, Indigenous affairs are certainly at the centre of the national consciousness. In fact, events have moved so quickly that we had a difficult time staying in front of them. During the last few months, important Indigenous rulings, legislation, actions, and hearings have dominated the national news. This would not have been a surprise to Olive. In February of 1991, as we drove through a heavy snowstorm along the frozen banks of the Red River, she predicted that Indigenous people were going to find their rightful place at the centre of the nation's past, present, and future. She further told me that I had an obligation to do what I could to contribute to this movement. When we reached Lower Fort Garry, she said, "You have seen injustice and now you have to do something about it. Some of us have been working on it but we can't go on forever." She was 70 years old then, and in spite of her protest she did go on to make many more contributions to help to fight against this injustice. The challenge that she issued to me is now passed on to you, the reader. In the pages of this text, you will find ample evidence of injustice and it is up to you to work together to do something about it.

William Newbigging

1 Origin Stories

CHAPTER OUTLINE

In the opening chapter we examine origin stories, taken from across Canada, to show how a critical reading of them helps us to gain understanding of the beliefs and diversity of Indigenous Peoples within Canada. We then discuss how these stories dovetail with what ethnohistory knows thus far about the origin of Indigenous Peoples in the Americas.

LEARNING OUTCOMES

1. Students will understand the importance of the oral tradition as it applies to the history of Indigenous Peoples within what has become Canada.

2. Students will learn to discuss how an ethnohistorical approach, including understanding the themes and concepts of the various oral traditions, enables us to overcome the challenges posed by an exclusively documents-based, classic historical approach.

3. Students will gain insight into the rich diversity of Indigenous Peoples within Canada.

4. Students will discover ethnohistorical evidence that supports the origin stories of Indigenous Peoples, as well as the gaps that still exist in the scientific evidence.

Introduction

Canadian history begins with the First Peoples. Indigenous Peoples have been here from time immemorial[1] and have contributed enormously to every aspect of Canadian life: political, social, economic, and cultural. Pride of place, however, has not meant a fair claim on the historical narrative of the country. There are many reasons for this but the most important one has to do with the conflict between the traditional, documents-based history of Eurocentric historians and the oral traditions of Indigenous Peoples within Canada. Other variables—such as bias, politics, economics, and nationalism—also influenced the incompatibility perceived to exist between classically trained historians and oral traditions.[2] Scholars have now come to practise a more inclusive and useful methodology, which has made it possible for Indigenous knowledge to be incorporated and accepted into the historical narratives taught at Western institutions. This approach is called **ethnohistory.** Ethnohistorians incorporate Indigenous voices into the historical narrative, using oral history, artwork, material culture, archaeological evidence, and etymology as source materials, and incorporate work from scholars in other disciplines such as linguistics, anthropology, and archaeology. Until very recently, most academic historians were non-Indigenous, but now Indigenous scholars are helping to transform the field through their greater knowledge of Indigenous languages and access to oral tradition and other cultural knowledge, as well as their ability to exert greater influence by virtue of their presence at academic institutions. Most importantly, more Indigenous language courses are now being offered and the field is being transformed as language reassumes its rightful place

Ancient Teaching - Maxine Noel : IOYAN MANI
Photo courtesy of Canadian Art Prints

***Ancient Teachings* by Ioyan Mani (Maxine Noel).** Maxine Noel signs her artwork with her Dakota Sioux First Nation name, Ioyan Mani, which translates as "Walk Beyond."

as a key to cultural knowledge. Through their work, ethnohistorians, both Indigenous and non-Indigenous, have worked hard to provide us with guidance as we attempt to rebuild the history of people who mostly did not keep written records, or who had their written records made for them by others. And yet, the efficacy of this approach is still debated in scholarly circles and in mainstream history. At its core, the rejection of Indigenous Peoples' history, as kept through oral tradition, has stemmed from colonial attitudes, which we will discuss in more detail in later chapters.

Often the best way to understand a culture is through exposure to its stories. The stories of the Indigenous Peoples of Canada contain universal human themes and symbols, but they also contain themes and symbolism unique to their tellers and to the ancient traditions of their tellers' peoples. By examining both the universal and the unique in the origin stories we can come to a greater understanding of how they understood the world around them. We can learn something about building relationships with the land, the waters, and the resources of this vast country. We can also learn something about the ways in which these peoples identified the necessities of life in what was sometimes an extremely difficult and even harsh climate.

The stories chosen in this opening chapter reveal, in the voices of the people themselves, many insights into the ways Indigenous Peoples within Canada understood their world and how this understanding was passed on from generation to generation. The rich oral tradition exists from sea to sea to sea, and it exists in a vast number of stories reflecting both the shared humanity of the people and the vast differences in climate and resources of the land. To demonstrate

Untitled, Jeffrey Veregge. Permission granted by artist.

Untitled by Jeffrey Veregge. Veregge, a member of the Port Gamble S'Klallam Tribe near Kingston, Washington, writes: "My origins are not supernatural, nor have they been enhanced by radioactive spiders. I am simply a Native American artist and writer whose creative mantra is best summed up with a word from my tribe's own language as: 'taʔčaʔx̣ʷéʔtəŋ', which means 'get into trouble'."

this we have chosen stories from all four cardinal directions: east, south, west, and north. The directions have significance in various Indigenous traditions, and are incorporated into a variety of Indigenous teachings. As explained by Elder Betty McKenna, from the Anishinaabe nation:

> We seek knowledge from those four directions. We get power from those four directions. They pull stuff into our lives. When we call out to them in prayer, they will bring things to us. The four directions came with creation. We didn't. We were the last thing created.[3]

The four stories included here begin to illustrate something of the richness and diversity of Indigenous cultures and offer a foundation upon which we might build a better understanding of the history of Indigenous Peoples within Canada.

The epistemological significance of the oral tradition cannot be gainsaid. Oral traditions preserve and promote knowledge and understanding, and the storytellers are the living storehouses of that knowledge. The themes of the stories teach lessons about the world and its necessities. The stories provide insight into ontology, that is, the nature of being, but also about the means of transmitting that knowledge to future generations. Thus, those listening to the stories are being educated about the world and about how knowledge is transmitted in the world. One listens to a story, learns the lesson of the story, and also learns how to transmit that lesson to the next generation through the story. The circle, that most central of all Indigenous Peoples' ontological metaphors, is thus made complete.

This is not to suggest, however, that the primary purpose of oral stories is necessarily didactic. To be sure, they teach the listeners about the world and a particular world view—about themselves—but at the same time they entertain and, depending on the story, they can amuse, strike fear, and otherwise draw on the wide range of human emotions. Indigenous Peoples within Canada remain strong adherents of oral traditions that have served them well for thousands of years, and these stories all exemplify the power of the oral tradition. We can only do so much justice to the oral tradition in a written format. For a better experience, we recommend visiting some of the suggested resources at the end of the chapter.

Oral History and Origin Stories

The best way to understand the history of Indigenous Peoples within Canada is to understand how they understood their world, and the best way to do that is to examine the layers of meaning in their oral histories and origin stories. This is not as easy or straightforward a task as it might seem. In the first place, the enormous diversity of cultures means that there are as many oral histories and origin stories as there are peoples. Even within confederacies, individual villages, clans, and even families had their own oral histories and origin stories and, as small differences matter, it is important to remember that these histories and stories hold very specific and important clues about how people understood their world. For example, the individual origin stories often refer to specific elements that, in turn, explain more universal concepts.

In this section we will first look at four specific origin stories—one from the east, one from the south, one from the west, and one from the north—and then will examine some of the larger

Steve Russell/Getty Images

Elder Gary Sault storytelling at the National Aboriginal Day and Indigenous Arts Festival at Fort York in Toronto. The tradition of storytelling continues in what is now Canada today. As one prolific example, Elder Gary Sault of the Mississaugas of the New Credit First Nation shares his knowledge through ceremony and story at major events across southern Ontario.

themes that appear in the oral histories. We will also consider how the oral tradition enriches our understanding of the past. The stories themselves, it should be noted, are in English translation and, as with all translations, nuances are lost and the beauty of the language is diminished. As the Italians say, "*traduttore, traditore*," or "translator, traitor," but that, too, loses something in the translation. Second, these stories are brief, written accounts of longer stories meant to be told by a storyteller and experienced over several hours or days. Still, by learning the stories and by examining the symbolism in its appropriate context, we have the best possible chance of overcoming the language difficulties occasioned by the need for translation. As we will see, words, names, and place names provide countless opportunities to understand aspects of the cultures of Indigenous Peoples that might at first seem unclear.[4]

The East: The Mi'kmaq of Listuguj

The origin stories of the peoples of eastern Canada often feature Glooscap as the creator. Glooscap himself was created when a bolt of lightning fused sand into the shape of a person. Glooscap was then made animate by the Creator. Glooscap made the natural features of the world and he made the animals who live in the world. The following is one story of Glooscap's arrival as related according to the tradition of the Mi'kmaq of Listuguj, who live at the mouth of the Restigouche River at the base of the Gaspé Peninsula, as told by Emanuel *Nàgùgwes* Metallic, Mi'kmaq of Listuguj.[5]

A very long time ago, our Mother the Earth was only a globe of water. In the Skyworld where the supernatural beings lived, the twins, Glooscap ("good") and Malsm ("weak"), were sent to earth in a large stone canoe. Where they landed, the canoe turned into land that we know today as Cape Breton. Glooscap set about and created all the animals and birds from the dirt. He made the animals much larger than they are today; in those days the beaver was as large as a bear. Likewise, Malsm created the badger, who represented evil because of its deceitful ways. Glooscap eventually killed Malsm.

Things continued to happen, like Glooscap's creation of human beings. It was from four arrows he shot at four different white ash trees that emerged the Passamaquoddy, Penobscot, Maliseet, and the Mi'kmaq peoples. He then set about teaching them what to eat and what to gather. Eventually, Glooscap had to leave. Before leaving towards the setting sun, he gathered and told them they could find him if they searched hard enough.

A number of important themes in this story help to explain the Mi'kmaw world view. In the first place, it is important to note that Glooscap created the four separate peoples in exactly the same way. There is no sense of hierarchy here. Second, Glooscap taught all the peoples about the resources of their territory. The link between knowledge and the tradition is thus made explicit in this origin story. Third, Glooscap made the beaver "as large a bear" in this story. The beaver was an important source of food and fur for the Mi'kmaq, and larger animals meant a kind of abundance. This may also be a reference to the "megafauna" that existed at the time the events of this story took place. This part of the story is very similar to other stories from other

INDIGENOUS LEADERS | Basil Johnston (1929–2015)

Few people have contributed to the preservation of Indigenous Peoples' past more than Basil Johnston. He was born on the Parry Island Indian Reserve and attended the St Peter Claver School for Boys in Spanish, Ontario, the largest residential school in the province. Johnston worked in education before joining the Department of Ethnology at the Royal Ontario Museum (ROM) in Toronto in 1969. It was during his time at the ROM that Johnston made his most significant contribution. He published several books that preserved Anishinaabe stories that might otherwise have been lost. He was also a keen student of language and gave hundreds of talks on elements of Anishinaabe-mowin. His most important publications—*Ojibway Ceremonies*; *Ojibway Heritage*; *By Canoe and Moccasin: Some Native Place Names of the Great Lakes*; and *The Manitous: The Spirit World of the Ojibway*—are still widely read in schools and universities across Canada. Johnston's efforts to preserve knowledge and language were of great significance. He understood very clearly the importance of language and oral tradition in the promotion and preservation of Indigenous Peoples' history and culture, and he worked to promote and preserve both.

Indigenous Peoples across Canada. Finally, Glooscap leaves to go west, or "towards the setting sun" as the storyteller expresses it. This, too, is a common theme in traditional stories across Canada and it is a specific acknowledgement of the movement of peoples as the land was settled following the retreat of the glaciers. As Glooscap finished his work in the east, he then went west, one supposes, to create new worlds there.

The South: The Kamiga Odaawak

At the time of their first contact with the Europeans, when the explorer Samuel de Champlain arrived at the mouth of the French River in the summer of 1615, the Kamiga Odaawak lived at the western end of Manitoulin Island and on the islands running along the limestone spur of the Penetanguishene Peninsula as far west as Mackinaw in the south and St Joseph Island in the north. They were the third largest of the four constituent nations who together formed the Odawaa Confederacy.[6] The Kamiga Odawaak were smaller in number than the Sinago Odaawak, who lived at the eastern end of Manitoulin, and the Kiskakon Odaawak, whose main village was at Nottawasaga in what is now called the Georgian Bay, but they were larger in number than the Nassauakueton Odaawak, who lived at Michilimackinac, on the coasts and islands of the strait where Lake Michigan's waters flow into Lake Huron. The following origin story comes from Doug Belanger of Batchewana First Nation.[7]

> One spring Namepich, the spirit keeper of the *namaybin*, or white suckers, told a female sucker to swim out of the water and onto the sand shore of a river. My people say this was the Thunder Bay River in Alpena, Michigan, and if you go there you can still see the place where this happened. It is called "The Sandies," I think. Now other people might tell you this happened somewhere else, but our story says it was the Thunder Bay River. The sucker laid her eggs in the sand where they were dried by the sun into the form of a woman who became mother to all of the Kamiga Odaawak.

The French were impressed by this story, and in their documents they always referred to the Kamiga Odaawak as les Outaouais du Sable, or the "Sand Odaawak" to distinguish them from the other three constituent groups of the Odaawa Confederacy.[8] Unlike the Kiskakon Odaawak and Sinago Odaawak, the Kamiga Odaawak did not name themselves after their ododam or totem; their name, which means sand or earth, is a reference to their origin story.[9] Within the Odaawa Confederacy, the Kamiga Odaawak were responsible for protecting the Michilimackinac gateway into Lake Huron and for maintaining good relations with the Bawating Ojibwa villages in the region of eastern Lake Superior. The Kamiga Odaawak invited members of the other three Odaawa nations to Bawating and Michilimackinac during the November whitefish run to participate in the fishing.

The origin story reveals something that, at first reading, might seem difficult to understand. The sucker does not seem to be a particularly noble animal. A bottom-feeding fish with a diet of aquatic insects lacks some of the obvious qualities one might expect to find in an animal used as a totemic symbol. The white sucker has neither the physical power of the bear nor the antici-patory industry of the squirrel. But the white sucker does have other, less immediately obvious qualities, and the oral tradition helps to explain the relevance.

Before contact with the French colonizers, the Kamiga Odaawak had lived at Bkejwanong, the area between Lakes Erie and Huron, present-day Canada's southernmost region. Some documentary records indicate this, but the oral tradition makes the location explicit.[10] The Michigan oral tradition of Makade-binesi or Chief Andrew J. Blackbird, as recorded in his History of the Ottawa and Chippewa Indians of Michigan (1887), refers to his own people, "the Undergrounds" (a reference to people who came from the sand or earth), living at Detroit.[11] Other oral sources—from Francis Assikinack and William Warren—also refer to the Kamiga Odaawak presence in Lake Huron.[12] The best source comes from the oral tradition as kept by Nin-da-waab-jig at Minishenhying Anishanaabe-aki.[13]

According to Nin-da-waab-jig, the presence of the Kamiga Odaawak at Bkejwanong (the area of the straits between Lakes Huron and Erie), specifically at Wauwi-Autinoong (also known as Lake St Clair), may be traced to the arrival of the ancient Anishnaabeg in the region sometime around 5,000 years ago.[14] Here, at Bkejwanong, the water of the Upper Great Lakes flows through the shallows and into the Lower Great Lakes. According to Nin-da-waab-jig, the water undergoes purification as it passes through the shallows. The bulrushes of the shal-low water help to add oxygen to the water. According to the tradition, this process was not only physical, but it was spiritual. On the physical level the rich plant life of the region pro-duced oxygen and absorbed impurities, but the Kamiga Odaawak tradition also teaches that there is a spiritual significance to the process. As Dean Jacobs of Walpole Island First Nation explains:

> As the water passed through Bkejwanong a circle was made complete. The water was made fresh and renewed. The white suckers have a role to play in this renewal. In the spring, when the rich plant life of the shallows begins to grow it is threatened by aquatic insects who devour the young plants as they begin to push through the lake bed. Just then, the white suckers swim into the shallow water to spawn and to feed on the aquatic insects. Thus they act as part of a larger circle of life which en-sures that the waters of the Great Lakes will remain pure.[15]

As the lakes were the source of whitefish—the most important Odaawa resource—there can be no doubt as to the importance of this process of renewal. Thus the white sucker assumes a central role in the health of the Great Lakes.[16] The lesson from the Kamiga Odaawak, then, has to do with conservation and with respect for the natural cycles of nature.

The West: Haida

The Haida (spelled "Xaada" in this story) origin story, like many on the Pacific coast and in northern Canada, features the raven as creator, but as an imperfect creator. The raven, now fairly common, was once a rare bird and perhaps this helped to give it a mysterious, super-natural quality. The Greek legend of Apollo makes reference to an equivocating raven oracle and the Book of Genesis relates the story of an unreliable raven messenger. Noah sends out a raven to learn if the waters from the Flood have subsided but it merely "went to and fro until the waters were dried up" (Gen. 8:7). Then, to gain a better understanding, he sends forth a dove. She "found no place to set her foot" (Gen. 8:8) and returns to Noah, but seven days later he sends the dove out again and she returns to the Ark with an olive leaf. In Norse mythology the ravens Hugin and Munin sit on Odin's shoulders to make daily reports on the state of the world. In his 1824 novel *St Ronan's Well*, the Scottish writer Sir Walter Scott calls an unreliable servant "a corbie messenger," "corbie" being the Scots word for raven.[17] The American poet Edgar Allan Poe makes explicit reference to supernatural associations in his 1845 poem "The Raven," and of course the shape-shifting Mystique character of the Marvel Comics and the *X-Men* films, whose alter ego is Raven Darkholme, employs this symbolism as well. Indeed, in Gord Downie and Jeff Lemire's animated *Secret Path*, the true story about a young boy who runs away from residential school only to die of the elements in an attempt to walk home, a raven plays a foreboding role. The universality of the symbolism remains unexplained, but there is no question about the centrality of the raven in the origin stories of the Indigenous Peoples of the Pacific coast and northern Canada. The following origin story, with Raven as the central character, is from the Council of the Haida Nation.[18]

Yaahl Sgalaalaanga (A raven song)

At one time the whole world was in darkness. The raven, yaahl, would fly over the ocean. He would fly and fly. That's all he would do. Then he saw something in the dark on the ocean. Then, through the misty pale darkness, he spotted something floating on the sea. It was a double-headed kelp. So he landed on it, and he decided to climb down, just as if it was a rope. As he climbed down he discovered that it was in fact a double-headed totem pole. So he climbed all the way down the shaft of the totem pole until he reached the bottom of the sea, and there, behind the totem pole was a longhouse. So, Raven walked in. He saw an old man busy at work. His head was bald and his old man's skin was pure white. He was like a seagull.

"Grandson, I have been expecting you," he said to Raven.

And Raven was pleased and proud to be treated so well. The old man took up two stones. One was black and the other was speckled. He told Raven, "Take this black rock as you are flying over the ocean and spit it down and it will become the seaward country. Take the speckled rock, bite it, spit it down and it will become Xaada Gwaay."

Now Raven often makes a few mistakes and when he took those stones, in his excitement, he mixed them up. After he chewed for a while, he dropped his first stone, the speckled stone, and it became the seaward country, now known as North

America. He took the black stone and threw down that and spat it down and it became Xaada Gwaay. But because he mixed them up Xaada Gwaay is smaller than North America. And that's the kind of thing Raven would do.

Now yaahl, the raven, was getting tired of only darkness. He had heard of a great sky-chief who was said to have all the light in the world. Raven decided that he would have to spy on the Sky Chief. He saw through the misty pale darkness that the chief had a daughter. And he watched as she went to get a drink of creek water. Now Raven could change his shape and could transfer into anything he wanted. So as she dipped her cup into the water, shape-shifter Raven turned himself into a hemlock needle and floated down the creek. The young girl scooped him up with her cup and swallowed him, and then he was inside her. The Sky Chief's daughter returned to her father's house, and not long after, yaahl was born as a child from her. As he was growing up, yaahl acted like any other child, and made a lot of noise when he didn't get what he wanted. And he knew his grandfather kept all the light in the world inside many bentwood boxes, and that's what he wanted.

Day after day he would cry, "Box, Box, Open the box!", until his grandfather opened one box.

There were 10 boxes, one inside each other, and after many days they finally came to the last one. Yaahl could see light shining through the edges of the bentwood box. (All the light in the world.) And he made so much noise that his grandfather finally opened it. It was a perfectly round ball of light brightly shining. And Raven played with it and rolled it all around the longhouse. The old chief saw how beautiful his wife and daughter were, and he was pleased with his grandson. But yaahl wanted to take the light away, and he changed back into his raven form. And he was a pure white raven. He snatched the white ball of light with his beak and flew away with it, up through the longhouse smoke hole when he became stuck and covered with soot, and turned completely black before he could fly away.

He flew as high as he could with the white light in his beak, but he couldn't fly high enough, so he had to break the perfect ball of light into pieces and then he spat them out into the sky. The small pieces became the stars and the large piece became the moon. And then he asked an eagle if he would take another large piece high up into the sky, where only the eagle can soar. And he did. And that became the sun. After then there was light in the world, but Raven has stayed black forever. Now that Raven could see everything, he wanted everything. And he heard about a chief that had all the salmon in the world, and he was very curious. After-all, he wanted to fill his world with good things to eat. And so he journeyed until he found this chief, his name was Beaver, Ts'ang. Once there, Ts'ang treated Raven as his guest and fed him plenty of fish. But he wouldn't let him see where the fish came from, and made Raven turn his back. So Raven watched Ts'ang closely in the reflection of a brightly polished mirror of argillite. And that's how he saw Ts'ang go behind his longhouse to a perfectly formed lake, overflowing with salmon. It was almost too much for Raven to hold himself back, but he managed.

Then, one day when the chief was busy, Raven could wait no longer. He gorged himself full of fish. And after he had his fill, he lifted up one corner of the lake and he rolled it up, just like a blanket. He rolled up the water, and he rolled up the fish, and any salmon that fell out he stuffed into his feathers. When the beaver chief returned he was *not* pleased with Raven, and started to chase him. But Raven flew into a tree. Ts'ang started to chew away at its base, and just as it was about to fall, Raven flew lightly to another tree. This made Ts'ang very angry, and he followed him there too, and chewed 'til that tree was ready to fall. And Raven, who was enjoying himself, flew again to another tree. This continued until Ts'ang was too exhausted to follow. And then Raven flew along the entire coast with his rolled up lake of fish. And he started to drop water and salmon wherever he was flying. In this way, raven created all the lakes and streams and rivers. And then with the last of the rolled up lake, and the salmon, stuffed in his feathers, he flew over Xaada Gwaay, and created all the lakes and rivers.

And so Raven shared the wealth, at least the wealth he couldn't keep in his beak. And this is just the way Raven created things, always a little by accident. Now that Raven had all the lakes and all the rivers and all the fish that he needed, he was looking around for some company. As he flew over Niikun, he looked down and he saw a giant shell. He wanted to have a closer look and so he landed beside it on the beach. It was a giant clam shell. Raven started poking it. "Ma, ma," he said. He poked it with his sharp beak. "Ma, Ma." After a while the shell started to open, slowly. Raven looked inside and saw many little eyes peeking out at him.

"Come here." But they closed it back up again, fast.

Raven was very disappointed. He sat there for a while, hoping the giant shell would open again. And slowly, very slowly, it opened again, bit by bit. He wanted to know who those eyes belonged to, and he wanted them to come and play with him. And as the shell opened, Raven could see that inside were creatures with black hair, but no feathers and no fur.

"How could they survive?" he thought.

And they made funny sounds that he couldn't understand. But he wanted to help them. He knew these were his people, and he liked them. They started to come out. All but one. He stayed behind. Raven tried to help him, and he reached in, but he accidentally killed him. And so when Raven created life, he also created death. But he was like their grandfather, and he wanted to help them. He had noticed there were no females, so he took them to a part of the island where the waves were high, and full of chitons [molluscs]. And when the chitons came close to the shore, the humans went into the waves. The chitons attached themselves to some of the males, and almost swallowed their sexual organs. Raven probably laughed a little at this too. Those males then became female, and so both male and female were now created. And they became the Xaadas. This is just one of our origin stories. The raven was mischievous and made mistakes. But he made things happen. And since the very first tree, there have been people here, because of the raven. We have stories about the tree too. Maybe another day, hey?

Although his creational, transformative nature is notable in this Haida tale, Raven is typical of the **trickster-transformer** found in many oral traditions. For example, Anansi (the Spider) originated in the tradition of the Ashanti of Ghana in West Africa, and stories of Anansi travelled with people from West Africa and appear in the oral tradition in Jamaica and other Caribbean countries. Coyote—the likely inspiration for "Wile E. Coyote" in the Road Runner cartoons—is found among various North American Indigenous groups, including the Navajo, Apache, and Hopi in the American Southwest, various Indigenous communities in what is today California, and Salish-speaking peoples in present-day Washington and southern British Columbia. In North American popular culture, Br'er Rabbit, from the folklore of African Americans in the American South, is another well-known trickster.

Bill Reid Foundation: http://www.billreidfoundation.ca/banknote/raven.htm

The Raven and the First Men by Bill Reid (1920–1998). In Haida culture, the Raven is the most powerful of mythical creatures. His appetites include lust, curiosity, and an irrepressible desire to interfere and change things, and to play tricks on the world and its creatures. The sculpture of *The Raven and the First Men* depicts the story of human creation.

This Haida story, like so many trickster-transformer tales, demonstrates the power of story-telling. An engaging storyteller can captivate her or his audience and can ensure that the essential elements of the story are committed to the audience's memory. Raven in this story has a sense of humour, at times tricks others, and is not always truthful. In other words, he is not perfect and occasionally responds to human appetites. This anthropomorphizes (gives human qualities to) Raven and makes him real to the audience. The effect of this is to give us some understanding of the ways in which the Haida people identified the necessities of their world: the land, the lakes, the rivers, and, perhaps most notably, salmon. Stories centred on Raven are common to Indigenous Peoples of the Pacific coast from California to Alaska, and also are popular among Na-Dené-speaking peoples of the Northwest interior in what is today Canada. Noteworthy, however, is how they are adapted to the particular environments of specific groups, so, for example, in the Haida tale Raven creates the specific landscape that the Haida call home.

The North: The Inuit of Sikusiilaq

The Inuit of Sikusiilaq (also known as Cape Dorset) on the southern coast of Baffin Island share the story of Sedna, the underwater goddess, with many of the peoples of Canada's Arctic region. Sedna's story is noteworthy because it describes the creation of the world, but it assumes that the people exist already. This is because the Inuit believe that their ancestors travelled from elsewhere to make their home in the Far North of what we now call Canada.

There are a number of variations of Sedna's story, but in essence it is the account of a young woman who refuses the offers of numerous suitors. Based on the version told by Victoria Mamnguqsualuk[19] (which when told in full can last well over an hour), the story goes like this.

Finally, after terrific pressure from her parents she accepts the proposal of a young man who claims to be an expert hunter and who promises to provide for her exceptionally well. She will have meat to eat and warm fur clothes and fur blankets to keep her warm against the harsh cold of the Arctic. Sedna goes with him to live on his island where she soon discovers that he is not a man at all but rather a raven disguised as a man. To make matters worse his hunting skills are limited to fish. Sedna is distraught to have been deceived and to have to make do with her fish diet. Finally her father learns of her fate and travels to the island to rescue Sedna. In order to do this he kills the raven and puts Sedna into his kayak to take her home.

The raven's friends are angered by this action and take their revenge by causing a huge storm. Terrified, Sedna's father throws her into the sea in order to save himself. She swims back to the kayak and grips on to its side. Her father, fearing she will now capsize his craft, tries to loosen her grip but Sedna will not let him. He then cuts off her fingers with his knife. Sedna swims to the bottom of the sea where she rules as an underwater goddess. From each of her bleeding finger joints issues forth a marine animal: a seal, a whale, a walrus, and so on. These, in turn, give birth to others of their type. Eventually there are so many animals the Inuit are attracted to come to hunt them and to live in the north.

This story provides a glimpse into the Inuit understanding of their history. They knew the powerful attraction of game drew their ancestors to come into the harsh climate and to thrive in conditions that others would have found intolerable. The emphasis in the story on the skill of the hunter is a theme at the very heart of Inuit culture. One of the most fascinating elements of the story, however, concerns the timing. Here we find an interesting example of seeing history over the "long term," as the French Annales School of history would have us see it.[20]

The ethnographer Norman Hallendy, who has lived for many years at Sikusiilaq, explains the importance of this view to the Inuit. He notes that his first interpreter, Pia Pootoogook, went out to interview the elders of Sikusiilaq in order to understand their concept of time. The elders explained to Pootoogook that they divided the past into six eras: "[t]he time before there were humans; the time of the earliest humans; the time of the Tuniit; the time of our earliest ancestors; the time when we lived on the land; the time when most Inuit moved into settlements."[21]

Sedna's story fits into this timeline between the "earliest humans" and the "Tuniit," this last being the word for the people who lived in the Arctic before the Inuit. The archaeological work at Sikusiilaq has uncovered evidence of the existence of these people. The Sikusiilaq Inuit word "Tuniit" means the first inhabitants.[22] According to the tradition, as the Inuit moved in, the Tuniit left. This Inuit timeline is a good example of how the oral tradition and the archaeological evidence support one another. In other words, it is yet another strong validation of the value and accuracy of the oral tradition.

Turtle Island and the Journey towards the Setting Sun

The four origin stories discussed in this chapter indicate something of the rich diversity of Indigenous Peoples within what has become Canada. The origin stories, one from each cardinal direction, were chosen to illustrate four important aspects of meaning. Sedna's story from the Inuit of Sikusiilaq shows the importance of natural resources, the vagaries of nature, and the Inuit sense of time and the slow process of evolution. The importance of history studied over long periods of time is also shown in the story and in the Inuit timeline. The Glooscap story of the Mi'kmaq of Listuguj also reminds us of the importance of resources, but it contains as well the importance of teaching. Just as the story teaches us, so does Glooscap within the story remind the people of the importance of teaching. In the Kamiga Odaawak story we are shown specifically how an origin story can help a modern listener to understand something that was left unexplained in the documentary record. Finally, in the Haida story, Raven is an imperfect creator. This is an explanation for the difficulties people encounter in the world and is a common theme in Indigenous Peoples' stories.

Although we can discern common themes (like the importance of natural resources and the vicissitudes of the natural world), the stories are a direct reflection of the important differences between the Indigenous Peoples of this vast land. Some similarities, however, deserve to be mentioned, and so we will close this chapter by making reference to two ideas that transcend these differences. The first of these is the story of Turtle Island, the second, the belief that people moved from the East to the West, towards the setting sun.

The Turtle Island story is the most common creation story, or in a sense a re-creation story, as it involves a flood, as do many other creation stories around the world. Variants of the Turtle Island story are told by people from the Maritimes, Quebec, Ontario, the Prairies, and the Territories. In an Ojibwa telling of the story, the world is flooded by water and all the land is covered by a deep ocean. Sky-woman is saddened by the flooded world and promises the animals that live in the water that she will make some land for them. She persuades a huge turtle to come from the deep to the surface and a number of the water animals come to rest on the turtle's shell. Sky-woman tells them that if one of them can bring her a piece of earth from the bottom of the sea she will make it into a rich land. One after another, the beaver, the fisher, the marten, and the loon try but fail to reach the bottom. Finally, the lowly little muskrat announces that he will try. Ignoring the derision of the others, the muskrat dives in and then, after a very long time, resurfaces, barely alive. In his paw he has a few grains of earth from the bottom of the sea and Sky-woman fulfills her promise and uses this bit of earth to create an island, which, in turn, gives rise to more and more land.[23]

In this story, we are encouraged to try. The world is a difficult and at times unpredictable place, but if we persevere we, too, can succeed like the little muskrat. The mockery in this parable—the laughter of the other animals when the muskrat announces his intention to try— is an important and recurring theme in Indigenous Peoples' storytelling. Arrogance is to be avoided at all costs, and to be full of oneself is a sure path to disaster.

Another well-known Turtle Island story is that of the Wendat people, and it is related here by one of their best-known historians, Georges Sioui (translated from the French).[24]

> The Wendat people believe, as do the other Iroquois people, that the earth where we all live was once an island upon which landed a woman from a celestial world. She was called Aataentisic. This celestial woman was called to land on the back of a turtle by the animals of the earth, though at the time, of course, there were only aquatic animals. By diving to the bottom of the water the most humble of these animals, the toad, had succeeded in gathering silt which the little turtle then spread on the great turtle's shell. Eventually there was enough of this silt to form the landmass of the Americas, the whole world as would be known by the First Peoples.
>
> Aataentsic, in visiting this island, found a house occupied by an old lady whom she immediately called Shutai, or grandmother. It was in the house of the grandmother that Aataentsic gave birth to a daughter, whom she had been carrying from the celestial world she had come from before her arrival. This daughter soon grew to become a young woman. Many suitors, who were in fact masculine spirits, came

to solicit the young woman's attention, but on the advice of her mother, the young woman chose the Turtle-spirit. This spirit left one of his arrows beside his sleeping love, and then, without her knowing it, came back and took it away. He was never seen again. Later, the daughter of Aataentsic gave birth to twin boys. The first was Tsestah, the man of fire, and he was destined to be the benevolent divinity of the Wendat people. The other was Tawiskaron, the man of flint, the creator and sower of traps, pitfalls, dangers, and difficulties in the life and in the environment of the Wendat people.

The themes of this story, although they belong to the Wendat world, are similar to those found in the Turtle Island myth from the neighbouring Anishinaabe world to which the Ojibwa belong. One theme in particular offers an important view into how the Wendat people understood their world. The twins Tsestah and Tawiskaron make clear that the world—that is, Turtle Island—is at once the source of all of our necessities and all of our troubles.

One final common theme in several origin stories is the movement of people towards the setting sun. This east–west movement is an important element in the stories of many Indigenous Peoples. The Glooscap story refers to it, as do some versions of the Anishinaabe Turtle Island story. Among certain peoples of central Canada, the ancestors are referred to as the Wabunukeeg, the "Daybreak People," a reference to their understanding that their ancestors came from the East.[25] Even among peoples whose ancestors do not appear to have migrated over great distances—such as the peoples of the Northwest—migration remains an important theme (for example, in the Tsimshian tradition).[26]

The stories in this chapter reflect the oral traditions of Indigenous Peoples from across Canada, but they are only a tiny sample, a brief introduction to the richness, diversity, and beauty of the tradition. Part of the richness of the oral tradition exists in the skill and creativity of the storyteller, and that is something that simply cannot be recreated in a written form. Winter was, and is, the storytelling season, and on long winter nights the elders, the living storehouses of Indigenous Peoples' knowledge, take hours to tell the stories that form the various traditions. To listen to a story is to take part in a living history, which immediately makes the listeners part of a process that exists as an unbroken circle to time immemorial.[27]

Origin Story from Ethnohistory

The origin story as written in ethnohistorical accounts is somewhat different but not contradictory to the ones above. New archaeological evidence found along the coast of BC indicates that members of the Heiltsuk Nation resided in what is now Canada as long ago as 14,000 years BCE,[28] while another site in Yukon has been dated at 24,000 years BCE, making it the oldest known site.[29] From physical and linguistic evidence, we know that humans were present in the Americas at least by 17,000 BCE, and perhaps by 50,000 BCE or even earlier.[30] Archaeologists are now in agreement that the general movement of many First Nations throughout the Americas was in a large clockwise direction.[31]

New discoveries and scientific breakthroughs are helping to improve our understanding of what we already know. While DNA evidence at first had archaeologists convinced that only one origin was possible for Indigenous Peoples, new evidence and better DNA analysis now suggest that there were a minimum of two separate origins for the First Peoples in the Americas,[32] which better fits the varied origins as described in different Indigenous traditions.

Two possible explanations for the northwestern origin of the First Peoples match the anthropological, ethnohistorical, and oral records. The first requires an American genesis, which is described in the traditions of some of the Indigenous Peoples of the Northwest. The tradition of the Gitxsan people maintains that their territory in the Upper Skeena River Valley is the original site of this American genesis and that all of the Indigenous Peoples can trace their ancestry to this origin. They see themselves as the people who never left.[33] Many other Indigenous Peoples in the Northwest share the tradition of having been born of the earth there.

Another possible explanation that fits with several origin stories is that the First Peoples arrived in the Americas from elsewhere. For a long time, the prevailing ethnohistorical theory was a land bridge, which allowed for a Pacific genesis and subsequent move to the Americas. At several periods during the late Pleistocene geological age this land bridge (known as **Beringia**) connected Asia and North America across the Bering Strait, and it is possible that some Indigenous Peoples, over the course of generations, crossed on foot during these times.[34]

The sea also offers an explanation for how people arrived in the Americas. In the Pacific, the Japanese current sweeping from the Asiatic coast eastward to the Americas provided a natural aquatic highway.[35] As described above, many origin stories of First Peoples include the arrival of people from elsewhere. The anthropological, geological, and archaeological evidence still being discovered is starting to help fill in some of the specifics that the origin stories do not provide.

Questions to Consider

1. What devices do the tellers use to help their audiences remember the key elements of the stories?
2. What is the significance of oral storytelling in Indigenous tradition?
3. What significance do the main themes have in the origin stories?
4. What has ethnohistory contributed to the discipline of history?

Recommended Readings

Augustine, Stephen, *Mi'kmaw Teaching Elder*. *"Four Directions Teachings."* http://www.fourdirectionsteachings.com/transcripts/mikmaq.html.

Crowshoe, Dr Reg, and Geoff Crow Eagle, *Piikani Blackfoot Teaching Elders*. *"Four Directions Teachings."* http://www.fourdirectionsteachings.com/transcripts/blackfoot.html.

Galloway, *Patricia. Practicing Ethnohistory: Mining Archives, Hearing Testimony, Constructing Narrative*. Lincoln: University of Nebraska Press, 2006.

Hallendy, Norman. *An Intimate Wilderness: Arctic Voices in a Land of Vast Horizons*. Vancouver: Greystone, 2016.

Lee, Mary, Cree (Nehiyawak) Teaching Elder. "Four Directions Teachings." http://www.fourdirection-steachings.com/transcripts/cree.html.

Llewellyn, Kristina, Alexander Freund, and Nolan Reilly, eds. *The Canadian Oral History Reader*. Montreal and Kingston: McGill-Queen's University Press, 2015.

Martin, Keavy. *Stories in a New Skin: Approaches to Inuit Literature*. Winnipeg: University of Manitoba Press, 2012.

McGhee, Robert. *Canadian Arctic Prehistory*. Toronto: Van Nostrand Reinhold, 1978.

Pauketat, Timothy. *The Oxford Handbook of North American Archaeology*. Oxford: Oxford University Press, 2015.

Pitawanakwat, Lillian, Ojibwe (Anishinaabe) Teaching Elder. "Four Directions Teachings." http://www.fourdirectionsteachings.com/transcripts/ojibwe.html.

Porter, Tom, Mohawk (Haudenosaunee) Teaching Elder. "Four Directions Teachings." http://www.fourdirectionsteachings.com/transcripts/mohawk.html.

Sassaman, Kenneth E., and Donald H. Holly, eds. *Hunter-Gatherer Archaeology as Historical Process*. Tucson: University of Arizona Press, 2013.

Sioui, Georges. *Les Wendats: une civilisation méconnue*. Sainte-Foy: Les Presses de l'Université de Laval, 1994.

2 At the Beginning

CHAPTER OUTLINE

As we have seen in the first chapter, the history of Indigenous Peoples within Canada is long, rich, and diverse. In this chapter we will examine the powerful geographic imperatives that helped to shape the different cultural adaptations across the country. We will turn to social organization and to the ecological basis for trade that connected nation to nation.

LEARNING OUTCOMES

1. Students will be able to understand the Indigenous Peoples' concept of their migrations across the North American continent.

2. Students will note the transition of many First Peoples from a hunter-gatherer economic strategy to an economic strategy that also incorporated agriculture.

3. Students will see how geography was the most important variable dictating economic choices.

4. Students will be able to identify aspects of the ecological basis for trade, which helped to forge relationships between different Indigenous Peoples.

TIMELINE From Time Immemorial to the 1200s

75,000–15,000 BCE
Ice Ages (Wisconsin glaciation), when Bering Strait land bridge was accessible for migration from Asia.

10,600–8700 BCE
Domesticated plants in Central and South America: gourds, avocados, beans, squash.

10,000–8000 BCE
Hunting of bison by means of drives and jumps begins.

7000 BCE
Earliest known domestication of corn, in central Mexico.

4300 BCE
Agriculture introduced in Northeastern Woodlands: squash.

3000 BCE
First local cultivated plant in Northeast: sunflower.

1000 ACE
Tobacco cultivated in Ontario; beans soon followed. Norse landing and brief settlement on northern tip of Newfoundland.

13,000 BCE
Bifacially flaked (fluted) stone points and knives dated to 11,000 years ago have been found and identified by archaeologists at both the Asian and North American sides of Beringia. Campsites of peoples of different cultural traditions scattered throughout North and South America. Northwest Coast culture established, based on salmon fishing and sea hunting—a sedentary culture with permanent settlements due to rich land and sea resources.[1]

8000 BCE
Migration of eastern Early Archaic peoples to western Plains and mixing with Plano (rippled flaking of spear and knife points) peoples creates Plains culture.

3500–2000 BCE
Olmec, the "mother" of American civilizations, in Gulf of Mexico region.

1500 BCE
Corn first cultivated in Canada, in present-day Ontario.

1200 ACE
Squash (and sunflowers) first grown domestically in Ontario, thus completing triad of the famous "three sisters" within Canada—corn, beans, squash.

Migrations, Movements, and Settlement

Whether born of the land or made from the land, the link between Indigenous Peoples and their ancestral territories is an undeniable manifestation of how they have always seen themselves (see Chapter 1). To understand the long-term relationship between the First Peoples and the land, we must also comprehend the waters and resources they relied on. In fact, some groups identified more closely with water than with the land and their mental maps included references to points on the shores of the seas, lakes, and rivers of Canada.[2]

Algonquian speakers who occupy so much of Canada's Subarctic forest, the **taiga**, at some point in time fanned northward from the Great Lakes, and the buffalo hunters of the northwestern Plains came from two directions, south and east. The Dene, on the other hand, began to move south after living in the Far North since about 9,000 years ago, following a volcanic eruption near White River.[3] Indigenous Peoples reached the southern tip of South America by at least 11,000 BCE. The forebears of the Inuit, the last of the Indigenous Peoples to settle in what is today Canada, spread eastward across the Arctic from Siberia. The High Arctic was the last region to be populated, sometime after 5000 BCE.

By 11,000 years ago—about the time of the last known mammoth and mastodon kills—campsites of peoples with different economic adaptations and cultural traditions were scattered throughout the Americas. In that period, and during the next 3,000 years or so, some 200 species of major animals disappeared from the two continents. We do not know what caused these extinctions, but whatever the reason, the disappearance of the giant mammals does not seem to have changed people's hunting patterns, as such game as bison and caribou had always been important. People survived for the same reason then as later: by being adaptable. The way of life that developed was based on the exploitation of a wide variety of food sources coupled with one of humanity's great strides forward in technology—the development of stone and bone tools.

Early Technology

Technology is the product of an accumulated fund of knowledge. Stone and bone tool technology reached its highest point of development in the Americas, in delicately crafted projectile points (for example, the development of **fluted points** around 11,200–10,500 BCE), seed grinding technology making a wider variety of seeds available for food, such as the small seeds of grasses and amaranths[4]) and, later, in the massive constructions of the Maya in Central America and the Inca in South America. The ancient city at Teotihuacan, featuring massive pyramids and a grand central avenue, was built around 2000 BCE and was one of the largest and most complex cities in the world at the time of its construction. Some of the Maya cities are even older.[5] The architectural and engineering skill of the early Maya people who built these cities rivals that of the great Roman architects and engineers.

The Incas in South America created the largest empire in the world during the century that spanned approximately 1430 to 1530; their "realm of the Four Quarters" incorporated more

The spear-thrower—atlatl—was a key part of the hunter's tool kit. The notched atlatl gave extra power to hurling a spear. An unusually elaborate weight, in the form of a plumed serpent holding a human head, is shown in this image. Debate exists around the benefits of these weights; they may have added to the effectiveness of the spear, or may have added to the atlatl's utility as a multi-purpose tool. Carved out of yew-wood with inlaid white-shell eyes, it has been radiocarbon-dated to 17,000 years ago. It was dredged up from the Skagit River, about 50 km south of the current Canada–US border, in Washington State.

than 200 ethnic groups. Working with stone required detailed and accurate observation on the one hand, and a workable social organization on the other.[6] In addition to the advanced engineering, and the learning to support that engineering, the Incas also possessed the ability to organize complex construction projects in formidable and remote locations. The famous citadel at Machu Picchu in what is now Peru occupies a site located on a mountain ridge some 2,500 metres above sea level. This would be an impressive technological feat even today. When it was built in the decades before the arrival of Columbus, it was unique.[7]

Cultural Adaptations and Resource Management

At the time of the first European contact with North America, that of the Norse about ACE 1000, most of the nations of the area that would become Canada were hunters and gatherers.[8] We know more about hunting activities than we do about gathering activities because hunting left recognizable debris that archaeologists could study, while gathering left very little. A number of well-known stories, however, have survived to the present. Most famously, we have many stories about the origin of maple sugaring.[9] As we shall see, various traditions have also carefully preserved the complex exploitation of plants for medicinal purposes.[10] The **hunter-gatherer** way of life evolved over thousands of years and grew out of an intimate knowledge of resources and the best way of exploiting them. From this knowledge of how and where plants would grow, North American people developed a new technology for managing food resources—farming.

Farming—The Three Sisters and Hundreds of Other Plants

There are no definite answers as yet as to why humans turned from collecting to cultivating plants in certain areas but not in others that seem equally suitable. The pressures of growing populations might have caused big-game hunters to turn to farming, but there is no physical evidence of this. Moreover, the switch in lifestyle was not all that sudden or complete.[11]

Furthermore, even though agriculture was closely associated with the development of permanent settlement, particularly as populations grew, the process of settling permanently in one location could (and did) begin without an agricultural base. What is essential for a sedentary way of living is an assured supply of food in one place, a situation not necessarily dependent on agriculture, at least in the period we are considering, when populations were usually small. Archaeological evidence indicates that permanent villages in the Americas date back to 15,000–13,000 BCE, before the domestication of plants. In the area that would become Canada, permanent settlement began at least 9,000 years ago.[12]

The exact timeline of the development and spread of agriculture in the Americas is not entirely known. Agriculture seems to have developed independently, within a span of a few thousand years at the end of the last Ice Age, in several widely separated regions of the globe: Mesopotamia, the monsoon lands of Southeast Asia, China, Mesoamerica, the Andes, and the Amazon. A sudden and unexplained jump in the atmosphere's carbon dioxide (CO_2), which occurred about 15,000 years ago, might provide the explanation. This increase in CO_2 made photosynthesis—the process by which plants convert sunlight into energy—more efficient, increasing growth rate and size. That might have triggered their domestication and the emergence of farming. Squash seeds found in a Mexican cave have been dated to 10,000 years ago.[13] The archaeological evidence shows that gourds were domesticated before corn, and so were squash and avocados. The first dates to 9000 BCE,[14] while the last two date to about 8700 BCE. Various beans, chili peppers,[15] and amaranth are at least as old. However, the Haudenosaunee origin story includes the cultivation of corn, beans, and squash (the **"three sisters"**) together since time immemorial. Whether Indigenous Peoples tried to domesticate these crops separately before realizing the advantages of cultivating them together, or whether the archaeological evidence is incomplete, is difficult to say. Probably, plant domestication began in several different places with various plants.

The plant world always has been the major source of medicines. (According to the Cherokee, animals brought diseases and plants provided the cures.) Recollect missionary Chrestien Le Clercq (c. 1641–after 1700) would report from Acadia, where he was from 1675 to 1686: "First Peoples are all by nature physicians, apothecaries, and doctors, by virtue of the knowledge and experience they have of certain herbs, which they use successfully to cure ills that seem to us incurable."[16] That this knowledge had roots that went deep into the past is not questioned. The process by which Indigenous Peoples acquired their herbal knowledge has not been shared to a wider audience, but there is no doubt about the results. Indigenous Peoples originally used more than 500 medicinal drugs that are still used today.[17]

Plant domestication could not have occurred without an extensive botanical knowledge already in place, as suggested by the vast number of plants used for medicinal purposes (see Historical Background box). It was no accident that agriculture developed first in warm, moderately rainy latitudes, where plant diversity was greatest and ecological conditions allowed the necessary freedom for experimentation. Northerners were no less skilful and experimental in exploiting their resources, but the restrictions of their environment meant that they had fewer options.

The people who hunted on the northwestern Plains, for example, harvested plants, such as the prairie turnip ("white apple"), which they had to observe carefully to determine the right time to gather it for drying and pulverizing for winter use.[18] There is also some evidence that they moved plant stocks from one location to another.

In the Northeastern Woodlands of North America, agriculture was introduced with the cultivation of squash around 4300 BCE, probably via southern trade, and the first local plant, the sunflower, was domesticated around 3000 BCE. Corn was the first cultivated food crop to reach what is now southern Ontario, and that not until after ACE 500. It remained the only crop for five centuries. Tobacco appeared about ACE 1000, with beans following somewhat later.

Squash (with sunflowers) did not reach southern Ontario until the thirteenth century, finally completing the triad of the famous "three sisters" in the northernmost limits of its range. The time this took could have been that needed for the plants to be adapted to a shorter growing season. By the sixteenth century, the triad—corn, beans, and squash—was being grown throughout agricultural America. As crops, the "three sisters" benefited the soil when sown together: beans capture nitrogen in the air and release it into the soil; squash roots are extensive and help prevent soil erosion; and the tall corn stalks provide the other plants with some protection from hail, damaging wind, and excessive sunlight. This gave the "three sisters" a sustainability and permanence lacking in modern agriculture.[19] As food they reinforced each other nutritionally when combined in diets.

First Peoples originally grew more than a hundred species of plants that are still routinely farmed today. They cultivated crops that would be grown as far north as the climate permitted and that, eventually, would extend production capacity in Europe, corn and potatoes being the best known, although tomatoes, peanuts, pineapples, and cacao (from which chocolate is made) are not far behind. Tobacco was grown for diplomatic, ritual, and some medicinal uses.

In all, the Wendat (as one example) at the time of contact were growing up to 17 varieties of maize and eight types of squash in the Great Lakes area. As well, they gathered more than 30 varieties of wild fruit and at least 10 kinds of nuts, besides other varieties of wild foods.[20]

Of these crops, corn (or maize) was the most important. If properly treated, it lasted over the winter and spring until the new crop began to ripen in summer. This Anishinaabe story gives us an idea of the proper preservation of corn:

> [A]lmost all the Anishinaabe people had a garden where they grew their food so they would be prepared for the coming winter months. I used to watch these men who made dried corn as I was very young and was not really useful in helping them with this activity. They seemed to enjoy the work with shucking the corn as it got to be dark; this was done when the corn was ripe. They would roast the corn over the fire with a stick pushed into the cob of corn. Then they would twirl this stick with the corn stuck to it over the fire, roasting the corn. As soon as one was finished they would put another ear of corn on the stick and begin roasting the corn. Then when the roasted corn cooled off enough they would remove the corn kernels from the cob. They would spread the corn kernels on [husks laid] on the ground and in direct sunlight so the corn would continue to dry.[21]

HISTORICAL BACKGROUND | The Puzzle of Corn

Corn presents a puzzle in tracing the early attempts at agriculture by the peoples of the Americas. By the 1500s, Indigenous Peoples were growing at least 150 varieties, adapted to a wide array of conditions.[22] However, if a wild corn once flourished, researchers have not found it. Two wild grasses related to corn—teosinte and tripsacum—still grow in the highlands of Mexico. Teosinte (the name is Mexican, meaning "mother of corn") can be crossbred with domesticated corn, but it needs equal hours of daylight and darkness and warm temperatures. Corn, in contrast, was being grown from Lake Huron all the way through to southern Chile when Europeans arrived.

The oldest site known where corn may have been developed as a crop is in central Mexico, where tiny cobs dated to 7000 BCE have been found. Stone tools for grinding corn appeared about 5,000 years ago and are still used today. The mortar and pestle also served the same purpose. Corn needed about a thousand years of selective breeding to produce the many varieties first encountered by Europeans. The main modification since has been for the cobs to become larger.

Corn cannot survive without human intervention, as it lacks the capacity to reproduce itself. It is among the most efficient crops in the world in terms of yield.[23] Its development is one of the world's great achievements in plant science.[24]

Animal Resources

Indigenous agriculture concentrated on plants rather than animals, but in terms of resource management in a broader sense, Indigenous Peoples exerted a lot of control over animals. Fishing played a part in these early resource management efforts. Classic Maya agriculturalists, for instance, were also fish farmers. North American farmers and hunters used fire to control directly the movements of animals, such as those of the buffalo on the Plains, and to modify vegetation, which in turn influenced the animals' feeding patterns. For instance, by the sixteenth century, the farming peoples of the Northeastern Woodlands of North America had transformed their habitat into one particularly suitable for deer—the so-called "deer parks."[25] There is ample evidence that stocks of game animals and fish were closely monitored and harvested accordingly.

Our Lives are in the Land, 48" x 60", Acrylic on Canvas, 2014. Permission granted by the artist.

Our Lives Are in the Land by Christi Belcourt (b. 1966), a Métis artist and activist. She explains: "The plants are teachers. They are connected to each other, and all other spiritual beings through the sacredness of life. When I remember who I am—a human being connected to all of life—I remember also that I am loved by the spirit world and our ancestors. And when I remember this, I remember to respect even the smallest of things."

Elaborate ceremonies were undertaken to preserve adherence to the practice of conservation and at all times the water was revered as a source of life and sustenance. The bodies of water themselves were revered for their abundance, and Indigenous Peoples did not take this abundance for granted. Reminders, in the form of ceremony, art, prayer, and stories—particularly trickster stories involving Raven, Nanibozhoo, Glooscap, and others, depending on the people—helped (and continue to help) Indigenous Peoples to remember the importance of resource conservation.[26] On the northwestern Plains, "where the sky takes care of the earth and the earth takes care of the sky,"[27] there were wide fluctuations in population of Indigenous Peoples, with considerable influxes from surrounding areas during seasonal hunts. The bison hunt provided the basis for these cultural patterns.[28] From about 7000 BCE to 4500 BCE, however, higher temperatures and drought decimated the herds of giant bison by cutting down on their food supply. Afterwards, the bison were of the smaller variety with which we are familiar today.

Hunters used both drives and jumps, depending on the conformation of the land. The greatest number of jump sites was in the foothills of the Rocky Mountains. Pounds were more common on the Plains. In Canada, most of the drive sites are in what is now the region occupied by the provinces of Saskatchewan and Alberta. One of the earliest jump sites, dated to more than 5,000 years ago, was **Head-Smashed-In** in southern Alberta.[29] It would continue to be used until the 1870s. This was an enormous site, so big that its use was an international affair. Recent archaeology has revealed 30 mazeways along which the buffalo were driven, and up to 20,000 cairns that guided the direction of the stampeding herds. Head-Smashed-In might also have been a trading centre, providing bison materials such as pemmican and hides in return for dried maize, manufactured goods, and possibly tobacco.[30] These forms of hunting called for co-operation and organization within bands but also between bands and nations.

In general, campsites were located on lookouts. Some found in Alberta include several hundred tipi rings, indicating long use. There may be more than a million such rings scattered throughout Alberta.[31] Medicine wheels, important for hunting rites, ringed the bison's northern summer range. Some were in use for at least 5,000 years.[32]

Whatever the type of communal hunting, strict regulation was involved. When several nations gathered for such a hunt, camp police enforced the rules. Penalties could include the destruction of the offender's dwelling and personal belongings.[33] In contrast, when herds were small and scattered, individuals could hunt as they pleased. This careful system of resource management was one of the first practices to be disrupted by European contact (see Chapter 3).

Cultural Adaptations and Geography

As groups of people spread to various regions across the northern half of North America they adapted to different climates and to the resources those regions provided. These vast geographic differences help us to understand the differences in cultural adaptations made by the groups of people who settled the area that would become Canada. Ecologists divide Canada into broadly defined ecological regions called biomes, ecozones, or biotic provinces, which differ immensely based on climate, flora, fauna, and soil types. These distinct regions, however, commonly have transitional zones between them that show some characteristics of both regions. Two ecozones cover most of what is now northern Canada. The tundra in the Far North is a region with an extremely cold climate, little vegetation, and maritime mammals such as polar bears, whales, walrus, and harp seals. Adjacent to the tundra, chiefly in northern Ontario around James Bay and Hudson Bay, but also, to a lesser extent, in northern Quebec and Manitoba, is the Hudson Bay Lowland. There are trees in this biotic province, mainly black spruce and tamaracks, but they tend to be smaller than members of these species growing in warmer climates. This relatively small region supports numerous migratory waterfowl and small mammals as well as some large mammals, such as moose, caribou, and, in the northern reaches, some polar bears.

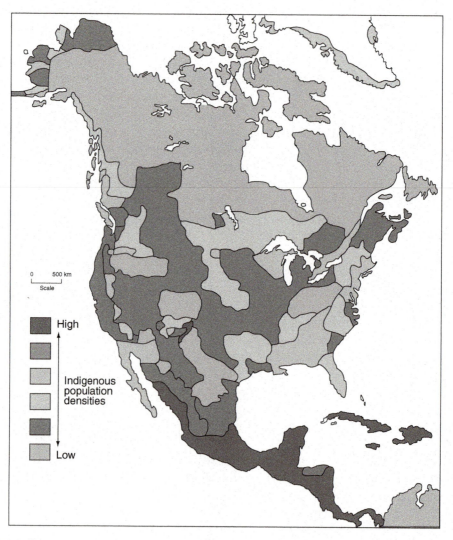

Map 2.1 Indigenous population densities in 1500 ACE.

© Carl Waldman, *Atlas of the North American Indian* (New York: Facts on File, 1985). Reprinted with permission of the publisher.

Map 2.2 Indigenous culture areas.

Waldman, *Atlas of the North American Indian*; R. Bruce Morrison and C. Roderick Wilson, eds, *Native Peoples: The Canadian Experience* (Toronto: McClelland & Stewart, 1986).

The boreal forest (taiga) extends from the Atlantic Ocean all along the rugged uplands of the Canadian Shield, through the northern reaches of the present-day Prairie provinces, and into northern British Columbia, the Northwest Territories, and Yukon. This densely wooded area of coniferous trees includes black spruce, white spruce, white pine, red pine, and eastern cedar, as well as a few broadleaf deciduous species such as white birch. The moose, the beaver, and the black bear are the most important of the region's animals. To the south is the Great Lakes transitional ecozone. The climate of this area of the Great Lakes and the St Lawrence

Valley is moderated by the huge inland seas that are the Great Lakes. As the name implies, the area includes the flora and fauna of both the boreal forest and the Carolinian forest to the south. The Carolinian species include broadleaf deciduous trees such as maple, ash, and oak. Deer are the most important large animal of the Carolinian forest.

To the west of the Great Lakes and south of the Shield and the boreal forest lie the grasslands of the Canadian Plains. This area is called the grasslands or prairie ecozone, although the agricultural development of the nineteenth and twentieth centuries has rendered it the most dramatically transformed region in the world. The grasslands that stretched from the woodlands in the east to the Rocky Mountains in the west supported massive herds of bison. Furthest west, along the Pacific coast, lies the temperate Pacific maritime ecozone. This region is dominated by huge mountains in the east and by the cedar forests of the coastal ranges in the west. It is populated by grizzly bears, elk, and bighorn sheep on land and by salmon and numerous other marine species in the coastal waters and rivers.

The environment of each of these biomes provided resources that in turn shaped the cultural adaptations of the particular groups who lived there. In the Far North the Inuit were hunter-gatherers. They hunted seals, walruses, whales, caribou, and muskox. Ivory from walrus tusks had a great value. The Inuit gathered edible seaweed called *kuanniq,* Arctic berries, bone, and soapstone. These comparatively meagre resources provided them with all they needed to eat and to clothe themselves. The harsh climate and their relative isolation helped to shape their world view. The culture of the Inuit is rich with tales of travelling vast distances to hunt and to find food. Relationships in Inuit communities were less formal or hierarchical than in other societies as people sought ways of adapting to their sparsely populated region.

The resources of the Hudson Bay Lowland and of the tundra–boreal forest transition zone to the west supported the Dene peoples, and to the east supported the Cree in the Hudson Bay region, as well as Inuit farther to the north in present-day Quebec and Innu to the east in Quebec and Labrador. These people hunted for caribou and other game, including waterfowl such as ducks and especially geese. They sought berries, grasses, roots, and tubers for use as nutrients, flavourings, and medicines. As with the Inuit, the relative isolation of the Omushkegowak and the Mushkegowuk, the Innu, and their adaptations to the region's extreme climate kept them in small family hunting groups with more informal social relations. Their stories, like those of the Inuit, focus on travel and hunting themes and identify the necessities of the world around them with reference to the environmental features that shaped their culture.

The Ojibwa people are a good example of a group who lived in the region of the boreal forest. The Ojibwa hunted for moose and beaver, gathered tubers, berries, and birchbark, and were active traders in the pre-contact period. The ecological basis for trade was more easily exploited by the Ojibwa than by those groups further to the north because of the relative proximity of trading partners. They traded the thick beaver pelts of the region north of Lake Superior to the Odaawa and Wendat peoples to the south. In return they received the agricultural products of those people: corn and tobacco. Like their northern neighbours, the Ojibwa lived in small, patrilocal family hunting groups and followed an annual round in search of different kinds of fish and game. Young couples lived with the male's family, probably because their economy was dominated by hunting, a primarily male pursuit according to the gender division of labour—though there is evidence that women also hunted small game such as birds and rabbits.

The Great Lakes transitional region was the most diverse of all of Canada's regions as it included the flora and fauna of two bordering ecozones. This meant that the Odaawak and the Wendats, who both lived in the region, had made complex cultural adaptations to their environment. They fished for the whitefish of the Great Lakes; they hunted the moose and beaver of the boreal forest and the deer of the Carolinian forest; and they practised agriculture, growing corn, beans, squash, and tobacco along the northern fringe of the growing zones for these crops. The Odaawak manufactured mats from the rushes of the Carolinian forest and birchbark canoes and boxes from the birch trees. The Wendats made wooden clubs, mortars, and pestles from the hardwood of the Carolinian trees. Both groups gathered blueberries, nuts, birchbark, and other non-timber forest products. Most importantly, their economic diversity gave both groups the impetus to trade, and this led to a relatively high level of contact with other groups (see more on trade below).

Both the Odaawak and Wendats held large feasts at specified times of the year to trade and to renew alliances with their neighbours. Both groups were matrilocal, as agriculture—an activity led by women—dictated living with the mother's family. Although they were similar in terms of their cultural adaptations, the Odaawa and Wendat peoples had important differences. The Odaawak spoke Anishinaabe-mowin while Wendats spoke an Iroquoian language, like the people of the Haudenosaunee Confederacy to the south and east. Like others who spoke an Iroquoian language, the Wendats lived in longhouses and relied more heavily on agriculture

INDIGENOUS LEADERS | Georges Sioui (b. 1948)

Georges Sioui was born in Wendake (Village-des-Hurons) in 1948 and currently is an associate professor in the Department of Classics and Religious Studies and Coordinator of the Aboriginal Studies Program at the University of Ottawa. In 1991 he received his Ph.D. in history from Laval University, making him the first person from a First Nations community to be awarded a doctorate in history in Canada. His first major publication, *Les Hurons-Wendats: une civilisation méconnue* (Laval University Press, 1994), was favourably received and provides much-needed balance to the history of the Wendat people. Sioui felt a strong personal imperative to do his part to set the record straight after his early exposure to the Jesuit interpretation of the Wendat past. Sioui, like others of his people, is very concerned with the powerful connections that exist between the Wendat and the geography of the Great Lakes–St Lawrence region. His beliefs, as expressed in all of his work, are strongly personal and he has long made an impassioned argument for what he terms autohistory, that is, a history written according to the oral traditions and personal experiences of the people themselves. For Sioui, such a history has very strong links to the land, waters, and resources of the places inhabited from time immemorial by Indigenous Peoples.

than did the people of the Odaawa nations. Both the Odaawak and Wendats were matrilocal, but the Odaawak were patrilineal while the Wendat nations were matrilineal, taking their clan identities from their mother's line and following the directions of their powerful grandmothers, the heads of the clans.

The Siksikawa of Niitsitapiikwan (the Niitsitapi Confederacy) in what is now southern Alberta cannot be understood without reference to the bison (buffalo), the most important resource of the grasslands. The Siksikawa, like the other peoples of the Plains, the Nakoda and Dakhóta, made shelters and garments from bison hides and subsisted on bison meat, either fresh or dried as pemmican. The Siksikawa also gathered berries, tubers, grasses, and other products of the grasslands. They lived in larger groups as bison hunting required the participation of large communities, and as a result they had a very formal social structure. Not surprisingly, the bison played a large role in Siksika storytelling, for if the entire community did not co-operate in the hunt the consequences could be dire.

Like all Indigenous Peoples, the people of the Niitsitapiikwan understood that the consequences of upsetting the delicate balance of the natural world were also dire. This is illustrated time and again in the oral tradition, and in particular in those stories describing the various schemes of the trickster: Napi or Old Man Coyote of the Siksikawa (see below), Weesakachek of the Nehiyaw, Nanibozhoo of Anishinaabe, and Glooscap of the Mi'kmaq and Wabanaki. Through these tales the importance of careful resource management is emphasized and re-emphasized.

In the moderate Pacific maritime region, people such as the Haida established large, palisaded, permanent villages. They built very large canoes out of giant cedar trees and fished the coastal waters. Haida culture is best represented by their exquisite totem poles, which were expressions of their beliefs and their warrior ethic as they sought to defend their territory and its rich resource base from external threats. Haida society was divided into two groups, the Raven and the Eagle, and each Haida family belonged to one or the other of these groups. Chiefs were usually the heads of the largest families within the groups and they were chosen according to a matrilineal succession. Membership in the family groups was claimed through the mother's family.[34]

Social Development

For a variety of reasons, including the geographic and economic determinants discussed above, social development varied throughout the Americas. While most Indigenous societies operated on an egalitarian basis, some societies, especially those that were more sedentary and had a rich resource base, such as on the west coast, developed complex hierarchies based on kinship.

Egalitarian and Hierarchical Societies

Economically **egalitarian societies,** which did not bestow status based on material wealth, did not separate authority from the group as a whole. In some cases, they even went to considerable lengths to ensure that such a separation did not occur. In those societies, available resources were open to all and their leaders used influence rather than force.[35] Free sharing ensured that the skills of, say, a superior hunter benefited the group rather than just the individual hunter. The power of chiefs depended on their ability to provide for their followers—status was based on merit, skills, public acclaim, or biological descent. The leaders' role was to represent the common will. With a few important exceptions, they did not use force, and they would have quickly lost their positions if they had tried.[36] This lent extreme importance to eloquence, the power to persuade. A chief's authority was "in his tongue's end; for he is powerful in so far as he is eloquent." Failure in this regard meant loss of position.[37] Among the Mi'kmaq—whose territory covered much of the coastal Atlantic region of what is now Canada—a chief could attract followers, but they were not subordinated to their leader's will,[38] except, perhaps, in time of war. Even in warfare, however, among many groups the individual was essentially his own leader. Perhaps most important of all, chiefs were expected to set an example for their people, in particular by being generous. Instead of gaining wealth through their positions, they could end up the poorest of the group because of the continual demands made on their resources.[39] This concept is illustrated in a Siksika trickster story:

> Old Man inveigled a fox into a conspiracy against four buffalo bulls. "My little brother," he said, "I can think of only one way to get these bulls. I will pluck all the fur off you except one tuft at the end of your tail. Then you will seem so funny to them that they will laugh themselves to death." This implausible scheme proved surprisingly successful: upon seeing the plucked fox the buffalo began to giggle among themselves. Rolling over in hysterics they soon laughed themselves to death. As the Old Man butchered his victims, the fox sat nearby, his back humped up, his teeth chattering in the icy air. When the last bull had been cut up, Old Man looked at the hairless fox and remarked, "It's pretty cold isn't it? Well we don't care for the cold. We've got our winter's meat and we'll have nothing to do but feast and dance and sing until spring." The fox did not reply. Old Man prodded him and the fox keeled over, frozen dead in the cold.[40]

Selection of leaders was based on qualification, although the sons of chiefs often succeeded their fathers. Besides the established leader, certain individuals, because of their particular skills and spiritual powers, could be chosen by social consensus to organize and lead such group activities as the buffalo hunt, a raid, or a seasonal transfer in the pursuit of food. However, the authority involved in such positions lasted only as long as the task or project at hand. Should a rival chief appear or factionalism result in a split, the dissident group could always break away and establish itself elsewhere. To avoid this factionalism, some groups, including the Anishinaabek of the Great Lakes, maintained both hereditary chiefs and chiefs chosen by consensus.

The general lack of quarrelling or interpersonal conflict in Indigenous communities impressed Europeans, who wondered how peaceful relations could prevail without the threat of force in the background. One European visitor reported in the eighteenth century that some chiefs were skilful leaders, as they knew "how to confine their commands within the limits of their power."[41] First Peoples, for their part, were not impressed when they saw Europeans being afraid of their captains, "while they laugh at and make sport of theirs."[42]

Such observations indicate how easy it was for Europeans to miss the subtleties of Indigenous social controls. Respect was exceedingly important, and within their spheres of competence, the chiefs did have authority.[43]

The Northwest Coast was the only area in what is now Canada where **chiefdoms** developed (such as those of the Haida, Nuu'chah'nulth, Kwakwaka'wakw, and Tsimshian). They had clearly marked class divisions between chiefs, nobles, and commoners based on wealth and heredity. There was also grading within each class.[44] Overriding class and even ethnic distinctions among the northern groups (Tlingit, Haida, and Tsimshian) was the division of each of these groups into two parts that researchers call "moieties,"[45] in turn subdivided into clans, which recognized descent only through the female line. Farther south, the Kwakwaka'wakw, Bella Coola, and Nuu'chah'nulth had no such moieties. They reckoned descent through both the female and

The Great Serpent Mound is an earthwork approximately 400 metres long in what is now southwestern Ohio. Radiocarbon dating has confirmed the long-held belief that this was built by the Adena people (ascendants of several Anishinaabe peoples, including the Giiwigaabaw, Myaamiaki, Mesquakie, Osaakii, and Shaawanwaki), and has helped narrow the date when it was built to approximately 300 BCE.

the male lines, and practised a ritual life characterized by secret societies. These traits were less evident among the Coast Salish. In general, their chiefs also had less power. The Salish word for "chief" translates best as "leader."

Chiefdoms varied considerably in their social complexities and centralization of authority. What they had in common was concern with rank based on lineage, through which their redistributive economies functioned. As well, they developed sophisticated artistic traditions, each in a different sphere (the Californians in basketry, the Northwest Coasters in woodwork, the Ohioans and Mississippians in stone sculpture and shell and copperwork, the east coasters in feather work and hide painting, and the Adena-Hopewell-Mississippian [*c.* 3000 BCE] in monumental earthworks).

Why some societies shifted from being egalitarian groupings of mobile peoples to become hierarchical sedentary or semi-sedentary chiefdoms, and eventually socially complex city-states, still puzzles historians.[46] There is impassioned argument in the discipline of history as to how humans became urbanized.

Trade and Alliance

As social development throughout the Americas varied, relationships between Indigenous Peoples also varied. Variations between hunting and gathering societies and those who picked up aspects of agricultural cultures created differences in resource strengths and needs, which encouraged co-operation and trade. The ecological basis for trade meant that the way of life of each was richer for their interchange. For example, the people who hunted buffalo on the northern Plains traded with various agricultural people who farmed along the Missouri River. This trade made it possible for each group to retain its specific character. Similarly, some farming peoples retained their hunting-gathering mode even as some of their neighbours developed into city-states, and, in one or two cases, empires.

The Indigenous Peoples of the Americas lived within cultural frameworks that met social and individual needs by emphasizing the group as well as the self. This was true even among those peoples, particularly in the Far North, whose groupings changed with the season and availability of food. Land, like air and water, was for the benefit of everyone, and so was communally owned. Because of the extensive coastline (the longest of any nation in the world), many of the First Peoples within what would become Canada had a maritime orientation. However, the great variety in the area's geographical regions (Arctic, Subarctic, Northeastern Woodlands, Great Plains, Plateau, and Northwest Coast) resulted in many variations on fundamentally similar ways of life.[47] For example, many of the Indigenous groups in central Canada had a lacustrine or a riverine orientation.

Trade and Gift Diplomacy:
An Important Part of Interactions

Uneven distribution of resources, and an ecological basis for trade, ensured that all of these people traded. In general, some people had access to greater agricultural opportunities while others had better hunting and fishing opportunities. Good relations, alliances, and the transfer of spiritual powers were of utmost importance in these exchanges, rather than economic considerations. However, there could be trade with an enemy if the parties could agree on a truce. Conflicts between the Haudenosaunee and the peoples of the Great Lakes were always resolved by re-establishing a trade.[48] They sealed agreements by an exchange of gifts and hostages, which led to the formation of blood ties. Alliances were less important in the Far North, where hostilities were expressed in chance killings or raids rather than in warfare.

Indigenous Peoples measured wealth either in material goods or in immaterial rights, such as those to certain songs, dances, or rituals. The principle of sharing prevailed as far as the basic necessities of life were concerned and a moral imperative to share was a distinctive feature of all Indigenous communities. The kinship groups divided up the village's hunting, fishing, and gathering territories. Acquiring prestige called for generosity. Individuals traded for goods to give away on ceremonial occasions, such as the potlatch on the west coast. **Gift exchanges**—"I give to you that you may give to me"[49]—were a social and diplomatic obligation. Indigenous Peoples presented gifts when people visited each other; on special occasions, such as marriage and name-giving; or for obtaining the return of prisoners of war. Status was important in these exchanges. The higher the rank of the recipients, the greater the value of the gifts.

Gifts also sealed agreements and alliances with other peoples.[50] Indigenous Peoples did not see treaties as self-sustaining. To be kept alive, treaties needed to be fed every once in a while by ceremonial exchanges. Later, during the colonial wars, periodic gift distributions would be essential in maintaining the alliances that proved so useful to the colonizing powers. Gift distribution helped to keep the alliances intact when periodic setbacks threatened to dismantle military co-operation that was of vital importance to both sides.

Trade goods could travel long distances. For instance, obsidian, valued for tools because of its keen cutting edge and also for ceremonial purposes because of its beauty, has been found on archaeological sites far from its place of origin.[51] The copper trade was also active. Various kinds of shells, depending on the region, were also much in demand for personal adornment and because of their commercial, diplomatic, and ceremonial value and use.

There is no archaeological evidence for the extent of the trade in perishable goods.[52] We know that Indigenous Peoples extensively traded oolichon oil (derived from candlefish), which they used as a condiment, from the Pacific coast into the interior along established routes that came to be known as "grease trails." In eastern Canada, trade dates back at least 6,000 years.

Allies and a Great League of Peace: Great Lakes Region, Huronia, and People of the Longhouse

At the time of first European contact, the Great Lakes region[53] held a vast range of Indigenous Peoples practising a wide variety of economic strategies. There were hunter-gatherers, agriculturalists, and many groups whose economic activities included hunting, gathering, agriculture, trade, and manufacture. Those who spoke Iroquoian languages and some Anishinaabek, such as the Odaawak of the Great Lakes—"land of the white pine"—had adopted agriculture, in addition to hunting, and were sedentary. Those who spoke Iroquoian languages lived in longhouses clustered in palisaded villages that had up to 1,500 inhabitants or more.[54] They moved their villages to new sites every 10 to 50 years when local resources, such as land and firewood, became exhausted. Apart from the Anishinaabe-speaking Odaawak, they spoke related languages.[55]

Sometime during the sixteenth century, or perhaps earlier, groups of people who spoke Iroquoian languages organized into confederacies that would have powerful impacts in regional politics.[56] The northernmost was that of the Wendat Confederacy,[57] an alliance of five nations. To the south, in what is now southern Ontario, was the confederacy of the Chonnonton people, about whom little is known. In the Finger Lakes region of today's central New York State was the Haudenosaunee Confederacy.

The Wendat Confederacy was concentrated between Lake Simcoe and the southeastern corner of Georgian Bay, an area of about 2,300 km². As far north as agriculture was possible with a Stone Age technology, the Wendat Confederacy had about 7,000 acres (2,800 ha) under cultivation. In **Wendake**,[58] "it was easier to get lost in a cornfield than in a forest."[59] The members of the Wendat Confederacy traded with the northern tribes, supplying them with corn, beans, squash, and tobacco, as well as twine for fishnets, in return for meat, hides, and furs. The beauty and bounty of the land were such that when the French first came to their country, the Wendat assumed it was because France was poor by comparison.[60]

By the end of the sixteenth century, Wendake counted an estimated 30,000 people—compared to 16,000 in the Haudenosaunee Confederacy[61]—who lived in up to 25 villages. The largest, Cahiagué, belonged to the Arendarhonon (Rock) nation[62] and may have had a population of 5,000. These villages were concentrated close to each other at the centre of Wendake. Cornfields formed a surrounding belt. Because of this, all Wendat people could understand each other, and their language was used in the northern trade networks.

Situated at a crossroads in the North American trading networks, Wendake dominated regional trade routes. It also dominated the political scene. It had surrounded the rival Haudenosaunee Confederacy with a system of alliances that extended as far as the Susquehannocks (Andastes, Conastogas), about 800 km to the south. Wendake apparently absorbed at least some of the St Lawrence Iroquoians who were dispersed during the sixteenth century, an event in which the Kanienkehaka of the Haudenosaunee Confederacy seem to have had a hand.[63] Despite this strength, however, Wendake would rapidly disintegrate before the realignment of forces brought about by the intrusion of European trade.

The Great Peacemaker, Dekanawidah, "Heavenly Messenger," whose name is always treated with great reverence, and his disciple, Hiawatha (Hionwatha), "One Who Combs," founded the Haudenosaunee Confederacy.[64] Its symbol was the White Tree of Peace, above which hovered an eagle, a very wise bird "who sees afar," indicating preparedness. According to tradition, Hiawatha dedicated himself to peace when he lost his family in an inter-tribal feud. The chairman of the Great Council bore the title Thadodaho (Atotarho), after the warlike chief whom Dekanawidah and Hiawatha converted to peaceful ways.[65]

The territory of the Haudenosaunee Confederacy (the People of the Longhouse) was larger than the lands of the Wendat Confederacy, although their population was smaller. The league's territory stretched from the Mohawk River in the east to the Genesee River in the west, a distance of about 180 km. It was a geographic position that would become strategically important to the European colonies on the east coast, as it controlled the major routes from the coast to the interior. Each member nation occupied its own villages, usually two or more. Each also had its own council, as did each group, whose council usually met in the nation's largest village. Women had the right to choose sachems (leaders selected from within certain families or clans)[66] and order their removal. Haudenosaunee social organization included division into phratries and clans, as on the Northwest Coast. The Great League of Peace was another name for the Haudenosaunee Confederacy.

Aside from the Northwest Coast, all the other nations whose land would make up Canada hunted and gathered food, although some were also at least partly agricultural and others had felt the influence of farming cultures. The Ojibwa,[67] for example, relied on an uncultivated crop, wild rice (*Zizaniaaquatica*). Wild rice, as is insinuated by the name, resists cultivation, but is an excellent source of nutrition when harvested from the wild. Their care of wild rice stands resembled farming, although their dependence on wild rice was much less than that of farmers on their crops—Iroquoians grew 80 per cent of their food requirements.[68]

The Nipissing and Omamiwinini, both allies of the Wendat Confederacy, did some planting, but they were too far north for this to be an important source of food. The Innu also seem to have practised some slash-and-burn agriculture.[69] The Gwich'in and related Han and Tutchone of present-day Yukon, like other hunting peoples, "encouraged" the growth of medicinal plants near their encampments.[70] The Mi'kmaq and Wuastukwiuk of the Atlantic coast, on the other hand, had at one point been an agricultural people but returned to hunting and gathering when the ecological changes wrought by the Little Ice Age (*c.* 1300–1850) made farming on the northern Atlantic coast unsustainable. According to their traditions, and confirmed by archaeology, they descend from a people who have been in the region for over 10,000 years.[71]

Hostilities

Inter-group hostilities were widespread in the Americas, but organized warfare was more common in the sedentary societies.[72] Indigenous Peoples did not fight to gain land or to subjugate others, but rather to protect access to natural resources, and then later to avenge the fallen. The Ojibwa historian Basil Johnston makes this connection between the importance of hunting and the subsequent connection to conflict abundantly clear in *Ojibway Ceremonies*:

> The Anishinabeg were primarily men of peace, visionaries who depended upon hunting for survival. Since the worth of a man was measured by his generosity and by his skill in the hunting grounds, bloodshed was not the final test of manhood in Anishnabeg society. Instead, the War Path was followed when it was deemed necessary to avenge an injury, whether real or imaginary, to oneself or to one's brother. It was a matter of pride never to let insult or injury go unpunished—but never was conflict begun for the purposes of conquest or subjugation.[73]

When an Ojibwa war party left its village the men gave a ritual address explaining the purpose of their participation. This example was recorded in the early nineteenth century: "I seek,

I seek our fallen relations; I go to revenge, revenge the slain, our relations fallen and slain, and our foes, our foes shall lie like them, like them they shall lie; I go to lay them low, to lay them low."[74]

Along the Northwest Coast the nature of warfare changed after contact with Europeans and the resulting epidemics and depopulation, but the underlying cause of conflict was the same: concern over resources. An exchange from the contact period makes this clear: "We see your ships and hear things that make our hearts grow faint. They say that more King-George-men will soon be here, and will take our land, our firewood, our fishing grounds."[75]

In the Far North, where competition over scarce resources was even more extreme, war parties sometimes set out to acquire people and possessions, especially canoes. (Those of the west coast were dugouts, the manufacture of which was slow and laborious.)[76] The members of the Haudenosaunee Confederacy, on the other hand, used prisoners as a means of maintaining their population numbers in the face of the high rate of attrition in their ranks caused by the cyclical warfare. Young men captured in battle were often subjected to a complex re-quickening ceremony in which they were given the identity and relations of a slain Haudenosaunee warrior. Those prisoners who refused to take part were summarily killed. Loot was a less important military objective.[77] In the Great Lakes region, wars were fought when scarcities of game animals forced rival groups to trespass into their neighbour's hunting territory. Reparations were a means of controlling killings resulting from blood feuds. Among traders such as the members of the Wendat Confederacy, this developed into an elaborate system.

Questions to Consider

1. How were the routines, assumptions, and compelling experiences of daily life shaped by adaptations to the various ecozones across Canada?
2. Discuss the ecological basis for trade that existed across the regions.
3. What explains the rise of egalitarianism among Indigenous Peoples?
4. With reference to ecological differences across the regions, explain the importance of trade among Indigenous Peoples.

Recommended Readings

Boatman, John. *My Elders Taught Me: Aspects of Western Great Lakes American Indian Philosophy*, Milwaukee: University of Wisconsin-Milwaukee, 1991.

Deloria, Vine, Jr. *Red Earth, White Lies: Native Americans and the Myth of Scientific Fact*. Golden, Colo.: Fulcrum, 1997.

Ellis, C. Douglas, ed. *Cree Legends and Narratives from the West Coast of James Bay*. Winnipeg: University of Manitoba Press, 1995.

Heyerdahl, Thor. *Early Man and the Ocean: A Search for the Beginnings of Navigation and Seaborne Civilizations*. New York: Vintage Books, 1980.

Hoffecker, John F. *A Prehistory of the North: Human Settlement of the Higher Latitudes.* New Brunswick, NJ: Rutgers University Press, 2004.

McClellan, Catharine. *Part of the Land, Part of the Water: A History of the Yukon Indians.* Vancouver: Douglas & McIntyre, 1987.

McGhee, Robert. *Canadian Arctic Prehistory.* Toronto: Van Nostrand Reinhold, 1978.

Sassaman, Kenneth E., and Donald H. Holly, eds. *Hunter-Gatherer Archaeology as Historical Process.* Tucson: University of Arizona Press, 2013.

Shutler, Richard, ed. *Early Man in the New World.* Beverly Hills, Calif.: Sage, 1983.

Weatherford, Jack. *Indian Givers: How the Indians Transformed the World.* New York: Crown Publishers, 1988.

Webkamigad, Howard. *Ottawa Stories from the Springs: Anishinaabe dibaadjimowinan wodi gaa bin-jibaamigak wodi mookodijiwong e zhinikaadek.* East Lansing: Michigan State University Press, 2015.

3 First Meetings

CHAPTER OUTLINE

This chapter describes the history of contact between the peoples of the North American continent and the peoples of the European continent and the United Kingdom. We will look at the ways these meetings began to disrupt the First Peoples across what would become Canada, and in particular we will examine some of the early reactions to the arrival of the newcomers.

LEARNING OUTCOMES

1. Students will be able to provide examples of the different kinds of contacts made between Indigenous Peoples and Europeans.

2. Students will gain a sense of the shifting nature of contact from the earliest encounters along the Atlantic coast with the Norse explorers until the arrivals of Basque, Portuguese, and French fishermen in the early years of the sixteenth century.

3. Students will gain further insight into the important differences in economic strategies that Indigenous Peoples employed.

4. Some of the early ontological differences between Europeans and Indigenous Peoples will be more readily understood through an appreciation of their first contacts.

TIMELINE First Contacts

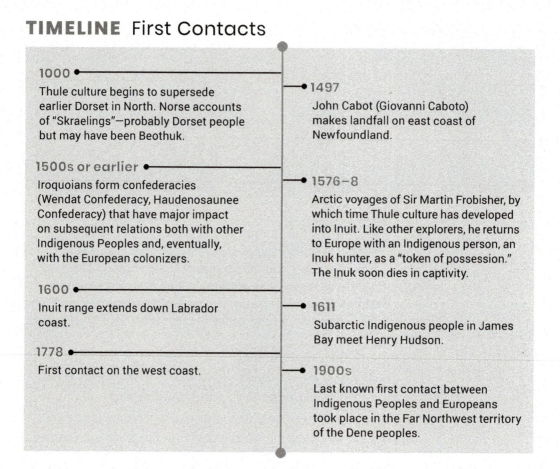

1000
Thule culture begins to supersede earlier Dorset in North. Norse accounts of "Skraelings"—probably Dorset people but may have been Beothuk.

1500s or earlier
Iroquoians form confederacies (Wendat Confederacy, Haudenosaunee Confederacy) that have major impact on subsequent relations both with other Indigenous Peoples and, eventually, with the European colonizers.

1600
Inuit range extends down Labrador coast.

1778
First contact on the west coast.

1497
John Cabot (Giovanni Caboto) makes landfall on east coast of Newfoundland.

1576–8
Arctic voyages of Sir Martin Frobisher, by which time Thule culture has developed into Inuit. Like other explorers, he returns to Europe with an Indigenous person, an Inuk hunter, as a "token of possession." The Inuk soon dies in captivity.

1611
Subarctic Indigenous people in James Bay meet Henry Hudson.

1900s
Last known first contact between Indigenous Peoples and Europeans took place in the Far Northwest territory of the Dene peoples.

Types of First Encounters

First contacts between Europeans and people from the Americas occurred over a period dating from the early eleventh century to the twentieth century.[1] In what is now Canada, the first meetings for which there is archaeological and anecdotal evidence began with the Norse about 1000 BCE[2] and continued as late as 1915, when members of the Canadian Arctic Expedition met isolated bands of Inuit who were completely unknown to the Canadian government.[3] In 1918, Royal North-West Mounted Police, while on a search for an Inuk, were still meeting people who had never seen a non-Indigenous person.[4] However, these Inuit knew of non-Indigenous people, as their ancestors had met them. In other words, first meetings with Inuit occurred, off and on, over a period of more than 900 years. The time span for such encounters with First Nations was about 400 years, with some Dene of the Far Northwest being among the last to meet white people early in the twentieth century.

We can define **first meetings**, of course, in a number of ways. One historian has listed three basic types: collisions, relationships, and contacts, all three of which rarely occur in a pure form.[5]

"Collisions" include the transmission of disease and the slave trade. Trade, evangelization, and colonial administration characterized the second type, "relationships." "Contacts" were encounters, for the most part short-lived, between Europeans and members of a non-European culture, and were usually peaceful, although they often involved ritual displays, such as flag- or cross-planting ceremonies, that could be interpreted as threats and that could lead to eventual collisions.

Contacts can be either pristine encounters—in which one or both sides had no previous knowledge of the other—or first encounters preceded by hearsay, the appearance of new trade goods through local networks, the spread of a new disease, or other evidence, such as the debris left behind by explorers. It is with these subtleties in mind that we will consider "first contacts" here.

The Cultural Exchange between the Americas and Africa and Eurasia

Questions about first contacts take on another character (and become heated) when we consider the possibility of overseas contact between the Americas and Africa and Eurasia before 1000 ACE. Answers arrived at in the present state of our knowledge must be considered as tentative, a pushing back of frontiers perhaps, but not final solutions.

If there were non-Indigenous influences at work in the Americas, they most likely came by the easiest and quickest route available—the sea. Long before the present era, the people of ancient southeastern China became known as Pai-Yueh, the Navigators. We can only speculate as to where these early sailors went. However, the peanut, an American plant, has turned up at two coastal Chinese sites dating to about 5300–4800 BCE,[6] and two varieties of chickens considered to be native to Asia were already established in America when the Spanish arrived.[7]

Chinese records tell of a search for islands in the Eastern (Pacific) Ocean where drugs for longevity could be found, as well as "magical beings and strange things." One such expedition, around 2200 BCE, resulted in 3,000 young men and women being sent a few years later. Their mission was to establish a trade in the longevity drug, but they were never heard from again. Likely we will never know for certain whether this account refers to the Americas. In 458 ACE, Chinese records tell us, the monk Hwui Shan, with four companions, sailed to the east and reached the land of Fu-Sang, believed to be in present-day Mexico, where he stayed for 40 years, returning to China in 499.[8]

In 1956, archaeologists discovered ceramics at Valdivia, in southwestern Ecuador, dated to 5200–4800 BCE, at that time by far the oldest-known such artifacts in the Americas. Their striking resemblance to Japanese pottery set off a wave of speculation that the Japanese introduced pottery-making to the Americas. Eventually, however, even older ceramics that had no resemblance to Valdivia ware came to light, ending that particular debate but leaving open the question of the origin of pottery in the Americas.[9]

In northeastern North America, another fully developed type of pottery called Vinette I by scientists and resembling ceramics from Asia appeared about 3000 BCE.[10] It could have resulted from local experimentations following exposure to the pottery of the mid-Atlantic region. Thus, pottery might have come into what is now Canada from Asia via Alaska and Yukon, or from the south into the east, both before 5000 BCE.[11]

The pottery problem has, if anything, fuelled the controversy over transoceanic contacts in general and their role in cultural diffusion in particular. The issue of the Japanese connection is far from dead, as a particular type of mace considered to be peculiar to Japan has surfaced in Ecuador, dated sometime before 1500 BCE. (Interestingly, in the Far North, the bow and arrow appeared about this time, or shortly before, and spread rapidly southward.[12]) Japanese and Indigenous Peoples are the only peoples to sing death songs. If there was a connection with other peoples, however, Indigenous Peoples were soon experimenting on their own.

As present, however, plants offer the strongest research evidence of early overseas connections between the Americas and other world areas. Accordingly, the scene now shifts to Southeast Asia, mainly Cambodia, southern India, and the Maldive Islands.[13]

The argument here is for a trade contact, mainly with Cambodian Khmers, around 400–1000 ACE. Prevailing winds and currents made such commerce possible, but it could not have lasted past the thirteenth century. Plant evidence indicates an early India–America connection. Both South America and Southeast Asia shared bottle gourds, coconuts, and some varieties of yams. Similarly, cotton, cultivated in Mexico and in Peru before 4500 BCE, seems to have connections to Asia. Some argue that this could have occurred by natural processes, but botanists see this as highly unlikely.[14] People appear to have been involved in the hybridization and cultivation of the domesticated plant that began in northwestern South America, probably Peru.[15] Maize (corn) has added to this botanical puzzle (see Historical Background box in Chapter 2).[16]

Not surprisingly, proponents of ancient contact between the Americas and overseas regions have eagerly supported these two cases. Since there is considerable resistance to the hypothesis of early contact before the time of European exploration, mainly on the grounds of insufficient sea-going technology at that time, the origin and development of gourds and cotton as crops remain unsolved problems.

Further west, we find Egypt and Phoenicia both being advocated for the honour of having reached the Americas. When archaeologist **Thor Heyerdahl** (1914–2002) looked for men who could recreate the ancient type of watercraft required to sail the South Atlantic, he found them at Lake Chad in North Africa and Lake Titicaca in the Andean highlands.[17] Heyerdahl has pointed out that Columbus reached the Caribbean by taking the ocean highway called the Canary Current. Carrying on a little further west, Spaniards later reached the Gulf of Mexico. It is in this region that the Olmec, the "mother" of American civilizations, appeared suddenly in a well-settled area about 3500 BCE during a time of natural disasters in and emigration from Afro-Eurasia. The Olmec influenced later city-states, such as those of the Mayas.

It is not always clear, however, in which direction the influences went. For instance, glyphic writing, once assumed to be an innovation of the Olmec in the Americas, was actually present centuries earlier, before 2600 BCE, at Monte Albán, in the land of the Zapotecs in present-day southwestern Mexico. This was one of the only two sites of the world where writing was indisputably invented. (The other was Mesopotamia, before 5000 BCE.)[18]

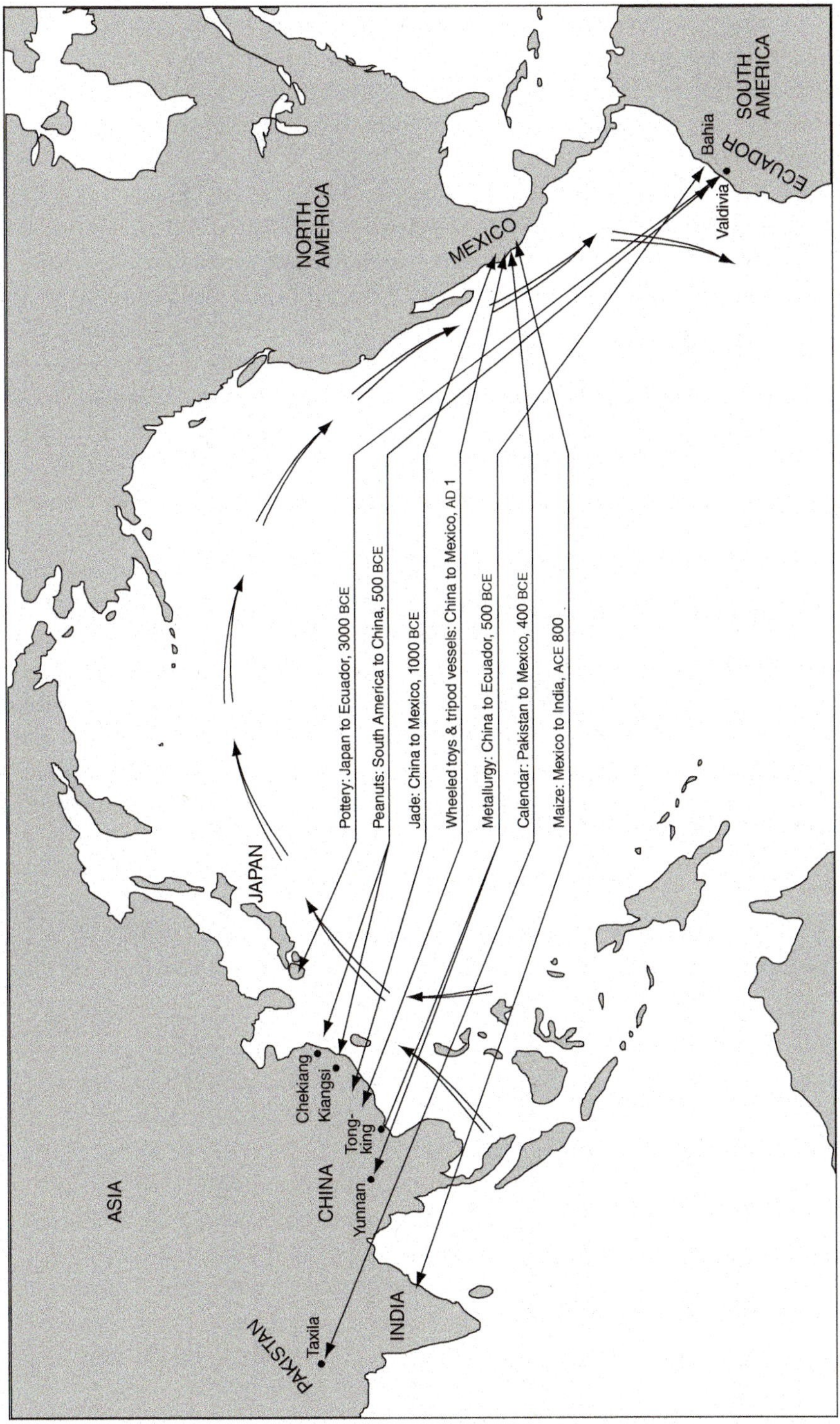
ASIA
CHINA
JAPAN
INDIA
PAKISTAN
Taxila
Yunnan
Tong-king
Chekiang
Kiangsi
NORTH AMERICA
MEXICO
SOUTH AMERICA
ECUADOR
Bahia
Valdivia
Pottery: Japan to Ecuador, 3000 BCE
Peanuts: South America to China, 500 BCE
Jade: China to Mexico, 1000 BCE
Wheeled toys & tripod vessels: China to Mexico, AD 1
Metallurgy: China to Ecuador, 500 BCE
Calendar: Pakistan to Mexico, 400 BCE
Maize: Mexico to India, ACE 800

Map 3.1 Transoceanic exchanges for which there is some evidence.

John Barber, "Oriental Enigma," *Equinox* 49 (Jan.–Feb. 1990): 83–95.

Heyerdahl saw no reason why early travellers, like the Spaniards at a later date, did not sail down the Pacific coast on sea-going rafts, built with balsa logs from Ecuador and equipped with sails. Heyerdahl saw the settlement of Easter Island—with its mysterious giant sculptured heads (some with carefully buried bodies), so different from the giant heads of the Olmec—as originating in the Americas.

As well, the peopling of Polynesia (including Aotearoa/New Zealand), even if largely originating in Southeast Asia as generally accepted, would have had to come via the Americas along the only route available with the available sailing technology—the Japanese Current. The sweet potato, widespread throughout the Pacific, is an American crop. As Heyerdahl saw it, Polynesia was the last region of the world to be populated by humans, and it was by way of the Americas. Genetic studies have revealed a close relationship between South American Indigenous Peoples and Polynesians.[19]

Whatever the outcome of these debates, one point is clear. Prehistory of the Americas was as filled with significant developments as that of Africa and Eurasia. Whatever the degree of overseas influence, the civilizations that evolved in the Americas were distinctively their own—and they likely had similar influence over the civilizations with whom they were in contact. For example, Indigenous Peoples of the Americas were the first masters of platinum metallurgy. Andean metal workers made skilful use of alloys. Peruvians manipulated sheets of gold, "the sweat of the Sun," and silver, "tears of the Moon," into desired forms with particular attention to surfaces and colour, a style called surface transformation.[20] Beaten metal work is even older in the Americas. The Old Copper Culture, in the Lake Superior region and to the south, dates to 6000 BCE. Europeans began very early in their relationship with Indigenous Peoples to benefit from the metallurgy of the Americas.

Varied as the cultures of the Americas were, they fit into a hemisphere-wide pattern and, like Europeans on the other side of the Atlantic, they shared a basic civilization. Scholars have characterized the Indigenous civilizations of the Americas as having "formidable originality."[21]

HISTORICAL BACKGROUND | The Norse and the Skraelings

The Norse who travelled to northern North America reported meeting Skraelings (from "skraelingjar," meaning small), who generally have been thought to be of the culture referred to as the **Dorset** by archaeologists.[22] The Norse thought of them possibly as folkloric creatures. They described them as "very little people," lacking in iron, who "use whale teeth for arrowheads and sharp stones for knives."[23] Another description refers to them as "small ill-favored men" with "ugly hair on their heads. They had big eyes and were broad in the cheeks."[24] The Norse said that the Skraelings were eager to trade the products of the hunt for weapons. That the Norse traded with the Skraelings has been inferred from the presence of European artifacts in Arctic archaeological sites, particularly burials. Even more fascinating was the discovery in Bergen, Norway, the Norwegian port for traffic with Iceland and Greenland, of a walrus figurine of Inuit workmanship. This find was made at an archaeological site dated to the thirteenth century. The written records give us no hint as to what the Skraelings thought of the Europeans.[25]

Norse settlements on northern Newfoundland and mainland Atlantic coasts did not last. There seem to have been four expeditions to Leifsbudir (Leif's booths, now thought to be the site near L'Anse aux Meadows) at the northern tip of Newfoundland, but hostilities developed between the local people and the visitors.[26] At sea, the **Little Ice Age** of about 1300–1850[27] caused the ice pack to thicken, interfering with shipping, which in any event had been irregular and was decreasing due to conditions in Europe. It eventually stopped, cutting off supplies from Norway on which the people's lifestyle (including diet) depended.[28] Eventually, the Norse abandoned their colonies.

The Inuit Meet the Kodlunas

The first recorded encounters with Europeans in the Americas took place in the eastern Arctic, perhaps some of them on Baffin Island, and along the North Atlantic coast of what is now Canada. Two of the peoples likely to have been involved, Dorset and Beothuk, have since disappeared. The Norse explorers who came took advantage of the mild climate of the so-called "Medieval Warm Period" to cross the North Atlantic in search of opportunities for trade, settlement, and conquest.[29]

During the time before the Europeans arrived, the ancestors of the modern Inuit were moving steadily eastward across the Arctic, displacing the earlier Dorset people. The **Thule**, as archaeologists have called them, reached the Atlantic coast sometime during the fifteenth century. The Dorset lingered in the northern Ungava until the fifteenth century. They also held out until about the same time in Newfoundland before giving way to the Beothuk, a proto-Algonquian people who followed a way of life based on the winter caribou hunt and the summer exploitation of sea and river resources. Some pockets of Dorset culture may have continued until the twentieth century on Hudson Bay.[30]

The Thule, like the modern Inuit but unlike the Dorset, possessed the bow and arrow, spear thrower, and sealskin-covered kayaks and umiaks. They used dogs as draft animals. They were the unchallenged masters of the tundra lands beyond the treeline, and other Indigenous Peoples seldom encroached on their domain.[31]

By the sixteenth century, the changing climate favoured the sea mammal-hunting activities of the Inuit, who were advancing eastward and southward down the North Atlantic coast as the weather turned colder and the Little Ice Age reached its most extreme point. When the Inuit met Frobisher during his Arctic voyages in 1576–8, they were already familiar with Europeans and their ships, as they had encountered them on hunting trips to the south.[32] There was no hint about wondering if Europeans were supernatural beings, any more than there had been on the North Atlantic coast when **John Cabot** (Giovanni Caboto) made landfall in 1497. The shock of first encounter seems to have dissipated very early in those northern regions, perhaps with the Norse, perhaps with later, unrecorded meetings. More shocks, however, would follow.

Frobisher brought back an Inuk hunter to England and displayed him as a "token of possession," proof that the explorer had found and claimed new lands for the Queen.[33] The Inuk soon died, but others followed. The Inuit back in the Arctic, for their part, maintained an

Jennie Williams, Nalujuk (2015). Photograph. Image courtesy of the artist.

Inuk artist Jennie Williams photographs Inuit in Nain, Labrador. She photographs people in their every-day environments and circumstances, working to document practices and traditions in the manner they are celebrated today in Labrador, including the tradition Nalujuk Night on Old Christmas (6 January), depicted here, in which adults dress as Nalujuit (bogeymen) and chase children (who, if they are caught, must sing to be released and receive candy).

oral tradition of the time when the kodlunas—as the Inuit called Europeans—visited them.[34] As well, they had carefully preserved odds and ends from Frobisher's visit, such as pieces of red brick and brass rings.[35]

Early English explorers referred to Inuit as "savages"—from the French word "sauvage" meaning natural or wild, but also meaning brutish, violent, and uncivilized—as well as "Indians"; in the eighteenth century, "Esquimaux Indians" was a common term. They were reported to "eate their meate raw" and also to "eate grasse like bruit beasts, without table or stoole, and when their hands are imbued in blood they lick them clean with their tongues." Although the English judged them to be "very tractable" and "easie to be brought to civility," they also considered Indigenous Peoples to be "Idolaters and witches," serious charges in an age when Europeans burned witches alive at the stake and when Christians tended to consider all non-Christians to be enemies.

The closest to sustained contact that developed between Indigenous Peoples of the eastern Arctic and Europeans during this period was through whaling.[36] This began along the Labrador coast and the Strait of Belle Isle, where Inuit met with Basque whalers, and later with French.

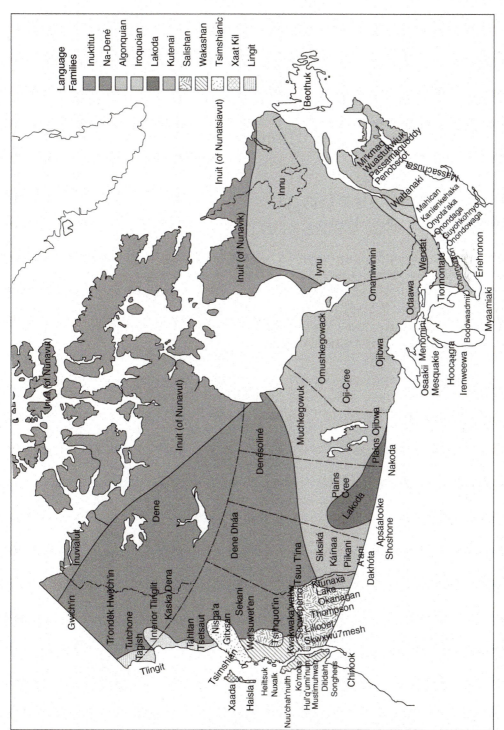

Map 3.2 Indigenous Peoples in and near what will become Canada at time of first contact with Europeans.

Alan D. Macmillan, *Native Peoples and Cultures of Canada* (Vancouver: Douglas & McIntyre, 1988); John Price, *Indians of Canada: Cultural Dynamics* (Scarborough, Ont.: Prentice-Hall, 1979)

These encounters introduced Europeans to Indigenous technology for deep-sea whaling, which from the seventh to the thirteenth centuries was the most advanced in the world. Combined with European deep-sea ships, that technology led to the growth of worldwide whaling.[37]

Arctic whaling would last until the first decade of the twentieth century. The resulting reduction of whale stocks severely affected Inuit domestic offshore whaling and led to changes in hunting patterns. On the positive side, the Arctic environment, which Europeans found unattractive in the extreme, protected Inuit territory. It would be the second half of the twentieth century before there would be a serious intrusion on Canada's northernmost lands and the people who live there (see Chapter 16).[38]

Subarctic Meetings— Different Perspectives

In 1611, more than a century after encounters had become sustained for the Inuit of the North Atlantic coast, a lone Iynu presented himself to **Henry Hudson** on the shores of James Bay.[39] On being given some tokens of friendship, he left to return with the skins of two deer and two beaver, which he offered in trade. The English obliged, and when they showed an inclination to bargain, the Iynu accepted the offer but indicated he did not like it. Picking up his goods, he departed, never to be seen by the English again.

This brief encounter suggests that the Iynu had a clear idea of the exchange rate he expected as well as of trading protocol, perhaps that of the north/south Indigenous networks, which at that time operated as far north as James Bay. Hudson's Bay Company (HBC) chief factor Andrew Graham (c. 1733–1815) reported that the first Indigenous Peoples to trade with Europeans in Hudson Bay were called Oupeeshepow.[40] He added that "they relate the arrival and wintering of the unfortunate Captain Henry Hudson, as handed down to them by the tradition of their ancestors."[41] Hudson seems to have been more eager to meet with Indigenous people than the latter were to meet the English following the encounter with the Iynu. Hudson's motive was simple: he wanted fresh meat. In this, he was disappointed, for "though the Inhabitants set the woods on fire before him, yet they would not come to him."[42]

The Iynu, for their part, have a startlingly different remembrance of their first trade with the English. In an episode that seems to have occurred somewhat later and to have involved a group rather than just an individual, they recall that the English wanted the fur clothing they were wearing and persuaded them to trade the clothes off their backs in exchange for European garments.[43] Explorers John Davis (?1550–1605) and **Jacques Cartier** reported similar incidents, although both men reversed the perspective. As they saw it, the Indigenous people were so eager for trade, they willingly parted with the clothes they were wearing, and not necessarily for European clothing.

The Iynu at the mouth of the Churchill River have an oral tradition of seeing strange signs and then meeting Europeans, who invited them aboard their ship. They were not afraid to accept, because from "the expression on the strangers' faces, they could tell they were welcome aboard."[44] Sporadic trade did not develop into a continuing relationship at this time, however. Violence all too often marked what contact there was, although contacts were usually peaceful at first.

The "Fish"—by Any Definition—Brought Europeans to the North Atlantic Coast, and Contact Turned into Conflict

Apart from the Inuit, the mainland Indigenous North Americans who have the longest history of contact with Europeans are the First Nations of the North Atlantic coast. This started with Cabot's visit, at a time when Christopher Columbus was between his second and third voyages and Spanish colonization of the West Indies was just beginning.

It was a contact that can best be described as casual, at least at first, although exchanges—of foods, agricultural produce, technology, and disease—occurred from the very beginning of contact in what has been called "the Columbian Exchange" (see Historical Background box). The Europeans had come not to colonize but to exploit the enormously rich fishing grounds, the whale runs up the Strait of Belle Isle between present-day Newfoundland and Labrador, and the walrus rookeries of what the French would call the Magdalen Islands in the Gulf of St Lawrence. Then as now, oil was big business, and with the adoption of Inuit hunting techniques, whales became the main source of supply, along with walrus. Fish was also in demand because the European religious calendar counted 153 meatless days a year.

Exploiting sea resources, especially the cod fisheries, did not involve the type of close or sustained contact with the local population

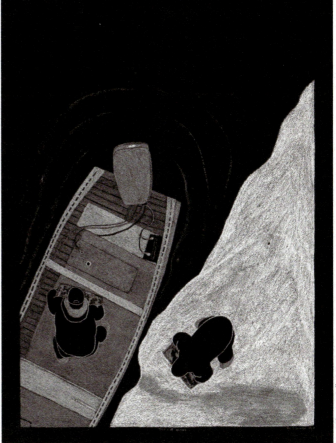

Dorset Fine Arts Gallery

A depiction of fishing in Kimmirut, Nunavut, by Inuk artist Tim Pitsiulak (1967–2016). Pitsiulak spoke of his artistic inspiration: "I am a hunter and I know the land and animals of the north. I am particularly inspired by the bowhead whale, because nobody really knows much about them. My inspiration to be an artist comes from my aunt, Kenojuak Ashevak, because she is the oldest and the best."

that the fur trade would later require. Until the fur trade began in earnest and European settlement got underway, the comings and goings entailed in the fisheries (a term that included whaling and seal and walrus hunting) allowed Indigenous Peoples and Europeans to pursue their separate lifestyles without much consideration for each other. By 1600, Inuit had expanded down the Labrador coast, occasioning sporadic hostilities throughout the French regime. By the 1690s, most French settlers in Labrador were on the south shore, numbering about 40 families. The English spread along Labrador's east coast into about 30 harbours and coves, some counting only one family each.[45]

By the second half of the eighteenth century, under the British, not only was settlement expanding even more, but also white trappers were competing with Inuit for fur and game resources. Hostilities increased, with each side raiding and killing as opportunities arose. The Inuit had the advantage of a huge hinterland, inhospitable to Europeans, to which they could retreat. The situation was such that Sir Hugh Palliser, governor of Newfoundland from 1764 to 1768, issued a proclamation in 1764 urging that the "Eskimo Indians" be treated as friends.[46] Less fortunate in this regard were the Beothuk.

The Beothuk Experience—Resistance and Genocide

We know very little about the **Beothuk**, who hunted on land and sea in what is now called Newfoundland. Not even their language is certain, although it may have been a variant of proto-Algonquian. They seem to have had an association with the Inuit. From earliest encounters, Europeans described the Beothuk as "inhuman and wild." At first, however, mutual tolerance—or, perhaps, a mutual distance—operated, and visiting Basques left fishing gear and boats in whaling ports over the winter without loss or damage.

The Beothuk people have usually been portrayed as being nervous of the European explorers. This is likely because the Portuguese explorer Gaspar Corte-Real took 57 Beothuks to be sold into slavery in 1500. This is an overlooked episode in the history of exploration, but it does throw light on the Beothuk reaction to the arrival of strangers.[47]

Eventually, thefts and hostile incidents accumulated into a feud that embittered both sides. The fishermen needed shore space for their drying racks ("flakes"). Often, they erected them on sites favoured by the Indigenous inhabitants for summer fishing. Mounting irritation between Beothuks and Europeans is only too evident in the references that have come down to us. According to France's top navigator at the time, the Beothuk had "no more God than beasts, and are bad people." The poet Pierre Crignon (c. 1464–1540) was no more complimentary: "Between Cape Race and Cape Breton live a cruel and rude people with whom we can neither deal nor converse."[49]

The Beothuk retreated as far as they could into the interior of the island, occasionally emerging in their cyclical rounds to attempt their traditional fishing, if the European presence did not frustrate them. Alternatively, they raided any European gear they could find.[50] Early in the

HISTORICAL BACKGROUND | The Columbian Exchange

The Columbian Exchange refers to transfers, whether of goods, disease, or technology and whether intentional or unintentional, between Europe and the Americas. The effects of these exchanges on the civilizations involved were profound.

DISEASES*	
Diseases endemic to the Americas	Bacillary and amoebic dysentery; viral influenza and pneumonia; arthritis; rickettsial (micro-organismic) fevers; viral fevers; American leishmaniasis (protozoan); American trypanosomiasis (parasitic protozoans); roundworms and other endoparasites; syphilis and pinta (both treponemal infections); and a mild form of typhus. Other illness attributed to arthritis, tuberculosis (especially spinal varieties), treponemal infections, Paget's disease (osteitis deformans), periostitis, acute osteomyelitis, and myeloma (bone cancer); dietary deficiency in maize-rich economies; anemia and dental problems
Diseases whose existence in the Americas before 1492 is debated	Malaria, yellow fever, pulmonary tuberculosis, venereal syphilis
Diseases that were certainly introduced by Europeans, Africans, and their livestock and animals	Smallpox, measles, influenza, bubonic plague, diphtheria, typhus, cholera, scarlet fever, trachoma, whooping cough, chicken pox, tropic malaria
Diseases that were probably introduced to Europeans by Americans	Syphilis
PLANTS	
American plants eaten by Europeans	Maize, many kinds of beans, peanuts, potato, sweet potato, sassafras, manioc (tapioca, cassava), squash, pumpkin, papaya, guava, avocado, pineapple, tomato, chili pepper, paprika, cocoa; soybeans originated in Southeast Asia, but some beans originating in the Americas include lima, pole, curry, kidney, French, navy (haricot), snap, string, and frijole
American non-food plants adopted by Europeans	Tobacco, rubber, some cottons, brazilin (dye from brazilwood tree), sisal (for rope)
Plants imported for consumption by Europeans	Wheat, chickpeas, melons, onions, radishes, salad greens, grapevines, sugar cane, orchard fruits (e.g., olives); bananas were brought from the Canaries in 1516

Continued

Plants imported for commercial reasons by Europeans	Sugar, cotton, rice, indigo (for blue dye), brazilin, cochineal (red dye extracted from the female Dactylopius coccus insect), achiote (yellow dye)
Plants imported by Europeans for livestock	Some forage plants and clover, although most would have travelled informally, in clods of mud, folds of textiles, etc.
Other plants imported by Europeans	Kentucky bluegrass, dandelions, daisies

ANIMALS	
domesticated animals brought to the Americas by Europeans	Horses, dogs, pigs, cattle, chickens, sheep, goats, cats, donkeys**
Accidental imports by Europeans to the Americas	Rats

Note: This is not a complete list.[48] Other examples of contributions to world culture are drugs such as quinine (used in malaria prevention and cure) and cocaine and precious metals. Europeans also adopted technology from the Americas, such as the canoe and whaling implements, whereas Indigenous Peoples embraced such things as metal knives and implements and, later, guns. In the first half of the sixteenth century, for example, the amount of silver and gold in circulation in Europe tripled. The amount that came from South America was 10 times the combined output of the rest of the world.

*There were at least 17 major epidemics between 1520 and 1600. Death toll estimates among Indigenous people across North America range from 30 per cent to 75 per cent. The earliest European accounts of the Americas all spoke of the "great multitudes" of people. Later, when colonization was gaining momentum, large stretches of territory were found unoccupied, as the spread of disease had preceded the European advance, and the notion of an "empty continent" gained currency.

**The Americas had some dogs and chickens. Horses had originated in the Americas but became extinct.

Noble David Cook, *Born to Die: Disease and New World Conquest, 1492–1650* (Cambridge: Cambridge University Press, 1998); Alfred W. Crosby, *The Columbian Exchange: Biological and Cultural Consequences of 1492* (Westport, Conn.: Greenwood Press, 1973); Bruce Trigger and Wilcomb E. Washburn, *The Cambridge History of the Native Peoples of the Americas*, vol. 1 (Cambridge: Cambridge University Press, 1996); Jack Weatherford, *Indian Givers: How the Indians of the Americas Transformed the World* (New York: Broadway Books, 1988); Nelson Foster and Linda S. Cordell, eds, *Chilies to Chocolate: Food the Americans gave the World* (Tucson: University of Arizona Press, 1992).

seventeenth century, an English admiral reported that operations were being hampered "because the Savages of that country . . . secretly every year come into Trinity Bay and Harbor, in the nightime, purposely to steale Sailes, Lines, Hatchets, Hookes, Knives, and such like."[51] Few early colonizers tried to establish a working relationship.

In the hard and unforgiving landscape of Newfoundland, the Beothuk reaction to contact is easy to understand. People (rightly) feared that their carefully managed resource base was being threatened by the newcomers. The different technologies possessed by these newcomers made the threat all the more worrisome. The increased presence along the south coast of Newfoundland by the Wabanaki and Mi'kmaw nations, and along the northwest coast by some Mi'kmaw fishing parties, served to heighten the tension. These peoples had been long-time trading partners of the Beothuk and had been welcome participants in the seal hunt. Eventually, however, they were encouraged, first by the French and then by British colonizers, to turn against the Beothuk in exchange for European weapons. The Beothuk fought back hard and, sadly, the reputation they left to history has suffered for the determined defence of their home.[52]

Once settlement began, the feuding turned into an open hunting season against the Beothuk. Official control was sporadic, a condition that benefited the fishing industry. Newfoundland was not declared a colony until 1824. By that time, there were practically no Beothuk left. One of the last of her people, Demasduit (Shendoreth, Waunathoake, Mary March, 1796–1819), was captured following a Beothuk raid of a salmon boat but died of tuberculosis before she could be returned to her people. Shanawdithit, who was Demasduit's niece, was deemed the "last known Beothuk" by European settlers and, like Demasduit (see Indigenous Leaders box), shared what she could of her people's language and customs before she died in 1829.[53]

Fur, Felt, and Spread of Disease

In the sixteenth century, the felt hat, which had been around for at least 200 years, became an essential fashion item in Europe. This created a strong demand for beaver fur, from which felt was made, so much so that the European beaver was trapped to near extinction. Then, in 1534, Frenchman Jacques Cartier sailed into the mouth of the river that he would name after Saint Lawrence and met men and women wearing the furs so coveted back in Europe. Cartier and others were quick to see the advantage in dealing more directly with these "New World" people than the fishermen had. European goods thus entered trade networks that had existed from time immemorial. Furs and the goods they were traded for would pass from hand to hand, carrying microscopic stowaways into the continent ahead of the white traders, so that European diseases, most notably smallpox, decimated groups of Indigenous Peoples long before they had direct contact with the newcomers.

INDIGENOUS LEADERS | Demasduit (1796–1819)

In March of 1819 a group of armed fur traders went to Red Indian Lake in Newfoundland to chase away the Beothuk people with whom they had been in conflict. One of the Beothuk women, Demasduit, was captured and her husband, Nonosabasut, was killed when he came to her aid. Demasduit was taken to St John's and there she spent the rest of her short life co-operating with her captors and asking to be returned to her family. She displayed no ill will to those who had killed her husband and taken her prisoner, but rather she provided the Anglican missionary John Leigh with as much information as she could for his compilation of a Beothuk vocabulary. She died while waiting to be returned to her people but her legacy lives in Leigh's work.

John Hewson, *Beothuk Vocabularies* (St. John's: Newfoundland Provincial Museum, 1978), 33–55.

Indigenous and European Ethos: Differences That Would Lead to Misunderstanding

The existing trade networks and sources of conflict were not the only barriers to understanding that existed between the First Peoples and the European colonizers. The difference between the American ethos and that of the Europeans was striking. Indigenous society was, for the most part, egalitarian. Its people viewed humans as part of a transcendent universal system. Europe, on the other hand, was a society of nation-states, patriarchal rule, and developing capitalism. Its people were convinced that humans were not only the centre of the universe but its controlling force.[54] As we will see when we come to the fur trade, European men would come to depend on Indigenous women in ways they must have found surprising.

Differences were particularly evident in attitudes towards land. For Indigenous Peoples, land existed for the benefit of all. For Europeans, it was private property, individually owned. In Europe, game was usually the property of the ruling classes and hunters who were caught taking game were charged and very harshly treated. In the Americas, game belonged to the entire community and skilled hunters were highly valued. At the time of first contact, however, differences were not as great as they would later become.

Some Europeans could and did adapt to Indigenous life, against the wishes of colonial officials. Even so, on first arrival, the Europeans did not see any resemblances to their own way of life.[55] As late as the end of the seventeenth century, Le Clercq could repeat in all earnestness the old saying that had been around since the days of Columbus, that Indigenous Peoples had neither faith, nor king, nor law.[56] How could they, since they were not dominated by patriarchal chiefs or captains with the power to command (recall the discussion of Indigenous Peoples' family and governing structures in Chapter 2)?[57] What was clear to Europeans from the start was that the first inhabitants were independent and so did not have a shared system of military defence. Individual nations banded together in confederacies, and those confederacies did defend one another, but this always took a great deal of time to organize. They did not have diplomatic mechanisms in place that would have allowed them to unite quickly to prevent the invasion and takeover of their lands. The tendency towards fragmentation had been effective for survival before prolonged European contact. Later, the colonizers would use the fragmentation that came with diversity as an instrument for European domination.

Questions to Consider

1. What patterns emerged from the earliest contacts between Europeans and Indigenous Peoples?
2. What were some of the causes of conflict between Indigenous Peoples?
3. What were some of the technologies the Indigenous societies of the Americas gave the world?
4. What were the some of the early difficulties that arose from contact?

Recommended Readings

Canadian Museum of History/Musée Canadien de l'Histoire. "Inuit and Englishmen: The Nunavut Voyages of Martin Frobisher." At: http://www.museedelhistoire.ca/cmc/exhibitions/hist/frobisher/frint01e.shtml.

Eber, Dorothy Harley. *When the Whalers Were Up North: Inuit Memories from the Eastern Arctic.* Montreal and Kingston: McGill-Queen's University Press, 1989.

———. *Encounters on the Passage: Inuit Meet the Explorers.* Toronto: University of Toronto Press, 2008.

——— and Pitseolak Ashoona, *Pitseolak: Pictures out of My Life.* Montreal and Kingston: McGill-Queen's University Press, 2004.

Grant, John Webster. *Moon of Wintertime: Missionaries and the Indians of Canada in Encounter since 1534.* Toronto: University of Toronto Press, 1984.

Marshall, Ingeborg Constanze Luise. *A History and Ethnography of the Beothuk.* Montreal and Kingston: McGill-Queen's University Press, 1996.

Morrison, R. Bruce, and C. Roderick Wilson, eds. *Native Peoples: The Canadian Experience*, 3rd edn. Toronto: Oxford University Press, 2004.

Paul, Daniel N. *We Were Not the Savages: A Micmac Perspective on the Collision of European and Aboriginal Civilization.* Halifax: Nimbus, 1993.

Trigger, Bruce G. *The Children of Aataentsic: A History of the Huron People to 1660*, 2 vols. Montreal and Kingston: McGill-Queen's University Press, 1976.

4 On the Eastern Edge of the Mainland

CHAPTER OUTLINE

In this chapter we will explore the history of contact and the early relations between the Indigenous Peoples of the Atlantic coast and the European colonizers. First we will examine the reaction of Donnakoh-Noh and the Stadakohnan people to the arrival of strangers from across the Atlantic. Then we will turn to see how the Mi'kmaw, Innu, and Wabanaki nations adapted to the important, dramatic, and rapid changes brought about by contact with the Europeans. Throughout this chapter we will examine the differing perspectives on important issues like landownership and exchange.

LEARNING OUTCOMES

1. Students will gain insight into of one of the great mysteries in Canadian history: the disappearance of the Stadakohnan and Hochelagan peoples, known to history as the "St Lawrence Iroquoians."

2. Colonization created great challenges for Indigenous Peoples, and students will gain an understanding of the way those challenges presented themselves from the very first contact.

3. The alliances forged between Indigenous Peoples and European colonizers date from the early contact period, and students will gain an awareness of the ways in which both sides attempted to defend their interests through the building of alliances.

TIMELINE Origins of the French Alliance

1534

The Iroquoian village Stadakohna, at present site of Quebec City, witnesses Jacques Cartier's first voyage to Canada. Two sons of Chief Donnakoh-Noh accompany Cartier on his return trip to France.

1535–6

Donnakoh-Noh's two sons return to Stadakohna with Cartier. Cartier then kidnaps the pair plus Donnakoh-Noh and other headmen and takes them back to Europe. They all die in France.

1541

Cartier's last voyage, with settlers to establish a colony. This attempted settlement lasts only two years. Hochelaga, at site of present-day Montreal, is largest Iroquoian settlement.

1603

Innu meet Samuel de Champlain at Tadoussac, at the mouth of Saguenay River. Champlain joins in celebration of Innu victory over Haudenosaunee. Innu Chief Anadabijou seals friendship pact with Champlain and French.

1608

Champlain founds Quebec on Stadakohna site; the Stadakohnan and Hochelagan villages are gone and the people driven away and killed in long war with Kanienkehaka and other members of the Haudenosaunee and likely, too, in battles with Mi'kmaq.

1610

Mi'kmaw Chief Membertou greets the French, who re-establish Port Royal (Annapolis Royal) in present-day Nova Scotia.

1627

Charter of La Compagnie des Cent Associés.

1629

Wabanaki envoy sent to Quebec to seek closer ties with French in trade and in their battles with the Haudenosaunee Confederacy.

1629–32

The Innu, who were in a dispute with the French, help the English gain control of Quebec.

1635

Death of Champlain ends, for a time, the alliance between Eastern Wabanaki and French.

1642

French establishment of Montreal; importance of Tadoussac as trading centre begins to wane, as does Innu hegemony in region.

1670s

Marriage of Pidianske, daughter of a Penobscot sagamore, to a French officer ends traditional hostility between Eastern Wabanaki and Mi'kmaq; both groups now allied with French.

Continued

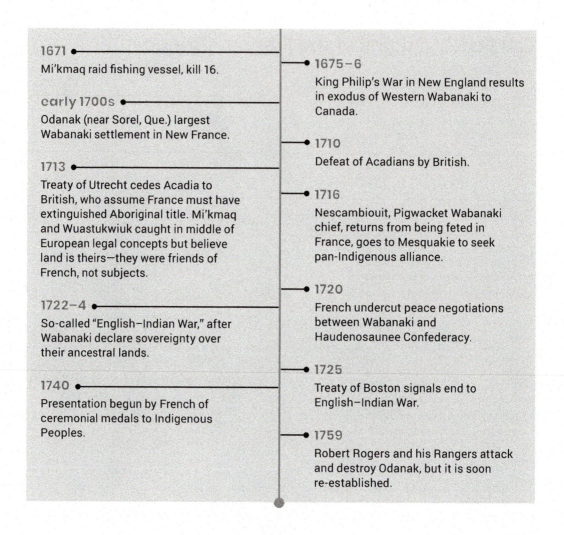

1671
Mi'kmaq raid fishing vessel, kill 16.

1675–6
King Philip's War in New England results in exodus of Western Wabanaki to Canada.

early 1700s
Odanak (near Sorel, Que.) largest Wabanaki settlement in New France.

1710
Defeat of Acadians by British.

1713
Treaty of Utrecht cedes Acadia to British, who assume France must have extinguished Aboriginal title. Mi'kmaq and Wuastukwiuk caught in middle of European legal concepts but believe land is theirs—they were friends of French, not subjects.

1716
Nescambiouit, Pigwacket Wabanaki chief, returns from being feted in France, goes to Mesquakie to seek pan-Indigenous alliance.

1720
French undercut peace negotiations between Wabanaki and Haudenosaunee Confederacy.

1722–4
So-called "English–Indian War," after Wabanaki declare sovereignty over their ancestral lands.

1725
Treaty of Boston signals end to English–Indian War.

1740
Presentation begun by French of ceremonial medals to Indigenous Peoples.

1759
Robert Rogers and his Rangers attack and destroy Odanak, but it is soon re-established.

The Voyages of Cartier

While coasting along the Gaspé during his first voyage to Canada (1534), Cartier met members of the Stadakohnan nation, St Lawrence Iroquoians presumed to have come from **Stadakohna**, a village on the present site of Quebec City. Cartier recorded:

> They go quite naked, except for a small skin, with which they cover their privy parts, and for a few old furs which they throw over their shoulders. . . . They have their heads shaved all around in circles, except for a tuft on the top of the head, which they have long like a horse's tail. This they do up upon their heads and tie in a knot with leather thongs.

Although Cartier claimed that these men showed great pleasure at meeting the French, "they had made all the young women retire into the woods, except two or three who remained, to whom we gave each a comb and a little tin bell, at which they showed great pleasure."[1] At this display of friendship, the Stadakohnan leader called the other women from hiding so that they, too, could receive gifts.

This friendliness would not last, however, particularly after Cartier persuaded Chief **Donnakoh-Noh** (d. 1539) to let his two sons, Tayagnoagny and Domagaya, go with him to France on his return voyage. Cartier's purpose was to train them as interpreters for the fur trade, in which he was successful. However, he apparently also expected them to act in the French interest when he brought them back to Stadakohna on his second voyage (1535–6), but the pair would prove to be true to their own.

Unfortunately, we do not have the story of this first contact from the perspective of the Stadakohnan people. Few extant stories offer an Indigenous perspective on the first contact with the Europeans, but the story of the floating island is a classic one, albeit one that is couched in the somewhat ponderous rhetoric of Silas Rand, a late nineteenth-century Baptist missionary to the Mi'kmaq. In this version, given by Mi'kmaw Elder Josiah Jeremy, some of the problems of trying to make sense out of momentous change are made clear:

> When there were no people in this country but Indians, and before any others were known, a young woman had a singular dream. She dreamed that a small island came floating in towards the land, with tall trees on it, and living beings,—among whom was a man dressed in rabbit-skin garments. The next day she related her dream, and sought for an interpretation. It was the custom in those days, when one had any remarkable dream to consult the wise men, and especially the magicians and soothsayers. These pondered over the girl's dream, but could make nothing of it. The next day an event occurred that explained all. Getting up in the morning, what should they see but a singular little island, as they supposed which had drifted near to the land and become stationary there. There were trees, on which a number of bears, as they supposed were crawling about. They all seized their bows, arrows, and spears, and rushed down to the shore intending to shoot the bears; what was their surprise to find that these supposed bears were men, and that some of them were lowering down into the water a very singularly constructed canoe, into which several of them jumped and paddled ashore. Among them was a man dressed in white,—a priest with his white stole on—raising his hand towards heaven, and addressing them in an earnest manner, but in a language they could not understand. The girl was now questioned respecting her dream. Was it such an island as this that she had seen? Was this the man? She affirmed they were indeed the same.[2]

Cartier was a better sailor than diplomat. The explorer had no doubt that he had "discovered" Canada,[3] as the north shore of the Gulf of St Lawrence was called. On his first visit, he had erected crosses of possession on the Gaspé and at Stadakohna.[4] Ironically, an account published later in France would describe Stadakohna as a seat of royal residence.[5]

During his second voyage, Cartier sailed up the river against the wishes of the Stadakohnan people, who controlled upriver traffic. The Stadakohnan chiefs responded by barring the Europeans from travelling up the river, the first example of a defensive strategy that would become a standard Indigenous response to the European onslaught. Territoriality was an important component of Indigenous Peoples' economic strategy—it was a vital component of resource management—and the Stadakohnan chiefs enforced their control over the river as a means of protecting their territory against the aggressive colonizing of the French explorers.[6] Cartier then kidnapped Donnakoh-Noh (see Indigenous Leaders box), his two sons, and other headmen, and took them back with him to France. None of them returned to their homeland.

Cartier's third and last voyage to Canada was in 1541, when he brought settlers for a colony that Lieutenant-General Jean-François de La Rocque de Roberval (c. 1500–60) was going to establish. Roberval, however, did not arrive until the following year. By then, the Stadakohnan people had become hostile, harassing Cartier and killing his men.[7] Cartier gave up after 10 months and returned home. Roberval did not fare any better. He was overly severe with his colonists and mistreated the Indigenous Peoples. He returned to France within the year after running out of food.[8] France's first attempt at colonizing the Americas had lasted less than two years: 1541–3.

Hochelaga was the largest of 14 villages on the north shore of the river, with about 50 longhouses and a population of 1,500. As with Stadakohna, it would later be described in grandiose terms.[9] But by the early seventeenth century, not one of these villages remained, and the language spoken at Quebec during the time of Cartier was "no longer heard in that region."[10] The people had become victims of a long war in which the Kanienkehaka were said to have been the aggressors (see Historical Background box).[11]

INDIGENOUS LEADERS | Donnakoh-Noh (d. 1539)

The history of Donnakoh-Noh provides us with the first Indigenous leader known to European historians. It also provides us with our first specific act of Indigenous resistance. On 24 July 1534 Jacques Cartier erected a cross some 10 metres high at the mouth of Gaspé harbour. Donnakoh-Noh came out to Cartier's ship and "pointing to the cross he made a long harangue making the sign of the cross with two of his fingers; and then he pointed to the land all around about, as if he wished to say that all this region belonged to him, and that we ought not to have set up this cross without his permission." Donnakoh-Noh was to head a long list of Indigenous leaders who confronted the newcomers with the courage of their convictions and determination to demonstrate a prior claim.

HISTORICAL BACKGROUND | The Disappearance of the Stadakohnan and Hochelagan People

The period just before the arrival of the Europeans seems to have seen warfare escalate to major proportions.[12] Cartier reported that 200 Stadakohnan people were killed in an encounter with the Mi'kmaq two years before his second voyage.[13] The Stadakohnan people fished in the Gaspé during the summer, and there may have been rivalry over access to ocean resources. Trade, traditional hostilities, and European-introduced epidemics might also have been factors. Furthermore, climatic changes caused by the Little Ice Age would have been disastrous for agriculture so far north. This could have made things worse for the Stadakohnan people, to the point where they were no longer able to resist the attacks of the Kanienkehaka warriors.[14]

However, accumulating evidence points ever more clearly to the dynamism of Iroquoians in late pre-contact times. Profound large-scale social and cultural changes had been underway long before the arrival of the Europeans. What happened afterwards may well have been, for the most part, a continuation of these processes and developments, with European-related factors playing only a small role.[15] The Stadakohnan and Hochelagan people probably withdrew westward, to join the Wendat Confederacy.[16]

Apparently, even though Europeans had been barred from travelling up the river, some of their trade goods had filtered into the interior through Indigenous networks. Soon, demand was growing faster than supplies.[17] Difficulty in obtaining items like iron axes might have been galling to the Haudenosaunee, especially the Kanienkehaka, who during the sixteenth century did not have direct access to European trade but who were keenly aware of neighbours, particularly those in Hochelaga, the village where today we find the city of Montreal, who did. Resorting to warfare to obtain what they could not get by peaceful means, they attacked the villages controlling the St Lawrence River, particularly Stadakohna. By the time **Samuel de Champlain** (*c.* 1570–1635) arrived on the scene in the early 1600s, the river was deserted except for roving Kanienkehaka war parties, which had spread such terror that other First Nations hardly dared to hunt in the area.[18]

The Innu and the Fur Trade

In contrast to the Beothuk and Stadakohnan people, Algonquian-speaking Innu and Mi'kmaq accommodated themselves comparatively peacefully to Europeans. It may have been the Innu who smoke-signalled Cartier at the mouth of the Strait of Belle Isle north of the Gulf of St Lawrence during his first voyage in 1534.[19]

According to oral traditions, particularly those of the Innu, the Haudenosaunee had pushed the Innu into the Subarctic before the arrival of Europeans. Later, the prospect of European trade lured these hunters of the northern interior to the coast. The Naskapi of Labrador exploited maritime resources as well as caribou. The Innu, living in the heavily forested interior but roaming as far as Newfoundland, depended mainly on moose in winter and freshwater fish in summer.[20]

When Champlain first met the Innu at Tadoussac in 1603, they were celebrating a victory over the Haudenosaunee with their allies, the Omamiwinini and the Wuastukwiuk. These raids and counter-raids continued until the mid-seventeenth century. In the meantime, Champlain joined in the victory celebrations at the invitation of Innu chief Anadabijou (*fl.* 1611) and sealed a pact of friendship with him and his people, which allowed the French to establish on Innu territory but did not involve land title.[21] Anadabijou's son and heir, Miristou, later known as Mahigan Aticq Ouche ("Wolf" and "Stag," indicating both cruelty and gentleness, d. 1628), would develop this relationship. The reason for his interest lay back in Europe: Canadian furs were in even greater demand following the Swedish capture in 1583 of Narva, the Baltic port through which Western Europe obtained furs from the Russians.

The Innu Control of the Early Trade

The French were quick to take advantage of the new source for furs through alliances with the First Nations who controlled the source of supply. They adopted Indigenous diplomatic protocol and negotiated these accords by means of gift distributions accompanied by feasting and speeches. The Innu, for their part, had a particular interest in cultivating the relationship, as **Tadoussac**, at the mouth of the Saguenay River on the Gulf of St Lawrence, was within their territory. Its location on the southern edge of the taiga and beyond the northern edge of agriculture, and its ease of access, had made it a favourite trading place for northern hunters and southern agriculturalists.

The Innu controlled the trade up the Saguenay. Therefore, they found themselves in an advantageous position as more and more European ships came to trade. Tadoussac became an outlet for interior trading networks that extended as far north as James Bay and as far west as the Great Lakes.[22] It was a position the Innu were to enjoy for more than half a century, until they were bypassed by the establishment of Quebec in 1608, nearly three decades after the St Lawrence had been reopened. Both sides benefited from the trade. In addition to furs, the Europeans got toggling harpoons for whaling, moccasins, maize, and potatoes. The Indigenous Peoples got knives, small mirrors, and other European manufactured goods. They also established the foundations for an alliance with a European power.

One item that had been popular since the early days of trading was the copper kettle. The gun, on the other hand, was not widely used by Indigenous Peoples. Until the end of the seventeenth century few people in the Northeast used guns for hunting, although they had adopted them for warfare long before that because of the terror they induced. As tools of hunting, however, guns of this period were unreliable, scarce, and dependent equally on shot and powder.

That the Innu prospered from this early access to a wide variety of trade goods is indicated by the quantity of presents received from chiefs of different nations at the installation in 1643 of Georges Etouat (d. 1648, a Christian convert, as his given name indicates) as "Captain" at Tadoussac.

Friction between Trading Partners

Trade occasionally led to disputes, violence, and even deaths.[23] Such incidents put strains on the alliance, and Champlain's insistence on European-style punishment rather than Indigenous-style reparations when Frenchmen were the victims did nothing to ease the tensions. When the French leader arrested an Omamiwinini man from the Kitche-sipirini nation on suspicion of murder, a displeased Chief Tessouat threatened reprisals.[24] In other cases, cultural misunderstandings led to unintended insults. One chief, who was offended with the inappropriate gift he

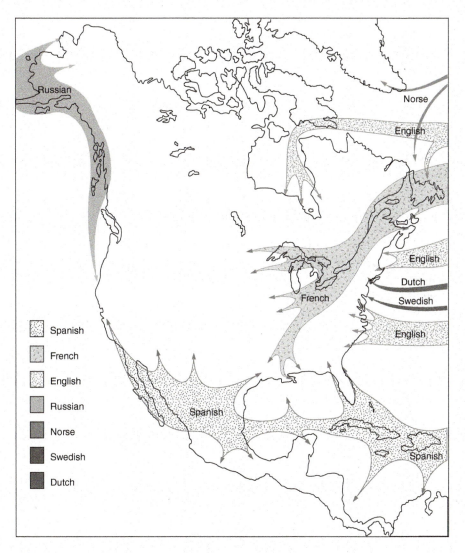

Map 4.1 European penetration of North America.

Waldman, *Atlas of the North American Indian*; Geoffrey Barroclough, ed., *The Times Atlas of World History* (Toronto: Fitzhenry & Whiteside, 1978), 161.

had received from a French captain during pre-trade ceremonies at Tadoussac, told his people to come aboard the ship and help themselves to what they wanted, paying what they wished.

Another problem area was the exchange rate. The flexibility of the French in this regard did not go down well. Once a rate had been agreed on, the Indigenous people expected it to be maintained for everyone. One chief, being offered a special deal for himself but excluding his people, indignantly turned it down with the words, "I am a chief; I do not speak for myself; I speak for my people."[25] Neither did they accept the concept of fluctuating prices according to supply and demand.

Perhaps the most serious problem of all, at least from a long-range point of view, was the overexploitation of resources that the trade encouraged. There were those, such as Jesuit historian Pierre-François de Charlevoix (1682–1761), who were appalled at the destruction. A "handful" of French had arrived, he said, in a land abounding with wildlife. Less than a century later, it was already noticeably less so.[26] Later, David Thompson would observe that in the West "Every intelligent Man saw the poverty that would follow the destruction of the Beaver, but there were no Chiefs to control it; all was perfect liberty and equality."[27] Understandably, traditional lifeways—including careful resource management—were not designed to withstand the forces of capitalist resource exploitation. Some Indigenous people were reported to have joined in the slaughter, killing even the breeding stock. Such examples, however, are more a reflection on the disruptive forces associated with European contact than they are evidence of some new movement away from the time-honoured practice of careful resource management.[28]

The Trade Shifts Westward

With the establishment of Quebec, it was not long before the Innu were replaced by the Wendat as main trading partners of the French (see Chapter 5). Tadoussac, once the hub of the Canadian fur trade, lost importance as the French penetrated further and further up the St Lawrence, finally establishing Montreal in 1642.

Despite their initially favourable trading position and the protection their Subarctic habitat afforded them, the Innu shared in the population decline that most Indigenous Peoples experienced after the arrival of Europeans. Outside the mainstream of colonial activity, the Innu pursued their traditional way of life with little modification or interference. They shared with the Inuit the advantage of a hinterland that was very large, relatively inaccessible, and forbidding to Europeans. It would be centuries before Western technology would be capable of exploiting economically the mineral and hydroelectric potentialities of this huge area. In the meantime, the Innu controlled, at least to a certain extent, the terms of their contact.

Who "Owns" the Land, and What Does Ownership Involve?

The coastal Mi'kmaq, like the Innu, quickly found advantage in the European presence.[29] This relationship began with the fisheries, which had first attracted European attention to the region. With their close relatives, the Wuastukwiuk, the Mi'kmaq willingly entered into the service of Europeans for a few goods or a little pay, doing "all kinds of work, such as cleaning and

http://www.alansyliboy.ca/petroglyph-humans

Little Thunder **by Alan Syliboy.** An established Mi'kmaw artist, Alan Syliboy's artistic vocabulary is inspired by the Indigenous petroglyphs of Nova Scotia. The character shown here, "Little Thunder," recurs in many of his works.

butchering whales."[30] They also hunted for marine mammals—walrus, seals, and small whales. Before the arrival of Europeans, they had depended primarily on marine resources, including cod and bass, as well as the deep-sea swordfish, and only secondarily on those of the forests.[31]

This pattern soon reversed itself, however, as the Mi'kmaq adapted to the fur trade. Their distinctive sea-going canoes, with gunwales swelling upward at the centre, were well adapted to coastal travel as well as for crossing the Gulf of St Lawrence and going to Newfoundland. By the beginning of the seventeenth century, Mi'kmaq were sailing European shallops (keel boats pointed at both ends).[32] They also continued their pre-contact involvement in the ecological basis for trade that existed between the hunters of the north and the agriculturalists of the south. One of the names by which the Mi'kmaq were known, "Taranteens," was said to mean "traders,"[33] and they treated their trading partners with courtesy.

An Indigenous custom that surprised early Europeans was that of respecting food caches and supply depots of others, even though unguarded. Like the Indigenous understanding of territoriality, this unwillingness to touch the resources of others must be seen in terms of the strongly held beliefs regarding communal property rights and conservation. A group of 79 Frenchmen moved temporarily, in 1605–7, from Ile Ste Croix to Port Royal (later known as Annapolis Royal). When they returned in 1610, they found that the Indigenous people had touched nothing and the paramount Mi'kmaw chief, Membertou (d. 1611), was there to greet them.[34] Trade flourished. For Europeans, the profits were great, since the goods offered for the furs brought by the First Nations cost a fraction of the value, in Europe, of the furs. In North America, the European trade items had a greater value as they could not be produced locally.

The Mi'kmaq used their deep understanding of their ancestral home to become superb seamen very quickly. During the eighteenth century, in their war against Britain, they were taking and sailing schooners as large as 70 tons.[35] By the nineteenth century, they were operating as commercial fishermen with their own vessels.[36] The Wuastukwiuk, also known as the "Saint John River Indians," shared a similar lifestyle. According to Spiritan Pierre-Antoine-Simon Maillard (c. 1710–62), the "Mickmakis and Mariquets, who, though different in language, have the same customs and manners . . . are of the same way of thinking and acting." Both groups interacted successfully with Europeans in the fisheries and the fur trade, and both became allies of the French, fought together during the colonial wars, and in general shared the same fate afterwards. This participation in the colonial wars ensured their survival in their ancestral lands. Nevertheless, they maintained a separate identity and sometimes acted separately.

English slave raids along the Atlantic coast had early aroused the hostility of the Mi'kmaq and pushed them into their alliance with the French. At the beginning, they fought for the traditional reasons of prestige and alliance, only to see their allies defeated. France's loss of Acadia in 1710 and the advent of British settlement soon put another cast on the conflict, which by that time was already a century old. At issue was a question that would permeate Indigenous–European relations: who owned the land, and what did ownership involve?

France believed that New France and Acadia were hers by right of "discovery."[37] As far as the French were concerned, the Indigenous Peoples did not own the land. The French merely allowed them to continue using it. The French monarch had been making grants of land to French subjects in Acadia at least since the beginning of the seventeenth century. Earlier, trading licences had also included land rights. The charter for **La Compagnie des Cent Associés** (1627) provided for Indigenous people who became Christian to be considered in all respects French, including proprietary and inheritance rights. Any property acquired, however, came by right of the French Crown, not by Aboriginal right.[38] Landownership had not become an issue earlier, however, in part because the French population was small. The French also depended on their allies, for reasons of the fur trade and war, and so took care to respect Indigenous villages and encampments.[39] Acadian colonists used areas of little interest to the Indigenous people.

That this did not extend to international recognition of Indigenous sovereignty was made painfully clear in the **Treaty of Utrecht of 1713**, when the French ceded Acadia to the English without mentioning their Indigenous allies. Britain, too, considered that she had gained from France clear sovereign title to the land. In fact, Britain believed the Mi'kmaq and their Indigenous neighbours had never possessed sovereignty anyway, being mobile or semi-sedentary peoples who had not organized into states recognizable to the British.

The original inhabitants of the land, however, did not share France and Britain's belief that France held a transferable title to the land. The Mi'kmaw view, indeed the view shared by all First Nations and Inuit, was that territory was held by the community. Rights to the land and resources—including the marine, lacustrine, and riverine rights—also included the responsibility to care for those resources. This view was not understood by the French or the British newcomers. French cartographers were frustrated in their efforts to delineate territory as their Indigenous sources sketched in circles as opposed to lines. The Indigenous understanding of their ancestral territories was unbroken but the newcomers struggled to come to terms with it.[40]

Far from being subjects of the French, the Mi'kmaq and Wuastukwiuk had welcomed them as friends and allies. They accepted the French king as their father, because he sent missionaries to teach them their new religion, but the idea that he had any claim on their lands, or that they owed him any more allegiance than they owed to their own chiefs, did not make sense to them. Periodically, they reminded the French that they had granted only use of their lands, which still belonged to the Mi'kmaq according to an older and more permanent concept of territoriality.[41] The Mi'kmaq also did not consider that their alliance with the French automatically implied their later subjugation to the British. As far as the Mi'kmaq were concerned, Acadia was their land, which they called Megumaage and which they had divided into seven districts under a system of chiefs and a paramount chief. As the Mi'kmaq saw it, the only right involving land that the British had gained through their conquest was the right to purchase from the Indigenous Peoples.[42]

Benefit and Cost of the English–French Rivalry

The English were well aware of the wisdom of maintaining good relations. It was not the First Nations' importance as allies that mattered so much as the difficulties they could cause if they were not.[43] Proclaiming George I as King of Acadia in 1762, the British asked the Indigenous Peoples for an oath of loyalty and to share their lands peacefully with the settlers they hoped would soon be coming.[44] In return, they promised more generous annual gifts than the French had been giving, but they relied mainly on offering better trade values at "truck houses" (trading posts run under government auspices). They also promised not to interfere with Indigenous Peoples' religions—by that time, many of them, particularly among the Mi'kmaq, were Catholic.

The Indigenous Peoples replied that they were pleased to have religious liberty but did not see why they had to have truck houses on their lands. They thought that trade could continue as it had in the past, mostly from shipboard. As for the oath of allegiance, they had never taken one to the French King and did not see why they should do so for the British. The Mi'kmaq wanted only to continue living in their territories without fear of English encroachment.

The French held a trump card in this contest to win the loyalty of the First Peoples: approximately a hundred missionaries who had worked in Acadia during the French regime. Canadian-born Antoine Gaulin (1674–1740) served from 1698 until 1731, retiring because of ill health. Maillard was in Acadia from 1735 until his death in 1762. The missions of Spiritan

Jean-Louis Le Loutre (1709–72), from 1737 until 1755, included Acadians as well as Mi'kmaq. The effectiveness of these missionaries stemmed at least in part from traditional Indigenous respect for shamans. France's identification of the importance of religion in First Nations leadership and their ability to turn religious sentiments in their favour were major factors in the success of the French with their First Nations alliances.[45]

One aspect of Christianity that resonated with some Indigenous groups was its use of ritual. Ritual was traditionally very important in Indigenous lives. In modifying the focus of ritual, the missionaries did not entirely change Indigenous preference in these matters.[46] In this, as well as in using their positions for political ends, French missionaries were so effective that in 1749 the exasperated English put a price on the head of Le Loutre.[47] In their turn, the British would adopt the French practice of using missionaries as agents of the state, particularly during the negotiations for the numbered treaties during the last part of the nineteenth century and the first part of the twentieth. Missionaries would also act as mediators in other areas until about mid-twentieth century. Meanwhile, the Mi'kmaq were far from passive in this struggle for control.

The Mi'kmaq soon learned to play the English off against the French and, eventually, to force the French to reorganize and increase their "gift" distributions (tools and equipment, guns, weapons and ammunition, food, clothing). In 1751, the Mi'kmaq successfully demanded that special gift distributions to meet their needs be incorporated into the regular ones.[48] The distributions, essentially Indigenous in their ritual character, came to be combined with the European custom of awarding titles and medals. Indigenous people had as much of a penchant for honours and prestige as Europeans. It would be difficult to overrate the importance both Indigenous Peoples and French colonizers attached to these ceremonies. Even the English, who had initiated the awarding of medals but who still looked on the annual gift distributions as a form of bribery, were drawn reluctantly into this form of diplomacy.[49]

Thus, although their traditional subsistence base was very quickly overexploited through the activities of the fisheries and the fur trade, the Mi'kmaq and Wuastukwiuk were able to substitute the goods and food they received from their allies to maintain their traditional lifestyle as long as the colonial wars, and consequently their own war, lasted. They were, however, severely reduced in numbers. The Mi'kmaw population, who might have numbered as many as 35,000 at the time of contact, had dropped to 3,000, and the Wuastukwiuk to 800. Membertou, the Mi'kmaw chief reported to have memories of Cartier, in 1610 said that in former times his people had been "as thickly planted as the hairs upon his head," but that after the arrival of the French they had developed bad habits in respect to food and drink, which had greatly diminished their numbers.[50] "Bad habits" do not tell the whole story, however.

Jesuit priest Pierre Biard wrote that more than half the population of Cap de la Hève died of disease in 1612, noting ominously, "One by one the different coasts according as they have begun to traffic with us, have been more reduced by disease." In 1617, an especially severe epidemic wreaked havoc among coastal peoples. By 1705, the rhetoric of extinction had taken hold among colonizers in the East. Some French colonizers believed that it was hardly worthwhile learning about the Indigenous Peoples, who, although once numerous, were now reduced to "almost nothing." It was reported that in 1,500 leagues of New France, the French outnumbered the Indigenous people by two to one.[51]

The Innu, Mi'kmaq, and Wuastukwiuk were the first to come into lasting relationships with the French. But the Wabanaki would become the most important of the French military allies and would contribute the phrase "French and Indians" to the colonial wars.

People of the Sunrise

The southernmost of the Atlantic coast peoples considered here are the Wabanaki, "Those Living at the Sunrise" (or "Dawnland People," among other variations).[52] The Wabanaki are closely related to the Mi'kmaq and Wuastukwiuk as well as to other Algonquin speakers to the south.[53] Their homeland is south of the present Canada–US border, but the dislocations caused by colonial wars and European settlement meant that many Wabanaki eventually found their home in what is now Canada.

The first of these people known to have come into contact with Europeans, in this case the French, were the Eastern Wabanaki. An account published in 1613 described between 10,000 and 14,000 souls living in 21 semi-permanent villages along 11 rivers in the region now known as Maine and New Hampshire. Bashabes (Betsabes, Bessabes, among other variations; d. 1616?) was the top man of 23 **sagamores**. Because of the nature of the soil and climate, and the availability of sea resources, the Eastern Wabanaki farmed less intensively than Iroquoians did.

European diseases soon took their toll here as elsewhere, wiping out or drastically reducing villages

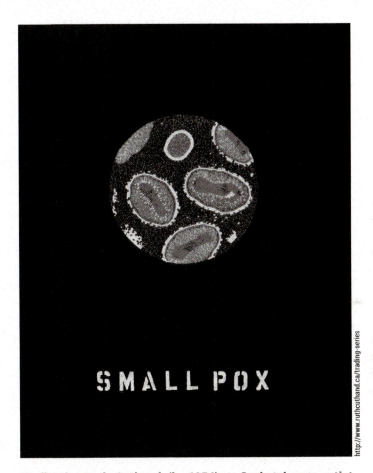

SMALL POX

http://www.ruthcuthand.ca/trading-series

Trading **by Ruth Cuthand (b. 1954), a Saskatchewan artist of Plains Cree and Scottish ancestry.** Of her work she writes: "Beads and viruses go hand-in-hand . . . . *Trading* is a series of 12 images of viruses brought by the Europeans and new disease that was brought back to Europe. Beads are a visual reference to colonization; valuable furs were traded for inexpensive beads. On the plains beads were a valuable trade item, they replaced the method of using porcupine quills. Obviously beads were quicker to use, covered large areas and came in a wide variety of colours. *Trading* examines both sides of European trade. Trade brought new items that revolutionized Native life. The downside was the decimation of many tribes through disease. Diseases quickly spread, arriving even before Europeans."

from a very early date. In 1616, Father Biard reported that there were no more than 3,000 souls in the region.[54] The influx of new trade goods also caused important social and political reverberations. The availability of iron tools and weapons—metal points for spears and arrows but above all swords, cutlasses, and even muskets—inflamed long-standing rivalries.[55] The first decades of the seventeenth century saw the Wabanaki, Mi'kmaq, and Wuastukwiuk all fighting each other. In ambushes at close range, muskets were devastatingly effective, with cutlasses and swords providing the *coup de grâce*.

The French seemed promising to the Wabanaki as trading partners and as allies, both in their traditional war against the Haudenosaunee Confederacy[56] and against the slave-raiding English. In 1613, when the English raided the French settlement of St Sauveur on the Penobscot River, the Wabanaki offered to help the beleaguered survivors.[57] They followed this up in 1629 by sending an envoy to Quebec to sound out the possibilities of developing these ties. Champlain was immediately interested, because the Wabanaki south of the Saco River were farmers and could possibly help provision his fledgling colony. Unable to help in the war against the Haudenosaunee Confederacy immediately, he promised to do so as soon as possible. In the meantime, he proposed a mutual assistance program involving food, supplies, and trade goods.[58]

The alliance proposal did not survive Champlain's death in 1635. The Wabanaki quickly took advantage of their access to European goods to develop their own trading networks. The French were annoyed enough to restrict Wabanaki visits to Quebec and, finally, in 1649, to warn them to stay away.[59] From this inauspicious beginning developed what became one of the most effective and long-lasting alliances in North American colonial history.

The Wabanaki Fight for Their Land

In 1642, Omamiwinini allies of the French had brought a Sokoki (Western Wabanaki) prisoner to Trois-Rivières under the impression he was a member of the Haudenosaunee Confederacy.[60] The French moved much faster to consolidate this new relationship than they had previously done with the Eastern Wabanaki. In 1651, a Jesuit missionary brought together various groups, including the Mahican (not usually included with the Wabanaki, but related), to form a solid front against their traditional enemies, the Haudenosaunee Confederacy, who were being particularly annoying to the French. The Haudenosaunee responded by intensifying their attacks.

The English taking of Acadia in 1654 and the growing intensity of the French–Haudenosaunee War severely restricted communication between French and Wabanaki. However, English settlement pressures from the south were increasing, pushing the Wabanaki into the French orbit, and France's re-establishment in Acadia in 1670 led to the development of the French–Wabanaki alliance. French officer Jean-Vincent d'Abbadie de Saint-Castin (1652–1707) consolidated this alliance in the 1670s when he married Pidianske (or Pidiwamiska; see box), the daughter of Madockawando (d. 1698), sagamore

INDIGENOUS LEADERS | Pidiwamiska (before 1658–c. 1720)

Although we know little about Pidiwamiska, she deserves to be recognized as one of the first in a long line of Indigenous women who married French colonizers. The demographic imbalance of more women on the Indigenous side—caused by endemic warfare—and more men on the French side meant that many Indigenous women would marry French colonizers over the course of the seventeenth and eighteenth centuries. The marriages worked politically, socially, and economically to consolidate the alliance between the French and Indigenous Peoples. Politically, French factions grew up around Indigenous families with French blood. Socially, French men became deeply entwined in their in-laws' families. Economically, the Indigenous women taught their husbands how to function in the North American environment. Pidiwamiska stands as leader of a cultural change that swept across the land that would become Canada.

of the Penobscots, "people of the white rocks country," reputedly the most powerful of the Wabanaki nations.

Now the Eastern Wabanaki and the Mi'kmaq were both allies of the French. The new situation did not produce unanimity within Wabanaki communities, however. Splits developed between pro-French and pro-English factions, leading to a new set of internal tensions. These tensions would increase with the quickening tempo of frontier warfare.

The exodus of the Western Wabanaki to Canada began as a trickle about this time.[61] It swelled into a major movement as a result of **King Philip's War**, 1675–6, the last major Indigenous push to expel the Europeans from New England. "King Philip" was the name the British used for Wampanoag chief Metacom (Metacomet). "That cataclysm in New England history"[62] destroyed the Indigenous presence in southern New England (the war was fought mainly in Massachusetts and Connecticut) and helped to ignite the simultaneous Maine War between the English and the Wabanaki. Clearly, the People of the Sunrise were caught in the middle of the ongoing French–English battles. The Wabanaki tried to prevent war but eventually had to take sides. They did not fight solely, or even mainly, as allies of the French but for their own lands. The English pushed them back sporadically until the final defeat of New France in 1760.

The Wabanaki Refuse To Be Pawns in a European Game

Early in the eighteenth century, **Odanak** on the St François River near Sorel, Quebec, became the largest Wabanaki settlement in New France. By the 1740s and 1750s, it was the main source for Wabanaki warriors fighting in border raids. This situation resulted in one of the most famous episodes in the annals of colonial warfare, the raid of Robert Rogers and his Rangers in 1759, in which they destroyed the village.

The French soon re-established Odanak but carefully settled the new arrivals into villages situated to act as buffers against parties of Haudenosaunee and English raiders, strengthening the defences of New France. An unplanned side effect of this policy was the promotion of smuggling between the French and English colonies, in which both the Wabanaki and the Haudenosaunee were active participants.[63] However, the French put aside their old objections that the Wabanaki competed with them in the fur trade. Instead, they now tried to lure the Wabanaki away from the English and to encourage raids against the latter.

The French were so successful in luring Indigenous Peoples to their side that the English began a counter-campaign. In this, they had two weapons: the promise of better deals in trade and, more important, the fact that the French had ceded Indigenous lands in the Treaty of Utrecht without even informing their Indigenous allies. The Wabanaki shared with the Mi'kmaq a stunned disbelief at the actions of their French allies. In words that would become all too familiar in later confrontations, the Indigenous Peoples asked, "by what right did the French give away a country that did not belong to them" and which the Indigenous Peoples had no intention of quitting?[64]

The English were thus able to persuade some refugees to return. Among these were the Eastern Wabanaki chiefs Mog (Heracouansit, "One with Small Handsome Heels," c. 1663–1724) of Norridgewock and Atecouando ("Deer Spirit-Power," fl. 1701–26). Atecouando set an example, bringing his people back to Pigwacket a decade after they had left for the St François River. Some Wabanaki even joined the English in fighting the Mi'kmaq.[65]

Regretting the Treaty of Utrecht, French officials tried to make up lost ground by arguing that the English in New England were "encroaching on [Wabanaki] territory and establishing themselves contrary to the Law of Nations, in a country of which the said Indians have been from all time in possession."[66] As for their own presence in Indigenous territories, the French pointed to their alliances to claim that they were there with the permission of the local people. With this encouragement, chiefs such as Wowurna ("Captain Joseph," fl. 1670–1738) of Norridgewock rejected the British claim to sovereignty over his people.[67] Others who had gone to the St Lawrence Valley reacted by returning to their ancestral homes and reasserting their sovereignty, even in the midst of growing English settlement.

The French would have preferred to keep the Wabanaki as a fighting force within their colony, where they would be easier to control. With strategic reasons in mind and also concerned with countering English manoeuvres, they tried to attract Mi'kmaq and Eastern Wabanaki to settle at Île Royale (Cape Breton; Oonumaghee to the Mi'kmaq), but with no success. Quite apart from the fact that Indigenous Peoples did not consider the island to be good hunting territory, the Wabanaki rejected the proposal that they move to serve their allies' political goals.[68] It would be 1723 before the Mi'kmaq, harassed by the English, finally agreed to establish at Mirliguèche on Île Royale if the French built a church for them.[69] The settlement did not last past 1750, however, when the mission moved to Sainte-Famille on Bras d'Or Lake, also on Île Royale.

The French also intensified their efforts to neutralize English commercial superiority. Their most effective means for achieving this was by carefully observing the annual feasting, speech-making, and gift distribution by which they maintained their alliances. According to Philippe de Vaudreuil (c. 1643–1725), governor-general of New France, 1703–25, "we treat our Indians as Allies, and not

> ### HISTORICAL BACKGROUND | The French and the Indigenous Peoples
>
> Throughout the history of New France, the French policy towards Indigenous Peoples was consistent: treat them with every consideration, avoid violence (this was not always successful), and transform them into Frenchmen.[70] They would reach these goals through gifts, military promotions, encouraging youth to accompany Indigenous people on their expeditions, and, as described above, religious indoctrination.[71]
>
> The French used these techniques throughout the period of New France, which formally ended with the 1763 Treaty of Paris. Another technique, tried early and later discarded, was to send "eminent and enterprising" Indigenous people to France "to amaze and dazzle them with the greatness and splendour of the French Court and Armie."[72] However, most of those sent proved not to be so easily impressed, and soon they learned to take advantage of these occasions to lobby in their own interests. Once, Versailles hosted six sagamores at the same time, all of them asking for help from the French against the English.[73] Yet another technique, as noted earlier, was ceremonial recognition, including presentation of appropriate gifts. The gifts offered on such occasions, mainly medals, were important influences on later negotiations.

as Subjects."[74] As with the Mi'kmaq, and allies generally, the awarding of medals and honours came to be an important element of these occasions, but reports of French ennoblement of Indigenous people are apparently more legend than fact (see Historical Background box).[75]

Vaudreuil had no doubt that France's ability to maintain a presence in the Northeast was due to the Wabanaki. Further, by winning the co-operation of the Wabanaki, the French "shall have completely provided for the security of Canada."[76] What started out as a commercial venture for the French ended up as the most politically important of all their First Nations alliances in New France.[77]

The Wabanaki Suffer in Their Allies' Defeat

In 1721, the Wabanaki delivered an ultimatum to Samuel Shute, governor of Massachusetts from 1716 to 1727. In it, the Wabanaki asserted their sovereignty over the territories east of the Connecticut River but said the English who were there could stay, provided no more came.[78] This was the start of the English–Indian War, a virulent three-year struggle that ended in the destruction of the Eastern Wabanaki town of Norridgewock (Narantsouak) in 1724[79] and the defeat of the Pigwacket in 1725.

The war ended with the signing of the **Treaty of Boston** in 1725 and its ratification at Falmouth (Portsmouth, New Hampshire) in 1727 despite belated French attempts to prevent it. Other ratifications soon followed in Nova Scotia. However, neither treaties nor ratifications ensured peace until the final defeat of New France, a situation the English tried to deal with by calling the Wabanakis "rebels."[80] Under the circumstances, the Wabanaki had no choice but to wind down their hostilities against the English over the course of the eighteenth century, even though they were as certain as ever of their rights.

The Wabanaki saw the land not in the terms of absolute ownership but as the right to control its usage and products. Atecouando (*fl.* 1749–57) of Odanak, for example, in 1752 challenged the authority of the British to survey Wabanaki lands without their permission, adding:

> We forbid you very expressly to kill a single beaver or to take a single stick of wood on the lands we live on. If you want wood, we will sell it to you, but you shall not have it without our permission.[81]

https://www.metmuseum.org/art/collection/search/35783

This wampum belt and powder horn was made by a member of the Penawapskewi(Penobscot) Nation *c.* 1779, which spanned the eastern border of the US and Canada, and is a member of the Wabenaki Confederacy, Wampum is made of leather, with beads made from shells. It was used as a living record of agreements between First Nations, and then between Indigenous Peoples and European trading partners. The art of making and exchanging wampum belts is still thriving today.

But the direction of events was clear. Ratifications to the 1725 peace had continued, as one group after another laid down arms despite continuing violations of their lands.

Such an act did not guarantee that the violations would stop, however, or even that individual Wabanaki would be respected. For instance, English hunters, who were never caught, killed and robbed Nodogawerrimet, the Norridgewock **sachem** (d. 1765), despite the fact that he had persistently worked for peaceful coexistence.[82] Wenemouet ("Weak War Chief," d. 1730), a Penobscot chief, tried to avoid special arrangements with either of the colonizing powers and to negotiate working relationships with both. Continuing settler encroachments undermined these efforts, however, and this played into the hands of the French by working to keep their alliance on a war footing.

The Pigwacket chief **Nescambiouit** ("He Who Is so Important and so Highly Placed Because of His Merit That His Greatness Cannot Be Attained, Even in Thought," *c.* 1660–1722) was one of several Wabanaki chiefs who realized that the First Nations' only hope of curbing European expansion lay in united action. Although he had been taken to France and honoured by Louis XIV for his efforts in the French cause, in 1716 Nescambiouit went to live with the Fox, whose recent defeat had not reconciled them to French penetration into the West. The French were able to abort Nescambiouit's pan-Indian initiative, as well as those of his associates, but were so worried by them that they limited Wabanaki travel into the *pays d'en haut* (the Great Lakes region) unless accompanied by the French.

In 1720, the Wabanaki and the Haudenosaunee exchanged wampum belts. Wampum belts—made originally from white and purple shell, served many purposes and like other elements of Indigenous culture their use spread from nation to nation. Among other things, they were used as invitations to discussion, as a promise, as mnemonic devices, as a declaration of truthfulness, and as a record of events.[83] Alarmed, the French moved quickly to stop the peace negotiations, believing that otherwise "the colony would be lost,"[84] even though they had signed a peace with the Haudenosaunee in Montreal in 1701. A pan-Indian alliance could only have worked against French interests, as, indeed, it would have done against those of any European colonizer.

For the Wabanaki, association with the French meant making the best of a bad predicament. Caught as they were in circumstances that defied their most creative efforts in war and peace, it is not surprising that they were eventually overwhelmed.

Questions to Consider

1. What became of the Stadakohnan and Hochelagan people?
2. What were the causes of friction between the Europeans and the Indigenous Peoples of the east coast?
3. What advantages did the French colonizers have over the English colonizers in terms of their relations with the Mi'kmaq?
4. In what ways did the French come to depend on their Indigenous allies?

Recommended Readings

Dickason, Olive Patricia. *The Myth of the Savage and the Beginnings of French Colonialism in the Americas*. Edmonton: University of Alberta Press, 1984.

Green, L.C., and Olive P. Dickason.*The Law of Nations and the New World*. Edmonton: University of Alberta Press, 1989.

Johnston, A.J.B., and Jesse Francis. *Ni'n na L'nu: The Mi'kmaq of Prince Edward Island*. Charlottetown: Acorn Press, 2013.

LeSourd, Philip, ed. *Tales from Maliseet Country: The Maliseet Texts of Karl V. Teeter*. Lincoln: University of Nebraska Press, 2007.

McBride, Bunny. *Women of the Dawn*. Lincoln: Bison Books, 2001.

Sleeper-Smith, Susan, ed. *Rethinking the Fur Trade: Cultures of Exchange in the Atlantic World*. Lincoln: University of Nebraska Press, 2009.

Tkaczuk, Diana Claire, and Brian C. Vivian, eds. *Cultures in Conflict: Current Archaeological Perspectives*. Calgary: University of Calgary Press, 1989.

Tremblay, Roland. *The Saint Lawrence Iroquoians: Corn People*. Montréal: Les Éditions de l'Homme, 2006.

Trigger, Bruce G., ed. *Handbook of North American Indians, vol 15: Northeast*. Washington: Smithsonian Institution, 1978.

———. *Natives and Newcomers: Canada's "Heroic Age" Reconsidered*. Montreal and Kingston: McGill-Queen's University Press, 1985.

Wiseman, Frederick Matthew. *The Voice of the Dawn: An Authohistory of the Wabanaki Nation*. Hanover, NH, and London: University Press of New England, 2001.

5 The Wendat Confederacy, the Haudenosaunee Confederacy, and the European Colonizers

CHAPTER OUTLINE

In this chapter we will examine the impact of the early colonizing efforts of the French and British on the Indigenous Peoples. The economic, social, and political impact was felt immediately, but the spiritual impact was more gradual and in the end more destructive to Indigenous lifeways. In particular, we will look at the role the Jesuits and other French colonizers had in the Haudenosaunee assault on **Wendake** in 1649. Finally, we will look at the establishment of British posts in the Far North and the changes that occurred as a result of the trade in furs.

LEARNING OUTCOMES

1. Students will gain an understanding of the pressures that caused the conflict between the Wendat Confederacy and the Haudenosaunee Confederacy.

2. We will see alternative views about the motivations for trade across the region and with the European colonizers.

3. Students will gain insight into the developing fur trade routes over the course of the seventeenth century.

TIMELINE From Champlain to the Hudson's Bay Company

1608
Samuel de Champlain establishes his habitation at Quebec.

1613
Tessouat turns Champlain around at Allumette Island in the Ottawa River.

1615
In response to 1609 invitation of Atironta, principal chief of the Arendarhonon, Champlain visits Wendake. He winters there after being wounded in battle between the Wendat Confederacy and the Haudenosaunee Confederacy. Champlain fought with the Wendat Confederacy to confirm the alliance.

1640s–50s
Haudenosaunee attacks bring end to Omamiwinini control of Ottawa River, the route from the Great Lakes to Quebec.

1649
Haudenosaunee warriors attack and rout the Wendat Confederacy: two Jesuit missionaries burned at stake; some of the Wendat nations burn their own villages as they flee Wendake. Some Wendat nations take refuge on Christian Island in Georgian Bay before moving to Ancien Lorette near Quebec; others go west to Chequamegon Bay in western Lake Superior. Later, they follow their Odaawa allies to Michilimackinac and then to le Détroit. Eventually, they settle in Ohio and Michigan and become known as Wyandots. Still others are captured and become adopted members of the Haudenosaunee Confederacy.

1609
Wendat leader Ochasteguin of the Arendarhonon and Omamiwinini leader Iroquet join forces to establish trade in meeting at Quebec with Champlain. Dutch established on what is now the Hudson River.
Champlain accompanies a Wendat, Innu, and Omamiwinini war party in their attack on a Kanienkehaka village.

1623
Dutch establish Fort Orange (Albany, NY).

1634
Jesuit missions in New France replace Recollects.
Smallpox epidemics begin to decimate Omamiwinini and Wendat peoples.

1642
Haudenosaunee begin river blockades to disrupt trade from Wendake to Quebec.

1668
English expedition to Hudson Bay.

1670
Hudson's Bay Company chartered, with monopoly trading rights over all lands (Rupert's Land) draining into Bay.

1670s
Ojibwa and Odaawa move south into former Iroquoian territories around Lake Ontario, Lake Erie, and southern Lake Huron; Cree expand further north and west.

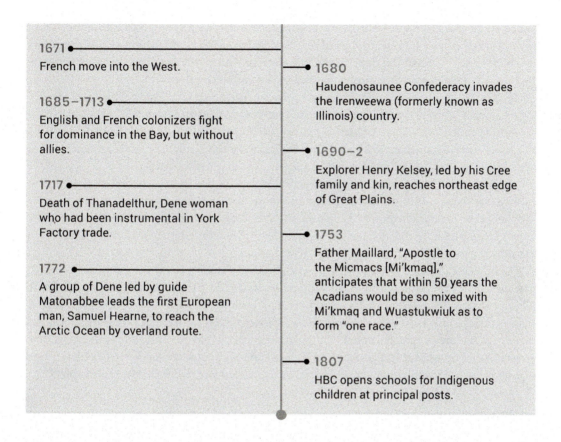

1671
French move into the West.

1685–1713
English and French colonizers fight for dominance in the Bay, but without allies.

1717
Death of Thanadelthur, Dene woman who had been instrumental in York Factory trade.

1772
A group of Dene led by guide Matonabbee leads the first European man, Samuel Hearne, to reach the Arctic Ocean by overland route.

1680
Haudenosaunee Confederacy invades the Irenweewa (formerly known as Illinois) country.

1690–2
Explorer Henry Kelsey, led by his Cree family and kin, reaches northeast edge of Great Plains.

1753
Father Maillard, "Apostle to the Micmacs [Mi'kmaq]," anticipates that within 50 years the Acadians would be so mixed with Mi'kmaq and Wuastukwiuk as to form "one race."

1807
HBC opens schools for Indigenous children at principal posts.

Jesuit Intrusions into Wendake[1]

The French establishment of Quebec in 1608 as the centre for the growing fur trade quickly attracted the attention of the Wendat Confederacy. The Wendat leader Ochasteguin (*fl.* 1609) joined an Omamiwinini delegation that was teaming up with the Innu to go and meet the French.[2] The Omamiwinini, with their leader Iroquet (*fl.* 1609–15), welcomed Wendat participation as it would enable access to the trade networks of the Great Lakes.[3] The interest these leaders had in meeting the French has long been the subject of historical debate. Some historians have suggested that economics, and access to European trade goods, was the underlying reason. Others have posited that security was the most important concern, that is, the Indigenous Peoples were concerned about the effects that French technology would have in terms of regional stability.[4] For Ochasteguin there may have been another reason. If the Stadakohnan survivors did join the Wendat Confederacy, then he would have been interested on behalf of his own constituents.[5] The result was the meeting with Champlain at Quebec in 1609, an event that changed the course of Canada's history.

Ochasteguin's people were the Arendarhonon, "the People of the Rock," occupying easternmost part of Wendake. The third newest members of the confederacy, which they probably joined about 1590 (well after European trade goods had begun filtering into the interior), they were also the second largest in population.[6] According to Wendat custom, Ochasteguin and members of his clan had the right, as the initiators, to control the new Wendat trade network. By 1615, all of the confederates were involved in this vast enterprise.

The largest nation in the Wendat Confederacy was the Attignawantan, "People of the Bear," a founding member of the confederacy. They would play host to the **Jesuits** and eventually would prove to be the most open to Christianity. Another founding nation that also was willing to accept Christianity was the Attigneenongnahac, "Barking Dogs" or "People of the Cord." The Arendarhonon, on the other hand, held to their traditional beliefs despite the best efforts of the Jesuits.

Most recent arrivals were the Tahontaenrat, "People of the Deer," who joined the Wendat Confederacy about 1610.[7] Like the Arendarhonons, they resisted Christianity. The possible fifth member, Ataronchronon, "People of the Marshes," in what is now called the lower Wye Valley, probably did not have a formal role in the confederacy and may have been a subsidiary group.[8]

The intense campaign of the Jesuits to persuade all to conform to the Christian norm caused tensions, as some Wendat converted and others resisted.[9] Tionnontaté leader Kondiaronk (Gaspar Soiaga, Souoias, Sastaretsi, known to the French as "Le Rat," c. 1649–1701) would later suggest that the only reason the missionaries wanted to convert Indigenous Peoples was to collect money from more people. He noted that the missionaries could not prove the existence of hell. As well, Kondiaronk (see Indigenous Leaders box) and his people contended with some traders who spoke of Christianity but cheated in the fur trade and stole from Indigenous people.[10]

INDIGENOUS LEADERS | Kondiaronk (*c.* 1649–1701)

Chief of the Tionnontaté Nation, Kondiaronk fought hard for his people during the second half of the seventeenth century. The French called him "Le Rat" and he is frequently mentioned in the official correspondence between the French officers in the Upper Great Lakes and their superiors in Quebec. Kondiaronk, along with his Kiskakon counterpart Koutaoiliboe, was one of the first practitioners of the diplomatic ploy of playing the French against the British. He is most famous for using all of his skills in warfare to prevent any peace between the French colonizers and the Haudenosaunee Confederacy. Kondiaronk kept the Tionnontaté Nation in close alliance with the Kiskakon Odaawa Nation and after the dispersal of the Wendat Confederacy he led the Tionnontaté people on a grand migration, first to Lake Michigan, then to Chequamegon, Michilimackinac, and finally Bkejwanong or le Détroit, as the French called it. He made certain that tobacco, the Tionnontaté's principal crop and trade item, was in good supply, and this was essentially the reason why he led his people to southern Lake Huron where it could be cultivated. He died at the Great Peace of Montreal in 1701, but not before giving a speech and making sure that the interests of his small nation were protected in the agreement.[11]

The Jesuits tried to ease the way to conversion by not interfering with local custom where there was no opposition to Christian values. This compromise, however, brought them into conflict with the French authorities and was only partially successful. Indeed, the French state found it difficult to determine exactly what the relationship between France and the Indigenous Peoples should or could be (see Historical Background box). Motives for conversion could be more related to preferential treatment in the fur trade than to religious conviction. In 1648, when only an estimated 15 per cent of the members of the Wendat Confederacy were Christian, half of those who were in the fur fleet had either converted or were preparing for it.[12] Commercial incentives were considerable—converts were considered to be French and so entitled to the same prices for their furs as Frenchmen, which were much higher than those paid to non-Christians[13]—but they must always be considered together with security concerns.

The influx of European goods seems to have strengthened the political and economic dominance of the Wendat at first. By late in the sixteenth century, these goods were penetrating inland by means of war, diplomatic exchanges, and trade.[14] French technology was useful for hunting, but also in warfare. The Wendat prospered but kept their traditional technology until their dispersal because the French were reluctant to trade guns to them as long as they were not converted.[15] This mixing of religious and economic considerations meant that the first Wendat warrior to obtain a firearm was the Christian Charles Tsondatsaa.[16] In 1641, the year of Tsondatsaa's baptism, the warriors of the Haudenosaunee Confederacy had 39 muskets, received in trade with the Dutch and the English. By 1643, the number had risen to 300. All of this is evidence of the important influence that European technology had in terms of regional security concerns and its potential influence on the conversion of the Wendat.

Lulled by the remoteness of Wendake from both the English and themselves, the French did not consider it necessary to arm the Wendat nations as they were doing at that time with the Wabanaki, whether they were Christian or not. Nor did they properly assess the role of the Wendat Confederacy in keeping the Haudenosaunee Confederacy in check. The cost to the French of these misjudgments would become evident by mid-seventeenth century, when the warriors of the Haudenosaunee Confederacy threatened the very existence of New France. The cost to the Wendat Confederacy would be even higher.

During the Quebec meeting of 1609, Atironta (*fl.* 1609–15), main chief of the Arendarhonons,[17] invited Champlain to visit Wendake. This pleased neither the Omamiwinini nor the Innu, both of whom traded with the French, and the Kichesipirini of Allumette Island[18] in the Ottawa River took action. By a series of ruses and fostered misunderstandings, their leader, one of several chiefs named **Tessouat** (Besouat, *fl.* 1603–13),[19] was able to delay the visit until the summer of 1615.[20] A later chief of the same name and the Kichesipirini also instituted a system of tolls along the river, which was so important to early trade and communication (see Indigenous Leaders box).

When Champlain finally visited Wendake in 1615, he confirmed the French desire for an alliance by joining with a Wendat war party in an attack on a Haudenosaunee village, probably

HISTORICAL BACKGROUND | French Law and Indigenous Peoples

A thorny question that the French never fully resolved during their regime concerned whether they should treat Indigenous Peoples as allies or as subjects of the French monarch. When dealing with other European nations, particularly the English, the French consistently denied responsibility for the behaviour of their allies on the grounds that they were sovereign. When it came to dealing with Indigenous Peoples, however, officials were not always clear as to what to do. As the colony became more secure, a consensus developed favouring the enforcement of French law, the imposition of which, however, was an extremely delicate matter.

The Indigenous Peoples saw themselves as free and sovereign, and did not take kindly to being put into French prisons for breaking laws they knew nothing about and would not have accepted if they had. As an eighteenth-century Spanish visitor to Louisbourg on Île Royale described the situation,

> These natives . . . acknowledged [the King of France] lord of the country, but without any alteration in their way of living; or submitting themselves to his laws; and so far were they from paying any tribute, that they received annually from France a quantity of apparel, gunpowder and muskets, brandy and several kinds of tools, in order to keep them quiet and attached to the French interest.[21]

that of the Onyota'aka.[22] The French leader was wounded in the knee and had to be carried back to Cahiagué, where he recuperated over the winter as the guest of Atironta. The French and the Wendat Confederacy formally concluded the alliance the following year at Quebec, with Atironta leading the Wendat delegation.

In 1626, the French sent a missionary to the neighbouring Chonnonton (known to the Wendat people as Attiwandaron, "People Who Speak a Slightly Different Language," and to the French as Neutrals because they managed to stay on peaceful terms with both the Wendat Confederacy and the Haudenosaunee), but the Wendat leaders saw to it that he did not stay long.[23] They viewed the move as unfavourable to their trading position.[24] On the other hand, when it suited their trading interests, they facilitated the movements of the Jesuits.[25] (This was not the first time the Wendat leaders had demonstrated their priorities when it came to trading. In 1633, they had executed coureur de bois Étienne Brûlé [c. 1592–1633] on the charge of dealing with their enemies, the Onondowaga.[26])

The Wendat alliance with the French confirmed the shift in importance of trade routes from north–south, as it had been before contact, to east–west. The immediate result of the French–Wendat alliance was a blossoming of the fur trade.[27] By plugging into the Wendat

Library and Archives Canada, C–005749

The French fanned the flames of rivalry among the First Nations, solidifying relations with the Wendat Confederacy and the Anishinaabek through military alliances against the Haudenosaunee Confederacy. This 1632 engraving represents a 1615 attack on a Haudenosaunee village. French infantry, to the left, are shown firing muskets in support of Wendat, who are attacking with bows and arrows and fire. At this time, the French did not provide firearms to their hosts.

trading network and convincing them to emphasize furs, the French developed the trade into the main economic activity of the north. Such commerce brought prosperity to everyone involved.[28] It also attracted the attention of the Wendat's rivals, the Haudenosaunee Confederacy, who did not have access to the lucrative trade and who resented the Europeans' alliance with their adversary.

Photograph by William Newbigging

Reconstructed longhouse at Crawford Lake, Ontario. The presence of corn pollen in the depths of the nearby meromictic lake led archaeologists to search for the remains of a Chonnonton village. The reconstructed longhouses and palisades are built on the site where the village remains were found.

The Wendat and Their French Allies Take the Offensive

The Wendat–French alliance confirmed the hostility between the French and the Haudenosaunee Confederacy. The Innu, Omamiwinini, and Mi'kmaq, along with the Wendat, had been fighting the **Haudenosaunee Confederacy** (called the Five Nations by the English and French) long before the arrival of Europeans. In trading with the Wendat and their various Anishinaabe allies, the French were stepping into a ready-made situation. This became evident in 1609, the year the Wendat called on Champlain. Then, the French leader found it necessary to confirm his intentions to ally with the Innu and the Omamiwinini by marching with them, and the Wendat, against the warriors of the Haudenosaunee Confederacy. Champlain would later claim to have fired a shot that brought down two chiefs.[29]

The animosity between the Haudenosaunee Confederacy and the French and their allies was reconfirmed the following year, in 1610, when Champlain again joined the Innu and the Omamiwinini, this time in repulsing a Haudenosaunee raiding party below Sorel.[30] With the sealing of the Wendat–French alliance in 1616, the war would escalate into the most famous

INDIGENOUS LEADERS | Tessouat and the Kichesipirini

Wendat trading sessions were "a pleasure to watch."[31] Delegations had to get permission to cross another's territory. As the traffic between the Great Lakes and Montreal increased, the Kichesipirini (known as Ehonkehronons to the Wendat people) of Allumette Island in the Ottawa River tried to discourage the Wendat from travelling to Montreal to trade with the French. Some historians have cast the Kichesipirini Anishinaabek as middlemen, attempting to make a profit by charging tolls, but there is a simpler explanation. In enforcing this policy, Chief Tessouat of the Kichesipirini was merely asserting what Donnakoh-Noh had done a century earlier and what countless others would attempt to do later: keep the French and their dangerous technology away from potential enemies. He asserted he was keeping the French trade for the Wendat Confederacy but this was merely subterfuge. He also claimed he could force the French back across the sea.[32]

Tessouat also tried to prevent the French from gaining access to the Great Lakes and in 1613 he turned around Champlain and his party at Allumette Island. Tessouat could not prevent the Wendat delegations from travelling the Ottawa River, nor could he hold Champlain off permanently, but he did try to impede the movement of French trade goods into the Great Lakes until he could solidify his position as gatekeeper and ensure the safety and security of his people. Increasing Haudenosaunee attacks eroded the position of the Kichesipirini of Allumette Island in the late 1640s and early 1650s, however. In spite of their complaints against the Kichesipirini chief and his people, the Wendat fur brigades were the first to suffer the consequences as the Haudenosaunee reduced and eventually eliminated the Kichesipirini control of the river.[33]

Indigenous–European confrontation in Canada's history. Champlain assumed that because his Indigenous allies were so firm in their attachment to the French, and because they so heavily outnumbered the Haudenosaunee, it would be easy to defeat them. As the Jesuit historian Pierre-François de Charlevoix (1682–1761) explained many years later,

> He [Champlain] had not foreseen that the Iroquois [Haudenosaunee], who for so long had been at odds with the Savages for a hundred leagues around them, would soon become allies with their neighbours who opposed France, and become the most powerful in this part of America.[34]

Amid Missionaries and Epidemics, the Wendat Edge towards War

The Wendat were eager to expand their trading operations to include the French, although neither they nor the French traders were enthusiastic about the arrival of missionaries.[35] But Champlain insisted: without missionaries, no trade. He arranged for missionaries from the Recollect order to come to New France in 1615. That same year, the Attignawantans accepted Recollect Father Joseph

Le Caron (*c.* 1586–1632) as the first missionary to Wendake.[36] The Jesuits would soon join the Recollects.[37] Among them was **Jean de Brébeuf** (1593–1649), who in 1626 was sent to the Wendat mission, which had been established in Wendake, because of his skill with languages. The Jesuits had high hopes of evangelizing the Indigenous Peoples quickly.[38] Instead, it would take Brébeuf nine years just to learn the Wendat language and compile a grammar.[39]

The attitude of the Jesuits was that "if once they can be made to settle down, they are ours."[40] Powerful trading interests, on the other hand, wanted to keep the Indigenous Peoples in the bush harvesting furs.[41] The Jesuits realized only too well that they also depended on

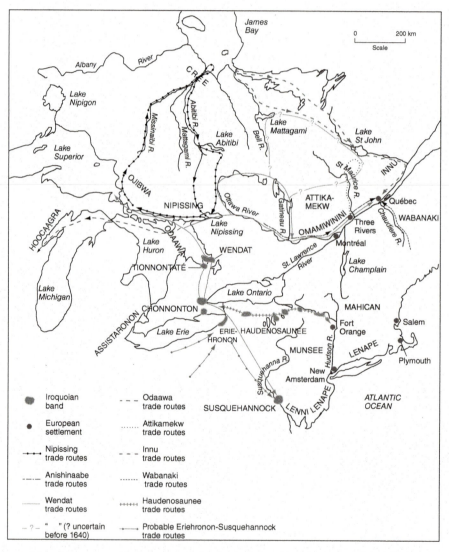

Map 5.1 Major central and eastern trade routes, first half of seventeenth century.

Bruce G. Trigger, *Children of Aataentsic*, vol. 1 (Montreal and Kingston: McGill-Queen's University Press, 1976).

the trade and so collaborated with it, but the tension remained unresolved.[42] Similarly, a certain tension developed over the mixing of races and the inevitability of intermarriage (see Historical Background box). These missionaries never completed the evangelization of the Wendat people, producing a few nuns among Indigenous women but not one priest among the men.[43] That is not to say, however, that the Indigenous people took no interest in their black-robed visitors.

One historian who has considered the reasons for the failure of the Christian missionaries is Georges Sioui. As a deeply spiritual Wendat scholar, Sioui offers a unique perspective:

> The Wendats (Huron) did not believe that they had been placed on the Great Island in order to dominate the rest of creation. The tradition reveals rather that they believed that they were created to bear witness to the infinite splendor and the infinite wisdom of the master of universe as well as that of his co-creators and to live in harmony.[44]

In general the apparent French interest in dominating the world around them did not sit well with the Wendat people. The Jesuits had to overcome the contradiction between their spiritual

---

HISTORICAL BACKGROUND | The Intermarriage of Indigenous People and French Colonizers

Although intermixing and intermarriage occurred independently of the formal kinship arrangements of the Indigenous Peoples, they were, nevertheless, closely linked. In Canada, the mixing of the races began long before settlement as a result of the fishing industries, particularly sea mammal hunting (classed as "fishing"), where Indigenous expertise was much in demand.[45] What began informally would later become official French policy.

The seventeenth-century permanent European settlements had few women. For one thing, Europe had barely recovered from the demographic disaster of the Black Death, and so nations such as France did not encourage emigration on any scale. The primary purpose of overseas expansion was resource exploitation; the settlement and growth of colonies in new lands were of secondary importance. Thus, the first groups that came out were largely male, sometimes selected for their particular trades skills. The official idea was that they would intermarry with the Indigenous population, producing a French population overseas.[46] The Church approved, as long as the brides first converted to Catholicism.[47] As Le Jeune observed, the aim was "to make them like us."

In short, Europeans needed to co-operate with Indigenous Peoples to establish a viable colony. Furthermore, when it came to selecting a mate, a First Nations or, later, a Métis woman had obvious advantages. The widespread and persistent belief that Indigenous people were really white, turning brown because of certain practices, eased concerns about intermixing for the French.[48] As well, French women sometimes married Indigenous men, though due to the demographic realities of the time, this was rarer.

teachings and the actions of French traders who seemed both avaricious and individualistic. Try as they might, the Jesuits were never able to convince all of the Wendat people of what the Jesuits argued were the benefits of conversion to the Christian religion.

Disease and Destabilization

The missionaries left during the brief English occupation of New France, from 1629 to 1632, and when France resumed control in 1633 the Recollects did not return. The Jesuits, however, did come back to the mission field. Hardly two years had passed after their return in 1634, however, when smallpox appeared among the Innu. It would soon reach the Wendat. Within four years, up to two-thirds of the population of these First Nations would be gone.[49] In the Indigenous view, somebody or something must be the cause. The Jesuits were the obvious suspects, particularly as they did not die of the contagion.[50] The Kichespirini drew the obvious conclusions and tried to scare the French away.[51] The French responded by threatening to withhold trade, a serious matter for the Wendat since the French were their only source for European goods.

As if disease were not enough, drought and forest fires added to their troubles. The opportunity was obvious for the Haudenosaunee to increase their attacks, although they, too, were suffering severely from the epidemics.[52] The Wendat looked to their old allies and trading partners, the **Council of Three Fires**—the Boodwaadmii, Odaawa, and Ojibwa—to help counter the threat from the Haudenosaunee, but the Three Fires Confederacy had little interest in mounting a large-scale attack against the Haudenosaunee Confederacy. For one thing, the three member nations were relatively safe from the Haudenosaunee threat. The Boodwaadmii were south and west of Lake Erie, the Odaawa lived in villages on Manitoulin Island and at Michilimackinac, and the Ojibwa were located along the north shores of Lakes Huron and Superior. The Haudenosaunee did not have the ability to attack at such a great distance and on so many fronts. Their one campaign against the Odaawa at Michilimackinac ended in disaster and starvation for the warriors. In addition, at the first sign of an advancing Haudenosaunee war party the threatened Ojibwa or Odaawa could jump into their canoes and go for help. As long as they kept an eye on the gateways into Lake Huron, the Odaawa and Ojibwa were impervious to the Haudenosaunee threat and they had little motive to help the Wendat by launching a pre-emptive strike. Meanwhile, the members of the Haudenosaunee Confederacy were looking to the south and east for an opportunity to join the fur trade.

For the Haudenosaunee, the new trade posed problems. For one thing, they had no allies with whom they could negotiate access to the French. Even when the Dutch set up at Fort Orange (Albany) in 1623, the Mahicans barred the Haudenosaunee. The Dutch, for their part, would have liked to have tapped into the northern trade, but the Haudenosaunee and Mahicans stood in the path.

The Haudenosaunee decided to try for the Dutch trade. This meant removing the Mahican barrier. They would also have to divert their raiding activities from the St Lawrence Valley.[53] Accordingly, they made peace with the Anishinaabek and the Wendat Confederacy in 1624 (which the French tried to prevent), removing the danger of enemy action from the rear and freeing themselves to attack the Mahicans, whom they finally defeated four years later. The Dutch, at first alarmed and uneasy, later accepted what had happened and opened trade relations with the eastern-most nation of the Haudenosaunee Confederacy, the Kanienkehaka, whom the French and English called the Mohawk.

On their eastern front, the Haudenosaunee established trade relations with the English. Now, they had two sources of goods. They also had shorter lines of communication, compared with the Wendat, deep in the interior, who had access only to the French. The Haudenosaunee played off the English against the Dutch, to the point where the Dutch, feeling threatened by both English and French, began to trade arms to the Haudenosaunee. In 1636, when some Anishinaabek tried to cross Haudenosaunee territory on their way to trade with the Dutch, Kanienkehaka warriors killed them. The Kichesipirini, led by Oumasasikweie (La Grenouille, "The Frog," *fl.* 1633–6), tried to turn French–Haudenosaunee differences to their own advantage, but their efforts backfired.[54] So ended the Kanienkehaka–Anishinaabe–Wendat agreement of 1624.

Meanwhile, French attempts to establish trade ties with the Haudenosaunee failed, so Champlain moved to strengthen his colony's defences. In 1633, he requested 120 men from France.[55] He established Trois-Rivières as a buffer for Quebec in 1634 and began to fortify the St Lawrence before his death the following year. The Haudenosaunee responded by building forts on the river from which to disrupt the fur brigades. Montreal, founded as a religious enterprise in 1642, quickly became a strategic outpost.

The die was cast. The French were committed to the fur-producing nations of the north for their own obvious commercial motives. The Haudenosaunee were committed to disrupting the northern trading networks for a combination of reasons, not the least of which was to keep threatened settler encroachment at bay. The war that would dominate the history of New France for a century was well on its way.

The Kanienkehaka and Onondowaga Succeed in Scattering the Wendat

Two member nations of the Haudenosaunee Confederacy (specifically, the Kanienkehaka and the Onondowaga, whom the French and English called the Seneca) began their blockades of the St Lawrence, Ottawa, and Richelieu rivers in 1642. These were successful enough that in 1644 and 1645, only one brigade in four made it to its destination.[56] In two years during the same decade, no brigades got through at all. In 1644, the French and some Kanienkehaka negotiated a peace, each side acting independently of its allies and, in the case of the Kanienkehaka, independently of the Haudenosaunee Confederacy.[57] It brought the short-term benefit of the second largest flotilla, 80 canoes, getting through in 1646. The cost was the killing of a Jesuit by holdout Kanienkehaka of the Bear clan.[58]

Two years later, in 1648, the Wendat Confederacy rallied, sending down 60 canoes, which picked up French reinforcements at Trois-Rivières.[59] It proved to be a hollow achievement. The brigade returned home to find three Wendat villages destroyed. The Haudenosaunee warriors had changed their tactics and now were attacking settlements instead of just the convoys, taking captives to replace Haudenosaunee population losses from war and disease. On top of that, the French were building fortifications in Haudenosaunee territory.[60]

The next year, 1649, when the Haudenosaunee warriors returned in force, the Wendat gave up, burned their 15 remaining villages, and dispersed. The Jesuits followed suit and abandoned their mission. The Jesuit dream of a new kind of Christian community in North America with a blend of French and Indigenous cultures was sent up in smoke. They also lost two of their missionaries to the fires of the stake, a common lot for captured enemies if they were not adopted.[61]

Among the Wendat, the greatest death toll came from starvation the following winter. About 5,000 died on Christian Island in Georgian Bay. Of those who survived, some joined with neighbouring Tionontati (called Petun by the French and Khionontateronon by the Wendat) and with the Kiskakon Odaawa. This group moved first to Chequamegon Bay in western Lake Superior and then to Michilimackinac, where they joined with the Kamiga Odaawa. As the Haudenosaunee threat diminished over the latter half of the seventeenth century, the Tionontati, Wendat, and Kiskakon Odaawa moved south to the area of Bkejwanong, the straits between Lakes Huron and Erie. There, the old distinctions between the Wendat and Tionontati peoples faded and they became known collectively as Wyandot. Several of their chiefs, among them Orontony (*fl.* 1739–50), entered into a trading relationship with the English.[62]

Of those who remained with the French alliance and continued to be known as "Huron" by the French, about 600 returned to their ancient territories along the north shore of the St Lawrence, eventually establishing Loretteville outside of Quebec (the ancient Stadakohna). Others fled to the Erie and Chonnonton, only to be defeated a second time by the Haudenosaunee. Most, however, went south to join the Haudenosaunee. Of those we know about, the Onondowaga took in the Tahontaenrat (Deer) as well as some Arendarhonon (People of the Rock), although most of the latter went to the Onondaga. A few got as far as Oklahoma. In later confrontations, the French would occasionally have the odd experience of fighting Haudenosaunee warriors who had once been their Wendat allies. When the Kanienkehaka accepted the surviving Attignawantan (Bear), however, they were taking in more than a conquered group of people.

Many of the Wendat-turned-Haudenosaunee had been previously exposed to Christian teaching. This gave the Jesuits leverage to intensify their evangelical campaign among the Haudenosaunee Confederacy. The campaign led to an out-migration from the Kanienkehaka villages to settlements around Montreal, as converts sought to be near their co-religionists.[63]

The dispersal of the Wendat Confederacy occurred 34 years after Champlain's visit and the arrival of the first missionary. From being the most powerful confederacy in the region, demographically, commercially, and militarily, in a little more than a generation the Wendat Confederacy was scattered far and wide, its villages destroyed, its cornfields reverting back to forest. It was far more than simply a defeat of a people. A complex commercial system had been brought down, the consequences of which would reverberate in the interior of the continent, reaching as far as James Bay in the Far North.

The fall of the Wendat Confederacy had far-flung consequences for both Indigenous Peoples and French colonizers. Wendake had been a breadbasket not only for the First Peoples but also for colonists. In New France, this led to an increase in land-clearing and in agriculture.

Politically, the dispersal of the Wendat Confederacy signalled a development that had been underway for some time. The French started off as a military force fighting on behalf of the Wendat and the Anishinaabek. Now, the Wendat and the Anishinaabek were fighting on behalf of the French.

The pattern of the fur trade was radically changed, also, as Montreal picked up where the Wendat Confederacy left off.[64] The annual brigades to Montreal, continued by the Odaawa along with remnants of the Wendat Confederacy, diminished and eventually ceased during the 1680s. Instead, the **coureurs de bois** fanned out from Montreal into the interior: the brigades were now going the other way. Despite the difficulties of inland travel—there were 38 portages between Montreal and Grand Portage, a distance of a thousand miles—it was an opportunity that the colony seized eagerly. The Jesuits reported that "all our young Frenchmen are planning to go on a trading expedition, to find the Nations that are scattered here and there; and they hope to come back laden with the Beaver-skins of several years' accumulation."[65] The east–west axis, fuelled with merchandise from Europe, now prevailed.

It was as part of this movement that Pierre Esprit Radisson (*c.* 1640–1710) and his brother-in-law, Médard Chouart des Groseilliers (1618–96?), penetrated north of Lake Superior during the 1650s with the indispensable aid of Odaawa and Wendat guides. Radisson did not record their names, but he mentions eight men of the Odaawa Confederacy in the Lake Huron voyage and two Wendat men in the Lake Superior voyage. In the Upper Great Lakes, Radisson and Groseilliers learned of the rich fur resources for which the Wendat had exchanged corn, beans, squash, and tobacco. The way was being prepared for the entrance of the Hudson's Bay Company, a quasi-governmental institution that would play a major role in the Canadian fur trade for two centuries.

In the meantime, the Council of Three Fires undertook a counter-offensive. By the end of the seventeenth century, it had driven the Haudenosaunee out of the entire Upper Great Lakes region and specifically from Wendake and the territories of the Tionontati and the Chonnonton. This led to the five members of the Haudenosaunee Confederacy agreeing to the 1701 Peace of Montreal.[66]

Wendake's Loss Is the Bay's Gain

While Europeans concentrated on the fur trade along the St Lawrence–Great Lakes systems, Indigenous Peoples were busy with their own networks, which stretched north to the Arctic and south to the Gulf of Mexico.[67] When the French finally reached Lake Mistassini in 1663, they became aware that enough trade goods were filtering through from the south to satisfy the needs of the northerners. This helps to explain why the French could not go through to the east side of James Bay by land until 1670. First Nations networks were coping with the increased volume brought about by the European trade.[68] The people saw no reason to encourage the French to come in.[69]

Four main trade routes stretched from the St Lawrence Valley to the north.[70] After the establishment of Quebec in 1608, however, the focus of the northern trade shifted west. The result was that the two routes from the Great Lakes to James Bay rose in importance. Wendake remained the hub of the north–south networks for 30 years, until it was destroyed in 1649. Haudenosaunee raiding parties then took advantage of the lack of Wendat protection, leaving the northern networks that had operated since distant times in disarray and cut off from access to trading goods from the south. In this realignment of forces, the Haudenosaunee Confederacy became the dominant Indigenous factor. They now controlled the main routes between the English colonies and the interior.[71] For most of the eighteenth century, the Haudenosaunee Confederacy would be the leading First Nations players in the Northeast.

In 1668, on the advice of Radisson and Groseilliers, an English expedition under the patronage of Charles II and his cousin Prince Rupert reached the shores of Hudson Bay.[72] Here they found that Indigenous Peoples who had once avoided contact were now eager to trade. The English organized the **Hudson's Bay Company** (HBC) and in 1670 granted it monopoly trading rights in those regions where the waters drained into the Bay. This territory, the 3.9 million square kilometres that forms the drainage basin of the Hudson Bay, was called Rupert's Land in honour of the royal sponsor of the expedition. The fact that this monopoly was granted to a commercial enterprise, with no thought given to the rights of the people living there from time immemorial, speaks volumes about the absolute neglect towards Indigenous land rights, resource rights, water rights, and especially sovereignty. There was no question of consulting the Indigenous Peoples involved.

That same year, the Company established Fort Charles on Rupert River. The local Cree were missing the supplies they used to receive through the Indigenous networks, and Fort Charles was an instant success. This resulted in the rapid spread of HBC forts around the Bay over the next 15 years. The French countered with their own forts in the interior but found the coureurs de bois more effective.

Trade Brings Changes, but Culture Remains Intact

The metal axe and cooking pot continued to be in demand as trade items.[73] The Europeans also soon assessed Indigenous preferences shrewdly enough to evolve the tomahawk, one of the first items developed by Europeans specifically for the Indigenous trade. Combining as it did the war axe with the peace pipe, it had connotations beyond the "practical" and fit with the Indigenous concept of the duality of nature, the dichotomy and interaction of life and death.

Brazilian tobacco was also an important trade item because even in the North, where tobacco did not grow, smoking was important for rituals.[74] Indigenous people also wanted decorative materials that they could not easily make themselves, such as mirrors and glass beads. These objects were adopted for use in religious and cultural celebrations, and so were highly valued.[75] Europeans quickly learned to appreciate certain aspects of Indigenous technology, such as the canoe, snowshoes, toboggan, and moccasins, to mention the best-known items, as well as their continued appreciation for the fashion of beaver furs.

By this time, the English had developed good relations with several nations along Hudson's Bay and throughout Rupert's Land, including the Omushkegowuk, the Iynu, and many others— all of whom the English referred to as "Cree." These nations would become more widespread as they prospered through the fur trade. The English, appreciating their hunting capabilities, found those whom they called Cree to be "of a humane Disposition."[76] Good relations were essential to the English, and the HBC post journals made little use of the word "savage," a term used so often in the settlements when referring to the Indigenous Peoples. The English of the HBC also knew that, at any time, the French—or anyone else on the scene—might make an offer and the Indigenous people might accept, destroying what the English were seeking to build. They had to secure the relationship, and they knew one way of doing so. It is important to note that the interests of the Hudson's Bay Company were those of a commercial nature, but that the interests of the New Englanders who participated in the Company's business included the acquisition of land and the expulsion of Indigenous Peoples, as the example of New England makes clear.

The First Treaties Formalized Trade Alliances

The English hoped to secure their position by entering into alliances, or "agreements."[77] The First Nations within Rupert's Land were willing partners in this. After all, they, too, were negotiating for alliances, without which trade was insecure. They did not understand, however, the "absolute propriety"—ownership—that the English believed they were acquiring.[78] The concept was completely foreign to them. Whatever the agreements were, Indigenous Peoples felt free to come to the posts, and one observer, at least, was under the impression that the HBC was paying them "rent"—probably a reference to the ceremonial gift exchanges and other rituals that accompanied trading.[79]

The English depended on the Indigenous **homeguards**, as they called them, who encamped near the forts, for food. This system helped to reduce shipping costs for the HBC, and helped protect the English from the uncertainties of shipping schedules. They tried to train their own men to hunt but at first were unsuccessful.[80] Here, too, feasts and gifts kept the relationship with the homeguards functioning. Even so, relations were not always easy.

Maintenance of the posts plus the demands of the fur trade eventually depleted game in some areas. Faced with starvation, Indigenous people turned to the posts for help. If such help was not given, ugly incidents could result. One occurred in 1832 at Hannah Bay, an outpost of Moose Factory, when starving Indigenous people raided it and killed its personnel.[81] These episodes were rare, however, in the North, but they do reflect the terrible harshness of the environment.

The Clash and Adaptation of Cultures

Neither side was impressed with the other's food. According to Samuel Hearne (1745–92), Indigenous people did not even like bread, "for though some of them would put a bit of it into their mouths, they soon spit it out again with evident marks of dislike; so that they had no greater relish for our food than we had for theirs."[82] Some individuals used this reaction to demonstrate their cultural superiority. Esquawino (Esqua:wee:Noa, *fl.* mid-eighteenth century), known to the English at Moose Fort as Snuff the Blanket, would hold his clothing to his nose when he entered the fort to avoid the smell. He refused to eat food prepared in the pots there.[83]

Vince Talotta/Getty Images

Johl Whiteduck Ringuette, chef and owner of Anishinaabe restaurant NishDish in Toronto. NishDish offers traditional Indigenous foods as part of Johl Ringuette's goal to bring traditions back to Indigenous people and keep food traditions alive while also encouraging discussion between Indigenous and non-Indigenous people. The restaurant also serves as a community hub, offering youth mentorship programs and a small market of Indigenous handmade goods. Johl Ringuette says of his restaurant, "It's really a reclamation of our food sovereignty, bringing back our food, what's best for our community."

On the other side of the picture, Hearne learned to appreciate some (though not all) Indigenous dishes.[84] He categorically dismissed the European belief that Inuit and First Nations of the Far North were cannibals.[85] Indigenous Peoples also eventually demonstrated dietary adaptability. They became so fond of prunes and raisins that they would "give a Beaver Skin for twelve of them to carry to their Children." But they continued to disdain cheese, believing that it was made of "dead Men's Fat."[86] Wendat (in common with Indigenous Peoples generally) did not like salt. In fact, they considered it to be poison (with some reason, the way Europeans were using it at the time) and refused to let their children touch it.[87]

The HBC sought at first to keep Indigenous people apart from Company "servants," as they called the men who worked for them. This, of course, turned out to be impossible. For one thing, the Company's minimum contact policy meant restriction of its access to the interior.

No European at that time could make such a trip without Indigenous people acting as guides and hunters.[88] As well, the presence of women in the trading groups that arrived at the posts sparked an interest among the servants, all of whom were male.

Women played a pivotal role in both trade and Indigenous societies within Rupert's Land generally. They fished and hunted small game, prepared maple sugar and other food, and made clothing. They also collected and prepared the materials needed to repair canoes—essential to all involved in the trade, whether Indigenous or European. John Tanner tells of an Odaawa woman named Netnokwa, who led trade negotiations.[89] **Thanadelthur** (d. 1717), a remarkable Dene woman, was captured by the Cree, escaped with another woman, and survived a year in the bush searching for York Factory, which she had heard about but had only a vague idea as to its location. Her companion died, and shortly afterwards a party from the factory found Thanadelthur. Taken to the post, she soon became invaluable as an interpreter and in persuading her people to come to the fort to trade despite the presence of their traditional enemies, the Cree.[90]

When the HBC relaxed its rule, at least unofficially, English exploration of the interior became possible. The need for new sources of furs, and particularly the aggressive expansion of the French, made such exploration necessary to the English. Henry Kelsey (c. 1667–1724) prepared for his extended voyage by living with Indigenous Peoples. During 1690–2, his Indigenous host family guided him to the northeastern edge of the Great Plains. There, he saw the great bison herds.[91] Similarly, **Samuel Hearne** met only failure in his attempts at northern travel until he accepted the advice of his Dene guide, **Matonabbee** (c. 1737–82). Thus, Hearne became the first European man to reach the Arctic Ocean overland, in 1772.[92]

Indigenous Imperatives to Trade

Even in trade, the HBC did not enjoy the control it would have liked. The Indigenous Peoples played the English against the French and were quick to recognize a better deal, but they were not businessmen in the same sense as Europeans. For one thing, they were not guided to the same extent by supply and demand in setting their prices.[93] Also, they accumulated goods to satisfy social obligations, rather than to denote status.

A disgruntled trader at Moose Fort described the entrepreneur Esquawino as "ye grand politician of all being a free Agent travelling about, sometimes to ye French, at others to Albany & this Fort, never drinks but has always his scences about him & makes ye best of his Markett at all places."[94] The English jailed the enterprising "Captain Snuff" on the charge of interfering with trade and stirring rebellion among the homeguard. Esquawino hanged himself because of loss of face.[95]

The HBC promoted contact only up to a point. The Company discouraged its men from teaching Indigenous children to read and write, fearing they would learn English trade secrets.[96] It would be a hundred years before it would recognize the value to the trade of Indigenous Peoples (particularly those born to its own employees) and launch a training program for them. By the 1790s there were increasing concerns about the growing number of children living at or near the posts. The London Committee—the businessmen in London who ran the Company—began to send spelling books and reading primers to the posts in order that the parents might educate their children. Soon, the Committee decided that formal education was necessary and in 1807 the Company opened schools at its main posts.[97] An early problem, however, was keeping the schoolmaster at his job. The fur trade was so much more lucrative than teaching.

A more serious problem, from an Indigenous perspective, concerns the curriculum. In addition to reading and arithmetic, "deportment" became an essential part of the curriculum. In other words, the girls (these schools taught both boys and girls) at the schools were given instruction in conduct so as to show them the "benefits" of an English way of life. The schools' focus on religious instruction was ominous as well, for this pointed the way towards the later residential schools. Students were taught the precepts of the Christian religion and they were expected to learn the church catechism and religious songs. All of this provided a foundation upon which the residential schools system would be built.[98]

The expanding presence of the English in North America disturbed the French at Quebec deeply, and they launched two encircling movements. The first one, in 1671, extended from the Great Lakes to the west and aimed at cutting off the English at the Bay from the interior; then, in 1699, the French moved to the south down the Mississippi, surrounding the Thirteen Colonies. The Haudenosaunee became alarmed, particularly with the first move. They saw it as an attempt to cut them off from the fur resources of the North. They responded by attacking the Irenweewa (the French called these people Illinois after their Odaawa allies told them their name was the Illinwe) in 1680 and stepping up their war against New France. Meanwhile, the French were doing their best to expand their own presence in North America.

National Territories Shift as the French Push beyond the *Pays d'en Haut*

The French moved to take possession of the West formally in 1671. To mark the occasion, they assembled 14 nations at the Jesuit mission at Sault Ste Marie to witness the ceremonies of possession—the raising of a cross and a post bearing the arms of France.[99] Although the First Nations knew of European interest in their lands, it is doubtful that they understood fully what the French were up to. Until that point, French relations with First Nations had been respectful of Indigenous land rights. With this westward expansion of the French, the First Nations gained a powerful new ally, one who would bring desired trade goods and who had promised to protect them from their enemies. As far as they knew, they had just concluded a good deal. The French learned, however, that the Haudenosaunee, whenever they came across a French metal plaque attached to a tree, tore it off and took it to the English. Thus, Jean Talon (1626–94), intendant of New France for two terms, 1665–8 and 1670–2, admitted the leaders of the Haudenosaunee Confederacy probably knew that the French were claiming the West as theirs.[100] On top of that, this huge expansion was presenting the French with problems of control—their people in the ***pays d'en haut***, the "upper country" of the Great Lakes beyond

Michilimackinac, did not always behave well. Officials realized the importance of the friendship of the local First Nations if they were to maintain a presence, and went to some trouble to keep the peace.[101]

In the 1670s, the French and the English were not the only ones expanding their territories. Ojibwa moved south from the north shore of Lake Huron into the former territory of the Wendat, the Tionontati, and the Chonnonton, all of whom the Haudenosaunee Confederacy had dispersed during the preceding decades. The Ojibwa and Nishnawbe-Aski pushed west, eventually moving onto the Plains into the territory of the Nakota, whom they pushed west and south. The Anishinaabe warriors fought hard against warriors of the Haudenosaunee Confederacy in skirmishes throughout the last decade of the seventeenth century.[102]

The Cree also expanded their territory.[103] By 1820, they were raiding in the Mackenzie Basin. To the north, the Dene contained them. To the south, they followed their Nakota (whom they called the Assiniboine) allies to take up life as buffalo hunters on the northern Plains.[104] The Cree/Nakota movement was partly linked to trade, at least in its later phase.[105] But the Siksikawa (called Blackfoot by the English) and their confederates, who controlled the central and southern Plains of present-day Alberta, stopped this movement.

In the Maritimes, the Mi'kmaq were not so fortunate. Advancing settlement was encroaching on them. They were in the throes of a war against the English, a confrontation that had begun early in the seventeenth century and would not end until the final defeat of France in 1760. Add to all this the century-long Haudenosaunee War against New France (which had ended in 1701) and Canada's "peaceful" frontier takes on the aspect of a wishful myth.

Questions to Consider

1. Why did Indigenous women seek French husbands?
2. In what ways did the Jesuits compromise the Wendat ability to defend themselves against the threat posed by the Haudenosaunee Confederacy?
3. Why did the Haudenosaunee Confederacy launch their attack on Wendake in 1649?
4. How did the Indigenous Peoples in what became Rupert's Land play the French against the English in the fur trade?

Recommended Readings

Bowden, Henry Warner. *American Indians and Christian Missions*. Chicago: University of Chicago Press, 1981.

Davis, Richard C., ed. *Rupert's Land: A Cultural Tapestry*. Calgary: Calgary Institute for the Humanities, 1988.

Francis, Daniel, and Toby Morantz. *Partners in Furs: A History of the Fur Trade in Eastern James Bay, 1600–1870*. Montreal and Kingston: McGill-Queen's University Press, 1983.

Houston, James. *Running West*. Toronto: McClelland & Stewart, 1989.

Jaenen, Cornelius J. *Friend and Foe: Aspects of French–Amerindian Culture Contact in the Sixteenth and Seventeenth Centuries*. Toronto: McClelland & Stewart, 1976.

Labelle, Kathryn Magee. *Dispersed but Not Destroyed: A History of the Seventeenth-Century Wendat People*. Vancouver: University of British Columbia Press, 2013.

Van Kirk, Sylvia. *Many Tender Ties: Women in Fur-Trade Society 1670–1870*. Norman: University of Oklahoma Press, 1983.

6 Some Indigenous–Colonial Wars

CHAPTER OUTLINE

The present chapter will cover the wars of the Haudenosaunee Confederacy and the system of alliances that evolved in response to threats both new and old. We will also examine the first efforts towards pan-Indigenism, again in response to the momentous changes. This chapter will address the important events both in the Great Lakes region and on the east coast, as Indigenous Peoples sought ways to accommodate the threats and the opportunities that arrived with the European colonizers.

LEARNING OUTCOMES

1. Students will understand the historical importance of alliance-building to Indigenous nations.

2. Students will gain insight into the difficult challenges posed by European colonization and they will gain understanding of the ways in which the various Indigenous alliances adapted to the changing diplomatic landscape.

3. Students will get an introduction to the Great Peace of Montreal that was held in 1701, possibly the most important diplomatic event of the contact era.

4. Students will see the differences that existed between the situations in the Great Lakes region and on the Atlantic coast.

TIMELINE From the Wars of the Haudenosaunee Confederacy to the End of the French Regime in America

1609–1701
The Haudenosaunee War, which ended with the Great Peace of Montreal.

1650
Kanienkehaka and Onondowaga join forces to defeat and disperse Attiwandaron villages to the west of the Niagara River.

1665
French sign peace treaty with Haudenosaunee nations , except for the Kanienkehaka, whose raids on French settlements have been especially unsettling.

1675
Onondowaga defeat the Susquehannock.

1687
Denonville sends dozens of captive Haudenosaunee warriors to France for service in galleys; 13 survivors eventually returned.

1693
French and Canadian militia warriors invade Kanienkehaka territory.

1710–38
The Mesquakie War (Fox War in English and Guerre des Renards in French), which involved French forces fighting alongside the Odaawak against the Mesquakie people of western Lake Michigan.

1716
French besiege Meskquakie village, killing an estimated 1,000 Indigenous people.

c.1720
Tuscarora migrate north to join the Haudenosaunee Confederacy. It is now called the League of Six Nations by the British colonizers.

1720s
Mesquakie war chief Kiala seeks alliance with Wabanaki (and Chief Nescambiouit), the Haudenosaunee , and Chickasaw.

1725
Mascarene's Treaty (Treaty No. 239) with Wabanaki after fall of Norridgewock, which details how Indigenous people must behave as British subjects.

1734
Kiala and three other Mesquakie leaders travel to Montreal to sue for peace: one chief pressed into galley service; Kiala sent as slave to Martinique, ends up abandoned on Guyana coast.

1749
Halifax established by English. Wabanaki and Wuastukwiuk of Saint John River ratify Mascarene's Treaty.

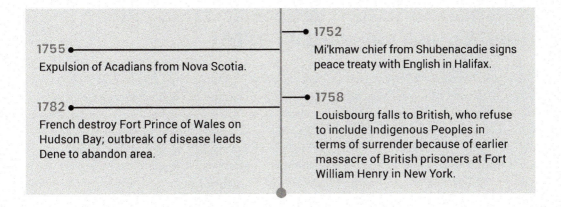

1755 — Expulsion of Acadians from Nova Scotia.

1752 — Mi'kmaw chief from Shubenacadie signs peace treaty with English in Halifax.

1782 — French destroy Fort Prince of Wales on Hudson Bay; outbreak of disease leads Dene to abandon area.

1758 — Louisbourg falls to British, who refuse to include Indigenous Peoples in terms of surrender because of earlier massacre of British prisoners at Fort William Henry in New York.

Alliances and Warfare

Unlike the British, who fought wars with Indigenous Peoples over land, and the Spanish, who saw Indigenous People as a slave labour force for gold and silver mines, French colonizers had a purpose for establishing amicable relationships with the peoples of northeastern North America. The French needed trading partners and they quickly came to view the Mi'kmaq, the Wendat Confederacy, and the Odaawa Confederacy of Lake Huron as allies. These alliances drew the French into war with the Haudenosaunee Confederacy (known to Europeans as the Five Nations Iroquois Confederacy), the ancestral enemies of the Wendat Confederacy and their Odaawa allies. From Champlain's first excursion with a Wendat, Innu, and Omamiwinini war party in 1609 to the **Great Peace of Montreal** in 1701, the French fought beside the Wendat and the Odaawak against the warriors of the Haudenosaunee Confederacy. For their part, the British waged endemic warfare against the Mi'kmaq of the east coast. Known as the Mi'kmaq War, this protracted conflict was fought over land and it lasted from about 1613 until 1761. It was a part of the Wabanaki wars (see Chapter 3). All of these wars were intermittent, sometimes with pauses that lasted for years.

Equalling, or perhaps even surpassing, the Haudenosaunee War in the intensity of emotion aroused was the Mesquakie War (1710–38), which saw French forces fighting in the region of western Lake Michigan after they came to terms with the Haudenosaunee in Montreal in 1701. The Mesquakie War concerned territory that became part of the United States, but it involved New France almost as deeply as the Haudenosaunee War had. The Mesquakie War began when the Ojibwa—allies of the Odaawak and therefore of the French—got into a series of disputes with the Mesquakie over encroachments into one another's ancestral hunting territories in the area between Lakes Michigan and Superior. The obligations of alliance thus drew the French into a conflict they did not want. The result of this war was defeat for the Mesquakie and a period of relative peace and prosperity for the Ojibwa and Odaawa nations of the Upper Great Lakes.[1]

Haudenosaunee War with the French and Their Allies (1609–1701)

The **Haudenosaunee War** was hard on both sides, but neither seemed able to stop.[2] The cyclical nature of the war, called the **Mourning War** by the members of the Haudenosaunee Confederacy, was ensured by the mutually held belief that warriors killed in battle could not enter the afterlife until they had been avenged in battle.[3] Both sides realized the futility of this belief, but it was difficult to eradicate. When the Omamiwinini war chief Pieskaret (d. 1647) killed 13 warriors of the Kanienkehaka in one engagement in 1645,[4] the leaders of the Kanienkehaka were ready to sue for peace. The French, feeling the effects of warfare in their fur trade, were willing to join the peace negotiations, but they handled the negotiations clumsily. Their failure to learn the rules of Indigenous diplomacy made matters worse. Not only did they hold meetings behind closed doors without the knowledge of allies and associates, but the peace agreement excluded their non-Christian allies as well.

The effect on the Indigenous Peoples when they learned the details of the French diplomatic shortcomings can easily be imagined. The treaty so displeased the excluded members of the Haudenosaunee Confederacy that it took all of the celebrated eloquence of a leading Kanienkehaka negotiator, Kiotseaeton ("The Hook," *fl.* 1645–6), with 17 wampum belts, to persuade even some of them to go along with its terms, at least for a while.[5] Among the main holdouts were the Onyota'aka. Not surprisingly, it did not take long for hostilities to resume, more intensely than ever, although the century of warfare was interwoven with attempts at peace.

Haudenosaunee Unity, Patched-Up Peace

In 1653, all the members of the Haudenosaunee Confederacy joined with each other to negotiate an accord. The French accepted the accord, even though their Indigenous allies were once more excluded from negotiating any peace terms. In the breathing space of a few years that followed, the Jesuits established a mission at Onondaga, the central village of the Haudenosaunee Confederacy, which would have important consequences in the future. In the meantime, the French allies received no respite. In the view of the French, the members of the Haudenosaunee Confederacy were not interested in peace until they obtained control of the flow of beaver from the region surrounding the southern half of the Great Lakes, deflecting flow to the Dutch and then the English.[6] This is a reflection of the French inability to understand Indigenous motivations. The Haudenosaunee leaders were more concerned with regional stability and Haudenosaunee security than with the trade in beaver pelts.

Except for a period in the mid-1650s, the four decades that followed the "patched-up peace" of 1645[7] saw the outlying areas of the colony, especially those around Montreal, become nearly impossible to farm. Sulpician missionary Dollier de Casson (1636–1701) described the "enemy all around us . . . [they] approach like foxes, fight like lions, fly away like birds." Haudenosaunee warriors, he wrote, thought nothing of passing a "whole day without moving, and hidden behind a stump" in order to dispatch a colonist.[8] "How can we fight a war against an invisible enemy?" one Jesuit complained. He added that unless they cut down all the forests, it would be impossible to stop the raids.[9] The exasperation with this type of warfare surfaced in a proposal that the Haudenosaunee be exterminated.[10]

By 1646, some Wendat leaders also doubted the wisdom of their alliance with the French. The benefits of the trade were great, but they blamed the French for the recent epidemics. Some found "that it costs them too dear, and they prefer to do without European goods rather than to expose themselves every year."[11] Meanwhile, the Haudenosaunee aimed to disrupt what they saw as a threatening alliance by raiding the Wendat villages, and in this they were very effective. A Jesuit missionary, observing these same techniques among the Wabanaki, said they made "a handfull of warriors more formidable than would a body of two or three thousand European soldiers."[12]

The Haudenosaunee attacks fuelled the anti-French faction among the Wendat. In 1648, a group of traditionalist Wendat men killed a young missionary assistant in the hope of ending the alliance and getting both French and Christianized Wendat expelled from Wendake, the ancestral homeland of the Wendat in what is now called southern Georgian Bay. This attempt by the traditionalist faction failed, however, and the pro-French faction prevailed. The Wendat gave the Jesuits a reparations payment said to have been the largest ever made by the confederacy.[13] That action, however, did not save the Wendat from dispersal the following year, a fate shared with their neighbours, the Tionnontaté, specialists in growing tobacco. That was only the beginning of a series of Haudenosaunee victories.

The Guerrilla Tactics of the Kanienkehaka

The **guerrilla warfare** waged by the warriors of the Haudenosaunee, based on surprise and speed of movement, was their preferred technique, particularly after they met with firearms. The only time the French faced a Haudenosaunee army on an open field was in 1609, when Champlain claimed that he had achieved deadly results from his one shot. Whether or not that account is true, Haudenosaunee warriors saw no virtue in exposing themselves to firepower they could not match. For the French, the tactics of the Haudenosaunee warriors were harder on nerves than on the lives of the colonists.[14] Dollier de Casson mentioned frequent skirmishes that wounded many but killed few. The Haudenosaunee Confederacy may have lost half their warriors to war and disease during the last two decades of the seventeenth century; the French, on the other hand, lost about 200 souls.[15]

To the French—indeed, to seventeenth-century Europeans in general—this type of warfare represented something new and, for a time, disconcerting.[16] At first, they tried to make a show of force in the European way. In 1665, they sent out the crack Carignan-Salières regiment, the pride of the French military establishment. Alexandre Prouville de Tracy, lieutenant general of America from 1663 to 1667, soon followed. The men of the Carignan-Salières regiment gave themselves *noms de guerre* or aliases as many of them had joined the army to avoid trouble in France. These names live on across Canada and many Métis people carry them today, an indication of the numbers of men who opted to stay in Canada and who went to the west, where they married Indigenous women. On 13 December 1665, the French signed a peace treaty at Quebec with four members of the Haudenosaunee, excluding the Kanienkehaka.[17]

As a result of Tracy's bold military enterprise against the Kanienkehaka villages in the autumn of 1666 and the French destruction of the corn crops and other supplies, the Kanienkehaka leaders sued for peace the following spring, in 1667. This time, the agreement held, at least for a while. The Haudenosaunee, who at that time were involved in wars from Virginia to Lac Saint Jean as well as in the West, needed time to adapt to this change in conducting international relations. The French also worked at coming to terms. In 1669, French officials executed three Frenchmen for killing an Onondowaga chief.

The destruction of their supplies apparently hit the Kanienkehaka hard. A few years later, the Onondowaga leaders presented La Salle, who was passing through their land, with 15 tanned deerskins in token of welcome. In a speech, an Onondowaga chief expressed the hope that the French would not burn their villages as they had done those of the Kanienkehaka a few years earlier.[18] At that point, they need not have worried. The Onondowaga were on the leading edge of western expansion, and many of them were trading with the English. In 1670, a worried intendant Talon estimated that the Haudenosaunee had diverted 1.2 million livres' worth of beaver. Therefore, it was important that the Onondowaga leadership not be antagonized.

French Invasion in the West

In 1673 Louis de Buade, Comte de Palluau et de Frontenac, governor general of New France, 1672–82 and 1689–98, enthroned in a sedan chair, headed up the St Lawrence to found a fort at Cataracoui, now Kingston. His intention was to ratify, and indeed to extend, the 1671 declaration made at Sault Ste Marie by the Sieur de Saint Lusson. This declaration effectively laid claim to the Upper Great Lakes region for King Louis XIV. At Cataracoui, Frontenac met delegates from the Haudenosaunee, who were much disturbed by Frontenac's presence. They saw it as a threat to their autonomy in the region of the Lower Great Lakes. To make matters even more unsettling, word came to the Haudenosaunee leadership that the Irenweewa leadership had allied themselves to the French. The Haudenosaunee were now feeling surrounded by potentially hostile forces.

In order to alleviate some of the pressure, the Haudenosaunee leadership negotiated a treaty with the Odaawak that same year. They promised to provide the Odaawak with trade goods in return for pelts.[19] It did not last past 1700, however, when the Haudenosaunee expeditions violated the treaty's terms by hunting in Odaawa territory. In the meantime, in 1680, the Confederacy's warriors invaded the country of the Irenweewa nations.

The French, for their part, again tried a European-style invasion of Haudenosaunee territory, this one organized by a new governor general, Joseph-Antoine Le Febvre de La Barre (in office 1682–5) and aimed at the Onondowaga (1684).[20] Illness broke out among the troops, however, forcing the army to encamp at a bay in Lake Ontario that became known as Anse de la Famine. There, the Haudenosaunee warriors found the French, disease-ridden and running out of food. Otreouti (Hateouati, among other variations, "Big Mouth," *fl.* 1659–88), Onondaga orator and chief, presented the Haudenosaunee terms. They would pay 1,000 beaver in return for damages from their raids. They were not, however, prepared to accept peace in the Irenweewa country, nor would they guarantee protection for French traders in the region. The French had no choice but to accept, a turn of events that angered officials in France. The government in Versailles quickly recalled Le Febvre de La Barre and sent out Jacques-René de Brisay de Denonville (governor general, 1685–9). Denonville was, after all, a professional soldier, so surely, the French believed, he could recoup this loss of honour.

In fact, Denonville's expedition against the Onondowaga (1687) had more casualties from disease than from fighting, but it was involved in one skirmish. Admittedly, it was an inconclusive ambush, but Denonville had at least engaged the Haudenosaunee warriors. He achieved this by adopting the Haudenosaunee tactics of surprise, surround, give way when pressed, and speed (a quick blow and rapid withdrawal).[21] The *raid-éclair* would contribute to the reputation of the Canadian militia as feared forest fighters in the cycle of French–English wars that began in 1689.

Denonville, like Tracy in 1666 against the Kanienkehaka, destroyed Onondowaga villages and food stores. He also captured a group of Haudenosaunee villagers and sent them to France as prisoners.[22] The ambush aroused a frightful row among the French colonizers. The Jesuits were especially angry, as they saw their years of difficult missionary work among the Haudenosaunee destroyed. Army officer Louis-Armand de Lom d'Arce de Lahontan (1666–before 1716), a caustic observer of the colonial scene, claimed that the French took prisoner friendly groups who came to settle around Fort Cataracoui. In fact, the royal government in France had long entertained the idea of transporting Indigenous prisoners to France, not just from New France but from the Caribbean also, and Denonville had acted under orders. In the end, though, the royal government in France backed down and returned the 13 survivors.

The Onodowaga suffered severely from the destruction of their stores by Denonville's troops, but they soon took revenge. Their raid on Lachine on an August dawn of 1689 saw 56 of 77 habitations go up in flames, killing at least 24 residents. They had caught the French completely by surprise, and the colony was stunned. More worrying for the French officials was the presence of an Odaawa witness to these raids. The peace settlement was bad enough, but the events at Lachine gave the Odaawak cause to wonder about the extent of French power. The strongest voice of discontent now arose from a prominent Sinago Odaawa named Ocheepik, whom the French called La Petite Racine. The Sinago Odaawak had always been the least enthusiastic towards the alliance with the French. They were responsible for the spiritual well-being of the nation itself and they equated the French with the zealous Jesuits. Ocheepik was a man in this tradition. He believed that relations with the French were best kept to a minimum: it was fine to trade furs for French weapons, but beyond that contact should be limited.[23]

In the summer of 1689 Ocheepik had gone to Montreal to attend the French–Haudenosaunee peace conference in order to report its outcome to the Odaawa council. Instead, he bore witness to the terrible ferocity of the Haudenosaunee attack and the pathetically inadequate French response. He returned to Michilimackinac and made his report to the general council that was called upon his return. The French were weak, he argued, and he stressed their inability to co-ordinate a defence of the colony. The Haudenosaunee warriors had been allowed to remain in the vicinity of Montreal for weeks and Governor Frontenac's bold assertions could do nothing to end their reign of terror. The Odaawa council resolved to set a moderate course. Two Onondowaga elders, Odaawa prisoners, were to be returned to their homes. This gesture was designed to threaten the French.[24]

War in Haudenosaunee Territory

For the next few years New France was in a virtual state of siege, with Montreal taking the brunt of the attacks. In 1691, Haudenosaunee warriors burned about 30 farms at Pointe-aux-Trembles, outside of Montreal. When the habitants captured a small group of Haudenosaunee warriors, they publicly burned three of them to death. The brutal lessons of warfare worked both ways.

During the 1690s, Frontenac was finally able to move the scene of war from New France or the territories of its allies and into the lands of the Kanienkehaka and Onondaga. The French inflicted heavy losses, and the Haudenosaunee leadership began to consider peace.[25] Their fear that the French would surround them was becoming a reality as the latter moved down the Mississippi and founded Louisiana in 1699. The French were encircling them also with alliances with western nations, particularly the Odaawak and the Myaamiaki (known to Europeans at the time as the Miami), who had fought very effectively for the French against the Haudenosaunee.[26]

The response of their English allies to Haudenosaunee requests for help was inadequate. The English provided few guns and little ammunition. The English were more concerned with their own security and were happy to let the warriors of the Haudenosaunee fend for themselves. For example, when the French and Canadians invaded Kanienkehaka lands in 1693, the forewarned English prepared for their own defence but neglected to warn their supposed Kanienkehaka allies. The latter suffered much damage and severe losses.[27] On top of that, the English and the French signed one of their periodic peace treaties in 1697 but did not include the Haudenosaunee in its terms. These actions are evidence of the lack of commitment shown by the British towards their allies. In fact, they show that there was no real alliance, and there would not be one until the American Revolution a century later. Both the English and the French claimed the Haudenosaunee as subjects. The Haudenosaunee, of course, did not see themselves as being subject to anyone.

Artful as always, the Haudenosaunee leaders signed a peace with the French in Montreal in 1701 in the face of English objections. Later that same year, they cemented their alliance with the English in Albany by ceding them lands in what would become southern Ontario.[28] The problem was that although the Chonnonton had occupied the area earlier, Odaawa, Ojibwa, Tionnontaté, and Wendat warriors had defeated the Haudenosaunee warriors in the region during the 1690s and had then established villages in the region the Odaawak called Bkejwanong and the French called *le Détroit*.[29] The English, apparently, were unaware of this. They also did not know that Haudenosaunee leaders, in a double twist, had negotiated with the French for their guarantee of hunting and fishing rights to that same region. Further, they assured the French of their neutrality in future wars but made no mention of this to the English. The Haudenosaunee negotiators were well aware that they could no longer put enough warriors in the field to challenge the Anishinaabe forces, the French *troupes de la marine* and militia forces living in the St Lawrence Valley, and the English forces all at the same time. European disease and endemic warfare had decimated their numbers.[30] On the other hand, Haudenosaunee leaders were playing both ends against the middle with great skill.[31]

In addition to diplomatic skill, the Haudenosaunee leaders had another ace in the hole—their access to English markets in Albany. During their hostilities against the French, they had been

INDIGENOUS LEADERS | Outoutagan (*fl.* 1698–1712)

One of the signatories of the 1701 peace was Outoutagan, or Jean Le Blanc as the French called him, a reference to his pale complexion. Outoutagan went to Montreal on 23 July 1701 in the expectation that the French would show support for the expansion of Odaawa territory around the Bkejwanong region. As soon as all of the delegates had arrived, Outoutagan of the Kamiga Odaawak presented Governor Callière with furs and, to the cheers of the entire assembly, Outoutagan declared the conference open. Of the four Odaawa **ogimaak, or chiefs,** at Montreal, Outoutagan bore the greatest responsibility for the success of the conference, and his meeting with Callière was the critical point of the conference. Outoutagan was the son of Le Talon, one of the most prominent Odaawak of the 1660s and 1670s. He was a strong supporter of the French, just as his father had been, and he was keenly aware of the prominence of the French alliance in the history of his own family. On more than one occasion he reminded the French governors of his family connection and the role his father had played in supporting the French in the past. Outoutagan was among the most perceptive of the Odaawa ogimaak, but he was also the most volatile. This last quality made him a diplomat of uneven quality.

Of all the private audiences he held, Callière's meeting with Outoutagan was the most delicate. Callière was able to convince most of the chiefs who sought private audiences with him that he was acting in their interest. The governor had a mild and engaging manner that led many of the delegates to believe his word even though he made too many promises to keep them all, and even though he blurred the important issues. Outoutagan was a more difficult case:

> Jean Le Blanc [Outoutagan] was the one who gave him [Callière] the most trouble. This Indian possessed great spirit, and though strongly committed to the French nation, he saw more clearly than was desired in a matter of this consequence.

Outoutagan informed Callière that the Odaawa leaders did not wish to see the various nations of the West relocated to the new fort that Cadillac had just completed at Detroit. He told the governor that Bkejwanong was Odaawa territory and the attempt to attract Boodwaadmii, Myaamiaki, and other nations would have grave consequences.[32]

careful to protect their position as suppliers in the English trading system. When the French market collapsed in 1696 because of oversupply, the Haudenosaunee leaders offered the French allies safe conduct through Haudenosaunee territories to New York markets—a brilliant move that deepened the crisis for the French in the West on both diplomatic and economic fronts. Their purpose was to allow the Anishinaabek into the English trade, but on Haudenosaunee terms.[33] Thus the Haudenosaunee maintained control in the trade and control over the access to European weaponry. This was a major diplomatic victory.

The Haudenosaunee Claim the Balance of Power, but Disease and Dissension Follow

The century of war shifted the balance of Indigenous regional power from Wendake to the Haudenosaunee territory south of Lake Ontario. The Haudenosaunee emerged with expanded territory, although not as much as they claimed.[34] Despite extensive adoptions of war captives, however, the population losses continued to mount. Between 1689 and 1698, the Haudenosaunee may have lost up to half of their fighting forces. Desertions to the Montreal settlements of converts contributed to this.[35] Remarkably, the Haudenosaunee still managed to keep their confederacy intact in the face of these losses and despite the relentless pressures of European settlement. The combination of these factors was changing Haudenosaunee society. For one thing, **longhouses** were being abandoned in favour of single-family living units. Even so, the Haudenosaunee identity remained strong.

With permission of the Royal Ontario Museum © ROM

The seventeenth-century Anishinaabe defeat of the Haudenosaunee as depicted around 1900 in porcupine quills on birchbark by Mesquab (Jonathan Yorke), from the Rama Reserve, Lake Simcoe. Mesquab took the design from a rock painting that once stood at Quarry Point, Lake Couchiching. Working from memory, Mesquab showed two Anishinaabe warriors dominating the Kanienkehaka in the centre. According to this picture, the Anishinaabe warriors had firearms while the Haudenosaunee warriors did not.

Paradoxically, the continued Haudenosaunee strength also assured the existence of New France, uniting the colonists and their allies and giving them a common purpose in the face of a common enemy. Indirectly, by destroying Wendake and dispersing the Wendats, the Haudenosaunee also facilitated the establishment of the English on Hudson Bay and forced the westward expansion of the French. These outcomes would soon lead to on-again, off-again battles between the French and the English in the North, which had a lasting impact on other Indigenous groups although they were not directly involved as allies.

The French historian of New France, Lahontan, held that it had never been in the interest of New France, either economically or politically, to eliminate the Haudenosaunee despite all the overheated rhetoric to that effect. In fact, by trying to destroy them, the French played into the hands of the English.[36] Other historians have agreed that the French failure to form a stable alliance with the Haudenosaunee Confederacy was a major factor in their 1760 defeat by the British.[37]

There is no way of knowing the war's toll for the Haudenosaunee. Hit by epidemics, particularly during the 1640s, they had compensated for their losses by incorporating defeated peoples. This was a technique they used very skilfully, but which the Jesuits later would be able to use to polarize Haudenosaunee society.[38] The death toll, however, eventually outran replacements, especially when the Haudenosaunee suffered mass defections as a result of the Jesuit missionary efforts. During the 1690s, two-thirds of the Kanienkehaka decamped for the two French missions around Montreal. Two factors were involved: the mass absorption of conquered peoples that had followed the dispersion of Wendake, and the work of the Jesuits.

Divisions within the Haudenosaunee communities became bitter as missionaries made inroads. Accusing the Jesuits of working for their destruction, traditionalists began a successful campaign to drive them out of Haudenosaunee territory, although they did not completely root out factionalism.[39] The Jesuits, for their part, encouraged converts to emigrate to such missionary villages as Sault St Louis (Caughnawaga, today's Kahnawake) and Prairie de la Madeleine (Kentake).[40] Within a couple of decades after the end of the conflict, the Haudenosaunee welcomed a new nation, the Tuscarora. The Haudenosaunee became known to the English as the **League of Six Nations.** The Tuscarora, fleeing from hostilities with settlers in the Carolinas, joined in 1722. This pattern of westward movement would become more and more common as the Anglo-American settlers pushed their frontier into the region of the Ohio River and the lower Great Lakes. As the Haudenosaunee laid down the gauntlet, however, their old allies the Mesquakie (whom the English called the Fox, the French called the Renards, and the Odaawa called the Outagami), one of the larger Anishinaabe groups of present-day Wisconsin, picked it up.

The Mesquakie War (1710–38)

The Mesquakie were old trading partners with the Haudenosaunee and were involved in the English trade network. They were the only Anishinaabe nation of the Upper Great Lakes who opposed the French, largely because they were on bad terms with the Odaawa and Ojibwa nations, important French allies. Although the scene of their war, what has come to be called the **Mesquakie War** (also known as the Fox War or Guerre des Renards), was far from the St Lawrence, in the *pays d'en haut*, it would become bitter, with the French forces determined to destroy people whom they deemed a dangerous threat to the French presence in North America.

Antoine Laumet *dit* Lamothe Cadillac (1658–1730) established Fort Pontchartrain (named after the Minister of the Marine) at Bkejwanong, the region between Lakes Huron and Erie. He won the support of the royal government by making the wild claim that this fort would replace Michilimackinac as the hub of the western trade.[41] Already the French were developing trade with the Dakota nations to the west of the Great Lakes. This had deeply disturbed their enemies, the Haudenosaunee and the Mesquakie. Cadillac must have been aware of this, but in order to demonstrate his apparent influence to his political supervisors, he invited the Mesquakie nations to establish villages around his fort—an invitation that outraged the Wendat, Odaawa, and Ojibwa peoples who had settled in the region in the 1670s and 1680s. This outrage turned into a riot in 1706 and the French officials eventually responded by finding a new position for Cadillac as the governor of Louisiana. In spite of the instability in the region, some of the Mesquakie nations accepted Cadillac's invitation in 1710, but the French at the fort were suspicious and watchful. Suspicion soon turned into anger as Mesquakie warriors began to attack French traders.[42]

Eventually other Mesquakie nations tried to leave their territory along northern Lake Michigan in order to establish villages among their Haudenosaunee allies, but the Odaawa and Ojibwa nations pressured the French to send forces to prevent this.[43] The Mesquakie responded in 1711 by preventing French traders from reaching the Mississippi and the Dakota nations to the west. Not only did they cut the French off from access to the southwest, but they also harassed the French allies on their hunting grounds. The French, again at the urging of their Odaawa and Ojibwa allies, retaliated, besieging a Mesquakie village for 19 days and killing about a thousand men, women, and children. If the French had hoped that this would cool the situation, they were mistaken.[44]

Finally, in 1716, the French sent out an army, possibly disguised as a trading delegation, the first French military expedition to penetrate so far west. Once more, the Mesquakie nations fortified themselves in a village, and the French destroyed it. The Fox–Wisconsin river system was once again open for traders. Ouchala (*fl.* 1716–27), the pro-French Mesquakie chief, led the peace negotiations. Among other terms, the Mesquakie agreed to hunt to pay the costs of the war. To ensure that the Mesquakie nations carried out these terms, the French took six hostages to Montreal, where two of them died of smallpox. Ouchala then delayed ratifying the agreement. By the time he did so, he was not able to prevail against the mutual recriminations concerning breaking the agreement.[45]

A good example of what the actual conflict looked like is to be found in the history of Francis Assikinack (1824–63), a nineteenth-century schoolteacher, Indian Department clerk, and historian. In this passage he describes the nature of an Odaawa war expedition:

> In commencing their journey, if by land, the leader put himself at the head of his party, consisting generally of from thirty to forty warriors. If they had to perform a part of their journey by water, he took his seat about the middle of the canoe, where he had to stand up and sing a war song as they started, with a rattle, or medicine ball in his right hand, made of hide, about the size of a cricket ball, having a small handle, and containing a few dry bones. When shaken it made a sharp sound, something like the noise of a rattlesnake. From the day of their setting out the war

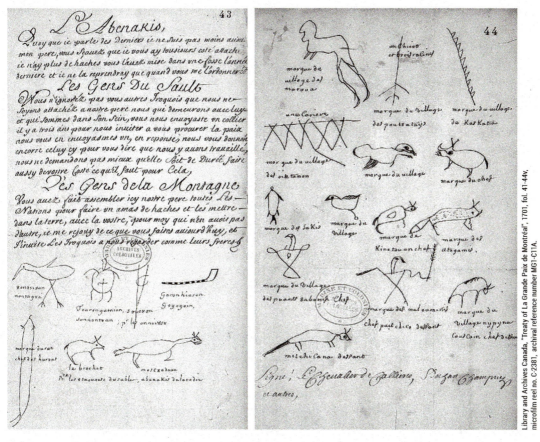

Folios from the Great Peace of Montreal (1701). 39 First Nations signed the Montreal peace treaty using the mark of each of their nations, along with the governor of New France. The Mesquakie mark is visible in the centre right of the right-hand page, signed by Chiefs Noro & Miskouensa (depicting a fox). As in the Indigenous Leaders box on p. 109, Outouagan along with Kinongé also signed the treaty to represent the Sable Odaawa. The Sable Odaawa mark is on the left page, centre (depicting a bear).

party fasted every day until noon. Their rules of war required them to be in perfect harmony with one another, never to make use of an expression which might wound the feeling of any of their party; and to abstain from all conversations about women and personal enemies at home.[46]

Kiala Works for Indigenous Unity, and the French Retaliate

A new governor general, Charles de Beauharnois de la Boische, in office from 1726 to 1747, set out to re-establish French control in the West. Two years after his appointment, in 1728, Paul Marin de la Malgue (1692–1753) became the French leader in the West, which he would dominate for the next quarter-century. In the midst of the bitter campaigns that followed, the Mesquakie, led by **Kiala** (Quiala, *fl.* 1733–4), moved to reaffirm their alliance with the Haudenosaunee.

Kiala was the war chief who headed the anti-French faction. He negotiated with the Chickasaw and Wabanaki, confirming old alliances and building new ones to counter the increasing French threat. Nescambiouit, the Wabanaki chief, was involved in these discussions (see Chapter 4). This greatly upset the French, who saw an attempt to encircle them, cutting them off from their allies and separating New France from Louisiana. Consequently, the French went on the offensive.

In 1730, the Mesquakie, harassed on all sides, sent two redstone axes to the Onondowaga, asking to come and live with them. In spite of French attempts to prevent it, the Onondowaga agreed, and the Mesquakie began their migration. Cornered in 1730 by the pursuing French under Nicolas-Antoine Coulon de Villiers (1683–1733),[47] they held out for 23 days before attempting a sortie.[48] By now, only a few hundred survived of the 1,300 Mesquakie people of a year earlier.[49] The French with their allies set about tracking down the remnants. Some groups fled west of the Mississippi. Villiers, one of his sons, and a son-in-law died in the fighting, setting off yet another punitive French expedition in 1734. This time, however, the French allies decided that matters had gone far enough. They refused to go along with the campaign, which, as a result, came to nothing.

In the meantime, in 1733, the remaining Mesquakie leaders had sued for peace. The following year, Kiala and three other Mesquakie leaders surrendered in Montreal. The French sent one of the chiefs to France for service in the galleys. They sent Kiala as a slave to Martinique but instead abandoned him on the Guyana coast. The Huron of Lorette—as the Wendat who settled at Quebec City called themselves—adopted his wife. The French scattered other Mesquakie prisoners among the missions. Thus ended Kiala's dream of uniting Indigenous Peoples from the Atlantic to the Ohio Valley.[50]

Some French allies went to Montreal to plead for their former enemies. They were having second thoughts: what was happening to the Mesquakie could happen to them. During this period, the Sauk reconsidered their position and became such firm allies of the Mesquakie that the two peoples ever since have been referred to together. In the final campaigns of the French, more of their allies sided with the Mesquakie and the Osaakiiwaki. As Beauharnois expressed it, "The Savages as a rule greatly fear the French, but they do not love them."[51]

Peace was finally achieved in 1738. The French confirmed it five years later, when Marin de la Malgue, who had stayed with the Mesquakie in the West, led another delegation to Montreal. The Mesquakie people were no longer the enemy. From a nation that had once counted at least a thousand warriors, they could now muster barely 250. Some Mesquakie warriors later joined the French and fought with them against the English, including the 1755 attack that annihilated the British army led by General Edward Braddock (1695–1755) and in the Battle of the Plains of Abraham in 1759.

What can we learn from these two conflicts? For one thing, the French were more effective against the Mesquakie than they had been for most of the war against the Haudenosaunee— because they had adapted to forest fighting techniques. The French had learned from their very first contacts to forge firm alliances with Indigenous Peoples. The English were much slower to recognize the importance of this form of diplomacy. In the Great Lakes area, however, the English had finally come to see the value of conducting diplomacy with the Indigenous people. The Indigenous Peoples, on the other hand, were beginning to realize the importance of allying with each other instead of with the invading Europeans. Although pan-Indigenism barely got a hesitant start, it was enough to give the French a severe fright.

The Mi'kmaq Defend Their Land (1713–61)

As the final round of the North American colonial wars got underway, the Mi'kmaq pitched into the fray on land and sea, asserting their right to make war or peace as they willed and reaffirming their sovereignty over their land, **Megumaage**. Between 1713 and 1760, they captured well over a hundred vessels, cruising in their captured ships before abandoning them, and forcing their prisoners to serve as crew. They had no use for ships of that size, just as they had no use for artillery. This activity peaked in 1722, the year the so-called English–Indian War broke out. Revivals of lesser proportions in the 1750s followed the establishment of Halifax in 1749 and the expulsion in 1755 of the Acadians, many of whom had blood ties with Indigenous people.[52]

The turning point came in 1725, when the Wabanaki sued for peace following the destruction of Norridgewock. The British took advantage of the situation to negotiate not only for peace (the Treaty of Boston) but also for a second agreement, Treaty No. 239 (also called **Mascarene's Treaty** after its main British negotiator), detailing how they expected Inidgenous Peoples to behave as British subjects.[53]

The treaties called for countermeasures, especially as the allies were complaining that the all-important gift distributions often did not have enough goods to go around. The French steadily increased the budget for this purpose. By 1756, it had reached 37,000 livres, not including "extraordinary expenses" entailed when employing Indigenous people.[54] Indigenous leaders would no longer accept promises of gifts to come. They would lead their allies only when they had goods in hand. What started as a matter of protocol to cement alliances and trade agreements ended as a means of subsistence for Indigenous Peoples and a form of protection for the French.

Even as the French spurred their allies to fight against the English, they did pause from time to time at the "*férocité inutile*" of some of their attacks. Sometimes, they even tried to curb them. In 1739, the governor of Île Royale, seeking to calm Mi'kmaw fears, asked them to keep the peace for the sake of the French King and themselves. The Mi'kmaq, on the other hand, worried that the French and English would unite to destroy them. They observed that if they had listened less to the French, they would be having less trouble with the English, who were taking their lands and destroying their fishing. They promised to be quiet for the present but warned that they would protect themselves against those who tried to destroy them.[55] A decade later, they would have reason to make good on their threat.

HISTORICAL BACKGROUND | War at Sea and on Land

Several characteristics distinguish the **Mi'kmaw War**. First, it was fought largely at sea. In addition, the part of it fought on land was the only case in Canada where an Indigenous group fought on their own lands for their own lands. In this aspect, the war in its later phases came to resemble the frontier wars in the US. Despite the fact that the Mi'kmaq and Wuastukwiuk have had one of the longest contacts with Europeans, and despite the protracted hostilities, they still are living on their ancestral lands, although only on a tiny fraction of what was once theirs.

The Mi'kmaq Declare War

When the British founded Halifax in 1749 in a district the Mi'kmaq called Segepenegatig, they once more failed to consult the Indigenous inhabitants. Asking "Where can we go, if we are to be deprived of our lands?" the Mi'kmaq adopted a European custom and formally declared war (see Historical Background box).[56] To the English, the Mi'kmaq were simply rebels.[57]

Mi'kmaw raids were effective enough for the governor to request more arms for the colonists, as "at present above ten thousand people are awed by two hundred savages." As the raids intensified, he issued a proclamation commanding the settlers "to Annoy, distress, take or destroy the Savages commonly called Mic-macks, wherever they are found."[58]

During this period, both French and English paid bounties for scalps at escalating rates, no questions asked.[59] In the midst of all this, for a brief period, the British officially encouraged marriages to Indigenous women.[60] They also gave in to the inevitable and began to be more generous in their gift distributions. This influenced the Wuastukwiuk and Wabanaki of the Saint John River, in 1749, to ratify Mascarene's Treaty. The French tried to answer this by sending René, a chief from Naltigonish, to act as a counter-agent, but without success.[61]

Despite their efforts, in 1752 the French received ominous news: a ranking chief from Shubenacadie had signed a peace treaty in Halifax.[62] This treaty was a major breakthrough, not only in its effect on the course of the Mi'kmaw War but also in the terms of the treaty itself. It guaranteed hunting and fishing rights for the Mi'kmaq and regular gift distributions. These gifts, later, would be transformed into annuity payments for surrendered lands.[63]

The Mi'kmaq, Wuastukwiuk, and Wabanaki See Their Allies Lose Ground

Further south, the fall of Fort William Henry (at Lake George, New York) in 1757—and the murder of English prisoners by French allies that followed—raised settler hysteria against Indigenous Peoples to such a pitch that when Louisbourg fell in 1758, the victorious British, under the brutal leadership of General Jeffery Amherst, refused to include the

Indigenous Peoples in the terms of surrender.[64] The Indigenous Peoples correctly saw this as not boding well for them, and when the British formally took over the fortress, not one was present.[65]

If the Indigenous factor had simply faded at Louisbourg, however, this was not true for Acadia generally. The British now had to make sure that the peace agreement included all chiefs and their people, if a general peace were to be achieved. It took the final defeat of the French in 1760 to accomplish this. A year later, they signed the peace. The Mi'kmaq, Wuastukwiuk, and Wabanaki of Acadia finally acknowledged British sovereignty. In return, they were assured that they would have the full protection of British laws just as any other subject "as long as the sun and the moon shall endure."[66]

In this long struggle, Mi'kmaq, Wuastukwiuk, and Wabanaki had shown themselves astute in turning imperial rivalries to their own advantage. After all, when it came to self-interest, there was not much to choose between the Indigenous Peoples and the colonial powers. The difference lay in the fact that both France and Britain were building empires, whereas Indigenous Peoples, after a brief initial period when some tried to use European alliances to expand their own territory, soon found themselves struggling to survive. Their ability to keep the colonial powers off balance became their most formidable weapon. In this, Louisbourg's role was vital.

For the French, whatever their original intentions for building the fortress, Louisbourg's greatest military usefulness turned out to be as a headquarters for the maintenance of Indigenous alliances and the encouragement of their guerrilla warfare. For the Mi'kmaq and Wuastukwiuk, it represented a reprieve from European economic and cultural domination, because as guerrillas they were able to dictate to a surprising extent their terms as allies, particularly with the French.

The spectre of French return to Canada continued to haunt the British until the defeat of Napoleon at Waterloo in 1815. In 1762 a French force captured St John's, Newfoundland, and held it for a couple of months, until they were defeated at the Battle of Signal Hill. Hearing this news, the Mi'kmaq became edgy, giving settlers a severe fright. Reports that French from the islands of St Pierre and Miquelon off the south coast of Newfoundland were secretly supplying the Mi'kmaq also fuelled these fears, but those rumours were never substantiated. It seems that the Mi'kmaq had gone to the islands, which remained under French control, looking for priests and supplies. The French were under orders to discourage such visits, on the ground that they would only annoy the British and would serve no purpose;[67] but they seem to have helped the Mi'kmaq anyway.

Thrown back on their own resources when traditional territories had long since been over-hunted, the Mi'kmaq were now desperately searching for a means of subsistence. Groups went to southern Newfoundland, where they had maintained sealing and fishing stations for centuries, alarming settlers and authorities alike. In spite of official attempts to dislodge them, however, they had come to stay.[68] This once assertive, far-ranging people on sea and land now had to take what they could get, and that was not very much. In fact, the process was in reverse. Settlers were now streaming into the homelands the Mi'kmaq had fought so hard to protect.

Questions to Consider

1. In what ways did the Haudenosaunee play multiple sides against one another in the late seventeenth century?
2. Define the term "Mourning War."
3. What were the causes of the Mesquakie War?
4. What were the war aims of the French and British in the Mi'kmaw War?

Recommended Readings

Assikinack, Francis. "Social and Warlike Customs of the Odahwah Indians," *Canadian Journal of Industry, Science, and Art* New Series, 3 (1858): 297–309.

Brandão, José Antonió. *Your Fyre Shall Burn No More: Iroquois Policy toward New France and Its Native Allies to 1701*. Lincoln: University of Nebraska Press, 1997.

Coates, Kenneth S., and William R. Morrison, eds. *For Purposes of Dominion*. Toronto: Captus University Publications, 1989.

Dickason, Olive Patricia. "Louisbourg and the Indians: A Study in Imperial Race Relations, 1713–1760," *History and Archaeology* 6 (1976): 1–206.

Edmunds, R. David, and Joseph L. Peyser. *The Fox Wars: The Mesquakie Challenge to New France*. Norman: University of Oklahoma Press, 1993.

Englebert, Robert, and Guillaume Teasdale, eds. *French and Indians in the Heart of North America, 1630–1815*. Winnipeg: University of Manitoba Press, 2013.

Hunt, George T. *The Wars of the Iroquois*. Madison: University of Wisconsin Press, 1967.

Jennings, Francis. *The Ambiguous Iroquois Empire*. New York: Norton, 1984.

Kenyon, W.A., and J.R. Turnbull. *The Battle for the Bay 1686*. Toronto: Macmillan, 1971.

MacLeod, D. Peter. *The Canadian Iroquois and the Seven Years War*. Toronto: Dundurn Press, 1996.

Richter, Daniel K. *The Ordeal of the Longhouse: The Peoples of the Iroquois League in the Era of European Colonization*. Chapel Hill: University of North Carolina Press, 1992.

7 The Struggle against British Colonialism

CHAPTER OUTLINE

The beginnings of the pan-Indigenous movement coincided with the fall of New France, an important subject in the present chapter. Indigenous Peoples quickly realized that their old tactic of playing one colonial power against the other was rapidly changing. In its place a complicated new political situation evolved in which the First Nations leaders had to negotiate a path between Britain and the newly emerging American nation. The immediate effect on the First Peoples who lived within what is now Canada was the beginning of the treaty system, as the Royal Proclamation of 1763 began a process still being negotiated to the present day. This beginning forms the second important subject of this chapter.

LEARNING OUTCOMES

1. Students will be able to define the concept of pan-Indigenism and will recognize its importance in the shifting political situation of the late eighteenth century.

2. Students will understand the significance of both the Royal Proclamation of 1763 and the Quebec Act of 1774 in subsequent treaty negotiations.

3. Students will gain insight into the severe difficulties confronting Indigenous Peoples in the early years of the British Regime.

TIMELINE From the Fall of New France to the Peace of Paris

1760
Fall of Montreal to British. British Commander-in-Chief Jeffrey Amherst ends trade ceremonies with First Nations.

1762
Pan-Indigenous alliance, led by Obwandiyag, Odaawa war chief, lays siege to Fort Detroit for five months.

1764
Peace conference at Fort Niagara formed by Sir William Johnson: 2,000 Indigenous people from 19 nations respond, but Obwandiyag does not go.

1765
Obwandiyag signs separate agreement but does not give up lands.

1769
Obwandiyag assassinated by a Peewaarehwaa (Peoria) man.

1775
British colonist invasion of what would become eastern Canada repulsed for two weeks by the Haudenosaunee Confederacy.

1776–83
Indigenous Peoples fight on both sides of US War of Independence.

1784
Haudenosaunee Loyalists granted Six Nations Reserve (Haldimand Grant) on Grand River in Upper Canada after cession of 3 million acres on Niagara Peninsula.

1760s–70s
Pan-Indigenous alliance, the Federation of Seven Fires, forms to resist loss of lands to settlers, but does not survive colonial distrust and US War of Independence.

1763
Treaty of Paris effectively ends French presence in North America. Proclamation of 1763 at least partially acknowledges Indigenous territorial rights. Nine British forts, including Fort Michilimackinac, fall to pan-Indigenous alliance in May–June. Neolin, "The Delaware Prophet," calls to drive Europeans back into the sea. Amherst proposes giving smallpox-infested blankets to the people of the Odaawa and Ojibwa Confederacies.

1766
Ratification of agreements at Fort Ontario, at which Obwandiyag dominates.

1774
Quebec Act brings Ohio Valley and Great Lakes region under Quebec jurisdiction; British colonists object that their "legitimate" expansion is being thwarted. This becomes a major cause for the Thirteen Colonies on the eastern seaboard to declare their independence from Britain.

1783
Peace of Paris to end conflict between Britain and Thirteen Colonies completely ignores Indigenous Peoples.

late 1700s–early 1800s
Millions of acres in present-day southern and central Ontario ceded by Ojibwa and Odaawa Confederacies.

Defeated by Peace

The defeat of France in the North America was a disaster for many Indigenous Peoples, from the east coast to the Great Lakes and even westward. Besides depriving them of their bargaining position between two rival powers, it also cut them off with brutal suddenness from trading partnerships that had become part of their economic strategies. To make matters worse, although the defeat of the French at Montreal in 1760 appeared to guarantee Indigenous Peoples protection for the lands they inhabited, colonial authorities did not honour the agreements.[1]

British Commander-in-Chief Jeffrey Amherst (1717–97) lost no time introducing economies after the fall of Montreal. Among the first items to be cut were the trade goods used to confirm the alliances. After all, now that the French were gone, the British did not think they needed their Indigenous allies. In Indigenous eyes, however, the annual trading ceremonies not only symbolized the renewal of English–Indigenous alliances, they also were the agreed-on price by which the Indigenous Peoples allowed the English to use their lands.

To complicate matters, Indigenous Peoples had come to depend on such items as guns and ammunition. **Sir William Johnson** (Warraghiyagey, "He Who Does Much Business"), British Superintendent of Indian Affairs from 1755 to 1774, strongly advised Amherst against the move,[2] but Amherst did not listen. The general situation was such, however, that some exchange remained a practical necessity and continued until 1858.

Britain had led her Indigenous allies to believe that once they drove the French out, encroaching settlers also would go and the Indigenous Peoples would get better trade deals. British officials, however, were rapidly losing control of their colonists and could not enforce any arrangements made on their behalf. More settlers than ever moved into Indigenous territories,[3] and Anglo-American traders raised their prices as they no longer had to worry about a competing supply of goods from the French.

During hostilities, the British co-operated with Indigenous leaders in limiting the liquor trade to preserve them as allies. With peace, they lost interest in protecting the Indigenous Peoples from the traffic that was so harmful to them yet highly profitable to the Anglo-American merchants.[4] Traders swarmed into Indigenous territory and operated outside of any recognized authority. The Indigenous Peoples were unable to control them, and colonial governments did not bother to do so.[5] Even though, in the words of Peter Wraxall, New York's secretary for Indian Affairs, 1750–9, trade was "the chief Cement which binds us together," it had its perils both for Indigenous Peoples and for white settler-colonizers. Nonetheless, trade was the "first Principle of our whole System of Indian politics."[6]

The First Peoples, on whichever side they chose, saw the struggle between the French and English as a threat to their delicate strategic balances and they started to worry about the associated dangers. As more than one chief remarked, no one had conquered the Indigenous Peoples. This land was their land, and they had allowed the Europeans to come and settle on it, but there had always been an understanding of mutual interest. The ceremonial exchange of trade goods symbolized the annual renewal of the alliances and the loss of one side had terrible consequences and implications for all Indigenous Peoples, which they recognized. Ojibwa chief Minweweh (Minavavana, *c.* 1710–70), "The One of the Silver Tongue," also known as "Le Grand Sauteur"), who fought alongside the French, voiced a general sentiment when he told the British: "Although you have conquered the French, you have not conquered us. We are not your slaves. These lakes, these woods and mountains were left us by our ancestors. They are our inheritance, and we will part with them to none."[7] The British, uneasily aware of Indigenous fears about losing their lands, eventually moved to reassure them by at least partially acknowledging their territorial rights in the **Proclamation of 1763**, which today is embedded in the Canadian Charter of Rights and Freedoms (Constitution Act, 1982, section 25[a]).

The British were unable to prevent their colonists from moving into territory that had been previously protected by the presence of the French, the Canadians (those settled in what was unofficially referred to as "Canada" though was still officially New France, which extended as far south as Louisiana), and the French allies. With the fall of New France, the British very quickly lost control of their own colonists and the Indigenous people paid the price. Even worse were the techniques the newcomers were using to "purchase" Indigenous lands and the extent of the lands involved. In 1756, Johnson warned about the effects of such practices. The fraudulent purchase of lands became an important element of the Royal Proclamation of 1763 as the British government attempted to regulate an issue that was becoming a crisis for Indigenous Peoples. As the First Peoples observed to George Croghan (d. 1782), a successful trader who for 15 years was Johnson's right-hand man, "in either case they would lose their Lands, & the consideration they got was soon spent, altho' the Lands remained," but in the hands of the non-Indigenous people.[8]

An Indigenous resistance loomed alarmingly close. At councils, nations met to share their grievances. Out of this coalesced the **Federation of Seven Fires** (also called the Seven Nations of Canada), an alliance network linking French mission Indigenous people: those Wendat and Haudenosaunee who had sided with the French.[9] The central fire was maintained at Kahnawake, where the members gathered every three years. The confederacy did not survive the dislocations of the US War of Independence or colonial distrust of anything that smacked of pan-Indigenism, a movement proposed by Obwandiyag aimed at uniting all First Nations against the British.[10]

Colonial officials knew the causes of Indigenous unrest, but they were unable to control their own colonists.[11] A British plan to control the traders by restricting trade to the posts and to eliminate rum failed, and Indigenous resentment reached the boiling point. Johnson, in alarm, called a general peace conference at Detroit in 1761. Just before it opened, he received a letter from Amherst forbidding ceremonial exchange. Johnson considered the decision so unwise he ignored it for the moment. The truth was not long in coming out, however, as other expected distributions did not take place. By the spring of 1762, Indigenous Peoples were short of ammunition and the lack of French blacksmiths meant that many of their firearms were unserviceable.

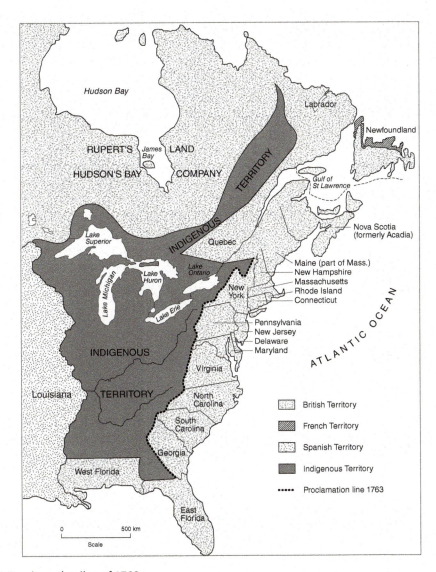

Map 7.1 Proclamation line of 1763.

© Carl Weldman and Infobase Learning, from *Atlas of the North American Indian* (New York: Facts on File, 1985). Reprinted with permission of the publisher.

Obwandiyag (Pontiac)

Out of this troubled situation emerged **Obwandiyag** (1712/1725–69), an Odaawa war chief. We do not know much about him, and we have only a vague idea of what he looked like.[12] His personality gave rise to contradictory reports. To some, he was imperious of manner, "proud, vindictive, warlike, and very easily offended."[13] However, Major Robert Rogers (1731–95), who went to Detroit in the fall of 1760 with 200 of his famous Rangers, and who had reason to be grateful to Obwandiyag for having prevented his warriors from attacking the British contingent, found him to be a man of "great strength of judgment and a thirst after knowledge."[14]

Obwandiyag seems to have supported a movement among the Indigenous Peoples that claimed a spiritual vision had called for a return to the ways of their ancestors. Like Nescambiouit of the Wabanaki and Kiala of the Mesquakie before him, Obwandiyag saw the need for united action against the Europeans. Also like Kiala, he was unable to achieve it on a large enough scale to change the course of events. Obwandiyag's challenge is most succinctly put by Makade-binesi (who published under the name Andrew Blackbird), the nineteenth-century Odaawa historian:

> According to our understanding in our traditions, that was the time the British Government made such extraordinary promises to the Ottawa tribe of Indians, at the same time thanking them for their humane actions upon those remnants of the massacre [he is referring to the capture of Fort Michilimackinac]. She [Great Britain] promises them that her long arms will perpetually extend around them from generation to generation. Or so long as there should be a rolling sun. They should receive gifts from her sovereign in shape of goods, provisions, firearms, ammunition, and intoxicating liquors! Her sovereign's beneficent arm should be even extended unto the dogs belonging to the Ottawa tribe of Indians.[15]

According to Major Rogers, Obwandiyag was prepared not only to accept British settlement but even to encourage it. He expected, however, to be treated with respect and honour.[16] Although he had fought on the side of the French, when Montreal fell Obwandiyag quickly moved to establish good relations with the British, on the strength of the latter's promises of better treatment. When that did not happen, he again turned to the French, this time those who had remained in the Old Northwest (the region surrounding the southern half of the Great Lakes, spanning modern-day Ohio, Indiana, Illinois, Michigan, and Wisconsin), but they had little to offer their former ally.

During the summer of 1762, a war belt and hatchet circulated through the Old Northwest, which represented a call to arms to all of the Indigenous Peoples in the region. Resentment had been building for well over a year, encouraged by the French residents still in the area. That fall, Onondowaga warriors struck the first blow by killing two Anglo-American traders. A month later, two British soldiers were killed in the Ohio Valley. Obwandiyag, after a series of wins against the English, tried to take Fort Detroit by a ruse, but his plan was betrayed. Obwandiyag then laid a siege that lasted five months.[17]

Obwandiyag appears to have supported a movement among the Indigenous Peoples that claimed a spiritual vision had called for the return to the ways of their ancestors. This was an early manifestation of **nativistic movements** by which Indigenous Peoples sought to cope with the invasion of their lands and missionary pressures against their way of life. **Neolin** ("One That Is Four," *fl.* 1760s), one of two known as "The Delaware Prophet," urged his people, the Lenni

Lenape, to abstain completely from contact with white people: "I warn you, that if you allow the English among you, you are dead, maladies, smallpox, and their poison will destroy you totally."[18]

The Ojibwa leaders Minweweh and Madjeckewiss (Machiquawish, among other variations, c. 1735–c. 1805) had better luck with a similar ruse against Fort Michilimackinac, at the Straits of Mackinac connecting Lakes Huron and Michigan. There, Ojibwa and Osaakiiwaki warriors organized a lacrosse game that allowed them to gain entrance to the fort and overwhelm its garrison. Between 16 May and 20 June 1763, nine British forts fell. The only posts in the war zone still in British hands were those at Detroit (Obwandiyag's men had given up their siege by the end of October), Niagara, and Fort Pitt.[19]

The British Response

An expeditionary force under Colonel Henry Bouquet (1719–65), a Swiss-born officer who had learned something from Indigenous tactics, rescued Fort Pitt. Bouquet taught his troops to move while firing, to form a circle when pressed, and to use the bayonet, a weapon that Indigenous warriors did not generally adopt. Despite the British success in this hard-fought engagement, by the end of the summer the Indigenous warriors of the resistance movement were in control of most of the Old Northwest. The system of garrisoned forts had not proven effective, and the result would be the most formidable Indigenous resistance that the British would face during the eighteenth century.

Neolin's call to drive the Anglo-Americans back into the sea seemed to be on its way to success. In his exhortations, he used a diagram painted on deerskin to show how Anglo-American settlers were blocking Indigenous Peoples from the enjoyment of their lands.[20] As his influence rose, so did that of Obwandiyag despite his failure at Detroit. Prominent as he was, however, Obwandiyag does not seem to have been the originator of the resistance, which was more in the nature of a spontaneous combustion.[21]

Amherst's Brutal Reaction

Amherst's immediate reaction was to underestimate both the scope and importance of this resistance. He did not have much regard for the capacity of the Indigenous Peoples to organize a large-scale resistance. When he was convinced, he reacted in ways that have made him infamous. He devised several plans aimed at a genocide, including distributing smallpox-infected blankets.[22] Those who were better acquainted with Indigenous Peoples counselled patience, knowing that they had no use for the forts they were taking; rather, they were after the supplies and hoped to drive the settlers out.

Indeed, the winter of 1763–4 passed without serious incident, as the Indigenous Peoples dispersed to their hunting grounds equipped with pillaged goods. When they began to run short, especially of ammunition, some groups voluntarily brought back prisoners in a gesture for peace. Others returned to their British alliance. The British, however, had revenge on their minds and sent out retaliatory expeditions, but they soon learned that revenge was a pointless and unrealistic

Small Pox Blankets, Bonnie Devine, 1995, mixed media on blankets, 5 pieces, 152 cm x 76 cm each. Collection of the Woodland Cultural Centre. Photo, Bonnie Devine.

Smallpox Blankets by Bonnie Devine (b. 1952), an Anishinaabe/Ojibwa member of the Serpent River First Nation and an associate professor at the Ontario College of Art and Design.

policy. First Nations losses during the resistance were probably low. In contrast, the settlers counted about 2,000 killed or captured and tremendous property damage. Despite the toll, however, Anglo-American settlement was not seriously deterred, and the fur trade had hardly been affected at all.

In July of 1764, Sir William Johnson attempted to restore stability to the Great Lakes region by assembling a peace conference at Fort Niagara. Over 1,700 delegates attended, mostly Wendat, Ojibwa, Odaawak, and Onondowaga. Johnson's policy was to meet with individual nations one at a time, in an effort to undermine the united front of Obwandiyag's movement. Obwandiyag himself did not attend. Johnson asked the delegates to return all prisoners and to break with Obwandiyag and his followers.[23]

The following year, 1765, Obwandiyag signed a separate agreement, in which he stipulated that France's surrender of its forts to the English did not mean that the English could automatically take over Indigenous land, as the French had been only tenants of the First Nations. He agreed that the British could reoccupy their forts, but hunting grounds must remain undisturbed.

When the final ratification of the agreements took place in July of 1766 at Oswego, Obwandiyag was a dominant figure. He made a strong claim for a renegotiated agreement with the British officials, and with Johnson in particular: "It is the will of the Great Spirit that we should meet here today and before Him and all present I take you by the hand and never will part with it."[24] This agreement did not have the full support of those who wished to continue the struggle against the British, and from then on Obwandiyag's influence diminished. Three years later, a Peewaarehwaa warrior assassinated him. Contrary to expectations, apart from some isolated killings, Obwandiyag's death did not ignite general warfare.[25] Still, the quiet that settled over the frontier was not a peaceful one for either the Indigenous Peoples or the Anglo-American traders and settlers.

The Kanienkehaka: Forced to Choose between the British and the Americans

First Nations had held the balance of power between two imperial rivals when France was present. Now, they found themselves jockeying for position between an imperial power, Great Britain, and her restive Thirteen Colonies (the colonies along the Atlantic seaboard spanning modern-day New Hampshire to Georgia), which would soon gain their independence as the United States of America. Under the earlier arrangement, both Britain and France had something to gain from alliances. In the new situation, only Britain at first found it useful to court such arrangements. In this regard, she had stepped into France's shoes, not always a comfortable fit. Indigenous leaders saw the opportunity to play the interests of the Anglo-Americans against those of the British, just as they had exploited the conflict between the French and the British in the past.

The **Quebec Act of 1774** brought the Ohio Valley and Great Lakes region under the jurisdiction of Quebec. This meant that the headquarters of the fur trade transferred from Albany to Montreal. (This shift in colonial administration superseded the arrangement contained in the Proclamation of 1763. Later, the argument would be made that it also abrogated the Proclamation's measures in respect to Indigenous lands, but this argument was not sustained. For further discussion of the Royal Proclamation, see below and Chapter 17.)

The British officials assured the Indigenous Peoples that they were protecting their territory against the illegal encroachments of settlers. The people of the Thirteen Colonies saw things differently: they felt that they were being deliberately thwarted from legitimate expansion. For them, the Quebec Act was one of the so-called "Intolerable Acts" and a provocation to launch their War of Independence. In 1775, Massachusetts entered into negotiations with members of the Wabanaki Confederacy. The following year, a group of Mi'kmaq signed a treaty at Watertown, agreeing to send men to the American army. Most of the people opposed this treaty, however, and the Mi'kmaq quickly disavowed it. Using the American precedent as an excuse, General Thomas Gage, commander-in-chief of the British forces from 1763 to 1775, ordered Guy Carleton, governor of Quebec, 1766–77, to use Indigenous warriors on the frontier. Instead, Carleton delayed. For one thing, the fur trade was booming, and Britain was building trading posts in the West.[26]

In what would become eastern Canada, the story was different. Americans invaded in 1775, bringing the Kanienkehaka of Kahnawake into the conflict. The Kanienkehaka warriors fought off two assaults but became (understandably) convinced that the British were sacrificing them to save their own troops, and consequently they went home. Even so, they had delayed the American invasion by nearly two weeks.

Members of the Haudenosaunee Confederacy were by now deep in the conflict despite efforts to maintain the neutrality they had decided on at the beginning of the century. This split the Confederacy. The Kanienkehaka, guided by the influential **Koñwatsi'tsiaiéñni** (Mary Brant, c. 1736–96) and her younger brother, the war chief **Thayendanegea** (Joseph Brant, 1743–1807), were pro-British.[27] (Thayendanegea had made a trip to England in 1775, during which he had been lionized by British society.) So were the Guyohkohnyo. The Onyota'aka—the "little brothers" of the Kanienkehaka—and the Tuscarora favoured the Americans.[28] The Onondowaga and Onondaga were divided. Lines were fluid, as inner dissensions increased. External relations also suffered, and attempts to form a united Haudenosaunee front got nowhere. As the Haudenosaunee leaders phrased it, the White Tree of Peace had been uprooted.[29] On top of that, the Haudenosaunee people had to face once more the unpleasant fact that siding with the losing side in a European-style war meant loss of lands.

The peace that Great Britain and the United States signed in Paris in 1783 completely ignored the First Nations. It made no provisions for their lands in the transfer of territory to the Americans. In particular, the cession of the Ohio Valley aroused a violent reaction on the part of British allies. Americans, on the other hand, flatly rejected proposals for the establishment of a separate Indigenous state. The Haudenosaunee leaders observed bitterly that they had not been defeated in the war, but they certainly were by the peace.

INDIGENOUS LEADERS | Koñwatsi'tsiaiéñni (Mary Brant, c. 1736–96)

The great matron of the Haudenosaunee Confederacy, Koñwatsi'tsiaiéñni was a Kanienkehaka woman of uncommon diplomatic and social ability. With her younger brother, Thayendanegea (Joseph), and her husband, Sir William Johnson, Koñwatsi'tsiaiéñni was responsible for leading the majority of the Haudenosaunee Confederacy into the alliance with the British against the American revolutionaries. Eventually this loyalist stance would lead the Haudenosaunee people to settle in the Grand River Valley in what is now Ontario. Koñwatsi'tsiaiéñni's greatest ability was in the realm of diplomacy. Her marriage to Sir William Johnson gave her considerable influence with British officials and Canadian settlers. Her prominent position in the Kanienkehaka nation gave her tremendous influence across the Haudenosaunee Confederacy.

She was truly a woman who lived comfortably in two worlds, and in some ways this example is her greatest legacy. She strove to manage her husband's estate and to keep her husband's household according to the standards of British colonial officialdom, and at the same time she was acutely aware of the colonial context and of the niceties of Indigenous diplomacy. After her husband's death she used her influence as head of the Haudenosaunee matrons to lead the Haudenosaunee warriors in the British cause. She had a particularly strong influence over the younger warriors and she had a great reputation among the entire confederacy. Her arrival at Fort Niagara in 1777 was seen as a pivotal moment in the difficult negotiations between the Haudenosaunee Confederacy and the British. Her capacity to move between the two worlds with seamless grace and skill certainly had a great deal of impact on the eventual Treaty of Paris, which brought the Revolutionary War to a close in 1783 and shaped the future of both Canada and the United States, as well as that of the Indigenous Peoples within these states. By keeping the Haudenosaunee in the alliance, Koñwatsi'tsiaiéñni made an enormous contribution to Canadian history and to the very existence of the border that now divides the two countries.

Posts and Proclamations

The British, in an effort to please their allies, did not evacuate the western posts as provided for in the treaty, a stance that led to prolonged wrangling with the Americans.[30] For Indigenous people dislodged by the war, the posts became a refuge, as 2,000 fled to them during the winter of 1784.[31] For the 5,000 or so Haudenosaunee refugees who congregated between the Genesee River and Niagara, the British negotiated with the Mississauga, a nation of the Ojibwa Confederacy on the north shore of Lake Ontario, and purchased land along the Grand River in Upper Canada (Ontario). (Although the original grant of 1784 has been much reduced since, the people of the Haudenosaunee Confederacy are still there.)

American pressure eventually forced the British to abandon the western posts, which they did in 1796. For the First Nations, this meant the loss of a buffer against the steadily increasing pressures from the east. On the positive side, however, the treaty provided for unhindered passage for Indigenous people over the border between Canada and the United States, and exempted them from taxes on personal goods. These have not been provisions that either side has

---

HISTORICAL BACKGROUND | Excerpt from the Royal Proclamation of 1763

And whereas it is just and reasonable, and essential to our Interest, and the security of our Colonies, that the several Nations or Tribes of Indians with whom We are connected, and who live under our protection, should not be molested or disturbed in the Possession of such Parts of Our Dominions and Territories as, not having been ceded to or purchased by Us, are reserved to them or any of them, as their Hunting Grounds—We do therefore, with the Advice of our Privy Council, declare it to be our Royal Will and Pleasure, that no Governor or Commander in Chief in any of our Colonies of Quebec, East Florida, or West Florida, do presume, upon any Pretence whatever, to grant Warrants of Survey, or pass any Patents for Lands beyond the Bounds of their respective Governments, as described in their Commissions; as also that no Governor or Commander in Chief in any of our other Colonies or Plantations in America do presume for the present, and until our further Pleasure be Known, to grant Warrants of Survey, or pass Patents for any Lands beyond the Heads or Sources of any of the Rivers which fall into the Atlantic Ocean from the West and North West, or upon any Lands whatever, which, not having been ceded to or purchased by Us as aforesaid, are reserved to the said Indians, or any of them.

And We do further declare it to be Our Royal Will and Pleasure, for the present as aforesaid, to reserve under our Sovereignty, Protection, and Dominion, for the use of the said Indians, all the Lands and Territories not included within the Limits of Our Said Three New Governments, or within the Limits of the Territory granted to the Hudson's Bay Company, as also all the Lands and Territories lying to the Westward of the Sources of the Rivers which fall into the Sea from the West and North West as aforesaid;

Continued

> And We do hereby strictly forbid, on Pain of our Displeasure, all our loving Subjects from making any Purchases or Settlements whatever, or taking Possession of any of the Lands above reserved, without our especial leave and Licence for the Purpose first obtained.

been careful to honour. The treaty did not apply to the Indigenous Peoples of Rupert's Land, the vast expanse to the north controlled by the Hudson's Bay Company.[32]

Long before the resistance, the British recognized that pressures on land, as well as "the shameful manner" in which trade was conducted in Indigenous territory, were inciting strong reaction. Following the defeat of France, even before the terms of the **Treaty of Paris** were concluded in 1783, officials moved to correct the situation by means of a series of proclamations.[33]

The first one, in 1761, issued to the governors of Nova Scotia, New Hampshire, New York, North and South Carolina, and Georgia, forbade them to grant lands or make settlements that would interfere with Indigenous Peoples bordering on those colonies. Settlers found to be unlawfully established upon Indigenous lands were to be evicted. There would also be no more sales of Indigenous lands without a licence, which would be issued only if the Commissioners for Trade and Plantations in London approved.

In 1762, Britain reasserted an earlier proclamation that the Mi'kmaq had a right to use the sea coast from Cape Fronsac "onwards." Hardly had this proclamation been issued, however,

Robert Houle, Premises for Self-Rule: The Royal Proclamation, 1994, photographic panel. Collection of the Winnipeg Art Gallery. Acquired with funds from the Canada Council for the Arts Acquisition Assistance Program. Photographed by Ernest Mayer.

THE ROYAL PROCLAMATION October 7, 1763 BY THE KING. A PROCLAMATION GEORGE R. Whereas We have taken into Our Royal Consideration the extensive and valuable Acquisitions in America, secured to our Crown by the late Definitive Treaty of Peace, concluded at Paris, the 10th Day of February last; ...And whereas it is just and re... to our Interest, and the Securi... the several Nations or Tribes... We are connected, and who live u... ould not be molested or distur... of such Parts of Our Domi... not having been ceded to or purchased by Us, are reserved to them, or any of them, as their Hunting Grounds. – We do therefore, with the Advice of our Privy Council, declare it to be our Royal Will and Pleasure, that no Governor or Commander in Chief in any of our Colonies of Quebec, East Florida, or West Florida, do presume, upon any Pretence whatever, to grant Warrants of Survey,...or upon any Lands whatever, which, not having been ceded to or purchased by Us as aforesaid, are reserved to the said Indians, or any of them. And We do further declare it to be Our Royal Will and Pleasure, for the present as aforesaid, to reserve under our Sovereignty, Protection, and Dominion,

Premises for Self-Rule: The Royal Proclamation by **Robert Houle (b. 1947)**, a widely regarded artist, curator, and educator and a member of the Saulteaux First Nations.

than the French blockade of St John's during the summer of 1762 rendered the reservation of coastal territories for the Mi'kmaq meaningless. The Proclamation of 1763 (see Historical Background box), following hard on the heels of the Peace of Paris of that same year, was slow in coming as a result of such continuing confrontations as the Mi'kmaw War. However, conflict in the Far Northwest speeded up the process.[34]

Even though the British originally saw it as a temporary measure, to make it operative they had to work out agreements as to where the boundaries lay between Indigenous territory and the colonies. The process took five years and involved 10 treaties.[35] The Proclamation provided that all lands that had not been ceded to or purchased by Britain and that formed part of British North America were "reserved lands" for the First Nations. In practice, this meant lands beyond the Appalachian Mountains to the border of what was Spanish-held territory, spanning about a third of the North American interior, although the Proclamation did not define its western boundaries. The British seem to have meant it to apply to the Maritime colonies as well, but those governments ignored it.[36] It did not apply to what was being called "Quebec" (the area that was the Old Northwest territory as well as what would become Upper Canada) or the west coast of North America, but did include lands within established colonies that had not yet been ceded, purchased, or set aside for Indigenous Peoples. It also did not apply to Rupert's Land, whatever its boundaries were, which was still under the jurisdiction of the HBC. Neither was it operative in the Arctic, which, in any event, had a different land-use pattern. The Crown reserved to itself the right to extinguish **Indian title**, resurrecting a policy legislated in Virginia in 1655 but that had fallen into disuse.

In the legal terminology of the day, "Indian title" meant rights of occupancy and use, not ownership. Britain assumed that she held underlying sovereign title. The areas that interested the Crown specifically were those that had potential for settlement. However, it wanted to prevent "unjust Settlement and fraudulent Purchase" of Indigenous lands, thus slowing the pace of colonization to keep the peace on the frontier. This protection did not extend to unceded Mi'kmaw and Wuastukwiuk lands, however, because the British still persisted in their view, dealt with in Chapter 4, that their title had already been extinguished twice over—first by French occupation and then by the Treaty of Utrecht.[37]

A question that arose later is whether the Proclamation recognized a pre-existing title or created it.[38] There was a movement in the courts towards the position that Aboriginal title preceded colonization, but recent decisions have seen Aboriginal rights as arising out of the Proclamation (see Chapter 16).

The English Approach to Treaties

The English, not trusting oral agreements, insisted on European-style written treaties. In relying on European traditions, they assumed that Indigenous societies had hierarchies and centralized authorities.[39] As this usually did not fit with the political realities of the communities they met, however, they, too, had to adapt. Sometimes, they entered into unwritten agreements, but they preferred not to.

Even with the written treaties, it is not clear what legal status the English gave them, even at the time. As far as we know, the English put none of these treaties through the procedure in the British Parliament that they usually did for international agreements, nor have Canadian courts acknowledged them as such. The colonizers admitted "Indian title" but did not agree as to what it included. They did agree, however, that a "savage" could never exercise valid sovereignty. Only peoples living within organized states could do that. Some Europeans further specified that the states had to be Christian. The legal nature of the treaties has never been fully clarified.[40]

The first British treaty that included First Nations in what is now Canada was the Treaty of Portsmouth, New Hampshire, signed in 1713 and involving Indigenous Peoples of the Saint John River, largely Wuastukwiuk but perhaps also some Mi'kmaq and others of the Wabanaki Confederacy. The treaty was for peace and friendship, similar to previous agreements. It also broke new ground by adding that the British would not interfere within the territories where they lived, and the Indigenous Peoples would enjoy "free liberty for Hunting, Fishing, Fowling, and all other [of] their Lawful Liberties & Privileges."[41]

The British repeated these provisions in the Treaty of Boston, 1725 (see Chapter 4). This treaty included Mi'kmaq of Cape Sable and other areas, as well as Wuastukwiuk. At the same time, the British took advantage of the disarray of the First Nations following the defeat at Norridgewock to insist on another agreement, Treaty No. 239 (Mascarene's Treaty).[42] Its purpose was to get Mi'kmaq, Wuastukwiuk, and the entire Wabanaki Confederacy to agree that the Treaty of Utrecht made the British Crown "the rightful possessor of the Province of Nova Scotia or Acadia according to ancient boundaries."[43]

That the British took such measures to get the Indigenous Peoples to "acknowledge His said Majesty King George's jurisdiction and dominion over the territories of the said Province of Nova Scotia or Acadia" and submit to him indicates the troubles they were having in this regard. However, the Indigenous Peoples did not accept that one could sign for all. At most, a chief could sign for his immediate band, and then only if its members agreed. In the case of the two treaties signed at Boston, this meant arranging ratifications and confirmations. Tracking down the chiefs and their bands was a slow process that at first did not much influence the course of the Mi'kmaw War.

As well, negotiations had to be conducted through interpreters,[44] who, as Recollect missionary Sagard observed, often missed the point either from "ignorance or contempt, which is a very dangerous thing as it has often led to big accidents."[45] Compounding the problems were grave difficulties in translating concepts, such as that of exclusive landownership, which had no counterpart in Indigenous languages. This situation was never satisfactorily resolved throughout the treaty-making period. As confusions—and deceptions—proliferated, so did suspicion and distrust on both sides.

Annuities first appeared in the Halifax Treaty of 1752, signed with the Shubenacadie band of Mi'kmaq. It promised regular gift distributions, probably an indication of the importance the British attached to this treaty, which was a major break in the prolonged hostilities with the Mi'kmaq. It also acknowledged the Mi'kmaq's right to "free liberty of Hunting and Fishing as usual" and "to trade to the best Advantage."[46] During negotiations, the Mi'kmaw chief, Major Jean-Baptiste (Joseph) Cope (Coppe, d. 1758/60), said that "the Indians should be paid for the land the English had settled upon in this country."[47] The British, however, were not yet ready to agree, at least in Nova Scotia, for reasons already noted. The peace established by the treaty soon ended, however, when Mi'kmaq killed two Englishmen.

The 1783 Treaty of Paris formally ended the presence of the French government and military in continental North America when, as one historian put it, they handed over the largest extent of territory ever covered "by any treaty dealing with the American hemisphere before or since."[48]

From "Peace and Friendship" to Land Transfers

After the 1763 Proclamation, treaties and administration took on a different character. Priorities changed—instead of being primarily concerned with peace and secondarily (if at all) with land issues, treaties now focused primarily on land. This was a direct result of the Proclamation's reservation to the Crown of the right to acquire Indigenous lands, which from then on would take place only by a treaty negotiated at a public meeting. The British would sign land cession treaties with the Indigenous Peoples of central and western Canada but not with those of the west coast, the Atlantic provinces, Lower Canada (Quebec), or the Arctic. Indigenous Peoples formally ceded about one-half of Canada's lands to the government.[49]

The year following the Proclamation saw two treaties negotiated in Upper Canada that gave the British use of the portage at Niagara Falls in return for a trade agreement. Other provisions were similar to those of earlier treaties in other areas. The First Nations were to keep the peace with the British, avoid helping the enemy, help in the defence of British posts and supply routes, and return prisoners of war.

The first was with the Wendat of the Bkejwanong region (where the cities of Detroit and Windsor are today), the other with the Onondowaga.[50] In 1781, the British renegotiated the second treaty with the Mississauga, whom the British now recognized as the rightful owners of the land in question, a strip six kilometres wide along the west bank of the Niagara River. The price agreed on by Wabakinine (Wabacoming, d. 1796) and other chiefs was "three hundred suits of clothing."[51] Further surrenders quickly followed. Between 1815 and 1825, Indigenous leaders signed nine treaties, giving up almost the entire peninsula between Lakes Ontario, Erie, and Huron.[52] At first, these treaties were for parcels of land for specific projects.

Until 1798, the government had no problem in obtaining surrenders for about three pence an acre in either cash or goods, although the value of "wild" land was estimated at from six to 15 pence an acre.[53] At that time, Upper Canada was the western frontier. The British did not record some of the transactions properly, and many were imprecise in their terms or in regard to boundaries, giving rise to later disputes. They soon formed the vast majority of the 483 treaties listed for Canada in 1912, although little more than 20 of the 30 or so major ones account for most of Ontario's geographical area.

A harbinger of the huge land cession treaties that would begin with the Robinson agreements of 1850 was the accord Wabakinine and other chiefs reached with Frederick Haldimand, governor of Quebec, 1778–86, for the Niagara Peninsula in 1784. By it, the Mississauga Ojibwa gave up their claim on three million acres of land (1.2 million ha) to the Crown in exchange for £1,180 in goods. The purpose was to provide land for the Haudenosaunee loyalists who had sided with the British during the American War of Independence and so had lost their land. Haunted by the fear of a Haudenosaunee resistance, the British had moved quickly to reassure Haudenosaunee loyalists that Britain had not abandoned them.[54]

By far the largest portion of the territory acquired from the Mississauga went to Thayendanegea and his followers. The Haudenosaunee received a tract six miles deep on either side of the Grand River beginning at its mouth—a total of 2,842,480 acres (1,150,311 ha), "which them and their posterity are to enjoy forever" (for further details, see Chapter 18). Known as the **Haldimand Grant**, it provided the land base for the Six Nations Reserve, as it is now known.[55] A 1785 reserve census enumerated a population of 1,843. The Kanienkehaka were in the majority, with 448 persons counted. The Onondaga accounted for 245, Onyota'aka, for 162, Tuscarora, 129, and Onondowaga, 78. Various others, including the Lenni Lenape and Muskoke, made up the rest.[56]

There followed a long struggle between the government and Thayendanegea as to land policies. Thayendanegea held that the Haudenosaunee had a **fee simple title**, which included the right to sell and lease to private individuals. He argued that the hunting way of life was no longer sustainable in that region and that the only source of income available to the Haudenosaunee was from the sale of parts of their grant. He also wanted to establish non-Indigenous farmers amid his people to teach them the settlers' agricultural techniques.

Thayendanegea eventually won his argument, but the result was a severe erosion of the original grant. Eventually, 381,480 acres (154,379 ha) were sold for three to six shillings an acre.[57] Thayendanegea lost considerably on all counts, as many of his transactions were never formalized legally. Besides, it was one thing to sell to private purchasers at high prices but quite another to collect from them.[58]

One effect of his dealings was to increase substantially the price of land.[59] The government, alarmed, went back to its former policy of curtailing Indigenous Peoples' rights to sell their lands. On top of all that, documents related to the original grant went missing, and a government survey of the reserve in 1791 ruled that it was much smaller than that described by the Haldimand Grant, stopping far short of the river's source.[60] The Simcoe Deed of 1793 confirmed what remained. Other Haudenosaunee leaders, with fewer followers, received smaller grants, such as that of Tyendinaga Reserve at the Bay of Quinte to Kanienkehaka leader John Deserontyon (Desoronto, Odeserundiye, c. 1740s–1811) and his band of 200.[61] Thus, the Haudenosaunee returned to the lands that other branches of their people had once occupied.

The Continuing Process of Land Cessions

Large-scale land cessions also became the order of the day for the Ojibwa and the closely related Odaawak between Lake Erie and the Thames River in Upper Canada. For example, in 1790, they surrendered two million acres (809,371 ha) for £1,200, and two years later ceded three million acres (1.2 million ha) for the same amount.[62] In the 1810s, cash payments gave way to annuities, which the administration considered to be more economical.

As already noted, the 1752 treaty with the Mi'kmaq introduced annual payments as a variation of reaffirming partnerships. By the early nineteenth century, annuities took the place of cash payments for land. Thomas Douglas, Earl of Selkirk (1771–1820), at Red River in 1817, was the first to use this new system. The following year, the Collingwood Treaty used it to settle for 1,592,000 acres (644,259 ha) ceded in return for a "perpetual" annuity of £1,200. Ojibwa chief Musquakie (Mayawassino, William Yellowhead, d. 1864) was one of the main negotiators.[63] His father had previously surrendered 250,000 acres (101,171 ha) in present-day Simcoe County. Annuities could be in the form of housing, equipment, and/or provisions instead of cash, as in 1822 when the Mississauga surrendered 2,748,000 acres (1,112,096 ha). In that case, the agreement was that each of the 257 band members would receive payments. Annuities were, indeed, very economical for the administration, as the Crown paid them from funds established with the proceeds of sales of surrendered lands.

Regulation of trade was another main concern of the British administration at this time. In the past, government had exercised its monopoly through government "truck" houses, which in Nova Scotia had been established in 1760, but that system did not pay for itself. In 1764, the government adopted a plan to implement a provision in the Proclamation of 1763 for the opening of trade to all. However, it restricted trade to designated locations, which in the North meant military posts.[64] As well, anyone who wanted to trade had to obtain a licence and post bond for good behaviour. These requirements proved to be highly unpopular with traders, who launched a vigorous—and ultimately successful—campaign against them.

The Proclamation also guaranteed that the government would continue to extend its authority further into Indigenous territory. The large-scale cessions of land in Upper Canada to the Crown were the prototype for a policy that would reach beyond the Great Lakes to the Petit Nord and into the Great Plains.

Questions to Consider

1. What were the objectives of the pan-Indigenous and nativistic movements?
2. In what ways did the Indigenous Peoples' world change in 1763?
3. Why did Obwandiyag fail to achieve his goals?
4. What choices did the Kanienkehaka leaders make during the Revolutionary War?

Recommended Readings

Blackbird, Andrew J. *History of the Ottawa and Chippewa Indians of Michigan.* Ypsilanti, Mich.: Job Printing House, 1887.

Calloway, Colin G. *Crown and Calumet: British–Indian Relations, 1783–1815.* Norman: University of Oklahoma Press, 1987.

Dixon, David. *Never Come to Peace Again: Pontiac's Uprising and the Fate of the British Empire in North America.* Norman: University of Oklahoma Press, 2005.

Dowd, Gregory Evans. *A Spirited Resistance: The North American Struggle for Unity, 1745–1815.* Baltimore: Johns Hopkins University Press, 1992.

————. *War under Heaven: Pontiac, the Indian Nations, and British Empire*. Baltimore: Johns Hopkins University Press, 2004.

Graymont, Barbara. *The Iroquois in the American Revolution*. Syracuse, NY: Syracuse University Press, 1972.

Kelsay, Isabel Thompson. *Joseph Brant, 1743–1807: Man of Two Worlds*. Syracuse, NY: Syracuse University Press, 1984.

McDonnell, Michael A. *Masters of Empire: Great Lakes Indians and the Making of North America*. New York: Hill and Wang, 2015.

Wallace, Anthony F.C. *Death and Rebirth of the Seneca*. New York: Vintage Books, 1969.

Washburn, Wilcomb. *Handbook of North American Indians, vol. 4: History of Indian–White Relations*. Washington: Smithsonian Institution, 1988.

8 Westward and Northward

CHAPTER OUTLINE

This chapter is devoted to the changes on the Canadian Plains and the Pacific coast as newcomers arrived and began a process of transformation of massive proportion. The introduction, by the Spanish, of the horse helped to change how the Indigenous Peoples adapted to their environment. It serves as a reminder that some changes were gradual and beneficial, while others were sudden and upsetting. This chapter will also provide a discussion of the arrival of European traders on the Pacific coast and of the various transformations that took place there as well.

LEARNING OUTCOMES

1. Students will be able to identify the economic strategies of the Indigenous Peoples of the northern plains.

2. Students will understand the nature of the economic and social changes that colonization began to force onto those peoples.

3. Students will gain insight into the ways in which change was first resisted as the process began to accelerate in the closing years of the eighteenth century.

TIMELINE The Plains Economy and the Bison Hunt

1600–1870
Development and flourishing of bison-hunting way of life.

1630
Indigenous Peoples on southern Plains own horses, after Spanish introduced horses a century earlier in Mexico.

1730s
Shoshoni using horses for raiding.

Mid-1700s
Cree communities, who had traded with HBC on the Bay and with French, and now established on Saskatchewan River, introduce guns to Plains culture.

1754–63
Seven Years War disrupts trade in the West.

1770
British traders back on Upper Mississippi and Saskatchewan after Seven Years War.

1774
HBC inland post of Cumberland House (west of The Pas, Manitoba).

1778
Captain James Cook sails into Nootka Sound on British Columbia coast. Cree guides take Peter Pond to the Athabasca country via Methye Portage, the third great route for fur resources (after St Lawrence and Hudson Bay).

1779
HBC Hudson House post (west of Prince Albert, Sask.).
Cree warriors attack independent traders at Eagle Hills Fort on the Saskatchewan.

1781–2
Epidemic takes heavy toll on Shoshone and Niitsitapi peoples.
The Niitsitapi Confederacy (also known as the Niitsitapiikwan)—now armed and on horseback—forces Shoshone off northern Plains.
A'ani people, weakened by epidemic, pushed south and east by Nakoda and Cree warriors.

1785
First trading ship—British—arrives on Northwest Coast.

1788
Pond establishes Fort Chipewyan for North West Company.

1791
A Haida chief, Koyah, disgraced by British, becomes enemy of fur trade and attacks ships and traders.

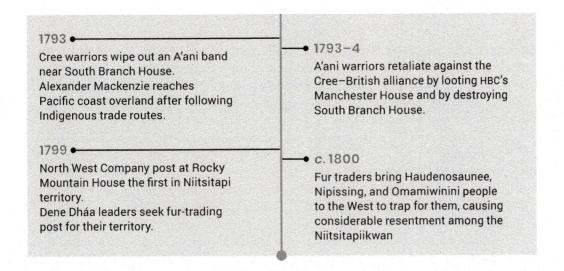

1793
Cree warriors wipe out an A'ani band near South Branch House.
Alexander Mackenzie reaches Pacific coast overland after following Indigenous trade routes.

1793–4
A'ani warriors retaliate against the Cree–British alliance by looting HBC's Manchester House and by destroying South Branch House.

1799
North West Company post at Rocky Mountain House the first in Niitsitapi territory.
Dene Dháa leaders seek fur-trading post for their territory.

c.1800
Fur traders bring Haudenosaunee, Nipissing, and Omamiwinini people to the West to trap for them, causing considerable resentment among the Niitsitapiikwan

On the Great Plains

By the early years of the eighteenth century, word spread throughout the western Plains of a strange animal, "swift as deer," that would become known to Cree people as Misstutim, "big dog." The use of horses for hunting bison on the Plains, which today is considered traditional, crystallized in Canada between 1700 and 1750, depending on locality. In southern Alberta, Saskatchewan, and Manitoba, it seems to have developed during the first half of the eighteenth century.[1] When Indigenous people began to own and ride horses after the Spaniards reintroduced them into the Americas is open to debate. About 1567, the Yaqui nations of Sonora in what is now the American Southwest rode horses and used them for food.[2] The Shoshone, seasonal residents of grasslands and Plateau, might have been the first on the northwestern Plains to acquire horses.[3] By the 1730s, they were using horses for raiding.[4]

Saukamapee, a Cree man who had married into a Piikani family, described to geographical surveyor **David Thompson** (1770–1857) his first encounter with the new arrival. Attacking a lone Shoshone man, Piikani warriors succeeded in killing his mount, then crowded in wonder about the fallen animal, which, like the dog, was a slave to man and carried his burdens.[5]

As for the Atlantic seaboard, horses were present since early in the seventeenth century but did not cross the Alleghenies until later. On the southern Plains, Indigenous Peoples owned horses by 1630 and may well have had some as early as 1600. Athapaskan-speaking Apache were raiding on horseback by the mid-seventeenth century.[6] Indeed, they evolved their own techniques for mounted warfare and buffalo hunting. Bison herds seem to have reached their great numbers not long before the arrival of Europeans.[7] The new character of the buffalo hunt influenced some peoples who were farming in the parklands, such as the Cheyenne and some branches of the Dakota, to abandon sedentary agriculture for the mobility of the chase.

People of the Niitsitapi Confederacy told stories of the power in the world around them. The story of the buffalo rock, recorded by the American naturalist and ethnologist George Bird Grinnell in 1892, is a fine example. When someone heard a peculiar faint chirp while travelling across the open prairie, the sound was said to have come from a buffalo rock. People would always look hard for the buffalo rock and when one was found there was much celebration. The story is worth giving in full as it reveals something about the Niitsitapi world view:

> Long ago, in the winter time, the buffalo suddenly disappeared. The snow was so deep that the people could not move in search of them, for in those days they had no horses. So the hunters killed deer, elk, and other small game along the river bottoms, and when these were all killed off or driven away, the people began to starve.
>
> One day, a young married man killed a jack-rabbit. He was so hungry that he ran home as fast as he could, and told one of his wives to hurry and get some water to cook it. While the young woman was going along the path to the river, she heard a beautiful song. It sounded close by, but she looked all around and could see no one. The song seemed to come from a cotton-wood tree near the path. Looking closely at this tree she saw a queer rock jammed in a fork, where the tree was split, and with it a few hairs from a buffalo, which had rubbed there. The woman was frightened and dared not pass the tree. Pretty soon the singing stopped, and the I-nis'-kim [buffalo rock] spoke to the woman and said: "Take me to your lodge, and when it is dark, call in the people and teach them the song you have just heard. Pray, too, that you may not starve, and that the buffalo may come back. Do this, and when day comes, your hearts will be glad."
>
> The woman went on and got some water, and when she came back, took the rock and gave it to her husband, telling him about the song and what the rock had said. As soon as it was dark, the man called the chiefs and old men to his lodge, and his wife taught them this song. They prayed, too, as the rock had said should be done. Before long, they heard a noise far off. It was the tramp of a great herd of buffalo coming. Then they knew that the rock was very powerful, and, ever since that, the people have taken care of it and prayed to it.[8]

Horse raiding became a favourite activity and was an accepted way of acquiring animals. Around 1800, some Niitsitapi men, raiding on the northern Plains, were seen riding horses with Spanish brands.[9] David Thompson described a spectacular raid in which a band of Nakoda disguised as antelopes made off with 50 horses from Rocky Mountain House.[10] The Nakoda people carried out such raids against their enemy, and thus, these were acts of war, not theft.[11]

With horses, running buffalo became universally favoured as a hunting technique. Mounted hunters chased the herds and killed animals with bows and arrows, or guns. Jumps began to fall into disuse between 1840 and 1850. In this earlier method dating back millennia, runners would lead a group of bison towards a cliff. Once there, other hunters would shout and wave robes and blankets, causing the confused animals to run off the cliff. A third group of hunters waited at the bottom and dispatched the wounded bison with spears (see Chapter Two). The last known use of a buffalo jump was by Niitsitapi hunters in 1873.[12] Pounds continued to be used until the end of the herds. In this method a hunter dressed in buffalo robes would lead the herd into a natural ravine or coulee, as they were known on the prairies, and then into a fenced enclosure built into a natural hollow. A large party of hunters then blocked the only exit and killed the animals.[13]

Horses became a symbol of warrior status, a key aspect of the social organization of the Niitsitapi Peoples. As always with the introduction of a new concept, this time the domestication of animals, changes brought disruptions to the established social conventions. Ownership of animals did not accord with long-held beliefs and customs. This led directly to problems as people tried to cope with a new concept, and it led to excesses. For example, in 1833 a Piikani chief, Sackomaph, owned between 4,000 and 5,000 horses, 150 of which were sacrificed on his death. On a more modest scale, an individual Siksika of Painted Feather's band was reported to have owned 50 horses. Among the Piikani, the number belonging to an individual could reach 300.[14]

First Winter, by Lauren Monroe Jr. Permission granted by artist.

First Winter by **Lauren Monroe Jr.** He writes, "In our art, we see the reclamation of our languages, cultures, and ultimately, our humanity as Indigenous people that the west tried to extinguish. By creating art, we as Indigenous artists are telling the world that we are still here, we are alive, and we will get back what we momentarily lost. We are still creating and dreaming like our ancestors have since time immemorial."

Horses, Firearms, and Disease: Shifts in Power Balances

At this time, all of the year-round residents of the northwestern Plains were Algonquian or Siouan speakers except the Shoshone, who spoke a Numic language, and the Tsuu T'ina, who spoke an Athapaskan language and who had broken away from the Dene Dháa, apparently not long before the arrival of Europeans. Eventually, the Tsuu T'ina became part of the **Niitsitapi Confederacy**, along with the Siksika, Káínawa, and Piikani, the most westerly and southerly of the confederates.[15]

Directly to the east of the Confederacy were the allied Algonquian-speaking A'ani, also known as Atsina, originally a division of the Arapaho who may have been the second to arrive in the region, after the Niitsitapiikwan.[16] Later, a fur trader, Matthew Cocking (1743–99), described A'ani customs and manners as similar to those of Europeans.[17]

If we exclude the Plains Ojibwa (sometimes called the Saulteaux), who reached the Plains by the late eighteenth century but who did not establish a major presence on the high Plains,[18] the newcomers in this northwestern region were the Plains Cree, who began to arrive early in the eighteenth century, possibly in association with their close allies the Siouan Nakoda, who preceded them. These peoples had long-established trading partnerships with the French and then the British and there is a possibility that they moved west as the European colonizers moved west, in order to maintain their old alliances. Another possibility is that there was a Cree presence in the West before contact and that it had been established as part of the ongoing movement westward that is described in the oral traditions of the peoples of the Great Lakes region. It is likely that the westward expansion of the trade encouraged an acceleration of a process that was already happening.[19]

But the early historic period saw the southwestern parts of the region being dominated by the raiding, mounted Shoshone. The Shoshone wore six-ply quilted armour and carried shields, but as yet did not have firearms. However, the sinew-backed bow was an efficient weapon, as were its arrows, tipped with stone or, later, with metal points. With the exception of the late-arriving Cree, Nakoda, and Plains Ojibwa, all of whom had earlier associations with the fur trade, the silent bow and arrow was the preferred weapon of the buffalo hunters.[20]

The appearance of the gun heralded the final phase of shifting Indigenous power balances on the northern Plains before the settlers arrived. The Shoshone first saw guns in the hands of their enemy, the Cree.[21] The Cree, trading with the English on Hudson Bay and with the French, by mid-eighteenth century were established on the Saskatchewan River and had been armed for some time. The Shoshone quickly discovered that this new weapon seriously lessened the advantage they had gained with the horse.[22]

There is argument as to the extent of the influence of the early smooth-bore gun on Plains warfare patterns.[23] However, there seems little reason to doubt that it had, at the very least, considerable psychological impact. For one thing, a musket ball was harder to dodge than an arrow or a spear. For another, when it hit, it made traditional armour obsolete. In the hands of a mounted warrior, as happened on the Plains, at close range even the smooth-bore musket could be overpowering.[24]

Before the Shoshone could get regular access to firearms, the Seven Years War (1756–63) disrupted trade in the West. By 1770, however, British traders were back on the Upper Mississippi and the Saskatchewan rivers and were beginning to penetrate into the Far Northwest. France as a power had all but disappeared from North America, and her jurisdiction over Louisiana had been transferred to Spain in 1762. This dealt a severe blow to whatever hopes the Shoshone might have had of obtaining enough guns to face their enemies. The Niitsitapi confederates, now mounted, already had access to British firearms, and by the end of the eighteenth century they pushed the Shoshone off the northern Plains.[25]

In achieving this, the Niitsitapi confederates had powerful help. Epidemics, especially that of 1781–2, took a heavy toll on the Shoshone.[26] By the turn of the century, the victorious Piikani warriors, who had been the confederates mainly involved in the struggle, were referring to the once-dreaded Shoshone as miserable old women, whom they could defeat with sticks and stones.[27] With the Shoshone threat gone and new fur trading posts in West, the fragile Niitsitapi alliance with Nakoda and Cree lost its main motivation, and the two expanding power groups came into collision.

The Siksika and Piikani Leaders Resist Efforts To Disrupt Trade Patterns

Horses altered not only the hunt, transportation, and warfare, but also—and perhaps most importantly—trade routes. While they were still allies, the Niitsitapi confederates had obtained their first European trade items through the Nakoda and Cree network rather than directly from Europeans. The French were the first they met,[28] and the French language had a lasting impact on communication in parts of the West, although the first meeting of the Niitsitapiikwan leaders known to written history was with HBC trader Anthony Henday (fl. 1750–62), whom the Cree trading captain Attikarish (Attickasish) led to them in 1754–5.[29] By then, the Niitsitapiikwan likely had horses[30] and were well into a period of expansion.

As the Piikani warriors pushed the Shoshone south and west, the Tsuu T'ina moved into the North Saskatchewan River basin, and the allied A'ani occupied territories vacated by the Niitsitapi confederates around the Eagle Hills. By 1770, the Niitsitapiikwan and their allies controlled the area along the eastern Rockies north of Yellowstone to the boreal forest.

The Niitsitapi confederates never took to trading with Europeans, as had the Cree and Nakoda. Not only were their needs being served adequately through the Indigenous networks, but they would have faced opposition if they had tried to penetrate Cree and Nakoda hunting territory that lay on the route to the Bay. There was also the fact that the demands of the fur trade conflicted with those of buffalo hunting. Late fall and early winter was the best season for trapping furs, as pelts were then in their prime. It was also the best time for killing bison and preparing winter provisions. Members of the Niitsitapiikwan ranged from the North Saskatchewan River to the headwaters of the Missouri in the south. They hunted bison from the Cypress Hills all the way west to the Rockies.[31]

Trapping was a family affair, whereas buffalo hunting involved the whole community. Of the Niitsitapi confederates, the Piikani people had the most beaver in their territory and, as a result, became the most active as trappers. The others, as well as the allies, became provisioners for the trade rather than trappers for furs. This independence of the Niitsitapi and the A'ani, combined with trading activities from its Montreal-based competitors in the West, spurred the Hudson's Bay Company to establish the inland posts of Cumberland House (near The Pas, Manitoba) in 1774 and Hudson House (west of Prince Albert) in 1779. By the time the **North West Company** (NWC) built Fort Augustus on the North Saskatchewan in 1795 and the HBC countered with Fort Edmonton that same year, trading posts ringed Niitsitapi territory.[32] The NWC was a group of floating fur trade partnerships that coalesced into "companies" founded by mostly Scottish and French colonial settlers based in Montreal, the first in 1779 and the second in 1783. In 1799, Nor'Westers built the first Rocky Mountain House, establishing a post within the Niitsitapi sphere of control.

Despite their unwillingness to meet the fur trade on its terms, the Niitsitapi and A'ani leaders complained that they were not being treated in trade as well as their enemies, the Cree, particularly in the case of firearms.[33] The traders did not help when they treated Indigenous Peoples badly, as happened all too often. The resulting tensions sometimes erupted into violence, as in 1781 when Piikani and Siksika bands burned the prairie around the posts. The traders believed they did it to scare game away and perhaps to force the traders to trade with them for provisions.[34] The establishment of the international border between Canada and the United States in 1818 further complicated what was already a complex situation.

Territoryscapes, 2009, Ska-Cheen acrylic and red earth on gallery wall, 25 feet tall approximately. Image Courtesy of Kamloops Art Gallery.

Territory Scapes by Tania Willard (b. 1977) of the Secwepemc Nation in present-day British Columbia. Willard is a curator and an artist in various media, and this work is part of her "Claiming Space" series. She writes: "Interconnectedness is the root system of my work as an artist. Land based art, community engaged practice, printmaking, painting are the mediums I most often work in, these ways of working are tied to me, I am tied to my ancestors, we are tied to the land."

When the Nor'Westers tried to cross the mountains to make contact with the Ktunaxa or Kutenai and the Secwepemc people, the Piikani became seriously alarmed, "for they dreaded the western Indians being furnished with Arms and Amunition."[35] David Thompson finally succeeded in building a post in Ktunaxa territory in 1807. At this, the Piikani raised a war party. Thompson was able to negotiate a peaceful settlement, but the delay cost the Nor'Westers the right to claim the mouth of the Columbia River for Britain.[36] That same year, Káínaa and A'ani warriors looted Fort Augustus. When the HBC built Peigan Post (Old Bow Fort) in 1832 in territory controlled by the Káínaa, the latter refused to let their old allies trade there. This forced the post to close two years later.[37]

The situation became worse when Americans—the "Mountain Men" of American western folklore—began trapping in Indigenous territory, an act the Niitsitapi leaders considered to be trespassing. Canadian **traders** had already, at the end of the eighteenth century, "brought in a great number of Iroquois, Nepissings, and Algonquins" to act as trappers for them, men who "with their steel traps had destroyed the Beaver on their own lands in Canada and New Brunswick."[38]

Since the Niitsitapi leaders would not allow them on their lands, the American newcomers went north and west, some going to the Upper Columbia, later moving down to the Lower Columbia and the Snake. If they encroached on Piikani lands, they were driven off in attacks that could be bloody.

Expansion, Prosperity, and War

In Canada, the opening of the rich fur resources of the Far Northwest—the Athabasca region—to European traders, and the growing market for buffalo robes shifted the trade's focus and brought about better relations between the Niitsitapiikwan and traders. The need for provisions for the Athabasca trade greatly increased the demand for **pemmican**, a product of the buffalo hunt. Pemmican, a highly concentrated food (made from fat, dried bison meat, and occasionally Saskatoon berries) that could be kept indefinitely, had the added advantage of being well suited for transport in small northern canoes.[39]

The new commerce placed a premium on the services of women, who prepared the hides and made pemmican and materials for repairing the traders' birchbark canoes. Where Niitsitapi women had usually married in their late teens, girls as young as 12 now did so. An increase in warfare meant women began to gradually outnumber men. Polygamy developed as a result, and so did a hierarchy among wives, with the senior wife usually directing the others.[40] Women taken in raids now tended to be kept by their captors rather than sold, a trend that grew stronger after the first third of the nineteenth century.

Commercialism and its emphasis on wealth disrupted other social institutions as well. Special-interest societies multiplied. The best known were connected with war and maintaining camp and hunt discipline. War as a way of life was a comparatively recent development. For the Niitsitapiikwan, warfare became a means of gaining wealth, making possible the elaborate ceremonies that became the route to prestige.

The A'ani were weakened by the ravages of the 1781–2 epidemic, and the Nakoda and Cree pushed them south and east. In 1793, Cree wiped out an A'ani band near South Branch House. Such incidents greatly intensified the resentment shared by the A'ani and the Niitsitapiikwan towards the trading success of the Cree and the Nakoda, which made possible the latter's superiority in arms.[41] In the eyes of the A'ani, HBC traders were, in effect, allies of their enemies. For that reason, they responded to the Cree raid by attacking the Company's Manchester House (on Pine Island in the Saskatchewan River), which they looted that same year. The following year, they destroyed South Branch House. Eventually, like the Shonshone, A'ani people were pushed south of the new international border.[42]

In contrast to the A'ani, the Cree and Nakoda were still expanding since their arrival on the Plains near the end of the seventeenth century. Although they also suffered severely from the epidemics (1776–7 had been particularly hard on them), their numbers were such that they were able to recover and continue their expansion.[43] In the southwest, however, the Niitsitapiikwan, their former allies when the Shoshone were a common enemy, stopped them. The Niitsitapi Confederacy and the Cree now considered each other their worst foe.

Neither the Cree people nor the Nakoda people who came from the woodlands of the east had trouble adapting to Plains life. By 1772, Cree were impounding bison, but they preferred the gun to the bow for the hunt, in contrast to peoples longer established on the grasslands. Buffalo hunting lessened dependence on the fur trade. The homeguards, so characteristic of the trading posts of the northern forests, were less apparent on the Plains.[44] Instead, buffalo hunters became provisioners for the trade.

Reduced dependence on the fur trade affected relationships with traders. In fact, the Plains Cree took part in one of the most widely remembered confrontations. It occurred in 1779 in reaction to the callous behaviour of a group of independent traders at Fort Montagne d'Aigle (Eagle Hills Fort), on the Saskatchewan between Eagle Hills Creek and Battle River. Cree warriors killed two traders and forced the rest to flee. The post was abandoned and apparently was never again reoccupied permanently. The incident also caused the abandonment that same year of the Nor'Wester Fort du Milieu and the HBC's Hudson House.

Nor was this an isolated occurrence. Cree warriors participated in another mêlée in 1781 at Fort des Trembles on the Assiniboine River that resulted in the death of three traders and up to 30 Cree warriors. Only the outbreak of the 1781–2 smallpox epidemic prevented large-scale retaliations against traders.[45] The much-vaunted peaceful co-operation that was characteristic of the fur trade in the northern forests was not so evident on the Plains.

In spite of this, the influences of the horse and the fur trade fostered a flowering of Plains cultures from 1750 to 1880. The horse made the buffalo hunt and the extension of overland routes easier. The fur trade made available a new range of goods and provided new markets for products of the hunt. This meant that as long as the herds lasted, Plains First Nations were able to hold their own and, indeed, to reach new heights of cultural expression. They were even able to overcome to a large extent the disasters caused by introduced diseases. They did not have time, however, to adjust to the disappearance of the herds on which all this was based. The dramatic suddenness of that occurrence catapulted events beyond their control.

In the Far Northwest

The invasion of the fur trade into the **Far Northwest**, today's Northwest Territories and British Columbia, received an enormous boost when the British eased restrictions at the interior posts in 1768. The westward movement began in the seventeenth century, when Cree and Nakoda peoples moved westward, in conjunction with the westward expansion of the fur trade. It ended in the voyage of Alexander Mackenzie (1764–1820) of the North West Company, who followed Indigenous trading routes from the Peace River down the Parsnip and Liard rivers to the Bella Coola River, reaching the ocean at Bentinck Arm in 1793.

The visit of Captain James Cook (1728–79) to Nootka Sound in 1778 has usually been considered the beginning of coastal movement. However, according to British Columbia geographer Samuel Bawlf, Sir Francis Drake (1541?–1596), while circling the globe in 1578–80, reached the mouth of the Stikine River where it cuts through the Alaska panhandle. He kept the visit secret, however, to hide it from the Spaniards, who were claiming the entire North American west coast.[46]

More than a century and a half later, in 1741, Vitus Bering (1681–1741) claimed Alaska for Russia. Spaniards arrived offshore in 1774, returning in 1789 to build a fort to protect their claims. They stayed until both Britain and Spain agreed to vacate the region in 1794. The British would soon come back, but not the Spanish (see Historical Background box).

Spearheading the Canadian involvement in both land and sea movements was the North West Company.[47] The NWC fought the Hudson's Bay Company at a severe disadvantage, however, as the latter had direct sea access to the fur providers through Hudson Bay, with the much slower land and river routes left to the NWC. In 1821, with the merger of the rival trading companies into a new Hudson's Bay Company with effective control over trade in a vast territory stretching from Hudson Bay to the Pacific, the HBC became active on the west coast. Its ship, *Beaver*, arrived in Vancouver in 1836, the first steamer to ply those coastal waters. In the meantime, Indigenous coastal trade networks flourished as Indigenous traders capitalized on European initiatives.

HISTORICAL BACKGROUND | The Lack of Indigenous–European Alliances in the West

The absence of colonial rivalry during the process of settlement was a mixed blessing for the Indigenous Peoples of the Pacific coast. For one thing, once trade dropped off, the First Nations and the Europeans had no common ground, and no alliances developed. Agricultural opportunities were limited and slow to appear so the only role for Indigenous Peoples in European settlements was as wage labourers in the fisheries and lumber camps.[48] Apart from the treaties that James Douglas negotiated (see Chapter 10), the settlers did not negotiate for the land they took. The idea that Indigenous Peoples had neither sovereign nor proprietary rights prevailed. The problems that resulted from such an attitude became acute with the discovery of gold on the Fraser and Thompson rivers in 1857.

The head start of the Cree in gaining access to European trade goods was substantial from a capitalist perspective. The Cree bands of Hudson Bay had a century to develop this new connection and to be influenced by European values before the people of the Far Northwest made their first shaky contact. Throughout all this time, however, Indigenous trade networks were operating. Likely, European merchandise worked its way deep into the interior long before traders did. Certainly, this was the case in the Great Lakes region.[49] Samuel Hearne, on his voyage to the Arctic in 1772, found beads of a type not traded by the HBC in an Inuit camp at the mouth of the Coppermine River.[50] Even though contact between Europeans and Indigenous Peoples was low-key during this period, however, it affected Indigenous relationships. Integration into an economy based on production for exchange, rather than for use, destabilized Indigenous ways of life. In some aspects, however, this new economy and what it brought to the Indigenous Peoples led to an intensification of traditional cultural activities.

As European weapons made their way westward with the trade, the nature of conflict changed. The Dene peoples not only fought Cree warriors but also came into conflict with one another. Thus, the Denésoliné contended with the T'atsaot'ine and Tłıchǫ peoples to keep them from direct access to the Hudson Bay posts.[51] Once the HBC posts moved inland, these hostilities lost their reason for being and stopped. The traditional enmity between the Cree peoples of the woodlands and the people of the tundra—the Inuit—had deeper roots, however, and continued far longer.

Another element adding to the complexity of this picture was the arrival of Haudenosaunee trappers, famed as rivermen, at the end of the eighteenth century. Mostly from Caughnawaga (Kahnawake) but also from Oka (Kanesatake) and St Regis (Akwesasne), most came under contract with the NWC, with a few coming on their own.[52] More than 300 arrived between 1800 and 1804. By 1810, they had concentrated along the eastern slopes of the Rockies in the Athabasca and Peace River regions, but by 1821 the movement was tapering off. Most of the newcomers had completed their contracts and were now "freemen."

Efficient fur hunters, the Haudenosaunee rivermen used the latest technology: metal traps. After the NWC joined with the HBC in 1821, the Lesser Slave Lake post accounted for more than a twelfth of the total returns for the Company that year, by far the largest quantity for a single post.[53] On such evidence, it is hardly surprising that the freemen faced accusations of over-trapping to the point of stripping the region of its fur resources. They intermarried locally, which usually meant with Cree or Métis, but later with settler European women.

The Europeans Push Further West, into the Plateau

The breaking of the mountain barrier into central British Columbia by Europeans presented a problem for the local Indigenous Peoples.[54] The Niitsitapiikwan controlled the easier passes to the south, and they feared that their enemies would obtain European firearms. But when the American Lewis and Clark expedition (1804–6) killed some of their people, distracting the Confederacy, David Thompson was able to push through Howse Pass,[55] only to find the pass under Piikani control. Finally, in 1811, Thompson was able to negotiate with the Tsuu T'ina for the use of the more northerly, longer, and more difficult Athabasca Pass. That would be the route for the European traders until 1841. By mid-century, the decline of the bison herds was becoming evident, however, influencing the Niitsitapi leaders to reconsider their position in regard to trade.[56]

The Ktunaxa of the Plateau, anxious to get direct access to trade goods, particularly guns, helped the traders. This was a new expression of an old rivalry with the Niitsitapi Confederacy, which long predated the arrival of European trade. In pre-contact days, this rivalry had surfaced over rights to hunt buffalo on the Plains. The Niitsitapi network was charging the Ktunaxa as much as 10 skins for an item that could be obtained for one at a post. Horses were the Ktunaxa's main stock-in-trade. These were much desired by the Piikani and other Plains peoples, who, as a result, took all the more care to see that the Ktunaxa did not gain access to the European traders.[57] In spite of Piikani efforts to prevent the trade, the Ktunaxa and other peoples of the interior slowly acquired arms.

Once Thompson established a post on the border between the Ktunaxa and the Salish territories, other traders quickly followed. Eventually, the Salish people of the interior were in a position to challenge the Piikani, and in 1810 and again in 1812 they defeated them. Piikani leaders blamed this defeat on the white men and vowed vengeance.[58] As on the Plains, the fur trade in its westward movement was not always peaceful as it encroached on established Indigenous trade networks, disrupted the time-honoured systems of trade and alliance, and reinflamed old enmities.

To the north, entrenched interests were less evident. The Dene Dháa people, an affiliate group of the Dene Confederacy, for example, sought out a fur-trading post on their own initiative in 1799. Their leader was an unusual chief, Makenunatane (Swan Chief, so-called because his soul could fly high like a swan), who seems to have realized that the new trade meant a shift in lifeways—for one thing, it called for individualized trapping rather than communal hunting for subsistence. This would obviously call for new rituals. Thus, he and his people wanted to learn about Christianity.[59] It is perhaps not surprising that the Dene Dháa still have a living prophet tradition.

Sea Otters and China Clippers

The sea otter motivated the opening of the fur trade of the Pacific coast, repeating—only more quickly—what had happened on the Atlantic coast nearly 300 years earlier with the beaver.[60] On the Northwest Coast shipboard trade was the main economic activity for a short but intense period, less than half a century. This is in contrast to the trade in Acadia and in the Gulf of St Lawrence, which thrived for over a century. In both regions, the trade depended on the hunting skill of Indigenous traders, which meant that participants followed Indigenous protocols. Contact on the west coast was comparatively peaceful but still resulted in an 80 per cent drop in the Indigenous population within a century.[61]

The sea otter trade began as a result of the activities of Captain Cook's crew at Nootka Sound.[62] The ship went on to China and there the British discovered the Chinese passion for sea otter fur. This gave rise to the China clipper traffic between Europe (or New England), the Northwest Coast, and China. Sea otter pelts were traded in China for silk, porcelains, and spices, as well as other items commanding high prices in Europe and in eastern North America. A single round trip could take more than three years, but if all went well it could realize a fortune.

The first trading ship arrived on the Northwest Coast in 1785. It was British. However, Americans ("Boston men") were soon dominant. During the following 40 years, until 1825, about 330 vessels flying a variety of national flags came into the region to trade. Of these, 60 per cent made only one visit, but 23 per cent made three or more visits. The peak trading years were between 1792 and 1812, but by about 1825 the sea otter was disappearing. The fur seal of the Pribilof Islands off the southwest coast of Alaska suffered a similar fate.

Times of Change—and Conflict—on the West Coast

It would be little more than half a century before non-Indigenous settlements would begin, in mid-nineteenth century. British Columbia remained predominantly Indigenous until the 1880s. Even then, however, all was not as before. More wealth meant more power for chiefs. Those who could quickly claimed monopolies and took over middlemen roles in the brief but highly profitable trade. Some became wealthy. In 1803, **Muquinna** ("Possessor of pebbles," *fl.* 1786–1817; see Indigenous Leaders box)[63] at Nootka Sound held a **potlatch** during which he gave away 200 muskets, 200 yards of cloth, 100 chemises, 100 mirrors, and seven barrels of gunpowder.

INDIGENOUS LEADERS | Muquinna (*fl.* 1786–1817)

Nuu'chah'nulth Chief Muquinna was one of the key figures at the time of contact with the Europeans in Nootka Sound. Muquinna was the chief of the Moachat group of the Nuu'chah'nulth nation and his particular group had its summer village at Yuquot, at the mouth of Nootka Sound, and its winter village at Tahsis at the very head of the Sound. Muquinna was adept at negotiating the strange and changing new world that the Europeans carried with them in their wake and he was among the most influential of all of the leaders on the Pacific coast in the late eighteenth century. He appears to have skilfully played the Spanish and British traders against one another—a strategy reminiscent of the Mi'kmaw strategy with the British and French on the other side of the continent, though generated independently—and negotiated the best deals for his people in the early contact period by managing this exchange. What we know of him, however, is taken entirely from the journals of the European traders so it is possible that they misinterpreted his status among the Nuu'chah'nulth because he occupied so strategic a location. Muquinna maintained an alliance with Wikinanish, the powerful and influential leader who lived nearby on Clayoquot Sound and whose people were also part of the Nuu'chah'nulth. Muquinna was certainly a capable trader but it is always important to note that the European journalists and traders assigned their own motivations to Indigenous Peoples. Muquinna certainly engaged in trade and negotiations with Captain James Cook and the Spaniard, Alexandro Malaspina, but we can be sure he had his own Nuu'chah'nulth motivations for doing so and these were not necessarily the same motivations that these two and others ascribed to him.

This prosperity, however, was short-lived for Muquinna and other chiefs in a similar position, for two reasons: the near extermination of the sea otter and the fact that the coastal regions quickly became glutted with trade goods. Even supplies of highly prized copper reached the saturation point around 1800. A third factor was the introduction of the HBC steamer *Beaver*, which made trade easier but also shifted much of its activity to the inside passage.

British North Americans did not appear on the scene until 1811, when Nor'Wester David Thompson arrived at the mouth of the Columbia to find Americans (largely former Nor'Westers) already building a post there. The HBC knocked out one competitor after another and eventually dominated the scene. In 1843, it established Fort Victoria in Songhees, or Coast Salish, territory, on Vancouver Island. By agreeing to supply the Russian posts with food, the HBC undercut the Americans. For the most part, these rivalries did not last long, in contrast to the prolonged confrontation in the *petit nord* and on the Plains.

As elsewhere in British North America, the European arrival on the Northwest Coast soon led to increased warfare. This, however, seems to have been of short duration, and in the maritime trade there were comparatively few incidents. Those that did occur included Indigenous retaliations against outrages committed against them, but the causes of many are now difficult to determine.[64]

One of the best-known incidents involved Koyah (Coya, Kouyer, "Raven," d. 1795?), a ranking Haida chief, and Captain Kendrick, leader of an American merchant expedition. Kendrick allowed too many Haida people aboard the *Lady Washington*, and some small items, including some of his personal linen, were pilfered. Kendrick seized Koyah and another chief, bolted each by a leg to a gun carriage, and threatened them with death until amends were made, which included trading all the furs in the village. Not satisfied when his terms were met, Kendrick further disgraced Koyah by whipping him and cutting off his hair, among other indignities.[65] Such a dishonour ruined Koyah's standing as a chief and turned him into an enemy of the fur trade. From then on, he attacked ships and traders whenever he could, including the *Lady Washington* in 1791. He lost his wife and two of his children in one of these episodes.[66]

Muquinna was more successful than Koyah when he overwhelmed the crew of the *Boston* in 1803, allowing only two to survive.[67] In this case, there seems to have been an accumulation of grievances, not the least of which was the fact that the fur trade was bypassing the Nuu'chah'nulth chief. His lavish potlatch of that year was never repeated.[68] The most successful of all Indigenous attacks on vessels was in 1811, when people from the Tla-o-qui-aht, members of the Nuu'chah'nulth nation, blew up the *Tonquin*, leaving no survivors.[69]

Indigenous Interest in Trade

From about 1806, crews began to winter on the coast. Year-round trade developed, and eventually posts were built. First Nation villages were built adjacent to forts, but for different reasons than the homeguards of the Northeast. When forts were built in their territory, nations assumed they had the right to control access to these new centres for trade. Thus, when the HBC moved Fort Simpson from the Nass River to the Tsimshian Peninsula in 1834, nine bands of Tsimshian lost no time in setting up camp nearby. Similarly, four bands of Kwakwaka'wakw converged on Fort Rupert soon after its construction on the northern end of Vancouver Island in 1849.

On the other hand, if the Indigenous people saw little advantage in having a fort in their midst and refused to trade, there was no point in trying to maintain it. An attempt to establish a fort among the Tsilhqot'in in 1829 met with this kind of reaction and closed after 15 years.[70] Other forts were maintained for even a shorter period. In such cases, the HBC had no alternative but to accept the situation.

The Company never did establish the complete control it would have liked in New Caledonia (what is now the central interior region of BC), although it did eventually establish interior posts. The Nor'Westers were the first on the scene, arriving overland across the Continental Divide to establish Fort McLeod on McLeod Lake in 1805, soon to be followed by others. The HBC became active in the area about 1824, following its amalgamation with the Nor'Westers three years earlier.

When coastal traders tried to extend their commerce up the rivers, particularly towards the north, they found themselves facing stiff competition from Indigenous traders. The extent of these networks surprised early traders when they found trade goods from the coast as far east as the Sekani of the Finlay and Parsnip rivers.[71]

In the Far Northwest, the Tsimshian and Tlingit were particularly aggressive in protecting their trade networks, and chiefs such as **Legaic** (Legex, Legaix) of the Tsimshian, who ran a strict monopoly over the Gitxsan on the Upper Skeena, and the Nisga'a Wiiseaks ("Shakes") on the Nass made it clear to whom they thought the trading rights on those rivers belonged.[72]

When the HBC sent combative ex-Nor'Wester Peter Skene Ogden (1790–1854) in 1834 to establish a post on the Stikine River, he backed down in the face of a threatened trade war.[73] Here again, the Company soon learned that in the short run at least it was wiser to co-operate with Indigenous networks than to compete with them. This policy paid off as the maritime trade declined and that between the coast and the interior stepped up. Still, HBC officers were not pleased when they learned of Kwakwaka'wakw traders buying furs at higher prices than the Company was paying and reselling them to Yankee traders—effectively cutting the HBC out of the deal. As always, Indigenous Peoples conducted business for their own reasons that were not necessarily aligned with the Company's interests, which frustrated the HBC.

Furs were not the only reason for the activity on the Northwest Coast. The HBC built Fort Rupert, for example, with an eye on the potential of nearby coalfields that the Kwakwaka'wakw had shown the whites in 1835. The intention of the Kwakwaka'wakw had been to work the mines themselves and sell the coal to the HBC.[74]

New Trade Networks Replace the Old, and Societies Are Disrupted

As elsewhere in the Americas, the social consequences of all this change could be drastic. European diseases seem to have been slower in appearing than on the east coast, and the resultant population drops, while severe, seem to have been proportionately somewhat less than what occurred in other regions of the hemisphere, which had drops in some cases of up to 95 per cent. The Northwest Coast population would reach its nadir in 1929, at 22,605,[75] after which it started recovering.

Library and Archives Canada, PA 95524

Nineteenth-century chiefs of the Wolf Crest of Git-lak-damaks, Nass River. Standing, beginning fourth from the left, Andrew Nash, John Nash, James Percival, Philip Nash, and Charlie Brown (right rear). Seated, second from the right, Mrs Eliza Woods and Matilda Peal, née Brown.

The connection between material wealth and rank, manifested in the potlatch, placed a premium on the control of trading networks. Chiefs who were well placed in this regard, such as Legaic of the Tsimshian or 'Kwah of the Wet'suwet'en (*c.* 1755–1840), both of whom had large interior networks, expanded their spheres of influence and became very powerful.[76] Others who depended mainly on the sea otter, such as Muquinna, did well for a while but then found their position undercut as the trade passed them by. In the boreal forests, on the other hand, material wealth was not a consideration in selecting peace chiefs, nor were these chiefs concerned with trading. Trading chiefs were a response to the European traders' preference for dealing with chiefs, and had little, if any, connection with the general problems of leadership with which the peace chiefs were involved.

In New Caledonia, one of the results of the increasing tempo of upriver trade was the spread of coastal cultures into the interior, reaching as far as the Wet'suwet'en on the interior Plateau. Dene people around Atlin and Teslin lakes in the North were so affected by these trends they became known as "interior Tlingit." Counterbalancing these were influences being brought in by the fur brigades coming from the east. Canoemen were often Haudenosaunee, some of whom reached the coast (and even Hawaii), but most settled in Oregon and northwestern Alberta.

Questions to Consider

1. What changes were brought about by the arrival of horses and guns in the West?
2. Why did the members of the Niitsitapi Confederacy resist the arrival of Europeans?
3. How did the arrival of traders affect relations among different Indigenous groups in the West?
4. What made the relations between Indigenous Peoples and newcomers distinctive on the west coast?

Recommended Readings

Abel, Kerry. *Drum Songs*. Montreal and Kingston: McGill-Queen's University Press, 1993.

Carter, Sarah. *Aboriginal People and Colonizers of Western Canada to 1900*. Toronto: University of Toronto Press, 1999.

Dempsey, Hugh A. *Indian Tribes of Alberta*. Calgary: Glenbow-Alberta Institute, 1986.

Fisher, Robin. *Contact and Conflict: Indian–European Relations in British Columbia, 1774–1890*. Vancouver: University of British Columbia Press, 1977.

Hyde, George E. *Indians of the High Plains*. Norman: University of Oklahoma Press, 1959.

McCormack, Patricia A. *Fort Chipewyan and the Shaping of Canadian History, 1788–1920s*. Vancouver: University of British Columbia Press, 2010.

Rich, E.E. *The Fur Trade in the Northwest to 1857*. Toronto: McClelland & Stewart, 1967.

Roe, Frank Gilbert. *The Indian and the Horse*. Norman: University of Oklahoma Press, 1951.

9 The British Alliance of 1812–14

CHAPTER OUTLINE

In this chapter we will examine the rapidly changing world of the early nineteenth century, with particular attention to the growing desire to present the expansionist Americans with a united front through the second great movement of pan-Indigenism. The role of the British, as ally against the Americans, and the difficult choices facing the peoples of the Great Lakes region form important themes throughout this chapter. In the end, the War of 1812 served as a partial victory for the Indigenous Peoples, and it enabled many of them to build a better life away from the threats associated with the westward push of American expansionism.

LEARNING OUTCOMES

1. Students will be able to see the difficult position that Indigenous Peoples' leadership found themselves in with the shifting alliance systems of the early nineteenth century.

2. Students will learn something of the importance of the ongoing efforts at a coordinated response to American expansionism.

3. Students will come to a better understanding of the towering figure of Tecumseh and his leadership role in the resistance to American expansion.

TIMELINE From the Peace of Paris to the War of 1812

1783
North Carolina confiscates all Indigenous lands; outcries lead to policy of purchase three years later.

1795
Treaty of Greenville demands huge land cessions to Americans, opens Ohio Valley to settlers.

1808
Tecumseh's brother, Tenskwatawa ("the Shawnee Prophet"), founds Prophetstown.

1812
17 July: Michilimackinac falls to Anishinaabe warriors and British, following strategy devised by Tecumseh and other First Nation chiefs.

15 August: Fort Dearborn (Chicago) falls to massacre by Main Poc's Boodwaadmii.

16 August: US General William Hull surrenders Fort Detroit after ruse concocted by Tecumseh.

13 October: Battle of Queenston Heights, led by the Kanienkehaka chiefs Ahyonwaeghs (whom the British called John Brant) and Teyoninhokarawen (whose British name was Major John Norton); British victory tempered by loss of General Isaac Brock, who had taken Fort Detroit with his friend Tecumseh.

1794
Pan-Indigenous alliance is defeated by American military forces in the Battle of Fallen Timbers; British fail to help the Indigenous Peoples.

1807
Death of Kanienkehaka war chief Thayendanegea (whom the British called Joseph Brant), and subsequent rise of Tecumseh.

1811
William Henry Harrison, Indiana governor, attacks Prophetstown while Tecumseh is away on pan-Indigenous mission.

1813
24 June: Battle of Beaver Dams, a Haudenosaunee Confederacy-led victory for British.

10 September: American naval victory on Lake Erie cuts British supply line to west.

5 October: At Moraviantown in southern Ontario, Tecumseh and his Indigenous allies save General Henry Proctor, who flees; Tecumseh, severely wounded, fights to death.

1814
5 July: Battle of Chippewa, in which Haudensoaunee warriors, led by Red Jacket, fight against Loyalist Haudenosaunee warriors under Teyoninhokarawen (Major John Norton). Treaty of Ghent ends hostilities between British and Americans.

Disruptions from the Peace of Paris

The Peace of Paris of 1783, which ended the American War of Independence, stunned Indigenous Peoples in the upper Middle West. The British had ceded the Ohio Valley—their lands—to the United States without any mention of Indigenous inhabitants, allies or otherwise. The dream of pan-Indigenous unity, which earlier in the century had inspired Nescambiouit of the Wabanaki and Kiala of the Mesquakie in their failed attempts to forge chains of alliances from the Great Lakes to the Atlantic, was now an urgent political goal.

In August of 1783, 35 nations assembled at Sandusky, in Ohio's Wyandot (Wendat) country, in the first of a series of councils to consider the matter. The Kanienkehaka leader Thayendanegea (Joseph Brant) lobbied hard for a confederation on the model of the Haudenosaunee Confederacy. Few delegates were willing to go that far, but realizing all too clearly the need for unity, some of them united in a loose confederacy.

Sir John Johnson (1741–1830), superintendent of Indians for the Northern Department,[1] assured the delegates that the Paris peace in no way extinguished their rights to lands northwest of the Ohio River. Spurred by this "Tomahawk Speech," as it has been called, the council agreed to hold to the line established by treaty in 1768. The Ohio River was now to be the boundary beyond which European settlement was not to spread. Settlers and even governments, however, showed little inclination to respect Indigenous rights. The new American government assumed that in winning independence it had automatically gained title to all territories east of the Mississippi, whether or not Indigenous Peoples were living on them.[2] In 1783, North Carolina confiscated all Indigenous lands within the state. Outcries were such that by 1786, the United States acknowledged the right of Indigenous Peoples to land and put a policy of purchase in place, but this did little to ease the situation. Not only was it poorly honoured in practice, but the Indigenous Peoples often simply did not want to sell.

In the battles that inevitably erupted, First Nations warriors twice defeated the Americans. The US then rallied a larger military expedition than ever and destroyed the coalition led by the Shaawanwaki chief Weyapiersenwah (Blue Jacket) in the **Battle of Fallen Timbers**, 1794. At Fallen Timbers, south of Detroit in northern Ohio, the pan-Indigenous coalition was served a double blow: not only did the British not come to the aid of their allies, but they also closed the doors of Fort Miami, their nearest fort to the battle scene.

Fallen Timbers effectively broke Indigenous resistance to the western advance of non-Indigenous settlement. The land cessions demanded in the **Treaty of Greenville** in 1795 made that clear. The continual loss of territory, even with cash compensation, was causing growing worry and resentment.[3]

The First Nations Defend the Canadas

The American push for land was not the only reason for worry. By 1808, the fur trade was in a depression.[4] Lacking other economic resources, Indigenous Peoples turned to their British allies for help. The British, caught in unresolved antagonisms in the wake of American independence—and by this time more aware of the usefulness of Indigenous allies to preserve their colonies in the event of future hostilities—were willing to comply. Between 1784 and 1788, they spent £20,000 a year on **gift distributions** to Indigenous Peoples, an expense supported by the fur barons of Montreal. As Montreal merchant James McGill (1744–1813) wrote to the governor, "The Indians are the only Allies who can aught avail in the defence of the Canadas. They have the same interest as us, and alike are objects of American subjugation, if not extermination."[5]

It was an ironic switch for the British. During the Seven Years War, they had complained bitterly about French maintenance and use of First Nations allies. When victorious, the British had tried to discontinue the practice with disastrous results (see Chapter 7). Now, 20 years later, they found themselves using the same tactics towards the Americans.[6]

Treaty Robe for Tecumseh, **an installation piece by Bonnie Devine (b. 1952).** Devine invites viewers to revisit the story of Tecumseh from a lens of social justice and integrity.

Bonnie Devine (b. 1952, Toronto). Treaty Robe, for Tecumseh (2013), cotton, linen, canvas, deer hide, megis shells, wood, acrylic and mixed media on paper.
Purchased with the support of the Canada Council for the Arts Acquisition Grants program /Oeuvre achetée avec l'aide du programme de Subventions d'acquisition du Conseil des arts du Canada and funds from the AGW Estate of Eleanor Wallace, 2014. 2014.002 . Image, courtesy of the Art Gallery of Windsor

In 1807, convinced that a conflict with the United States was inevitable,[7] instructions from London came to the colony to ensure the loyalty of the peoples of the west. Remembering the support they had received from the Haudenosaunee (particularly the Kanienkehaka) during the recent war with the Americans, the British concluded that Indigenous support was vital to the preservation of Britain's remaining North American colonies.[8] The very people whose pleas for help Britain had ignored at the Battle of Fallen Timbers in 1794, the British now tried to win over to their cause.

Indigenous Peoples, for their part, needed all the help they could get in their efforts to preserve their territories. In the early post-independence period in the United States, even the unreliable British seemed preferable to the aggressively expansionist Americans.

Tecumseh

The death of Thayendanegea (Joseph Brant) in 1807 opened the way for **Tecumseh** ("Shooting Star," "Panther Crouching in Wait," *c.* 1768–1813), part Shaawanwaki, part Cree, to move onto centre stage. Having lost his father and a brother to the Americans in the ongoing US frontier wars, he became an advocate of pan-Indigenism. He had refused to participate in the Treaty of Greenville, which opened the Ohio Valley for American settlement. Like other Indigenous leaders, Tecumseh sided with the British, not because he liked them particularly but because he saw them as the lesser of two evils.

As with Obwandiyag, Tecumseh was linked with a prophet, in his case his brother, **Tenskwatawa** ("Open Door," Lalawethika, 1775–1836). More widely known as the Shawnee Prophet, Tenskwatawa took his name from the saying of Jesus, "I am the door."[9] His nativistic religious revival prepared the way for Tecumseh's own pan-Indigenous movement, with its doctrine that land did not belong to particular nations but, rather, to Indigenous Peoples as a whole. As a result, he argued, no single nation had the right to give up land on its own. This should be done only by all the nations of the region in council.[10] His was an Indigenous answer to the Proclamation of 1763, which held that Indigenous lands could be ceded only to the British Crown. It was also a challenge to the policy of divide and rule.

Although no authentic portrait of Tecumseh exists, there are verbal descriptions of his appearance. Apparently, he cut a striking figure, combining a fine physique with a great sense of style. He dressed in the manner of his people but with a flair that drew the admiration of both Indigenous and non-Indigenous people. His personality was equally impressive, combining a passionate concern for his people with a genius for strategy. As his friend **General Isaac Brock** (1769–1812) observed, if he had been British, he would have been a great general.[11] Tecumseh is widely regarded as the greatest of all Indigenous leaders during the period of resistance to European settlement.[12]

Tecumseh challenged the cessions of territory the Americans were obtaining, particularly those that **William Henry Harrison**, governor of Indiana Territory from 1800 to 1812, wrung from Indigenous Peoples. He visited as many nations as he could, urging them to unite to prevent further encroachment. His proposal was a radical departure from traditional Indigenous inter-national politics, yet Tecumseh made remarkable headway towards realizing his vision of an alliance from Lake Michigan southward.[13] As the influence of Tecumseh and Tenskwatawa spread, the British became interested, and the Americans, apprehensive.

Tecumseh gained the support of the Boodwaadmii, Ojibwa, Shaawanwaki, Odaawak, Hoocąągra, and Giiwigaabaw. He had less, but some, success with the Lenni Lenape, Wendat, Mamaceqtaw, Myaamiaki, and Piankeshaw, among others. The Maskó:kí, who had been strong supporters of the British in the recent war, felt particularly betrayed by the peace (their first reaction to the news had been to call it a "Virginia lie"[14]), so very few joined. Tecumseh's appeal was to the younger warriors. Older chiefs tended to oppose him, fearing that his proposed pan-Indigenous council would further erode the lifeways that had been undermined by the arrival of the Europeans.

Despite such opposition, however, other factors came to Tecumseh's aid. The loss of markets for furs caused hardship among those who had adapted to the trade, a situation aggravated among Great Lakes Anishinaabek by crop failures two years in a row and the disappearance of game because of drought.

By this time, the British had developed a cadre of trader/agents who had learned how to negotiate with Indigenous Peoples, following the example of the French. Among these was the Irishman Matthew Elliott (*c.* 1739–1814), who lived with the Shaawanwaki for many years,

INDIGENOUS LEADERS | Tenskwatawa (1775–1836)

The Shaawanwaki spiritual and political leader Tenskwatawa gave an intellectual and spiritual depth to the pan-Indigenous movement of the early nineteenth century. His call for unity was deeply rooted in the traditional beliefs and world view of his people. His life was not without personal struggles and in fact in his youth he had been tempted to give in to the seemingly inevitable changes being forced on his people. He abused alcohol and he turned his back on his traditional beliefs. One day, however, he experienced a series of visions and he turned his life around. He changed his name to Tenskwatawa, the "Open Door," and he began to teach that the revitalization of elements of traditional beliefs was crucial to the survival of the Indigenous Peoples. Tenskwatawa believed that the Great Spirit would protect the Indigenous Peoples from the evils of American settlement as long as the people reverted to their earlier ways and beliefs.

After 1805 many Indigenous people from across the Great Lakes region came to the Ohio Valley to hear his message and to join the growing pan-Indigenous movement centred on the village of Prophetstown in Indiana Territory, which Tenskwatawa founded in 1808. Even when Prophetstown fell to troops led by Governor Harrison in the Battle of Tippecanoe in November 1811, revealing the all-too-human limits of his power, he still retained a large following. Tenskwatawa continued to wield some influence and he continued to provide a spiritual grounding for the political and military career of his brother, Tecumseh. By 1812 Tenskwatawa had become persuaded that the best course of action was to form a stronger alliance with the British against the expansionist Americans. Tecumseh relied heavily on Tenskwatawa's reputation in order to win other Indigenous Peoples over to that point of view.

married among them, and was so assimilated to the Shaawanwaki way that the British did not completely trust him. Once dismissed from Indian Affairs on unproven charges of corruption, he was called back in 1808 as superintendent at Amherstburg, on the Detroit River in extreme southwestern Upper Canada near Detroit, because of his connection with the strategically located Shaawanwaki. One of his first actions was to arrange a council at Amherstburg that attracted 5,000 Anishinaabek and other Indigenous Peoples.

Another influential figure was the Scot Robert Dickson (c. 1765–1823), whose flaming red hair and beard became part of western folklore. He was a brother-in-law of Yanktonai Dakota chief Red Thunder. A long-time trader, Dickson was British agent for the peoples living west of Lake Huron. His was a hard-headed approach that earned him the reputation of being tough but fair, tempered by a strong streak of generosity, although he tended to favour the various Siouan-speaking peoples. Nevertheless, he played a major role rallying the western Indigenous Peoples to the British cause, to which they remained loyal during the war.[15]

But the British were more interested in fostering trade than in provoking war. For one thing, the deadly struggle with Napoleon in Europe had left them with neither the troops nor the resources for more military campaigns. Tensions were mounting, however, particularly between Harrison and Tecumseh. Tecumseh was especially annoyed when the governor ordered land surveys, and he moved to prevent them. Harrison bided his time but then seized the moment in 1811 when the Shaawanwaki chief was away rallying southern nations to his cause. Harrison attacked Prophetstown, at the confluence of the Wabash and Tippecanoe rivers, and the ensuing battle was less a victory for the Americans than it was a personal defeat for Tenskwatawa.[16] This bloodshed damaged his influence.

For Tecumseh, the attack ended his plan to delay military action until the Indigenous Peoples and the British could gather enough forces to deal a decisive blow to the Americans. For the British, it confirmed their suspicions that the Canadian border was not safe from American aggression.

Gains and Losses

The last of the colonial wars in North America, the **War of 1812–14** has been classed as a continuation of the American War of Independence.[17] For Britain and the US, it was an inconclusive contest that left important matters, such as those relating to Indigenous Peoples, as unresolved as they had been before the fighting. For the First Nations, it was a turning point. The Haudenosaunee Confederacy (then called the Six Nations Iroquois) who fought for the British fought on their own terms, for their own objectives. Unfortunately, the factionalism that had seen some members of the Haudenosaunee Confederacy move to the Grand River and others remain in New York continued to plague the Haudenosaunee, and at times they found themselves confronting one another on the field of battle. The Haudenosaunee military contribution to the British war effort in 1812–14 was tremendous. They had retained their old skill at small-scale warfare, which the French had called *la petite guerre* and which the Americans feared. In fact, American fear of the Haudenosaunee warriors played an important and sometimes crucial role in the war. Similarly, in the West, the Odaawa and Ojibwa allies fought for their own objectives and with similar results. They, too, had preserved their war tactics and weapons, and they, too, inspired fear in the American armies.

Indigenous participation in the War of 1812 was important and even decisive. The Indigenous allies were the key factor in Great Britain's successful defence of Upper Canada.[18] In the West, it was largely an Indigenous-led war. For instance, the fall of **Michilimackinac** on 17 July 1812 to British and Anishinaabe forces was an Anishinaabe victory. Its strategy, worked out by Tecumseh and other chiefs, had been that of surprise.

The psychological effect of the Michilimackinac victory was enormous, well beyond its broader military significance. Indigenous Peoples now flocked unreservedly to the British flag. Elliott and Dickson had no trouble raising 4,000 warriors. The Michilimackinac victory also had an impact on General William Hull (1753–1825), US commander at Detroit, whose fear of Indigenous people was well known. He proclaimed that "no white man found fighting by the side of an Indian will be taken prisoner."[19] A ruse led him to believe that British forces on his flank included 5,000 Indigenous warriors, and Tecumseh reinforced it by using the old trick of marching his warriors again and again past a vantage point in full view of the Americans.

Tecumseh then cut American communication lines, and Hull, convinced that the situation was hopeless, surrendered on 16 August without firing a shot. Tecumseh and General Brock rode together into the fallen fort.[20] When Hull learned what had happened the day before at Fort

Dearborn (Chicago), when Main Poc's Boodwaadmii killed most of the garrison, he probably felt justified. American officials disagreed, however, and court-martialled the hapless Hull.

These successes, especially the fall of Detroit, encouraged leaders of the Haudenosaunee Confederacy, previously set on neutrality, to join British forces. They were a major factor in the British success at **Queenston Heights**, on the Niagara Peninsula, on 13 October 1812, when they arrived at a critical moment on the field of battle led by the Kanienkehaka war chief **Teyoninhokarawen (Major John Norton**, *fl*. 1784–1825) and Ahyonwaeghs (whom the British called John Brant or Henry Tekarihogen, 1794–1832), youngest son of Thayendanegea and Ohtowaʔkéhson (Catherine Brant), likely head woman of her clan.[21] Again, the American fear of Indigenous warriors had its effect, and the invasion was repelled. The Americans fled across the river. But the cost was high for the British, as they lost Brock.[22]

Tecumseh cut an American force to pieces near Fort Meigs, Indiana, on 5 May 1813.[23] On the Niagara Peninsula, the **Battle of Beaver Dams**, on 24 June 1813, was a Haudenosaunee victory. According to Teyoninhokarawen, "The Cognauguaga [Caughnawaga, of the Haudenosaunee Confederacy] Indians fought the battle, the Mohawk [Kanienkehaka] got the plunder and [Lieutenant James] Fitzgibbon [1780–1863] got the credit."[24] But as the months wore on, Tecumseh began to lose the initiative. He was able to get some Maskó:kí to open war in the south, but their confederacy was split to the point of civil war. In 1814, the Americans destroyed what was left of their confederacy.[25] In the meantime, the American naval victory on Lake Erie, 10 September 1813, cut the British supply line to Fort Malden (Amherstburg), the main British centre for gift distribution, endangering Indigenous alliances in the West. To complicate matters, a rift was growing between the First Nations and their British allies.

Teyoninhokarawen explained the nature of the British alliance from his own unique per-spective at a Great Council Fire held at the Grand River in June of 1812:

> You know that the preferring to live under the protection of the King, rather than fall under the power or influence of the Americans,—induced us to fix our habitations in this place. If the King is attacked, we must support him, we are sure that such conduct is honourable;—but how profitable it might be to submit to these Mighty Men without resistance, we can by no means ascertain;—We know that We would feel it highly disgraceful, and we remember what has been the fate of those who have thought that a passive inoffensive Demeanour would be sufficient protection. Witness the peaceable People of Conestogue butchered at Lancaster,—the harmless Moravian Delawares, murdered at their own Village on Muskingum,—and many other instances that clearly demonstrate a manly resistance to be the strongest sec-urity against armed enemies like them, who invade us with their host of new made soldiers, only confident of awing by the pomp of military parade and numbers. We know them to have always been the Enemies of the Aboriginal Nations.[26]

The British general who succeeded Brock, Henry Proctor (1763–1822), did not attract the admiration of Tecumseh. His frustration with the British general was understandable, in that the Shaawanwaki chief had by this time assembled one of the largest Indigenous "armies" the Great

> **HISTORICAL BACKGROUND** | Moraviantown
>
> In 1792, the Moravian Brothers established a village for refugee Lenni Lenape on the Thames River near the future international border. Although they called it Fairfield, it became popularly known as Moraviantown. Not only was it successful (for one reason, the Lenni Lenape were traditionally agriculturalists), it was even more prosperous than surrounding colonial settlements. Looted and burned by the Americans in the War of 1812, the town was rebuilt as New Fairfield in 1815 but never fully recovered. Beset by the usual problems of settler encroachments, which became steadily more serious, many Indigenous people left for the American Middle West. The colonial authorities also refused to grant the Lenni Lenape clear title to the land. In 1903, the government turned New Fairfield over to the Canadian Methodist Episcopal Church, a move the Lenni Lenape resented.

Lakes had ever seen, estimated at 2,000–3,000 warriors or even more. The contrast with the British force was glaring—it counted only about 800 men. When Proctor finally made a stand at **Moraviantown** (Historical Background box) in southern Ontario on 5 October 1813, Tecumseh and his warriors did the fighting, saving the general's life. Tecumseh, severely wounded, fought until his death. Proctor fled.

The End of Tecumseh's Movement

Warriors of more than 30 First Nations had fought under Tecumseh. Now he was dead, and his loss would be hard to overestimate. No leader was able to fill his role as a catalyst for pan-Indigenous action. With his passing also went the remains of Tenskwatawa's nativistic movement. Effective Indigenous participation in the war, however, did not end with the defeat at Moraviantown.[27] Warriors continued fighting until the end of the war, sometimes in large numbers. But the underlying unity of purpose that Tecumseh had evoked was greatly weakened.

The British tried to fill the void by enshrining Tecumseh's memory as an icon. They gave Tecumseh's son, Paukeesaa, a commission in the British army. His brother, Tenskwatawa, received a sword and pistols as gifts of the Prince Regent and was named principal chief of the Western Nations, and the British heaped his sister, Tecumpease, with gifts of condolence. But ceremonial protocol could not transform a memory into a new Tecumseh. The British also could not disguise the fact that they were not fully committed to the war, locked as they were in the struggle in Europe with Napoleon. Britain's wooing of the First Nations in this particular case sprang not so much from humanist or ideological conviction as it did from the need to use all means possible to maintain and preserve her positions in two different parts of the world at once, a circumstance not lost on her North American opponents.

The Americans moved to take advantage of the situation and to turn the First Nations to their side of the fighting, and they were able to persuade some groups. On 5 July 1814, a contingent of the Haudenosaunee Confederacy, largely Onondowaga under Red Jacket, fought on the American side at the Battle of Chippewa, north of Fort Erie on the Niagara Peninsula, against British forces that included 200 men of the Haudenosaunee Confederacy and 100 western Anishinaabek under Teyoninhokarawen (Major Norton). The battle saw Haudenosaunee warriors once more pitted against Haudenosaunee warriors, as had happened in the American War of Independence. This time, the First Nations fighting on the Canadian side sustained their heaviest losses.

These casualties, incurred in fighting what was now seen as a newcomers' quarrel, shocked the entire Haudenosaunee Confederacy.[28] The pro-American members sent a deputation to discuss with the pro-Canadian members a new, and more inclusive, policy of neutrality. As a result, only a few warriors remained to fight the Battle of Lundy's Lane, although other Indigenous warriors continued to fight in other theatres.

The British had learned their lesson from the Treaty of Paris of 1783. During the negotiations for the **Treaty of Ghent**, 1814, which formally ended the war, they tried to bargain for the establishment of an "Indian territory," the boundaries of which would follow those fixed at the Treaty of Greenville (1795). The Americans absolutely refused to agree to this proposal. The most they would accept was to recognize Indigenous lands as they had been before hostilities—in legal terms, the status quo ante bellum.

To suggest that this was a disappointment for Indigenous Peoples in the US is to put it mildly. All their battles, very often successful in individual cases, had not earned them back any lost territories. Additionally, despite the assurances of the Treaty of Ghent, Indigenous Peoples continued to lose land. Métis communities in the Great Lakes area were overwhelmed and even occupied militarily.[29] By 1817, forced removal of Indigenous Peoples from their lands began in the Ohio Valley, a policy that would reach a peak with the Trail of Tears for the Cherokee in the 1830s.

In some instances, Indigenous Peoples themselves decided to migrate. The Boodwaadmii did so in the years 1835–40, when they left their Great Lakes homelands to settle in central and southern Ontario, where they still are today.[30] Some Onyota'aka of the Haudenosaunee Confederacy settled around Muncey, Ontario, around 1840. Even though the Onyota'aka had sided with the Americans during the War of Independence, they had been deprived of most of their lands in New York.

Indigenous Peoples were not the only ones on the move during this time. Settler expansion was dramatic—the population of what would become Canada tripled from approximately 750,000 in 1821 to 2.3 million by 1851. In Upper Canada alone, it rose by a factor of 10, to reach 952,000. By this time, Indigenous Peoples east of the Great Lakes were already a minority in their own lands. By 1812, they formed about 10 per cent of the population of Upper Canada.[31]

For Indigenous Peoples within Canada, the War of 1812–14 was the end of an era.[32] As long as the colonial wars lasted, they had been able to maintain their positions in return for war service. The loss of that bargaining tool put them at a serious disadvantage. Post-war governmental reorganization reflected this change: in 1830, "Indian administration" was shifted from the military to the civilian arm. New conditions, however, demanded new adaptations.[33] Adaptation, of course, had always been the key to Indigenous survival. The circumstances might have changed, but the requirement to work out satisfactory life patterns under prevailing conditions remained the same. Traditional values and culture would find new life and new forms in rising to these challenges.

Questions to Consider

1. What role did Tecumseh play in the conflicts between the British and the Americans?
2. What advantages did the British gain from their Indigenous allies?
3. Why did Haudenosaunee, Odaawa, and Ojibwa warriors fight against the Americans?
4. Where did the various peoples move after the War of 1812–14?

Recommended Readings

Allen, R.S. *His Majesty's Indian Allies*. Toronto: Dundurn Press, 1993.

Benn, Carl. *The Iroquois in the War of 1812*. Toronto: University of Toronto Press, 1998.

Dowd, Gregory Evans. *A Spirited Resistance: The North American Indian Struggle for Unity, 1745–1815*. Baltimore: Johns Hopkins University Press, 1992.

Edmunds, R. David. *The Shawnee Prophet*. Lincoln: University of Nebraska Press, 1983.

———. *Tecumseh and the Quest for Indian Leadership*. Boston: Little, Brown, 1984.

Paxton, James. *Joseph Brant and His World*. Toronto: Lorimer, 2008.

Stanley, G.F.G. *The War of 1812: Land Operations*. Toronto: Macmillan, 1983.

Sugden, John. *Tecumseh's Last Stand*. Norman: University of Oklahoma Press, 1985.

Tanner, Helen Hornbeck, ed. *Atlas of Great Lakes Indian History*. Norman: University of Oklahoma Press, 1987.

10 The "Indian Problem": Isolation, Assimilation, and Experimentation

CHAPTER OUTLINE

The misguided concept of assimilation—trying to make Indigenous people into Euro-Canadians—forms a central theme in this chapter. Over the course of the nineteenth century the British government, with the strong support of the Anglican Church, attempted to force a program of assimilation on the Indigenous Peoples living within what we now call Canada. This took various forms and was pursued with varying degrees of effort according to time and place. In all cases it failed. History, language, tradition, geography, and strongly held cultural beliefs kept the forces of assimilation in check throughout the century, and eventually Indigenous assimilation faded from the official agenda. Although this was positive in a few cases, the overall effect of governmental neglect was devastating in other ways.

LEARNING OUTCOMES

1. Students will gain an understanding of the response to attempted assimilation across Canada.

2. Students will learn something of the overwhelming pace of change that confronted Indigenous leaders in the nineteenth century.

3. Students will gain insight into the role of such leaders as Kahkewaquonaby, Mikak, and Legaic.

TIMELINE From the First Reserve to the Gitxsan Uprising

1637
First Indigenous "reserve," at Sillery, near Quebec City.

1769
Moravians receive land grant on northern Labrador coast.

1784
New Brunswick separated from Nova Scotia; refuses to recognize the only land grant to Indigenous Peoples previously made in the colony.

1820
Whalers operating on east side of Baffin Island.

1827
Grape Island settlement of Ojibwa in Bay of Quinte founded by American Methodist missionary William Case.

1830s–40s
Upper Canada administration, over Haudenosaunee protests, gives Grand River Navigation Company the Six Nations Reserve's funds and land, and the company floods more Haudenosaunee territory before going bankrupt. (Haudenosaunee ultimately lose a 1948 court decision over the matter.)

1836
Grape Island project relocated to Rice Lake at Alderville, Ont.

Anglican Herbert Beaver the first permanent west coast missionary, at Fort Vancouver.

Sir Francis Bond Head, lieutenant-governor of Upper Canada, arranges large land surrenders by Ojibwa in Manitoulin chain and on Bruce Peninsula (the Saugeen Tract).

1765
Moravian missionary Jens Haven intercedes to ease conflict between Labrador Inuit and Europeans, who had forced Inuit up the Labrador coast.

1771
Haven founds first mission at Nain, which includes trading post.

1812
Selkirk colony for white settlers established at Red River, site of the largest Métis settlement in the West.

1825
Miramichi fire in northern New Brunswick destroys 6,000 square miles of prime forest, the resource base of subsistence for countless Indigenous people.

Britain grants land along Credit River to Métis Methodist minister Peter Jones and his Mississauga converts.

1835
Indian Affairs agent T.G. Anderson begins Ojibwa settlement project at Manitowaning on Manitoulin Island; project eventually deemed a failure, but Ojibwa remain, founding village of Little Current.

1838
Only 1,425 Mi'kmaq listed as living in Nova Scotia.

1840s
HBC establishes posts in Far Northwest.

Continued

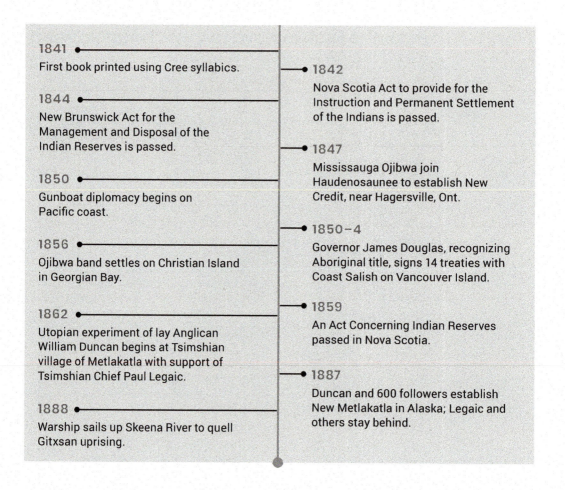

1841
First book printed using Cree syllabics.

1842
Nova Scotia Act to provide for the Instruction and Permanent Settlement of the Indians is passed.

1844
New Brunswick Act for the Management and Disposal of the Indian Reserves is passed.

1847
Mississauga Ojibwa join Haudenosaunee to establish New Credit, near Hagersville, Ont.

1850
Gunboat diplomacy begins on Pacific coast.

1850–4
Governor James Douglas, recognizing Aboriginal title, signs 14 treaties with Coast Salish on Vancouver Island.

1856
Ojibwa band settles on Christian Island in Georgian Bay.

1859
An Act Concerning Indian Reserves passed in Nova Scotia.

1862
Utopian experiment of lay Anglican William Duncan begins at Tsimshian village of Metlakatla with support of Tsimshian Chief Paul Legaic.

1887
Duncan and 600 followers establish New Metlakatla in Alaska; Legaic and others stay behind.

1888
Warship sails up Skeena River to quell Gitxsan uprising.

Assimilating the "Vanishing Indians"

Two destructive ideas concerning Indigenous Peoples dominated British civil administration for North America in 1830. First, it was believed that they were disappearing. At the start of the nineteenth century, it was estimated that there had been about 18,000 Indigenous people in Upper and Lower Canada (later Ontario and Quebec). This figure did not include the peoples living to the north of the Upper Great Lakes. Twenty years later, the number had dropped to 12,000, lending support for the popular myth of the "vanishing Indian." In contrast, between 1818 and 1828, the non-Indigenous population doubled.

The second notion was that Indigenous Peoples should either move to communities isolated from whites or else assimilate. Agriculture[1] and education, entrusted to missionaries, would achieve **assimilation**. In the patronizing words of a colonial secretary, the aim was "to protect and cherish this helpless Race . . . [and] raise them in the Scale of Humanity."[2] Sir John Colborne, lieutenant-governor for Upper Canada, suggested in 1829 that the best way of financing the assimilationist program would be through the leasing and sale of Indigenous lands. Sir James Kempt, governor of Lower Canada, 1828–30, agreed. Indigenous people must become self-supporting citizens within the cultural framework of colonial life. The old hunting ways were doomed. In other words, the Indigenous Peoples would be expected to pay their own way into the assimilation that was being forced upon them. It was expected that colonial governors would mainly, but not entirely, work out details. The administration of "Indian affairs" in the Canadas changed radically between 1828 and 1845.

In 1829, the government separated the administration of Indian affairs, as it was called, in Lower Canada from that of Upper Canada, leaving most of the experienced personnel in Upper Canada. Administrators recruited some Indigenous people as interpreters and clerks, but none at the policy-making level. Major-General H.C. Darling, Indian Affairs' chief superintendent, 1828–30, in his 1828 report on Indigenous conditions—the first such for the Canadas— advocated model farms and villages as the best means of assimilating Indigenous Peoples, and this policy had enough support to go forward.[3]

Model Villages Would Immerse Indigenous Peoples in Euro-Canadian Culture

The nineteenth century was the era of Utopian experiments—attempts to create communities that would reflect Victorian ideals of the good life. For Indigenous Peoples, these **model villages** would become an instrument for the inculcation of Euro-Canadian values, or so it was hoped. These experiments all were in Canada West (as Upper Canada was called after the Act of Union in 1841), but they drew much of their inspiration from the long-established Indigenous villages of Canada East (formerly Lower Canada). The inhabitants of these earlier villages were officially Christian and living sedentary lives, an "achievement" the British hoped to copy in Canada West.[4] In fact, they already had the examples in Canada West of two successful Christian Indigenous villages, Credit River and Grape Island.

A Mississauga-Welsh Métis and Methodist minister, **Kahkewaquonaby** (Peter Jones, "Sacred Feathers," 1802–56), was very successful converting his people to Methodism.[5] In 1825, government officials offered to build a village of 20 houses for the converts on the west bank of the Credit River and to help them get started as farmers. The Mississauga of the River Credit were under heavy pressure to make the change to agriculture and looked to Kahkewaquonaby to help them find their way into this strange new world.[6] They selected him as chief at the age of 27, an unusual honour. Officialdom wanted Kahkewaquonaby's people to switch to Anglicanism, but the people did not relate to that denomination's structured institutionalism, and they resisted. Concerned about the ties that Methodism had to Radical Republicans in America[7] at the time, the government refused the band's application for a deed[8] and even tried to move the settlement to Manitoulin Island, farther from American influence, a move the people were able to prevent. Eventually, at the invitation of the Haudenosaunee leaders of the Six Nations, the Mississauga of the River Credit established New Credit near Hagersville, Ontario, in 1847.[9]

In another instance, an American-born Methodist missionary, William Case (1780–1855), using American funds, established a village in 1827 on Grape Island in the Bay of Quinte, 10 km east of Belleville. Case ran the project like an army camp. Even so, for a while it worked. In 1836, the project moved to a more suitable location at Alderville, on Rice Lake. Two other settlements launched by Indian Affairs, at Coldwater and the Narrows (near Orillia) in 1829, had shorter lives. They both were under the direction of Thomas G. Anderson (1779–1875), Indian Affairs agent. By 1837, financial problems had become acute, and both settlements were abandoned. Ojibwa Chief John Aisance (Ascance, Essens, *c.* 1790–1847) cited fraud. In 1856, his band moved to Christian Island in Georgian Bay.[10]

INDIGENOUS LEADERS | Kahkewaquonaby (Peter Jones, 1802–56)

Kahkewaquonaby or "Sacred Feathers" was a man with a foot in three different worlds, Anishinaabe, Haudenosaunee, and British. He was the son of a prominent Mississauga Ojibwa woman named Tuhbenahneequay and a retired Welsh surveyor named Augustus Jones. Augustus was married to a prominent Kanienkehaka woman named Sarah Tekarihogen and Kahkewaquonaby spent a good deal of time with his step-mother's Haudenosaunee relations. By the time he was 11 he had been sent to school in Stoney Creek, where he became immersed in settler culture. He learned to speak, read, and write in English. When he was 15 he moved to the Six Nations reserve at Grand River with his family.

More by accident than by design, Kahkewaquonaby fell into Methodist Christianity and he began to work as a missionary. His firm belief was that Indigenous Peoples would bene-fit in the changing world of the nineteenth century by adopting settler beliefs and customs, and he saw Methodist Christianity with its evangelizing ways as a path towards progress for both the Anishinaabe and Haudenosaunee peoples. Not all would agree, of course, and Kahkewaquonaby had a difficult time in winning converts among people who preferred their old customs and beliefs. In some sense Kahkewaquonaby was fighting against the great move-ments of the past few decades, which saw Indigenous Peoples flock in force to the teachings of Neolin and Tenskwatawa. Nevertheless, Kahkewaquonaby persevered and he worked hard to win converts to Methodism. He became highly successful at his calling, and by the 1830s he had converted thousands to his religion.

The First Peoples who participated in the model villages were perhaps the most committed to their success and to education in particular. Both Indigenous Peoples and the British government saw schooling as the key to the future, but where Indigenous Peoples viewed education as a tool for adaptation, administrators saw it as a means of assimilation—and official goals were not always realistic. Combined with a deep pessimism about Indigenous capabilities "to rise to civilization," it was easy for British administrators to see failure when difficulties arose. The fact that the survival rate of these projects was as good as it was speaks volumes for the determined efforts of the Indigenous people to make the best of a very difficult situation. In *Sacred Feathers*, historian Donald B. Smith showed how Kahkewaquonaby (Peter Jones) personified this struggle:

> [He] lived in a period of oppression for Canada's native peoples.... For three decades Peter Jones fought back: to obtain a secure title to the reserves, a viable economic land base for each band, a first-class system of education, and Indian self-government. The white politicians largely ignored him ... others today fight the political battles that Peter Jones began.[11]

"The Greatest Kindness We Can Perform"

At least one high official saw attempts at assimilation as a waste of time. **Sir Francis Bond Head**, lieutenant-governor of Upper Canada from 1836 to 1838, reasoned this way: hunters showed little if any inclination to become farmers. Model villages implanted more vices than they eradicated. Therefore, the "greatest kindness we can perform towards these Intelligent, simple-minded people is to remove and fortify them as much as possible from all Communication with the Whites." He thought Manitoulin, the world's largest freshwater island, and its surrounding region would make a satisfactory refuge, as it was "totally separated" from non-Indigenous people.[12] Bond Head took advantage of the British ploy of gift distribution at Manitoulin Island in 1836 to arrange two major land cessions. He then convinced a number of Ojibwa leaders to sign over "the twenty-three thousand islands" of the Manitoulin chain on the promise that the Crown would protect the region as Indigenous territory.[13]

The second agreement (1854) was with the Saugeen Ojibwa of the Bruce Peninsula.[14] After warning them that the government could not control squatters moving into their territory, Bond Head promised that if they would move either to the Manitoulin Island region or the northern end of Bruce Peninsula above Owen Sound, the government would provide them with housing and equipment. Under pressure, the Ojibwa signed over 1.5 million acres (607,028 ha), the **Saugeen Tract**, leaving them with "the granite rocks and bog land" of the remainder. Few took advantage of the Manitoulin Island offer. Bond Head wanted the whole of the Bruce Peninsula but settled for what he thought he could get without argument. Using similar tactics, he proceeded to obtain other surrenders to the south.

These huge, peaceful surrenders greatly impressed the imperial government. The Aborigines' Protection Society,[15] a British Society formed in 1837 to protect the interests of Indigenous Peoples across the British Empire but also to promote assimilation, saw the deals as an exchange of 3 million acres (1,214,057 ha) of rich lands for "23,000 barren islands, rocks of granite, dignified by the name of Manitoulin Islands." The Ojibwa attitude was ultimately one of helplessness in the face of the settler juggernaut. Their "Great Father was determined to have their land." In fact, at issue was more than land; despite a Royal Declaration in 1847 acknowledging the Saugeen Ojibwa title to their aquatic territory and traditional fishing grounds around the Saugeen Peninsula, it was not long before the colonial government came to regard the Ojibwa's aquatic territory as public waters and to favour non-Indigenous interests over those of the Ojibwa people.[16] Saugeen discontent reached the point of passing the wampum belt to take up the hatchet. Warned that they could not prevail against the whites, they replied:

> We know that very well; but don't you see that we are all doomed to die; all our land is taken from us, and we think that if we kill a few of the white people they will come and kill us off, and then there will be an end of us.[17]

More Than Land Lost to Colonial Interests

During this period, the Haudenosaunee leaders of the Six Nations became embroiled in a different sort of problem. Faced in the 1820s with a scheme to develop the Grand River for navigation, they did their best to oppose it on the grounds that parts of their lands would be flooded and their fisheries ruined.[18] In spite of protests, the government agreed to help the Grand River Navigation Company by using Six Nations funds to buy its stock. Between 1834 and 1847, the Upper Canadian administration (and, after 1840, that of the Union of the Canadas) helped the company to the tune of $160,000 from band funds without the consent of the Haudenosaunee. Not only that, it granted 369 acres (149 ha) of Haudenosaunee land to the company, in addition to the flooded areas, again without band consent.

In the 1830s and 1840s, the company built five dams, five locks, and a towpath on the lower Grand River despite growing protest from the Haudenosaunee. Then, unable to compete with the railways, it went bankrupt, leaving the Haudenosaunee holding worthless stock they had never wanted in the first place. Their attempts at restitution got nowhere. The impasse continued after Confederation, when the Canadian government refused to accept responsibility, a position the courts upheld.[19] An attempt to settle out of court proved fruitless.

Overall, demand for land drove the colonies' relations with their Indigenous hosts and led to the creation of reserves—lands reserved for the use of Indigenous Peoples. Further south,

European immigrants were fleeing overcrowding and famines in Europe, pro-British refugees were arriving on promise of a reward for their loyalty to the Crown, and colonial governments were gazing ever more intently at what "vacant" reserve land was left.

Indian Administrations

Arctic and Subarctic People Contend with Missionaries, Whalers, and Fur Traders

The Inuit had two main arenas for association with whites—the comparatively mild Labrador coast since the sixteenth century and the central and western Arctic since early in the nineteenth.[20] The hostilities between the Labrador coast Inuit and Europeans, carried over from the French regime, had driven the Inuit northward. In 1765 the conflict was eased, although not ended, through the efforts of Moravian missionary Jens Haven (1724–96), known to the Inuit as Ingoak ("Inuit friend").[21]

In 1769, the Moravians received a land grant of 100,000 acres (40,469 ha). Haven launched his first mission at Nain in Labrador two years later. An influential Inuk woman, **Mikak** (Micoc, c. 1740–95), helped him win local support (see Indigenous Leaders box). Mikak was one of the Indigenous people who had been sent to London in the hope that she would be impressed with English might and would influence her people to stop harassing English fishing operations. She proved, however, to be very much her own woman and she decided how to interpret the colonizing ambitions of the British government for herself.[22] Three other land grants followed, as the Moravians expanded their operations. When they combined trading with their missionary work, however, they found themselves in competition with the Hudson's Bay Company, a situation that peaked in the second half of the nineteenth century. The Moravians eventually abandoned trade to the HBC in 1926.[23]

In the central and western Arctic, whaling was the attraction, at first mainly for English and Scottish. By 1820, whalers were operating on the east side of Baffin Island and moving westward. By shortly after mid-century, Americans dominated whaling off the west coast of Hudson Bay as well as in the western Arctic. Their main target was the bowhead whale, sought for its oil but especially for its baleen ("whalebone"), much in demand to create the tightly corseted feminine silhouette then so fashionable.[24]

Individual enterprise was the order of the day, particularly in the western Arctic. There was no systematic organization of whaling operations and no government supervision.[25] For the Inuit, the association could be profitable in the short run, as they hired out to the whalers. They also benefited from the debris (such as wood and metal) the outsiders left behind. In the long run, however, the adoption of the gun and trade goods (including foods such as flour, sugar, and tea)[26] led to a decline in traditional hunting skills and a consequent lessening of self-sufficiency. Introduced diseases made the situation worse. The combined effects of these factors would become severe later in the nineteenth century.

The massive pressure on whale populations had begun to affect the availability of the sea mammals. Although whale meat was only one item of diet,[27] obtaining it was the ultimate challenge for the hunter—very important to self-esteem and prestige within one's community. More significant, the commercial slaughter of whales and walrus, at its peak from 1868 to 1883, resulted in widespread starvation.[28] In the extreme climate of the Arctic, even a small change in the ecological balance could produce drastic results. By 1900, the population of Inuvialuit of the western Arctic had declined sharply. Gradually their numbers recovered as the population was augmented by the arrival of Inuit peoples from further west.[29] This was only one indication of the dislocations resulting from contact that would eventually be more widespread.[30]

None but the Inuit were interested in settling permanently in the Arctic, so the British did not raise the question of land, leaving the Inuit to pursue their own lives in their own ways. Non-Indigenous intrusions were few and scattered. The HBC, in fact, did not establish a permanent post in the High Arctic until early in the twentieth century. During the 1840s, however, the Hudson's Bay Company began establishing posts in the Far Northwest despite serious doubts as to the legality. The first was Peel River Post, which would later become Fort McPherson in the Northwest Territories.

The HBC then pushed westward into the Yukon,[31] where the Indigenous Peoples were already trading with Northwest Coast groups and with Russians on the Pacific coast. Locals were pleased to have access to the new trade goods, but coastal traders such as the Tlingit did not take kindly to this double invasion of their trading domains.[32] When the HBC established Fort Selkirk where the Pelly and Yukon rivers meet, in the homelands of the northern Tutchone, the Tlingit defended their commercial interests by wrecking the post and defying both British and Russians. In the midst of that three-cornered fight, the missionaries arrived—the Anglicans in 1861, with the Roman Catholics hard on their heels a year later.[33] To the south and east, of course, the missionaries had arrived several decades earlier, but one, **William Duncan**, sought the isolation of the northern coast for his missionary experiment at **Metlakatla**.

The Mi'kmaq Continue the Fight for Their Land

In 1829, Shanawdithit, the last Beothuk person known to Europeans, died of tuberculosis, leaving no officially recognized Indigenous peoples in Newfoundland, although the Miawpukek First Nation of Mi'kmaq at Bay d'Espoir maintained a presence on the south coast. In Nova Scotia, the 1838 census cited only 1,425 Mi'kmaw people, and there were concerns about further population decline. The government of Nova Scotia recognized no Aboriginal territorial rights, apart from the right to hunt and fish "at the pleasure of the sovereign" (see Chapters 4 and 7). If individual Mi'kmaq wanted land, they had to apply for grants like anyone else. What they received, however, were licences of occupation "during pleasure." An Order-in-Council set aside 20,050 unsurveyed acres (8,114 ha) for this purpose,[34] but neither lands nor locations were good, and none were near Halifax, once a favoured hunting ground.[35]

These lands were not reserved for specific bands, which would most often be the case in other parts of what would become Canada (see Historical Background box). All Indigenous Peoples in the province were equally entitled to all reserves, a system that stayed in effect until 1960.[36] Even so, non-Indigenous squatters, whom the government was unable (or unwilling) to control, continually invaded them. Even worse, homesteaders' tickets of location sometimes overlapped reserves.[37] Some chiefs, such as Andrew Meuse (*fl.* 1821–50, chief near Annapolis Royal), lobbied hard for their people with some results. Meuse, for example, won the right for his people to pursue their traditional hunt of the porpoise.[38]

In 1842, Nova Scotia created the post of Indian commissioner to supervise the reserves. The commissioner saw to it that chiefs were acknowledged publicly by making them militia captains. He also provided them with surveys of their reserves to help them organize distribution of lands among their people. The first holder of the new post was Joseph Howe (1804–73),

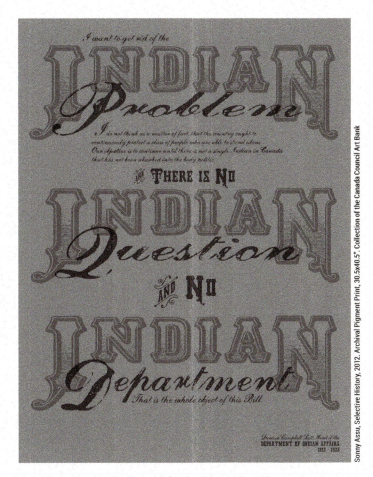

Sonny Assu, Selective History, 2012. Archival Pigment Print, 30.5x40.5". Collection of the Canada Council Art Bank

Selective History **by Sonny Assu (b. 1975)** critiques the use of historically oppressive language by the Canadian government to proliferate the notion of the "Indian Problem."

who later opposed Confederation. Frustrated by lack of public and administrative support and by anti-Indigenous sentiment, he lasted in the position only about a year. Failure of the potato crop in 1846–8 added to the woes of both the colony and the Indigenous people.

It was not until 1859 that the government enacted legislation under which established squatters could buy the lands they had already taken, with the proceeds placed in a fund for Indigenous relief. Henceforth, too, the government stated that it would eject squatters, regularize surveys, and give plots to individuals. However, very few of the squatters paid anything for their lands, and none paid in full.[42]

Soon, the government announced that the boundaries of the reserves had been established beyond dispute. By 1866, reserves totalled 20,730 acres (8,389 ha) for 637 Indigenous families. At that time, not many Mi'kmaq were farmers. Furthermore, they objected to the

INDIGENOUS LEADERS | Mikak (*c.* 1740–95)

The importance of language is illustrated beautifully in the story of Mikak, an Inuk woman who knew that in order to advocate for her people she would have to learn to speak the language of the newcomers. When the Moravian Brethren, an old Protestant order that experienced a revival in the eighteenth century, sent missionaries to Labrador, two of them encountered the young Inuk woman, Mikak. As the missionaries had worked in Greenland among the Inuit there, they were able to communicate with her in her own language. Mikak understood the power of language right away and she immediately set about learning. Two years later she was taken prisoner by some English fishermen but her captors quickly recognized that she had a gift for language—they taught her English and she taught them a few words of Inuktitut. In 1768, she was taken to England, presumably in order to impress her. Mikak began advocating for her people as soon as she arrived. She was taken to court and she had the chance to meet with the Moravian missionaries she had first met in 1765. She seems to have seen them as a means to support the interests of her own people and she began to advocate on their behalf. She used her voice well and when she returned to Labrador she worked to establish better relations between her people and the newcomers, and directly or indirectly, she was instrumental in furthering trading along the Labrador coast.[39]

HISTORICAL BACKGROUND | The Kanienkehaka of Kahnawake

Reserves in the modern sense (lands set aside for Indigenous Peoples' continued use upon surrender of most of their territory)[40] did not appear until after the Proclamation of 1763. Under the French regime, which did not recognize Aboriginal title, lands were granted to missionaries "for the benefit of the First Peoples." This meant that Indigenous Peoples, such as the Cree and Ojibwa in the North, were powerless to act when their lands were invaded by loggers and settlers, as were the Mi'kmaq of Restigouche with respect to their fishing grounds.

Although their problems were not a priority for the new British government, involved as it was in confronting the French, the Kanienkehaka won their point in one case. In 1761, when the Jesuits took the stand that as the seigneurs of Caughnawaga (Kahnawake) they had the right to sell portions of its lands, Kanienkehaka leaders complained to General Thomas Gage, military governor of Montreal from 1760 to 1763. Remembering that the Kanienkehaka warriors had been allies of the British in the recent war, the soldier governor saw to it that the Jesuits were deprived of all interest in the reserve, which was turned over to the Haudenosaunee.[41] This action was ratified in 1764 by James Murray, governor of Quebec, 1763–6. Gage's action would stand Kahnawake in good stead in the future.

division of reserves into individual leaseholds, preferring to continue their custom of holding lands in common.

In 1830, the New Brunswick government counted fewer than a thousand Mi'kmaq, Wuastukawiuk, and Wabanaki. Those of the white pine stands of the Miramichi had been devastated by a disastrous fire in 1825, which destroyed 6,000 square miles (15,540 km²) of prime forest along with their subsistence base. When New Brunswick was separated from Nova Scotia and became a colony in 1784, it had refused to recognize the only land grant of the previous administration, 20,000 acres (8,094 ha) along the Miramichi River to John Julian and his band. By the time the administration confirmed the grant in 1808, it was half its original size.[43]

As in Nova Scotia, the uncontrolled influx of Loyalists aroused resentment. In this case, troops had to be called in. The administration of affairs related to Indigenous Peoples was as haphazard as in Nova Scotia. When lands set aside for them finally were listed, in 1838, 61,293 acres (24,804 ha) were counted and divided among 15 reserves. Here, also, there was difficulty with squatters who refused to budge from Indigenous lands.[44] The lieutenant-governor

Heffel Fine Art Auction House

In the late 1880s, the Tsimshian were wealthy and powerful enough to rival the Hudson's Bay Company—and to hold their own in a power struggle with missionary William Duncan. In this drawing by Tsimshian artist Fredee Alexcee (1853–1940s), Legaic is presiding over a pole-raising ceremony while standing on the stairway leading to the entrance of his residence. The elevated doorway signals that it was a "sky-house," indicating Legaic's lofty position. The stairway symbolizes the World Tree, the channel between the underworld, earth, and sky. Two attendants hold coppers, thus displaying Legaic's wealth.

of New Brunswick urged that Indigenous people be treated as children—an idea widely accepted at the time—thereby limiting their legal rights and preventing them from handling their own affairs.

Moses H. Perley, Special Commissioner for Indian Affairs, 1841–8, sounded the alarm that Indigenous lands were shrinking fast.[45] Perley played a major role in drafting the 1844 Act for the Management and Disposal of the Indian Reserves in this Province. By the time it was passed, however, it was so altered that his efforts to protect Indigenous wishes and interests were thwarted. The colony would reallocate reserves on the basis of 50 acres (20 ha) per family. The "surplus" would be sold "for the benefit of the Indians." By 1867, Indigenous holdings had been boosted—theoretically—to 66,096 acres (26,748 ha). In fact, 16 per cent of that acreage had been sold, usually at ridiculously low prices, and squatters still occupied 10,000 acres (4,047 ha). The only thing that saved First Nations from losing all their land was the fact that much of New Brunswick was unsuitable for agriculture.[46]

The situation was even worse in Prince Edward Island. In 1767, it had been divided among 66 absentee British proprietors, with nothing left for its Indigenous inhabitants. Numerous petitions gave rise to much debate, during which the Mi'kmaq raised the point that although they had once "raised the tomahawk" against the British, they had put it down on being promised fair treatment. "They promised to leave us some of our land—but they did not—they drove us from place to place like wild beasts—that was not just."[47]

An 1856 law provided for a commissioner appointed to look after Indigenous affairs. In 1859, the colony set aside 204 acres (83 ha) on the Morell River the only such successful transaction on the island.[48] Eventually the Aborigines' Protection Society bought Lennox Island, 1,400 acres (567 ha) just off the northwest coast of PEI, for the Mi'kmaq. The group raised funds for the project in Britain and completed the sale in 1870. They provided money to settle seven Indigenous families. Four years later, almost 90 acres (36 ha) were under cultivation.

Ominous Signs on the Prairies

On the prairies, the buffalo-hunting way of life was in full swing during the first half of the nineteenth century, but indications of things to come were becoming increasingly evident. The fur trade was in decline, as were the herds of buffalo.[49] Herds could still impede travellers on occasion,[50] but already in the 1830s shortages had begun in certain areas. For two years in a row (1848–9), they were increasingly serious.[51] As early as the beginning of the nineteenth century, the Saulteaux Ojibwa and others, on their own initiative, began to take up agriculture.[52] Their traditional ways of life, however, were still essentially intact.

As in other parts of Canada, the arrival of missionaries in the West led to increased social tensions. Chiefs such as Peguis (Begouais, Pegouisse, "Destroyer," "Little Chip," baptized William King, 1774–1864) of the Saulteaux Ojibwa at Red River became actively disenchanted with the treaty they had signed with Selkirk in 1817.[53] The Métis also were becoming uneasy about their land rights.

Confusion in the laws matched this mixture of cultures. Three legal systems were in effect: Canadian,[54] British, and Indigenous. The 1821 Act for Regulating the Fur Trade had given the HBC a 21-year monopoly for "trading with the Indians in all such parts of North America, not being part of the lands or territories hitherto granted to the said Governor and Company of Adventurers of England trading to Hudson's Bay, and not being part of any of His Majesty's Provinces in North America."[55] The lack of clarity in this wording gave rise to uncertainty and disputes.[56]

Some years later, the mixing of cultures was instrumental in the rise of a religious movement among the Hudson Bay Cree between the Churchill and Albany rivers, in 1842–3. A newly developed system of written language for the Cree probably played a special role in the movement, which combined Christian and traditional Indigenous elements and was led by **Abishabis** ("Small Eyes," d. 1843) and his associate Wasiteck ("The Light"). They claimed they could provide their people with the knowledge to find the road to heaven, since they had been there themselves; they even provided a sketch map.[57]

In the end, Abishabis was killed by his own people as a windigo (a being with an overweening appetite who preys on humans) because of his increasingly unacceptable behaviour, which had included murder. His movement was a reaction to the presence and teachings of Europeans but it also vividly illustrated the creative response of Indigenous religions in merging the new teachings with their own beliefs. As we have seen, the rise of Indigenous prophets in response to outside pressures was widespread among Indigenous Peoples—the prophet Neolin was associated with Obwandiyag; Tenskwatawa added a mystic element to Tecumseh's campaign; towards the end of the nineteenth century the Ghost Dance movement, originating in a vision of the Paiute prophet Wovoka, rose on the American Great Plains and found its way to the prairies of Canada; and a recent example of the prophet movement has been among the Dene Dháa of the Northwest.

Gunboat Diplomacy on the West Coast

By 1852, there were 500 settlers on Vancouver Island. Although the Proclamation of 1763 did not apply beyond the mountains, Governor **James Douglas** at first tried to deal with the land question based on an "unequivocal recognition of Aboriginal title."[58] Between 1850 and 1854, he signed 14 agreements with Coast Salish bands on Vancouver Island, paying in blankets and other goods rather than in cash for surrenders. On Salish insistence, he also stopped settlers from enclosing unpaid-for lands. The land area involved in the agreements was limited (about 3 per cent of the island's area), as settlement was slow. By 1855, there were only 774 British settlers living on Vancouver Island, clustered around Fort Victoria and Nanaimo.[59]

When Douglas ran out of funds, however, neither the colony nor Britain would send more. Both paid lip service to Aboriginal title, but neither would pay for it. Douglas then did the next best thing. He had reserves surveyed for Indigenous Peoples that included their village sites and burial grounds, as well as their cultivated fields and "favorite places of resort," such as fishing stations. These reserves, although small by central Canadian standards (west coast First Nations, being non-agricultural and largely dependent on the sea, did not need as much land, according to officials), took the Indigenous groups' preferences into account to some extent. When allotments proved to be too small, Douglas had them increased. Once, when Indigenous people at Langley wanted to relocate their village, he had a new reserve surveyed for them.[60]

Despite Douglas's paternalistic attempts to work with First Nations, by that point the nations there had already suffered heavy losses. Not surprisingly, stories from Northwest Coast First Nations emphasized loss and disruption in the nineteenth century. The overall effect of the disruptions brought by colonization was the splintering of peoples into much smaller groups. The Wai Wei Kum oral history provides a telling example. The Tlaaluis split from the Kwiakah, but both groups identified as being Laich-Kwil-Tach of the southern Kwakwaka'wakw, itself a branch of the Kwakwaka'wakw:

> Eventually, likely in the early part of the 19th century, the Tlaaluis moved to *Saaiyouck* at Arran Rapids, opposite Stuart Island. This move effectively gave control of the passageway between Vancouver Island and the mainland to the Laich-Kwil-Tach, preventing all north to south movement without Laich-Kwil-Tach knowledge. In the mid-19th century the Tlaaluis were attacked while living at *Saaiyouck*, likely by people from the north. This attack decimated their numbers so greatly that they were forced to rejoin their Kwiakah relatives. The Kwiakah, once again including the Tlaaluis, returned to *Saaiyouck*, maintaining control of the passageways to the south.[61]

These divisions are evidence of the disruptions of the nineteenth century.

In addition, partly in compensation for the small size of the reserves, Douglas let Indigenous people buy Crown lands on the same conditions that applied to settlers.[62] He managed this despite Colonial Office instructions that white settlement should have priority. In other words, Douglas tried to balance Indigenous and settler rights.[63] The weakness of Douglas's policy, according to one historian, lay in its dependence "on his own personal qualities and that it was never codified in any legislative enactment."[64] Therefore, when Douglas retired in 1864, the Colonial Office could ensure that his successors gave settlers' interests priority. A new Commissioner of Crown Lands, Joseph W. Trutch (1826–1904), also appointed in 1864, thought Indigenous Peoples had no more rights to land "than a panther or a bear" (to use a journalistic expression of the period). His reductions of reserve sizes for the benefit of settlers have left a continuing legacy of litigation.[65]

Even during Douglas's day, relations between settlers and Indigenous people were uneasy, and violence erupted early. In 1844, some Coast Salish men killed livestock belonging to Fort Victoria, then attacked the fort when trade was suspended. It took a show of force to restore peace. In 1850, the period of coastal **gunboat diplomacy** was launched in Canada.[66] After the Newitty, a branch of the Kwakwaka'wakw, killed three runaway sailors, a government warship destroyed a village and 20 canoes. The following year, another warship destroyed another village. There were no arguments about how the government would pay for these expeditions, as there were when it came time to pay Indigenous Peoples for land.[67]

Then, in 1852, two youths, one Cowichan and the other Snuneymuxw, killed an HBC shepherd. Douglas persuaded Cowichan and Snuneymuxw chiefs to give up the persons involved. The murderer and his accomplice were tried and hanged in 1853, the first such criminal trial in the West. Tensions mounted, and settlers, alarmed at the continuing frontier wars in the United States, feared an Indigenous uprising. The sudden appearance of a group of peaceful Indigenous people was enough to send settlers fleeing. When a white settler was murdered in 1856, 400 sailors and marines set out to capture the guilty Cowichan.

Meanwhile, discontent had been bubbling in the region of the Skeena for a number of years. At issue were land and social issues. Trutch expressed official sentiment in 1872 when he told a Kitkatla delegation representing one of the Tsimshian nations, "the days are past when your heathenish ideas can be tolerated in this land."[68] In 1888, however, reports of an uprising were reaching Victoria. A Gitxsan chief, Kamalmuk (known to the settlers as Kitwancool Jim), had followed Gitxsan custom by killing a medicine man believed to have caused the death of several people, including the chief's own child. The chief's brother then married the medicine man's widow and, as far as the Gitxsan were concerned, the matter was settled.

Not so in the eyes of the colony's authorities, however. The Colony of British Columbia's standing police force (established in 1858) were sent to arrest Kamalmuk but shot him in the back, killing him instead. Gitxsan outrage aroused fears of an attack in the colony. The government sent a gunboat and additional police to the scene. A "war correspondent" from the *Victoria Daily Colonist* went along as well.[69] The presence of the warship so far upriver impressed the people, who had never seen anything like it. A series of meetings with the chiefs of the area emphasized the point that British law was to prevail. The chiefs agreed, and after 1890 the government no longer used gunboats for this purpose.

During the first half of the nineteenth century, the situation of Indigenous Peoples within what is now Canada varied widely from coast to coast, as this survey makes evident. With the ending of the colonial wars and the decline of the fur trade, however, the era of partnership between Indigenous Peoples and Europeans came to an end. If adaptation had been the key to Indigenous survival in the past, it now became the password that would give Indigenous Peoples entry into the future.

Questions to Consider

1. What challenges were faced by Kahkewaquonaby (Peter Jones) and others who called on Christianity to help Indigenous Peoples adapt to a changing world?
2. Why did Sir Francis Bond Head see assimilation as a waste of time?
3. What difficulties confronted Governor James Douglas as he tried to accommodate the peoples of the west coast?
4. What were the troubling signs, both for Indigenous Peoples and for settlers, in the West?

Recommended Readings

Bockstoce, John R. *Whales, Ice, and Men: The History of Whaling in the Western Arctic*. Seattle: University of Washington Press, 1986.

Bringhurst, Robert. *A Story as Sharp as a Knife: The Classical Haida Mythtellers and Their World*. Lincoln: University of Nebraska Press, 2002.

Gough, Barry M. *Gunboat Frontier: British Maritime Authority and Northwest Coast Indians, 1846–1890*. Vancouver: University of British Columbia Press, 1984.

Harring, Sidney L. *White Man's Law: Native People in Nineteenth-Century Canadian Jurisprudence*. Toronto: University of Toronto Press, 1998.

Smith, Donald B. *Sacred Feathers: The Reverend Peter Jones (Kahkewaquonaby) and the Mississauga Indians*. Toronto: University of Toronto Press, 1987.

———. *Mississauga Portraits: Ojibwe Voices from Nineteenth-Century Canada*. Toronto: University of Toronto Press, 2013.

Upton, Leslie F.S. *Micmacs and Colonists: Indian–White Relations in the Maritimes, 1713–1867*. Vancouver: University of British Columbia Press, 1979.

11 Towards Confederation for Canada, Towards Wardship for Indigenous Peoples

CHAPTER OUTLINE

The deep problems caused by the experimental nature of British administration over the course of the nineteenth century form the central theme of this chapter. Various policies were tried out by British officials but they varied widely according to time, place, and even the individual administrators. In British Columbia, for example, the measured leadership of Governor Douglas softened the hard policies made by a distant regime. The other important theme of this chapter concerns resistance. Indigenous Peoples did not submit meekly to the often outrageous demands of an imperial power, and the spirit of resistance shines brightly at such locations as Seven Oaks, Mica Bay, the Chilcotin Valley, and Red River.

LEARNING OUTCOMES

1. Students will gain insights into the nature of the problems caused by the regional approach taken by British administrators.

2. Students will have a better understanding of the legislative attempts to force assimilation on Indigenous Peoples in the nineteenth century.

3. Students will understand the context of the Métis unrest that shook the country in the latter part of the nineteenth century.

4. Students will have a better understanding of the growing nineteenth-century movement towards resistance across the country.

TIMELINE From Seven Oaks to the Uprisings

1816
Cuthbert Grant leads Métis in Battle of Seven Oaks after Métis unrest and hardship following export embargo.

1839
Crown Lands Protection Act declares Indigenous lands to be Crown lands.[1]

1840
Act of Union of Upper and Lower Canada.

1842–4
Bagot Commission examines "Indian administration," as it was then called.

1845
Métis leaders sign petition asking for definition of their status.

1847
Métis leaders petition London for recognition of rights, declaration of colony free of HBC control.

1850
Commissioner of Lands position created in United Canadas.[2]

Robinson Superior and Robinson Huron treaties: lands surrendered are twice the area of all previous land cession treaties in Canada West.

1850–1
An Act for the Better Protection of Lands and Property of Indians in Lower Canada is passed. Similar legislation for Upper Canada follows.[3]

1851
Métis again petition for colony, just as Vancouver Island had become colony in 1849.

1857
An Act to encourage the Gradual Civilization of the Indian Tribes of the Canadas[4] is introduced by John A. Macdonald.

Palliser scientific expedition to report on conditions for living, settlement in Plains region.

Fraser River gold strike.

1858
"Fraser River War" as Salish outraged by invasion of their territory by 25,000 gold-seekers.

1859
Act Respecting Civilizing and Enfranchisement of certain Indians passed in United Canadas.[5]

1860
Indigenous administration passed from British Colonial Office to the colonies.

1862
Manitoulin Island cession. Dakhóta uprising in Minnesota followed by hangings at Fort Snelling, largest mass execution in US history.

1864
Tsilhqot'in War: after raids and killings, five Tsilhqot'in men sentenced and hanged.

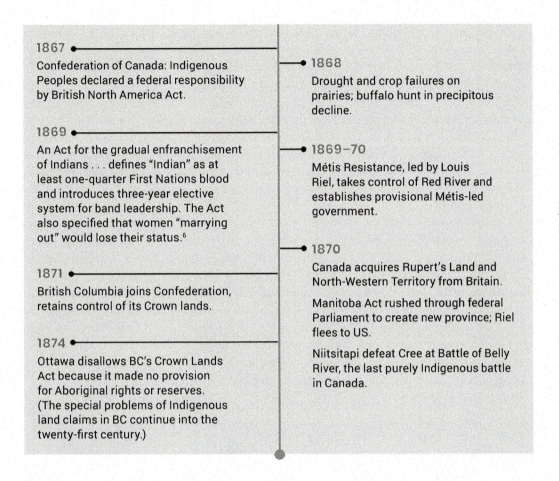

1867
Confederation of Canada: Indigenous Peoples declared a federal responsibility by British North America Act.

1868
Drought and crop failures on prairies; buffalo hunt in precipitous decline.

1869
An Act for the gradual enfranchisement of Indians . . . defines "Indian" as at least one-quarter First Nations blood and introduces three-year elective system for band leadership. The Act also specified that women "marrying out" would lose their status.[6]

1869–70
Métis Resistance, led by Louis Riel, takes control of Red River and establishes provisional Métis-led government.

1870
Canada acquires Rupert's Land and North-Western Territory from Britain.

Manitoba Act rushed through federal Parliament to create new province; Riel flees to US.

Niitsitapi defeat Cree at Battle of Belly River, the last purely Indigenous battle in Canada.

1871
British Columbia joins Confederation, retains control of its Crown lands.

1874
Ottawa disallows BC's Crown Lands Act because it made no provision for Aboriginal rights or reserves. (The special problems of Indigenous land claims in BC continue into the twenty-first century.)

"White Man's Burden" or Indigenous Burden?

During the 1830s, Britain held a parliamentary inquiry into the conditions of Indigenous Peoples throughout the Empire. The British widely recognized that they had deprived First Nations, as well as other Indigenous Peoples across their vast Empire, of their lands. They did not, however, generally agree on what they should do about it—or even admit that they should do anything at all.

The committee report was clear: unregulated frontier expansion was disastrous for Indigenous Peoples, who almost without exception lost their lands.[7] Trespass was only part of the problem. Another concern was that Indigenous Peoples were losing their land, particularly through devious leasing practices.[8] Curbing settlers was tough politically, particularly in areas where they were needed for defence. In an attempt to correct this situation, in 1839 Britain legally declared Indigenous Peoples' lands to be Crown lands, a decision that had consequences beyond landownership.

At that time, most political rights where land was concerned extended only to property holders. Indigenous Peoples, on the other hand, held their land in common (apart from some individuals who had accepted the European way). Making the Crown the guardian of their lands, in effect, excluded most Indigenous people from political rights,[9] which supported the belief that they were like children, in need of paternal protection.[10] Popular imagination during the nineteenth century romanticized this into the **"white man's burden."**[11]

By 1830, British Indian administration, as it was then called, was 75 years old and desperately underfunded. Its main interest was acquiring land. In fact, the government paid so little attention to Indigenous affairs that the Act of Union (1840) forgot to make provision for it—or for the payment of annuities for earlier land cessions, an oversight that was not corrected until 1844.

Although transferred to the civil arm in 1830, the Indigenous policy of the two Canadas continued to be administered from London until 1860, through the lieutenant-governor of Upper Canada, who was also given the title of superintendent-general of Indian Affairs. The superintendent-general, therefore, had to act both for the Crown and for the Indigenous Peoples. Inevitably, the two roles came into conflict.[12] As well, funding for Indigenous administration came from five different sources. It was also uncertain, to say the least, reflecting the lack of importance now given to Indigenous affairs. This attitude would deepen until well into the twentieth century. Although Britain transferred the responsibility of the administration of Indigenous affairs and relations to Canada in 1860, it was two years before a single administration was set up. Even then, unification was not complete.[13]

HISTORICAL BACKGROUND | From Marginalization to a New Vision

As with Confederation, no one thought to consult—or even inform—the Inuit before Privy Council issued a proclamation in 1880 transferring Britain's Arctic territories to the Dominion. Similarly, when Newfoundland joined in 1949, no mention was made of the Innu and Inuit of Labrador or of the Mi'kmaq of St George's Bay and other regions. The government did not extend the right to self-government, which the colonies had so vigorously and successfully claimed for themselves, to its Indigenous Peoples. The government did not give Indian status to the Mi'kmaq, who had been accustomed to fishing and sealing in Placentia and St George's Bay from time immemorial, and who had migrated to the St George's Bay area since the fall of New France. Only in 1984 did the province establish its first reserves, and as of 2017, only one Mi'kmaw community (Conne River, Samaijij Miawpukek reserve) had official recognition as a band on the island of Newfoundland with a land base. The Qalipu Mi'kmaq First Nation, established by the government in 2011 to provide Indian status and certain Aboriginal rights to others of Mi'kmaw heritage throughout the island of Newfoundland, does not have a reserve.

Making matters even more confusing, in the mid-1800s Britain developed the concept of regional approaches.[14] This meant almost as many policies as there were colonies. In the Maritimes, it was one of "insulation"; in the Canadas, "amalgamation"; in Rupert's Land and on the Northwest Coast, support of HBC administration. In other words, centralized imperial administration was not coping very well with the many local problems of colonial government, and the voices of the Indigenous Peoples were either not being heard or were being ignored. This policy failure would have repercussions into the twenty-first century, and Indigenous people were often the last to know of changes in policy and in effective authority over their affairs (see Historical Background box).

Who Is an "Indian"?

In the meantime, reports were pouring in from other investigations into Indigenous affairs (there were three between 1839 and 1857). The most important was that of the **Bagot Commission** of 1842–4, named after chief commissioner Sir Charles Bagot (1781–1843).[15] It described a lack of direction in Indigenous administration and urged centralized control for the British North American colonies—the opposite of what the Colonial Office was practising. It also reaffirmed the 1763 Proclamation's position that Indigenous Peoples had rights of possession in regard to land, including the right to compensation for surrenders. These points were not always being honoured. The Commission recommended, among other things, that

- reserves be surveyed and boundaries publicly announced;
- a system of timber licensing be instituted for reserves;
- all title deeds be registered and considered binding; and
- Indigenous Peoples be taught European techniques of land management and provided with livestock, agricultural implements, furniture, and the like in lieu of the presents that the British government had distributed in the years following the Conquest.

The commissioners thought that bands should be allowed to buy and sell land, at least between themselves. This, they believed, would encourage Indigenous Peoples to adopt individual freehold ownership in place of their traditional communal ownership, which the commissioners considered "uncivilized."[16] Finally, they urged that banks be established on reserves and that more schools for Indigenous Peoples be established, with the co-operation of various religious denominations. The report described Indigenous people as "an untaught, unwary race among a population ready and able to take every advantage of them."[17]

Identifying goals was one thing; doing something about them proved to be something else again. Easiest to achieve were the department's reorganization and centralization under the civil secretary as superintendent-general for Indian Affairs and the measures to improve the protection of Indigenous lands. More controversial was the gradual stop to gift distributions,[18] which Indigenous Peoples resisted. Budgetary considerations prevailed, however, and the gifts ended in 1858. Indigenous opposition to individual landownership was not surprising, not only because of their entrenched customs but also because, invariably, they lost a lot of land following its imposition.[19]

In 1850 and 1851, the Canadian legislature approved two land acts incorporating some of Bagot's recommendations.[20] Passed hurriedly because loggers were invading reserved lands, these measures made it an offence for private individuals to deal with Indigenous Peoples concerning their lands. However, it was still unclear what "Indian title" actually meant. In 1850, the government also created the post of Commissioner of Indian Lands.[21]

The next year, Canada East (Quebec) set aside 230,000 acres (93,079 ha) for the creation of Indigenous reserves and acquiesced to the distribution of up to £1,000 a year. However, only 170,012 acres (68,801 ha) were actually granted.[22] Furthermore, the Commissioner, not the individual First Nations, had control over leasing and rentals.[23] In the meantime, largely because of the amount of property involved, the government decided that it needed to define who, exactly, was an "Indian." The 1851 Act for Canada East, accordingly, undertook the task—without consulting Indigenous communities—and came up with these criteria (presented using language from the Act):

- all persons of Indian blood reputed to belong to the particular body or tribe of Indians interested in Indian lands or their descendants;
- all persons intermarried with any such Indians and living among them, and their descendants;
- all persons residing among such Indians, whose parents on either side were or are Indians of such body or tribe, or entitled to be considered as such; and
- all persons adopted in infancy by any such Indians, and residing in the village or upon the lands of such tribes or bodies of Indians and their descendants.

The administration quickly decided that this definition was too inclusive, however, and revised it, once more without Indigenous input. This time, it excluded newcomers living within Indigenous communities and newcomers married to Indigenous women. It also distinguished between **status Indians**—those who were officially registered—and **non-status Indians**.[24] Status Indian women married to men who were not status Indians kept their status, but their children did not have the right to claim it. The provision allowing non-Indigenous women married to status Indians, in the language of the provision, to gain status and to pass it on to their children stayed in: in other words, the male line determined ancestry. This more restrictive definition would prove problematic as well. Men and women were treated unequally. Children were left vulnerable to discrimination. Status could be lost through these discriminatory provisions. Clearly, the legislation was flawed and these flaws would lead to serious problems.

Inquiry followed inquiry. Concerned about charges that its "civilizing" program was not working, the Canadian government named a commission to investigate. It resulted, in 1857, in An Act to Encourage the Gradual Civilization of the Indian Tribes of the Canadas, which introduced the idea of giving Indigenous people land and the right to vote in exchange for surrendering their treaty rights.[25] The commissioners also set out a plan to achieve this, most of which would be in effect until 1960. Eligible were males 21 years of age and over, able to read English or French, minimally educated, and "of good moral character and free from debt," who had passed a three-year probation. By those standards, many in the white community would not have been eligible.[26] The successful candidate would receive 20 ha of taxable reserve land.

Indigenous Peoples rallied in rejecting the Act. They correctly saw the measure as an attempt to destroy Indigenous communities and their way of life. At the same time, it would break up their reserves, allotment by allotment. By 1876, only one candidate had been enfranchised.[27] Two years after the 1857 Act, an Act for Civilizing and Enfranchising Indians still encouraged enfranchisement and consolidated earlier legislation pertaining to Indigenous Peoples but dodged the issue of reserves.[28]

In 1860, the United Canadas took over Indigenous administration from Britain's Colonial Office. The Commissioner of Crown Lands became chief superintendent of Indian Affairs, but the deputy superintendent actually did the job. Although Indian Affairs would not become a full department until 1880, it received its first full-time head in 1862: William Prosperous Spragge, who that same year had assisted William McDougall (1822–1905, Commissioner of Crown Lands, 1862–4) in negotiating the Manitoulin Island surrender. Spragge held his post until his death in 1874. Yet again, Indigenous Peoples had not been consulted.

More Land Surrenders

Throughout the Canadas, tensions were increasing, while the resources to maintain the Indigenous way of life shrank. As overexploitation of land progressed, the concept of family hunting territories took on a new importance. What had started among Indigenous Peoples as a custom of asking permission to hunt on another's territory became an enforced requirement.

The discovery of mineral deposits north of Lake Superior led the government to permit mining without considering the interests of the Ojibwa people of Batchewana or Garden River. Chief Shingwaukonse (Little Pine, 1773–1854) of Garden River, near Sault Ste Marie, and other Ojibwa leaders went to Toronto and demanded that the revenues from the mining leases be paid to them as the owners of the region. They got nowhere.[29] Three years later, in 1849, another request, this time for a land settlement, again drew no response. The Ojibwa took matters into their own hands and moved to close the Quebec and Lake Superior Mining Company operation at Mica Bay by force. Within three weeks, troops were on the scene to quell the "rebellion," sometimes called the Michipicoten War.[30]

One of the two commissioners sent to investigate the situation was Thomas Anderson, of the Upper Canadian model village experiments, by now chief superintendent for Indian Affairs. The commissioners found the Ojibwa eager to sign a treaty with the government, and even willing to let the government decide the amount of compensation. Despite their confidence in the "wisdom and justice of their Great Father," however, the Ojibwa were clear-sighted about their objectives. The negotiations were not simple, but out of them arose the practice of including provisions for reserves in the treaties, setting the pattern for the future. Indigenous Peoples had long had this idea, but up to this time the various colonial assemblies had not set aside lands for Indigenous Peoples on a regular basis. In the Indigenous view, reserves were not something the government granted them. These were lands that they had not shared with the newcomers.[31]

Reserves were "the cradle of the Indian civilizing effort—and the means of securing the White man's freedom to exploit the vast riches of a young dominion."[32] For that reason, establishing large reserves in isolated areas came to be seen as counterproductive. Instead, they should be small and close to white settlements to help First Nations people to learn white ways.[33] Chief negotiator for the treaties was ex–fur trader William Benjamin Robinson (1797–1873). His mandate: to obtain rights to as much land as possible for as little as possible from Penetanguishine along the north shore of Lake Huron and across to Batchawana Bay on the eastern shore of Lake Superior and down to Pigeon River. Payment was to be by annuities, and each band would be permitted to choose a site for its own reserve. Hunting and fishing rights would continue over the entire surrendered area. Furthermore, there were to be no gift distributions. Indigenous etiquette required an exchange of gifts on such occasions, however, so Robinson had to compromise on this.[34]

The Lake Superior chiefs signed on 7 September 1850 and the Lake Huron chiefs two days later. Some chiefs would claim later they were pressured into signing and threatened to appeal to London. The land surrendered was twice the area of the land given up in all previous treaties combined in Canada West,[35] extending north to the height of land separating Rupert's Land from Canada. By now, virtually all of Canada West was clear of Aboriginal title. The two **Robinson treaties** confirmed the pattern that had been developing since the Proclamation:

- Negotiations were at open and public meetings.
- Lands were "surrendered" only to the Crown.
- A schedule of reserves to be held in common was annexed to each treaty.
- Each member of the signing band received annuities.
- Finally, Indigenous Peoples retained "full and free privilege to hunt over the territory now ceded by them and to fish in the waters thereof as they have heretofore been in the habit of doing," except for those portions sold to private individuals or set aside by the government for specific uses.

One of the points that bothered the dissident chiefs was the small size of their annuities—£500 to £600—compared to those being handed out in southern Ontario. Robinson replied that southern Ontario lands were good for agriculture. In northern Ontario, on the other hand, the lands were of little or no use for farming. Robinson did not refer to the ecological effects of mining in the mineral-rich region.

Another point that quickly drew attention was the nature of the "surrender." Indigenous Peoples did not claim absolute ownership of the lands, only the right to their use. How could they surrender them to the Crown, or to anyone else for that matter? Yet another complication lay in the fact that since the Crown already claimed underlying title, what was it accepting from the Indigenous Peoples? Questions like these would lead to a series of court cases (Chapter 17).

The influence of the Robinson treaties would soon be evident in the next major cession, that of Manitoulin Island. The region had been set aside as a reserve by the 1836 treaty with the Odaawa, in the expectation that those living to the south would move there. But by 1860, only 1,000 people had moved in, with 3,000 acres (1,214 ha) being farmed. Under pressure to open more land for settlement, the government ended the project.[36]

The treaties notwithstanding, the question of protection for Indigenous lands remained essentially unsolved as settler encroachments continued in agriculturally attractive areas. Legislation enacted a year before Confederation gave the government the sole right to sell reserved lands that the Indigenous Peoples were not using—and to do so without consulting them. Neither were they included in discussions leading to the Confederation created by the British North America (BNA) Act of 1867. None of the signatories even raised the question of their partnership.

Wards of the State

With the creation of the Dominion of Canada in 1867, Nova Scotia, New Brunswick, Quebec, and Ontario kept control of Crown lands within their borders. So did Prince Edward Island and British Columbia when they joined a few years later. Saskatchewan and Alberta, after they were created in 1905, did not gain that control until 1930. Indigenous Peoples became a federal responsibility in the section of the BNA Act on "Indians and lands reserved for Indians," the only reference in the Act to Indigenous Peoples within Canada. This separated their administration from that of Crown lands. Indigenous people continued in a distinct legal category, that of **wardship**. They could, if they chose, step out of this category to attain the rights and responsibilities of other Canadians, but the price was high.

According to one historian, reserves were the main institution that the Dominion inherited from colonial administrations.[37] From the Indigenous perspective, the main inheritance was the tradition of the treaties to regulate relations between them and settlers, primarily in connection with land. Whites confidently expected that Indigenous people would eventually be assimilated. As Sir John A. Macdonald (Prime Minister of Canada, 1867–73, 1878–91) observed in 1887, "the great aim of our legislation has been to do away with the tribal system and assimilate the Indian people in all respects with the other inhabitants of the Dominion as speedily as they are fit to change."[38]

Canada acquired Rupert's Land, including the southern portion of present-day Nunavut[39] and the North-Western Territory (present-day Yukon, portions of today's western and northern Northwest Territories, and parts of northern Saskatchewan, Alberta, and BC), in 1870. This vast expanse was designated the North-West Territories. Manitoba became the fifth province that same year. British Columbia joined Confederation in 1871, and Prince Edward Island became the seventh province in 1873. These expansions meant that in four years, Canada's recognized Indigenous population increased from 23,000 to more than 100,000 (estimates that may be low), from 0.7 per cent of the population to 2.5 per cent.[40] Each area had a separate history made up of a distinctive set of experiences. All of these governments, however, shared a habit of passing laws in the interests of the dominant society without consulting Indigenous Peoples who might be affected by these laws.

This pattern was in place in 1868, when the new Dominion formed the Department of Secretary of State and gave it responsibility for Indigenous Peoples until 1873, when the Department of the Interior took over Indigenous administration. "Indian affairs" involved control of Indigenous lands and property (including resources) as well as funds. High on the department's priority list was the consolidation of the various laws inherited from previous administrations, a comparatively simple task in the East, where the Indigenous population was too small to be deemed an important political consideration.

On the prairies and in British Columbia, however, Indigenous people still were in the majority, and so could mount an effective resistance. The situation became even more diverse when Britain handed over her Arctic territories to the Dominion in 1880. The year following Confederation, Indian Affairs reaffirmed its "guardianship policy." It also introduced a three-year elective system for bands and somewhat extended the powers of chiefs and band councils, but Indian Affairs could still override them. Cabinet could also depose chiefs or band councillors. The cabinet decided, on the recommendation of the superintendent-general, which bands were ready for the three-year elective system, a step that it could take without the band's consent.[41] Once more, it used individual landholdings carved out of reserves to reward enfranchisement, this time by means of "location tickets" that carried with them rights of inheritance.[42] Those who became enfranchised lost the right to be classed as Indians, according to the terminology, but they maintained their treaty rights (other than treaty payments) and their right to live on a reserve. This meant, among other things, that they could hold a business licence, buy liquor, and send their children to public schools.

The government confidently expected that these new provisions would undermine resistance to **enfranchisement**. However, by 1920, only about 250 Indigenous people had chosen to enfranchise.[43] Later, more people accepted the vote as the government eased the Act's requirements.

Marrying Out

The 1869 Act for the Gradual Enfranchisement of Indians expanded features of the 1851 legislation that treated men and women differently.[44] In the language of the Act, if a registered Indian man married a non-Indian (non-registered or not Indigenous) woman, she gained Indian status, which she passed on to their children. In contrast, if a woman who was registered as a status Indian married a man who did not have Indian status, she lost her status and all rights associated with that status. Their children would also not qualify for status. If a woman with status did marry a man with status, but from a different First Nation or band, she and her children became a member of her husband's First Nation or band and lost any claim to her own. Another provision added a "blood quantum" requirement to the definition of an Indian. To qualify, a person born after the passing of the Act must now have at least one-quarter First Nations blood.[45] In that case, the one-quarter First Nations wife of a husband who was not a registered member of any First Nation could claim Indian status, but her children could not.

These measures aroused strong opposition. The General Council of Ontario and Quebec Indians lobbied hard for the rights of First Nations women, but nothing came of their efforts.[46] The Indian Act of 1876, essentially a consolidation of the legislation considered in this and the previous chapter, would keep these features[47] (see Chapter 12).

The Acts of 1868 and, in particular, 1869 were designed to break down established forms of government on the grounds they were "irresponsible." The elected band council would be the instrument to achieve this.[48] It was hardly surprising that, with the exception of the Kanienkehaka band living to the north of Lake Ontario (the Mohawk of the Bay of Quinte), bands resisted by refusing to exercise even the limited powers given to them. Meanwhile, on the other side of the continent, Indigenous Peoples were facing a threat of a different sort.

The West Coast and the "Tsilhqot'in War"

If white settlement was impinging on Indigenous power on the west coast, the discovery of gold overwhelmed it. A precursor was the mini-rush in 1850–3 on the Queen Charlottes (Haida Gwaii), followed by another of similar proportions on the Stikine in 1862. Fortunately for the First Nations involved (Haida and Tsimshian, respectively), both proved to be of short duration. Even so, confrontations led Governor Douglas to assert British authority with shows of force. Soon, news spread of the gold deposits of the Fraser River in 1857 and the Cariboo in 1862. This time, the strike was huge.

The Salish of the Fraser had been quietly mining the placer gold for years and trading it instead of furs at HBC posts, but they were overwhelmed in 1858 when 25,000 gold-seekers flooded into Victoria. In short order, 10,000 men were panning for gold along the Fraser. Outraged at this invasion of their territory, Salish chief Spintlum confronted the miners. A hysterical press in Victoria reported the "Fraser River War" as a massacre of miners. The actual tally was 30 Indigenous people and two whites killed. Again, Douglas asserted British power, announcing that British law applied to all, Indigenous people as well as miners. He tried to win Indigenous co-operation by appointing some of their leaders as magistrates, but this did nothing to alleviate the havoc being wreaked on their way of life.

The mining operations needed to extract the hard-rock gold of the Cariboo strike, deep in the interior, meant the building of roads for the transport of equipment and supplies. Proceeding with all possible haste and no consideration for the damage to the Indigenous hunting-and-gathering economy, the invaders interfered with Indigenous salmon weirs, raided villages, and even looted graves. As the Indigenous people saw it, the non-Indigenous interlopers were destroying their subsistence base, so it was up to them to replace it, but the road gangs turned away Indigenous people who asked for food. On top of all this, 1862 also saw smallpox among the Tsilhqot'in, a Dene-speaking people of the interior ranges of the Coast Mountains.

Matters quickly came to a head. In 1864, the Tsilhqot'in, the main victims of these developments, sent out war parties to attack road gangs. After several bloody encounters in which 13 non-Indigenous people died, government forces tricked eight insurgents, including chiefs Tellot, Alexis, and Klatsassin, into surrendering. Five received death sentences and were quickly hanged en masse. One was sentenced to life imprisonment.[49] The judge acknowledged, however, that the treatment they had received from the usurpers had provoked them. The following year, the looting of Indigenous graves became illegal. Despite the fears of the whites, no generalized Indigenous war developed.

Governor Douglas's touch was sorely missed after he retired in 1864. Where he had accepted Indigenous requests for as much as 200 acres (81 ha) per Indigenous householder, the new chief commissioner of lands and works, Joseph Trutch, set the ceiling at 10 acres (4 ha).[50] On the prairies, Indigenous people were being allowed 160 acres (65 ha). Non-Indigenous people could

INDIGENOUS LEADERS | Klatsassin (d. 1864)

The terrible threats of 1864—hostility, disease, and cheating—provoked a strong response from many of the Indigenous Peoples of the west coast. In Clayoquot Sound, the trading vessel *Kingfisher* was taken and its crew killed. In the interior, the Tsilhqot'in people were threatened with death after a settler accused some of them of stealing supplies. A group under the leadership of their chief, Klatsassin, decided that they needed to oppose the settlers by force in order to defend their lives and their land. Klatsassin was a man of great influence: physically strong, forcible, and brave, Klatsassin was a representative of the spirit of resistance, which drove people across the region to oppose the new officials who replaced the retired Douglas. Klatsassin led a group of men on a mission of violent direct action in the spring of 1864, designed to persuade the settlers to leave. Instead, he was tricked via messenger into attending what he saw as a meeting out of which his life and freedom were to be guaranteed if he were to attend, and what the British expedition leaders saw as full surrender. Klatsassin was executed by the British officials along with four of his companions. Klatsassin remains a powerful symbol of resistance and a heroic defender of a way of life that was under terrible threat.

pre-empt 160 acres and purchase an additional 480 acres. Beginning in 1865, Trutch, in a program of "adjustments," took away much of the reserve land set aside for First Nations. The following year, he issued an ordinance preventing First Nations people from pre-empting land without written permission from the governor.[51] In 1870, First Nations lost altogether the right to pre-empt. What was left was the right of individuals to purchase lands from non-Indigenous people. Since the Indigenous people saw the land as theirs already, this was not a "right" they appreciated. Predictably, resentment rose.

When British Columbia entered Confederation in 1871, it kept control of its Crown lands, the only western province granted this privilege up to that time. This did not bode well for the Indigenous Peoples, even though the agreement gave Ottawa the responsibility for Indigenous administration and provided for the necessary transfer of lands to the federal authority. Again, no one consulted the Indigenous Peoples, although they still outnumbered the newcomers at the time and would continue to do so until the mid-1880s.[52]

One of the first acts of the new province was to deprive First Nation members of the provincial franchise, which they did not regain until 1949. With the exception of the adhesion to Treaty Eight in its northeastern corner, no post-Confederation treaties were signed in the province. British Columbia did not even create a ministry of Native Affairs until 1988.

Almost immediately, Ottawa and British Columbia were locked in a battle over the size of allocations for reserves. The federal government thought that a family of five would need 80 acres (32 ha), but BC thought that 10 acres were enough. In 1873, the administrations worked out a compromise of 20 acres (eight ha) per family, regardless of size, but it pleased no one. In 1874, the federal government disallowed BC's Crown Lands Act because it did not make provision for First Nations reserves, but British Columbia continued doling out lands to First Nations people in minimal lots. By the last decades of the century, the 90 reserves established for the Kwakwaka'wakw totalled 16,500 acres (6,680 ha), an average of 183 acres (74 ha) per reserve.[53]

The Métis Challenge

Hardly had Confederation been accomplished than the federal government came face to face with a situation that had been brewing for a long time in the Northwest: the demands of the Métis for recognition. The Métis of Red River saw themselves as a "New Nation," neither First Nations nor newcomer but a distinctive blend of both that incorporated farming, buffalo hunting, and the fur trade.

The Métis way of life developed under the economic umbrella of the trade and in the isolation of the Northwest. They built their log cabins where they fancied, usually along riverbanks without formal arrangements with the HBC—in fact, often without the Company's knowledge. At Red River, in the District of Assiniboia, a Métis sense of identity had crystallized with the troubles that developed after the coming of the Selkirk settlers in 1812—in the clash of cultures and, above all, in the rivalries of opposing fur-trading interests. The amalgamation of the North West Company and Hudson's Bay Company made the Métis the largest element in Red River's population,[54] empowering them to act decisively when things took a turn for the worse—which they soon did.

First, the War of 1812 interrupted Red River's supply lines. Two years later, food shortages led to a ban on the export of provisions without a special licence—the Pemmican Proclamation of 1814. This greatly disturbed the Métis, for whom trade in pemmican—a high-protein mixture of dried meat and berries—was an important economic activity. They reacted by conducting a series of raids against the Red River colony.

In the spring of 1816, after a winter of starvation during which an unknown number of people died, the Métis Nor'Wester captain **Cuthbert Grant** (c. 1793–1854) assembled 60 buffalo hunters and attacked an HBC brigade bringing down pemmican. They then captured and ransacked Brandon House, an HBC post, and took the pemmican to Red River. At Seven Oaks, Robert Semple (1777–1816, governor-in-chief of Rupert's Land since 1815) and 21 settlers challenged them. By the time the smoke cleared, Semple and his men were dead. Only one Métis had been killed, and Grant's prestige among his people soared. The most popular Métis account of this event has been preserved in this song, often referred to as the national anthem of the Métis, which was composed by Pierre Falcon (1793–1876) to commemorate the Battle of Seven Oaks:

> Oh, people do you wish to listen
> To a song that tells a true story?
> How on June 19 a band of brave Bois Brulé
> Advanced like brave warriors towards the English?
> When we met two of our men yelled a warning:
> "There are the English who wish to attack us."
> We stopped immediately and like honourable men

Sent a messenger saying:
"Englishmen stop for a moment we want to talk to you!"
The English leader, like a madman, ordered his soldiers to fire.
The first shot came from English pistols—they missed the messenger.
We shot the English captain first, then killed nearly all his army,
Only four or five escaped.
Do you know who wrote this song?
It is Pierre Falcon the poet of Red River![55]

A gathering of Métis leaders at Qu'Appelle Valley that same year named Grant "Captain General of all the Half-Breeds."[56]

As the buffalo herds dwindled, and farming loomed closer as an alternative to the fur trade, both the hunt and traditional communal values began to give way to those of the individual. More Métis became wage labourers, and their relative position within the fur trade hierarchy declined. Now, most were at the level of menial labour rather than at that of the officer class, where some had been earlier. The Métis saw the HBC monopoly as leading to the "utter impoverishment, if not the ruin, of the Aboriginal people." They were also upset at the appointment in 1838 and subsequent actions of the anti-French Adam Thom (1802–90) as recorder (a judgeship) for Assiniboia.

The prospect of the government encouraging white settlement spurred the Métis (particularly those who were French-speaking) to become more militant. In 1845, 977 of them signed a petition to Alexander Christie, governor of Red River and Assiniboia, 1833–9, and of Assiniboia, 1844–9, claiming special rights by virtue of their Indigenous blood. The governor told them that they had no more rights than those enjoyed by all British subjects.

Two years later, in 1847, Alexander Kennedy Isbister (1822–83) took their petition to England. Isbister, had been born at Cumberland House, was the grandson of chief factor Alexander Kennedy and Aggathas, a Cree woman.[57] This time, the Métis asked that the HBC charter be declared invalid and that Red River (reorganized into the District of Assiniboia in 1836) be declared a colony. This petition gave rise to spirited exchanges in the British Parliament. Powerful forces opposed monopolies in principle, but the colonial secretary could not imagine Indigenous Peoples capable of self-government. Only those regions that had enough white settlers to ensure they would have control should have colonial status. The Métis could have appealed to the Privy Council but only at their own expense. Their meagre resources strained, they formally dropped the issue in 1850. Other petitions on other issues would follow.

In 1849, the year Vancouver Island became a colony, the Company in effect lost the power to enforce its monopoly. The Métis kept up their campaign against Thom, and in 1851 HBC Governor Sir George Simpson withdrew him from office. Simpson also gave in to demands that the Métis have a wider representation on the Assiniboia Council but managed to fudge its execution. As HBC control eroded, a Canada West group that would later call itself **Canada First** began a campaign to annex Red River to Canada. With Confederation, the Canada Firsters became strident, adding yet another challenge to the fundamentals of the old order of the "custom of the country," with its elements of Indigenous law. The Métis were divided on the issue. As the Métis were waging their war of words with the HBC and London for recognition, they continued actual hostilities in the field against their long-standing enemies, the Dakota.[58] An 1851 confrontation, the Battle of Grand Coteau, from which they emerged victorious, proved to be even more important than Seven Oaks in encouraging their sense of identity. More problematic, however, was the international border. At first, US officials let them cross over in pursuit of buffalo by virtue of their Indigenous blood. Now, however, the American attitude was stiffening, and the Métis were finding themselves excluded from hunting south of the border.

The clamour became such that the British Parliament established a select committee in 1857 to examine British policy in the Northwest and to determine if the region (particularly the prairies) had potential for anything other than the fur trade. The British Royal Geographical Society also sent out a scientific expedition under Captain John Palliser (1817–87) to report on the region. Canada West, not to be outdone, organized its own expedition. Toronto professor Henry Youle Hind (1823–1908) and engineer S.J. Dawson (1820–1902) went out to determine the best route for transportation and communication to facilitate annexation.

The result was that mainland British Columbia was separated from HBC administration and became a Crown colony in 1858. On the other hand, the government did not deem Red River, with its predominantly Métis population, ready for such a status.[59] The disappointment in Red River was profound. As for the Indigenous Peoples, their fears for the future had not been calmed. Already, they wanted a treaty.

Confederation Brings Centralization— and Western Isolation

When Confederation became a reality, four western Cree and Saulteaux Ojibwa chiefs agreed among themselves about the extent and limits of their land claims in preparation for the negotiations they foresaw in the not-too-distant future.[60] A Saulteaux Ojibwa band in Assiniboia allowed settlers onto their lands only on the condition that a permanent agreement be negotiated within three years.[61]

In Red River, changing social customs added to the tensions of the political scene. Victorian standards influenced those of the frontier, leading to a series of sex scandals. These, in turn, erupted into open defiance of HBC authority.[62] As the whites were at each other's throats, the balance of power fell to the Métis, the settlement's largest armed force.[63] The 1862 Dakhóta uprising in Minnesota also had repercussions in Red River, as ragged and starving refugees (largely Dakhóta) drifted in from the fighting. In the spring of 1863, 600 of them appeared, bringing the medals they had received from the British for their active alliance in the War of 1812.[64] Dakhóta had been fleeing in small numbers into Canada since the 1820s. Now, however, the problem became acute, as the people of Red River had to provide for their former enemies. When the HBC, as a representative of the British, pledged friendship with the Dakhóta, Peguis (who died in 1864 at age 90) and his people felt betrayed. That same year, 1864, a group of Saulteaux Ojibwa attacked a refugee Dakhóta encampment.

Amid these swirling tides of change, Red River's isolation from Canada became more evident than ever. This was the era of railroad building, but there were no immediate plans for the Northwest, and communication was slow. It was faster and easier to communicate via the United States. Obviously, the HBC could no longer control the reins of power, but the Colonial Office steadily refused to set up a Crown colony. Prime Minister Macdonald reluctantly agreed to negotiate for the purchase of Rupert's Land and to extinguish Indigenous land rights once the region was under Canadian control, but he hoped the HBC would do this before the transfer.

These were rough years for many reasons, not just political ones. Drought and grasshopper plagues brought crop failures. The buffalo hunt was also declining and becoming more distant. The fisheries were at low ebb. In 1868, even the rabbits were at the bottom of their cycle. That was also the year Ontario decided to build a road from the northwest angle of Lake of the Woods to Fort Garry. The project proceeded with more haste than foresight: the government did not always clear Aboriginal title, nor did it heed Indigenous claims to fees for the right of way and for timber used. There were even conflicts arising between ancestral patterns of First Nations land use and more recently evolved Métis lifeways. In addition, protests soon developed over wages. Several Métis claims provide evidence that the government was discriminating against Métis workers by offering unequal wages. Wages were paid in scrip (temporary paper currency), which could only be redeemed at a store owned by the leader of the Canada Firsters.[65]

In spite of all these difficulties, a land rush was obviously developing—and settlers were staking claims to land without regard for Aboriginal rights. The rush for land threatened the settlement pattern that had developed spontaneously among the fur trade families of Red River: river frontage farms with long, thin ribbons of land stretching back into woodlots. The pattern mirrored that of the old Quebec regime. This system assured each holder of access to the river, the main transportation route. Throughout all this, there was no official effort to consider the needs of the people of Red River.

The slowness of the Canadian government to act, however, was not lost on an interested spectator to the south. Minnesota offered $10 million for HBC lands but was refused. In 1868, the state protested the impending transfer of HBC lands to Canada without a vote of the settlers (with no mention of Indigenous people, who were in the vast majority) and passed a resolution favouring annexation to the United States. That same year, Britain set up a provisional government for Rupert's Land. William McDougall, who had negotiated the Manitoulin Island surrender of 1862 and who was now actively working for the annexation of the North West to Canada, became the first lieutenant-governor in 1869. His job was to "report upon the state of the Indian tribes now in the Territories" and to make suggestions as to how the nations could best be protected and "improved."[66]

Meanwhile, Ottawa continued oblivious to the situation in Red River. The new North West Council it appointed was English and Protestant in composition, without representation of the region's French-language element. Even the English-speaking settlers protested this. In the meantime, another figure was making his voice heard: **Louis Riel** (1844–85), a young and charismatic Métis[67] who had attended the Collège de Montréal for several years. A natural leader, with a strong sense that the Métis of Red River were, indeed, a "New Nation," he represented the opposing force to Canada First. When in 1869 the English-speaking Métis William Dease (*fl.* 1855–70) organized a meeting demanding that the payment for Rupert's Land be made to First Nations and Métis people as rightful owners of the land, not to the HBC, Riel attended as an observer. He was already a member of the **Comité National des Métis**, which had been organized to defend Métis rights with the active support of Abbé Joseph-Noël Ritchot (1825–1905) of St Norbert.

The transfer of lands and authority from the HBC to Canada was scheduled for 1 December 1869, still without official consultation with the people. When word reached Red River that McDougall and his entourage were coming before the scheduled date of transfer, Riel and the Comité acted to defend their interests. They blocked the border on the Pembina Trail, by which the official party must travel, and on 31 October refused to let them enter Assiniboia. McDougall had been warned but had not believed that matters would come to that. The new Dominion had finally come face to face with the new nation whose existence it had steadfastly refused to acknowledge.

Concerned about the land transfer from the HBC to Canada, and the power vacuum that would result, Métis leaders organized a government that could respond effectively to the needs of both Indigenous people and newcomers. Seen here are Louis Riel (seated, centre) and his councillors, 1869–70. In front, left to right, are Bob O'Lone and Paul Prue. Seated are Pierre Poitras, John Bruce, Riel, W.B. O'Donoghue, François Dauphinais. Standing in the rear are Le Roc, Pierre de Lorme, Thomas Bunn, Xavier Page, André Beauchemin, Baptiste Tereaux, and Thomas Spence.

Red River Takes a Stand

The Métis were not the only ones who viewed the transfer with mistrust. Resident HBC officers, like the Métis, had not been consulted on the terms of the transfer, and the government had made no provision for any claims they might have had. They resented English indifference to their fate and wondered about Canada's ability to hold the union together, especially in view of the US purchase of Alaska in 1867. Trade was flourishing between Red River and points south of the border.[68] In the American view, it was only natural that the North West should become part of the United States, joining it with Alaska. The English-speaking settlers were also unhappy at what was happening but were not prepared to go as far as the Comité National.

The day after Riel and the Comité turned McDougall back, a roll call revealed 402 men, all bearing arms and prepared to support Riel. Later that day, 100 more were reported to have arrived. Discipline was strict: no alcohol. Two days later, 2 November, Louis Riel informed the HBC officer at Fort Garry that the fort was under the protection of his men, a move that forestalled a Canada First plan to take over. It also ensured the Comité's control over Red River, at least until federal troops arrived, which could not be before spring. McDougall, cooling his heels in Pembina, compounded his errors. In a snowstorm on 1 December, the day originally scheduled

Untitled by **Sherry Farrell Racette,** a Métis artist and scholar who is an associate professor of Native Studies and Women's and Gender Studies at the University of Manitoba. On 10 December 1869, Louis Riel assembled a party of Red River residents in the courtyard of Fort Garry. On this day the newly formed provisional government raised it flag and demanded their rights as loyal citizens of the Crown.

Illustration from Calvin Racette, *Flags of the Métis*, illus. Sherry Farrell Racette [Regina: Gabriel Dumont Institute, 1987], at: http://www.metismuseum.ca/media/document.php/12153. Flags%20of%20the%20Metis.pdf

for the formal transfer of Rupert's Land to Canada, he crossed the border into Canada and read the proclamation of the transfer. Thus, HBC authority formally ended without any effective official authority to take its place. McDougall tried to correct this by commissioning John S. Dennis (1820–85), surveyor and militia officer, as "lieutenant and conservator of the peace," authorizing him in the Queen's name to put down the Métis by force. The Canada Firsters greeted this with enthusiasm, but the English-speaking settlers refused to co-operate. A group of Saulteaux at Lower Fort Garry under Chief Henry Prince (Miskoukeenew, "Red Eagle," 1819–1907, son of Peguis) felt otherwise. They announced they were ready to fight for the Queen. Some Dakhóta people also joined the Canada Firsters.

A week later, on 8 December, Riel issued the "Declaration of the People of Rupert's Land and the North-West," stating that "a people, when it has no government, is free to adopt one form of Government in preference to another, to give or to refuse allegiance to that which is proposed."[69] On 10 December, residents hoisted the Métis flag. On the 27th, they established the first provisional government, with Riel elected president. Riel and his Métis were in control of Red River without having shed a drop of blood.

Back in Ottawa, Prime Minister Macdonald learned on 25 November of the Métis blockade. His immediate reaction was to advise his representative in London not to complete the transaction with the HBC until Canada could be assured peaceful possession of the North West. He then sent a message to McDougall, warning him that he was, in effect, approaching a foreign country under HBC control and that he could not force his way in. When McDougall chose to follow the line of the Canada Firsters and to go ahead anyway, he created a political vacuum in Red River. Macdonald had seen the consequences, both nationally and internationally, all too clearly: the United States might acknowledge this provisional government.[70]

What followed is etched in Canadian historical lore. McDougall never did gain entry to Assiniboia and had to return to Ottawa. Riel formed a second provisional government on 8 February 1870, which was more broadly representative of Assiniboia's community than the first had been. In the meantime, the rowdy behaviour of some Canada Firsters led to the execution by court martial of Orangeman Thomas Scott on 4 March.[71] This inflamed racial passions between English-language Protestants and French-language Catholics. Quebec, which had remained aloof, as it had seen the Métis as "savages," now came to their defence. Macdonald moved quickly to meet with a Red River delegation. The two parties agreed on terms, and Macdonald's government rushed the Manitoba Act, which created the province of Manitoba (see Historical Background box), through Parliament. It obtained royal assent on 12 May.

McDougall fought hard to have the bill rejected, and he was on solid legal ground. The Act had to be amended hastily to make the new province constitutional. Apart from the Selkirk Treaty, Aboriginal title to lands had not been extinguished. This pushed the federal government into negotiating the first of the numbered treaties of the West in 1871 and 1872. In a move to forestall a raid from Ontario, Macdonald sent a military expedition to Red River in 1870 under Colonel G.J. Wolseley (1833–1913). The newly appointed A.G. Archibald, lieutenant-governor, 1870–3, was supposed to arrive ahead of the troops. The Métis were counting on this. Unfortunately, it happened the other way around.

Despite the unfinished state of both the Dawson Road and the transcontinental railway, and the need to negotiate rights of passage with the Ojibwa, through whose territory the expedition had to pass,[72] the military expedition arrived first. Riel, forewarned, went into hiding.[73] The behaviour of the troops in the settlement did more damage than all the previous months of uncertainty. During the 10 months of the resistance, the Métis had served when needed to keep the peace as volunteers, even providing their own arms and ammunition. Their conduct had been exemplary. Now, they had to endure verbal and physical abuse, in two instances to the point of being killed. Wolseley's expedition was Britain's last official military action in present-day Canada.

Canada was divided on Riel. Ontario demanded that he be brought to justice. Quebec answered in his defence. Macdonald was able to announce in all truth that he had no idea as to the Métis leader's whereabouts, which he hoped would calm the situation. The Fenians, who were conducting sporadic raids from across the border, hoped for Métis help, particularly as one of them, William B. O'Donoghue (d. 1878), had been one of Riel's top aides. The Métis leader refused, however. In 1871, Archibald publicly shook his hand in thanks, a gesture that cost the lieutenant-governor his office.

The Red River crisis of 1869–70 and the question of amnesty that arose out of it were the first serious racial controversies the Dominion faced. Although the English–French confrontation took centre stage, the underlying First Nations–Métis–non-Indigenous division had been the major factor. Great Britain might have lobbied for the creation of an Indigenous buffer state in the US during the negotiations for the Treaty of Ghent in 1814, but when it came to creating a Métis domain within her own colonies, she had not been up to the challenge.[74]

Neither the Indigenous Peoples of the North-West Territories nor the government had any reason to believe the racial issue was settled. Settlers of European descent were arriving every day in the North West, and the trickle was turning into a flood. Both sides could look to the south, to the violence of the American West, for a glimpse at what the future might be. Canada's vision of a nation from sea to sea did not include disputes over who owned the land when the next wave of settlers arrived. Indigenous Peoples wanted to safeguard their rights while they still were in the majority. The answer for both lay in treaties.

HISTORICAL BACKGROUND | The New Province of Manitoba

Riel suggested the name of the new province: "Spirit Strait" of the Crees, "Lake of the Prairies" of the Assiniboine. "Manitoba" stood for self-government and was already in use for the region. Macdonald made the "postage stamp" province as small as possible, 11,000 square miles (28,490 km²). He guaranteed the province official equality of French and English and a separate school system. Crown lands were to be under Dominion control, with 1.4 million acres (566,560 ha) being reserved for the unmarried children of the Métis, an area close to the size of Prince Edward Island. The Dominion would respect all existing occupancies and titles, including those of Indigenous Peoples, a principle more easily stated than honoured, as events would prove.

Questions to Consider

1. What were the findings of the Bagot Commission?
2. What were the specific aims of the 1857 Civilizing Act?
3. Account for the disturbances at Mica Bay in the middle of the nineteenth century.
4. What led to the crisis in the Red River settlement?

Recommended Readings

Burton, Antoinette. *The Trouble with Empire: Challenges to Modern British Imperialism*. Oxford: Oxford University Press, 2017.

Chute, Janet. *The Legacy of Shingwakonse*. Toronto: University of Toronto Press, 1998.

Ens, Gerhard. *Homeland to Hinterlands: The Changing World of the Red River Metis in the Nineteenth Century*. Toronto: University of Toronto Press, 1996.

—— and Joe Sawchuk. *From New People to New Nations: Aspects of Metis History and Identity from the Eighteenth to the Twenty-first Centuries*. Toronto: University of Toronto Press, 2015.

Getty, Ian L., and Antoine S. Lussier, eds. *As Long As the Sun Shines and Water Flows*. Vancouver: University of British Columbia Press, 1983.

Howard, James H. *The Canadian Sioux*. Lincoln: University of Nebraska Press, 1984.

MacLeod, Margaret, and W.L. Morton. *Cuthbert Grant of Grantown*. Toronto: McClelland & Stewart, 1974.

Pannekoek, Frits. *A Snug Little Flock: The Social Origins of the Riel Resistance of 1869–70*. Winnipeg: Watson & Dwyer, 1991.

Reid, Jennifer. *Louis Riel and the Making of Modern Canada: Mythic Discourse and the Postcolonial State*. Winnipeg: University of Manitoba Press, 2012.

12 The First Numbered Treaties, Police, and the Indian Act

CHAPTER OUTLINE

The history of the treaties that shaped the nature of the relationship between the central government and the Indigenous Peoples of northern and western Canada forms the substance of this chapter. We will examine the different views held by the First Peoples and the Canadian authorities on the nature and meaning of the treaties and will look at some specific examples of how the treaties were made. Throughout the chapter we will pay close attention to the underlying problems that those different perspectives helped to create and how those different perspectives are reflected in the Indian Act.

LEARNING OUTCOMES

1. Students will gain a clear understanding of the ways in which various peoples understood the importance of the treaties.

2. Students will be able to define the terms used in the language of the treaties.

3. Students will gain insights into the unsettled historical context under which the treaties were made.

4. Students will learn about the difficulties caused by the lack of a coherent Crown position on governance in the period leading to the Indian Act.

TIMELINE From Treaty One to Cultural Interference

1871

Treaty One (Stone Fort Treaty) with Saulteaux Ojibwa, Mushkegowuk, and others in southern Manitoba.

Treaty Two (Manitoba Post Treaty) with Saulteaux Ojibwa, Nishnawbe-Aski, and Cree peoples, in central Manitoba.

1874

Treaty Four with bands in southern Saskatchewan and western Manitoba.

1875

Treaty Five with bands in northern Manitoba.

1877

Treaty Seven, signed with Siksika leaders at Blackfoot Crossing, covers southern Alberta and opens lands for completion of transcontinental railway.

1880

Indigenous administration becomes a separate department within Department of the Interior.

1885

Franchise Bill introduced by Macdonald with aim of Indigenous assimilation.

1895

Thirst dances (sun dances) of the Plains Cree, Nakoda, and Siksika peoples banned. Like the potlatches, these continue secretly.

1873

Treaty Three (Northwest Angle Treaty) with Ojibwa and Nishnawbe-Aski of northwestern Ontario and southeastern Manitoba.

North West Mounted Police force created.

Cypress Hills Massacre: American wolfers cross border after some horses were stolen and slay 20–30 Nakoda people encamped at sacred meeting place.

1876

Treaty Six with Cree and Nakoda peoples of central Saskatchewan and Alberta includes provision of a "medicine chest" that becomes the legal basis for free health care for status First Nations and some Inuit.

Indian Act passed, a consolidation and revamping of pre-Confederation legislation from the Canadas.

1884

Potlatch feasts of Northwest Coast groups banned.

1890s

Ghost Dance spiritual movement of Dakhóta people in the United States, which anticipates return of the bison herds and disappearance of white man, spreads to Dakhóta reserves in Saskatchewan and Manitoba.

The Varied Meanings of "Treaty"

Treaties characterized relations between Europeans and Indigenous Peoples from the very beginning. By the 1870s, however, the government saw them as contracts for the final, once-and-for-all means of opening up Indigenous lands for settlement and development by extinguishing Aboriginal land title. Indignous groups missed this at first, because by their custom, agreements were not necessarily permanent. Instead, they were subject to changing conditions that could call for renegotiation and renewal. Even pacts of peace and friendship undertaken to last forever had to be renewed from time to time with appropriate ceremonies to keep them "alive."

Government representatives soon mastered Indigenous figures of speech for negotiations, borrowing such phrases (among others) as "as long as the sun shines and the water flows." When negotiators used these terms in treaty language, Indigenous people expected the Crown to keep its word.[1] In the Indigenous view, the treaties they were now negotiating with the Canadian government would help them to adapt to the demands of the modern world within the framework of their own traditions. In return, they agreed to be loyal subjects of the Crown, respecting its laws and customs. Missionaries were prominent in a number of these negotiations, sometimes as agents of the government, at other times as mediators.

In the context of Indigenous relations with the Canadian government in Ottawa, a treaty has been defined as a compact or set of fundamental principles that formed the basis for future negotiations between one or more Indigenous groups and the Crown.[2] In the government view, the treaties granted privileges. In the Indigenous view, they protected rights.[3] In some areas, settlement had preceded treaties, and this influenced the government's decisions. As can be imagined, in such cases settler reaction to Aboriginal land rights was usually openly hostile. The accompanying Historical Background box provides a brief synopsis of the history of treaties in Canada.

Again, negotiations were far from being either simple or easy. As S.J. Dawson, the engineer for the Canadian expedition to the West led by Henry Youle Hind, described it:

> Anyone who, in negotiating with these Indians, should suppose he had mere children to deal with, would find himself mistaken. In their manner of expressing themselves they make use of a great deal of allegory, and their illustration may at time appear childish enough, but in their actual dealings they are shrewd and sufficiently awake to their own interests, and, if the matter should be one of importance, affecting the general interests of the tribe, they neither reply to a proposition, nor make one themselves, until it is fully discussed and deliberated upon in Council by all the Chiefs.

Treaties One, Two, and Three: Ontario and Manitoba Land Surrendered

Treaty One is called the Stone Fort Treaty because negotiations took place at Lower Fort Garry, which was built of stone. The Saulteaux Ojibwa, Mushkegowuk, and others in southern Manitoba around Portage la Prairie and Winnipeg petitioned Lieutenant-Governor Archibald for a treaty

HISTORICAL BACKGROUND | Treaties in Canada

By the time of Confederation, various governments had already negotiated 123 treaties and land surrenders in British North America with Indigenous Peoples. Between 1860 and 1923, 66 treaties were signed, covering a little more than half of Canada's Indigenous Peoples. The Proclamation of 1763 gave Canada the right to negotiate for land title in the West. This led directly to the **numbered treaties**, which began with Treaty One in 1871 and ended with Treaty Eleven in 1921. (Other treaties had proper names.) Between 1923 and 1973, the government negotiated no new treaties because of legislation banning the use of band funds for land claim actions. By the time of the James Bay and Northern Quebec Agreement in 1975, the number of such actions had approached 500.[4]

In acquiring Rupert's Land, to which the terms of the Proclamation of 1763 did not extend, the Canadian government promised to negotiate with the Indigenous Peoples within its de-cided borders for the extinguishment of their title and the setting aside of reserves for their exclusive use.[5] It considered Indigenous Peoples to have the right to use the land for such pur-poses as hunting and fishing. Title did not include either sovereignty or ownership in fee simple.

Even such limited rights were not universally acknowledged, however. The idea—developed in the sixteenth century—that Indigenous Peoples had no land rights at all was still alive, as officials made clear during negotiations. In this view, treaties were a moral, not a legal, obli-gation.[6] In practical terms, they were a means of avoiding conflict. In any event, Canada's promise to Britain to honour the provisions of the Proclamation of 1763 led directly to the 11 numbered treaties negotiated between 1871 and 1921.

The government moved to clear an area of Aboriginal title when the land had significant value or when there were political considerations. Thus, when Manitoba became a province and settlers were already moving in, it moved quickly to extinguish Aboriginal title. Canada could not afford to repeat the costly frontier wars of the United States.

Mounting demands from Indigenous Peoples led to the Robinson Huron and Robinson Superior treaties negotiated in 1850. Similar agitations were now developing in the West. A.G. Archibald, as lieutenant-governor of Manitoba and the North-West Territories, responded in 1870 by sending out a representative to investigate the Indigenous position.[7] However, the first attempt to reach an accord in Manitoba that year ended in failure. What was more, added Dawson, negotiators had to be very careful about what they said, as "there are always those present who are charged with keeping every word in mind."[8] Once, a Fort Frances chief repeated to him, word for word, what Dawson had said two years earlier.

in the fall of 1870. Signed on 3 August 1871, it included 16,700 square miles (43,253 km²). On 21 August 1871, the Saulteaux Ojibwa, Cree, and other bands in central Manitoba signed Treaty Two, also called the Manitoba Post Treaty. Through the treaties, the government was justifying its creation of Manitoba but also preparing the way for white settlement.

The question of delegates became a concern during the negotiations for Treaty One when a chief complained he could "scarcely hear the Queen's words." As it turned out, the HBC's

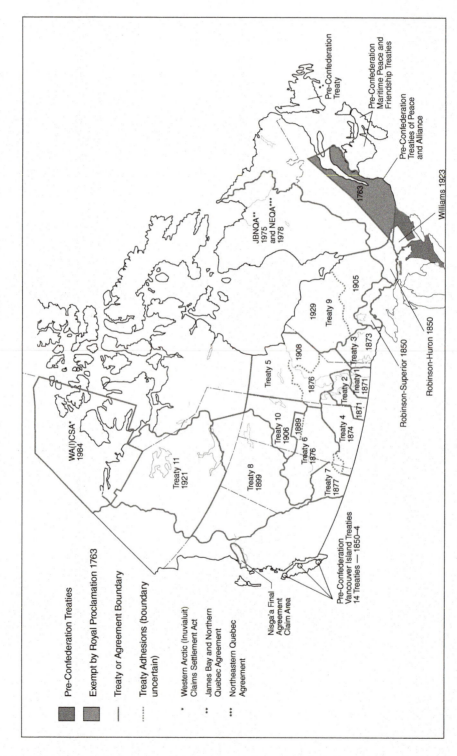

Map 12.1 Areas covered by treaties and agreements.

Alan D. Macmillan, *Native Peoples and Cultures of Canada*; Wilcomb E. Washburn, *History of Indian–White Relations* (Washington: Smithsonian Institution, 1988); *Report of the Royal Commission on Aboriginal Peoples*, 2, part 2: 483.

imprisonment of four Anishinaabek for breach of a service contract was the cause of his hearing loss. The government released the prisoners, who attended the meeting, and the chief's hearing improved.[9]

The Indigenous Peoples opened negotiations by claiming reserves amounting to about two-thirds of Manitoba. Archibald and Wemyss Simpson, then Indian Commissioner, termed this "preposterous." They countered with 160 acres (65 ha) per family of five, and an annuity of $12, and they threatened the Indigenous Peoples with being swamped by settlers without any compensation if they did not agree.

The chiefs were disturbed. They could not see that the Crown offer would benefit their children. What would happen, one chief asked, if Indigenous people had more children after they settled down? Archibald replied that the Crown would provide for them from lands further west, forgetting that other Indigenous Peoples already occupied those lands. Was it really fair, another chief asked, to allow the same amount of land for them as for settlers, considering the differences in their circumstances and ways of life? And what about help in getting started in this new life? The Crown promised schools and schoolmasters, ploughs and harrows. The chiefs thought there should be more: clothing, housing, and agricultural equipment. They got the impression that the Crown negotiators agreed.

The terms for Treaties One and Two were similar: $3 for each person and an annuity of $15 per family of five, prorated for families of different size, payable in goods or cash. The Crown stood firm on its offer of 160 acres per family of five, which the Indigenous Peoples reluctantly accepted. It agreed to maintain a school on each reserve and said it would ban liquor sales on reserves. Archibald promised hunting and fishing rights in his opening speech, but these did not appear in the treaty's final draft. Neither was there any provision for the farm implements, livestock, and clothing that had been a part of the verbal agreement, although the Crown expected the Indigenous Peoples to take up farming. Even so, the terms that Ottawa accepted had exceeded original instructions.

The chiefs later complained that the Crown was not honouring oral promises made during negotiations. Eventually, in 1875, the Crown revised the two treaties, but it still did not give all that had been promised. After that, officials were much more careful about what they said during negotiations.

During the first treaty negotiations, the Crown gave surprisingly little thought to the terms of the expected surrenders. Officials paid more attention to the ceremony that would surround the negotiations, expecting to overawe the Indigenous Peoples and thus reduce their demands. On the contrary, the chiefs forced major changes in the Crown's offerings.[10] During these discussions, they raised most of the issues that appeared in later treaties. Their success is a measure of their skill in negotiating, given that the Crown could, and did, impose a "take-it-or-leave-it" approach.[11] In two instances, those of Treaty Nine signed in 1905–6 and the Williams treaties of 1923, the Ontario and Canadian governments had worked out the terms before opening negotiations with the chiefs.[12]

The Saulteaux Ojibwa of the Lake of the Woods district signed Treaty Three, the Northwest Angle Treaty, on 3 October 1873. Most of the 55,000 square miles (142,450 km^2) it dealt with were in Ontario, except for a small part in southeastern Manitoba. It cleared title to the Dawson Road and also provided for the railroad right-of-way.

The Nishnawbe-Aski knew that theirs was "a rich country." As Chief **Mawedopenais** of Fort Frances put it, "the rustling of the gold is under my feet where I stand."[13] Making the point that it was "the Great Spirit who gave us this; where we stand upon is the Indians' property, and belongs to them," he observed that settlers had already robbed them of their lands, "and we don't wish to give them up again without getting something in their place."[14]

After prolonged and difficult negotiations, and several refusals by Ojibwa chiefs to sign, its final terms were more generous than those of the previous two treaties. The negotiators also made provision for the continuation of hunting and fishing rights and included agricultural equipment and supplies. Schools would be established, and the sale of liquor on reserves would be banned. A request by the Indigenous Peoples that they be granted free passes on the Canadian Pacific Railway was rejected out of hand.[15]

The Métis were influential in the negotiations of Treaty Three. This was the first of the numbered treaties specifically to include them, which took place at the request of Mawedopenais after some official hesitation.[16] Similarly, during the bargaining for Treaties Four and Six, the Indigenous Peoples requested that their "cousins" be included. At first, the Crown accepted this and set aside land for the Métis of Rainy River. However, after the Red River Resistance, Ottawa amended the Indian Act, excluding "halfbreeds" from both the Act and treaties.[17] In spite of this, the Métis continued to be influential in the negotiations.

The better terms of Treaty Three reflected the greater familiarity of the Indigenous Peoples of the area with the governmental negotiating process and their greater political assertiveness. Alexander Morris (1826–89), who had succeeded Archibald as lieutenant-governor of Manitoba in 1873, made four attempts over three years before they agreed to sign.

Mawedopenais, chief of the Fort Frances Anishinaabek, made an important call for transparency in the closing speeches marking the signing of Treaty Three. He knew the importance of transparency in consensus-building, and consensus-building remains the very core of Indigenous Peoples' governance. At the end of the Treaty Three negotiations, Mawedopenais borrowed from white rhetoric:

> Now you see me stand before you all: what has been done here today has been done openly before the Great Spirit and before the Nation, and I hope I may never hear anyone say that this treaty has been done secretly: and now in closing the Council, I take off my glove and in giving you my hand I deliver my birthright and lands. And in taking your hand, I hold fast all the promises you have made, and I hope they will last as long as the sun goes round and the water flows, as you have said.[18]

Many times, the Euro-Canadians would later reflect on the implications of the rhetoric they used so freely during negotiations.

In the meantime, Treaty Three set precedents for later treaties, particularly where agricultural equipment and livestock were concerned. Eventually, in 1881, the government extended the boundaries of Manitoba to include those areas ceded by Treaties One, Two, and Three. In the case of Treaty Three, this would lead to a confrontation with Ontario and to Canada's first court case involving Aboriginal rights (a phrase that came into popular usage in the 1960s), *St Catherine's Milling v. The Queen* (Chapter 16). Other court cases would soon follow.

The Liquor Trade

The transcontinental railroad was inching its way from sea to sea. The bison were receding, and settlers were exerting more and more pressure on First Nations and Métis lands. Ottawa was aware of the growing instability in the West, and the possibility of the American frontier wars extending into Canada filled the Canadian government with alarm. Under the BNA Act, law enforcement was a provincial responsibility, however, and so a federal force would be able to operate only in those areas not yet organized into provinces. Alternatively, it could come to an agreement with those provinces that did not have their own police.

Macdonald's original plan was to use Métis for at least half of the rank and file of a federal police force for the West, under British officers, following the British colonial model. The conflict of 1869–70, in particular Ontario's violent reaction to the Métis initiative, led him to drop the idea, and the **North West Mounted Police** (NWMP), created in 1873, was initially composed of settlers of British heritage.[19]

Almost immediately, an incident brought the new force into action. The **Cypress Hills**, near the international border where the Alberta/Saskatchewan border would eventually be drawn, was a sacred area for Indigenous Peoples, where hostile nations could camp in peace. It was also a favourite resort for American traders, men whose stock-in-trade was liquor,

Library and Archives Canada, C-020038

Tȟatȟáŋka Íyotake (Sitting Bull), chief of the Hunkpapa Dakȟóta, who came to Canada in 1877 with 4,000 followers after the Battle of Little Big Horn, 1876. Tȟatȟáŋka Íyotake and his people were denied a reserve, and famine forced his return to the US and surrender in 1881.[20] He was killed while being arrested in 1890 as part of the American government attempt to quell the nativistic Ghost Dance movement.

Marilyn Angel Wynn/Getty Images

Spirit Warriors **by Colleen Cutschall (b. 1951)**, a Lakhóta artist originally from Pine Ridge, South Dakota, but who for many years has lived and worked in southwest Manitoba. As the centrepiece of the Little Bighorn Battlefield National Monument in present-day Montana, her sculpture in iron helped change the site from a tribute to General Custer to a memorial where Indigenous people could honour the warriors, women, and children who died in the battle.

as well as for hunters/trappers called "wolfers" because of the skins they usually obtained. The "wolfers" were widely despised by Nakoda and Plains Cree peoples because they used strychnine to poison bison meat as a means of obtaining wolf pelts. The poison killed dogs belonging to the Indigenous people and it entered the regional ecosystem.[21]

A group of these wolfers at Fort Benton, Montana, had some horses stolen. Their search for those they considered guilty brought them to the Cypress Hills. There, they attacked a Nakoda camp, killing 20 or 30 people and sexually assaulting a large number of women.[22] In the charges and countercharges that followed, it was never established that the Nakoda were, indeed, the original culprits. In fact, the weight of evidence was to the contrary. Later, it would be established that the horse thieves had been Cree.[23] What was clear at the time was the need for a law enforcement agency in the region. That year, 1873, nearly 100 Indigenous people died in fights caused by the social instability in the region, and by the failure of the Crown to protect them from the lawless traders coming into the region from across the border.[24]

Canada promptly sent out 150 North West Mounted Police to confront traders and wolfers, whose forts were bristling with cannons, according to rumour. The trip was hard. Many of the animals that formed part of the equipment train died, and at one point the expedition got lost. Among the local guides who came to its rescue was Jerry Potts (Ky-yo-kosi, "Bear Child," 1840–96), son of a Káínaa woman and an American fur trader.[25] The Mounties finally arrived at Fort Whoop-Up, a trading post, to find only one trader, who invited the police in to dinner.

Until 1885, the main tasks of the Mounties were to prevent the excesses of the rogue American traders and establish good relations with the Indigenous Peoples. They were successful on both counts. Canada at that point was on good terms with the Cree, an inheritance from the HBC. The attitude of the Niitsitapiikwan, however, was uncertain. Superintendent James F. Macleod (1836–94) set about cultivating a relationship with one of its chiefs, **Isapo-Muxika** (Crowfoot, *c.* 1830–90), and soon became a personal friend.[26]

Clearing the Way for European Settlement—Treaties Six and Seven

Treaty Six, signed in two ceremonies at Forts Carlton and Pitt in 1876, included a provision to maintain a **"medicine chest"** for the benefit of the First Nations. This became the basis for free health care for status First Nations and some Inuit.[27] It also provided for rations in case of famine, important now that buffalo had become scarce.

INDIGENOUS LEADERS | Isapo-Muxika (*c.* 1830–90)

Isapo-Muxika was not a hereditary Siksika chief. He was born of Káínaa parents, but after his father died and his mother married a Siksika man, he became Siksika. His courage and his success in battle gained him a position of authority among his adopted people. In 1865, with the death of the chief of his band, Nookskatos, Isapo-Muxika became a minor Siksika chief, leading the Moccasin band. Perhaps owing to his own outsider status, Isapo-Muxika attempted to establish relations with all of the people in the Canadian West: the Métis, Euro-Canadian fur-traders, missionaries, and the North West Mounted Police.[28]

Isapo-Muxika's importance to history dates from the 1870s, when American traders arrived selling whisky and rifles. Aware of the dangers, Isapo-Muxika took steps to welcome the arrival of the NWMP as an ally against this destructive and divisive trade. His leadership allowed the First Nations of western Canada to avoid some of the worst excesses of the illegal trade that led to terrible fighting in the American West. The process of settlement in Siksika territory took place without violence thanks in large measure to the spirit of co-operation that Isapo-Muxika developed with the NWMP. Such co-operation could not have existed without his status as a great and courageous leader. His friendships with other First Nations leaders, especially **Pītikwahanapiwīyin** ("Poundmaker," *c.* 1842–86), and his insistence on consultation and consensus-building enabled him to maintain an influence far beyond the Siksika Nation.[29]

Abraham Wikaskokiseyin ("Sweetgrass," d. 1877),[30] chief of the Fort Pitt Crees and leading spokesman during the Treaty Six negotiations, told officials, "We hear our lands were sold and we do not like it. We don't want to sell our lands. It is our property, and no one has the right to sell them."[31] Other chiefs believed that the Europeans had borrowed the land, as it could not be bought. In any event, Wikaskokiseyin signed the 1876 treaty. His people, however, felt that he had signed their lands away without consulting them properly, and they killed him.[32]

Treaty Seven, signed the following year at Blackfoot Crossing, near Gleichen, Alberta, attracted Canada's last great gathering of independent Plains First Nations. It cleared the way for the construction of the railroad, among other items. Isapo-Muxika agreed to sign on the advice of a shaman, who told him the treaty would change his life and that of his people: "What you will eat from this money will have your people buried all over these hills. You will be tied down, you will not wander the Plains. The whites will take your land and fill it."[33] But in spite of these consequences, there was no alternative. With the signing of this treaty, the Canadian government had seemingly secured its western settlement frontier.

Not all Indigenous Peoples were enamoured of the treaties. When administrators had sent gifts to smooth the way for Treaty Six negotiations, the most famous and influential of the Plains Cree chiefs, Mistahimaskwa ("Big Bear," c. 1825–88), had retorted, "We want none of the Queen's presents. When we set a trap for a fox we scatter meat all around but when the fox gets into the trap we knock him on the head. We want no baits. Let your Chiefs come to us like men and talk to us."[34] Pītikwahanapiwīyin, nephew of Mistawasis and adopted son of Isapo-Muxika, told Treaty Six negotiators, "This is our land. It isn't a piece of pemmican to be cut up and given back to us in little pieces. It is ours and we will take what we want."[35]

Assimilation through Legislation: The 1876 Indian Act

In 1873, the government set up separate boards to deal with Indigenous affairs in Manitoba, the North-West Territories, and British Columbia. But Confederation called for centralization, so two years later it replaced the boards with the old superintendency system. This, in turn, called for more legislation. Indigenous Peoples, already the most regulated of peoples in Canada, would become even more so. The government would now interfere with their lives at every turn, down to, and including, the personal level.

The **Indian Act** of 1876 consolidated and revamped earlier legislation into a nationwide framework that was still fundamentally in place in the early twenty-first century. Its original goal of encouraging assimilation was overlooked in the repression that followed the 1885 revolt (see next chapter) but was recovered in 1951. But the Act's fundamental purpose—to assimilate Indigenous people—has stayed a constant. Furthermore, "the right of Indians to control the actions of the Department" would not be recognized "under any circumstances."[36]

Measures for protection of reserve lands and resources were taken directly from the 1850–1 Acts, although somewhat strengthened, and the enfranchisement provisions of 1857 were kept and expanded. Now, any member of a First Nation who got a university degree qualifying him as a minister, lawyer, teacher, or doctor could become enfranchised and get a location ticket without going through the otherwise mandatory three-year probation. The regulation depriving a First Nations woman of her status if she was married to a Canadian who did not have Indian status also stayed on the books.

One measure that came in for revision was the definition of an Indian. According to the new definition, he or she was "a person who pursuant of this Act is registered as an Indian, or is entitled to be registered as an Indian" or a person of First Nations blood reputed to belong to a band and entitled to use its lands.[37] Incidentally, a person could be registered without having signed a treaty. It also defined other terms for the first time, such as "band," "member of a band," and "reserve" (see Historical Background box).

In 1869, the government instituted an elective system for the selection of chiefs and band councils in First Nations government.[38] The new system, however, was not traditional among Indigenous Peoples and met with considerable resistance. The government's goal was administrative uniformity, but it also wanted to speed up assimilation by eliminating local and traditional systems of government. According to the Act of 1876, the chief's period of office was three years, but Indian Affairs could remove him at any time for "dishonesty, intemperance, or immorality." The Indian Affairs agent also paid the bills, and so he was obviously in

Glenbow Museum and Archives, NA–532–1

Payipwat, in 1885. One of the major leaders of the Plains Cree at the time of the treaty signings on the prairies, he remained loyal to the Crown during the 1885 troubles.[39] This contrasted with his long record of fighting for better treaty terms, the right to choose the location of his reserve, and the right to practise traditional religious rituals. Twice arrested and imprisoned for his persistent efforts, he was finally deposed by the government in Ottawa in 1902. His followers remained loyal, however, and refused to select a successor until after his death in 1908.

> **HISTORICAL BACKGROUND** | Defining Bands, Band
>   Members, and Reserves
>
> According to the Indian Act of 1876, a **band** is a body of Indigenous people for whom the
> Crown has set aside lands for their common use and benefit; for whom the government is
> holding monies for their common use and benefit; or whom the Governor-in-Council has de-
> clared a band. A member of a band is a person whose name appears on a band list or who is
> entitled to have his/her name appear on such a list. A **reserve**, within the meaning of the Act,
> is a tract of land that the Crown has set aside for the use and benefit of a band.

a position of power. The Haudenosaunee Confederacy opposed the new system because of its obvious interference with autonomous choice for forms of government.

Lands held in trust by the Crown for First Nations peoples could not be taxed, mortgaged, or seized for debt by any person other than a First Nations person or a band. This severely reduced access to development capital.[40] A First Nations person who held property under lease or outside of the reserve could be taxed. In Manitoba, the North-West Territories, and Keewatin District (today, the mainland central Arctic, which is part of Nunavut, plus portions of northern Ontario and Manitoba bordering on Hudson Bay), Indigenous Peoples who signed a treaty could not acquire lands by homestead or pre-emption. This was to prevent them from claiming both a share of a reserve and a homestead. The superintendent-general retained the right to grant allotments on reserve lands in fee simple as a reward for enfranchisement. Most bands resisted the measure and refused to approve location tickets or to sell or lease their lands, even for a limited period.[41]

An Upward Spiral of Regulation

The bureaucratic administration of Indigenous Peoples did not become a separate department until 1880. Even then, however, it continued to be within the Department of the Interior, where it stayed until 1936. The Minister of Interior was also superintendent-general of Indian Affairs, but effective power lay with the deputy superintendent-general. To the superintendent's power to impose the elective system whenever he thought a band was ready for it was added the power to designate only elected officials as band spokesmen. The Crown would not recognize or deal with traditional leaders.

In 1884, the government banned the elaborate feasts of the Northwest Coast First Nations, known under the general label "potlatch,"[42] along with dances associated with religious **Tamanawas rituals**. In the case of the potlatches, the argument was that their "giveaway" aspect went against the concept of private property.[43] This criminalization of cultural practices was a key step in the Canadian government's mission of cultural genocide that they considered to be necessary in order to encourage assimilation. As provincial court judge Alfred Scow pointed out in front of the Royal Commission of Aboriginal Peoples:

> This provision of the Indian Act was in place for close to 75 years and what that
> did was it prevented the passing down of our oral history. It prevented the passing

down of our values. It meant an interruption of the respected forms of government that we used to have, and we did have forms of government be they oral and not in writing before any of the Europeans came to this country. We had a system that worked for us. We respected each other. We had ways of dealing with disputes.[44]

Towards the end of the nineteenth century and into the twentieth, missionaries also started a campaign to remove totem poles, seeing them as symbols of an undesirable belief system.

In 1895, the government, in effect, prohibited the **thirst dances** ("sun dances") of prairie First Nations.[45] The result was to drive the dances underground, as the government could not effectively enforce the prohibition. At this time, Dakhóta reserves such as the Wahpeton at Round Plain, Saskatchewan, and Wood Mountain, Manitoba, were also holding the **Ghost Dance**, which had originated in 1889 from the prophecy of Wovoka (Jack Wilson), a Paiute spiritual leader in Nevada who foretold a peaceful end to white expansionism. This expectation, and the Ghost Dance, quickly spread among First Nations throughout much of the American West. **Millenarianism** was another type of mystical movement, rooted in Christianity, that also appeared from time to time.[46] These movements worried officials, because they strengthened the peoples' inner resources to withstand the intensifying attacks on their culture, and such beliefs found fertile soil in the difficult circumstances the Indigenous people were facing: loss of land and a way of life; the virtual disappearance of the bison; increasing starvation and poverty.

In the meantime, some Indigenous Peoples became skilled in fighting these bans through legal channels.[47] On 21 February 1896, *The Daily Colonist*, Victoria, published a petition signed by three elders of the Na'as band asking for the restitution of their customs:

> If we wish to perform an act moral in its nature, with no injury or damage, and pay for it, no law in equity can divest us of such right. We see the Salvation Army parade through the streets of your town with music and drum, enchanting the town.... We are puzzled to know whether in the estimation of civilization we are human or fish on the tributaries of the Na'as River, that the felicities of our ancestors should be denied us.[48]

Traditions were far from disappearing. In fact, the ceremonies, traditional cultural practices, and values of various Indigenous groups were thriving—and still being disparaged by officials—some 40 years after these bans. As late as the 1930s, government reports continued to blame the apparent resistance to the agricultural model for economic self-support on the continuation of traditional ceremonies.[49]

The Indian "Advancement" Act

An Act for Conferring Certain Privileges on the More Advanced Bands of Indians of Canada, with the View of Training Them for the Exercise of Municipal Affairs—this was the official name of the Indian Advancement Act. Its purpose was to transform band regulations into municipal laws. Passed in 1884, it gave band councils limited powers of taxation, subject to the approval of the department; responsibility for public health; and the power to enforce bylaws. It also reduced the number of band councillors to six, even though traditional First Nations councils were large.[50] The Act replaced the three-year election system, in effect since 1869, with annual elections, considered necessary for the municipal type of government the Act was preparing the bands for.

Taking as few chances as it could, the Act stated that chiefs deposed by the Governor-in-Council (i.e., the Governor General affirming a decision of the federal cabinet) on grounds of dishonesty, intemperance, or immorality could not be re-elected immediately. The decision as to which bands qualified rested with the Governor-in-Council. Bands considered not "advanced" enough for this system were mostly in the West. In effect, the powers of the superintendent-general, or his designated agent, to direct the band's affairs had been greatly increased. He could call for and supervise elections, and he could summon and preside over band meetings.[51]

Indigenous Peoples across Canada considered these new measures just another attempt "to force white ideas on the red men."[52] In all, only nine bands adopted the new system, some of them under pressure. By 1906, the government incorporated what was left of the Indian Advancement Act into the Indian Act (see Chapters 14 and 15 for a discussion of later changes to the Indian Act), but it remained the case that Indigenous and Canadian views of the Act differed considerably.

In the meantime, on the prairies, Indigenous unrest was growing, as fewer and fewer bison were available. The Métis were also unhappy about their land situation. The government responded by amending the Indian Act once again (in 1884), this time to make incitement of First Nations or Métis people to riot an offence and to ban the sale or gift of ammunition to First Nations and Métis people in Manitoba and the North-West Territories.[53] Obviously, the government had clear warnings of what was to come.

The Franchise Bill

Still pursuing the integration of Indigenous people, Macdonald introduced the Franchise Bill into Parliament in March of 1885, four days before the outbreak of the Northwest Rebellion. With Indigenous Peoples east of the Great Lakes in mind, Macdonald proposed the franchise for all males who were British subjects and who met certain minimum property qualifications, whether or not they held land individually. Indigenous Peoples of Ontario and Quebec, he said, might not be contributing to the general assessment of the country,

> but they have their own assessment and their own system of taxation in their own bridges and roads, they build their own school houses. They carry on the whole system in their own way, but it is in the Indian way, and it is an efficient way. They carry out all the obligations of civilized men . . . in every respect they have a right to be considered as equal with the whites.[54]

He added, however, that the First Nations of the North-West Territories and Keewatin, Manitoba, and "perhaps" British Columbia were not yet ready for the measure. They should be excluded unless as individuals they were occupying separate tracts of land.

The bill aroused strong opposition on the grounds that First Nations in general were not paying taxes. The cry went up that it would allow the "wild hordes" led by the likes of Mistahimaskwa and Pītikwahanapiwīyin to go "from a scalping party to the polls."[55] Macdonald was able to get the bill passed, but the Liberals revoked it in 1898, claiming that it was "an insult to free white people in the country to place them on a level with pagan and barbarian Indians."[56]

Clearly, the country was not prepared to accept Indigenous people on an equal footing. When it came to choosing between Indigenous people and whites, the interest of the latter usually would be provided for. In the situation brewing in the West, the conflict of interests was moving steadily towards violence. The political machinations in Ottawa were terrible provocations that could easily have led to an escalation of violence. It would be amazing how little violence there was, and of what short duration.

Questions to Consider

1. What mistakes did the Canadian government make in the treaty process?
2. What led to the troubles at Cypress Hills?
3. Why did some Dakhóta communities come to Canada?
4. What were the main provisions of the 1876 Indian Act?

Recommended Readings

Atleo, Richard. *Tsawalk: A Nuu-chuh-nulth World View*. Vancouver: University of British Columbia Press, 2005.

Cardinal, Harold, and Walter Hildebrandt. *Treaty Elders of Saskatchewan*. Calgary: University of Calgary Press, 2000.

Daschuk, James William. *Clearing the Plains: Disease, Politics of Starvation, and the Loss of Aboriginal Life*. Regina: University of Regina Press, 2014.

Dempsey Hugh A. *Crowfoot: Chief of the Blackfeet*. Edmonton: Hurtig, 1972.

Ewers, John C. *The Blackfeet: Raiders of the Northern Plains*. Norman: University of Oklahoma Press, 1989.

Kehoe, Alice B. *The Ghost Dance*. Toronto: Holt, Rinehart and Winston, 1989.

McNab, David T. *Circles of Time: Aboriginal Land Rights and Resistance in Ontario*. Waterloo, Ont.: Wilfrid Laurier University Press, 1999.

Peterson, Jacqueline, and Jennifer S.H. Brown, eds. *The New Peoples: Being and Becoming Métis in North America*. Winnipeg: University of Manitoba Press, 1985.

Sherwin, Allan. *Bridging Two Peoples: Chief Peter Jones, 1843–1909*. Waterloo, Ont.: Wilfrid Laurier University Press, 2013.

Talbot, Richard. *Negotiating the Numbered Treaties: An Intellectual and Political Biography of Alexander Morris*. Saskatoon: Purich Publishing, 2009.

13 Time of Troubles

CHAPTER OUTLINE

Conflict over natural resources was a problem that was aggravated by the arrival of European immigrants. In this chapter we shall see that this was particularly true in western Canada, where the decline of the bison led to conflict between Siksika and Cree peoples and more generally between the Métis and the First Nations. Ultimately, the conflict pitted European settlers against everyone else. Conflict became more pronounced as the focus shifted away from the bison and other natural resources to include land title. Worse still, the completion of the Canadian Pacific Railway led to an exponential increase in European settlers and to a deepening crisis for the Indigenous Peoples of the vast Canadian prairie.

LEARNING OUTCOMES

1. Students will learn the social and economic effects of the decline of the bison herds.

2. Students will understand the underlying causes of the resistance movements and the actions of 1870 and 1885.

3. Students will gain insight into the suffering that followed the arrival of waves of European immigrants into the West.

TIME LINE From the Disappearance of the Bison to the 1885 Conflicts

1859
Cree hold series of councils in Qu'Appelle region over dwindling bison herds and massive Métis involvement in hunt.

1872
St Laurent founded along South Saskatchewan River by Gabriel Dumont and other Métis.
Batoche, another Métis settlement, founded near St Laurent.

1880
Louis Riel is instrumental in getting Montana First Nations to allow Indigenous people within Canada to hunt on both sides of the new border; Indigenous people from within the Canadian border raid horses of their traditional southern enemies, which breaks brief alliance.

1884
Ottawa amends Indian Act to cut off sale or gift of ammunition to Indigenous Peoples in Manitoba and North-West Territories.
Mistahimaskwa calls a thirst dance on Pītikwahanapiwīyin's reserve—more than 2,000 participate.
Dumont and other Métis ride south to Montana on 4 June to ask their former leader, Riel, to return to help them in gaining rights that have been often promised but never given.
Mistahimaskwa losing influence to Cree war chiefs, who advocate violence to regain independence.
16 December: Riel petitions Ottawa for all people of West—First Nations, newcomers, Métis—to be treated with full dignity as British subjects.

1870s
Groups of Métis leave Red River to form new settlements to north and west.

1871
Cree leaders conclude treaty with Siksika leaders to allow them to hunt in Siksikawa territory.

1878
John Norquay elected as Manitoba's first and only Métis premier, though he identified with his Orkney heritage.

1881–8
Edgar Dewdney, lieutenant-governor of North-West Territories, seeks to divide First Peoples just as Cree chief Mistahimaskwa seeks to unite them.

1882
Mistahimaskwa, leader of largest band of Plains Cree, forced finally to sign Treaty Six in order to get rations for his starving people after he has tried to form Indigenous alliances against white intrusion. He is made to take an isolated reserve.
US military sent to confiscate horses and equipment of Indigenous people living within Canada hunting south of the border; border crossings restricted.

1884–5
Hard winter due to two straight years of poor crops for First Nations and Métis on western Plains.

Continued

1885

Ottawa acknowledges Riel petition but is prepared only to set up a commission.
8 February: Riel replies: "In 40 days they will have my answer."
8 March: Riel announces intention to set up provisional government.
18 March: Métis seize Indian agent and other officials and occupy church at Batoche, cut telegraph lines from Regina to Prince Albert.
19 March: Riel proclaims provisional government.
26 March: Métis attack NWMP sortie at Duck Lake, killing 12. Riel, armed with crucifix, stops pursuit of routed police.
End of March: Pītikwahanapiwīyin's and Minahikosis's people leave reserves, head towards Battleford.
2 April: Mistahimaskwa's war chiefs pillage HBC stores at Frog Lake, killing nine. Mistahimaskwa stops onslaught in time to save HBC representative as well as other settlers who had sought refuge at fort.

15 April: Mistahimaskwa takes NWMP's Fort Pitt in peaceful surrender.
24 April: Métis ambush Canadian militia, led by F.D. Middleton, at Fish Creek.
2 May: Pītikwahanapiwīyin's sleeping camp attacked, and Pītikwahanapiwīyin halts pursuit of fleeing militia.
9–12 May: Middleton and militia defeat entrenched Métis, who run out of ammunition, at Batoche.
15 May: Riel surrenders.
26 May: Pītikwahanapiwīyin surrenders.
2 July: Mistahimaskwa walks into Fort Carlton to surrender.
16 November: Riel, convicted of treason, is hanged at Regina.
17 November: Six Cree and two Nakoda men hanged at Battleford. Pītikwahanapiwīyin, Mistahimaskwa, Kāpeyakwāskonam sent to prison; all die soon after release.
Pass system introduced to restrict First Nations individuals to their own reserves.

Now That the Bison Are Gone

The bison, once "countless" because they were so many, were rapidly becoming "countless" because there were none left to count. The problem was particularly difficult for Indigenous Peoples to accept. The key to their adaptability had always been a careful and consistent approach to resource management, and over time people had developed a complex and spiritual relationship with the animal world. The wanton slaughter of the bison herds both by newcomers and by peoples who had lost their connection to the careful relationships of the past was thus as incomprehensible as it was damaging. The suddenness with which the decline was occurring made the decline much worse.[1]

The Cree were among the first people to be affected by the decline of the bison herds. Alarmed, they held a series of councils in the Qu'Appelle region in 1859 in which they maintained that the pursuit of bison should be restricted to Indigenous Peoples. They saw the HBC expansion onto the prairies as part of the problem. They wanted trade but did not like to see their lands invaded by newcomers who also hunted there. If the newcomers wanted meat, pemmican, or hides, they should trade for them from the Cree hunters.[2]

Kevin McKenzie, Father, Son and Holy Ghost II (detail), liquid plastic, carbon fiber, neon, 2017, each component 34" x 34" x 14".

Resurrection by Kevin McKenzie (b. 1961), a Cree/Métis artist from Saskatchewan.

The Trials of the Métis Continue

Many **Métis** had already accepted agricultural or wage-earning options into their lifestyle as the bison herd vanished (see Historical Background box). Other problems arose, however, so that the transition for them, too, became painful, if not quite as drastic as it would be for First Nations. The fur trade, dominant for 200 years, had in many aspects reinforced the cultural and economic positions of First Nations and Métis in the Canadian West. As the trade declined, and as newcomers helped themselves to territory in disregard for the rights of the Métis and First Nations, resentment grew into action.

In 1872, the Métis asked Lieutenant-Governor Archibald to protect them against settlers occupying their land. Archibald had previously rejected their proposal that a block of land be reserved for their use, as was being done for First Nations who signed treaties. The federal government also opposed the idea, claiming that the Métis should apply for land on an individual basis, as European settlers did. In Manitoba, after all, speculators had acquired most of the land set aside for "children of the half-breed heads of families" for only a fraction of its value. Did they want the same thing to happen in the North-West Territories, where not more than a quarter of the grants were actually occupied and improved by Métis?[3]

HISTORICAL BACKGROUND | Shifting Populations

The total population of First Nations in the Canadian West is estimated to have been about 35,000 in 1870 (a figure considered by some to be too high), the Métis, about 10,000–12,000, and newcomers, fewer than 2,000. Epidemics and swelling waves of immigration quickly changed these proportions, however. By 1883, European newcomers heavily outnumbered First Nations and Métis populations.[4]

The Indigenous population on the Plains was highest during the summer, when bison herds were at their largest. Bison did not have long-distance migratory movements, congregating instead where the feeding was most attractive.[5] The shrinking of the herds had the effect of increasing the ceremonial aspect of the hunt, and shamans able to call the animals gained in importance and prestige. Bison were central to the ceremonial life of Plains Indigenous Peoples.

It is not clear whether Ottawa told the Métis about its position concerning treating them as individuals rather than as communities. In any event, groups scattered from Red River to establish independent settlements, a pattern that had been in effect for some time (see Chapter 11). The difference was that now farming was replacing bison hunting. The best known of these groups was led by the bison-hunt captain, **Gabriel Dumont** (1838–1906), reputed to speak six Indigenous languages, in addition to French and English.[6] In 1872, he led his group north to colonize an area about 45 to 50 km long and some 10 km wide, including a stretch of the South Saskatchewan River and Duck Lake. Its southern boundary was Fish Creek.[7] One of the reasons for choosing this site was that it already had a mission, **St Laurent**, founded in 1871 by Oblate Alexis André (1833–93). Each family had a "ribbon" lot with river frontage of about 200 metres, following the Red River pattern. Nearby were another two missions, St Louis and St Antoine de Padoue. The settlement connected with the latter dated to 1872 and was called after its founder, trader François-Xavier Letendre *dit* Batoche (*c.* 1841–1901). **Batoche** was the commercial centre for the cluster of Métis settlements, referred to collectively as South Branch, straddling the Carlton Trail (the main route to Edmonton) as well as the South Saskatchewan.

Ottawa, in the meantime, had already decided on the square survey as the settlement pattern for the West. However, anyone who had settled in the region before 1870 could keep the original boundaries. In the case of the Métis, who used ribbon lots, this was important. After 1870, settlers had no legal right to special consideration, although the government instructed surveyors to accommodate special claims as best they could. Usually, this took place to the satisfaction of both parties, but at South Branch this did not happen, some say in error. The Métis could not gain recognition of their land claims based on Aboriginal right, as the government had already denied them that, nor could they accomplish this based on prior settlers' rights, as the law considered them to be squatters. On the other side of the picture, the Métis were negligent about filing claims for patent.[8]

Gabriel Dumont and the St Laurent Council

On 10 December 1873, Dumont called together the St Laurent Métis, who numbered more than 300, to discuss setting up a governing body. (Later, its population would swell to 1,500.) They unanimously elected Dumont president and chose eight councillors. The new body enacted 28 basic laws modelled on those that governed the bison hunt, with the added right to raise taxes. The regulations covered issues such as labour and employment conditions and the settlement of disputes but did not mention theft (apart from horses) or violent crimes such as assault, manslaughter, or murder, all of which were extremely rare among the Métis at that time.

St Laurent was off to a promising start. Encouraged, Dumont visited other South Branch communities suggesting that they do the same. He hoped that they could eventually work out a self-governing plan, at least for South Branch and perhaps for the whole Northwest, until the time when the North-West Council established by Canada would actually be ready to govern. When that happened, the St Laurent council assured federal officials, it would

Glenbow Museum and Archives, NA–1063–1

Gabriel Dumont, a bison-hunt captain who was fluent in French, English, and many Indigenous languages, was instrumental in the settlement of and in creating a viable government for the St Laurent Métis settlement in Saskatchewan—an administration that the Canadian government would not accept. Later, he was Riel's military leader and strategist during the Northwest Rebellion of 1885.

resign in favour of Ottawa's authority. However, the other communities were not well enough organized to rise to the challenge. In the meantime, the decrease of bison caused the St Laurent council to tighten its regulations. It asked the North-West Council to adopt its measures for the whole region. And then, other events intervened.

That summer, 1874, a party of bison "free hunters" arrived in the area the St Laurent settlers considered to be theirs. Dumont and his men, including some Cree, confronted the intruders and told them they were trespassing and breaking local laws. When the hunters refused to accept this, the Métis issued fines and confiscated their equipment and supplies as set out in the St. Laurent regulations. The hunting party proceeded to the nearest HBC post, Fort Carlton. There, they complained to the chief factor, Lawrence Clarke, who then reported the incident to Lieutenant-Governor Morris as an unwarranted attack, maybe even an open revolt against Canada.[9]

The HBC, for its part, had been uneasy about St Laurent from the beginning, particularly as Dumont had offered his services to Riel during a visit in 1870.[10] The press did not improve matters: "Another Stand Against Canadian Government Authority in the Northwest," one headline screamed. Ten thousand Cree were reported to be on the warpath. Fort Carlton was said to have fallen, and six members of the North West Mounted Police killed. A detachment of the NWMP under Superintendent Leif Crozier (1847–1901) went to the St Laurent council on 20 August 1875 to discuss the matter.

Crozier examined the council's laws and pronounced them sensible for local conditions. Neither did Edward Blake, federal Minister of Justice, 1875–7, see anything wrong with them. He observed that the very fact they had been necessary pointed to the need for establishing a properly constituted government on the prairies. The council agreed to disband as a formal body, and the police said they would have no objections to the bison hunt being regulated along the suggested lines. But it was 1877 before the North-West Council enacted hunting laws, too little and too late to save the herds.

Deprived of their council and thus of the ability to act on their own, the Métis asked the government for schools, or at least for help in getting them established. The Canadian government, as usual, was slow but eventually agreed to help. The Métis also wanted two representatives on the North-West Territories Council. In response, the government appointed Pascal Breland (d. 1896), a long-time member of the Assiniboia council but a man whom the Métis did not admire.

Growing Unrest

In 1878, Manitoba elected its only Métis premier, the English-speaking John Norquay (1841–89). By that time, the flood of immigration was changing Manitoba into an increasingly English-speaking community. This transition was capped by the language legislation of 1890, which transformed Manitoba from the officially bilingual province established in 1870 in accordance with Riel's dream into a unilingual English one.[11] Premier Norquay, who identified with his Orkney rather than his Cree background, started the process. Cree remained an important language but it was ignored in the legislation.

Land title continued to be a problem, and there was no agreement among the Métis as to how to solve it. Some petitioned on the basis of Aboriginal right. Others wanted land grants like those awarded under the Manitoba Act and asked the government to help them in changing over to farming, as it was helping First Nations. St Laurent wanted the surveyors to recognize its river lot system. Officials said this was not necessary, as the Métis could easily divide the square survey into the desired river lots, but the Métis were seeking government recognition of their system, not just an adaptation. To add to the confusion, survey maps were slow in appearing, so the Métis could not make legal claims. In 1884, a government inspector came out, but he arrived at no solution the Métis could accept. When they had been ignored before, during the political vacuum created by the ending of the Hudson's Bay Company's government, they had got results by taking matters into their own hands. Now, in the midst of a world economic crisis (1883), they met once more to consider their course of action.

At St Laurent, on 30 March 1884, 30 Métis met at Abraham Montour's house. They recalled that Lord Lorne (John Douglas Sutherland Campbell, Governor General, 1878–83), during his 1881 tour of the West, had promised to bring the Métis situation to the attention of the government, but nothing had happened. The Métis cry was similar to that of the First Nations: "the government stole our land, and now is laughing at us." A few weeks later, at another meeting, the group decided to invite Riel back from his Montana refuge, where he was teaching school. On 4 June 1884 Dumont and some companions rode south to get their leader.[12]

This Is Our Life, This Is Our Land
Mistahimaskwa and the Appeal for Pan-Indigenous Resistance

In 1870, the HBC lands were transferred to Canada. When Indigenous Peoples responded with increasing militancy, Ottawa cut their rations, its main weapon for bringing the people into line. The year of the Cypress Hills Massacre, 1873, **Mistahimaskwa** ("Big Bear") clashed with Gabriel Dumont when the Métis leader tried to direct the hunt on the High Plains.[13] Half Ojibwa, half Cree, Mistahimaskwa led the largest band of Cree on the Plains at that time, about 2,000 souls. As a young man, he had been noted for his ability to shoot accurately under the neck of his horse while riding at full tilt. Of impressive presence, he did not like dealing with newcomers.

Like Tecumseh and Nescambiouit before him, he worked for pan-Indigenism. He saw that unless Indigenous people united in the face of non-Indigenous settlement, they were lost. Refusing official gifts being distributed prior to Treaty Six negotiations, he said he did not want to be baited so that the government could put a rope around his neck (Chapter 12). He was referring not to death but to loss of freedom.[14]

Mistahimaskwa did not like the terms being offered for Treaty Six. In particular, he disliked the provision that Canadian law would become the law of the land. As he saw it, the people would lose their autonomy under this treaty. Accordingly, he refused to sign in 1876 but eventually was forced to do so in 1882, at Fort Walsh, to get rations for his people. By then, it was too late for him to have any impact on the treaty's terms.

Mistahimaskwa's campaign to unite Indigenous Peoples and to get better treaty terms had seriously alarmed Ottawa, causing officials to increase their efforts to find chiefs, such as Mistawasis ("Big Child," d. 1903) and Ahchacoosacootacoopits ("Star Blanket," *c.* 1845–1917), willing to negotiate. Of those who did negotiate, only Wikaskokiseyin and Minahikosis ("Little Pine," *c.* 1830–85) had reputations that came close to that of Mistahimaskwa. Minahikosis held out for three years, but finally, his starving people persuaded him. He signed in 1879.[15]

Another holdout was Kamiyistowesit ("Beardy," *c.* 1828–89) of the Parklands People. Like other dissenting chiefs, he maintained that since the Europeans had caused the bison to disappear, it was now their responsibility to provide for Indigenous Peoples. Beardy carried his objections to the point of threatening to seize the trading post at Duck Lake, in his band's hunting territory, if the government did not meet his demands for support. Authorities responded by sending an NWMP detachment to reinforce the threatened post. The NWMP fed 7,000 from its own rations, an act Ottawa considered to be encouraging the holdouts.

A Plains Cree chief who got along reasonably well with whites was **Pītikwahanapiwīyin ("Poundmaker")**, an adopted Siksika chief.[16] He inherited his name from his father, a Nakoda shaman renowned for building pounds. Pītikwahanapiwīyin was a forcible advocate for his people. Faced with government reluctance to go beyond the short term (in fact, it considered the First Nations' concern for their children and grandchildren to be little more than a smoke-screen), he observed, "From what I can hear and see now, I cannot understand that I shall be able to clothe my children as long as the sun shines and water runs."

In the end, he was one of those who signed in 1876, although he continued to hunt and did not accept a reserve until 1879. By then, all in the Treaty Six area except Mistahimaskwa had bowed to the inevitable, but all had not accepted reserves. In the final accounting, the signers of Treaty Six did better than those of Treaty Four, winning such concessions as the "medicine chest" clause (although it would be 1930 before there was an on-reserve nursing station, at Fisher River, Manitoba) and also the promise of relief in the event of famine or pestilence. But the price was an enormous area of land, 815,850 km².

Looming Preventable Disaster

By 1876, the only place in Canada where there were enough bison left to pursue the old way of life was the Cypress Hills. There were larger herds in Montana, but local Indigenous Peoples kept them from moving north by setting fire to the grass along the border. As a result, Canadian Plains peoples converged on the Cypress Hills, a movement that peaked in 1877–9.

Although most of the bands had selected reserves, and some were getting started in their new way of life with government assistance, there were delays in surveying sites and in providing supplies and equipment. It was a standoff. As long as there were bison around, and the Indigenous Peoples wanted to hunt them, why move faster with the new program? The warnings of the NWMP, missionaries, and settlers of a looming but preventable disaster produced no results. As early as 1877, there were complaints that needed equipment was not arriving. Those

Indigenous Peoples who wanted to get started in their new way of life, and there were many, were, more often than not, frustrated by misguided bureaucratic paternalism compounded by ineptitude. As one anthropologist noted, it is easy, with hindsight, to criticize the government's handling of the situation, for which it had no precedent,[17] but the fact remains that when Indigenous Peoples objected, as in the case of Mistahimaskwa, the government blamed them for the problems.[18]

Indigenous Peoples set old hostilities aside, as Siksika, Plains Cree, and Dakhóta consulted on measures to regulate the hunt. In 1880, Mistahimaskwa and Minahikosis headed south to the remaining bison range on the Milk and Missouri rivers. There, they met with Riel. The Métis leader persuaded the Indigenous Peoples in Montana—southern Nakoda, Piikani, Apsáalooke, and A'ani—to let the northerners hunt on their reservations. The alliance fell apart, however, when the Indigenous people from Canada gave in to the temptation to raid the horses of their hosts, who, after all, were still traditional enemies. In 1882, the US army confiscated the horses and equipment of the Indigenous people from north of the border and sent them back. From then on, the authorities restricted border crossings.

Meanwhile, Mistahimaskwa and other Plains Cree chiefs were discussing a plan to select reserves next to each other, which would have resulted in an Indigenous territory. The reserves they chose took in much of what is now southern Alberta and southern Saskatchewan. They almost succeeded, but the government in Ottawa realized what was going on and prevented it, although it meant violating treaty provisions for freedom to select reserve locations. It also meant uprooting already established Indigenous farmers.[19] Even though Mistahimaskwa was finally forced to take a reserve in an isolated location in 1882, he did not

INDIGENOUS LEADERS | Edward Ahenakew

Much of what we know of the culture and philosophy of the Plains Cree is thanks to the efforts of Edward Ahenakew (1881–1961), a great-nephew of Pītikwahanapiwīyin. Ahenakew was the first Cree student to attend the University of Saskatchewan, in 1910, and he was ordained as an Anglican priest in 1912. He moved north and began to work on the reserves of northern Saskatchewan, particularly at Onion Lake where he became an early champion of First Nations health care. Travelling extensively by dogsled in winter and by canoe in summer, he brought comfort and strength to the Cree people during the ravages of the influenza pandemic in 1918–19. His experiences led him to medical school at the University of Alberta. Poverty prevented him from graduating, but his contributions did not end. He quickly became the great champion of Cree culture. He wrote a Cree–English dictionary and he collected stories and published them throughout his long and productive life. These stories, published together posthumously in 1973 as *Voices of the Plains Cree*, remain a key source for the history and culture of the Cree people. It is a magnificent contribution and a lasting tribute to a man who, at a ceremony to grant him an honorary doctorate of divinity, was called the "Martin Luther King of the Cree."

give up. With other chiefs, he continued to try to get reserves as close together as possible around Battleford.

Since 1880, the government in Ottawa had enforced a policy of work for rations, except for the orphaned, sick, or aged. Furthermore, it interpreted the famine clause of Treaty Six to mean that only a "general" famine warranted free rations. The daily allowance for individuals was 13 ounces (383 grams) of flour, three ounces (99 grams) of bacon, and six ounces (170 grams) of beef. Later, Lawrence Vankoughnet, deputy superintendent-general of Indian Affairs, 1874–93, and such agents as Hayter Reed (1849–1936), who succeeded Vankoughnet, 1893–7, ordered this reduced. Reed did not mention in his reports that Indigenous people were starving, perhaps because he saw it as a result of laziness and immorality. To the Cree, Reed was "Iron Heart."[20]

Mounting food shortages led to desperate actions, and Indigenous people began to kill the cattle that were supposed to get them started as farmers and ranchers.[21] Even government agents realized that stopping rations of offenders would not solve the problem, and so they used fines instead. In 1883, three Cree chiefs, Sehkosowayanew ("Ermineskin"), his brother Keskayiwew ("Bobtail"), and Samson (inheritor of the mantle of Maskepetoon), wrote to Prime Minister Macdonald, who also held the Interior portfolio and thus was superintendent-general:

> If no attention is paid to our case now we shall conclude that the treaty made with us six years ago was a meaningless matter of form and that the white man has doomed us to annihilation little by little. But the motto of the Indian is, "If we must die by violence, let us do it quickly."[22]

Even Pītikwahanapiwīyin, who had co-operated at first, became disgruntled. He consulted with Mistahimaskwa, who thought it would be a good idea to go to Ottawa to see if someone was really in charge of Indian Affairs, and if so, to deal with him directly. Despite his reputation among whites as a troublemaker, the record indicates that Mistahimaskwa opposed violence and even prevented it on occasion. He recognized that negotiation was the way to work out constructive measures. First, though, the Indigenous Peoples had to get together and agree among themselves.

In 1884, Mistahimaskwa called a thirst dance to be held on Pītikwahanapiwīyin's reserve. More than 2,000 participated, the largest united effort managed by the Cree. Mistahimaskwa's aim was to get Indigenous Peoples to select a single representative for a term of four years who would speak for all. He also wanted the Cree to join in obtaining a single large reserve on the North Saskatchewan. He argued that Ottawa had unilaterally changed Treaty Six from what it had agreed to during negotiations: "half the sweet things taken out and lots of sour things left in." They needed a new treaty, as well as a new concept for establishing reserves.

As Mistahimaskwa laboured to unite Indigenous Peoples, Edgar Dewdney, lieutenant-governor of the North-West Territories, 1881–8, worked to divide them, using food as an instrument to keep the people quiet. In 1884, he invited Isapo-Muxika to visit Regina and Winnipeg, where the Siksika chief received a royal reception.[24] On seeing the size of the

My 4th Great Grandfather, Chief Maskepetoon, © George Littlechild.

Chief Maskepetoon **by George Littlechild (b. 1958),** a widely acclaimed Plains Cree artist. Maskepetoon ("Broken Arm," c. 1807–69) was a Cree chief noted later in his life as a peacemaker and a convert to Methodism. He was killed when he entered a Niitsitapi camp, unarmed, to seek peace between the Crees and the Niitsitapiikwan. The sketch at the centre of Littlechild's artwork is by the well-known nineteenth-century western artist, Gustavus Sohon.[23]

settlements, Isapo-Muxika became all the more convinced that violence was useless. Dewdney also provided for the arrest of any First Nations person found on a reserve not his own without official approval. He was determined that never again would Mistahimaskwa or any other chief convoke a large assembly. That this view violated the law—not to mention basic human rights—was overlooked in the fear of an Indigenous war. The police view simplified

Glenbow Museum and Archives, NA-1104-1

Isapo-Muxica with his family, 1884.

the situation: "the government would not permit armed bodies of men, whether First Peoples or Whites, to roam the country at large."[25]

Although confrontations were increasing, up to this point there was remarkably little violence. Ottawa persisted in the view that the situation in the West was really not its responsibility. In contrast, Indigenous Peoples believed that settlers should pay for having provoked disaster.

Armed Resistance in the West

The first Métis resistance, in 1869–70, occurred with the passing of the HBC as governing power in the region and the transfer of its lands to Canada. The second, the **Northwest Rebellion** in 1885—this time an uprising—occurred with the passing of the bison. It also coincided with the completion of the Canadian Pacific Railway, which would bring in greater numbers of settlers than ever.

Two years of poor crops (1883–4) meant that the winter of 1884–5 was hard. At the same time, Ottawa seemed to lose its sense of direction, and it disarmed the North-West Territories militia.

Meanwhile, Mistahimaskwa was having his own problems, as his war chiefs gained influence at his expense. His son Ayimisis (Imases, "Little Bad Man," 1851–1921) and Kapapamahchakwew ("Wandering Spirit," *c.* 1845–85) advocated violence as the only way of regaining independence.[26] Mistahimaskwa recognized that violence was useless but was so involved trying to develop pan-Indigenism that he had lost touch with his people. Conditions were so obviously unsettled that, in 1884, Ottawa banned the sale or gift of "fixed ammunition" or "ball cartridges" to Indigenous people of Manitoba and the North-West Territories.[27] That this went against the treaties was either overlooked or brushed aside.

In spite of all this uncertainty and unrest, Riel's return in 1884 did not trigger a call for violence. Riel repeatedly stressed his peaceful intentions, even as he maintained that the North-West Territories should be a self-governing province and that Indigenous Peoples should be treated better. He also said that white settlers were being charged too much for land.

The Métis wanted Riel to replace Pascal Breland on the North-West Council. The settlers, however, were not so sure. They were worried about Riel's relations with Indigenous Peoples. Although Mistahimaskwa did not join up with him, he told Riel he was confident the Métis leader would not forget First Nations people in his fight for Métis rights. Vankoughnet, deeply suspicious of Mistahimaskwa, cut his band's rations. The people were becoming hungrier and hungrier. Even co-operative chiefs such as Mistawasis and Ahchacoosacootacoopits were complaining,[28] and rations were not the only issue.

As Riel pointed out in his petition to Ottawa on 16 December 1884, the people of the West had every right to be treated with the full dignity of British subjects, which was not happening. In his list of complaints, he included those of Métis, First Nations, and Europeans. This time, the government in Ottawa acknowledged receipt of the petition. The Métis were so jubilant that on New Year's Day 1885 they honoured Riel at a banquet and presented him with a house, some money, and an illuminated address thanking him for his efforts on their behalf. Their optimism was premature.

As it turned out, the most that Ottawa was prepared to do was to establish a commission to list Métis living in the Northwest in 1870 and their claims. At first, it was not empowered to do

In 1869–70:	In 1885:
The HBC had no effective police or military to enforce its decisions.	The NWMP was very much a presence on the northwestern Plains.
Government troops did not arrive until after the passing of the Manitoba Act, 1870.	Troops arrived at Qu'Appelle a week after Riel set up his provisional government.
Riel and the Catholic Church worked closely together.	Riel had assumed a new spirituality, which strained his relations with the Catholic Church.
Métis held the balance of power in Red River and were the settlement's effective armed force; white settlers were a small minority.	White settlers heavily outnumbered the Métis.

anything about them. Dewdney realized this was too little too late. He modified the message before relaying it to the Métis, but the ploy did not work. On 8 February, Riel replied, "in 40 days they will have my answer." The religious implications of that response were obvious, as the seasonal Lenten fast, which occurred at this time of year, lasted 40 days. Riel's relations with Father Alexis André were already strained, and he was beginning to see himself as a prophet. Aware of the anomaly of his position as an American citizen, he offered to return to the US and leave the Métis to work out their own problems. They refused to let him go and, at a secret meeting, agreed to take up arms if necessary "to save our country."

On 8 March, Riel announced his intention to set up a provisional government and presented a 10-point Bill of Rights.[29] Two days later, the Métis began a novena.[30] By this time, Riel had broken with Father André. Both the novena and Riel's "40 days" ended on 18 March. The Métis seized the Indian agent and other officials, and occupied the church of St Antoine de Padoue at Batoche. They cut the telegraph lines from Regina to Prince Albert but left those to Battleford intact.

The next day was St Joseph's Day, St Joseph being the patron saint of the Métis. Riel proclaimed his provisional government, and the people armed themselves. Kāpeyakwāskonam ("One Arrow," c. 1815–86), chief of the Willow Cree whose reserve was the closest to South Branch, butchered all the cattle on his reserve and joined the Métis. (Later, he claimed that he had been threatened by Dumont and forced into his action.) Riel, emulating events of 1869–70, sent a summons to Fort Carlton on 21 March, calling on it to surrender.[31]

Five days later, on 26 March, Crozier attempted a sortie from the fort with 100 Mounties and volunteers to seize a strategic supply point. The Métis met him at **Duck Lake**, a place they had chosen. Within 15 minutes, 12 of Crozier's men were dead and 11 wounded. Five Métis and one Cree were killed. Riel, armed with a crucifix, stopped the pursuit of the routed police, preventing an even worse bloodbath. As the defeated column returned to the fort, reinforcements of 100 men arrived. With this protection, the fort was evacuated to Prince Albert. Thanks to Riel's restraint, there was no further action at this point.

Hard on the heels of these events, Pītikwahanapiwīyin's and Minahikosis's people left their reserves and headed for Battleford, headquarters for distributing supplies. Settlers took fright and fled into the fort. The Cree looted the abandoned houses and stores during the last two days of March. Minahikosis, who had been in poor health for several years, died just afterward.[32]

Mistahimaskwa's war chiefs took matters into their own hands and looted HBC stores at Frog Lake on 2 April. Nine people died in the incident, including the agent, two priests, and settlers. Mistahimaskwa stopped the bloodshed in time to save the HBC representative and the women and children.[33] Most of the settlers in the area were able to take refuge in Fort Pitt, an NWMP garrison, which then surrendered to Mistahimaskwa. The chief allowed the soldiers to leave, then took over the fort on 15 April.

The call to arms that these events raised brought a quick response across Canada. Since the railway was not completed, transporting troops and supplies meant loading and unloading 16 times before reaching Regina. Even so, by 6 April, **Frederick Dobson Middleton**

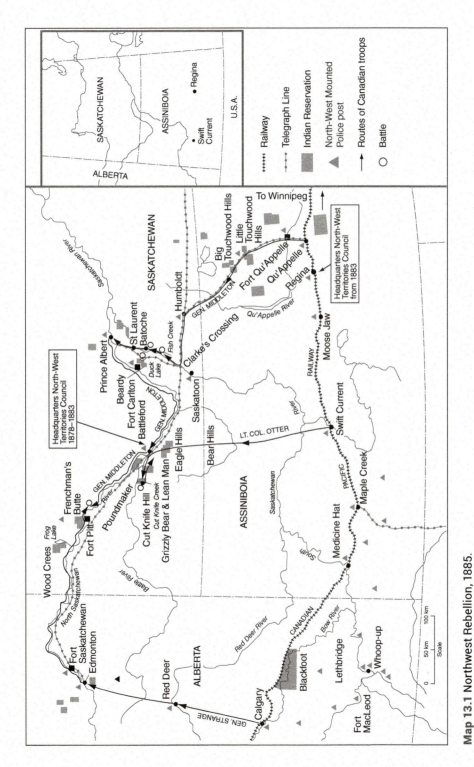

Map 13.1 Northwest Rebellion, 1885.

Adapted from D.G.G. Kerr, *Historical Atlas of Canada*, 3rd rev. edn (Toronto: Nelson, 1975).

Legend:
- Railway
- Telegraph Line
- Indian Reservation
- North-West Mounted Police post
- Routes of Canadian troops
- Battle

Inset map labels:
- SASKATCHEWAN
- ASSINIBOIA
- ALBERTA
- U.S.A.
- Regina
- Swift Current

Main map labels:
- SASKATCHEWAN
- ASSINIBOIA
- ALBERTA
- Saskatchewan River
- North Saskatchewan River
- Battle River
- Red Deer River
- Bow River
- Qu'Appelle River
- South Saskatchewan River
- Touchwood Hills
- Little Touchwood Hills
- Big Touchwood Hills
- To Winnipeg
- Headquarters North-West Territories Council from 1883
- Headquarters North-West Territories Council 1878–1883
- Fort Qu'Appelle
- Qu'Appelle
- Regina
- Humboldt
- GEN. MIDDLETON
- St Laurent
- Batoche
- Fish Creek
- Clarke's Crossing
- Prince Albert
- Beardy
- Fort Carlton
- Battleford
- Duck Lake
- Saskatoon
- Eagle Hills
- Bear Hills
- Moose Jaw
- RAILWAY
- LT. COL. OTTER
- Swift Current
- Frenchman's Butte
- Fort Pitt
- Poundmaker
- Cut Knife Hill
- Cut Knife Creek
- Grizzly Bear & Lean Man
- Wood Crees
- Frog Lake
- Fort Saskatchewan
- Edmonton
- Red Deer
- Medicine Hat
- Maple Creek
- PACIFIC
- CANADIAN
- Calgary
- GEN. STRANGE
- Blackfoot
- Lethbridge
- Fort MacLeod
- Whoop-up
- GEN. MIDDLETON
- River

Scale: 0 50 km 100 km

(1825–98), commander of the Canadian militia, and his troops were marching north to Batoche from Qu'Appelle. From Swift Current, Colonel William Dillon Otter (1843–1929) headed for Battleford on 13 April, and from Calgary, Major-General Thomas Bland Strange (1831–1925) set off for Edmonton, where he arrived on 1 May.[34]

On 24 April, Middleton ran into Dumont's ambush at **Fish Creek**, South Branch's southern boundary, but the Métis fired prematurely and Middleton was saved. To the west, on 2 May, Otter attacked Pītikwahanapiwīyin's sleeping camp at Cutknife Hill. Pītikwahanapiwīyin repelled the attack but refused to let his warriors go off in pursuit, saving Otter and his men from rout. The following week, 9–12 May, Middleton and 850 men confronted entrenched Métis, about 350 strong, at Batoche. After three days, the Métis ran out of ammunition. It was the only clear defeat of the Métis during the uprising, but it was decisive. When the Canadian forces burned and looted after the battle, even Riel's opponent Father André made an indignant protest.[35]

Riel surrendered on 15 May, Pītikwahanapiwīyin on 26 May. On 2 July, Mistahimaskwa and his youngest son, Pimee, walked into Fort Carlton to surrender to a startled sentry. The rebellion's toll: 53 non-Indigenous people killed and 118 wounded, and about 35 Cree and Métis people killed. Less than 5 per cent of the Indigenous population of the Northwest had been involved.[36]

Immediate Consequences

During the revolt, the residents of Wolseley, Manitoba, passed a motion to send to Ottawa:

> It is now time for the Government to take decisive action, and that their first shall be that orders be issued to hang Riel to the first tree when he is caught; but, if there must be delay, that it shall only be long enough to capture Dewdney and hang the two together.[37]

The government, however, turned its anger not against its own representatives but against those who had protested the treatment they had received. The government charged or considered charging more than 200 individuals, most for treason-felony against an empire that had conscripted First Nations and Métis into its orbit without consulting them and, in the case of the First Nations, without granting them citizenship. In the end, 84 trials were held, 71 of which were for treason-felony, 12 for murder, and one (Riel's) for high treason.

Of the 19 Métis convicted, Riel was charged with treason; he was hanged on 16 November 1885.[38] Most of the other Métis prisoners were convicted on the lesser charge of treason-felony. Eleven were sentenced to seven years, three to three years, and four to one year each. Most of the captured and accused First Nations individuals (all Cree except for two Nakoda) were charged with treason-felony, but some were tried for murder as well as other offences. Eleven were sentenced to hang. Three later had their sentences commuted to life imprisonment. The other eight were hanged together at North Battleford on 17 November, one of the two largest mass hangings in Canada's history.[39] Prison sentences ranged up to 20 years for manslaughter and 14 for arson.

Prison terms were virtual death sentences. Mistahimaskwa, Pītikwahanapiwīyin, and Kāpeyakwāskonam all had to be released before their three-year terms were up and died within the year. Mistahimaskwa pleaded for amnesty for his band. Many were hiding in the woods, and winter was setting in. (Some of Mistahimaskwa's followers went to Onion Lake, where they were fed at government expense until relocated on a new reserve in 1887.) Mistahimaskwa served a year and a half of his sentence before his health broke. Eventually, all of the Indigenous Peoples convicted of treason-felony were pardoned before their sentences were up. Pītikwahanapiwīyin was at least spared one indignity as a prisoner. Through the intercession of his adoptive father, Isapo-Muxika, his hair was not cut. Pītikwahanapiwīyin, true to his conciliatory yet unbending nature, made an eloquent speech at the trial following his surrender after the Northwest Rebellion. It is worth quoting:

> The bad things they have said against me here are not true. I have worked only at trying to keep the peace. This spring, when my Indians, the halfbreeds and the white men fought, I prevented further killing. As soon as I heard what had happened at Batoche I led my people and went to the white man and gave myself up.

Mistahimaskwa and Pītikwahanapiwīyin in detention. Mistahimwaska's hair was cut as a means of making him appear less Indigenous, and as a form of humiliation; at the request of his adoptive father, Isapo-Muxika, Pītikwahanapiwīyin was spared this indignity. Both men died shortly after their release from prison.

If I had not done so, there would have been plenty of bloodshed. For this reason I am here . . . I will not excuse myself for saving the lives of so many people even if I must suffer for it now.[40]

After the Conflict

The South Branch Métis, particularly those of St Laurent, had fought to be recognized as a colony, but with special status that would acknowledge their Aboriginal rights and distinctive lifestyle. Although they shared grievances with both First Nations and white settlers, the Métis considered themselves to be separate and distinct. Each group was fighting for itself, although they had a common enemy: a distant and uncomprehending bureaucracy. One of the ironies of the conflict was that it undid the progress made during the decade when Mistahimaskwa and other chiefs had worked for the autonomy and self-government of their people.

As for the government in Ottawa, its hostility towards those perceived by officials as inferior—because they were "others," strangers—has been a historical constant. In 1885, Indigenous people might have been appreciated on their own merits in philosophical or artistic circles, but in the political arena they were expected to conform to the dominant power. For the Métis, such attitudes reduced and even ignored the role in which they could have excelled, as mediators between the First Nations and the newcomers. Lord Dufferin, who had been governor general from 1872 to 1878, was one of the few who appreciated this. He attributed Canada's comparative rarity of frontier wars to the influence of the Métis.[41]

Controversy over the personality of Riel and, above all, over the roles of the government and the Métis in the confrontation is still very much alive among Canadian scholars. Riel's declaration of rights, labelled revolutionary at the time, seems mild today: he was asking for more liberal treatment for First Nations and newcomers as well as for the Métis. More heated is the argument over whether the government provoked the uprising to solve its problems in constructing the transcontinental railway. Thomas Flanagan asserted that "Métis grievances were at least partly of their own making" and that "the government was on the verge of resolving them when the Rebellion broke out."[42] On the other hand, Doug Sprague stated that the uprising "was not the result of some tragic misunderstanding, but of the government's manipulation of the Manitoba Métis since 1869" for political reasons.[43] The jury is still out. What there is no doubt about is that the defeat at Batoche ended for half a century the Métis struggle for recognition as a people.[44] And it would be a century before that struggle regained a momentum close to that of the days of Riel.[45]

In practical terms, land transfers were made more flexible, and registration of deeds simplified. The North-West Territories gained representation in the House of Commons, with Assiniboia getting two members and the regions that would become Saskatchewan and Alberta one each. In 1887, the Territories got two members in the Senate. This was no mere recognition of the rights of the people living there to representation. The government of Canada had, in fact, set as its goal the destruction of traditional forms of government as well as the division of First Nations communities, and the machinery needed to accomplish this was already in place.

Questions to Consider

1. What were the immediate effects of the disappearance of the bison?
2. What did the transfer of land from the HBC to Canada mean for the people of the Northwest?
3. What were Louis Riel's hopes for the region?
4. What were the consequences of the Battle of Batoche?

Recommended Readings

Bumsted, J.M. *Louis Riel vs. Canada: The Making of a Rebel.* Winnipeg: Great Plains Publications, 2001.

Carter, Sarah A. *Lost Harvests: Prairie Indian Reserve Farmers and Government Policy.* Montreal and Kingston: McGill–Queen's University Press, 1990.

Dempsey, Hugh A. *Big Bear: The End of Freedom.* Vancouver: Douglas & McIntyre, 1984.

Flanagan, Thomas. *Riel and the Rebellion.* Saskatoon: Western Producer Prairie Books, 1983.

Lytwyn, Victor. *Muskekowuck Athinunuwick: Original People of the Great Swampy Land.* Winnipeg: University of Manitoba Press, 2002.

The Northwest Resistance Digitization Project: A Database of Materials held by the University of Saskatchewan Libraries and the University Archives, http://library.usask.ca/northwest/contents.html.

Payment, Diane. *Batoche (1870–1970).* St Boniface, Man.: Editions du Blé, 1983.

Reid, Jennifer. *Louis Riel and the Creation of Modern Canada: Mythic Discourse and the Post-Colonial State.* Winnipeg: University of Winnipeg Press, 2012.

Siggins, Maggie. *Riel: A Life of Revolution.* Toronto: HarperCollins, 1994.

Sluman, Norma. *Poundmaker.* Toronto: Ryerson Press, 1967.

Woodcock, George. *Gabriel Dumont.* Edmonton: Hurtig, 1975.

14 Repression and Resistance

CHAPTER OUTLINE

The resistance of the 1870s and 1880s had serious and terrible consequences for the First Nations and Métis of western Canada. Two issues
became increasingly prominent. The first was the ongoing loss of land and
resources to the new immigrants and the second was the concerted effort to
force assimilation through residential education. These processes caused
terrible pain across the country but they also led to other, more sophisticated forms of resistance. Indigenous soldiers won great respect for their
impressive participation in the First World War and the momentum gained in
that conflict carried over to the formation of the League of Indians of Canada
in 1919, an important step towards national political organization.

LEARNING OUTCOMES

1. Students will learn about the aftermath of the resistance of the 1880s.

2. Students will gain insight into the kinds of interference perpetrated by
   the Department of Indian Affairs.

3. Students will understand the different motivations of those who supported the establishment of residential schools.

4. Students will become aware of the negligent treatment of Indigenous
   veterans after the First World War.

TIMELINE The Growth of Organized Resistance, from 1890 to the 1958 Indian Act Revisions

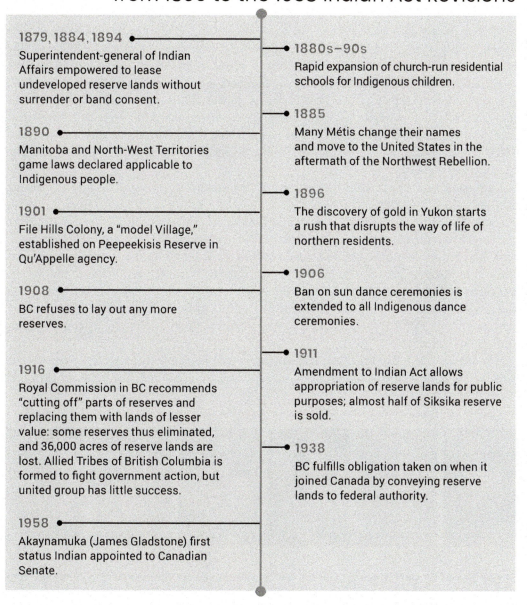

1879, 1884, 1894
Superintendent-general of Indian Affairs empowered to lease undeveloped reserve lands without surrender or band consent.

1880s–90s
Rapid expansion of church-run residential schools for Indigenous children.

1885
Many Métis change their names and move to the United States in the aftermath of the Northwest Rebellion.

1890
Manitoba and North-West Territories game laws declared applicable to Indigenous people.

1896
The discovery of gold in Yukon starts a rush that disrupts the way of life of northern residents.

1901
File Hills Colony, a "model Village," established on Peepeekisis Reserve in Qu'Appelle agency.

1906
Ban on sun dance ceremonies is extended to all Indigenous dance ceremonies.

1908
BC refuses to lay out any more reserves.

1911
Amendment to Indian Act allows appropriation of reserve lands for public purposes; almost half of Siksika reserve is sold.

1916
Royal Commission in BC recommends "cutting off" parts of reserves and replacing them with lands of lesser value: some reserves thus eliminated, and 36,000 acres of reserve lands are lost. Allied Tribes of British Columbia is formed to fight government action, but united group has little success.

1938
BC fulfills obligation taken on when it joined Canada by conveying reserve lands to federal authority.

1958
Akaynamuka (James Gladstone) first status Indian appointed to Canadian Senate.

More Consequences for the Cree . . .

Mistahimaskwa and Pītikwahanapiwīyin were in prison, and Minahikosis was dead. Deprived of their leadership, the Cree now found even their remaining chiefs under attack. The government in Ottawa wanted all those who had not given unwavering support to the government to be deposed. Others could stay in office until their deaths, but they would not be replaced. The goal was the destruction of Indigenous forms of government and the splitting of Indigenous communities. The government increased the numbers of Indian agents and strengthened the North West Mounted Police (NWMP). Cree horses, guns, and carts were impounded, and annuities of those who were implicated in the uprising were discontinued for five years.[1] The government also introduced a **pass system** to keep western First Nations people on their reserves (and Métis people off of them). The argument was that the rebels had violated their treaty rights and thus had lost them.[2]

Ten years later, the NWMP was reporting that Indigenous Peoples "found wandering aimlessly about the prairie have been induced to return to their respective reserves."[3] What amounted to hysteria among cattlemen and settlers contributed to the repression. In 1906, the ban on certain sun dance practices was extended to include all types of Indigenous dancing. The dances continued anyway, but in hiding. Restrictions on the movements and customs of Indigenous people remained until well into the twentieth century, and not just on the prairies. In Dawson, Yukon, Indigenous people were also subjected to a curfew. By 1923, those who wished to move to a city needed a permit. Although the measures were illegal, the government justified them as necessary to protect the Indigenous people from evil non-Indigenous influences.[4]

For the decade following 1885, Indigenous people accepted these growing repressions without violence. When it did erupt, it was on the part of individuals. Between 1895 and

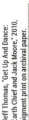

Jeff Thomas, "Get Up And Dance: Earth Chief and Jack Moore," 2010, pigment print on archival paper.

Get Up And Dance

***Strong Hearts* by Jeff Thomas (photos by Jeff Thomas and Edward Curtis).** Thomas, who self-identifies as an urban Iroquois, writes: "When I saw my first powwow in the mid-1970s I was struck by the powerful sense of self the dancers exhibited on the powwow grounds. I also saw a link to the images made in the early twentieth century by Edward S. Curtis but, unlike the Curtis subjects, which are usually photographed against a plain backdrop and seem frozen in time, I was interested in pulling back the curtain to show the background activities that led up to the dance. I was determined to find social meaning beyond the tourist-like veneer of the event."

1897, for example, a member of the Káínaawa, Si'k-okskitsis ("Charcoal" or, literally, "Black Wood Ashes," 1856–97), and a Cree called Kahkeesaymanetoowayo ("Almighty Voice" or "Voice of the Great Spirit," grandson of Kāpeyakwāskonam ["One Arrow"], 1874–97), killed five policemen. The death toll was the result of the police trying to track them down, in separate pursuits.[5]

In 1896, a group of Tsuu T'ina defied police attempts to get them to leave Calgary, and the police were becoming steadily more uncomfortable with the task of restricting movements. As early as 1893, a police commissioner issued a circular warning about sending First Nations people back to their reserves without legal justification. However, some Indian agents continued to enforce the pass system—described as selectively applied tyranny—until the mid-1940s.[6]

. . . and for the Métis

After the 1885 Rebellion, many Métis, fearing identification as such, changed their names. Others fled to the US, particularly Montana, where they became known as "Canadian Cree." Some joined the Cree under Mistahimaskwa's son Ayimisis, who had also fled south, and were admitted to reserves. Still others fled north, particularly to the Mackenzie River area.

For those who remained in Canada, land title continued to be a tortured question. The government dealt with Métis land claims—without consultation—by Orders-in-Council. Where First Nations gained special status through the treaties that extinguished their Aboriginal rights, the Métis did not see long-term benefits with the settlement of their claims. Of the 566,560 ha set aside in Manitoba for the Métis, only 242,811 had been distributed to them by 1882.[7]

The Manitoba Act of 1870 had acknowledged Métis entitlement to land but provided for the extinguishment of that title through grants of reserved land. In 1874, Ottawa introduced **scrip**, a substitute for legal tender, which provided for either a specified amount of land or its equivalent in cash. The great majority of the Métis agreed to scrip, as many lived in regions that were marginal for agriculture.[8] For them, it seemed better to sell their scrip, often for very little. There are records of scrip sold to speculators for as little as half its face value. Fortunes were made by land speculators at the expense of the Métis, called "half-breed scrip millionaires" at the time.[9]

The Métis also faced a dilemma. If they took treaty—and those who lived near Indigenous communities sometimes had the option of being included in a treaty—they became legally First Nations, and many felt that they were a separate people.[10] If they took scrip, they moved into the non-First Nations camp. Culturally, the line between the two classifications was far from clear-cut, but the legal distinction was enormous. For one obvious point, responsibility for status Indians was (and is) solely that of the federal authority. The Métis, on the other hand, even though they finally were recognized as an Indigenous people in the Constitution Act, 1982, had to wait till the *Daniels* decision of the Supreme Court of Canada in April of 2016 to receive the same rights as status Indians. This unanimous decision ruled that the federal government has the same responsibility to Métis and non-status Indians as it does to status Indians and Inuit.[11]

The troubles of 1885 galvanized Ottawa into action on Métis land claims. Four days after the encounter at Duck Lake, on 30 March, the government empowered the first of a series of commissions to extinguish Métis land claims. A few weeks later, Métis operating river lots of 40 acres (16 ha) were allowed to buy that land at a dollar an acre, then select 160 acres (65 ha) for a homestead.

Treaty Nine (1905–6) did not include Métis, but Treaties Ten (1906) and Eleven (1921) did. In the case of Treaty Eleven, the Métis of the Mackenzie River District each received $240 in cash because of the lack of suitable farmland.[12] The government instructed the land claims commissions to encourage Métis who had taken treaty and who were living on reserves to withdraw and take scrip. Many did, at least partly because of difficult conditions on reserves, where people were living on the meagre amounts distributed by the government.

The Growing Power of the Department of Indian Affairs

The Klondike gold strike of 1896 catapulted northern Indigenous Peoples to centre stage. The confrontations of the Fraser gold rush repeated themselves, as fortune hunters flooded into Yukon, intent on their personal quests and without regard for the rights of the local people. As the government hurriedly prepared to negotiate Treaty Eight, a question arose: should the Métis be included with First Nations? Most Métis were against the suggestion, so the government established two commissions, one to negotiate treaty with the First Nations, the other to work out scrip for the Métis.[13] Still intent on encouraging as many as possible to enter treaty, the government first negotiated the treaty. It took two years to hammer out terms with Cree, Denésoliné, Dene Dháa, Sekani, and others.[14] For the Métis, the offer was for $240 in cash or 240 acres (97 ha) of land.

When it came to issuing scrip, officials once again tried not to make it payable to the bearer, but speculators who had come expecting to make a killing refused to accept such scrip. The Métis then also refused to accept it and threatened to influence First Nations against taking treaty. Officials knuckled under and offered scrip payable on demand. Similarly, when officials tried to postdate scrip issued to children until their age of maturity, parents insisted that it be payable immediately. The first $240 scrip was sold for $75, and soon the price dropped even lower.

During the summer of 1899, the commission issued 1,195 money scrips worth $286,000 and 48 land scrips for 11,500 acres (6,070 ha), about half of them at Lesser Slave Lake and others at Fort Vermilion, Fort Chipewyan, and Peace River Crossing.[15] Only a fraction of the benefits went to the Métis. In 1900, two new commissions dealt with the Métis of Saskatchewan and those parts of Manitoba that had not been included in its original boundaries.

After the 1885 confrontations, the Department of Indian Affairs assumed more and more control over the lives of Indigenous Peoples. Soon, they would not have a free hand even in such personal matters as writing a will or, in the West, selling their own grain or root crops.[16] At the same time, agents' power grew and became more arbitrary. Eventually, they directed farming operations, administered relief in times of need, inspected schools and health conditions on reserves, enforced department rules and provisions, and presided over band council meetings. In effect, they directed the political life of the band. Agents did not vote at those meetings, but they could, and did, influence proceedings.

The main problems facing Indigenous people were a continuation of old ones. The biggest problem remained the ongoing, unauthorized use of reserve lands and resources such as fish, game, minerals, timber, and non-timber forest products. In 1890, furthermore, Manitoba and the North-West Territories declared their game laws applicable to Indigenous Peoples. By doing this, they were ignoring the treaties that guaranteed hunting and fishing rights on Crown lands, which led to a series of court cases. While Indigenous people fought the erosion of their land and sovereignty, however, the government policy continued steadfast in its push towards assimilation, which found its focus in the West, as it had further east, in education.

Assimilation through Education

Indigenous leaders had asked for schools on their reserves during treaty negotiations. Many saw them as a means of preparing their children for the new way of life that lay ahead. The final draft of Treaty One had contained a promise that the government would "maintain a school on each reserve hereby made, whenever the Indians of the reserve should desire it."[17] What they foresaw was a partnership with the newcomers as they worked out their own adaptations.[18] Officials and their supporters, however, saw another purpose for schools: assimilation. When the government in 1879 commissioned Nicholas Flood Davin, a lawyer and journalist who would later become the first MP for Assiniboia West, to recommend a course of action for western Indigenous education, administrators advised him not to use the schools in the East as a model.[19]

Eastern Schools—"Little or No Good"

The government had already started schooling in the Canadas—day and boarding schools—within a couple of decades of the War of 1812. As with their western counterparts later on, Indigenous leaders also took initiative towards education. Chief Shawahnahness (*fl.* 1833) of the St Clair River Ojibwa wanted his children to learn to read and write so that white traders would not be able to cheat them. Chief Shingwaukonse ("Little Pine") was so convinced of the importance of a school, or "teaching wigwam" as he called it, at Garden River that he postponed harvesting to go fundraising in southern Ontario. Prominent converts like Kahgegagahgowh (George Copway 1818–69) and the Reverends Shahwundais (John Sunday, 1795–1875), Sowengisik,

(Henry Bird Steinhauer, 1818–69), and Kahkewaquonaby (Peter Jones, 1802–56) also were active in promoting education within their communities.[20]

When Kahkewaquonaby toured England in the 1830s and 1840s to raise money, he promoted the idea of schools run by Indigenous people that would produce "men and women able to compete with the White people, able to defend their rights in English, under English law."[21] In 1846, Ojibwa Chief John Aisance from Beausoleil Island, who had fought with the British during the War of 1812, asked Captain Thomas G. Anderson, a former fur trader and veteran of the same war, for a local school during treaty negotiations, but noted that his band had moved "four times, and I am too old to remove again."[22] At this meeting, Anderson expressed the expectation that First Nations would be running their own schools within 25 years, and the chiefs pledged a fourth of their annuities to cover the cost of education during that time period.[23] Within a decade, many would believe that the First Nations were not getting their money's worth. In setting up schools, the government turned to those who had experience and independent sources of income, and could muster people willing to work in remote areas for low pay: the churches.

Like the government, mission-minded churches had not been idle. New France, after all, had made abortive attempts at boarding schools as part of its assimilation policy. In 1787, the **New England Company**, a non-sectarian Protestant organization, founded several schools, including an "Indian college" at Sussex Vale, New Brunswick. Its original aim was to teach useful trades to Mi'kmaw children through apprenticeship, but instead, the children ended up as a cheap source of labour for local farms and businesses. By 1826, the Rev. John West (d. 1845), who worked for both the Anglican Christian Missionary Society and

Hill & Adamson. Rev. Peter Jones (b). PGP HA 420. Courtesy of the National Galleries of Scotland

Kahkewaquonaby (the Rev. Peter Jones) travelled to Britain in 1845 to raise funds for Ojibwa schools. He had hoped for schools run by Indigenous people that would help them defend their rights. That's not what he got. This photograph, possibly the earliest studio camera study of an Indigenous man from what is now Canada, was taken in Edinburgh.

the Hudson's Bay Company, was able to say, "little or no good has accrued to the Natives from the Establishment at Sussex Vale."[24]

Undaunted, the New England Company blamed the Mi'kmaq, claiming that a more "advanced" group would do better. To prove its point, it moved its operation to the Six Nations reserve at Grand River and several other nearby communities, such as the Bay of Quinte (Grape Island, later Alderville) and Garden River, where the New England Company financed existing Anglican and Methodist stations (see Chapter 10).[25]

A network of schools was already in place, then, when colonial governments were ready to address the education issue.[26] The advantages of a partnership with the missionaries, who could raise funds independently and provided the labour, were obvious. The administration favoured **residential schools** over **day schools**, as it believed they speeded the process of assimilation.[27] There were two types of residential schools. Boarding schools were usually located on reserves and catered to students between the ages of eight and 14 years. Industrial schools, off reserves, had more elaborate programs and took in students until the age of 18. Curricula combined basic subjects with a half-day of "practical" training. For boys, this involved agriculture, crafts, and some trades, and for girls, the domestic arts.

A school for Haudenosaunee children from the Six Nations reserve had existed for some time near Brantford, not far from the Grand River reserve, amid opposition mainly from among the 20 per cent of reserve residents who followed the **Longhouse religion** of Onondowaga chief Ganiodaio (Shanyadariyoh, "Handsome Lake," d. 1815), which combined elements of the Christian religion and the traditional Haudenosaunee belief system.[28] By 1829, it had become a "mechanic's institution," known as the Mohawk Institute. More successful in attracting children than many of the other schools, by 1867 the Mohawk Institute had 90 students. In 1869, it would hire its first Indigenous teacher, Isaac Barefoot, and send five of its students to Helmuth College in Brantford for further education.[29] This success would not last.

From the beginning, many reserve parents refused to send their children away to school, and most of the students who enrolled were either orphans or from destitute families, whose needs were great. As time went on, funding dropped, and in 1898 the New England Company withdrew all support from the Mohawk Institute. As conditions deteriorated, parental resistance increased, prompting Hayter Reed, superintendent-general of Indian Affairs, to blame the problems on the fact that the children were spending too much time on academic work and were being allowed to go home for vacations. A later school administrator overworked the children in an attempt to save money. **Frederick Ogilvie Loft**, founder of the League of Indians of Canada, said of his time at the Institute, "I recall the times when working in the fields, I was actually too hungry to be able to walk, let alone work."[30]

Rebellion against the schools took many forms. On 19 April 1903, Institute residents set fire to the main building. Later, they burned barns and the playhouse. The government rebuilt the school, and Haudenosaunee leaders responded by creating the Indians' Rights Association, which succeeded in getting public curriculum taught in reserve day schools.[31] In 1913, a father sued the Mohawk Institute over the treatment his daughter had received at the hands of the principal. He won only a partial victory in court, but the principal was later fired. Other New England Company schools fared even worse.[32]

Any improvements to physical and sanitary conditions at the schools, however, were inadequate towards helping them gain acceptance in Indigenous communities. Separation from family was a major issue; "outing"—the practice of hiring students out as servants or manual labourers, with the schools collecting pay—was another; curriculum, yet another. Although students in industrial schools were supposed to spend a half-day at schooling and a half-day learning a useful trade, lack of funding meant that residents spent most of their time at manual labour. As well, to keep numbers—and grants—up, schools often admitted children who were too young to learn a trade.[33]

All of this Davin dutifully ignored, and he consulted with no Indigenous people before completing his report. The administration had seen potential for industrial schools in Ontario because, in their view, the Indigenous population was "advanced" enough to benefit from

The Scream (2017), Kent Monkman. 84" x 126", Acrylic on canvas.
Reproduced with permission of artist.

***The Scream* by Kent Monkman (b. 1965)**, a widely known and controversial First Nations artist of Cree and Irish ancestry. Monkman says: "History is a narrative; it's a collection of stories sanctioned by the ruling power, and reinforced through words and images that suit them. That was the whole point of taking on history painting: to authorize these moments that have been swept under the rug for generations."

them. In 1879, Davin recommended the same structure as beneficial to the "warlike" peoples in the West.[34]

Industrial Schools in Western Canada

Despite the lack of success already seen in the East, the government in Ottawa quickly decided it would be more economical to develop the already existing schools run by the churches than it would be to create its own system, an arrangement that would last until 1969. Although education was a provincial responsibility under the BNA Act, Indigenous Peoples came under federal authority. The treaties, furthermore, committed the federal government to providing and maintaining schools and teachers on reserves. In practice, this meant that most Indigenous children were to be educated in schools run by the department.

An 1883 Order-in-Council marked the beginning of the first three industrial schools to open on the prairies: at Battleford and Qu'Appelle in the North-West, and at High River in the southern portion of what would become Alberta. The money came from the existing Indian Affairs budget, which reduced the amount available for relief—at a time when hunger was widespread on the prairies. Before the turn of the century, seven more schools would open, repeating the same story that had been told in the East.

Almost from the start, the school at Battleford was plagued by lack of funding, truancy, and low staff morale. As local parents refused to send their children, the Department of Indian Affairs recommended that the school start with "orphans and children who have no natural protectors."[35] When the Northwest Rebellion broke out, the students were scattered. By the late 1880s, opposition to the school had grown to the point where its viability was being questioned. Dunbow School at High River, which Oblate Father Albert Lacombe (1827–1916) left in 1885 after a brief and unsuccessful tenure, did not fare much better.[36]

Qu'Appelle's viability was least questioned of the initial three, in part because of its distance from the Rebellion and in part because of the tireless efforts of its first principal, Father Joseph Hugonnard (1848–1917), to wrest funding from the government.[37] Even so, throughout the lifespan of the industrial schools, Indigenous parents criticized them and resisted sending their children. At a meeting on the Muskowpetung reserve in northern Saskatchewan early in the twentieth century, parents protested the secrecy surrounding sickness at the Regina school, its use of pupils as labourers, and the breakup of home circles.[38] The children resisted by running away, stealing—often food—and, finally, committing arson. Parents refused to send their children to the point where the government started using the pass system to prevent parents from using their time off the reserves to interfere with their children's schooling. One mother attacked Father Hugonnard with a knife to give her children time to escape into the woods.[39]

In 1910, Cree parents from the Beardy and Okemasis reserves filed a complaint against St Michael's Industrial School at Duck Lake. In particular, they protested the school's practice of

INDIGENOUS LEADERS | Frances Nickawa (1891–1927)

Resistance took many forms and some Indigenous people realized that the campaign to improve conditions across Canada required greater education and awareness of the Indigenous people themselves. One such person was Frances Nickawa of Split Lake, Manitoba. Like others in her community she was taken away to Norway House Indian Residential School. A bright and outgoing girl, she quickly caught the attention of Hannah Riley, the school's sewing teacher. Riley adopted Frances and in 1907 the two moved to Vancouver, where Riley had accepted a position in an orphanage. In Vancouver, Frances began to perform as a soloist and elocutionist in churches across the city. She gave beautiful and moving renditions of Cree stories to larger and larger audiences and soon her fame began to spread. In 1919 she went on a rail tour across western Canada to much acclaim. By 1920 she was on the road full-time, performing first across eastern Canada and then abroad in Britain and finally in Australia. Her songs and stories helped raise awareness of Indigenous people in general and of the Cree in particular. Frances Nickawa always said that she was "Cree to the core," and she helped to raise interest and awareness of her people across Canada and the British Empire.

Jennifer S.H. Brown, "Frances Nickawa: A Gifted Interpreter of the Poetry of Her Race," in Sarah Carter and Patricia McCormack, eds, *Recollecting: Lives of Women of the Canadian Northwest and Borderlands* (Edmonton: Athabasca University Press, 2010), 263–86.

"outing" students to the community. The parents argued that the school should send graduates back to their families. The Indian agent agreed, calling the practice "slavery." That same year, he reported that half the children who attended St Michael's died, usually from tuberculosis, before reaching the age of 18.[40] But the Oblates who ran the school fought the parents' petition for a day school, and St Michael's remained open.

Further west, Indigenous people had been the majority in British Columbia through much of the nineteenth century, and Governor James Douglas had more or less left them alone. By the 1870s, however, the European population was growing, and the government started encouraging missionaries to found schools. Eventually, the size of the Indigenous population, combined with furious competition among the Christian denominations, would see the creation of more industrial schools in BC than anywhere else in Canada, most run by the Roman Catholic Oblates, who already had a strong presence in the West.

Like industrial schools elsewhere, BC institutions were plagued by overcrowding and underfunding, which often led them to abandon their stated purpose: to teach young Indigenous people a trade. Methodist-run Coqualeetza (St Paul) School near Chilliwack took children out of classes to do drudge work when it was short-staffed. Most of the graduates of the Anglican-run school at Lytton ended up as unskilled farm labourers.[41]

Even so, there were success stories, often the work of exceptional individuals. The Káínaa leader Akaynamuka (James Gladstone or "Many Guns," 1887–1971, Canada's first Indigenous senator, named in 1958) remarked,

> Over the years I have been grateful for the education I received, and I have always been impressed about St Paul's mission and Calgary Industrial School. In those days, we had dedicated teachers ... even today you can tell the Indians who went to those schools before 1905. They have been the backbone of our reserves.[42]

Mike Mountain Horse, who attended Calgary Industrial School at the same time as Akaynamuka and later became prominent in the Indian League of Canada, agreed; however, most disagreed with this assessment. According to author Eleanor Brass (1905–92), who grew up in the **File Hills Colony** (see Historical Background box), a boy who was in an industrial school for 10 years spent only four in the classroom,[43] and parents who kept their children away from these schools understood that the schools were teaching more than a trade.

In 1888, the Indian agent at Alert Bay, BC, noted that parents disliked the local school because it meant "the downfall of all their most cherished customs," and the principal at Alert Bay cited the elders as the reason for low school attendance. As one historian has

HISTORICAL BACKGROUND | The File Hills Colony

The idea of model villages did not die in the nineteenth century. The File Hills Colony was established in 1901 on the Peepeekisis reserve at Indian Head in what would soon become the province of Saskatchewan. It was the special project of W.M. Graham, the resident agent. His idea was to extend the training young Indigenous people received at government schools,[44] ensuring that they would not "regress" to their Indigenous ways by returning to their own families and communities. He assigned individual lots, with a portion of the colony being left for hunting and community pasture. Some colonists were able to handle as many as six or seven lots. Others found that the farming life was not for them, and picked up and left.

Graham controlled those who stayed to the point of even having their marriage partners chosen for them. He strictly limited visits between households and banned such gatherings as powwows or dancing of any kind. (This did not mean that there were no such occasions, only that they were held secretly.) In the 1930s, however, it began to lose its younger population. Although many admired the project, the government never repeated the experiment.

noted, "Respect for other cultures was not included in the training of the nineteenth-century missionary."[45] The practice of changing students' names served to strip them of their identity, and some schools referred to students by number. A boy who attended Qu'Appelle Industrial School later recalled having his braids cut off without explanation, leaving him wondering if his mother had died because, in the Nakoda tradition, haircutting is associated with mourning.[46]

The decades of the 1880s and 1890s witnessed the rapid expansion of industrial schools. Increasing costs, however, soon gave rise to second thoughts. Industrial schools cost money that the government was unwilling to pay. Clifford Sifton, who became Minister of the Interior and superintendent-general in 1896, did not see that Indigenous people had "the physical, mental or moral get-up" to compete with non-Indigenous people on equal terms.[47] Accordingly, he considered industrial schooling for Indigenous people a waste of time and effort.

By the turn of the twentieth century, enthusiasm for industrial schools had waned. Rising costs and poor administration, including charges of abuse to students, led to a gradual phasing out of the program. As early as 1897, the government had admitted that there was little practical difference between boarding and industrial schools, except that the latter received more government money per capita. Over the next few decades, it would accept that the industrial schools were not bringing about the hoped-for quick assimilation, and one by one they were closed or converted to boarding schools. By 1923, there was one type of boarding facility acknowledged under the general name "residential school."

The Right to Choose a Chief

As the nineteenth century drew to a close, confrontations continued over the imposition of the elective form of government[48] and strong Indigenous resistance made it impractical to insist on annual elections. The Cowessess band illustrates the struggles that arose. At its own request, the band went on the three-year elective system in 1887. However, Hayter Reed, the agent from 1881 to 1893, did not approve of the chief elected a few years later, who was an advocate of traditional ways.[49] In 1894, Reed, now deputy superintendent-general of Indian Affairs, denied the band the right to hold another election. In the end, the Cree persistence won out, and the Cowessess band finally held its elections.[50]

As time went on, resistance against government by imposition grew. Bands refused to exercise their police and public health powers, or to spend band funds for those purposes. In response, the department gave the superintendent-general the power to carry out these functions using band funds. The government let some bands, mainly in the Prairie provinces, continue choosing their chiefs by their traditional methods. The department, in approving the chiefs so selected, saw them as appointees. By 1900, there were four systems of band government: three-year elective (Indian Act), one-year elective (Advancement Act), hereditary (Yukon, NWT, and in varying numbers in the provinces), and appointed.[51]

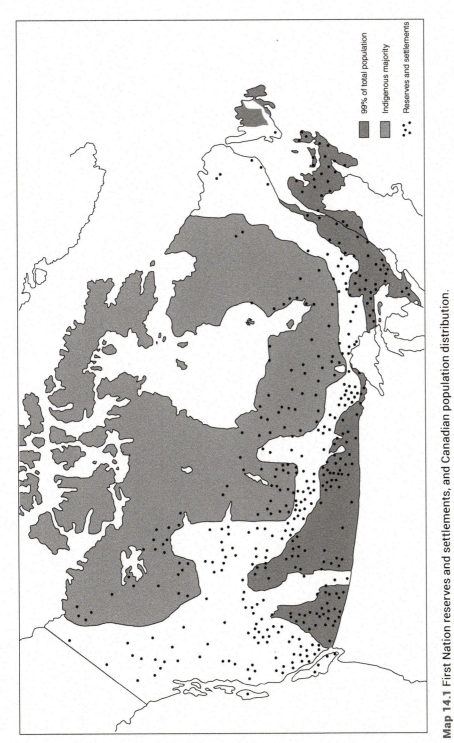

Map 14.1 First Nation reserves and settlements, and Canadian population distribution.

Report of the Royal Commission on Aboriginal Peoples, 2, part 2: 450; adapted from Russel Lawrence Barsh, "Canada's Aboriginal Peoples: Social Integration or Disintegration?" Canadian Journal of Native Studies 14, 1 (1994), and used with the permission of Brandon University, Brandon, Manitoba.

Legend:
- 99% of total population
- Indigenous majority
- Reserves and settlements

The Battle over Reserved Lands

As the government reserved lands for First Nations, it also made provisions for the surrender of these lands by lease or sale. In theory, reserve lands could be surrendered only by a majority of male reserve residents over the age of 21 at a meeting specially called for the purpose. When band councils resisted the leasing of lands even for a limited period, the government handed the power to allot reserve lands without band consent to the superintendent-general (1879, 1884, 1894).[52]

Band councils continued to fight the imposed regulations. The administration responded in 1898 by granting the superintendent-general overriding powers. Soon, the government gave itself the power to remove First Nations from any reserves next to or partly within a town of 8,000 inhabitants or more. In effect, this abolished the St Clair Ojibwa reserve at Sarnia, Ontario, and the Songhees reserve at Victoria, BC.

The policy of establishing reserves near towns was abandoned. Land was now so valuable that the policy took second place. Instead, more comments were being heard about removing First Nations to remote areas as settlers flooded in. Their increasing demands, along with those of developers and railway companies, influenced Indian Affairs to decide that many of the reserves were too large for the number of people living on them—and their populations were declining. Reserve lands beyond immediate requirements came to be regarded as "surplus" and thus open to negotiations for surrender to the Crown. Those in favour of this claimed the sales were providing First Nations with cash to get started in their new lives as farmers or ranchers. An amendment to the Indian Act in 1911 empowered municipalities or companies to expropriate Indigenous land for roads, railways, or other public purposes, with up to half of the proceeds to be paid directly to band members.[53]

In Ontario, such deals had taken off after the War of 1812, when the Crown gained some 2.8 million ha of Indigenous lands.[54] As the tide of immigration moved westward, the Prairie provinces became the major scene for such activity. The period between 1896 and 1911 saw 21 per cent—more than one-fifth—of reserve lands on the prairies thus surrendered.[55] In 1910–11, almost half of the Siksika reserve in Alberta was sold for more than a million dollars. In spite of the cash inducement, however, First Nations were seldom either eager or unanimous about surrendering. Far more often, they accepted deals only reluctantly and after persuasion. And matters did not stop there.

Commissions and Expropriations

The surrender initiative did not yield the expected benefits for the Indigenous Peoples, however, and resistance grew. The St Peter's band in Manitoba and Piikani leaders in Alberta publicly called for the overturn of surrenders but were unsuccessful. Clifford Sifton, superintendent-general of Indian Affairs, 1896–1905, said that the consent of the First Nations concerned was necessary but did little to ensure that this happened.[56] The result was that surrenders were eventually phased out in favour of leases.

In British Columbia, the continuing deadlock between the province and Ottawa over Indigenous lands gave rise to the Joint Commission for the Settlement of Indian Reserves in the Province of British Columbia to investigate and act on the problem. This it did, off and on, from 1876 to 1910.[57] Other initiatives included a Squamish delegation to Edward VII in London (1906), a petition to the Canadian government (1909),[58] another petition, which elicited Prime Minister Sir Wilfrid Laurier's promise of help (1910),[59] a Royal Commission (1913–16),[60] and a petition by the Nisga'a to the Judicial Committee of the Privy Council in London (1913). The action of the Nisga'a had been spurred by BC's adamant refusal to discuss Aboriginal rights or to allow the Royal Commission to consider the issue. In 1908, the province had refused to lay out any more reserves.[61] The Privy Council said it could consider petitions only if they came from the courts of Canada.

The Royal Commission of 1916 recommended the "cutting off" of specified reserve lands[62] and their substitution with larger areas of lesser value, costing the First Nations 36,000 acres (14,569 ha) of more valuable land and eliminating entire reserves.[63] This led to an increase in the sizes of reserves—if not their land value—but the First Nations bitterly opposed the cut-offs.[64] They refused to appear before the Commission, and in 1916 they organized into the **Allied Tribes of British Columbia** to fight the Commission's recommendations and to assert Aboriginal right.

In spite of the spirited resistance of Allied Tribes leaders, including Squamish chief Andrew Paull (1892–1959) and Haida Rev. Peter Kelly (1885–1966), BC approved the Commission's report in 1923. Ottawa followed a year later.[65] In 1926, the Allied Tribes carried their petition to the Privy Council in London but were intercepted by the Canadian High Commissioner, who promised to deliver the documents on their behalf, but he did not. The following year, a Special Joint Committee of the Senate and House of Commons issued a "final settlement" in which it held that BC's First Nations had "not established any claim to the lands of British Columbia based on Aboriginal or other title."[66] The committee recommended that the First Nations be granted $100,000 a year as compensation for the lack of treaty rights but opposed letting BC First Nations use the courts to settle claims. Three days before hearings began to entertain the grievances of the Allied Tribes, the government strengthened the existing prohibitions against using band funds for land claim actions without departmental approval; now, outside fundraising was also banned, a measure that remained in law until 1951.[67]

Soon after, the Allied Tribes collapsed, but by 1931 Paull had organized the Native Brotherhood of British Columbia, which later became the North American Indian Brotherhood (NAIB). Finally, in 1938—67 years late—British Columbia fulfilled the terms of its Act of Union by transferring 592,297 acres (239,694 ha) to the federal authority.

The First World War and New Pressures on Land

The First World War (1914–18) had seen a renewed wave of pressures on Indigenous lands. Once more, the government had amended the Indian Act so that it could take or lease reserve lands for agricultural production without band permission—financing the projects out of band funds.

To add even more insult to injury, the Indigenous Peoples in question were at the bottom of the priority list for using the equipment bought for the projects. The Káínaa of southern Alberta led the protests, but without result.[68]

Indigenous Peoples across the land contributed in many ways to the war effort. The Káínaa raised substantial amounts for the Red Cross despite poverty on the reserves.[69] About 4,000 Indigenous soldiers served in the armed forces. As veterans, however, Indigenous soldiers soon discovered they were not getting the same benefits as other veterans. In the words of one official: "These returned Indian soldiers are subject to the provisions of the Indian Act and are in the same position as they were before enlisting."[70] Despite some improvements, the equal treatment they received in the armed forces (including the right to vote) would not extend into civilian life, and the meagre benefits that veterans received—land settlements and agricultural loans—were meaningless to Indigenous veterans.[71]

Overseas, there was no pass system to prevent Indigenous troops from different parts of Canada from meeting one another, comparing experiences, and discussing shared problems. Chief Frederick Ogilivie Loft, a Kanienkehaka officer in the Forestry Corps, was so moved by what he heard from fellow soldiers that, on his own initiative, he met with the Privy Council in London to find out what it could do. They told him they could not respond to the petition of an individual but advised him to go back home and build an organization that could speak on behalf of Indigenous Peoples.[72] He founded the **League of Indians**.[73] In November of 1919, Chief Loft wrote to chiefs and band councils across Canada to urge them to join the League of Indians of Canada. In his letter of invitation, he provided details of the need, noted the opportunity afforded by the military service of so many Indigenous soldiers, and also enclosed the Constitution of the League adopted at Sault Ste Marie at the First Congress of 2–4 September 1919. His letter recalls earlier attempts to benefit from unity and strength in numbers:

> We as Indians from one end of the Dominion to the other are sadly strangers to each other; we have not learned what it is to co-operate and work for each other as we should; the pity of it is greater because our needs, drawbacks, handicaps and troubles are all similar. It is for us to do something to get out of these sad conditions. The day is past when one band or a few bands can successfully—if at all—free themselves from the domination of officialdom and from being ever the prey and victims of unscrupulous means of depriving us of our lands and homes, and even deny us the rights we are entitled to as free men under the British Flag.
>
> As peaceable and law-abiding citizens in the past, and even in the late war, we have performed dutiful service to our King, Country and Empire, and we have the right to claim and demand more justice and fair play as a recompense for we, too, have fought for the sacred rights of justice, freedom and liberty so dear to mankind, no matter what their colour or creed.
>
> The first aim of the League then is to claim and protect the rights of all Indians in Canada by legitimate and just means; second absolute control in retaining possession or disposition of our lands; that all questions and matters relative to individual and national well-being of Indians shall rest with the people and their dealing with

the government shall be by and through their respective Band Councils at all times to be consulted, and their wishes respected in like manner as other constituted bodies conducting public affairs.[74]

His proposals included giving Indigenous people the vote without losing their special status, allowing them greater control over band funds and properties, and improving the standards of education for Indigenous children. His efforts led to police surveillance and his being branded by Indian Affairs officials as an agitator.

By the 1920s, League leadership was predominantly western. Miistatosomitai (Mike Mountain Horse) and Ed Ahenakew were moderates, but later leaders were more radical.[75] The League lobbied against the pass system, petitioned for additional programs, and asserted an Aboriginal right to hold thirst dances. By the 1930s, better schooling and assistance for Indigenous farmers had been added to its list of demands. Aid to farmers was a long-standing issue. The Indian Commissioner for the Northwest Territories (now Manitoba), Hayter Reed, had been a proponent of the "peasant farmer" policy, whereby Indigenous people who took up farming would have to sow and harvest by hand. He went so far as to prevent Indigenous farmers from using modern equipment. This kept Indigenous farms in a "state of underdevelopment," according to his biographer.[76] As early as 1893, the Pasquah and Muscowpetung bands had petitioned the House of Commons to correct this inequity.[77]

Eventually, the League succumbed to pressure from without and within, and inside the organization the diverse and sometimes divergent agendas of status versus non-status Indians and Métis, and of radicals versus moderates, strained relations. By the 1940s, Loft, in his seventies and in failing health, was unable to hold the League together, and it faded from the political scene. But the need for a pan-Indian organization was recognized.

Questions to Consider

1. Why did Indigenous leaders Kahgegagahgowh, Shingwaukonse, and Kahkewaquonaby request education?
2. What did those who supported the Longhouse religion hope to achieve?
3. By whom were residential schools favoured over day schools? Why?
4. What were the findings of the 1916 Royal Commission?

Recommended Readings

Brass, Eleanor. *I Walk in Two Worlds*. Calgary: Glenbow Museum, 1987.

Carter, Sarah A. *Aboriginal People and Colonizers of Western Canada to 1900*. Toronto: University of Toronto Press, 1999.

Chute, Janet E. *The Legacy of Shingwaukonse*. Toronto: University of Toronto Press, 1998.

Dempsey, Hugh A. *Charcoal's World*. Saskatoon: Western Producer, 1978.

Johnston, Basil. *Indian School Days*. Norman: University of Oklahoma Press, 1988.

Metatawabin, Edmund. *Up Ghost River: A Chief's Journey through the Turbulent Waters of Native History*. Toronto: Vintage, 2015.

Miller, Christine, and Patricia Chuchryk, eds. *Women of the First Nations: Power, Wisdom, and Strength*. Winnipeg: University of Manitoba Press, 1996.

Miller, J.R. *Shingwauk's Vision*. Toronto: University of Toronto Press, 1996.

Milloy, John S. *A National Crime: The Canadian Government and the Residential School System, 1879–1986*. Winnipeg: University of Manitoba Press, 1999.

Sellars, Bev. *They Called Me Number One: Secrets and Survival at an Indian Residential School*. Vancouver: Talonbooks, 2012.

Winegard, Timothy. *For King and Kanata: Canadian Indians and the First World War*. Winnipeg: University of Manitoba Press, 2012.

15 Tightening the Reins: Resistance Grows and Organizes

CHAPTER OUTLINE

The process of developing a more organized resistance grew exponentially over the course of the twentieth century at both the local and national levels. At the local level, individual First Nations—notably Haudenosaunee from the Six Nations of the Grand River—attempted to bring international pressure to bear on the government of Canada. At the national level, the process that had begun with the attempts to organize the League of Indians began to bear fruit. Reaction in favour of the Hawthorn Report and opposed to the White Paper is illustrative of the growing strength of organized resistance. This growing strength is also to be found in the ability of the Métis and of First Nations women to speak with greater authority.

LEARNING OUTCOMES

1. Students will gain a more detailed view of the federal government's assimilationist policies.

2. Students will learn something of the participation of Indigenous soldiers in the First and Second World Wars and about the renewed activism that the participation gave rise to.

3. Students will gain insights into various other resistance movements, including those of the Haudenosaunee Confederacy and the Métis.

4. Students will learn about the efforts to give Indigenous people greater control over Indigenous education.

5. Students will understand the key differences between the Hawthorn Report and the White Paper.

TIMELINE The Growth of Organized Resistance, from 1890 to the 1985 Indian Act Revisions

1890
Indian agents empowered to enforce anti-vagrancy laws.

1896
Land set aside in Alberta for exclusive use of Métis at Saint-Paul-des-Métis.

1914
Indigenous people forbidden to perform traditional dances in traditional clothing at fairs and stampedes.

1920
Indian Act amendment leads to enfranchisement (and loss of Indian status) of nearly 500 Indigenous people in less than two years.

1922
Armed confrontation between Haudenosaunee members and the RCMP.

1923–4
Haudenosaunee leaders take their claim to sovereignty to League of Nations; case is dropped after British intervention at League of Nations.

1924
Ludger Bastien first Indigenous member elected to Quebec legislature.

1930
L'Association des Métis d'Alberta et des Territoires du Nord Ouest organized.

1936
Department of Mines and Resources absorbs Indigenous administration.

1938
Alberta's Métis Population Betterment Act leads to creation of 10 Métis colonies, of which eight still exist.

1951
Major changes to Indian Act, granting women the vote in band council elections, allowing secret ballot, limited but greater Indigenous control of band affairs, less sweeping ministerial powers.

1958
Tyendinaga Reserve on Lake Ontario first to gain complete control of band funds.

1966
Hawthorn Report criticizes centuries-old policy of assimilation and presents view of Indigenous people as "citizens plus" because of their original inhabitancy.

1967
Indians of Canada Pavilion at Expo 67 brings plight of Canadian Indigenous Peoples to public consciousness.

1969
Federal government White Paper proposes end of Indian Act, termination of treaties, and that First Nations be treated equally with all other Canadians.

1970
Supreme Court rules in *Drybones* that Indigenous people have right to drink alcohol in public.

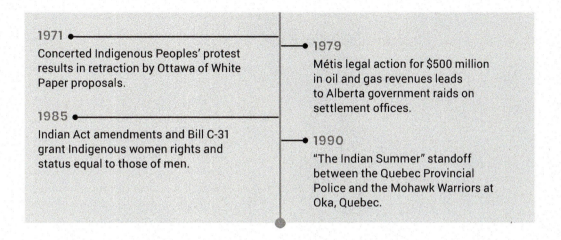

1971
Concerted Indigenous Peoples' protest results in retraction by Ottawa of White Paper proposals.

1979
Métis legal action for $500 million in oil and gas revenues leads to Alberta government raids on settlement offices.

1985
Indian Act amendments and Bill C-31 grant Indigenous women rights and status equal to those of men.

1990
"The Indian Summer" standoff between the Quebec Provincial Police and the Mohawk Warriors at Oka, Quebec.

Assimilate "Them" and They Cease to Exist?

As the police pulled back from having to enforce the pass system (see Chapter 14) that restricted the movements of western Indigenous people, the department moved to strengthen the other means it had already called into play to achieve the purpose. In 1890, it had empowered Indian agents to enforce the Criminal Code's anti-vagrancy provisions. Then, in 1914, it strengthened the bans on "giveaway" ceremonies central to the potlatch (1884) and the endurance rituals of the thirst dance (1895). Now, Indigenous people could not even appear in "Indigenous clothing" or perform their traditional dances at fairs and stampedes. Finally, the government prohibited such dances in any type of dress unless the department gave written approval.[1] This was a direct blow to Indigenous Peoples' sense of community. Administrators saw any encouragement of Indigenous culture as undermining its assimilation policy. Encouraged by missionaries, during the 1920s the RCMP conducted raids and confiscated personal effects at their discretion.

Another aspect of this drive towards assimilation was **compulsory enfranchisement**—the power given to the superintendent-general to enfranchise Indigenous people he considered qualified, whether or not they wanted to become voters. As well, these individuals would receive title to the reserve lands they occupied and their share of band money. In effect, to the government, enfranchisement meant an end to an individual's status under the Indian Act. The government also eased the way for Métis who had taken treaty to get the vote and paved the way for Indigenous women married to non-Indigenous men[2] to give up their First Nations status.

Brian Jungen installation view, Kunstverein Hannover, Hannover, Germany, 2013. Courtesy of Catriona Jeffries, Vancouver.

Totem Poles by Brian Jungen (b. 1970), one of Canada's most widely acclaimed Indigenous artists, whose background is Swiss and Dene Dháa. Jungen employs repurposed materials, in this case golf bags, to point to the disjuncture between traditional Indigenous culture and values and modern consumer society.

Although the government designed these measures with the Indigenous Peoples east of the Great Lakes in mind, the alarm and hostility they aroused spread from coast to coast. The Haudenosaunee Confederacy found wide support when they petitioned the Governor General against these arbitrary moves towards enfranchisement.[3] The department's purpose was clear enough: "to continue until there is not a single Indian in Canada that has not been absorbed into the body politic and there is no Indian question, and no Indian Department."[4] In other words, the government's goal was total cultural capitulation, the extinction of Indigenous Peoples as Indigenous Peoples.[5] Walter E. Harris, who as Minister of Citizenship and Immigration was responsible for Indian Affairs from 1950 to 1954, expressed the hope that the Act, even when revised, would be only temporary, as the "ultimate goal of our Indian policy is the integration of the Indian into the general life and economy of the country."[6]

The government's approach of treating the Indigenous people as minors to be assimilated led to resistance and defiance, both covert and open. The Department of Indian Affairs (DIA) became more arbitrary, and Indigenous Peoples refused to co-operate. Time and again, they demonstrated they were prepared to suffer rather than be treated like children. The government paid lip service to consultation, but in practice it could not bring itself to listen and actually take into account what Indigenous Peoples were saying.[7]

On an individual level, decorated war veteran Francis Pegahmagabow (1891–1952; see Indigenous Leaders box), an Ojibwa from the Parry Island reserve (now Wasauksing

INDIGENOUS LEADERS | Francis Pegahmagabow

Francis Pegahmagabow is representative of the great sacrifice made by Indigenous soldiers in the two world wars. In the First World War, Indigenous volunteers were second only to British-born Canadians proportionally, and not by much. Francis Pegahmagabow remains one of Canada's most decorated soldiers and the most decorated Indigenous soldier. He was one of those rare individuals who volunteered at the outbreak of war in 1914 and fought until the armistice in 1918. Along the way he fought with skill and great courage in the 1st Battalion of the famed First Canadian Division. He fought at Second Ypres in April of 1915 when German troops used poison gas for the first time; he fought and was injured in the Somme in 1916; he fought and helped turn the tide in the Battle of Passchendaele in the autumn of 1917. In all of these battles and in many others he risked his life to get supplies of ammunition or to leave cover to drive back determined enemy soldiers. He was awarded the Military Medal and subsequently was awarded two bars. All of his decorations may be seen in the Canadian War Museum in Ottawa. His reputation in the First Canadian Division was outstanding and when the veterans returned to Canada a number of them lobbied on behalf of Indigenous Peoples, thanks to their first-hand experience of fighting alongside men like Francis "Peggy" Pegahmagabow.[8] Later, as chief of the Parry Island reserve, he fought against the Indian agent system, for Indigenous control of resources, and for ownership of Georgian Bay islands that the Ojibwa of Wausauksing claimed had not been ceded in the Robinson Huron treaty. On National Aboriginal Day in 2016 a sculpture of him was unveiled in Parry Sound before a large audience including Assembly of First Nations National Chief Perry Bellegarde.

First Nation), and others challenged government authority to such an extent that in 1933 Indian Affairs set as official policy that Indigenous people could not contact the department directly. All correspondence had to go through the Indian agent, who often wrote off complaints to their superiors as having come from either chronic complainers or outside agitators.[9]

The process of more and stiffer regulations continued until the onset of the Great Depression in 1929. Meanwhile, prices for fur and fish plummeted, putting Indigenous people on welfare rolls.[10] In 1936, Indigenous administration was shunted off to the Department of Mines and Resources, which was more concerned with industrial development than with the social problems of Indigenous groups and individuals. The administration now encouraged northern Indigenous Peoples in their traditional hunting and trapping activities,[11] as these enabled them to be self-sufficient.[12] Even if Indigenous people could afford the new and larger farm machinery, which rarely was the case, their farms usually were too small to make effective use of it. This situation became acute after the Second World War, with the result that many Indigenous people gave up farming.

For King and Country (2015), Barry Ace, Canada Council Art Bank, Photographer: Brandon Clarida.

For King and Country (2015) by Barry Ace (b. 1958), who is a member of M'Chigeeng First Nation on Manitoulin Island, utilizes cultural markers such as porcupine quills, deer hide, and glass beads. The piece denounces the policies of the federal Indian Act, which denied the vote to Indigenous people, many of whom fought overseas during the First and Second World Wars.

More Social Engineering: Residential Schools and Beyond

By the turn of the twentieth century, enthusiasm for industrial schools had waned. Rising costs and poor administration, including charges of abuse to students, led to a gradual phasing out of the program. Investigations in 1907–9 revealed that 28 per cent of the students who had attended Sarcee Boarding School between 1894 and 1908 had died, mostly from tuberculosis.[13] New regulations and financing arrangements led to some improvement.[14] Still, charges of student abuse continued to surface.

The year of compulsory enfranchisement, 1920, was also the year for strengthening compulsory school attendance to ensure that all First Nations children between the ages of seven and 15 attended. Ten years later, the government stiffened regulations still more. By this time, First Nations children could be committed to boarding schools and kept there until the age of 18 on the authority of the Indian agent, a measure far in excess of any applied to all other Canadians. These regulations might have been responsible for statistics reported by Duncan Campbell Scott (1862–1947), the deputy superintendent-general from 1913 to 1932, indicating that school attendance rose from 64 per cent in 1920 to 75 per cent in 1930. This was mostly due to residential schools—by the

1930s, there were more than 80.[15] To Scott, these figures were proof that Indigenous Peoples were on their way to becoming "civilized."[16]

Other statistics, however, tell a different story. In 1930, three-quarters of Indigenous pupils across Canada were in Grades 1 to 3. Only three in 100 went past Grade 6. By mid-century, the proportion of students beyond Grade 6 had risen to 10 per cent, an improvement but only one-third of the comparable level of other Canadian children. As late as 1951, 40 per cent of Indigenous children over the age of five were reported to be without formal schooling, in spite of regulations for enforced attendance.[17]

Throughout all this, Indigenous Peoples were not allowed to contribute to the content of studies or to exercise any control over schools, although some petitioned to have more emphasis on classwork and less on "practical" training such as farming. Many students were abused. In some schools, authorities implemented a series of nutrition experiments that led to malnutrition and suffering. More research is being done into this dark area.[18] The schools eventually also banned the use of Indigenous languages and the practice of traditional religions. The attempt to ban Indigenous languages was one of the most serious and damaging elements of the program geared towards cultural genocide.[19] Language was, and is, the foundation upon which all other cultural aspects are built.

When Indigenous people proved they were as adept as other Canadians at their own game, the result could be hostility and rejection instead of acceptance. In the words of John Tootoosis, who headed the Federation of Saskatchewan Indians in the late 1950s and 1960s, they were caught between two cultures but a part of neither:

> When an Indian comes out of these places it is like being put between two walls in a room and left hanging in the middle. On one side are all the things he learned from his people and their way of life that was being wiped out, and on the other are the white man's way which he could never fully understand since he never had the right amount of education and could not be part of it. There he is, hanging in the middle of the two cultures and he is not a white man and he is not an Indian. They washed away practically everything an Indian needed to help himself, to think the way a human person should in order to survive.[20]

In the Far North, at least one residential school incorporated a few Indigenous instructors and some culturally appropriate education. The Anglican school at Shingle Point, Yukon, had two Inuit hunters on staff to teach the boys hunting and fishing techniques. The girls received lessons in the domestic arts within the framework of Arctic conditions. It is important to note, however, that Inuit children did not attend residential schools with any consistency until the 1950s.[21]

The parliamentary investigations that preceded the 1951 revision of the Indian Act rejected Indian Affairs' education policy as it then was and proposed instead that Indigenous children be integrated into public schools. Ten years later, of the 38,000 Indigenous students in school, almost one-fourth were attending provincially controlled institutions. The total proportion of Indigenous pupils beyond Grade 6 had doubled.[22] By this time, however, some were advocating autonomous Indigenous schools, separate from those of the dominant society. It was at this time, too, that many Indigenous children were taken from their homes and communities and placed in foster care or adoptive homes. In all, 15,000 Indigenous children were adopted into Canadian families in the 1950s, 1960s, and 1970s. The cultural loss was even more pronounced among these **"Sixties Scoop"** children than it was for Indigenous children who were sent to residential school.

Apologies, Reparation, and Growing Indigenous Control

Most of the residential schools still operating had closed during the 1970s. The harm they left in their wake eventually led to lawsuits by former students seeking damages for their compulsory school attendance and the treatment some had received, and by 2003, thousands of lawsuits had been filed against the churches and individuals involved. The Anglican Church, through Archbishop Michael Peers, initially had issued an apology in 1993 for the personal harm caused by the residential schools. As Archbishop Peers stated, "I am sorry, more than I can say, that we were part of a system which took you and your children from home and family." The Anglican Church led the way when it finalized a negotiated settlement with the federal government in late 2002 committing $25 million to reparations. The Presbyterian Church, which had been responsible for fewer schools, offered a formal apology in 1994. The United Church, having previously made a general apology in 1986, issued a formal apology in 1998. Finally, in April 2009, following a private meeting in Rome with a small delegation of residential school survivors, including AFN National Chief Phil Fontaine, the Pope expressed his "sorrow" on behalf of the Roman Catholic Church, which had been responsible for about 75 per cent of the residential schools in Canada. Although the apologies from the churches in the 1990s met with a cool reception,[23] they preceded any formal apology or announcement of reparations from the federal government (see Chapters 18 and 19).

In December 2003, a unanimous ruling by the British Columbia Court of Appeal that the federal government held 100 per cent liability in the case of the school at Port Alberni[24] moved this issue forward on the government's agenda. In May 2005, the federal government signed an agreement with the Assembly of First Nations outlining the basis on which the government and the AFN would work together to resolve claims and appointed retired Supreme Court Justice Frank Iacobucci to oversee the process.[25] The first results of that process are discussed in Chapter 19.

Blue Quills, near St Paul, Alberta, in 1970 became the first school in Canada to be controlled by an Indigenous band.[26] In 2015, it evolved into University nuhelot'įne thaiyots'į nistameyimâkanak Blue Quills.[27] The early success of Blue Quills encouraged others to follow its example; in 1973 the Métis community at Ile à la Crosse in northern Saskatchewan took over the local school.[28] The following year, the Ojibwa of Sabaskong Bay in northern Ontario began the process of taking over their elementary school; three years later, in 1977, they were running the secondary school also.[29] Today, Indian Affairs encourages bands to take over full or partial administration of reserve schools, although its funding policy is not always consistent with this goal. By 2010, Canada counted 518 schools being operated on reserves by Indigenous Peoples.[30]

As of August 2017, encouraging signs are evident as the movement towards Indigenous control over Indigenous education gains traction. This is not to say that the forces of change have had an easy time, but Indigenous-run schools are chalking up good records.[31] The intensity and duration of the campaign to promote Indigenous education reflects the importance accorded to this aspect of cultural protection and development. Control of education, especially language education, goes to the heart of the movement for self-government.

In 2011, the National Panel on First Nations Elementary and Secondary Education in Canada found that conditions in the schools themselves were below the national standard and that reform was necessary. The Panel's report, delivered to the Minister of Aboriginal Affairs and Northern Development and to the National Chief of the Assembly of First Nations, made five recommendations: to create a First Nations Education Act; to create a National Commission for First Nations Education; to develop regional First Nations Education Organizations (FNEO); to ensure adequate funding; and to establish a framework for accountability and reporting.

These recommendations are gradually being implemented, but the process has been anything but smooth. On 7 February 2014, Prime Minister Stephen Harper and Shawn A-in-chut Atleo, National Chief of the Assembly of First Nations, announced changes to the proposed First Nations Education Act. The proposed Act, now called the First Nations Control of First Nations Education Act, would adopt the recommendations made by the AFN during the Special Chiefs Assembly held in December 2013. These provisions included: recognition of First Nations and treaty rights; sustainable funding; reciprocal accountability with no unilateral federal oversight; and continued meaningful dialogue and consultation. As part of the agreement, the government committed an additional $1.9 billion for Indigenous education—$1.25 billion over three years for First Nations schools across Canada, with annual increases of 4.5 per cent, $500 million over seven years for infrastructure, and $160 million for an implementation fund. In addition to the increased funding, the proposed Act would establish new guidelines for education standards that are comparable to provincial standards. Most importantly, the Act would facilitate the development of First Nation education authorities and incorporate language and culture programs. Finally, the First Nations Control of First Nations Education Act would also repeal the provisions in the Indian Act related to residential schools, a measure of great symbolic importance.[32]

In early May 2014, after Atleo resigned suddenly as National Chief on 1 May, the federal government announced that it was not going to attempt to move forward with the legislation until there were parties to work with. Atleo had come under sharp criticism from some regional chiefs and other Indigenous leaders, as well as the grassroots, for having given away too much and, more generally, for being too conciliatory towards the federal government in Ottawa and too close to Prime Minister Harper. Specifically, critics of Atleo and of the proposed legislation he had championed believed that the Act would give too much control to the Minister of

Aboriginal Affairs and did not protect treaty rights, and that the extensive consultation claimed by the government and the National Chief certainly had not reached the grassroots or many First Nations.[33] More recently, in August of 2017, the province of Ontario signed the Anishinabek Education Agreement with the Anishinabek Nation, which paves the way for Indigenous control of Indigenous education in Ontario. The hope is that this agreement will provide a model for agreements with the other provinces and territories.[34]

Organized Action and a Revised Indian Act

Early attempts at pan-Indigenous political unity had been led by such figures as the Wabanaki's Nescambiouit, the Mesquakie's Kiala, Thayendanegea of the Kanienkehaka, and, more recently, the returned First World War veteran Fred Loft, the Kanienkehaka founder of the League of Indians. Yet, the effective beginning of Indigenous Peoples' activism in Canadian politics can be dated to a trip to Ottawa in 1943 by Andrew Paull and Dan Assu of the Native Brotherhood of BC to protest taxation of BC's Indigenous fishermen and price ceilings on sockeye salmon.[35] At this time, and even though they were not citizens, Indigenous soldiers were serving in the armed forces during the Second World War in proportionately higher numbers—up to 6,000—than any other segment of the general population, repeating a pattern that had been evident during the First World War. An unexpected area in which they had a unique advantage in the Second World War was that of language. Indigenous languages were particularly useful for transmitting sensitive information—codes can be broken, but languages have to be learned. Canadian **"code talkers"** used Cree; Americans used Lakhóta, Navajo, and Comanche.

The Second World War brought social upheaval and, with it, a change of attitude. When Indigenous soldiers returned to civilian life, the restrictions and inequities of their lot on reserves became glaringly evident. In response, veterans' organizations and church groups mounted a campaign that resulted in the establishment of a Joint Senate and House of Commons Committee on the Indian Act, which held hearings from 1946 to 1948.[36] Indigenous leaders were highly critical of the first draft of the proposed revisions. Led by Akaynamuka (James Gladstone) of the Káínaa First Nation, they claimed that the draft, instead of entrenching their rights, actually would erode them.

Faced with such protests, the government set about revising the revisions. This time, it heard witnesses, the first time for such consultations at that level.[37] Treaties and treaty rights concerned the Indigenous Peoples most. They wanted these left in place, but with the freedom to govern themselves. Land claims were not far behind. For the government, the goal continued to be assimilation.

The revised Act of 1951 can hardly be called revolutionary, but it still heralded the dawn of a new era. Not since the first Indian Act was the minister's power as limited as it became in 1951—but he still had veto power. The new Act did not allow bands to establish their own forms of government, but it did increase their measure of self-control.[38] In fact, with few exceptions the band could now spend its monies as it wished, unless the Governor-in-Council expressed reservations. This meant, for example, that it could now fund lawsuits to advance claims. It would be 1958, however, before any bands had complete control over their funds.

The government also repealed anti-potlatch and anti-dance measures.[39] It dropped compulsory enfranchisement and restrictions on political organizations, both of which were not working out, in any event. Political organizations, such as the Allied Tribes of British Columbia, had been functioning since early in the twentieth century.[40] A case was fought all the way to the Supreme Court in 1970 for Indigenous people to win the right to drink in public.

Although the 1951 Act moved towards self-government, it did not go nearly far enough to satisfy such groups as the Haudenosaunee Confederacy, who were claiming sovereignty as actively as ever. Even moderates were critical of the revised Act. How could the Act make full citizens of Indigenous

Akay-na-muka (James Gladstone), of the Káínaa First Nation, Alberta, was the first "treaty Indian" appointed to the Canadian Senate. His daughter, Pauline Dempsey, adjusts his headdress while his wife, Janie, looks on. The occasion was his retirement, at age 83, in 1971.

people, they asked, if they were not going to be allowed the responsibilities that go with citizenship? The 1951 amendments also explicitly excluded Inuit from the Act, despite the 1939 *Re: Eskimo* ruling of the Supreme Court of Canada declaring Inuit as "Indians."[41]

A second joint committee for the review of Indian Affairs policy sat from 1959 to 1961. This time, land claims surged to the forefront, and the committee responded by repeating a recommendation of the first joint committee in 1951, that a claims commission be established. That would not happen until 1969 (see Chapter 17). Meanwhile, Andrew Paull and Dan Assu's 1943 petition on fishing rights had triggered a chain of events that eventually led to the formation in 1968 of the **National Indian Brotherhood**. Originally only for "treaty Indians," soon it was acting on behalf of Indigenous groups across Canada. It lasted until 1982, when the **Assembly of First Nations** emerged as the national voice for status Indians.[42]

The Hawthorn Report

The centennial of Canada's Confederation in 1967 presented too good an opportunity to miss. At Expo in Montreal, Indigenous Peoples, with the support of Indian Affairs, erected a pavilion in which they publicly expressed, for the first time on a national scale, dissatisfaction with their treatment.[43] The general public reacted with stunned disbelief that people in Canada were being treated this way. Most Canadians had no way of knowing what was happening on the reserves and in the North. Canada, in celebrating the centennial of its Confederation, had simply not thought to include Indigenous Peoples as founding members.

The obviously marginalized position of Indigenous Peoples, in the North as elsewhere, had earlier spurred the federal government, in 1963, to appoint anthropologist Harry B. Hawthorn to investigate their social, educational, and economic conditions. His report, which appeared in 1966, listed 151 recommendations. It stated that an Indigenous person should not be forced to "acquire those values of the majority society he does not hold, or wish to acquire," and that the department should assume a more active role as advocate for Indigenous interests.[44] The report supported the Indian Act but recommended changes. It also revealed that their average per capita annual income was less than half that of other Canadians. Indigenous education was also far below the national average. Hawthorn urged that Indigenous people have the opportunity to study in their own languages. He observed that school texts were often not only inaccurate on the subject of Indigenous Peoples, they were usually insulting.[45]

Concerning self-government, Hawthorn noted that, between 1951 and 1964, only about a quarter of the bands that Canada counted at that time had passed any bylaws, largely because the Governor-in-Council could veto any band decision. When it came to money bylaws, fewer than 50 bands were deemed "advanced" enough to exercise this power. In other words, outsiders were running the reserves.

According to Hawthorn, Indigenous Peoples reacted by orienting themselves primarily to kinship and other groupings. Band councils persisted only because the government insisted on dealing through them. By complying with the system, bands assured themselves of more generous welfare grants, but the price was that they could not make decisions affecting their lives. This pattern of dependency took such root that, in some cases, even urban bands actually voted against local autonomy. Acceptance of welfare also weakened communal activities.[46]

Indigenous organizations and leaders received the **Hawthorn Report** well. As the report explained, "in addition to the normal rights and duties of citizenship, Indians possess certain additional rights as charter members of the Canadian community."[47]

The 1969 White Paper and Some Consequences

In 1969, Ottawa came up with what was described—although not by most Indigenous people—as a "breathtaking governmental recipe for equality." This was the **White Paper**, a proposal designed to break "the pattern of 200 years" and to abolish the existing framework of

Indigenous administration, widely criticized for setting First Peoples apart and hindering their development.[48]

In fact, rising administrative costs were at the heart of this government initiative, although it was, in part, a response to the American Indian Movement (AIM, or "Red Power"), which had arisen in Minnesota in 1968 and was spreading into Canada, challenging the administration to allow Indigenous Peoples a greater say in running their own affairs. The government, therefore, announced it was going "to enable the Indian people to be free—free to develop Indian cultures in an environment of legal, social and economic equality with other Canadians."[49] In other words, instead of Hawthorn's "citizens plus," Indigenous people were to become like all other Canadians. Their special status would end. The White Paper did not recognize Aboriginal rights and, in effect, treaties would be cancelled. When the government announced the new policy, it hit a solid wall of opposition. The National Indian Brotherhood (NIB) said flatly that the proposals were not acceptable:

> We view this as a policy designed to divest us of our aboriginal, residual, and statutory rights. If we accept this policy, and in the process lose our rights and our lands, we become willing partners in culture genocide. This we cannot do.[50]

Later in 1969, the government named Dr Lloyd Barber, vice-president of the University of Saskatchewan, as commissioner for First Nations land claims but did not initially authorize him to deal with Aboriginal rights (see Chapter 17). This reflected Prime Minister Pierre Elliott Trudeau's personal rejection of the concept of Aboriginal right at that time. The NIB rejected Barber's office as an outgrowth of the White Paper. The government's 1970 hiring of a Cree lawyer from Calgary, William I.C. Wuttunee, a former chief of the National Indian Council of Canada and now a supporter of

John Kahionhes Fadden drawing

***Deskaheh* by John Kahionhes Fadden.** Deskaheh (Levi General), who travelled on a Haudenosaunee passport, gained support in Europe for Haudenosaunee sovereignty, but London intervened to make his appeal to the League of Nations futile. Upon his return in early 1925, after more than a year in Geneva and London, he was denied entry to Canada and spent the few months before his death later that year at the Tuscarora reservation near Niagara Falls, New York.

the White Paper, inflamed the opposition. Wuttunee was banned from several reserves, including his own, Red Pheasant.[51]

The official Indigenous response to the White Paper was *Citizens Plus* (known as the "Red Paper"), written by the Indian Association of Alberta. Rejecting wardship, it still advocated special status, but as defined by the treaties.[52] Eventually Trudeau conceded that the government had been "very naive . . . not pragmatic enough or understanding enough." He might also have added that his government did not want to face the political difficulties associated with according "Citizens Plus" status to Indigenous people while French Canadians were demanding, and being refused, something similar. His government formally retracted the White Paper on 17 March 1971.

The Haudenosaunee Struggle for Autonomy

The Haudenosaunee Confederacy has a long record of arguing for autonomy, so it is not surprising that they deeply resented the restrictions imposed by the Indian Act of 1876, and particularly by its later amendments, without any Indigenous input. They rejected the authority of the department and the Act it administered. The main advocates of self-government were the hereditary chiefs, who in 1890 petitioned Ottawa for recognition of their autonomy and exemption from the Indian Act. They were rebuffed, as they had been in 1839 when they sought to be governed according to their own laws. An 1890 amendment to the Indian Act empowered the department to set up an elective system without the approval of the Indigenous Peoples involved. In the department's view, the hereditary form of government did not fit the needs of the modern world. Among the Haudenosaunee, supporters of the new system, called "Dehorners,"[53] tended to be younger and Christian. Traditionalists were mainly older followers of the Longhouse religion. In the ensuing power struggle, the traditionalists, led by **Deskaheh** (Levi General 1873–1925), of the Guyohkohnyo won the day.[54]

With the close of the First World War, the Haudenosaunee of the Six Nations of the Grand River First Nation near Brantford, Ontario, established a committee to campaign for sovereignty. The government countered with an amendment to the Indian Act that abolished traditional governments. A Haudenosaunee petition to the Supreme Court of Canada and to the Privy Council in London got nowhere and aroused little public concern. However, there was much more public sympathy for the Haudenosaunee cause in Europe than in Canada.

An armed confrontation between Haudenosaunee members and the RCMP in 1922, in which shots were fired, led the Haudenosaunee Confederacy to take their case to the newly formed League of Nations. Canada, on the other hand, argued that it was a domestic matter and thus beyond the League's jurisdiction. At about this time, Deskaheh, waging an effective campaign in London, issued a pamphlet entitled "The Redman's Appeal for Justice." In it, he stated that all the Haudenosaunee Confederacy was asking for was home rule, much as the colonies had done a century earlier. Estonia, Ireland, Panama, and Persia (Iran) rallied to the Haudenosaunee cause. Norway, the Netherlands, and Albania joined them, but then London intervened, charging that "minor powers" were interfering in the British Empire's "internal affairs." The League of Nations dropped the case in 1924. A direct appeal by Levi General to George V brought no result.

In the meantime, Canada appointed an investigator to examine the question of government on reserves as well as charges of mismanagement of Haudenosaunee trust funds. The investigator recommended an elective system. The government implemented the decision without delay and without a referendum, imposing an elective council on the Haudenosaunee Confederacy and abolishing the hereditary one. The Kanienkehaka rebelled. The next few years saw a traditionalist revival that included an attempt to re-establish links within the Haudenosaunee Confederacy that had been severed 150 years earlier. Providing the spark was Paul Diabo's 1926 arrest in Philadelphia as an illegal alien. Seeing their historical right to free passage between the US and Canada threatened, the Grand Councils at Onondaga and Six Nations of Grand River argued successfully before the US courts that their existence as nations had been challenged. The following year, the Grand Council met at Kahnawake, near Montreal.[55] Under the hereditary system, women had an important voice in the selection of chiefs, but the elective system did not give women the vote. Ironically, at about this time (1924), a chief of the Loretteville Wendat, Ludger Bastien (1879–1948), became the first Indigenous member to be elected to a provincial legislature, that of Quebec.[56]

Deskaheh's death in 1925, shortly after his return from Europe, dealt a heavy blow to the Haudenosaunee independence movement, but the movement did not die. In 1942, the Kahnawake council, near Montreal, asked that their tribal laws replace the Indian Act. Haudenosaunee leaders from various reserves mounted a campaign against the 1951 changes to the Act, claiming that they were dictatorial and would slow their progress as a nation. During that same decade, Kahnawake took the Canadian government to court over lands seized for the St Lawrence Seaway. Despite their resistance, the Haudenosaunee Confederacy lost 1,300 acres (526 ha), including river frontage.[57] This was a cultural and economic blow for a people famed for their river expertise. (Indeed, in the late nineteenth century, when the British needed canoemen for their expeditionary force up the Nile River to relieve Khartoum, they recruited mainly at Kahnawake.[58]) The Kanienkehaka finally won a $1.5 million settlement in 1963 after 17 years of bitter negotiations.[59] Later, after losing an island to Expo 67, the Haudenosaunee leaders moved against the Canadians living on the reserve and evicted about a thousand of them in 1973 on the grounds of overcrowding.[60]

The result of all this was the deterioration of the band's relationship with the Quebec provincial police, to the point that in 1969 it established its own independent police force. Called **Peacekeepers**, this force eventually became the official law enforcement agency on the reserve.[61] Later, the **Warrior movement** would gain support among those who felt that the Peacekeepers did not take a strong enough stand.[62]

The Warriors gained a reputation for strong action within the community and they were seen as a powerful force for greater autonomy. When the RCMP raided Kahnawake's cigarette stores[63] in 1988, the Warriors rallied the Haudenosaunee Confederacy to block the south entrance to

Mercier Bridge, located on reserve land and connecting the Island of Montreal with the south shore. The standoff lasted 27 hours, with armed Warriors patrolling the bridge, "the first instance of armed native resistance in Canada's recent history."[64] The RCMP responded by describing the Kanienkehaka as "violent."[65] The government charged 16 persons with smuggling.

Thus was the stage set for the "Indian summer" of 1990, when Kahnawake again blocked the bridge in support of Kanesatake in its confrontation at Oka (see Chapter 17 for details). Although the blockade was brief, the standoff lasted 78 days, a member of the Quebec provincial police was shot and killed, and the two besieged communities were virtually cut off from the outside world. The Canadian Police Association called the Kanienkehaka "terrorists."[66] The behaviour of the Canadian government once more drew the censure of the international community.

Alberta Métis

As has already been noted, Métis considered that their Indigenous heritage gave them a right to land (see Chapters 12 to 14). Furthermore, most did not accept that this right could be extinguished by treaty. As European newcomers settled the West, the Métis became more and more scattered in small, impoverished bands. In 1895, Father Albert Lacombe approached Ottawa with a proposal to establish a reserve for Métis where they could learn how to farm. The government approved, seeing this as an alternative to scrip while also avoiding special status, but contributed only $2,000 to the project.

Saint-Paul-des-Métis was established the following year, 1896. It was the first tract of land set aside for the exclusive use of the Métis. The first year, 30 families from across Alberta and Saskatchewan moved to St Paul. By 1897, there were 50 families. Two years later, the Grey Nuns were operating a boarding school like those for First Nations. Farmsteads were allotted quickly, but far away from each other so that the colony was dispersed. This worked against community cohesiveness. On top of that, the promised livestock and equipment did not appear. This, plus the general underfunding, discouraged the Métis and they drifted away. In 1908, the government ended the Métis leases and, two years later, threw the reserve open for French-Canadian settlement.

The government blamed the Métis for the project's failure. The Métis claimed that even though the government had not fulfilled its obligations, many of their number had succeeded. The real issue, they said, was the prospect of a Canadian Pacific Railway route through the region, which raised the value of the land. That was why Euro-Canadian settlers were clamouring to have it opened for general settlement. As the Métis saw it, church, government, and French Canadians had combined to ensure the settlement's failure.

Although some became successful farmers, most of the Métis moved north, squatting on unsurveyed Crown lands where they could hunt, trap, and fish. The Métis settlements that sprang up tended to be on the fringes of newcomer settlements. These were the "road allowance people," living hand-to-mouth on Crown land that had been set aside for future highway construction.[67] Alberta's Métis population at this time—the 1920s—has been variously estimated at from 12,000 to 75,000.

The onset of the Great Depression meant that Métis who had been barely eking out an existence now faced disaster. In 1930, they organized l'Association des Métis d'Alberta et des

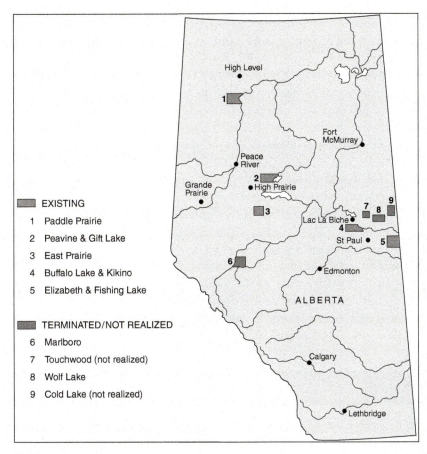

Map 15.1 Métis settlements in Alberta.

Adapted from *Metisism, A Canadian Identity* (Edmonton: Alberta Federation of Metis Settlement Associations, 1982).

Territoires du Nord Ouest. The first president was Joseph Dion (1888–1960), who was teaching on Keehewin Indian reserve (now Kehewin Cree Nation). In his book *My Tribe the Crees*, he presented an Indigenous view of the 1885 rebellion. In 1940, the Association was reorganized and its title changed to the Métis Association of Alberta through the efforts of Malcolm Norris (1900–67) and James Brady (1908–67).[68] Taking up the cause of land settlement projects for Métis, l'Association des Métis reported that by the end of October 1933, 348 families had been resettled in northern Alberta. Still, misery was widespread. The Association's efforts caught the attention of the provincial government, which agreed to a public inquiry, and a commission under Alberta Supreme Court Judge Albert Freeman Ewing (1871–1946) was struck.

As the Commission saw it, the only way out of the situation was for the Métis to change their way of life to conform to the dominant society. It did not see that the government had a legal obligation to help them—that had ended with the issuance of scrip—but there were humanitarian considerations. Ewing opposed special status, as had been granted First Nations.

Already, the Métis Association of Alberta had presented the provincial government with a list of 11 possible sites for Métis colonies. Taking its cue from this, the Commission proposed the establishment of farm colonies on good agricultural land, near lakes with plentiful stocks of fish and with access to timber for building. There was no provision for self-government.

The report of the **Ewing Commission** also recommended that northern hunting and trapping Métis each be granted 320 acres (130 ha) of land to be held on the same basis as if they were in the colonies. They should also be allowed free hunting and fishing permits, as well as preference in acquiring them in areas where there was danger of game depletion.

The Métis Population Betterment Act of 1938 implemented the Ewing Commission's recommendations. At that time, it was the most advanced legislation in Canada relating to the Métis. The Act was also unusual in that the government had written it in collaboration with Métis representatives. However, amendments were one-sided on the government's part, and these were not long in coming. In 1940, the definition of Métis was restricted. In 1941, another amendment gave the provincial cabinet the power to create game preserves on the settlements. By the next year, the minister could raise an annual tax. In 1943, the government established a Métis population betterment trust account. It became a fund in 1979.[69]

HISTORICAL BACKGROUND | Defining Métis

The Ewing Commission accepted the definition of Métis given by the Métis Association of Alberta: "anyone with any degree of Indian ancestry who lives the life ordinarily associated with the Métis." The Association would later extend its definition to include anyone who considered himself/herself a Métis and whom the community accepted as such, a position supported by the Royal Commission on Aboriginal Peoples (RCAP).[70]

Eventually, when Alberta amended its Métis Population Betterment Act in 1940, it defined a Métis as "a person of mixed white and Indian ancestry having not less than one-quarter Indian blood" who was not "either an Indian or non-Treaty Indian as defined in the Indian Act." It designed this definition to restrict the numbers of people eligible for provincial benefits. In 1996, the RCAP came out in support of the view that Métis are in the same category as other Indigenous Peoples under the Constitution Act (BNA Act) of 1867. This position was strengthened with the ruling in *R. v. Powley* in 2003, which affirmed the existence of Métis as a distinct Indigenous people.[71] In 2016, as we have seen in the previous chapter, the *Daniels* decision by the Supreme Court of Canada made it clear that the term "Indians" in section 91 (federal powers) of the Constitution was meant to include Métis and non-status Indians. With regard to the Métis specifically, the RCAP stated that their national culture was "conceived in Quebec, gestated in Ontario, and born on the western Plains."[72]

Initially, the province selected 12 locations in central Alberta and opened 10 of these for Métis settlement. Eventually, two of the colonies were closed so that by the end of the century there were eight, comprising 539,446 ha. The two closings, particularly that of Wolf Lake in 1960 over the protests of a dozen resident families, illustrated a weakness of the settlements: the Métis held their lands on leases. They did not have underlying title.

Originally, each of the settlements dealt individually with the provincial government. As this proved unsatisfactory, the Alberta Federation of Métis Settlement Associations was formed in 1975 to co-ordinate administration and also to prevent more closures.[73] Problems continued, however. A legal action started by the Métis against the government for an estimated $500 million in oil and gas revenues from settlement lands culminated in 1979 with raids organized by the provincial Department of Social Services on six of the eight settlement offices, confiscating files pertaining to the suit. The provincial ombudsman handled the dispute, deciding that some of the files were provincial property but that others should be returned to the settlements. The matter had been handled badly, and the Métis were owed an apology. The ombudsman urged that the Métis be given more control in running their own affairs and that more be hired in government service.[74]

At this time, the Alberta government moved responsibility for the Métis from Social Services to Municipal Affairs and created a committee under Grant MacEwan to review the Métis Betterment Act. MacEwan had been lieutenant-governor of the province from 1965 to 1974. His report in 1984 strongly supported self-government and urged that title to Métis lands be transferred to the settlements.[75] The province partially implemented these recommendations. In 1989, it granted title to 512,000 ha of land, approved limited self-government, and established a cash settlement of $310 million over 17 years.[76] In the 1990s, the provincial government passed legislation establishing a Métis land base, local government, and funding to the Métis Nation of Alberta, formerly the Métis Association of Alberta, for the development of social services and other programs.[77] Mineral rights, including royalties on oil and gas wells, still went to Ottawa.

Indigenous Women Fight for Rights

As in the larger Canadian society, women's rights among Indigenous Peoples were slow in being dealt with, although people like Mary Two-Axe Earley (1911–96) of Kahnawake and Nellie Carlson of Saddle Lake in Alberta had been raising their voices since the 1950s in protest against discriminatory provisions of the Indian Act.[78] It was particularly galling that the Act linked a woman's status to that of her husband. This meant that a Euro-Canadian woman acquired Indian status on marrying a status Indian, but a status Indian woman lost hers when she married anyone without Indian status.

In 1981, as a result of a complaint by Sandra Lovelace of Tobique reserve in New Brunswick, the United Nations Human Rights Committee found the Indian Act in breach of human rights. The Canadian government granted bands the power to decide whether a woman would lose status on marrying a non-Indigenous man.[79] Not until the 1985 amendment to the Indian Act (Bill C-31), however, did women obtain the right to keep their status on marrying anyone without

CP/Bill Brennan

Jenny Margetts (1936–91), left, of Edmonton, and Monica Turner of Geraldton, Ontario, both of Indian Rights for Indian Women, speak to reporters during a demonstration in front of the Parliament buildings, 1973. Margetts fought a lifelong battle against sex discrimination in First Nations band membership and also promoted Indigenous language and cultural courses in public schools.

status and to pass that status on to their children. Also reinstated were persons who had lost their status through such actions as enfranchisement or having obtained a university degree.[80] In effect, Bill C-31 sounded the death knell of the official policy of assimilation but it was an imperfect piece of legislation. An attempt was made to address the oversights in 2010. Bill C-3, The Gender Equity in Indian Registration Act, did not adequately address the problems that arose from ignoring the rights of the grandchildren of the affected women. Activist Sharon McIvor continues to refuse to tolerate this injustice.[81]

It was estimated that about 50,000 persons would be eligible for reinstatement under the new legislation but that fewer than 20 per cent would apply. A year later, 42,000 had applied, far exceeding expectations. By 1997, the number had reached 100,000.[82] Most have not moved to reserves. Crowded conditions have been a limiting factor, but the prevailing sentiment among Indigenous Peoples is that the legislation was imposed on them. The original injustice was not of their making, any more than the law aimed at its correction. In view of this position, the department redefined Indigenous Peoples into two categories, those who are registered federally and those whose bands have accepted them as members. This made it possible to be a band member without being registered, or vice versa.[83]

Questions to Consider

1. Who is most culpable for the harms caused by the residential schools—governments, churches, individuals, or all Canadians?
2. What steps are being taken towards greater Indigenous control in Indigenous education?
3. What were the main recommendations of the Hawthorn Report?
4. What accounts for the political activism of the Haudenosaunee Confederacy?

Recommended Readings

Alfred, Gerald R. *Heeding the Voices of Our Ancestors: Kahnawake Mohawk Politics and the Rise of Native Nationalism*. Toronto: Oxford University Press, 1995.

Alfred, Taiaiake. *Peace, Power, Righteousness: An Indigenous Manifesto*. Toronto: Oxford University Press, 1999.

Brownlie, Robin Jarvis. *A Fatherly Eye: Indian Agents, Government Power, and Aboriginal Resistance in Ontario, 1918–1939*. Toronto: Oxford University Press, 2003.

Castellano, Marlene Brant, Lynne Davis, and Louise Lahache. *Aboriginal Education: Fulfilling the Promise*. Vancouver: University of British Columbia Press, 2013.

Campbell, Maria. *Halfbreed*. Toronto: McClelland & Stewart, 1973.

Coates, Kenneth S., and William R. Morrison, eds. *Land of the Midnight Sun: A History of the Yukon*. Edmonton: Hurtig, 1988.

Forte, Maximilian, ed. *Who Is an Indian? Place and Politics of Indigeneity in the Americas*. Toronto: University of Toronto Press, 2013.

Fournier, Suzanne, and Ernie Crey. *Stolen from Our Embrace*. Vancouver: Douglas & McIntyre, 1997.

McInnes, Brian D. *Sounding Thunder: The Stories of Francis Pegahmagabow*. Winnipeg: University of Manitoba Press, 2016.

Paquette, Jerry, and Gérald Fallon. *First Nations Education Policy in Canada: Progress or Gridlock?* Toronto: University of Toronto Press, 2010.

Titley, E. Brian. *A Narrow Vision: Duncan Campbell Scott and the Administration of Indian Affairs in Canada*. Vancouver: University of British Columbia Press, 1986.

York, Geoffrey, and Loreen Pindera. *People of the Pines: The Warriors and the Legacy of Oka*. Toronto: Little, Brown and Company, 1991.

16 Development Heads North

CHAPTER OUTLINE

The treaty process of the nineteenth century came to an end in Canada's North, where the issues were complicated by broader ethnic diversity. The people of Canada's Far North, the Inuit, are one of three groups—along with the First Nations and the Métis—recognized as Indigenous Peoples by the federal government. This chapter will examine development in the North in relation to the members of the Dene Confederacy and the Cree, and also the Inuit. From the process of treaty negotiations, we will move into the creation of a new territory, Nunavut, created in 1999 as a separate jurisdiction for the Inuit.

LEARNING OUTCOMES

1. Students will understand the nature of the economic and social changes that transformed the peoples of the Arctic.

2. Students will understand how the treaty process continued into the early twentieth century.

3. Students will learn why the geopolitical jurisdiction of Nunavut was established.

TIMELINE Arctic Developments, from the Transfer of Jurisdiction to the Creation of Nunavut

1880
Jurisdiction of High Arctic transferred to Canada by Britain.

1883
Railway reaches Calgary.

1891
Railway reaches Edmonton.

1892
Sir Wilfred Grenfell begins medical missionary work on Labrador coast.

1893
HBC closes last Yukon post.

1895
NWMP establish first permanent post in Far North, in Yukon.

1898
Yukon becomes separate territory—just in time for Klondike gold rush.

1899
Treaty Eight, covering northern Alberta, northwest Saskatchewan, northeast BC, and parts of Yukon and NWT, is signed as a result of the Klondike gold rush.

1900s
Collapse of Arctic whaling industry.

1902
Entire band of Sadlermiut, perhaps the last remnant of earlier Dorset culture, perishes on Southampton Island.

1905–6
Treaty Nine (James Bay Treaty), covering northern Ontario, and Treaty Ten in northern Saskatchewan, which clears the way for settlement with creation of province of Saskatchewan.

1920
Tłįchǫ people refuse Treaty Eight payments because of attempts in recent legislation to restrict their hunting and fishing rights.

1921
Treaty Eleven, covering much of Northwest Territories.

1924
Two Inuit found guilty and hanged on Herschel Island for 1921 murder of police officer, five others.
Indian Act amended to include Inuit (later to be excluded by 1951 revisions).

1930s
Reindeer herd introduced in western Arctic.

1934
Relocations of Inuit to "more suitable" communities and hunting and fishing grounds begun in Arctic; they would fail.

1939
Supreme Court rules that all Inuit are a federal responsibility.

Continued

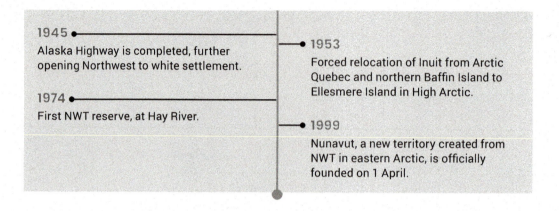

1945 • Alaska Highway is completed, further opening Northwest to white settlement.

• 1953 Forced relocation of Inuit from Arctic Quebec and northern Baffin Island to Ellesmere Island in High Arctic.

1974 • First NWT reserve, at Hay River.

• 1999 Nunavut, a new territory created from NWT in eastern Arctic, is officially founded on 1 April.

Trade and Self-Sufficiency

As it happened in the southwestern regions of Canada, so it happened in the Northwest. Canadian jurisdiction expanded through the fur trade, followed by missionaries and, later, the police. After it joined with the North West Company, the Hudson's Bay Company founded posts all over the Subarctic northwest of British North America. This expansion continued after the Company's surrender of Rupert's Land to Britain in 1869 and its transfer to Canada in 1870. However, by 1893, the Company had closed its last post in Yukon, in the face of competition from Americans (following their purchase of Alaska) and also from whalers.[1]

At first, the appearance of newcomers, mainly fur traders and missionaries, did not radically alter subsistence patterns, although changes did occur with the emphasis on fur hunting in the boreal forest and whaling in the Arctic, and the availability of trade goods. Metal goods, such as knives, kettles, and axes, soon proved useful, as did nets, twine, and, of course, firearms. Even as they traded for these items, however, the First Nations and the Inuit (the collective name for the people of the Arctic as defined in the 1982 Canadian Constitution) retained a large degree of self-sufficiency. But with time, industrialization slowly invaded the North, and the way of life changed.

Southerners Come to the North to Stay

In the second half of the nineteenth century, transportation was being revolutionized as missionaries and gold-seekers opened new routes to the North. Earlier attempts at discovering passage by sea across the North had largely failed (see Historical Background box). In the south, the railway reached Calgary in early 1883 and Edmonton in 1891. Trips that had once taken weeks and months or even years now took days. Trappers and prospectors were quick to take advantage of the new situation. By 1894, non-Indigenous trappers were established at Fort Resolution, north of the sixtieth parallel. According to a Fort Chipewyan elder, there were

> white trappers all over the place, and we were on very friendly terms with them. I went trapping with them many times. . . . I would guide them and show them how to trap. They were very thankful for that as they took their pelts home.[2]

Some non-Indigenous trappers, however, started using poison. This was completely unacceptable to the Indigenous people, as we have seen in Chapter 12 with the strong reaction against the American wolfers that resulted in the Cypress Hills Massacre.[3] The reaction was such that the government banned the practice, but enforcement was difficult, to say the least. Indigenous resentment mounted as northern resources soon showed the effects of increased exploitation.[4] In addition, trade added the uncertainties of the marketplace, and subsistence in the North, never easy, began to become problematic. The winters of 1887–8 and 1888–9 saw so many people die of starvation that Ottawa sent relief through the HBC and the missions. This situation would be repeated with increasing frequency. It was 1938 before the Northwest Territories Council restricted trapping licences to territory residents.

HISTORICAL BACKGROUND | The Northwest Passage

For centuries the British searched for a passage across the top of North America that would provide a shortcut to the riches of the Far East. In fact, these failed explorations, dating back to Martin Frobisher in 1576 (who did return to England with an Inuk captive), led to the European mapping of Canada's Far North—renaming the North with European names, as was their custom. The most famous attempt was the final expedition of Sir John Franklin (1786–1847) of 1845–8, which likely became ice-bound, with all of the men starving or freezing to death or dying of scurvy.[5] In turn, the disappearance of Franklin and his men led to many expeditions in the following years that, though failing to discover either Franklin or the **Northwest Passage**, did continue to add to the British mapping of the Arctic. Eventually, the wrecks of the HMS *Erebus* and the HMS *Terror* were found, in 2014 and 2016, by using the Inuit oral history collected by Louie Kamookak of Gjoa Haven.[6] The first explorer to navigate the Northwest Passage successfully was the Norwegian Roald Amundsen in 1903–6 in a tiny ship, the ***Gjoa***. An RCMP icebreaker, *St Roch*, completed a west-to-east passage in 1940–2 and in 1944 completed an east-to-west passage in a single summer. But the commercial attraction of finding the Northwest Passage had died with Franklin—until in recent years, with climate change and the diminished extent of Arctic sea ice, some shipping from an Arctic mine to the Far East traversed the Passage, and large cruise ships in the summer have navigated the Passage and provided a boost to the economies of some Inuit communities.

The association between government and missionaries would last until the 1940s. The government also provided some medical care. Ottawa's official position, however, was that it had no responsibility towards people who had not signed a treaty, and it saw no reason for one in those distant regions.

When the North West Mounted Police (NWMP) arrived in Yukon in 1895 to establish their first permanent post in the Far North their instructions were "not to give encouragement to the idea they [the Indigenous Peoples] will be received into treaty, and taken under the care of the government."[7] Official belief that Indigenous people were waiting for the chance to live off government handouts did not take into account the deep satisfaction of living off the land, despite its difficulties.[8] The police would enforce the law of the dominant society but also perform such governmental tasks as recording vital statistics, distributing mail, and collecting customs duties.

Two Views of Inuit/Newcomer Contacts

Missionaries had one view of the relations between the Inuit and the non-Indigenous population; the government, represented by the NWMP, had another view. The police came to the North in response to pleas from missionaries, who were deeply disturbed by the free flow of liquor. They agreed that liquor was a problem. Otherwise, they thought the missionaries were more concerned about the welfare of Indigenous people than of non-Indigenous people.[9] Charles Constantine of the NWMP (in Yukon as inspector, 1894–7; as superintendent, 1897–1902) could not see that Inuit society was disintegrating, as the missionaries claimed.[10]

In the western Arctic, more than 1,000 whalers were wintering at Herschel Island, occupying their off-season in living and trading with the 500 Inuvialuit, as the Inuit of the region were called. When gathered for trading, some camped near the whalers, others on islands scattered along the coast. At first, this was highly profitable for both sides, each within the terms of its own culture. For example, 100 primers (a device to detonate the main charge of a firearm) that cost 10 cents in New York traded in the Arctic for one muskox skin that sold in the south for $50. When accused of overpricing their goods, traders pointed to their heavy costs.[11] Even so, the trade built fortunes never before seen in the North. The Inuit obtained otherwise unavailable (or very rare) items that made their lives easier. They eagerly sought the new goods, not foreseeing, any more than did the non-Indigenous people, that the use of these goods would eventually help to disrupt both the ecological equilibrium and their social organization.[12]

The growing likelihood of violence and open disregard for authority finally persuaded the government of Canada to act. It organized Yukon, stretching from the Subarctic into the Arctic, into a district in 1895; three years later, it became a separate territory, under a commissioner named by the federal Minister of Mines and Resources and an appointed council of up to six members.[13] In the western Arctic, the newcomer population numbered about 500, drawn there by furs and minerals. Indigenous people numbered about 2,600. Already, there had been a severe decline in the Indigenous population, estimated to have been about 8,000 at the beginning of the nineteenth century.

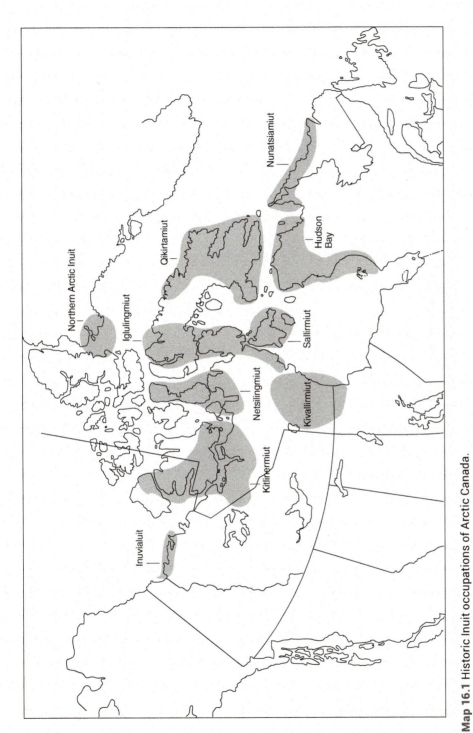

Map 16.1 Historic Inuit occupations of Arctic Canada.

Adapted, with the permission of the Canadian Museum of Civilization, from Robert McGhee, *Canadian Arctic Prehistory* (Ottawa: Canadian Museum of Civilization, 1990).

Police protests to the contrary, the missionaries' fears for the Inuvialuit were realized. Disease and the disruption of lifestyle took their toll, and by 1920 there were no more of the original Inuvialuit in Yukon.[14] Some survived around Tuktoyaktuk in the NWT, but most modern Inuvialuit moved in from Alaska. Local disappearances occurred in other areas as well, particularly where white whalers were active. Their lack of regard for the resource led to the collapse of the whale population and to the destruction of a way of life that had existed for millennia. For example, in 1902 an entire band of 68 Sadlermiut (believed by some to be the last of the Dorset people)[15] died of starvation and disease on Southampton Island.[16] To make matters worse, the whaling industry collapsed early in the twentieth century, triggered by a change in women's fashions and the increased use of petroleum products instead of whale oil. What saved the Inuit from total economic disaster was a new fashion, white fox skins.

Northerners Seek Treaty

First Nations and Métis in the North had been agitating for a treaty since the 1870s despite their fear of the restrictions it could impose and their distrust of non-Indigenous people. As the Cree leader Moostoos (c. 1850–1918, "The Buffalo") put it during Treaty Eight negotiations at Lesser Slave Lake, "Our country is getting broken up. I see the White man coming in, and I want to be friends. I see what he does, but it is best that we should be friends."[17] The government in Ottawa, however, held fast to its view that a treaty was unnecessary. It saw little prospect of either industrial development or significant white settlement north of the sixtieth parallel.[18]

As had happened at other times and places, Indigenous people were terribly upset by having their trading networks invaded. The Tlingit, for example, controlled the main routes between the coast and the interior, the Chilkoot, Chilkat, and Taku passes. They had long regulated the trade in the region.[19] That was not a position they could maintain, however, when the 1896 strike at Rabbit Creek, later known as Bonanza Creek, set off the **Klondike gold rush**. Ironically, of the three persons who made the strike, two were Tagish—Skookum Jim and Dawson (Tagish) Charlie—as was Kate, the wife of the third, George Carmack.[20] Whether they wanted it or not, the old way was gone forever as one of the most rapid migrations and economic expansions in history began.[21]

The first thing the government of Canada did was reassert its sovereignty. In Yukon, it reinforced the police force to nearly 300 men. The Indigenous people, for their part, were becoming increasingly uneasy. They felt it was unjust "that people who are not owners of the country are allowed to rob them of their living."[22] Miners rafted logs down the river, destroying Indigenous fishing weirs and crowding Indigenous villages out.[23] The influx of fortune hunters who were willing to take the law into their own hands added to the resentment already felt against non-Indigenous trappers. The situation threatened to go out of control, and in 1897 the police set up patrols.[24]

On the whole, Indigenous people saw the police presence as positive, except when the NWMP began in 1896 to enforce blanket legislation against hunting "wood buffalo." Indigenous people depended on the wood bison as a food source. Apparently, this was the only such regulation applied to Indigenous people at that time, but this turnabout on the part of the government reinforced Indigenous doubts as to its good faith. Such regulation without regard for local conditions could result in severe economic hardship, especially when game depletion reduced options.[25]

Treaty Eight (1899)

"The Trail of '98" saw the influx of gold-seekers reach serious proportions. By the end of 1898, almost 800 prospectors, most of them Americans, were wintering on the banks of the Mackenzie River.[26] Contemptuous of Indigenous people, they shot their horses and dogs, interfered with traplines, and exploited fish and game resources at will. The police were too few and the area too large for them to cope with the situation.[27] In June 1898, several hundred alarmed First Nations and Métis individuals gathered at Fort St John in northeastern British Columbia and announced they would no longer let anyone, even police, pass through their territory until a treaty was signed. This time, the government in Ottawa agreed.

It was not enough, however, for First Nations and Métis to ask for treaty to be included, even if they were suffering hardship.[28] The initial lack of militancy on the part of most of the Yukon Indigenous Peoples in defence of their rights encouraged the government to exclude most of their territory from the negotiations. The Oblate missionary turned historian, René Fumoleau, thought it likely that "Ottawa was afraid that the Indigenous Peoples would put too high a price on their rich land."[29]

The treaty commissioners, headed by David Laird, were soon impressed with the "keenness of intellect" and "the practical sense" of the northerners in pressing their claims. "They all wanted as liberal, if not more liberal terms, than were granted to the Indians on the Plains."[30] The northerners, worried about the increasing frequency of famine, were united in wanting help during such periods. They urged that the government care for the aged and needy. They also asked for schools but wanted no interference in their religious beliefs. By this time, most of the Indigenous people concerned were Roman Catholics.

By far the most important point the treaty commissioners had to deal with was the Indigenous fear that hunting and fishing rights would be curtailed, as was already happening in the case of the wood bison. This was vital for a people living in a land where agriculture, or even ranching, was not generally viable. Provision of ammunition and twine for making nets relieved Indigenous worries to some extent. The matter of selecting reserved land was left for the future.[31] As with earlier negotiations, the First Nations, not the government, introduced most of the forward-looking parts of the treaty terms.

After two days of negotiations at Lesser Slave Lake, the treaty was signed. The government considered that the treaty not only extinguished Aboriginal title, it also provided that Aboriginal **usufructuary right** would be "subject to such regulation as may from time to time be made by the Government, and excepting such tracts as may be required for settlement, mining, lumbering, trading, or other purposes."

The Indigenous groups had quite another view. They all held that the negotiators had guaranteed their rights to hunt, fish, and trap without restriction.[32] An elder later recalled,

> Moose is our main source of livelihood on this earth. Not like the white man, the King; he lived mainly on bread, he said. But the Indian lived on fish, ducks, anything. The King asked the Indian what he wanted for a livelihood. The Indian chose hunting and fishing not to be limited. As long as he lived.[33]

The First Nations and Métis did not agree with the government, however, as to what they had given up in return for the recognition of this right. In fact, the topic of landownership was not made explicit during negotiations. In the eyes of one member of the Denésoliné, "the white man never bought the land. If he had bought it, there would have been very large sums of money involved."[34]

There were other points of disagreement as well. The Indigenous Peoples believe they had been assured of health care and social services, but these items do not appear in the written document. Furthermore, provisions that were included, such as aid to start farming where feasible, were not always honoured, at least not in the ways the First Peoples thought they should be. To them, Treaty Eight was essentially a peace and friendship treaty. In 1913–15, when the government moved to survey the Treaty Eight area, and particularly the individual allotments, the Indigenous people reacted with mistrust and fear, seeing this as a threat to their liberty of movement.[35] At Fort Resolution in 1920, the Tłı̨chǫ refused to accept their treaty payments as they had become unhappy about attempts to restrict hunting and fishing. They won recognition of their special position in a signed agreement and accepted the treaty payments. Then, the document disappeared.[36]

In the Northwest Territories, the first reserve was created at Hay River in 1974. In British Columbia, one was established under Treaty Eight at Fort Nelson in 1961, although the province had been laying them out since the 1850s. In 1979, Ottawa set aside 7,284 ha in Wood Buffalo National Park for the Fort Chipewyan Cree, following a breakdown of negotiations with Alberta. The Cree had requested 36,422 ha. The same band signed in 1986, when it received 4,970 ha of reserve land with full mineral rights as well as hunting, fishing, and trapping rights, and $26.6 million in cash. The Métis of the region could either enter treaty at the time of signing or take scrip. In the latter case, they received either 97 ha of land or $240 in cash.

Treaties Nine, Ten (1905–6), and Eleven (1921)

The prospect of mining development and the need to clear railway right-of-way in northern Ontario finally influenced Ottawa to agree to Indigenous demands for a treaty, which had begun as far back as 1884.[37] Treaty Nine (James Bay Treaty)[38] involved 336,300 km². Adhesions in 1929–30 covered territories included in Ontario when the province's final boundary was established in 1912. Treaty Ten, in northern Saskatchewan, was negotiated to clear land title for the province, created the year before, in 1905.[39]

In the Northwest Territories, the years following the signing of Treaty Eight saw conditions go from bad to worse, particularly in the region north of Great Slave Lake and along the Mackenzie River. Even though it was outside the Treaty Eight area, Indian Affairs opened an agency at Fort Simpson in 1911 "to distribute relief and to carry out experiments in farming." The agent arrived that summer with two horses, four oxen, and 10 tons of equipment and supplies. Despite being so far north, the experiment went reasonably well, and the suspicions of the Indigenous Peoples were allayed. Their lifestyle remained unchanged, adapted as it was to northern conditions.[40]

In 1908, the HBC established its first permanent post north of the Arctic Circle. Between 1910 and 1920, spurred by the growing presence of independent traders, it opened 14 more.[41] The years 1915–20, a period of international tension, war, and revolution, saw the fur market peaking in value at the same time as the use of currency replaced the old barter system. Indigenous traders, having no experience with this new form of buying and selling, were easily cheated. As well, the post-First World War influenza epidemic hit the North hard, particularly the Inuit. In 1920, the fur market crashed.

As with Treaty Eight, First Nations and Métis agreed to sign Treaty Eleven only after the government and Bishop Gabriel Breynat (1867–1954) assured them of complete freedom to hunt, trap, and fish.[42] For the Dene, the treaty was one of peace and friendship. The negotiators assured them this was their land. "You can do whatever you want," they told

Chief Samson Beardy (standing) and Commissioners Walter C. Cain and Herbert N. Awrey (seated at table) during negotiation of Treaty Nine payments, northern Ontario, 1929.

Library and Archives Canada, PA-094969

the Dene; "we are not going to stop you." When the government failed to honour the terms of the treaty, a disenchanted Breynat publicly campaigned against the way the northern Indigenous Peoples were being treated, a campaign that Father Fumoleau later carried on.[43] In 1973 the Dene filed a caveat in Alberta claiming Treaties Eight and Eleven were fraudulent. With the aid of retroactive legislation, the government later denied that they had had the right to file the caveat.

By now, the isolation that had protected the North for so long was broken. The final blow came during the Second World War with the construction of the **Alaska Highway**, completed in 1945. Yukon Indigenous Peoples helped to lay out its route. In so doing, they opened up their territories to non-Indigenous settlement.[44] By the 1950s, Indigenous people were no longer free to hunt and fish as they pleased. In some regions, they had to register their traplines.[45]

Changing Views on Jurisdiction

Although Europeans had been present in the eastern Arctic, off and on, since the eleventh century, and with increasing frequency since the seventeenth, the first permanent official presence occurred in the western Arctic when Canada sent the NWMP in 1903 to establish posts at Herschel Island and Fort McPherson. The Eastern Arctic Patrol was not instituted on a regular basis until 1922, although there had been occasional government voyages since the late nineteenth century. For most Inuit, first experiences with the new order were through the police, who represented the government until the mid-1950s, when the Department of Northern Affairs and Natural Resources took over.

In the Arctic, problems of first contact were worked out in terms of the Criminal Code rather than of land, as had occurred to the south. The Canadian officers were under orders not to meddle with Indigenous customs as long as they were "consistent with the general law." Canada also tempered its justice with cultural considerations when two Oblate missionaries were killed in 1913 near Bloody Falls on the Coppermine River. The two Inuit involved, Uluksuk and Sinnisiak, believed they were acting in self-defence when the priests made threatening gestures during an altercation. After being found innocent in the first trial, a judge sentenced both to be hanged, but this was commuted to life imprisonment. The two men were released after two years and became guides and special helpers to the police.[46]

However, when a police officer was shot to death in 1922, while investigating the deaths of a newcomer and four Inuit, the government felt that it had to set an example. A trial was held at Herschel Island, and the two Inuit found guilty, one of them about 16 years old, were hanged in 1924. This was the first hanging in the Arctic.[47] It dramatically illustrated the newcomers' emphasis on the offence and punishing the offender. In the Inuit way, the focus was to preserve the equilibrium of the community.[48] Insisting that the Inuit abide by Canadian law led to what was widely recognized as social injustice; by 1945, some Canadians believed that the Criminal Code should not apply to the Inuit.

With respect to administration, official reaction was to lump Inuit with First Nations. The first mention of Inuit in Canadian legislation occurred in 1924, when the Indian Act was

Leena Alivaktuk Very Proud Inuk, Barry Pottle. Permission Granted by Leena Alivaktuk and Barry Pottle.

Leena Alivaktuk, Very Proud Inuk!, **by Barry Pottle (b. 1961),** from his recent *Awareness Series*. Pottle, an Ottawa-based Inuk artist originally from Nunatsiavut, the homeland of Labrador Inuit, says: "The Eskimo Identification Tag (Disc number) was developed by the Government of Canada in the 1940/50s as a means of identifying Inuit for census purposes. From my understanding, Inuit of the Eastern and Western Arctic traditionally had one name which created confusion for government officials, especially if Inuit were identified as having the same name as another community member. It was only in 1970 that Project Surname commenced. The Eskimo Identification Tag program allowed the Government to list the name of each individual with a unique number which was effectively a precursor to the Social Insurance Number of today. Inuit people either wore or had to memorize their Eskimo Identification Number. Exhibiting both the E-numbers and portraits of my fellow Inuit gives me the opportunity to bridge the gap between a number and a person—it gives voice and identity to Inuit, to recent history."

amended to include them. This drew comment from Arthur Meighen, who was between his two terms as Prime Minister (1920–1 and 1926):

> I should not like to see the same policy precisely applied to the Eskimos as we have applied to the Indian. . . . After seventy-five years of tutelage and nursing . . . the Indians are still helpless on our hands.[49]

Perhaps it was because of such sentiments that the government did not apply the Act to Inuit when the Arctic came under Canada's flag. The Inuit came under Canadian jurisdiction as ordinary citizens, because the government had signed no treaties with them. However, regarding liquor, the police treated the Inuit the same way they did the First Nations, arguing that they were "morally," if not legally, the wards of Indian Affairs.[50] In 1927, Inuit affairs were transferred to the Northwest Territories, but the people still starved as game diminished. Quebec took Ottawa to court to get it to accept responsibility for the Inuit within its provincial borders. Historically and politically, Inuit had been habitually classed as First Nations, as Quebec proved in court. Its *coup de grâce* was to produce official correspondence, dated in 1879, in which Inuit were referred to as "Indians."[51] In 1939, the Supreme Court of Canada ruled that, for administrative purposes, the Inuit were "Indians" (i.e., fell under the umbrella of First Nations) and therefore a federal responsibility.

In 1950, the year the Inuit got the federal vote, an Order-in-Council vested authority for the Inuit in the Minister of Resources and Development. Administration for the Inuit was kept separate from that for First Nations. For example, there is no national registry for Inuit as there is for First Nations, and the Inuit were specifically excluded from the Indian Act when it was revised in 1951.[52] In other words, the status of Inuit was not acknowledged in policy until 1996 when the Royal Commission on Aboriginal Peoples explicitly identified the Inuit as a people owed "mutual recognition, mutual respect, sharing, and mutual responsibility," according to the language of the report.[53]

Ironically, Quebec experienced a change of attitude in 1960 and began actively claiming jurisdiction over the Inuit within its borders, a process it formalized with the establishment of a provincial ministry, Direction générale du Nouveau Québec, in 1962.[54] At one point, federal and provincial authorities were building rival schools.[55] In the meantime, officials remained convinced that Indigenous people must be encouraged to maintain their traditional way of life, as otherwise they would degenerate.[56] In the 1920s, two very large game preserves were established for exclusive Indigenous use, one in the Back and Thelon river basins, the other on Victoria and Banks islands. The latter became the Arctic Islands Game Preserve in 1926, when it was extended to cover all Arctic islands. The Thelon Wildlife Sanctuary, established in the central Arctic in 1927 and expanded in 1956, is Canada's second largest protected area, today straddling Nunavut and the NWT—and is more than twice the size of Belgium.[57]

New Strategic Significance

A turning point in official evaluation of the Arctic took place during and after the Second World War, when its strategic importance in world geopolitics became glaringly evident. The crucial roles of its weather stations and the Distant Early Warning radar line—the **DEW Line**—to military operations caused authorities to take another look at the land and its people.

When the government introduced family allowances and old age pensions, for instance, it hesitated to include the people of the Arctic. In the end, it did not send them cheques. Instead, it arranged credit at HBC posts for designated food supplies.[58] The requirement that the children attend school led the government to construct the necessary buildings in the 1940s and most of these were open by the 1950s. This effectively ended the old reliance on missions but brought a new set of problems.

The destruction of the natural subsistence base in the Far North in the twentieth century proceeded faster than replacements, although there were successes, such as the programs to rehabilitate beaver and muskrat in trapped-out areas.[59] The collapse of the white fox market, 1948–50, when the rest of Canada was experiencing an economic boom, highlighted once again the widespread and complex changes sweeping the Far North. The difficulties of the trapping industry increased even more with the campaign of the anti-fur lobby.[60] Into the twenty-first century, it was again in a severe depression.

Throughout this period, the policy of "encouraging" Inuit to relocate to areas selected by the government was in full force.[61] At first the relocations were co-ordinated with the fur trade. Indian Affairs informed the HBC in 1934 that if it wished to continue its operation in the North, it must assume responsibility for Indigenous welfare without expense to the department.[62] That failures in relocation resulted is hardly surprising. The Inuit were much better equipped to determine their own living requirements than were outsiders.

The considerations that guided the selections for **relocation** did not always match the conditions the Inuit needed for survival. This was illustrated by a series of attempts that began in 1934,

INDIGENOUS LEADERS | Susan Aglukark

Susan Aglukark (b. 1967) is an Inuk musician who has won great acclaim in Canada and internationally for her unique blend of traditional Inuit themes and elements of contemporary musical forms. The winner of multiple Juno awards, a recipient of the Queen's Diamond Jubilee Medal, and a member of the Order of Canada, Aglukark has been an inspiration for young people across Canada. Aglukark has not taken her fame lightly, but rather she has used her musical talent and the reputation it has won her to promote a number of humanitarian concerns. She serves as a special adviser to the Collateral Damage Project, an organization devoted to creating a protective dialogue on the issues of suicide and mental health. One of her songs, "Kathy," deals with the issue of suicide in youth. From 2008 to 2011, she served as the chair of the Arctic Children and Youth Foundation, an organization whose primary "objective is to champion activities that will improve lives and provide greater opportunities for the Children and Youth throughout Arctic Canada." She is also the founder of the Arctic Rose Fund, an effort to establish food banks across Arctic Canada. Her message of caring for young people is universal and it lives in both her music and in her speaking engagements.

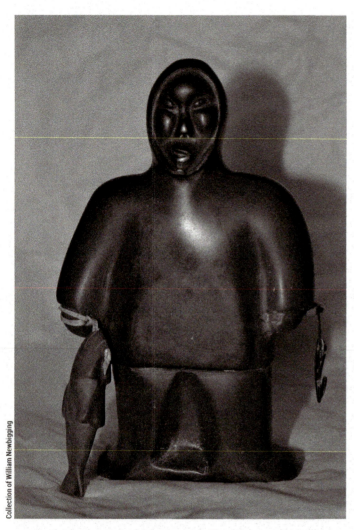

Untitled by Samwillie Mickpegak (1922–2002). This steatite carving with leather and cotton string was given to co-author Bill Newbigging by a former nurse at the Hamilton Sanatorium. Mickpegak, an Inuk from Kuujjuaraapik (Disc Number E9312), was one of hundreds of convalescent tuberculosis patients from the Far North who made these carvings.

when the government transported 22 Inuit from Cape Dorset, 18 from Pond Inlet, and 12 from Pangnirtung to Dundas Harbour. What appeared to officials to be a suitable location, however, turned out to have ice conditions in winter that impeded both hunting and dog-team travel needed to maintain traplines. After two years, the Inuit had to be evacuated. Some went back to their home bases, but others tried life in still another location. In the succeeding years, the government transported Inuit to one site after another (Croker Bay, Arctic Bay, Fort Ross, Spence Bay), each one of which proved to be unsuitable for the hunting and trapping way of life that officials were convinced must be preserved.[63] This shifting of the Inuit population reached its peak from 1958 to 1962 but continued at least to the end of the 1970s.[64] Game continued to diminish, and Inuit continued to die of starvation and disease as they were shuttled back and forth.

By the mid-1950s and early 1960s, the Inuit had the highest rate of tuberculosis in the world, an ironic situation at a time when the government was establishing an elaborate health-care system in the Arctic.[65] By 1952, the largest population of Inuit in the country was to be found in the Sanatorium in Hamilton, Ontario. The legacy of this event is to be found in the soapstone carvings made by those who were convalescing.[66] Sometimes, in the case of children who had been sent to southern Canada for treatment, southern families adopted them without informing their parents.[67]

Still convinced of the need to relocate, the government considered, and rejected, a plan to move the Inuit to the south. The North needed its people for a new reason: to support Canada's claims to sovereignty. Spurred by this imperative of international politics, the government began in 1953 to move Inuit from Inukjuak (Port Harrison) in Arctic Quebec to Ellesmere Island in the High Arctic, where game resources were untouched. As well, it brought Inuit in from Pond Inlet, northern Baffin Island. In all, nearly 90 Inuit were relocated to Grise Fiord and Resolute Bay in a forced move to which they did not become reconciled. Not only that, but the game resources available were not what the new arrivals were used to. In the view of historian Shelagh Grant, concern about its sovereignty in the Arctic had been Canada's main motivation for the resettlement policy, which she termed a "misadventure." The Inuit put it more strongly. As they see it, they have been the subjects of a failed social and political experiment.[68]

Nunavut ("Our Land") Is Born

The creation of the territory of Nunavut out of the Northwest Territories on 1 April 1999 was a dramatic moment for the country. Comprising more than 2.2 million km², better than a fifth of Canada's entire surface, Nunavut is the largest land claim settlement in the country's history. The agreement involved the surrender of Aboriginal title on the part of the Inuit (who comprise about 85 per cent of a total Nunavut population of 35,944, as of the 2016 census) but gave them ownership in fee simple of 350,000 km², an area half the size of Saskatchewan,[69] the largest private landholding in North America. Nunavut's official languages are English, French, and Inuktitut, and its flag depicts on a white ground a red inukshuk with a blue North Star. The agreement also included a cash settlement of $1.17 billion over 14 years.

The idea for the creation of a northern jurisdiction administered in co-operation with the Inuit developed after the Second World War and came under active consideration beginning in 1978 as a result of a proposal by Inuit Tapirisat, a national organization representing the four regions of Nunatsiavut (Labrador), Nunavik (northern Quebec), Nunavut, and

Inuk elder Ekalool Juralak lights a traditional "qulluliq" at the dedication of the Nunavut legislature in Iqaluit on the day before Nunavut officially became a territory.

Inuvialuit (NWT).[70] The concept received a major boost in 1985 when the Royal Commission on the Economic Union and Development Prospects for Canada (the Macdonald Commission) supported it on the grounds that regional governments adapted to particular circumstances, cultural and otherwise, would better meet the needs of the Canadian North.

That same year, 1985, the project received unexpected outside support when the United States sent the *Polar Sea* through the Northwest Passage without permission from Canada. This was the second such infringement on the part of the Americans (the first occurred in 1971), who wanted those waters to be declared international. Since the Inuit and their forebears have been in the region for more than 1,000 years, the creation of a self-governing territory was seen as the best possible way of strengthening Canada's claim to Arctic sovereignty. The Northwest Territories endorsed the idea by a margin of 54 to 46 per cent in a plebiscite held in 1992, which led to an accord being signed that same year for the creation of the new territory.[71]

The project took final shape in 1993 with the **Nunavut Land Claim Settlement** and, finally, with the federal Nunavut Act. The territory was given a new style of "public government," more or less on the elective provincial model but with greater decentralization.[72] In one major aspect, it differs from the party-oriented governments to the south in that in some areas it follows the Inuit practice of reaching decisions by consensus. Indigenous traditions have also influenced the justice system, worked out in co-operation with the Royal Canadian Mounted Police.[73]

Challenges include the training of lawyers and administrators, and housing shortages compounded by rising costs, particularly of fuel and transportation.[74] At the turn of the century, widespread poverty and high unemployment showed no signs of easing, resulting in labour unrest, and the youth suicide rate was the highest in the world.[75] Still, for Inuit elder Nancy Karetak-Lindell, the first elected MP for Nunavut, the creation of the territory has given her people back their lives.[76] In fact, by 2017 there was evidence that Karetak-Lindell was right. The Nunavut Economic Development Strategy, developed in 2003, is now bearing fruit. In 2012, this plan was updated and in February of 2014 the Nunavut-Sivummat Conference was held in order to complete the process of updating the Strategy. Similarly, in the summer of 2012 a number of regional public policy forum roundtables were held across the territory and these have resulted in new development partnerships between Inuit groups and developers. In addition, for the past several summers luxury cruise lines, working in close co-ordination with Nunavut tourism and arts officials, have made upwards of a dozen annual transits of all or part of the Northwest Passage, which has brought many thousands of dollars to Indigenous artists throughout Nunavut and to communities along the route, such as Cambridge Bay and Pond Inlet.

The proposal for the establishment of Nunavut is best given in the words of the chair of the Inuit Land Claims Commission, John Amagoalik. His account of the process reveals much about the strong desire for an Inuit jurisdiction within the federal framework:

> When we first presented our Nunavut proposal to the Government of Canada, they indicated that they did not want to deal with political development at the land claims table. They very much wanted to negotiate land claims and to leave political development on "another track." Those were their words. The Inuit wanted to keep the two things together. We made it very clear that we could not sign any agreement

that did not include the commitment to create Nunavut. At that point we agreed to disagree. But we agreed to start negotiating the details of the land claims agreement while we were pursuing Nunavut through the political arena. We made it clear that when the land claims agreement was ready to be signed, the creation of Nunavut would have to be brought in, if it was ready to be part of the land claims agreement. In the twenty years that it took to negotiate the land claims settlement, the two went along parallel lines. We were negotiating the claims here, and we were pursuing Nunavut through other means.[77]

Questions to Consider

1. How did life change in the Arctic after the Klondike gold rush?
2. How did the northern economy adapt to the collapse of the whaling industry?
3. Why did the government become so interested in relocating people across the Arctic?
4. Why was Nunavut created?

Recommended Readings

Abel, Kerry. *Drum Songs: Glimpses of Dene History*. Montreal and Kingston: McGill-Queen's University Press, 2005.

Alcantara, Christopher. *Negotiating the Deal: Comprehensive Land Claims in Canada*. Toronto: University of Toronto Press, 2013.

Bennett, John R., and Susan Rowley. *Uqalurait: An Oral History of Nunavut*. Montreal and Kingston: McGill-Queen's University Press, 2008.

Bussidor, Ila, and Üsten Bilgen-Reinart. *Night Spirits: The Story of the Relocation of the Sayisi Dene*. Winnipeg: University of Manitoba Press, 1997.

"Dene Nation History." http://denenation.com/history.

Dorais, Louis-Jacques. *The Language of the Inuit: Syntax, Semantics, and Society in the Arctic*. Montreal and Kingston: McGill-Queen's University Press, 2015.

"Louie Kamookak." https://www.louiekamookak.com.

North, Dick. *The Lost Patrol*. Vancouver: Raincoast Books, 1995 [1978].

Pitseolak, Peter, and Dorothy Harley Eber. *People from Our Side*, trans. Ann Hanson. Montreal and Kingston: McGill-Queen's University Press, 1993.

Tester, Frank James, and Peter Kulchyski. *Tammarniit (Mistakes)*. Vancouver: University of British Columbia Press, 1994.

Zaslow, Morris. *The Northward Expansion of Canada, 1914–1967*. Toronto: McClelland & Stewart, 1988.

17 Canadian Courts and Aboriginal Rights

CHAPTER OUTLINE

Aboriginal and treaty rights form the central subject of this chapter. To demonstrate the centrality of the issue of Aboriginal rights, we will examine the difficult events of the Oka Crisis, or the "Siege of Kanesatake" as some Haudenosaunee leaders prefer to call it. We will also examine a number of important court cases—*Sparrow*, *Adams*, *Sioui*, and *Delgamuukw*—to demonstrate how Aboriginal rights are defined by the Supreme Court of Canada. Finally, we will look at aspects of the Canadian justice system to learn about the differing concepts of justice.

LEARNING OUTCOMES

1. Students will be able to define the term "Aboriginal right."

2. Students will understand the context that led to establishment of the Indian Claims Commission of 1970.

3. Students will learn about the causes and outcomes of the Oka Crisis of 1990.

TIMELINE Treaties from Louis XV to the Nisga'a Final Agreement Act

1717
Louis XV grants seigneury at Oka (Kanesatake) to Seminary of St Sulpice as an "Iroquois mission" (as described in the grant).

1721
Nearly 900 Haudenosaunee members move to area of Sulpician mission.

1781
Kanienkehaka leaders at Kanesatake go to court to prove proprietorship of land held by Sulpicians but lose their case.

1841
British confirm seminary's title at Oka.

1875
Sulpicians obtain court order to dismantle Methodist church at Oka.

1868
Haudenosaunee and Omamiwinini leaders, citing Oka seminary's tyranny and oppression, unsuccessfully petition Ottawa for clear title to the land and their village.

1885–9
St Catherine's Milling v. The Queen: Judicial Committee of the Privy Council, in complex jurisdictional case between Ontario and Ottawa, upholds validity of Proclamation of 1763 but claims that British, by setting foot in North America, gained title to all Indigenous lands.

1877
Haudenosaunee protesters burn the Catholic church at Oka.

1912
Privy Council upholds Oka seminary title in ongoing land dispute.

1936
Sulpicians sell most of Oka land to Belgian real estate company, which begins to sell parcels of land.

1961
Kanienkehaka leaders at Kanesatake request that land be formally declared a reserve, but get no response.

1969–77
Indian Claims Commission headed by Dr Lloyd Barber.

1970
Federal Fisheries Act restricts Aboriginal right.

1973
Supreme Court split decision on Nisga'a land claim case (*Calder*) opens way for greater recognition of Aboriginal rights, although Nisga'a technically lose in court.

1974
Gull Bay band of Ojibwa organizes reserve police force.

1975
Comprehensive claim by Kanesatake residents for Aboriginal title rejected by Ottawa.

Continued

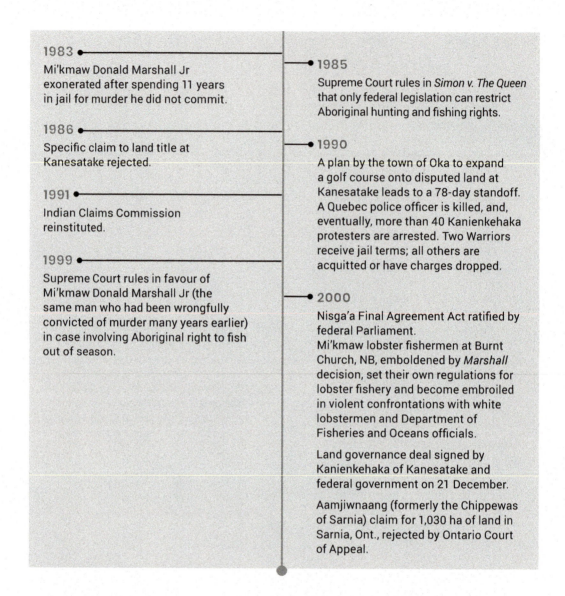

1983
Mi'kmaw Donald Marshall Jr exonerated after spending 11 years in jail for murder he did not commit.

1986
Specific claim to land title at Kanesatake rejected.

1991
Indian Claims Commission reinstituted.

1999
Supreme Court rules in favour of Mi'kmaw Donald Marshall Jr (the same man who had been wrongfully convicted of murder many years earlier) in case involving Aboriginal right to fish out of season.

1985
Supreme Court rules in *Simon v. The Queen* that only federal legislation can restrict Aboriginal hunting and fishing rights.

1990
A plan by the town of Oka to expand a golf course onto disputed land at Kanesatake leads to a 78-day standoff. A Quebec police officer is killed, and, eventually, more than 40 Kanienkehaka protesters are arrested. Two Warriors receive jail terms; all others are acquitted or have charges dropped.

2000
Nisga'a Final Agreement Act ratified by federal Parliament.
Mi'kmaw lobster fishermen at Burnt Church, NB, emboldened by *Marshall* decision, set their own regulations for lobster fishery and become embroiled in violent confrontations with white lobstermen and Department of Fisheries and Oceans officials.

Land governance deal signed by Kanienkehaka of Kanesatake and federal government on 21 December.

Aamjiwnaang (formerly the Chippewas of Sarnia) claim for 1,030 ha of land in Sarnia, Ont., rejected by Ontario Court of Appeal.

Treaty Three and the *St Catherine's Milling* Decision

Canada's first **Aboriginal rights** court case gave rise to two statements that set legal precedents in Canada. One concerned Aboriginal rights, the other, provincial rights. At the time, provincial rights aroused the greater passion. Indeed, Aboriginal rights were considered almost incidental, although they were at the very heart of the dispute. These rights cover the pieces that the treaties did not mention. Aboriginal rights can refer to claims on resources such as fish, game, timber, non-timber forest products, minerals, and water. In Aboriginal rights cases Indigenous Peoples are generally called upon to demonstrate continuous usage of the resources in question.

St Catherine's Milling v. The Queen arose from the long-standing dispute between Ontario and the federal government over the location of the province's northwestern boundary.[1] The Indigenous Peoples whose lands were concerned were neither consulted nor brought to the witness stand in the ensuing court action. In 1884, the Privy Council in London decided in favour of Ontario. The federal government was not so easily defeated, however. It delayed enacting the enabling legislation to put the decision into effect. Ontario responded by filing a legal suit in the High Court of Ontario against the federally licensed St Catherine's Milling and Lumber Company for illegal logging on provincial lands.

The argument boiled down to this: exactly what had the Dominion obtained from the First Nations in Treaty Three?[2] The lumber company, and hence the government in Ottawa, argued that before the Crown acquired land title—through purchase rather than conquest—First

---

HISTORICAL BACKGROUND | Indigenous Peoples' "Ownership" of Land

Misunderstanding and misrepresentation of Indigenous concepts of "ownership" have been perpetuated to this day, in that it is claimed that Indigenous people did not "believe" in "ownership." This misrepresentation of a concept has led to real-world consequences for Indigenous people, as will be discussed throughout the chapter. The pressure of non-Indigenous claims to their territories has led First Peoples to articulate traditional concepts in terms understandable to non-Indigenous people. Indigenous Peoples' cyclical and holistic ways of viewing the world translate into land being held as common property by the community as a whole. First Nations have an undivided interest in the land. Everyone, as a member of the group, has a right to the whole. Furthermore, the right to the use of land belongs not only to the living but also to those who have gone before as well as to those who will come. Neither does this right belong exclusively to humans; rather, it is inherent to other living things and objects imbued with a spiritual presence, such as animals, plants, and rocks.

When Indigenous Peoples signed treaties and land agreements, they could not give up absolute ownership of the land, because they never claimed it for only themselves. The Crown, to claim absolute title, would have to obtain surrenders from past generations as well as those of the future. As far as First Nations are concerned, when they signed treaties, they were not alienating their lands but sharing them.[3] They were astonished at the idea that their hunting and fishing rights originated with the Proclamation of 1763. In their view, those rights had always existed. The treaties confirmed an already existing situation, subject to limitation only in areas where settlement had occurred.

Nations had been owners of the land but subject to the restriction that they could sell only to the Canadian government. Neither provinces nor individuals had the right to buy lands from First Nations. The Proclamation of 1763 specifically referred to "lands reserved for Indians." Because of the wording of the Proclamation, treaties were an essential prerequisite for the expansion of colonial settlement in British North America, and only the federal authority could engage in that activity.

Oliver Mowat (1820–1903), Premier of Ontario, appeared for the province. He was blunt: "We say there is no Indian title in law or in equity. The claim of the Indians is simply moral and no more." Property, so the argument went, was just something created by law. Since First Nations had no rules or regulations that could be considered laws, they had no title to their ancestral territories that the Crown could recognize. There could be no such thing as Aboriginal title independent of the Crown's law.

During the course of the province's arguments in *St Catherine's Milling*, Indigenous Peoples were described as an "inferior race . . . in an inferior state of civilization" who had "no government and no organization, and cannot be regarded as a nation capable of holding lands."[4] Indigenous Peoples' understanding of "owning" or "holding" land has always been rather different. Ironically, in an essential respect this view is not unlike the "trustee" position the government took towards its holding of lands for the Indigenous Peoples (see Historical Background box).

Three weeks after the first hearing, on 10 June 1885, the Chancellor of Ontario, John Alexander Boyd (1837–1916), presented his decision. His statement on Indigenous Peoples rights set a precedent for Canadian courts in its thoroughness. By that date, the Northwest Rebellion was effectively over. Pītikwahanapiwīyin had surrendered, and only Big Bear was still at large. Two of Boyd's sons had volunteered against Riel. Boyd described Indigenous people as having no fixed residence, moving around as they needed. "As heathens and barbarians it was not thought that they had any proprietary title to the soil, nor any claim thereto as to interfere with the plantations, and the general prosecution of colonization."[5] As legal ownership of the land had never been attributed to them, Treaty Three First Nations had not conveyed any such rights to the federal government. Therefore, the licence the Dominion had granted to St Catherine's Milling Company was invalid.

According to Boyd, in legal terms Treaty Three also was meaningless. If they so chose, Indigenous Peoples could treat with the Crown for the extinction of their Aboriginal right of occupancy. But if they refused to do so, the government could go ahead with settlement and development of the country, displacing Indigenous Peoples if necessary. Boyd's decision was maintained through three appeals, the final one to the **Judicial Committee of the Privy Council** (1888). The *St Catherine's Milling* decision was still in effect in 2017 despite some monumental legal battles since.[6]

As for the First Nations of Treaty Three, they did not fare well. Ottawa and Ontario could not agree on the promised selection, location, and extent of reserves. For some, it would be a generation, or even several generations, before their reserves were confirmed. For others, the process was still going on into the twenty-first century. Neither has the exact nature of First Nations' interest in reserve lands been fully defined.

During Treaty Three negotiations, Mawedopenais, Fort Frances chief, had repeated a sentiment that Indigenous leaders had been expressing in various terms ever since the first arrival of Europeans in North America: "This is what we think, that the Great Spirit has planted us on this ground where we are, as you were where you came from. We think where we are is our property." He added that the Great Spirit had provided the Indigenous Peoples with the rules "that we should follow to govern us rightly."[7] Mississauga Kahgegagahbowh (George Copway) was even more categorical: "The hunting grounds of the Indians were secured by right, a law and custom among themselves. No one was allowed to hunt on another's land, without invitation or permission." Repeated offences could result in banishment from the group.[8]

Nearly Three Centuries of Confrontation at Oka

An even older but still only partially resolved case was that of the Haudenosaunee of **Oka** against the Seminary of St Sulpice.[9] It dated from Louis XV's 1717 grant of a seigneury to the Sulpicians on the Ottawa River where it meets the St Lawrence, about 30 km west of Montreal, on the condition that it be used as a Haudenosaunee mission.[10] The grant left unresolved, however, the question of whether the Sulpicians were the sole proprietors or trustees.[11] In 1721, nearly 900 Haudenosaunee people, mainly Kanienkehaka, moved to the new location at Lake of Two Mountains, with funds provided by a private benefactor.[12]

As far as the Haudenosaunee were concerned (particularly the Kanienkehaka, who predominated), this was their territory and they went to court in 1781 to prove their proprietorship. Their evidence was the "Two-Dog Wampum" belt (the dogs, at each end of the belt, were the protectors of their land, represented by 27 beads). The court rejected their claim.[13] That the Haudenosaunee position at Oka aroused concern was evident in the fact that the British felt it necessary to issue a special ordinance in 1841 confirming the seminary's title. Encouraged by this support and now much less enthusiastic about its missionary role, especially as the Haudenosaunee were deserting Catholicism in favour of Methodism, the seminary pressured the Haudenosaunee to leave. The Sulpicians brought in French-Canadian settlers to replace them.[14]

In 1853 and 1854, the department set aside lands for the Omamiwinini at Maniwaki, Quebec, and for the Haudenosaunee at Doncaster, Ontario. Some moved to the new locations, but most rejected the compromise.[15] The situation boiled over in 1868, when both the Omamiwinini and Haudenosaunee, led by new Haudenosaunee chief Onasakenrat (1845–81),[16] petitioned Ottawa for clear title to the land and to their village, Kanesatake.[17] The result was the arrest and jailing of three chiefs, including Onasakenrat (who would end up in jail eight times on land-related charges), and an Order-in-Council in 1869 reaffirming the seminary's title.

Another inquiry, this one in 1878, found that the seigneury was the property of the seminary.[18] Faced with the Haudenosaunee refusal to accept this decision, the department arranged for the seminary to buy land in the Township of Gibson, Ontario, as compensation for the Haudenosaunee and as a solution to the problem. Although the seminary built houses on the newly acquired lands and offered lots for each family, few finally agreed to the move. For one thing, no one had consulted them as to the location of the new reserve. For another, they considered the compensation too little.[19]

This rejection led to still another report, in 1883. It spoke of a deep-seated public conviction that "although the Indians may not have a legal claim to the lands, as owners thereof, they are nevertheless entitled to compensation for the loss of lands which they had been led to suppose were set apart for their benefit."[20] In the meantime, not all was confrontation. Between 1886 and 1910, Kanienkehaka and non-Indigenous leaders collaborated on a reforestation project to stabilize the region's sandy soil. It became a model for other such efforts in the province.[21]

Since neither side would budge on the land issue, the case was eventually fought out in the courts, with the government in Ottawa paying the expenses of both sides. In 1912, the Privy Council decided in favour of the seminary but suggested that a charitable trust that could be enforced be set up for the Haudenosaunee.[22] Then, in 1936, the seminary, faced with a financial crisis, sold most of its seigneury, including the forest at Oka, to a Belgian real estate company.[23] The company set up a sawmill operation and began to sell off the land for agricultural development. This upset the Haudenosaunee so much that, in 1945, the alarmed department bought the seminary's unsold lands, except those used for religious purposes, plus an additional 500 acres (202 ha) of woodland for fuel, and assumed responsibility for the Haudenosaunee.[24]

All this took place without input from the residents of Kanesatake, who continued to press their claims. Their request in 1961 that the land in question be formally declared a reserve brought no response. They followed up in 1975 with a comprehensive claim asserting Aboriginal title, which the department rejected. The Haudenosaunee came back two years later with a specific claim, but it, too, was eventually rejected in 1986. The Haudenosaunee, for their part, continued to reject proposals that they settle on nearby federal lands. In the meantime the Warrior movement—described as the defence arm of the Longhouse religion but not universally accepted as such—was steadily gaining ground.

That the problem was not only unresolved but had intensified became dramatically evident in the summer of 1990, when the town of Oka announced it was going to expand a golf course, built in the 1950s, into the disputed area. The Haudenosaunee responded by barricading the location. Quebec police tried to storm the barricade, failed, and one police officer was killed.[25] Kahnawake residents, about 30 km away, came to the support of their kin by blocking highways crossing their reserve, as well as the Mercier Bridge, one of the main access routes to the Island of Montreal. The standoff at Kanesatake lasted for 78 days. Quebec tried to cut off food supplies to the holdouts, a move the Haudenosaunee thwarted with the aid of the Red Cross.[26]

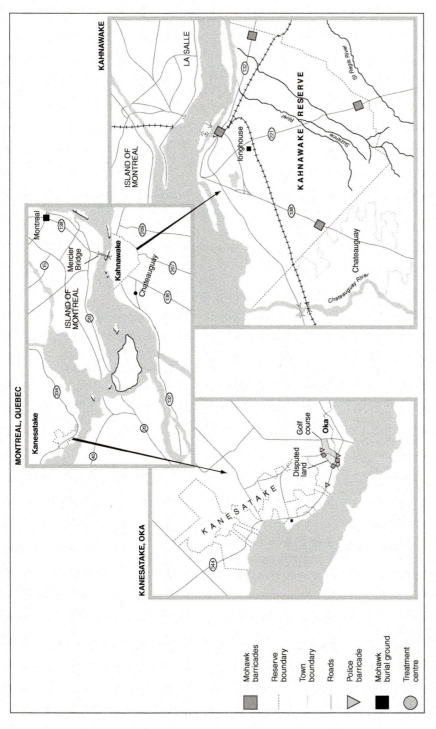

Map 17.1 Kahnawake, Oka, Mercier Bridge.

Associated Press Graphic, 1990; Rick Horning, *One Nation Under the Gun* (Toronto: Stoddart, 1991).

Ellen Gabriel became the face of the Oka Crisis thanks to her role as media spokesperson for the Haudenosaunee. She has continued to engage in high-profile activism and remains a model for calm but forcible assertion of rights. Her description of her activism before, during, and after the Oka Crisis is well worth noting:

> I began my activism before the "Oka Crisis" of 1990, not that it was noticeable. Perhaps the best way to describe my awakening to the situation all Indigenous Peoples experience was when I was a teenager in the mid-70s, reading *Akwesasne Notes*. There in the *Notes* was an article regarding the Black Hills and how the Hopi and Navajo peoples were trying to stop uranium mining in their territory. I remember reading a quote from an elder that digging uranium out of the earth was like pulling the lungs out of Mother Earth. It was a statement that touched me as I had never heard anyone speak in such a way to defend the rights of Mother Earth.
>
> As a child growing up in the 60s and witnessing the peace and love movement of the "Hippies" my curiosity was piqued on issues like women's rights, anti-war movements and of course love. I was disturbed in listening to the news on television about the assassination of Martin Luther King [Jr.] from racism and narrow-mindedness. I would think that this was wrong, to hate someone simply because of their race.
>
> The sad thing was at that time mainstream media never covered any "Native" issues. It was only community newspapers like *Akwesasne Notes* that reflected the realities of [being] Onkwehón:we [Indigenous], at least that I knew of. The AIM movement was heralded by many of the youth in my community but like any movement that becomes too strong, it becomes divided by government authorities spewing their propaganda to a public only too willing to believe the myths about "wild and savage" Indian peoples.
>
> In the spring of 1990, I joined other community members in Kanehsatà:ke to fight against the expansion of the 9-hole golf course on the last of our communal lands. Our barricade lasted 6 months with one of its most memorable moments in our history, manifested through an SQ [Sûreté du Québec] raid against the people of Kanehsatà:ke's barricade on July 11th. A botched raid whereby they attempted to eliminate us in order to silence our voices through the use of force. It was a summer of hundreds if not thousands of human rights violations that remain unanswered to this day.
>
> The extreme measures that Quebec and Canada took to criminalize the two affected Mohawk communities of Kanehsatá:ke and Kahnawake reinforced my idea that being born Onkwehón:we meant to be constantly attacked, especially if one holds strongly and firmly to the beliefs of our ancestors.
>
> Since the Oka Crisis of 1990, or as I prefer to call it the Siege of Kanehsatake, I have travelled throughout the world speaking about the Siege, but as well about Indigenous Peoples' rights, history, culture, traditions and realities of Indigenous

John Kenny, *The Gazette*, Montreal

Ellen Gabriel (right) on the blockade at Kanesatake in the summer of 1990. Her calm and courageous demeanour won support from all segments of Canadian society.

peoples of this Turtle Island. I have participated in negotiations with government both provincially and federally and participated in various international forums. I have listened to Indigenous elders, youth and people from throughout Mother Earth on the problems they have been experiencing because of colonial practices like the Indian Act and the Indian Residential School System. But as well, I have heard from the frontline workers, community activists, professionals and academics who have solutions to restore peace and strength to our nations.[27]

In the end, the province asked the federal government to send in the army. In the trials that followed, two Kanienkehaka men were found guilty of 29 of 56 charges: Ronald Cross (known as "Lasagna," 1957–99) was sentenced to four years and four months and Gordon ("Noriega") Lazore to 23 months. A third, Roger Lazore, was acquitted. Of 39 Kanienkehaka

David Cooper/Getty Images

Rebecca Belmore stands in front of her wood megaphone *Speaking to Their Mother* in 2014. Belmore (b. 1960), an Anishinaabe originally from northwestern Ontario, explains: "This artwork was my response to what is now referred to in Canadian history as the 'Oka Crisis.' During the summer of 1990, many protests were mounted in support of the Mohawk Nation of Kanesatake in their struggle to maintain their territory. This object was taken into many First Nations communities—reservation, rural, and urban. I was particularly interested in locating the Aboriginal voice on the land. Asking people to address the land directly was an attempt to hear political protest as poetic action."[28]

men brought to trial a few months later, five were freed for lack of evidence. The rest were acquitted.[29]

More than a decade later there was still no agreement on what had been learned from Oka.[30] On the positive side, the crisis heightened public interest in the situation of Indigenous Peoples in general. Another positive development has been Ottawa's increase in funding for land claim settlements, somewhat speeding up a still all-too-slow process.[31] More specifically, the federal government has continued an already launched policy of buying land in the disputed area to prevent another confrontation. Finally, 10 years after the crisis, it signed a land governance deal with Kanienkehaka leaders on 21 December 2000, which some people have hailed as a step towards self-government.[32] The underlying specific land claim, however, remains to be met nearly 30 years after the Oka Crisis came to a head in 1990.[33]

Hunting, Fishing, and Other Resource Claims

In other cases before the courts, there has been more accommodation with regard to hunting and fishing rights than in the matter of land rights. Even so, the record is inconsistent. In Nova Scotia, for instance, a series of cases beginning in the 1920s found against hunting and fishing rights,[34] based on the understanding that Indigenous sovereignty had never been recognized. That decision was upheld in appeals.[35] On another level, in 1970, the federal Fisheries Act did away with the treaties of 1725, 1752, and 1779. That situation remained until 1985, when the Supreme Court ruled that the 1752 agreement was still valid. In the eyes of the Mi'kmaq, the new decision meant that their rights were neither outdated nor set aside.[36] Although the courts have upheld the validity of the 1752 treaty, they have not upheld its status as an international treaty.[37]

Similarly, other provincial courts have in general upheld usufructuary rights—but based on treaty, not on Aboriginal rights. A major exception has been Quebec. Since it had no treaties to override its legislation, it has claimed the right to regulate hunting and fishing. In New Brunswick, on the other hand, Mi'kmaq resistance in 1981 led to 400 heavily armed provincial police, backed by bulldozers and helicopters, raiding the Restigouche reserve community and confiscating 250 kg of salmon and more than 75 nets. A second raid followed two days later, in which tear gas was used and the bridge linking the reserve to Campbellton, New Brunswick, was blocked. The Mi'kmaq in their turn blockaded the four roads leading into their reserve. After the police left the reserve, the two sides reached an agreement on fishing rights.[38] Federal game laws, on the other hand, have prevailed over treaties. In other aspects of Aboriginal rights, the courts have been less tolerant of Indigenous claims. For example, in British Columbia in 1969, Frank Calder, founder and president (1955–74) of the Nisga'a Tribal Council (later the Nisga'a Nation),[39] maintained that his people's Aboriginal title had never been extinguished and that they had not ceded their territory to Britain. In ***Calder v. Attorney General***, he repeated what another spokesman had told a Royal Commission in 1888:

> What we don't like about the government is their saying this: "We will give you this much land." How can they give it when it is our own? We cannot understand it. They have never bought it from us or our forefathers. They have never fought or conquered our people and taken the land in that way, and yet they say now that they will give us so much land—our own land. . . . It has been ours for a thousand years.[40]

As a result, Calder argued, provincial land legislation was invalid.

The BC Supreme Court ruled, however, that any rights Indigenous Peoples had at time of contact were overruled by the mere enactment of white man's law, in spite of the fact that none of the legislation stated that fact. In 1973, the Supreme Court of Canada upheld the ruling on a technicality.[41] Pierre Trudeau (Prime Minister, 1968–79 and 1980–4), assessing this judgment, conceded that Indigenous Peoples might have more rights than he had recognized in the White Paper of 1969 (see Chapter 15).[42] He entrenched Aboriginal rights without definition in

INDIGENOUS LEADERS | Harold Cardinal (1945–2005)

Richard Siemens © University of Alberta

As he became more engaged in negotiations with the federal government in his early twenties as the leader of the Indian Association of Alberta, Harold Cardinal also helped to shape policy. His most lasting contributions, however, are his publications, beginning in 1969 with *The Unjust Society: The Tragedy of Canada's Indians*. This book was written as a direct challenge to the 1969 White Paper, which urged the assimilation of Indigenous Peoples and argued for the abolition of status. Cardinal, of Cree ancestry, pointed out that this strategy would deprive Indigenous Peoples of their hard-earned rights. He argued that implementation of the ideas proposed in the White Paper would be akin to rewriting history. He argued

Harold Cardinal, Honorary Doctor of Laws, University of Alberta, 1999.

that cultures could only be protected under the structures that had evolved through negotiation over the centuries. Well-written and passionate, *The Unjust Society* quickly found a large audience and many Canadians were convinced by Cardinal and alarmed by the evident injustice inherent in the White Paper. After publication of *The Unjust Society*, governments could no longer manage to ignore Indigenous perspectives. Academics and policy-makers referred constantly to Cardinal's powerful book. Notably, he was also the principal author of *Citizens Plus*, the "Red Paper" produced by the Indian Association of Alberta, and, in 1977, published *The Rebirth of Canada's Indians*.

Throughout his life, Dr Cardinal studied and worked in the fields of policy development and education, and in his later years he earned a law degree from Harvard University. His contributions to the First Nations of Canada and to public life in general were enormous.

the Constitution of 1982 despite a determined assault by the provincial premiers to prevent it. This partial constitutional victory for Aboriginal rights did not mean acceptance by the courts, however, as the *Bear Island* case illustrates.

At issue in *Attorney General of Ontario v. Bear Island Foundation*, 1984, was the legal nature of the continuing interest of the Teme-agama Anishnabay (Bear Island people) in their ancestral lands, about 4,000 square miles (10,360 km²) in and around Lake Temagami (100 km north of North Bay, Ontario), against a provincial government that wished to open up the area for resource and tourist development. When the Teme-agama claim finally came before the court, Justice Donald Steele ruled that the British Crown had acquired its rights in Canada by conquest, first against the French (he did not explain how that related to Aboriginal title) and then against Obwandiyag (Pontiac) in 1763. He made no mention of the First Nations and Métis allies who had fought for the British on those occasions. The "primitive level" of First Nations' social organization, the judge wrote, meant that "the Indian occupation could not be considered true and legal, and that the Europeans were lawfully entitled to take possession of the land and settle it with colonies."[43] Judge Steele's decision was upheld in 1989 on the basis of new evidence to the effect that during the Robinson negotiations the Teme-agama had sold their land for $25.

The British North America Act gave the federal government responsibility for "Indians and lands reserved for Indians," a responsibility that time and again has not been fulfilled. However, "all lands, mines, minerals and royalties" from the land were to be the proprietary interest of the four provinces that first made up Confederation. (The Prairie provinces gained control of their natural resources in 1930.) This separation of powers has meant that the provinces have a vested interest in opposing Aboriginal land claims.[44] Thus, there were (and are) serious concerns as to the adequacy of existing systems—whether by direct negotiation with the government or through the courts—to deal with Indigenous claims, dating back to the nineteenth century.

In 1890 formal arbitration was attempted with the establishment of a board to deal with disputes between Canada and the provinces of Ontario and Quebec. Indigenous Peoples were allowed little opportunity to participate, and in only one case were they permitted even to select their own lawyers. During its decade of existence, the board heard about 20 cases dealing with disputes over financial matters and lands. It succeeded in settling only three of these cases; the courts later reversed two other decisions.

In the wake of the 1969 White Paper, the first hint of a change in Prime Minister Trudeau's position came during the second year of the Indian Claims Commission, in 1970, when its terms of reference were broadened to include comprehensive claims (claims arising in non-treaty areas). This opened the door for the Indian Claims Commissioner, Lloyd Barber, to consider Aboriginal rights. Although government policy did not officially change until after the Nisga'a (*Calder*) decision in 1973, and the Commission's life was short (it lasted until 1977), Barber won praise because of his even-handed approach and willingness to listen to all sides.[45]

In his final report, Barber observed that it was up to the Indigenous Peoples to establish their claims, rather than waiting for others to do the right thing by them. He did not, however, resolve the basic principles for evaluating claims or determine the kind of mechanism that would be best for their resolution. A joint National Indian Brotherhood/cabinet committee, established in 1975, lasted for only three years before the First Nations withdrew. A Canadian Indian Rights Commission did not last much longer. Reconciling national and regional priorities was a major difficulty. It would be 1991 before the present Indian Claims Commission was established.

The department has consistently considered the courts to be a last resort for dealing with claims. As far as the Indigenous Peoples are concerned, litigation presents hazards, not the least of which is cost. While restrictions against First Nations raising funds for such a purpose were removed in 1951, departmental funds available to them for research cannot be used for litigation without departmental consent.[46] Other aspects of the problem are considered in Chapter 18.

CP PHOTO/Fred Chartrand

A Gitxsan dance group performs outside the Supreme Court of Canada at the opening of the Gitxsan-Wet'suwet'en appeal (*Delgamuukw*) in 1997.

Turning Points and Setbacks

Three court cases, taken together, have been widely viewed as representing a turning point in a more inclusive Canadian legal approach to Aboriginal right.[47] In the first, *Sparrow v. The Queen* (1990), the Supreme Court found that Aboriginal fishing, land, and hunting rights for food, social, and ceremonial purposes had priority over later legislation.[48] This interpretation of Aboriginal right was supported in *The Queen v. Adams* (1996), when the Supreme Court of Canada ruled that George Weldon Adams, a Kanienkehaka fisherman, had a right to fish for food in Lake St Francis,[49] contrary to Quebec fishery regulations. In the *Sioui* case (1990), the Court ruled that a 230-year-old safe-conduct was in effect a treaty and so took precedence over later laws.[50] The rights in question relate to self-government, a result of what has been called "the Indians' historic occupation and possession of their tribal lands."[51]

This trend received a sharp check in March of 1991, however, when Justice Allan McEachern, in ***Delgamuukw v. British Columbia***, rejected the claim of the Gitxsan and Wet'suwet'en to Aboriginal right over traditional lands in northern British Columbia, a resource-rich area about the size of Nova Scotia that had never been ceded by treaty and whose people had never been

---

HISTORICAL BACKGROUND | The Nisga'a Treaty

The **Nisga'a Final Agreement Act** (Nisga'a treaty) was ratified by Parliament in 2000 after 22 years at the bargaining table and nearly 200 years of lobbying on the part of the Nisga'a (see Chapter 18). The decision to accept oral history as evidence in court helped to bring it to a conclusion. The agreement gave them self-governing rights to 1,900 km^2 of land (8 per cent of the area they originally claimed) in exchange for giving up their tax-free status under the Indian Act. Hailed as a breakthrough marking "a new understanding between cultures,"[52] the basic land claim of the Nisga'a had been enormously strengthened by the Supreme Court's decision regarding oral evidence.

---

conquered. In 1997, the Supreme Court of Canada overturned the judgment with the argument that the lower courts had not given enough weight to oral tradition. In the Court's opinion, the laws of evidence must be adapted to place oral history on an equal footing with other types of evidence accepted in law, instead of being classed as hearsay, as was the prevailing practice[53] (see also Historical Background box).

The Supreme Court of Canada reached an explosive decision in 1999 when it acquitted **Donald Marshall Jr** (1953–2009), a Mi'kmaw from Nova Scotia, of charges concerning the taking and sale of fish as a treaty right outside of the regulated season. This decision led to out-of-season fishing by other Mi'kmaw fishermen in the region. Non-Indigenous fishermen reacted against the differential restrictions by destroying lobster traps belonging to the Burnt Church band in New Brunswick's Miramichi Bay. The confrontation escalated in spite of a clarification from the Supreme Court that "the treaty right . . . can be contained by regulation," a qualification the band did not accept.[54]

The government finally brokered an agreement by which the Burnt Church band agreed to stop fishing on 7 October 2000, more than three weeks earlier than they had planned. By then, however, the lobsters had already started their seasonal migration to colder waters, making them harder to catch. Also by then, Mi'kmaw fishing gear had been seized, a Department of Fisheries and Oceans boat had rammed a Mi'kmaw boat broadside, turned round and rammed it again, demolishing it and hurling its Mi'kmaw occupants into the water, and several Mi'kmaw fishermen had been arrested.[55]

Another landmark decision, this one applying to hunting, was that of the Ontario Court of Appeal, when it ruled early in 2001 that the Métis, as a distinct Indigenous people, have the constitutional right to hunt for food out of season and without a licence. The jubilant reaction of the Métis had less to do with hunting than with the fact that this was the first time a Canadian court of appeal recognized the legal existence of the Métis nation, even though it stopped short of defining the Métis as a people. Justice Robert C. Sharpe stated, "While I do not doubt there has been considerable uncertainty about the nature and scope of Métis rights, this is hardly a reason to deny their existence." He added that in spite of their 1982 constitutional recognition, there has been no serious effort anywhere in Canada to deal with Métis rights.[56]

In fact, even as Justice Sharpe made this observation the Manitoba Métis Federation (MMF) was fighting for the land rights they had been guaranteed in the Manitoba Act of 1870. In 1981 the MMF launched its case, but when it was finally heard in 2007 it failed on a number of procedural grounds. The court found that there was a lengthy delay in implementing the land provisions of the Manitoba Act and that the delay was due to government error. The court also ruled, however, that the Métis failed to demonstrate that they held their land collectively and that the claims had been filed too late. The Manitoba Court of Appeal heard the case in 2010 and upheld the trial judge's finding that the MMF had no standing to bring the case. Finally, on 8 March 2013 the Supreme Court of Canada ruled. The Court granted the MMF's appeal and held that the Crown had "failed to implement the land grant provision set out in s. 31 of the Manitoba Act of 1870 in accordance with the honour of the Crown." The Supreme Court also granted the MMF costs throughout.[57] A Memorandum of Understanding was issued in 2016, with talks beginning in late 2017.[58]

Indigenous Peoples within the Canadian Criminal Justice System

Public awareness that the justice system has not served Indigenous people well has also grown. At the beginning of the twenty-first century, Indigenous people were three times more likely to go to jail than non-Indigenous Canadians. This was dramatically illustrated by the Donald Marshall case in Nova Scotia. Marshall, a Mi'kmaw, was convicted in 1971 for a murder he did not commit and was jailed for 11 years before being exonerated in 1983. A subsequent investigation pilloried the justice system for failing Marshall at every turn.[59] Similarly, in Alberta a Royal Commission found that "Systemic discrimination exists in the criminal justice system. There is no doubt that aboriginal people are over-represented in this system and that, at best, the equal application of the law has unequal results."[60] Former Indian Affairs Minister Tom Siddon (in office, 1990–3) agreed that Canadian justice in general has displayed "inadequate sensitivity" to the particular needs of the Indigenous Peoples.[61]

On the other side of the picture, on 6 October 2000, Canada's first Indigenous court opened on the Tsuu T'ina reserve just west of Calgary. With Indigenous judges, prosecutors, and peacemakers, it is geared to recognize Indigenous traditions, values, languages, and customs. Chief Roy Whitney saw it as "providing the opportunity to create our own system of justice."[62] In 1990, the death of Neil Stonechild, last seen in police custody, and the deaths of other Indigenous men in Saskatoon led to criminal convictions for local police officers and the most extensive investigation of Indigenous people and the justice system to date.[63] The calls for a separate Indigenous justice system have arisen from the recognition that traditional Indigenous culture and values are in some ways at odds with the British-derived system in place in Canada (Table 17.1).

Instituted on 15 November 2001, armed with a $2.5 million budget, and chaired by Alberta lawyer and former MP Wilton Littlechild, the Commission on First Nations and Métis Peoples and Justice Reform undertook a thorough examination of the criminal justice system. In its final report, released in June 2004, the Commission cited racism as central to Indigenous people's mistrust of police services and recommended better screening of police candidates;

Table 17.1 Two Justice Systems

Justice System	British Justice Adversarial	Traditional Indigenous Justice Non-confrontational
Function of justice	Ensure conformity, punish deviant behaviour, and protect society	Heal the offender, restore peace and harmony to the community, reconciliation between offender and victim/family
Guilt	European concept of guilty/not guilty	No concept of guilty/not guilty
Pleading guilty	The accused has the right against self-incrimination; thus, it is not seen as dishonest to plead not guilty when one has actually committed the offence	It is dishonest to plead not guilty when one has committed the offence (values of honesty and non-interference)
Testifying	Witnesses testify in front of the accused as part of the process	Reluctance to testify, as it is confrontational to testify in front of the accused
Truth	Expectation to tell the "whole truth"	It is impossible to know the "whole truth" in any situation
Witnesses	Only certain people are called to testify in relation to specific subjects	Everyone is free to have their say; witnesses do not want to appear adversarial and often try to give answers that will please council, often changing their testimony
Eye contact	Maintaining eye contact sends the message that the individual is telling the truth	In some Indigenous cultures, maintaining eye contact with a person of authority is a sign of disrespect
Verdict	The accused is expected to show signs of remorse during proceedings and on receiving a guilty verdict	The accused must accept what happens without any signs of emotion
Incarceration/probation	Means of punishing and rehabilitating the offender	Indigenous offender has the responsibility to make restitution to the victim

The calls for a separate Indigenous justice system have arisen from the recognition that traditional Indigenous cultures and values are in some ways at odds with the British-derived system in place in Canada.

Source: "Aboriginal Peoples and the Criminal Justice System," special issue of the *Bulletin of the Canadian Criminal Justice Association* (Ottawa, 15 May 2000), from Corrine Mount Pleasant-Jette, "Creating a Climate of Confidence: Providing Services within Aboriginal Communities," in *National Round Table on Economic Issues and Resources* (Ottawa: Royal Commission on Aboriginal Peoples, 27–9 Apr. 1993). Reproduced by permission of the Canadian Criminal Justice Association.

more First Nations and Métis officers, legal aides, and judges; and better training for existing police forces. Other recommendations included an independent complaints investigation agency, a "therapeutic court" that would deal with social issues, and allowing individual communities to deal with some cases that under the current system would appear before the courts.

The Commission also recommended that alternatives to prison sentences be sought, with input from First Nations and Métis elders. Another promising development was pioneered earlier by Ontario's Gull Bay band (Ojibwa) when it organized its own reserve police force in 1974, a first for Canada. Others have followed suit, with encouraging results: a drop in the crime rate on reserves serviced by their own police.[64]

Still, the legal position of First Peoples in Canada is determined not only by the Indian Act but also by the Constitution and the treaties. Despite the Canadian Charter of Rights and Freedoms, which in theory overrides all other statutes, the Indian Act continues to define Aboriginal rights even as "it reflects so little faith in the Indians."[65] Far from viewing Indigenous people as equals, however, its goals of protection and assimilation have led to an emphasis on control rather than development.[66] Initiative and enterprise have been stifled, ensuring poverty and underachievement. Even with enfranchisement, Indigenous people, whether veterans or otherwise, did not have access to equality of opportunity and social benefits. In the words of Cree spokesman Harold Cardinal, the Indian Act has "subjugated to colonial rule the very people whose rights it was supposed to protect."[67] As of 2017, the Trudeau government is proposing to do something about this, though it remains to be seen what changes will take place.

Questions to Consider

1. What caused the Oka Crisis?
2. Why is *St Catherine's Milling* a landmark case?
3. What is the long-term significance of the *Delgamuukw* case?
4. What finally brought about the resolution of the Nisga'a land claim?

Recommended Readings

Asch, Michael. *On Being Here to Stay: Treaty and Aboriginal Rights in Canada*. Toronto: University of Toronto Press, 2014.

Cardinal, Harold. *The Unjust Society*. Vancouver: Douglas & McIntyre, 1969.

Cardinal, Harold, and Walter Hildebrandt. *Treaty Elders of Saskatchewan*. Calgary: University of Calgary Press, 2000.

Clark, Bruce A. *Native Liberty, Crown Sovereignty*. Montreal and Kingston: McGill-Queen's University Press, 1990.

McNab, David T. *Circles of Time: Aboriginal Land Rights and Resistance in Ontario*. Waterloo, Ont.: Wilfrid Laurier University Press, 1999.

Miller, J.R. *Compact, Contract, Covenant: Aboriginal Treaty Making in Canada*. Toronto: University of Toronto Press, 2009.

Mills, Antonia. *Hang on to These Words: Johnny David's Delgamuukw Testimony*. Toronto: University of Toronto Press, 2005.

Steckley, John L. *Indian Agents: Rulers of the Reserves*. New York: Peter Lang, 2016.

Wiebe, Rudy, and Yvonne Johnson. *Stolen Life: The Journey of a Cree Woman*. Toronto: Alfred A. Knopf, 1998.

18 The Road to Self-Government

CHAPTER OUTLINE

The main subjects of the present chapter concern Indigenous Peoples' strides towards self-government and the advances in economic development during the second half of the twentieth century and into the first decades of the twenty-first century. We will also look at constitutional reform, a key component of the struggle for self-government. As we shall see there have been both successes and failures in this area. We will discuss the Royal Commission on Aboriginal Peoples, an extensive inquiry that was created to propose possible ways forward, as well as the attempts at a First Nations General Assembly. Finally, we will consider the implications of the policy direction announced by the Justin Trudeau government in August of 2017 following his promise in February of that year to review all federal laws and policies as they relate to Indigenous people.[1]

LEARNING OUTCOMES

1. Students will gain insight into the land claims process.

2. Students will gain an understanding of the strong connections between lands, resources, and governance.

3. Students will be able to follow the stages on the long process towards Indigenous self-governance.

TIMELINE Self-Government Initiatives from 1933 to 2017

1933
Lubicon Cree band in northern Alberta, missed in Treaty Eight signing, applies for land settlement.

1966
Indigenous administration and northern resources management combined in Department of Indian Affairs and Northern Development (later called Department of Indian and Northern Affairs).

1970
Mercury pollution of English-Wabigoon River system in northwestern Ontario, which devastated Grassy Narrows and Whitedog reserves since 1950s, is traced to Reed Paper Company mill at Dryden, Ontario.

1972
Cree and Inuit of northern Quebec get injunction to stop James Bay project, but it is suspended on appeal.

1975
James Bay and Northern Quebec Agreement reached between governments and Inuit and Cree of northern Quebec falls short of entrenching rights for Indigenous Peoples in the region.

1983
Report of the Special Parliamentary Committee on Indian Self-Government (Penner Report) urges distinct form of Indigenous self-government.

1940–79
Reserve site established for Lubicon Cree, but resource explorations and provincial road on Lubicon land create problems still unresolved.

1968
Smallboy's Camp, a traditionalist encampment on Crown land in southern Alberta, is established by hereditary Cree chief Johnny Bob Smallboy.

1971
Inuit Tapirisat of Canada formed in response to announcement of Quebec's proposed James Bay hydroelectric project.

1974–7
Mackenzie Valley Pipeline Inquiry (Berger Inquiry) sets new standard for listening to and accounting for Indigenous concerns about development projects.

1976–7
Len Marchand first Indigenous federal cabinet minister.

1982
Patriation of Canadian Constitution; Constitution Act, 1982 recognizes and affirms "existing aboriginal and treaty Rights."

1984

Cree-Naskapi Act of Quebec, hailed as the first self-government legislation for First Nations, replaces Indian Act for regions it covers.

Western Arctic Claim Agreement extinguishes Inuvialuit Aboriginal title in exchange for $55 million and ownership of 96,000 km².

1990

Manitoba MLA Elijah Harper withholds vote on ratification of Meech Lake Accord, effectively killing agreement that would have given Quebec special status while ignoring First Nations.

1995

Standoff over disputed land on shore of Lake Huron between Chippewas of Kettle and Stony Point First Nation and Ontario Provincial Police results in shooting death of Ojibwa activist Dudley George.

1997

First Nations Bank of Canada begins operations in Saskatoon.

1999

Loon River band signs land settlement agreement.

2002

Ta'an Kwach'an Council Agreement.

2005

Carcross/Taglish First Nation Final Agreement, Kwanlin Dün First Nation Final Agreement, Tlicho Agreement, Westbank First Nation Self-Government Agreement.

1983–7

Three First Ministers' Conferences on Indigenous rights, mandated in Constitution Act, 1982, accomplish little.

1989–90

Woodland Cree break from Lubicon band, gain band status, and cut deal with federal and provincial governments.

1991

Loon River people break from Lubicon band, gain band status.

1991–6

Royal Commission on Aboriginal Peoples concludes with five-volume, 3,537-page report including 440 specific recommendations.

1996

Report of the Royal Commission on Aboriginal Peoples published.

1998

Formal government regret expressed for residential school abuses and $350 million healing fund established.

2000

Nisga'a Final Agreement.

2004

Kluane First Nation Final Agreement.

Continued

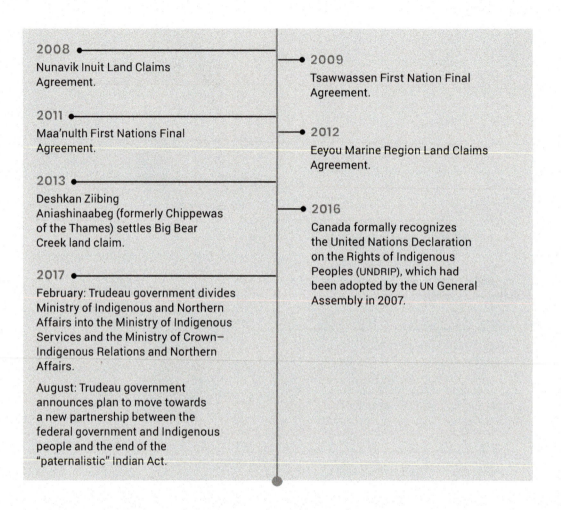

2008
Nunavik Inuit Land Claims
Agreement.

2009
Tsawwassen First Nation Final
Agreement.

2011
Maa'nulth First Nations Final
Agreement.

2012
Eeyou Marine Region Land Claims
Agreement.

2013
Deshkan Ziibing
Aniashinaabeg (formerly Chippewas
of the Thames) settles Big Bear
Creek land claim.

2016
Canada formally recognizes
the United Nations Declaration
on the Rights of Indigenous
Peoples (UNDRIP), which had
been adopted by the UN General
Assembly in 2007.

2017
February: Trudeau government divides
Ministry of Indigenous and Northern
Affairs into the Ministry of Indigenous
Services and the Ministry of Crown–
Indigenous Relations and Northern
Affairs.

August: Trudeau government
announces plan to move towards
a new partnership between the
federal government and Indigenous
people and the end of the
"paternalistic" Indian Act.

The Ongoing Government–
Indigenous Relationship

The White Paper had been withdrawn. This meant that in the 1970s the Indian Act still was
in effect. Thirty years later, at the turn of the century, the government still had the legal right
to make unilateral decisions, even to the point of terminating treaties. As early as 1971, however, it was funding Indigenous political organizations to act as forums for policy discussions.[2]
This, of course, was a complete turnabout from its move in the 1920s to curb such organizations
by cutting their funding.

    In other areas, such as social assistance programs, the government has seemingly abandoned
its expectation that Indigenous Peoples would assimilate to white ways. Where it once saw

reserves as temporary expedients for easing them into non-Indigenous society, now it sees the reserves as homelands that First Nations and Métis have a right to control. It will take a long time to rectify the poor social conditions that have developed on many of them,[3] and settling land claims has been seen as key to economic development.

At the close of 1990, 500 to 600 **specific claims**[4] were outstanding, some of them not having been resolved for 15 years or more. The struggle of the Lubicon of northern Alberta (see Historical Background box), for example, began during the 1930s, when the Great Depression drove many non-Indigenous people into their land. About 100 of the outstanding claims had been settled by the end of the century. The Indian Specific Claims Commission, with increased funding to speed up the process, was established in 1991 in response to the Oka Crisis. Despite some success, it has also met with frustrations, often complicated by the **division of powers** between the federal government and the provinces.[5]

In 1973, the Canadian government, responding to various Indigenous land claims, re-affirmed its continuing responsibility for First Nations and Inuit under the BNA Act. It also referred to the Proclamation of 1763 as "a basic declaration of the First Nations interests in land in this country." It recognized the loss of traditional use and occupancy of lands in BC, northern Quebec, Yukon, and the Northwest Territories in areas where "Indian title was never extinguished by treaty or superseded by law." For those areas, the government offered to negotiate a settlement involving compensation or benefits in return for relinquishment of the Indigenous interest.

By now, however, Indigenous people were more interested in entrenchment of their rights than in extinguishment. In 1975, the Joint Council of Chiefs and Elders adopted the Declaration of the First Nations:

> We, the original peoples of this land know the Creator put us here.
>
> The Creator gave us laws that govern all our relationships to live in harmony with nature and mankind.
>
> The laws of the Creator defined our rights and responsibilities.
>
> The Creator gave us our spiritual beliefs, our languages, our culture, and a place on Mother Earth which provided us with all our needs.
>
> We have maintained our freedom, our languages, and our traditions from time immemorial.
>
> We continue to exercise the rights and fulfill the responsibilities and obligations given to us by the Creator for the land upon which we were placed.
>
> The Creator has given us the right to govern ourselves and the right to self-determination.
>
> The rights and responsibilities given to us by the Creator cannot be altered or taken away by any other Nation.

By the end of the twentieth century, the Canadian public, in general, was supportive of the Indigenous position, particularly in regard to land claims.[6]

HISTORICAL BACKGROUND | The Lubicon Cree

One of the best-known and longest-standing claims, which remained unsettled in 2017, is that of the Lubicon Cree band of the Treaty Eight area in oil-rich northern Alberta.[7] Missed at the treaty signing, the band did not apply for a land settlement until 1933. Ottawa, responding in 1939, promised a reserve. In 1940, both federal and provincial governments approved a site at the western end of Lubicon Lake, but the site was never surveyed, and disputes arose about band lists. A judicial inquiry in 1944 did not lead to a settlement acceptable to the band. There matters remained until 1952, when mining and oil explorations expanded into the Lubicon's area. In 1979, the band's attempt to prevent the construction of a road into the area failed.

By 2014, the province of Alberta had issued licences for over 2,600 oil and gas wells on the traditional territory of the Lubicon Cree. That territory is now criss-crossed by over 2,400 km of pipeline. On 29 April 2011, one of these pipelines ruptured and spilled an estimated 28,000 barrels of crude oil into wetlands about 10 km from the Lubicon community of Little Buffalo. More than 70 per cent of Lubicon territory has been leased for future resource extraction and this includes oil sands extraction development projects. The people are worried. A 1990 complaint to the United Nations Human Rights Committee has gone unheeded by the government of Canada despite subsequent United Nations complaints, the latest at this writing being in 2016. Concerns about health and sanitary conditions have been raised by the Lubicon Cree and then ignored by the governments of Alberta and Canada. Although Alberta openly admits that vast revenues have been generated by the projects, the Lubicon Cree have not enjoyed the benefits.[8]

Bernard Ominayak took over the band's leadership in 1978 and has remained chief ever since. In 2013, he was unanimously acclaimed chief for yet another term. He has attempted to work with the other governments and with private enterprise but he is not playing on a level field. Ominayak announced an agreement between the Lubicon band and Petro-Canada allowing for oil exploration under certain conditions on lands claimed by the band, but this was not accepted by most members of the community. As of 2017, there is still no agreement with Petro-Canada.

The Push for Resources Underscores the Need for Self-Government

Developing technology has meant greater industrial attention to northern resources. In 1957, John George Diefenbaker (1895–1979) led the Conservatives to an overwhelming victory with his vision of the "New North." His model was a colonial one: improve

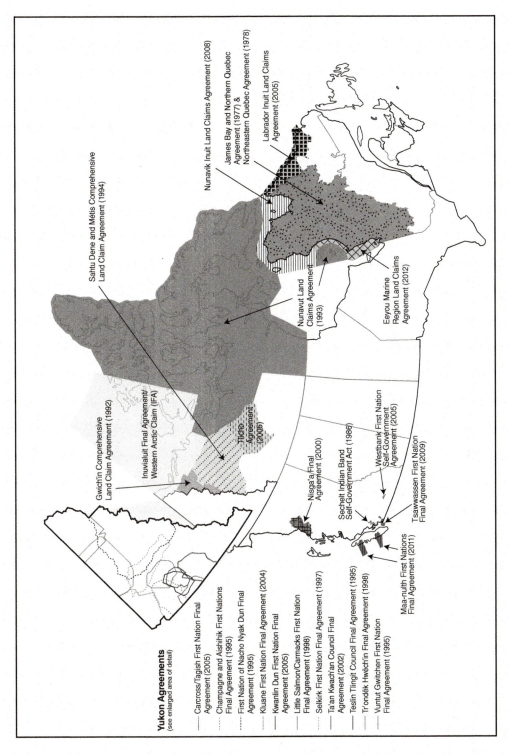

Map 18.1 Major comprehensive claim areas.

Adapted from Indian and Northern Affairs, *Comprehensive Land Claims in Canada*, April 2014, Comprehensive Claims Branch, DIAND, Ottawa.

transportation to the North, in particular the northern reaches of the provinces, so that people and industrial know-how could come in to exploit northern resources and ship the benefits south. Changes in federal procedure also reflected this attitude. In 1966, Indigenous administration and northern resources management were combined in the Department of Indian Affairs and Northern Development, which is how matters stood at the end of the twentieth century, except that the name had been shortened to Indian and Northern Affairs. Industrialization continued in the earlier pattern with little consideration for the needs of northern peoples.

In the 1950s, for example, the water supplies of the Grassy Narrows and Whitedog reserves in Ontario's Treaty Three area showed signs of mercury pollution, but it was 1970 before the cause was discovered. The Reed Paper Company was dumping methyl-mercury at its Dryden, Ontario, mill into the English-Wabigoon River system. The contamination forced reserves to close their commercial fisheries. Eventually, the Ojibwa called in specialists from Minamata, Japan, where a similar situation had occurred, to assess what was happening. They confirmed mercury poisoning.

The Ojibwa then found out that treaty assurances provided little protection. When Reed announced plans for a new mill in 1974, the people had to prepare their own case on land use and forest management. In the midst of the public scandal, an agreement for the new mill, containing some provision for environmental protection, was signed in 1976.

The discovery of oil at Prudhoe Bay, Alaska, in 1968, seven years after oil exploration had begun in the Canadian High Arctic, led to a proposal for a pipeline running south down the Mackenzie Valley for 2,400 miles (3,800 km) to connect into existing pipeline systems, crossing regions covered by Treaties Eight and Eleven. Three years later, in 1971, Quebec announced its plan to develop the James Bay watershed in that province as a gigantic hydroelectric project in a region where no treaties had been signed. In neither case was thought given to consulting the peoples of the regions involved.[9] After all, in the past, railways had been built, dams constructed, and whole villages relocated without any such consultations, but times had changed. Now, even the churches, traditional instruments for assimilation and upholders of government policy, were questioning the high social price of economic development undertaken without regard to local situations.

Quebec launched the James Bay project without consulting the First Nations and Inuit who would be affected. The Inuit reacted by forming a number of associations,[10] which Tagak Curley and Meeka Wilson co-ordinated in 1971 under a new organization, Inuit Tapirisat of Canada. It became a major voice for Inuit across the Arctic as they worked towards political and economic control while preserving their culture, identity, and way of life.

Quebec already had a record of refusing to delay development projects pending the resolution of Indigenous claims. In 1972, Judge Albert Malouf granted the Grand Council of the Crees (Quebec) and the Northern Quebec Inuit Association an injunction to halt the James Bay hydroelectric project, only to see it suspended on appeal a week later. The Quebec Court of Appeals eventually ruled that Aboriginal rights in the territory had been extinguished by the HBC charter of 1670. The uproar stirred by these events was unprecedented. Besides speeches, meetings, and public demonstrations, the Cree and Inuit held theatrical evenings in which they put on performances that ranged from the traditional to the contemporary. After they reached an agreement, Billy Diamond, chief of the Waskaganish band of James Bay Cree, observed: "It has been a tough fight, and our people are still very much opposed to the project, but they realize that they must share their resources."[11]

The **James Bay and Northern Quebec Agreement** of 1975[12] left the Inuit and Cree communities of Quebec with substantial control of their own political, economic, and social affairs, although the final say still rested with the government.[13] More generous than the numbered treaties, the accord still fell far short of entrenching Indigenous rights. As far as the Indigenous Peoples involved are concerned, the expectations to which it gave rise have not been met.[14] Critics have pointed to the price: the flooding of 10,500 km^2 of once productive hunting land without consideration of wildlife factors. Their point was dramatically reinforced in 1984, when Hydro-Québec inadvertently drowned 10,000 caribou by releasing a large volume of water during their migration. On top of everything else, expected contracts for hydroelectric power did not materialize.

The La Grande River phase of the project was completed by 1986 and the Laforge River phase was mainly completed by the end of 1996. The proposed final phase of the project, referred to as the Great Whale, was suspended when the State of New York withdrew its offer to purchase power from Hydro-Québec in reaction to Cree opposition to Great Whale. In 2002, Quebec signed the "Peace of the Braves" agreement with the Grand Council of the Crees to allow for the diversion of the Rupert River. After lengthy studies and in spite of protests, this project was completed in 2009.[15]

Another case that underscores the difficulties encountered between developers and Indigenous Peoples wanting to preserve the integrity of their traditional territory concerns the Kitchenuhmaykoosib Inninuwug First Nation (KI). In 2006, this northwestern Ontario First Nation was sued by Platinex, an exploratory drilling company that held an unencumbered 100 per cent interest in 81 mining leases covering approximately 12,080 acres (4,892 ha) of the Nemeigusabins Lake Arm of Big Trout Lake. The leaders of KI resisted this proposed development in order to safeguard and preserve their traditional land, culture, way of life, and core beliefs. The decision, released by the Ontario Superior Court on 22 May 2007, ordered a consultation protocol; a timetable; and a Memorandum of Understanding between KI, Platinex, and Ontario. Further, the Court held that consultation funding was necessary and that the Court would supervise the process. KI immediately protested, noting that the fiscal imbalance between the parties would render the process unfair. Six community leaders were jailed on 17 March 2008 for contempt of court after protesting what they argued was an unfair judgment. They were freed on appeal on 23 May 2008.[16] An Omamiwinini band, the Algonquins of Barriere Lake in southwestern Quebec, north of Gatineau, found themselves in a similar resource conflict situation and it, too, remains unresolved. The Quebec government placed an interim mining moratorium in 2011, but that was lifted again in 2016, resulting in further clashes between the Omamiwinini and industry.[17]

Mackenzie Valley Pipeline Inquiry

In 1974, Prime Minister Pierre Trudeau appointed Justice Thomas Berger to chair the **Mackenzie Valley Pipeline Inquiry**. In carrying out his mandate, Berger not only decided to consult the people directly, he broke with tradition by seeing to it that the media covered the hearings. Public interest was intense, as southern Canadians learned about life in the North, many of them for the first time. A witness to the hearings reminded them that northerners, too, had a way of life to protect:

> I wonder how people in Toronto would react if the people of Old Crow went down to Toronto and said, "Well, look, we are going to knock down all those skyscrapers and high rises . . . blast a few holes to make lakes for muskrat trapping, and you people are just going to have to move out and stop driving cars and move into cabins."[18]

When Berger's report appeared in 1977, it became a best-seller.[19]

Berger's recommendation that the pipeline be put on hold for 10 years to allow time for Indigenous concerns to be considered was a shocker to many Canadians, accustomed as they were to development being given top priority. Eventually, large quantities of natural gas were discovered in Alberta and British Columbia, providing more easily available sources of fuel.[20] In 1985, an oil pipeline running about half the length of the Mackenzie Valley, from Norman Wells to northern Alberta, was completed, two years before Thomas Berger's recommended moratorium would have ended.

The lapsing of the moratorium revived interest in the original proposal, but with a difference. This time, the Indigenous people, instead of opposing it, indicated support, provided that they could be major participants. This turnabout was influenced by dramatic price increases for oil and gas. The Inuvialuit of the western Arctic, whose land claim was settled in 1984, lost no time in taking advantage of this favourable turn of the market and negotiated four oil and gas concessions that netted them $75.5 million.[21]

On the Political Front

The period between the rejection of the 1969 White Paper and the patriation of the British North America Act in 1982 was marked by protest and confrontation, bureaucratic dissension, and policy confusion.[22] This came to a head in a 1974 clash between west coast Indigenous people and an RCMP riot squad in Ottawa that disrupted the opening of Parliament. About 200 Indigenous people had come from Vancouver—the "Native Peoples' Caravan"—in what was supposed to have been a peaceful protest against poor living conditions. Nervous authorities called out the riot squad and then brought out the military, the first time the government used such measures against Indigenous demonstrators.[23]

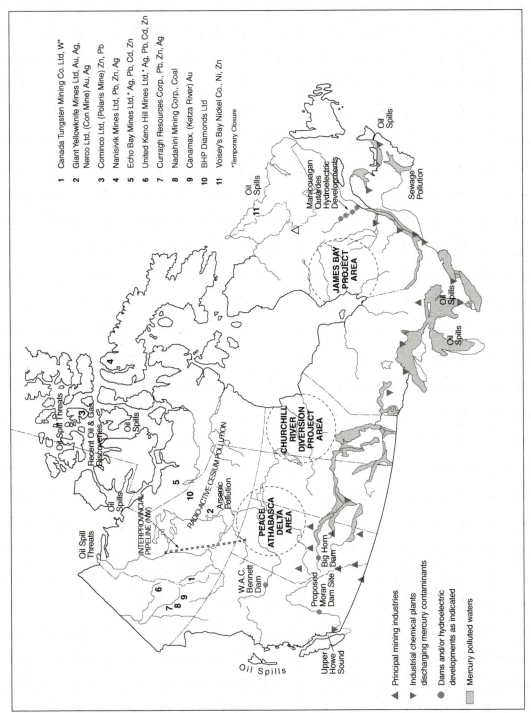

1   Canada Tungsten Mining Co. Ltd, W*
2   Giant Yellowknife Mines Ltd, Au, Ag,
    Nerco Ltd, (Con Mine) Au, Ag
3   Cominco Ltd, (Polaris Mine) Zn, Pb
4   Nanisivik Mines Ltd, Pb, Zn, Ag
5   Echo Bay Mines Ltd,* Ag, Pb, Cd, Zn
6   United Keno Hill Mines Ltd,* Ag, Pb, Cd, Zn
7   Curragh Resources Corp., Pb, Zn, Ag
8   Nadahini Mining Corp., Coal
9   Canamax, (Ketza River) Au
10 BHP Diamonds Ltd
11 Voisey's Bay Nickel Co., Ni, Zn

*Temporary Closure

▲ Principal mining industries
▼ Industrial chemical plants
    discharging mercury contaminants
● Dams and/or hydroelectric
    developments as indicated
▨ Mercury polluted waters

Map 18.2 Principal industrial development areas and effects on Indigenous Peoples.

Canada, *Aboriginal People of Canada and Their Environment* (Ottawa: NIB, 1973); Canada, *Looking North: Canada's Arctic Commitment* (Ottawa: DIAND, 1989).

The negotiations that preceded patriation and the adoption of the Constitution Act, 1982, saw considerable Indigenous political activity. As a Dene leader observed, "While others are trying to negotiate their way out of Confederation, we are trying to negotiate our way in."[24] First Nations, Inuit, and Métis, concerned that Aboriginal rights be enshrined in the new Constitution and convinced they were not being given a fair hearing in Canada, sent delegation after delegation to Britain and Continental Europe to press their cause. At one point, 300 Indigenous people went to Britain to present their case to the Queen, but at the request of the short-lived Tory government of Joe Clark (1979–80) they were denied an audience.

Eventually, when the **constitutional patriation** was accomplished in 1982, Indigenous Peoples won recognition of "existing" Aboriginal rights but without a definition of the term. However, there was provision that such rights could not be harmed by anything in the Charter of Rights and Freedoms.[25] Its recognition of the Métis as an Indigenous people was a consequence of their earlier recognition by the Manitoba Act of 1870. As a concession to Indigenous Peoples for having been excluded from the constitutional negotiations, the government made provision for three conferences between Indigenous leaders and Canada's first ministers.

These conferences, held in the mid-1980s, made clear that, constitutionally, the Indigenous role is at best advisory. Whatever the justification for Indigenous self-government, it rests at the local level. When it comes to constitutional matters that concern the country as a whole, the final say rests essentially with the federal Parliament and provincial legislatures. The term "constitution" as used here is a European political concept. It provides "a set of rationally conceived and formalized rules for the exercise of political powers and, equally important, for the restraint of political power."[26] For Indigenous Peoples, the Constitution not only embodies their internal sovereignty but also symbolizes the aspiration for self-determination for the people.

Indigenous Peoples were not only moving towards a demand to be granted self-government, they also wanted to win recognition that their own viable governments existed long before the arrival of Europeans. Cree lawyer Delia Opekokew elaborated: "Aboriginal right," she wrote, "recognizes our ownership over lands we have traditionally occupied and used and our control and ownership over the resources of the land—water, minerals, timber, wildlife and fisheries." What was more, she added, such a right "recognizes our Indian government's sovereignty over our people, lands and resources."[27] In 1983, this position received a powerful boost from the Report of the Special Parliamentary Committee on Indian Self-Government, known as the **Penner Report** after the committee's chairman, Keith Penner, Liberal MP for Kenora, 1968–88. The report urged that Indigenous Peoples be allowed to establish their own level of government, distinct from those of the municipality and the Indian Act. A major result would be the reinforcement of Aboriginal rights.

Hopes were high at the launching of the first of the three constitutionally mandated First Ministers' Conferences on Indigenous affairs in 1983. As Inuit delegate Zebedee Nungak cheerfully put it, "We're here to do constructive damage to the status quo."[28] That was just what some of the provincial premiers feared, however. Brian Mulroney (Conservative Prime Minister, 1984–93), at first apparently enthusiastic about resolving the question of Aboriginal rights, pulled back, so that the third and last of the conferences, in 1987, was even more frustrating than the first two.

Not many weeks later, Mulroney and the provincial premiers signed the Meech Lake Accord, recognizing Quebec as a distinct society and granting that province special status, to be ratified within three years. The disillusionment among the Indigenous Peoples was profound. What the government had denied to them was now being given to Quebec. The special status idea had doomed the Hawthorn Report because the government of Pierre Trudeau worried about people in Quebec demanding special status. Now, the government of Mulroney was proposing just that. The injustice was not lost on Indigenous leaders.

Indigenous Peoples rallied. When the opportunity presented itself to kill the Accord by legislative means, they took it. All of the provincial legislatures had to ratify the agreement. **Elijah Harper**, an Anishinaabe chief from Red Sucker Lake and the only Indigenous member of the Manitoba legislature (NDP, Rupertsland),[29] withheld his vote on the grounds that procedural rules were not being followed. The Speaker of the House agreed, observing that the Accord was too important "to open the door for some future legal challenge because all the rules weren't obeyed." The matter had been introduced to the legislature at the last minute. Harper's delaying tactics meant that the 23 June 1990 deadline could not be met, and so the Accord died.[30]

Elijah Harper, then an NDP member of the Manitoba legislature, holds an eagle feather for spiritual strength as he uses delaying tactics to prevent the 1990 Meech Lake Accord from being ratified. Eagles are regarded as the most favoured of the Creator's animals, and the fact that they often lay two eggs has given them a special association with the number two. In this case the reference is to two cultures, Indigenous and non-Indigenous.

CP PICTURE ARCHIVE/Winnipeg Free Press/Wayne Glowacki

The stalling of Aboriginal rights at the constitutional level has to some extent been counterbalanced by an inching towards recognition at local levels.[31] Between 1913 and 1954, the deputy minister of the Department of the Interior and a council consisting of missionaries, an HBC trade commissioner, and an RCMP commissioner governed the three districts of Keewatin, Mackenzie, and Franklin in the Northwest Territories. Following epidemics that swept through the Dene and Inuit, the government transferred political control to the Department of Indian Affairs and Northern Development. The NWT government has seen a dramatic increase in

Indigenous participation since it became fully elective in 1975. Indigenous participation has influenced the character of the Legislative Council, which has abandoned the party system in favour of Indigenous consensus politics. In other words, the move is towards decentralization. Yukon, on the other hand, has had an elective council since 1908, but its government is more centralized than that of the NWT.[32]

Northern Self-Government

The Cree-Naskapi Act of Quebec, 1984, was a result of the Penner Report, as well as being a consequence of the James Bay and Northern Quebec Agreement (JBNQA) and its related accords of 1975–8. Hailed as the first **self-government** legislation for Indigenous people in Canada, the Cree-Naskapi Act replaced the Indian Act for the regions it serves and establishes the communities as corporate entities, over and above their members' legal existence as individual persons.[33] However, disagreement soon arose as to the extent to which Ottawa had implemented the agreed-upon funding formula. The government maintained in 1988 that it had effected 80 per cent of its commitments. Chief Henry Mianscum of the Mistassini band took an opposite view: "probably 70 per cent of that Agreement hasn't been implemented."[34]

The Western Arctic Claim Agreement (Inuvialuit Final Agreement) was also reached in 1984.[35] It extinguished Inuvialuit **Aboriginal title** to the western Arctic in return for ownership of 96,000 km^2 stretching up to Banks Island, along with payments of $45 million in benefits and $10 million for economic development. The administration of all this came under the umbrella Inuvialuit Regional Corporation (IRC), organized the following year. Its concerns include wildlife conservation and management, as is generally the case in these northern agreements. Its business arm, the Inuvialuit Development Corporation, bought a transportation firm for $27 million with a virtual monopoly on barge transportation in the Canadian Arctic. Among their many enterprises, the Inuvialuit are exclusive owners of the government-set muskox quotas for their region.[36] Similarly, Indigenous business activities and entrepreneurialism, both on a band level and individually, have increased significantly in recent years.

In Yukon, after nearly two decades of negotiation, an Umbrella Final Agreement was signed in 1993 whereby the territory's 14 bands retain ownership of 44,000 km^2 and receive compensation of $260 million while avoiding complete extinguishment of Aboriginal title. Besides protection for wildlife, the agreement also creates a constitutional obligation to negotiate self-government.[37]

The federal government, however, is far from conceding that entrenchment of Aboriginal rights is a feature of land claim settlements. This was dramatically illustrated by the cancellation of the Dene/Métis Western Arctic land claim agreement late in 1990,[38] after the Dene/Métis demanded to renegotiate a clause in the preliminary agreement that required the surrender of Aboriginal and treaty rights in return for the settlement. As the Dene put it, "Our laws from the Creator do not allow us to cede, release, surrender or extinguish our inherent rights."[39]

Getting Out of the Way of Self-Determination

The federal government, meanwhile, has been making room for some First Nations to exercise their rights to self-determination at the municipal level, in line with the long-held legal opinion that if Indigenous Peoples have the national vote they should be allowed to run their own affairs at the local level. In 1986, for example, the 650-member Sechelt band assumed legal and political control in fee simple of a reserve of 10 square miles (26 km²), 50 km north of Vancouver, after a decade of effort on their part. Alberta's tiny but wealthy Sawridge band also has negotiated a self-government agreement, and others have followed suit. In 1990, Dene Georges Erasmus, the Assembly of First Nations' National Chief, 1985–91, described the Indigenous vision of the new order of things as one of "sharing, recognition, and affirmation."[40] In contrast, at the same time, Chief Ben Michel of the Innu argued that "an attack on the economic base of Canada" would not be an insurrection. Rather, he said, it would be an exercise in sovereignty, at least for the Innu, who have never surrendered it.[41]

The Royal Commission on Aboriginal Peoples Announced

A consequence of the Oka crisis was Prime Minister Mulroney's announcement in 1991 of the **Royal Commission on Aboriginal Peoples** (RCAP) to investigate and report on the situation of Indigenous people across the country. Mulroney appointed seven commissioners, but none of the four Indigenous members represented the western numbered treaties. Of the two co-chairs, Georges Erasmus was formerly president of the Dene Nation, Northwest Territories, and more recently National Chief of the Assembly of First Nations. René Dussault was a judge of the Quebec Appeals Court. It was "the first time in modern history that the non-Aboriginal people have sat down with Aboriginal people and together . . . reviewed where they've been together and tried to chart a course on where they want to go."[42] It would be the most thorough official investigation ever undertaken of Indigenous life in Canada.[43]

In the meantime, the ending of the Oka standoff did not mean the end of tensions and demonstrations, as Indigenous leaders continued their arguments for a larger constitutional role for their people.[44] Protests in various forms, such as occupations of land or offices, or the erection of barricades at strategic places, erupted sporadically across the land. In January 1993, six teenagers in the Innu community of Davis Inlet, Labrador, tried to commit suicide. The incident quickly blew up into an international scandal: "Tragedy at Davis Inlet. The near-suicides of six teens display the hollowness of government promises to improve the community," according to a headline in *The Gazette*, Montreal.[45] The Innu of Davis Inlet finally were relocated in 2003 to a new community, Natuashish, built at a cost of more than $150 million on the Labrador mainland near their former island community.

BC's First Land Claims Agreement: The Nisga'a Treaty

British Columbia's position in relation to the Indigenous people who lived within its created borders was for a long time unique in Canada. For one thing, apart from the 14 small treaties on Vancouver Island negotiated by Governor James Douglas, 1850–4, and the overlap of Treaty Eight into its northeastern corner in 1899, the province had not negotiated treaties with the First Nations who lived there. Not recognizing Aboriginal rights, it denied having any outstanding obligations that could be settled by way of land claims. It maintained this position until 1990 when—following court rulings, federal pressure, and a change in public attitude—it agreed to open talks. Two years later, the newly formed New Democratic government promised to resolve the 47 open claims, which covered most of the province. This raised the hopes of Indigenous leaders, whose sometimes overlapping demands soared to encompass more than 110 per cent of the province's land. The government responded by announcing that only 5 per cent would be available for settling claims.[46]

The Nisga'a were the first of BC's claimants to have their case heard. A nation of 5,500 in the Nass Valley and spreading to the northwest, they had filed their claim 70 years earlier.[47] Originally, it involved 24,000 km^2 of the northern part of the province. Finally, after intensive negotiations (behind closed doors for the final two years), the Nisga'a agreed to accept 1,930 km^2.[48] The land turned over to the Nisga'a, to be communally owned in fee simple, is valued at $100 million and remains exempt from provincial property and resource taxes; however, it is a fraction of what was once theirs.

The persistence of the Nisga'a had paid off. Parliament ratified their treaty in 2000. The *Calder* case of 1973 (Chapter 17) set the scene. Although that decision had gone against the Nisga'a on a technicality, the judges had agreed that the First Nation did indeed have Aboriginal title to its ancestral lands. From there, the Nisga'a never stopped pressing, first the federal government, then, after 1990, the provincial government as well. The discussions were neither simple nor easy. At one point, they broke off entirely.

It took a tragedy to break the deadlock: the shooting of an activist from the Chippewas of Kettle and Stony Point First Nation. In 1995, a land occupation at Ipperwash, Ontario, saw Canada's first Indigenous casualty in a land claim standoff, Dudley George.[49] An Ontario provincial court found Police Sergeant Kenneth Deane guilty of criminal negligence causing death but Deane spent no time in jail.[50] The prospect of spreading violence very quickly brought the negotiators back to the table, and the terms of British Columbia's first land claim preliminary agreement soon were settled.[51] Not surprisingly, in view of its past policies, BC faces the largest roster of unsettled **comprehensive claims**[52] of any of the provinces. As of 2000, the number had climbed to 51. Across the country at the same time, there were more than 1,000 claims in process in various categories. By 2012, a number of major claims had been settled, including four in Yukon alone. Since then, four comprehensive claims have been settled: the Yale First Nation Final Agreement in British Columbia was signed on 13 April 2013 and received royal assent in Parliament on 19 June 2013; the Tla'amin Final Agreement in British Columbia was signed on 11 April 2014 and received royal assent on 19 June 2014; in Manitoba, the Sioux Valley Dakota Nation's self-government agreement received royal assent

BC Premier Glen Clark and Nisga'a Tribal Council President Joe Gosnell shake hands before signing the Nisga'a Final Agreement in Terrace, BC, 27 April 1999. The historic ratification of the Nisga'a Treaty and Nisga'a Constitution won a majority vote by the Nisga'a Nation on 6 November 1998 after 113 years of negotiations.

in Parliament on 4 March 2014 and came into effect on 1 July 2014; and the Délı̨nę First Nation's self-government agreement was signed on 18 February 2015 but is not yet in effect.[53]

The Royal Commission on Aboriginal Peoples Report

The commissioners' five-volume, 3,537-page report, when it finally appeared, was stunning in its size and the scope of its proposals for Canada and Canadians. It involved a fundamental re-organization of the country's social and political institutions in relation to Indigenous Peoples. In the commissioners' words:

> We advocate recognition of Aboriginal nations within Canada as political entities through which Aboriginal people can express their distinctive identity within the context of Canadian citizenship. . . . At the heart of our recommendations is the recognition that Aboriginal peoples are peoples, that they form collectives of unique character, and that they have a right to governmental autonomy.[54]

In other words, the relationship between Indigenous and non-Indigenous people is central to Canada's heritage. With this in mind, the commissioners identified four key issues: the need for a new relationship between Indigenous and non-Indigenous Peoples, self-determination through self-government, economic self-sufficiency, and healing for Indigenous Peoples and communities. They made 440 recommendations detailing specific measures to achieve these goals, including:

- An Indigenous parliament—the House of First Peoples—elected as a third order of government to advise the federal and provincial legislatures on matters relating to Indigenous Peoples.
- The merging of 1,000 or more separate bands, Inuit villages, and Métis settlements into 60 to 80 Indigenous nations entitled to self-government. Indigenous Peoples should be recognized as possessing a unique form of dual citizenship, as citizens both of an Indigenous nation and of Canada.
- The enactment of an Aboriginal Nations Recognition and Government Act to establish criteria for the recognition of Indigenous nations and to complete a citizenship that is consistent with international norms of human rights and with the Canadian Charter of Rights and Freedoms.

HISTORICAL BACKGROUND | Willie Dunn

Against the context of hard political negotiation one finds a powerful cultural context. Willie Dunn (1942–2013) was a Mi'kmaw filmmaker, activist, playwright, and folksinger. His song "Son of the Sun" proposed a view of Indigenous culture and the importance of customary usage in beautiful and elegant simplicity:

Son of the Earth	The Gun and the Sword
Soul of Life	Buried the Hatchet
Children of Worth	Buried the Stake
Daughters of Starlight	Bow to Each Other
Daughters of Mirth	Peace to Make
Sisters of Sunlight	The Earth Supplies
Sisters of Earth	And Nature Feeds
Brothers of Nature	But we turn away
Brothers of Old	For Artificial Needs
And the Story I'm Told	Down to Earth
I had a Dream	Stay a While
Of my own Accord	The Sun is Shining
They laid to Rest	Sit there and Smile

In addition to self-government, the recommendations dealt with such matters as co-management of wildlife resources, keeping Indigenous customary usage in mind when establishing national parks, ownership and management of cultural historic sites, and even a proposal for the establishment of an electronic worldwide information clearing office. In the view of the RCAP, there are four dimensions to social change in reference to Indigenous people: (1) healing; (2) improving economic opportunity; (3) developing human resources and Indigenous institutions; and (4) adapting mainstream institutions to both Indigenous and non-Indigenous needs.[55]

On the subject of self-government, the commissioners proposed for urban Indigenous people a "Community of Interest Government." Such a government would operate based on voluntary membership within municipal boundaries, with powers delegated from Indigenous national and/or provincial governments.[56] The Commission commended Quebec for its hunter income support programs, which were developed as part of its northern land claim agreements.[57]

Self-Government in Any Context

Even as the commissioners were hammering out their recommendations, some of them had already been realized, at least in part. Others were in the process of being met. A notable example is the northern Quebec community of Oujé-Bougoumou.

Oujé-Bougoumou, counting between 500 and 600 persons at the turn of the twenty-first century, was one of the nine northern Quebec bands listed under the James Bay and Northern Quebec Agreement of 1975. The United Nations has recognized the village as one of 50 world-class models that integrates traditional concepts with modern engineering techniques and architectural designs.

It was not always like this. The Oujé-Bougoumou's troubles had started in the 1920s, when their territory became the focus of mining development. There followed a period during which the government displaced the Cree time and again as they got in the way of mining interests. It would take years of persistent effort on the part of such individuals as Chief Jimmy Mianscum. Eventually, in the 1980s, they won recognition as a band and renamed themselves the Oujé-Bougoumou Cree Nation. After still more administrative battles, and with a new chief, Abel Bosum, they chose a site at Lake Opémisca, hired one of Canada's leading architects (Douglas Cardinal, of Siksika/Métis heritage from Alberta), and set about building yet another village. When negotiations with the federal and provincial governments collapsed, they declared jurisdiction over their territory of 10,000 km². As Indigenous leaders across the country rallied to their cause, Quebec (1989) and Ottawa (1991) finally signed deals. In the words of Bosum, from "the very beginning, our objective has been to build a place and an environment that produces healthy, secure, confident and optimistic people."[58]

In an urban context, the Tsuu T'ina Nation administers and is developing land adjacent to Calgary, Alberta, as is the Nippissing First Nation at North Bay, Ontario. The Squamish

INDIGENOUS LEADERS | Ovide Mercredi

Ovide Mercredi (b. 1946) is a former National Chief of the Assembly of First Nations and one of the strongest proponents of self-government and constitutional reform in Canadian history. Mercredi first came to national attention as an advocate for the Cree in northern Quebec at the time of the proposed Great Whale hydroelectric project. In 1989 he became a vice-chief of the Assembly of First Nations representing Manitoba, and in this capacity he became a key adviser to Elijah Harper during the Meech Lake Accord debates. In 1991 he was elected to a first term as National Chief of the Assembly of First Nations. He was elected to a second term in 1994. As a firm believer in non-violent protest, Mercredi played a key role as a mediator in the Oka Crisis of 1990 and again at Gustafsen Lake in 1995 when a Sun Dance ceremony led to a land dispute and to armed confrontation. Throughout his career, Mercredi has been a forceful and eloquent voice for the inherent right to self-government. His work on constitutional reform represents his long-term vision for Canada's future. His 1993 book, *In the Rapids: Navigating the Future of First Nations*, provides a clear glimpse of what that vision is. His latest projects have included consulting with the Law Society of Upper Canada to reflect on how the Society addresses Indigenous people, in particular their complaints and issues.[59]

Assembly of First Nations. Used with permission

Indigenous leader Ovide Mercredi gave a stirring speech at the Crown–First Nations Gathering in January of 2012. See indiancountrytodaymedianetwork.com/2012/05/28/aboriginal-leader-ovide-mercredis-stirring-anticolonialism-speech-115251.

Nation Capilano Indian Reserve, including its business park, is situated entirely within the city of Vancouver. In Saskatchewan, on the other hand, bands have targeted nearby cities for the creation of satellite reserves within the city limits but affiliated with the parent reserve. Their purpose is to provide centres of business activity and social service distribution for areas of the cities, such as Prince Albert, with large Indigenous populations.[60] While many Indigenous bands and individuals have embraced and taken advantage of the opportunities provided in modern society, others have sought and found strength in a retreat from that society and a return to more traditional practices.

Directly related to the RCAP—in fact, launched within three weeks of its report—was Canada's first Indigenous bank. The First Nations Bank of Canada began operations in Saskatoon in 1997 as a co-operative enterprise involving the Saskatchewan Federation of Indian Nations, the Saskatchewan Indian Equity Foundation, and the Toronto-Dominion Bank. Matthew Coon Come, National Chief of the Assembly of First Nations, 2000–3, an original board member, saw the benefits as including a greater degree of Indigenous economic control and greater sensitivity to the needs of First Nation communities and businesses, as well as an opportunity to share in the profits.[61]

On the political front, an initiative of Ronald Irwin (Indian Affairs Minister, 1993–7) to amend the Indian Act to give Indigenous Peoples more control over their own affairs met with an angry reception on the part of Indigenous leaders, who felt that the proposed measures did not go far enough and that the Act should be abolished. National Chief Ovide Mercredi moved quickly to warn Ottawa that implementing the RCAP recommendations was its "last best chance" to improve the lot of marginalized Indigenous Peoples, thus avoiding rising remedial expenditures for social and economic ills, not to mention the possibility of violence. The bill died on the order paper when a federal election was called for 2 June 1997.

The idea behind the bill was not dead, however. In January 2001, Robert Nault, Irwin's successor as Minister of Indian Affairs, proposed supplementing the Indian Act with a **First Nations Governance Act** (FNGA). The proposed Act would give bands increased powers to levy taxes on reserves, as well as the right to garnish wages and seize assets. Nault saw the proposed measure as a step towards self-government. The reaction of Indigenous leaders was predictable: unless they would be involved in working out the new format, it would not get the support it needed to succeed.[62] Many First Nations leaders opposed the legislation, first, because it did not recognize the inherent right of self-government, and second, because it was seen as an attack on existing Aboriginal and treaty rights. For its part, the federal government claimed that the proposed Act would increase the accountability of both First Nations and their governments. However, discussions about how the proposed Act would improve education, health care, and housing and eradicate poverty revealed obvious disagreements regarding the achievement of these important goals.

The opposition to the proposed FNGA rose steadily, and included many non-Indigenous groups. Amnesty International and the Anglican, Catholic, and United churches of Canada joined the Assembly of First Nations in condemning the proposed legislation. As Grand Chief

Matthew Coon Come noted, the FNGA would "leave a legacy of shame, a legacy of despair, and a legacy of colonialism when we were looking for a legacy of hope for our future generations."[63] Opposition focused on the federal government's failure to address self-government and on the vagueness that appeared to threaten treaty rights and Aboriginal rights. Under Bill C-7 there was no explicit reference to the right of self-government. In the final analysis the FNGA related more to federal legislation and policy issues—to a desire to streamline an administrative quagmire—than to important constitutional rights. Its aim was federal housekeeping, not a new deal for Indigenous Peoples within Canada.[64]

In some sense the failure of the FNGA was the failure of a federal government that had effectively run its course and lacked good new ideas for the country. Nonetheless, once Paul Martin had replaced Chrétien as Liberal leader and Prime Minister, and after having eked out a minority government in the 2004 election,[65] he and Indigenous leaders took action to improve economic development, self-sufficiency, and education within Indigenous communities. The **Kelowna Accord** of November 2005, brokered by Prime Minister Martin and Indigenous leaders, was to provide some equity for Indigenous people after the failure of the FNGA. Unfortunately, the Kelowna Accord, which had promised $5 billion over its initial five-year phase for economic development, education, and various other services, fell by the wayside after the election of a minority Conservative government in February of 2006.

At this point, the initiative to replace the Indian Act shifted away from the federal government and to Indigenous communities across Canada. Many organizations have advanced the cause of self-governance. The foremost among them is the First Nations Governance Centre, an organization staffed by Indigenous professionals. Education is the primary activity of the Centre and workshops are held in general governance areas: leadership; policy development; strategic planning; transparency and community engagement; and constitution drafting. More specialized workshops are held in areas of particular concern to Indigenous governance. These areas include culture and tradition in governance; territorial rights; and governing traditional lands.[66] By 2014, various self-governance models had taken form.

Recently established agreements with the Kwanlin Dün First Nation in Yukon, various First Nations in Manitoba, and with the Anishinabek Nation (the political body representing forty First Nations in Ontario) provide models for new government-to-government relationships based on partnership and mutual respect. Another model exists in Nunavut, where the democratically elected territorial government is responsible for all citizens regardless of ethnicity but the reality is an Inuit-led government. An agreement-in-principle was signed for a similar public (but mainly Inuit) government, the Nunavik Regional Government, in northern Quebec. This proposal was put to a referendum in April 2011 and was rejected by over 65 per cent of voters.

Self-government, as it evolves, will require economic reform and economic development, something that, as we have seen, a number of communities have achieved. But others have not, and they continue to live in conditions of poverty unimagined by most Canadians. After the Martin government was defeated by the Conservatives under Stephen Harper, governance was moved off the agenda, at least as a one-size-fits-all exercise. It was replaced by policies favouring

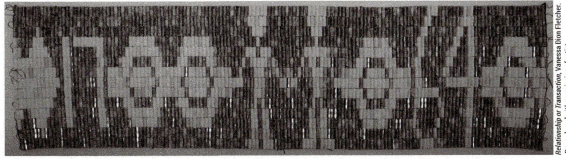

Relationship or Transaction **by Vanessa Dion Fletcher, an artist of Boodwaadmii and Lenape ancestry.** Dion Fletcher explains that her work "is a reproduction of Western Great Lakes Covenant Chain Confederacy Wampum Belt. This belt depicts two figures holding hands in the centre flanked by pentagons and the date 1764. My reproduction is made using $5 bills as the quahog (purple) beads and replica $5 bills as the whelk (white) beads."

privatization. Eventually an omnibus bill, C-45, was proposed by the Conservatives and passed as the Jobs and Growth Act in December of 2012. This Act had serious implications for Aboriginal rights, self-governance initiatives, and the environment. The proposal to modify the old Navigable Waters Protection Act of 1882 meant the deregulation of waters flowing through First Nations lands. This alone was cause for serious concern. In some quarters Prime Minister Harper's government was seen as moving towards a Canadian version of the Dawes Act in the United States. The Dawes Act of 1887 entitled the US President to establish surveys of tribal land (as it is called in the United States of America) and to divide it into allotments for individuals. The problems at Caledonia, Ontario (see Chapter 19), were caused by just such an approach. Some leaders have even seen Harper's policies as an attempt to drive people from the reserves.

Concerns, Hopes, and Fears

It surprised no one that Indigenous leaders hailed the RCAP report as an "inspiring road map to the future," all the more because it so clearly expressed the Indigenous position.[67] Erasmus denied an early criticism that the Royal Commission "listens only to Indians,"[68] saying that the Commission was neither an Indigenous organization nor an advocacy group.[69] Towards the end of the twentieth century, Indian Affairs was involved in self-government and jurisdictional negotiations at 81 tables across the country, involving about half of all First Nations.

In general, Indian Affairs acknowledged the need to build a new partnership with Indigenous Peoples, as well as to strengthen their communities to enable them to govern themselves.[70] It also acknowledged that "the inherent right of self-government is an existing Aboriginal and treaty right."[71] Early in 1998, Jane Stewart, Minister of Indian Affairs and Northern Development,

1997–9, officially expressed the government's regret for the residential school abuses and announced a $350 million healing fund to help those who had suffered. At the same time, Stewart announced an action plan called "Gathering Strength" to develop a partnership with the Indigenous leaders to carry out needed reforms in general administration.

The reaction of Indigenous leaders was mixed, to say the least, particularly as the Minister of Indian Affairs, not the Prime Minister, had made the statement of regret.[72] Still, the department was able to report a year later that it had developed with the Assembly of First Nations an agenda to correct the situation and that, in fact, this agenda was already in operation at national, regional, and community levels. AFN National Chief Matthew Coon Come, however, said the apology was not good enough. Instead, he asked for a national Truth and Reconciliation Commission to be established by Order-in-Council to act as a national forum for venting feelings and working out problems that have resulted from the residential school experience.[73] The Truth and Reconciliation Commission, as we shall see in the next chapter, made its final report in December of 2015.[74]

On the matter of self-government, matters were complicated by the diversity of circumstances of each case.[75] Fiscal restraint means that federal funding must be achieved through reallocation of existing resources, which involves taking the interests of other Canadians into account. Where their jurisdictions or interests are affected, provincial or territorial governments must be included in negotiations. In general, three-way (federal, provincial, Indigenous) processes seem to be the most effective. First Nations leadership has also accepted its share of responsibility in mapping out the future; Coon Come expressed this at an Indigenous health conference held in Ottawa. In a speech entitled "Our Voice, Our Decisions, Our Responsibility," he made the point that solutions to the social ills that plague the Indigenous

Past, Present, and Future of the Anishinaabe People, Christian Chapman. Reproduced with permission of the artist.

***The Past, Present, and Future of the Anishinaabe People* by Christian Chapman.** "When my family adopted your family, we became relatives, and that cannot be undone. . . . [The Queen] is the one we adopted. She and her children received the right to occupy this territory alongside my family."—Christian Chapman

communities cannot all come from outside. "We are the ones who have to do something. We must act." High on his list of priorities was leadership accountability. In his words, "we need to clean up our own act."[76]

In another realm involving Indigenous Peoples' control of their future, the AFN National Chief, Phil Fontaine, at the end of June 2005, on the twentieth anniversary of Bill C-31 becoming law, called for a joint First Nations–government process to establish Indigenous citizenship. Fontaine stated that Bill C-31 "has not resolved any of the problems it was intended to fix and has . . . created new problems." Gender discrimination continues, for example, and the status Indian population "is declining as a direct result of Bill C-31." The National Chief emphasized,

> It is morally, politically and legally wrong for one government to tell another government who its citizens are, and we are calling for a process to move citizenship to the jurisdiction where it properly belongs . . . with First Nations governments. . . . Canada is in a clear conflict of interest . . . because the number of registered Indians creates financial implications for the government.[77]

The gender discrimination in Bill C-31 was brought to the British Columbia court of Appeal in 2010, which led to Bill C-3, though it was stalled until 2015 when the Superior Court of Quebec also ruled that the Federal Government must amend the Indian Act to remove the ongoing gender discrimination. This was further deferred until December 2017, when Bill S-3 came into effect under the Trudeau government. Bill S-3 makes important strides, but it has still not removed all gender discrimination within the Indian Act.

As illustrated by the path of Bills C-3 and S-3, difficulties and different priorities brought the process to a crawl during the Harper government—though the Truth and Reconciliation Commission was officially established during this time (see Chapter 19).

Most noticeable in the absence of positive forward momentum under the Harper administration was Canada refusing to adopt the **United Nations Declaration on the Rights of Indigenous Peoples** (UNDRIP), which was adopted by the United Nations in September of 2007 (see Chapter 19). This has changed with the government of Justin Trudeau. The announcements by the Trudeau government concerning the new relationship between Indigenous people and the federal government are evidence of this change. The Trudeau government has made it clear that the relationship is a main priority of his government.[78] In May of 2016, Canada announced its unqualified support for UNDRIP at the United Nations, and in February of 2017, Trudeau announced the government's intent to review all federal laws and policies as they relate to Indigenous people. In June 2017, on National Aboriginal Day—since renamed National Indigenous Peoples Day—he issued the clearest statement yet on the importance his government places on the relationship:

> No relationship is more important to Canada than the relationship with Indigenous Peoples. Our Government is working together with Indigenous Peoples to build a nation-to-nation, Inuit–Crown, government-to-government relationship—one

based on respect, partnership, and recognition of rights. We are determined to make a real difference in the lives of Indigenous Peoples—by closing socio-economic gaps, supporting greater self-determination, and establishing opportunities to work together on shared priorities. We are also reviewing all federal laws and policies that concern Indigenous Peoples and making progress on the Calls to Action outlined in the Final Report of the Truth and Reconciliation Commission.[79]

In late August of 2017, Trudeau announced the splitting of the Ministry of Indigenous and Northern Affairs into two ministries: the Ministry of Indigenous Services and the Ministry of Crown–Indigenous Relations in accordance with a recommendation of the RCAP. He chose two of his most capable ministers to lead the new ministries. At a news conference following the cabinet shuffle he noted that bigger changes still were planned: "We are demonstrating with this change today that we are serious about taking the right steps to move beyond the Indian Act, but doing it in partnership and collaboration with Indigenous Peoples."[80] Reactions to these announcements have been mixed, but hopeful.[81] The willingness to work on a true nation-to-nation basis is the furthest any Canadian government has ever gone towards working with Indigenous Peoples towards self-governance.

Questions to Consider

1. What makes the situation of the Lubicon Cree unique?
2. Explain the connections between the Penner Report and the Cree-Naskapi Act.
3. What were the key recommendations of the Royal Commission on Aboriginal Peoples?
4. What steps towards self-government have been made since 1996?

Recommended Readings

Asch, Michael. *Home and Native Land: Aboriginal Rights and the Canadian Constitution*. Toronto: Methuen, 1984.

Cardinal, Harold. "Nation-Building as a Process: Reflections of a Nihiyow (Cree)," in Paul Depasquale, ed., *Natives and Settlers Now and Then: Historical Issues and Current Perspectives on Treaties and Land Claims in Canada*. Edmonton: University of Alberta Press, 2007.

Goddard, John. *Last Stand of the Lubicon Cree*. Vancouver: Douglas & McIntyre, 1991.

Hedican, Edward J. *Ipperwash: The Tragic Failure of Canada's Aboriginal Policy*. Toronto: University of Toronto Press, 2013.

Hornig, James F., ed. *Social and Environmental Impacts of the James Bay Hydroelectric Project*. Montreal and Kingston: McGill-Queen's University Press, 1999.

King, Sarah J. *Fishing in Contested Waters: Place and Community in Burnt Church/Esgenoopetiti*. Toronto: University of Toronto Press, 2013.

Samson, Colin. *A Way of Life That Does Not Exist: Canada and the Extinguishment of the Innu*. St John's and London: ISER Books and Verso, 2003.

Shkilnyk, Anastasia M. *A Poison Stronger Than Love: The Destruction of an Ojibwa Community*. New Haven: Yale University Press, 1985.

19 Reconciliation and Revitalization

CHAPTER OUTLINE

The final chapter of this text examines the themes of reconciliation and revitalization. Reconciliation is evident in the formal apology for the many harms of the residential schools and in the work of the Truth and Reconciliation Commission of Canada. Revitalization may be seen in the continued advances made in self-governance, Aboriginal and treaty rights, economic development, and in the increased sharing of Indigenous knowledge. We will look specifically at some important Supreme Court decisions and at continued activism at Caledonia and in the Idle No More movement.

LEARNING OUTCOMES

1. Students will learn the significance of a number of Supreme Court decisions.

2. Students will see how oral history is used in court cases.

3. Students will learn something of the context of continued activism.

4. Students will understand the importance of the United Nations Declaration on the Rights of Indigenous Peoples.

TIMELINE From the Patriation of the Canadian Constitution to Idle No More

1982
Patriation of Canadian Constitution; Constitution Act, 1982 recognizes and affirms "existing aboriginal and treaty rights."

1990
Supreme Court rules in *R. v. Sioui*. In this case, a document signed in 1760 by General James Murray, military governor of Quebec, which guaranteed the Huron the free exercise of their customs and religion, was held to be a treaty.

1997
Supreme Court overturns British Columbia Appeal Court decision in *Delgamuukw v. British Columbia*. The most important element in this case was the Court's allowance of oral history on an equal footing with other types of evidence.

2003
In September, with the decision in *Powley*, the Supreme Court affirms that Métis have rights that are recognized and protected by Canada's Constitution.

2007
On 19 September, the federal government announces a $1.9 billion compensation deal for an estimated 80,000 former residential school students.

1990
Supreme Court rules in *Sparrow v. R.*, the first case in which the Court dealt with section 35 of the Constitution Act, 1982, which recognizes and affirms "the existing aboriginal and treaty rights of the aboriginal peoples of Canada."

1996
Supreme Court rules in *R. v. Adams*, another Aboriginal rights case that supported the right to resource use as found in *Sparrow*.
Van der Peet case helps to define Aboriginal rights, determining that fishing rights do not necessarily extend to the right to sell catch commercially.

2000
The Canadian government ratifies the Nisga'a Final Agreement Act, granting 1,900 km^2 to the Nisga'a.

2005
In October, Henco Industries decides to develop the Douglas Creek Estates adjacent to the Six Nations Reserve, which later causes clashes between residents of Caledonia, near Hamilton and Brantford in southern Ontario, and Haudenosaunee members of the Six Nations.

2008
On 11 June, the Prime Minister of Canada makes a statement of apology to former residential school students in the House of Commons.

Continued

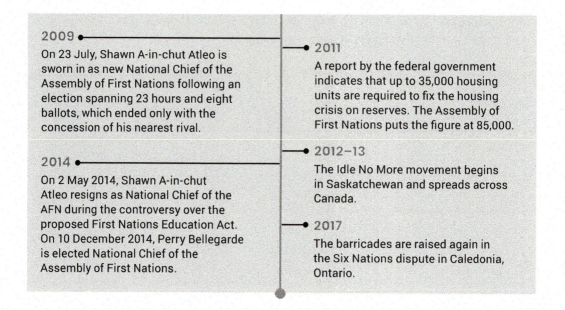

2009
On 23 July, Shawn A-in-chut Atleo is sworn in as new National Chief of the Assembly of First Nations following an election spanning 23 hours and eight ballots, which ended only with the concession of his nearest rival.

2011
A report by the federal government indicates that up to 35,000 housing units are required to fix the housing crisis on reserves. The Assembly of First Nations puts the figure at 85,000.

2014
On 2 May 2014, Shawn A-in-chut Atleo resigns as National Chief of the AFN during the controversy over the proposed First Nations Education Act. On 10 December 2014, Perry Bellegarde is elected National Chief of the Assembly of First Nations.

2012–13
The Idle No More movement begins in Saskatchewan and spreads across Canada.

2017
The barricades are raised again in the Six Nations dispute in Caledonia, Ontario.

An Apology

On 11 June 2008, the Prime Minister of Canada rose in the House of Commons and made history with three words: "We are sorry." His statement and those made that day by the leaders of the other parties in Parliament, and the responses by the leaders of five national Indigenous organizations mark a watershed in Canada's Indigenous history. The apology was made for the damage wrought on stolen children, their families, and their communities by the residential schools since the late nineteenth century. Harper's introductory comments are worth quoting:

> I stand before you today to offer an apology to former students of Indian residential schools. The treatment of children in these schools is a sad chapter in our history.
>
> For more than a century, Indian residential schools separated over 150,000 aboriginal children from their families and communities.
>
> In the 1870s, the federal government, partly in order to meet its obligation to educate aboriginal children, began to play a role in the development and administration of these schools.
>
> Two primary objectives of the residential schools system were to remove and isolate children from the influence of their homes, families, traditions and cultures, and to assimilate them into the dominant culture.
>
> These objectives were based on the assumption aboriginal cultures and spiritual beliefs were inferior and unequal.
>
> Indeed, some sought, as it was infamously said, "to kill the Indian in the child."
>
> Today, we recognize that this policy of assimilation was wrong, has caused great harm, and has no place in our country. . . .[1]

Although Harper's apology met with mixed reviews, many Indigenous people were glad of the positive step towards an improved relationship that it represented. Others cautioned that the Prime Minister was acting in the interest of resource development and that he was only trying to improve relations in order to facilitate economic projects. Some of the early hope for change began to fade a few years after the apology. On 11 June 2012, a stained-glass window by Métis artist Christi Belcourt was unveiled at the House of Commons to commemorate the fourth anniversary of the apology. The Assembly of First Nations National Chief Shawn Atleo noted at the time that any goodwill created by the apology was being lost: "I think its symbolism is just fine. What's really required is action. Real change."[2] He warned that Indigenous people across Canada were becoming impatient with the slow progress being made in discussions about poverty, housing, resource-sharing, and education. Some of this impatience would fuel the Idle No More movement of 2012–13.

Although the change has been slow in coming, there are positive signs that improvements are being made. This chapter will examine some of these signs. Across Canada one of the most important and cherished Indigenous traditions is oral history, the passing of a people's storehouse of knowledge from one generation to the next. The historic 1997 decision by the Supreme Court of Canada in *Delgamuukw v. British Columbia* overturned a decision of the British Columbia Court of Appeal and ruled that oral history must be considered "as a repository of historical knowledge for a culture."[3] Other Aboriginal and treaty rights cases continue to push the legal and administrative agenda towards fairness and healing. The priority of resource allocation that came from the landmark **Sparrow v. R.** case of 1990 is a good example of a step forward. This case involved Ronald Sparrow, a member of the Musqueam Indian Band of the Coast Salish, who

HISTORICAL BACKGROUND | Samson Cree Nation

In 1989 legal proceedings were instituted in the Federal Court of Canada by the **Samson Cree Nation** against the federal government with regard to the royalties from oil and gas revenues that the federal government holds in trust for the band. The Samson Cree Nation, part of Treaty Six in central Alberta, sought to have the federal government, in particular the Department of Indian Affairs, declared in breach of its treaty, trust, fiduciary, and other obligations and duties with respect to the management of the oil and gas revenues relating to the Pigeon Lake reserve. The sums of money involved were huge—a reflection of the demand for oil and gas—and the case points to the critical need for Indigenous development corporations that will have the real interest of Indigenous people at heart.

Finally in 2007, the Federal Court of Appeal held that the Crown was a trustee and had fiduciary obligations, but the majority of the Court ruled that the Crown had acted "reasonably." The dissenting judge, Justice J. Edgar Sexton, found that the Crown did not meet its duties as a trustee. Justice Sexton agreed with the claims brought by the Samson Cree Nation that it had been the victim of "inferior and discriminatory treatment." Justice Sexton found that

Continued

this treatment was in violation of section 15 of the Canadian Charter of Rights and Freedoms. Most interestingly, he blamed the Indian Act. Specifically, he noted:

> Concluding that the Crown has no duty or power to invest the Indian moneys would subject Indians, who must deal with the Crown as their trustee, to inferior treatment merely because of their Indian status and membership in an Indian band. This would appear to constitute discriminatory treatment on the part of the government in violation of subsection 15(1) of the Charter on the basis of race, or national or ethnic origin.[4]

HISTORICAL BACKGROUND | Treaty Land Entitlement

One area where progress is being made concerns Treaty Land Entitlement in western Canada. Land claims in the West had long been hampered by the shifting nature of responsibility. The boundaries of the province of Saskatchewan were different when the treaties were signed than they are at present. When the Hudson's Bay Company sold the huge tract of the Northwest known as Rupert's Land to Britain in 1869 and it was transferred to the new Confederation of Canada in 1870, these transactions occurred without consideration of the land rights of the region's people. Naturally, leaders of the Indigenous Peoples involved complained of this violation of a policy established as far back as the Royal Proclamation of 1763. The federal government recognized that a number of First Nations did not receive the reserve lands they were entitled to under the original surveys for the numbered treaties, but it did little about this situation until 1930 when it signed the Natural Resources Transfer Acts with the provinces of Manitoba, Saskatchewan, and Alberta.

By this agreement, responsibility for outstanding treaty land obligations shifted from Canada to these provinces at the time they finally gained control over their Crown lands, minerals, and resources. One of the most important aspects of Treaty Land Entitlement involves water and riparian rights. Water courses, construction and changes to fish habitat, pollution, and rights over lake and riverbeds have been a major concern to Indigenous leaders. Water is as important, and in some communities more important, to Indigenous lifeways than land. The Treaty Land Entitlement Agreement acknowledges this.[5]

In 1992, by the Saskatchewan Treaty Land Entitlement Framework Agreement, 25 Saskatchewan First Nations, the federal government, and the provincial government moved to ensure that all of the First Nations receive the amount of reserve land to which they are entitled. Saskatchewan provides the Crown land for sale; the federal government provides the funds to purchase the land; and the First Nations select and purchase the land for the reserves. The Manitoba Treaty Land Entitlement Framework Agreement, following the exact pattern as the Saskatchewan agreement and for the exact same reasons, was signed in 1997. As of August 2016, Saskatchewan and Manitoba had made the most progress in the Treaty Land Entitlement process, with 90 per cent of such transactions having taken place in these two provinces.[6]

had used a fishing net larger than allowed by law. The Supreme Court found that under section 35 (1) of the Constitution Act, Indigenous fishing, land, and hunting rights for food, social, and ceremonial purposes had priority over later restrictive legislation, and Sparrow was acquitted.

On the other hand, there is still work to be done. The ongoing (as of 2017) Douglas Creek land claim in Caledonia, Ontario, is an example of the challenges that need to be confronted. Although the Ontario Provincial Police seem determined not to repeat the tragic events of Ipperwash, the Douglas Estates land claim remains a volatile and difficult situation and has excited a great deal of media and public attention. Similarly, the lawsuit brought by the Samson Cree Nation in central Alberta (see Historical Background box) against the federal government reveals that high-stakes claims create special problems that need to be addressed with fairness and resolve. Treaty Land Entitlement has been one method of beginning to right past wrongs, especially in Saskatchewan and Manitoba (see Historical Background box).

Delgamuukw, Oral History, and Legal Sequencing

As we saw in Chapter 17, Justice Allan McEachern ruled to reject the Aboriginal rights claim of the Gitxsan and Wet'suwet'en to 58,000 km^2 of their traditional lands in northern British Columbia. The case relied heavily on oral history and on the testimony of more than 100 witnesses. McEachern, Chief Justice of the Appeal Court of British Columbia, denied the existence of Aboriginal rights of ownership, but in 1997 the Supreme Court of Canada overturned the judgment and found that oral history evidence had not been given sufficient weight in the original trial. Justice Brian Dickson stated, "Claims to aboriginal title are woven with history, legend, politics, and moral obligation."[7] In addition to the obvious importance of a land claim of such a vast size, the *Delgamuukw* case is of special significance in terms of the importance placed by the Court on oral history. With a few exceptions—including pictographs and wampum belts— most Indigenous history lives in the memories of the people. Stories are told and passed on from one generation to another, and from time immemorial these stories have constituted the storehouse of people's knowledge.[8]

From the very first contacts between Europeans and Indigenous Peoples, oral history has played an important role. When Samuel de Champlain travelled up the Ottawa River in the summer of 1613 in his first attempt to visit the Wendat in their villages, he kept a careful record of his travels and noted several elements of oral history. When he landed at Allumette Island the Kitchesipirini chief Tessouat invited him and his party to a feast. Later, Champlain complained bitterly about the Algonquin habit of repetition and he marvelled at how long his hosts discussed matters of import.[9] What Champlain saw and heard that night was the careful repetition of facts that would enable his hosts to remember events long after Europeans—and others trained in the written tradition—had forgotten them.

Oral histories take many forms and can be repeated as stories. Some of them were recorded. Two famous examples of oral histories that were written down in the nineteenth century are those of Francis Assikinack and Andrew Makade-binesi (published as Andrew J. Blackbird).[10]

Francis Assikinack was an Odaawa historian from Manitoulin Island who published his oral histories at the urging of the chief clerk for the Indian Department, Daniel Wilson. Assikinack had been educated at Upper Canada College in Toronto and came to understand the importance of the written word in the changing world around him. His histories are clearly written and factual. Makade-binesi, another Odaawa historian who had been sent away to get a European education, is often used as an example of the validity of oral history. In one section of his history Makade-binesi refers to a group of people as Stockbridges, a term that referred to a New England town where they had been sent after being forced off their ancestral land. By the time Makade-binesi wrote his history this term had gone out of use completely and the only way Makade-binesi could have known it was from the oral tradition he had learned from his parents and from his extended family.[11] This kind of validation is not possible in most cases because of the paucity of written sources.

The Supreme Court ruling to allow appropriate weight to oral history testimony reveals that the Court has come to accept what historians have known for some time: oral history provides the best way to overcome the evidentiary shortcomings of the written record and the best way to find the Indigenous perspective. Cases that have benefited from this acceptance include that of the Nisga'a, where the Court allowed a great deal of oral history testimony to help clarify the issues around the Nisga'a land claim in British Columbia, a case that was extremely complex.[12]

Caledonia Land Claims

One complex case still awaiting a resolution is the **Douglas Creek** dispute in Caledonia, Ontario. Like many Indigenous issues, the problems at Caledonia have deep roots. Before we can hope to understand what seems to be an ill-conceived fiasco on the part of the Henco property developers, we first must examine the history of the Haudenosaunee people in the Grand River region. In many ways the story of the settlement of the Haudenosaunee on the Six Nations Reserve, the so-called **Haldimand Tract** along the Grand River, resonates with some of the critical themes of Canadian history: settlement; the clash of cultures between the Europeans and the Indigenous people; the clashes between French and English; and worries over American expansionism. At the heart of the story is one of Canada's most famous Indigenous leaders, Thayendanegea.[13] The territory in question, the Haldimand Tract in what is now southern Ontario, lies west of the Niagara Peninsula, north of Lake Erie, south of Lake Ontario, and east of Lake Huron.

For the loyalty of the Haudenosaunee allies to the British Crown the British government informed Thayendanegea that the Haudenosaunee people would be accommodated as soon as possible with a new home. Such a home had a number of very specific requirements. The Grand River region, from its source to its mouth, fit the bill perfectly. The soil and climate of the region were nearly identical to old Iroquoia, in present-day upstate New York. The crops would thrive just as they had further east. Deer and other game were abundant, all the more so because the region had not had many human visitors since the end of the seventeenth century. Second-growth forests were plentiful and there was a lot of choice for village sites close to these forests. Most importantly, the area was available for settlement. The land was purchased by the British from the Mississaugas, recently arrived in this area from their ancestral homeland in northern Lake Huron. Their economic orientation to the resources of the lakes was ill-suited to this tract of land.[14]

Accordingly, on 25 October 1784, the governor of Quebec, Sir Frederick Haldimand, made the so-called Haldimand Proclamation. Acting for the Crown, Haldimand conveyed to the Kanienkehaka "and such others of the Six Nations Indians as wish to settle in that quarter" the Grand River tract of land as restitution for their losses in the Revolutionary War. Haldimand's grant was quite specific and the Haudenosaunee were authorized to settle along the banks, from its head to its mouth "six miles deep from each side" of the Grand River.[15] In the early spring of 1785, Thayendanegea led a group of 1,843 Six Nations people from Lewiston, New York, across the Niagara to their new home.[16]

What appears to be a clear and unequivocal document, however, soon gave rise to a set of controversies that still rage today. The agents of the British Crown, from Haldimand forward, asserted that the land granted was not transferable and that the Haldimand Proclamation did not recognize the political sovereignty of the Six Nations Confederacy. Understandably, Thayendanegea interpreted matters differently. He argued that the Proclamation was a de facto recognition of Haudenosaunee sovereignty and that the title to the land was, therefore, held in what British law called "an estate in fee simple." To prove this, he quickly sold and leased huge sections of the Grand River to British settlers.[17]

These actions alarmed the Crown. In 1793 the lieutenant-governor of the new province of Upper Canada, John Graves Simcoe, drafted the "Simcoe Patent," a document stipulating that all land transactions in the Haldimand Tract had to be approved by the Crown. Thayendanegea simply ignored Simcoe and his "Patent" and continued to invite British settlers into the Haldimand Tract. Somewhere between Haldimand's grant and Simcoe's action, Thayendanegea and other Haudenosaunee leaders began to change their minds about the presence of British settlers. In the early days they had been invited in as a means of demonstrating Haudenosaunee sovereignty, but as time went by Thayendanegea realized the extent of the huge changes sweeping across the region. Simcoe was inclined to allow Thayendanegea to have his own way as he feared losing the Haudenosaunee as military allies.[18]

In 1834, the first inquiry into the situation in the Haldimand Tract was held. The Crown determined that Thayendanegea had acted illegally, but by then it was deemed too costly and difficult to move all of the British settlers from their farms. In response to the ongoing problems, the Superintendent of Indian Affairs, Samuel Peters Jarvis, went to the Onondaga Council House in January 1841 and suggested the Haudenosaunee voluntarily surrender their lands (save some reserve lands and the areas of the villages, a total of about 20,000 acres or 8,100 ha) back to the Crown so that the Crown could administer the Haldimand Tract "for their exclusive benefit and interest." Jarvis argued that one contiguous reserve would allow for more economical construction of schools, churches, and other public buildings. The chiefs agreed, but the agreement did little to alleviate the confusion that resulted from Thayendanegea's earlier interpretation of the Haldimand Proclamation.[19] After Jarvis got the Haudenosaunee to surrender their lands the ownership question of most of the land that had been sold and leased was resolved, at least in the eyes of the Crown. Various interests in the Haudenosaunee continued to maintain a different point of view.[20]

Following the Order-in-Council of 1843 that affirmed the surrender, a delegation of Haudenosaunee chiefs appealed to the government to grant an additional 35,000 acres (14,175 ha). This was affirmed, and in 1847 the reserve was formally established at approximately 55,000 acres (22,275 ha), although subsequent surrenders reduced its size to 44,900 acres (18,185 ha). The government also forced squatters off the reserve land, but many of them simply returned. The particular land in question at Caledonia falls into this grey area. It was never legally surrendered, but as long as the descendants of the original British settlers were on the property, nothing was done. When the land was sold to Henco Industries for development, the trouble started.[21]

In 2006, the Ontario government negotiated the purchase of the Douglas Creek Estates property from Henco Industries for $21.1 million, and a year later the federal government contributed $15.8 million towards the Ontario purchase. Nonetheless, bitterness between some residents of Caledonia and the Haudenosaunee people has not entirely subsided, and a final resolution of this land issue that dates back more than two centuries must await the resolution of many other specific land claims relating to the Haldimand Tract that have been filed over the past several decades. Since 2006, very little has changed. The Haudenosaunee first brought litigation against Canada and Ontario in this matter in 1995. The Haudenosaunee wanted answers about the ways in which the Crown managed and disposed of its land, money, and other assets. In 2009, the Haudenosaunee formally reactivated the 1995 litigation and the claims are now before the courts. In February 2010, the mayor of Haldimand intimated that the province of Ontario had decided to "give the land back to the Six Nations" but no formal announcement of any such decision was made. In July 2011, the Attorney General of Ontario, Chris Bentley, announced a $20 million settlement for the people of Caledonia in response to their class-action lawsuit, but there is still no word on a solution for the Haudenosaunee. In the summer of 2017 the barricades went back up in response to the difficulty in finding a solution.[22]

Photo by William Newbigging

The landscape of present-day Caledonia.

The Residential Schools Settlement Agreement, 2007

An agreement to compensate the estimated 80,000 recognized survivors of designated Indian residential schools was ratified by the federal government on 19 September 2007. This agreement was not only for those who attended and survived but also for those who did not survive or who have since died. The issues surrounding the profound damage to individuals, communities, and cultures caused by the residential schools have been the focus of the **Truth and Reconciliation Commission of Canada**, but this symbolically important body got off to a less than encouraging start. Ontario Court of Appeal Justice Harry S. LaForme of the Mississauga of New Credit First Nation was appointed to head the Commission in May of 2008 and began his work in June of 2008, but in October of that year he resigned, citing the insubordination of the other two commissioners, who, among other things, were less interested than Justice LaForme in the reconciliation aspect of the Commission's mandate. These two commissioners held on to their positions, without a chair, until January of 2009, when they finally stepped down.[23] A reconstituted Commission was established in June of 2009, headed by **Justice Murray Sinclair**, the first Indigenous judge in the Manitoba court system.

The Commission was charged with a clear mandate. It was directed first to discover the truth about what happened in the residential schools and then to inform Canadians about the truth of what happened in the residential schools. In order to accomplish these two missions, the Commission used the records held by those who operated and funded the schools, including the Anglican Church and the Roman Catholic Church, and oral testimony. This last came from both the officials who operated the schools and, of course, from the students, their families, and their communities. In some cases, the Commission even required evidence from anyone "personally affected by the residential school experience and its subsequent impacts."[24]

The Commission's main hope was to promote healing. The idea was to help the survivors, in particular those who were First Nations, Inuit, and Métis, to heal through truth. A broader hope was that truth and healing would lead to reconciliation and to improved relationships between Indigenous people and the Government of Canada (and, by implication, all non-Indigenous Canadians). Truth, it was hoped, would lead to an ongoing process of reconciliation for both the individual survivors and for the entire country.[25]

The most important part of the process involved gathering statements, and the Commission's largest task was to collect testimonials from the individual students and family members in a sensitive manner. The official mandate of the Commission made this explicit:

> The Commission shall provide a safe, supportive and sensitive environment for individual statement taking/truth sharing.
> The Commission shall not use or permit access to an individual's statement made in any Commission processes, except with the express consent of the individual.[26]

As of March 2014, when the last meetings were held in Edmonton, the Truth and Reconciliation Commission had gathered more than 6,200 testimonial statements ranging in length from several minutes to several hours. Most of these statements were videotaped (or in some cases audiotaped), and they provide a vital historical collection of the entire residential schools experience.[27]

The September 2007 agreement with the federal government was to provide at least $1.9 billion to residential school survivors. The last federally run residential school had been closed in 1996 in Saskatchewan.[28] There have been many painful stories and memories from Indigenous persons of a legacy of mental, physical, and even sexual abuse. The path to a settlement agreement with the federal government and the Canadian churches that ran these schools took over 10 years from the time, in January of 1998, when the federal government announced an **Aboriginal Action Plan**, which called for a renewed partnership with many Indigenous people and Indigenous organizations to recognize the past mistakes and injustices.[29]

With many lawsuits related to the residential schools still pending, the federal government proposed payments for all former residential school students who were alive as of 30 May 2005. The proposal included an initial payout of $10,000 plus $3,000 for each year the student attended the school. However, this proposal included a provision that such an offer would release the government and the involved churches from all further liability relating to the Indian residential school experience, except in serious cases of sexual abuse or any physical abuse. For this purpose the **Independent Assessment Process** (IAP) was set up to address these serious cases of abuse.[30]

In the current deal, each eligible person who attended a designated residential school was expected to receive about $28,000. Not everyone, however, was happy with the agreement or its payment, and legal actions remain outstanding. Some survivors had to fight the government to gain access to their school records. While the Indian residential schools settlement brought some closure for the federal government and the churches accused in the lawsuits, financial compensation can never equal the suffering and anguish. The long-term damages to Indigenous individuals, families, and communities are incalculable.[31]

The experience of residential school is best left to the people who were most affected. This story, by Allan Saganash Jr, is typical of the thousands of sad stories across Canada:

> My story starts at home. The year was 1957. The family was somewhere in the bush on my dad's hunting ground. We were like maybe 80 miles from the little island known as the Waswanipi Post.
>
> It was sometime on a cold crispy day in the latter part of January while I was playing outside in my rabbit fur outfit, my mom suddenly picks me up and takes me inside the winter camp. I remember her saying that someone was coming from the lake on snowshoes. Our visitor was Bertie Happyjack. He was with my brother Wally Saganash.
>
> It has always been my understanding even at six years old (I would be seven in March) that when you had visitors everyone was happy. But this time something was wrong. Everyone in that winter camp was crying. Only children cried I thought.

I was not old enough to completely understand what was going on therefore I was not told that our visitor had brought some very bad and disturbing news that shocked everyone in that winter camp.

The news was that my brother had died while attending the residential school in Moose Factory, Ontario. Someone from the federal government agency had told Bertie Happyjack, who knew where our camp was to go and inform William Saganash that his son John Saganash had died and that he was buried on December 6, 1956.

John was my older brother, he was my best friend, my companion, my idol. He was the person in my life that paid the most attention to me."

Rose Cameron, a former residential school student, is now a highly successful university professor in the Department of Social Work at Algoma University in Sault Ste Marie. Her story reveals her desire to overcome the terrible challenges that the system imposed upon her:

At the age of six, I was placed in the Cecilia Jeffery Presbyterian Residential School in Kenora, Ontario, along with many other Saulteaux-Anishinabe children from the northwestern Ontario Treaty #3 area. While in this institution my mother died in a tragic accident. It was not until much later, when I began researching her genealogy, that I was astonished to learn that both of my parents and many of my aunts and uncles had also attended this same residential school.

Life at the residential school was a combination of alienation and fear while trying to adapt and make sense of a foreign environment. I was often separated from my two older sisters, who also resided at the school, and I had to quickly learn how to interact with complete strangers in the dormitory. In order to help protect me from corporal punishments that were handed out by the supervisors, my older sisters told me not to speak in our Saulteaux-Anishinaabe language with others since it was against the rules, but only speak to them in private. I was also instructed to listen to the supervisors and to obey their orders.

On the positive side, my exposure to the residential school system provided me with an opportunity to become aware of life outside of my First Nations community. I had more to eat there than at home and in order to survive in that arena I had to adapt and learn new lifelong skills such as self-discipline and social interaction. It would later occur to me that the residential school philosophy and practice was indoctrination by assimilation, but with subservience; that the system had no intended goal regarding equality and respect. As a young adult I contemplated my residential school experience, and I began to understand how racism plays out in society. Equally important for me, my experience at the residential school informed me about how to understand both the western and Saulteaux-Anishinaabe realities. I then embarked on a journey of self-determination and completed high school, college, and earned five university degrees, including a Ph.D. in Social Work at the University of

Students at Shingwauk residential school, Sault Ste Marie, Ontario, 1955.

Toronto. Residential school for me, ironically, did not defeat me with institutional racism, but through my own self-determination it empowered me towards success.[32]

Of course, many students did not survive or overcome the residential school experience, but even through tragedy there have been moments of powerful healing and reconciliation, and of steps towards a better future. When Tragically Hip front man Gord Downie (1964–2017), widely acclaimed for chronicling the mundane events of Canadian history, was diagnosed with inoperable brain cancer in late 2015, he set himself one final task: to memorialize the life, death, and spirit of Chanie Wenjack, a 12-year-old Anishinaabe boy who died of exposure in 1966 when he ran away from Cecilia Jeffery Residential School in Kenora in an attempt to return to his home at Ogoki Post, nearly 1,000 km distant. Downie's *Secret Path*, a song cycle, graphic novel, and animated film, profoundly affected many thousands, and led to the Assembly of First Nations honouring him in a special blanket ceremony where he was given the Lakhóta spirit name Wicapi Omani ("Man Who Walks among the Stars"). At that time Wicapi Omani noted that Canadians should not celebrate the last 150 years as a nation but the next 150 years—the seven generations that will be needed for healing: "We must walk down a path of reconciliation from now on. Together, and forever."[33]

Shingwauk Residential Schools Centre

Residential school survivors return to Shingwauk, 2002.

Missing and Murdered Indigenous Women and Girls

One of the most important elements in reconciliation concerns the disproportionate number of Indigenous women and girls who are victims of violent crime. One of the "Calls to Action" published by the Truth and Reconciliation Commission makes this clear:

> 41. We call upon the federal government, in consultation with Aboriginal or-
> ganizations, to appoint a public inquiry into the causes of, and remedies for,
> the disproportionate victimization of Aboriginal women and girls. The inquiry's
> mandate would include: i. Investigation into missing and murdered Aboriginal
> women and girls. ii. Links to the intergenerational legacy of residential schools.[34]

In December of 2015, the newly formed government of Prime Minister Justin Trudeau announced a national inquiry.[35]

In spite of the importance of the work—indeed, it is difficult to imagine a more important area of inquiry—and the qualifications of the commissioners, the **National Inquiry into**

Missing and Murdered Indigenous Women and Girls has had a great deal of difficulty. In part, this can be explained by the task of managing competing demands: the Inquiry must reconcile the need to make broad-based structural recommendations, and at the same time it must answer specific questions about specific cases.[36] One of the commissioners and several staff members have left the Inquiry and, at the time of writing, its future success is in doubt. What is not in doubt, however, is the level of interest and concern that this issue has captured. The national media have been actively following the story, and Indigenous and non-Indigenous groups across Canada are demanding action.

Fred Lum/© Copyright The Globe and Mail Inc.

REDress Project by Jaime Black, a Métis multidisciplinary artist from Winnipeg. Of her REDress Project, she explains that it "focuses around the issue of missing or murdered Aboriginal women across Canada. It is an installation art project based on an aesthetic response to this critical national issue. The project seeks to collect 600 red dresses by community donation that will later be installed in public spaces throughout Winnipeg and across Canada as a visual reminder of the staggering number of women who are no longer with us. Through the installation I hope to draw attention to the gendered and racialized nature of violent crimes against Aboriginal women and to evoke a presence through the marking of absence." (www.redressproject.org)

The United Nations Declaration on the Rights of Indigenous Peoples

The publication of the Truth and Reconciliation Commission final report on what happened at residential schools helped to raise the profile of Indigenous issues on a national scale. On an international level, a number of developments have made governments more inclined to address the long-standing challenges faced by Indigenous Peoples within what is now Canada. The most important of these is the United Nations Declaration on the Rights of Indigenous Peoples (UNDRIP) of 2007.[37] In November of 2015, the new Prime Minister of Canada, Justin Trudeau, asked the Minister of Indigenous and Northern Affairs, Carolyn Bennett, to implement the Declaration. Other members of the new cabinet were also given this mandate. In May of 2016, the minister announced that Canada is a "full supporter, without qualification, of the Declaration."[38]

Part of the response to the UNDRIP may be seen in the Trudeau government's actions supporting Indigenous self-government that we examined Chapter 18. In fact, when Bennett addressed the United Nations General Assembly in April of 2017 she made this connection explicitly: "In direct response to the Declaration, the Prime Minister has mandated the Minister of Justice and Attorney General for Canada to chair a working group to review all federal laws and policies related to Indigenous Peoples, to reverse the colonial and paternalistic approaches. This is about breathing life into Section 35 of Canada's Constitution which formally entrenches the rights of Indigenous People in Canadian law, and yet for far too long has not been lived up to."[39] She also noted that the work of identifying priorities in this effort was being undertaken in consultation with leaders of the First Nations, Inuit, and Métis. As noted in the last chapter, it is too early to tell whether these discussions will lead to the desired changes. In fact, concerns were raised early on by the Justice Minister, Jody Wilson-Raybould, about the difficulties implementation would involve, but the effort looks to be sincere. Having noted that, the current government continues to allow questionable fossil-fuel infrastructure projects against the will of First Nations affected by them. Time will tell.[40]

Economic Development

Shawn A-in-chut Atleo of the Ahousaht First Nation on the west coast of Vancouver Island was elected as the new National Chief of the Assembly of First Nations in July of 2009, following a potentially divisive and extended (eight ballots over 23 hours) election process. After campaigning on the importance of education, economic reform, and First Nations unity, Atleo explained, "We know economic independence is political independence; economic power is political power."[41] Achieving such independence and power will be the challenge in the years to come.

Although Atleo was re-elected to a second term in July of 2012, he failed to maintain the confidence of First Nations people across the country and resigned his position in the spring of 2014, following criticism from the grassroots and some regional leaders over his support of the proposed First Nations Control of First Nations Education Act (see Chapter 15). A rare meeting in mid-May of 2014 of the "Confederacy of Nations," a group of regional leaders designated by the AFN charter to meet in crisis situations, dismissed this proposed legislation, sought to take over the education file and negotiate with the federal government, and voted to strip the AFN executive of its powers for the time being.[42] In December of 2014, the AFN elected Perry Bellegarde, Atleo's rival in the previous campaigns, and the issue of First Nation control over education—which is so central to social and economic development—was put on hold.[43]

The obligation to consult that was expressed by the Supreme Court in the *Delgamuukw* case has proved useful in ongoing economic development. Although the Supreme Court has become somewhat more conservative in its interpretations of Aboriginal rights, consultation has led to new opportunities and to a new way of promoting economic development. For example, in November of 2013, Premier Christy Clark of British Columbia and Premier Alison Redford of Alberta drafted a framework for an agreement to allow pipelines carrying Alberta bitumen to cross British Columbia. This agreement was necessitated by a proposal to build the Northern Gateway pipeline from Alberta to the deepwater port of Kitimat on British Columbia's coast. In addition to environmental concerns, the two premiers agreed that any such pipeline proposal was to be made in consultation with Indigenous leaders. Most importantly, they agreed that all legal requirements with regard to Aboriginal and treaty rights had to be met and that First Nations had to be provided with opportunities to benefit economically from any proposed projects.

Although it is true that the premiers were responding to the changing political climate and to the consultation requirements of the *Delgamuukw* case, it is important to remember that increased Indigenous authority over the land and its resources goes back even further. In the 1980s and 1990s, First Nations in British Columbia led the way by protesting logging in Clayoquot Sound on Vancouver Island. Logging companies, hoping to harvest much of the old-growth temperate rain forest in Clayoquot Sound, met strong opposition from Indigenous groups and environmentalists. The Nuu'chah'nulth were particularly strong in their opposition to the proposed logging, and they made sure that their peaceful protests and their blockading of logging roads got national and international media attention. The Clayoquot Sound protest marked an impressive beginning to a growing alliance between environmental groups and Indigenous people, and it served as an inspiration for other Indigenous leaders hoping to assert greater authority over the land and its resources.

Development continues to play an important role in the evolving relations between Indigenous Peoples and the federal government. The Harper government pressed for economic development, and in particular resource exploration and mining, on First Nations land. A short film, "Our Community, Our Future: Mining and Aboriginal Communities," was produced in 2011 by Natural Resources Canada and made available in English, Cree, French, Ojibwa, and Oji-Cree. The film examines the mining sequence from exploration through operation and eventual closure and rehabilitation. The message is clear: the federal government is attempting to help create business opportunities in Indigenous communities. The motivations and the desirability of some of this encouragement are rather less clear.

For their part, Indigenous Peoples across Canada are pressing for greater economic opportunities in more traditional areas of economic activity. Fishing has long been the most important economic activity of many Indigenous communities, and the management of the Indigenous fishery is critical to economic development. The National Indigenous Fisheries and Aquaculture Forum, first held in Dartmouth, Nova Scotia, in 2011, provides opportunities for the sharing of information and the development of economic strategies from coast to coast. Issues such as loss of habitat (from pollution, construction, and the introduction of exotic species), priority of allocation (since the *Sparrow* case), sustainability, and resource co-management have crucial importance for the future of Indigenous fisheries. Since 2003, the Aboriginal Aquaculture Association has worked to help communities develop thriving sustainable fisheries based on aquaculture.

Idle No More

Housing is one area of economic development that has lagged behind. In 2011, a federal government report noted that between 20,000 and 35,000 new housing units would need to be built in Indigenous communities across Canada to resolve the housing crisis. The Assembly of First Nations responded immediately, claiming that the number of required units was closer to 85,000. As the national media reported the story—and as images of dilapidated and overcrowded

www.aofrc.org/a/6a00e5539o7a7f88330174421104e3970c-450wi

Resource management remains the critical issue in Indigenous economic development. Here, Robert Madahbee and Maureen Peltier stand next to a posted sign describing management conditions in the fishery at Sucker Creek, Aundek Omni Kaning First Nation, on Manitoulin Island, Ontario.

houses were televised—outrage grew across the country. In November 2012, a "teach-in" was held in Saskatoon to discuss the governance and environmental concerns with Bill C-45 (see the Indigenous Leaders box). The session was entitled "Idle No More" and was intended to call attention to environmental and sovereignty issues. The media attention given to the housing and infrastructural problems on reserves quickly gave the Idle No More movement a much broader appeal.

A "National Day of Action" was declared for 10 December 2012, and the next day the movement found its media profile raised when Attawapiskat Chief Theresa Spence announced that she was going on a hunger strike to protest the infrastructural and housing crisis in her community. Attawapiskat had suffered terrible flooding problems in 2009 and sewage and toxic waste forced many from their homes. Attawapiskat thus encapsulated the environmental, governance, and infrastructural issues that the Idle No More organizers had been anxious to publicize. The movement, and the national media attention, soon focused on the small camp on Victoria Island in the Ottawa River at Ottawa, where Theresa Spence stayed during her hunger strike. By the time Chief Spence ended her fasting on 24 January 2013, the Idle No More movement had gained important momentum. Although Chief Spence was not a part of Idle No More, her actions helped to draw attention to the issues that many Canadians had ignored and to sustain the movement's momentum.

By the end of 2013, however, the movement had been transformed and its relevance to Indigenous issues had diminished. In some ways the movement became of a victim of its own success and the lack of cohesion, brought about by both its grassroots origins and its lack of a single mandate, which resulted in its splitting into various special interests. Many Idle No More activists have now moved on to the Indigenous Nationhood Movement, attracted by the latter group's focus on reclaiming traditional lands and re-establishing traditional forms of government. The simple truth might be that the diversity of issues involving Indigenous Peoples within what is now Canada is simply too complex for one activist movement to address.[44] In a December 2013 article entitled "Idle No More, One Year Later" the *Toronto Star* called the movement a wave of change and concluded that the next wave will not be called Idle No More, but that activism and calls for change would continue in a different form.

Increased Sharing of Indigenous Knowledge

The most compelling recent development in the history of Canada's First Nations has been the evolving focus on **Indigenous knowledge**. There is a real effort to discover and to share knowledge and epistemology that is not based on the Western tradition. In other words, there is an ongoing effort to move outside of the universities to build a knowledge system based in Indigenous communities. Language is the key to knowledge and is crucial to knowledge dissemination. Some First Nations are already offering intensive language immersion programs,

INDIGENOUS LEADERS | Jessica Gordon and Idle No More

The Idle No More movement began as an e-mail exchange between four women from Saskatchewan: Jessica Gordon from Pasqua First Nation in Treaty Four Territory, Sylvia McAdam from Treaty Six, Nina Wilson from Treaty Four White Bear Territory, and Sheila McLean, a non-Indigenous woman. The dialogue at first concerned the need to make a stand against Bill C-45, the omnibus bill that proposed, among many other things, changes to land, resource, and water management on First Nations lands. Gordon named the movement "Idle No More" as a reminder "to get off the couch and start working."

As its first order to business, Gordon and her friends decided to organize a teach-in at Station 20 West, the newly opened community enterprise centre in Saskatoon, on 10 November 2012. From the outset the group employed social media tools to get their message to Canadians, and soon people across the prairies were organizing rallies and protests under the Idle No More banner. The environmental concern quickly gave the movement an even bigger base of support. Protests, flash mobs, and rallies were held across Canada and even, in some instances, in the United States. Gordon and her friends understood the power of grassroots and the need to build consensus, for in the Indigenous world consensus is foundational to all decision-making.[45]

which require learners to live on a reserve and to use Indigenous language in both formal learning settings and in informal living.

In some communities, institutes have been established to give greater administrative control to Indigenous knowledge dissemination. The Six Nations Polytechnic in Ontario is one example where Indigenous community-based learning thrives outside of the mainstream university system. Kwantlen Polytechnic University in British Columbia is another. Both have strong language-driven cultural programs for the dissemination and preservation of Indigenous knowledge. Of course, that knowledge is shared to the advantage of non-Indigenous Canadian society.

The spread of Indigenous knowledge is being promoted more vigorously by the mainstream Canadian university system. Most universities now offer at least some Indigenous courses, and it is safe to say that all Canadian universities offer courses with Indigenous content. In 1996, only a handful of Indigenous learning programs were to be found in Canadian universities, including at Calgary, Lakehead, Laurentian, McMaster, the Saskatchewan Indian Federated College, and Trent. The majority of Canadian universities now have Indigenous studies programs, and as of 2016, some schools such as the University of Winnipeg and Lakehead University have made courses with Indigenous content mandatory for all students.[46] A great need to preserve and promote Indigenous learning in Canada continues, and it is the firm hope of the authors that this text will inspire some students to take up this challenge.

INDIGENOUS LEADERS | Daphne Odjig

The Woodland-style artist Daphne Odjig (1919–2016) was one of Canada's greatest and most influential artists. She is often referred to as the driving force behind the Indian Group of Seven. She was born on Wikwemikong First Nation into a family of mixed Odaawa and Boodwaadmii heritage on her father's side. Her mother, whom her father met while he was serving in the Canadian Expeditionary Force during the First World War, was English. Back on Manitoulin Island, the young family lived first with Daphne's paternal grandfather, Jonas Odjig, and he introduced his granddaughter to the traditional art forms of the Anishinaabe people. He taught her to paint.

Her father, Dominic Odjig, was something of a war artist and he captured scenes from the destruction in France and Belgium. Her mother, Joyce Peachey, was a skilled embroiderer, and Daphne refers to her "three powerful influences" repeatedly in her book, *A Paintbrush in My Hand*.

Although her artistic style is thoroughly Woodland, there are strong influences from the wider art world. Odjig always acknowledged a debt to Picasso for his "synthetic cubism," and in 1986 she was invited by the directors of the Picasso Museum in Antibes, France, to paint a memorial to the Spanish master. Odjig drew her subjects from the natural beauty of the Canadian wilderness and gave them life by her powerful visual references to Indigenous art, culture, and ideas. Some of her paintings reflect her strong commitment to political activism and her belief that art makes the world a better place. In the ancestral tradition of her father's people, Daphne Odjig was a storyteller. Her paintings tell stories, relating how the Anishinabek interpreted the world around them and the ways in which they identified its necessities. Later, when she moved west, she drew on themes from the Crees of northern Manitoba and from the Indigenous cultures of the west coast. Her art truly spans both Canada and the Indigenous Peoples who live within its borders.

Randy Quan/Toronto Star via Getty Images

Daphne Odjig stands in front of her 1991 painting *Bond with the Earth* in 2001. In an interview with the CBC, Odjig said "I paint what comes from my heart—how I feel and what I've experienced through life . . . If there's any Aboriginal children around, I hope it motivates them that they too can accomplish what they want to be."[47]

Questions to Consider

1. Why is oral history so vital in First Nations claims cases?
2. What difficulties does the Missing and Murdered Indigenous Women's Inquiry face?
3. What has been the task of the Truth and Reconciliation Commission of Canada?
4. What was the significance of Canada adopting the United Nations Declaration on the Rights of Indigenous Peoples?

Recommended Reading

Bone, Robert M. *The Canadian North: Issues and Challenges*, 5th edn. Toronto: Oxford University Press, 2016.

Elsey, Christine. *The Poetics of Land and Identity among British Columbia Indigenous Peoples*. Halifax: Fernwood, 2013.

Graymont, Barbara. *The Iroquois in the American Revolution*. Syracuse, NY: Syracuse University Press, 1972.

———. "Thayendanegea," *Dictionary of Canadian Biography Online*.

Havard, Gilles. *The Great Peace of Montreal*. Montreal and Kingston: McGill-Queen's University Press, 2001.

Innes, Robert. *Elder Brother and the Law of the People: Contemporary Kinship and Cowessess First Nation*. Winnipeg: University of Manitoba Press, 2013.

Johnston, Charles M. *The Valley of the Six Nations*. Toronto: University of Toronto Press, 1964.

Kelsay, Isabel Thompson. *Joseph Brant: Man of Two Worlds*. Syracuse, NY: Syracuse University Press, 1984.

Manuel, Arthur, and Grand Chief Ronald Derrickson. *The Reconciliation Manifesto: Recovering the Land, Rebuilding the Economy*. Toronto: Lorimer, 2017.

Merasty, Joseph Auguste, with David Carpenter. *The Education of Augie Merasty: A Residential School Memoir*. Regina: University of Regina Press, 2015.

Miller, J.R. *Shingwauk's Vision: A History of Native Residential Schools*. Toronto: University of Toronto Press, 1996.

———. *Residential Schools and Reconciliation: Canada Confronts Its History*. Toronto: University of Toronto Press, 2017.

Talaga, Tanya. *Seven Fallen Feathers: Racism, Death, and Hard Truths in a Northern City*. Toronto: House of Anansi, 2017.

Epilogue

If any one theme can be traced throughout the history of the Indigenous Peoples within Canada, it is the persistence of their identity. The ancestors of First Nations, Inuit, and Métis lived on this continent long before explorers from other continents first came to North America. For thousands of years before this country was founded, they enjoyed their own forms of government. Diverse, vibrant Indigenous nations had ways of life rooted in fundamental values concerning their relationships to the Creator, the environment, and each other, in the role of elders as the living memory of their ancestors, and in their responsibilities as custodians of the lands, waters, and resources of their homelands. *These lifeways were disrupted and undermined by the arrival of Europeans, but not forgotten or forsaken.*

The confident expectation of Europeans that First Nations were a vanishing people, the remnants of whom would finally be absorbed by European-descended Canadian society, has not happened.[1] If anything, Indigenous Peoples are more prominent in the collective conscience of those who reside within this nation than they have ever been. Adaptability has always been the key to their survival; it is the strongest of Indigenous traditions. Despite concerted efforts of generations of Canadian governments, Indigenous Peoples have remained distinct cultural groups, have retained their rights to self-determination, and have preferred to remain as such even at the cost of social and economic inequality.[2]

In this edition of the text we have attempted to support this spirit of resilience by underlining the strength and importance of language as a means of cultural adaptability. Specifically, we have tried to do this in two ways: first, we gave privilege to Indigenous voices wherever possible, and, second, we used autonyms as opposed to names invented by European colonizers.[3] This has not been an easy task as it has involved compromise and translation. Translation, as we mentioned in the introduction, is never as good as the original. As Dr Johnson famously observed, "You may also translate history in so far as it is not embellished with oratory, which is poetical."[4] There is the rub. This history is full of oratory as we attempted to accommodate two traditions, one written and the other oral. By including as many Indigenous voices as possible we have also had to accept that many would be in translation.

The importance of using Indigenous languages goes well beyond the simple desire for inclusivity. First, Indigenous languages throw light on difficult historical problems by helping to allay the evidentiary shortcomings that plagued the early study of the Indigenous past. One example here will suffice to make this point. When scholars first tried to identify the so-called "fire-people" or "fire nation" that one finds described by Champlain and Sagard and in numerous places in the *Jesuit Relations*, they could not come to a consensus. Some posited that the Asistagueroüon (according to Champlain's spelling) or Assistaronon (according to Sagard's spelling) was a reference to the Boodwaadmii, and others argued that the reference must be to the Mascouten people.[5] Other candidates were also put forward by other historians.[6] The Anishinaabe words, however, leave no room for debate. "Boodwaadnad" means those who light fires and the Boodwaadmii refer to themselves as the fire-keepers.[7] Mascouten was thought by the Jesuits to mean "people of the prairie," and indeed the Anishinaabe word for prairie is "mshkode."[8] By paying closer attention to Indigenous languages, we can arrive at a much more accurate account of the Indigenous past.

Second, the increased use of Indigenous voices and Indigenous language also helps us to overcome the problems associated with Eurocentricism. Again, one example will suffice. The Jesuit Pierre-François-Xavier de Charlevoix famously asserted that the "les Algonquins & les Abénaquis pratiquoient autrefois une espece de Pyromancie. [In the past, the Omamiwinini and the Wabanaki peoples practised a kind of pyromancy.]"[9] For this misunderstanding we must blame both Charlevoix's Jesuit prejudice but also his linguistic misunderstanding. The word "autrefois," meaning in the past, is the key. It tells us that Charlevoix did not witness this so-called pyromancy but that he had heard of it, and assigned the term "pyromancy" to what had been described to him. Unfortunately, we do not know where he heard this or how he (mis)understood what he heard. This kind of confused evidence must not be allowed in the court of history.

Many students who feel an inclination to study an Indigenous language are deterred by the complexities of the grammatical structures and the difficulties of pronunciation arising from the unfamiliar phonemes. No such obstacles prevent students from learning vocabulary, however, and the study of Indigenous vocabulary pays rich dividends in increased understanding and deeper insight. Language remains the key, and education is the key to language preservation. The stalled First Nations Control of First Nations Education Act, introduced in Parliament in February of 2014, could yet be revived and may yet be instrumental to efforts concerning language preservation. This, however, is open to doubt, and the issue of education remains highly contentious, as we saw in Chapters 15 and 19.

One of the ways in which we have attempted to help circumvent the issues of translation in Indigenous self-representation is through incorporating more Indigenous art into the new edition. There has been growing international recognition of Indigenous art, especially since the Second World War. West coast art has long been appreciated—dating back to the days of first meetings in the eighteenth century, in fact—but that of other regions has been slower in gaining acknowledgement. In the 1940s, largely through the efforts of Toronto artist James A. Houston, Inuit learned printmaking. Carving in soapstone and ivory and the creation of tapestries also were encouraged; with the support of the Canadian government, the Hudson's Bay Company, and the Canadian Handicrafts Guild and the development of co-operatives to handle production and marketing, Inuit art became known worldwide. Another success story that developed somewhat later, that of Eastern Woodlands art, favours painting over printmaking, although both forms are practised.[10] Crafts such as porcupine quill work, beading, embroidery, and leather work have also come into their own and are much in demand. Most recently, contemporary artists who blend Indigenous traditions with contemporary concerns and aesthetics, often including the incorporation (and sometimes parody) of Western influences and materials, have become popular. In the literary, musical, and theatrical arts also, Indigenous people are winning respectful attention. Indigenous artists have also used art, and the platform that artistic attention provides, to further the message of self-determination for Indigenous Peoples. The renovated Canadian and Indigenous Galleries at the National Gallery of Canada are one recent example of this.[11] The message is clear: Indigenous Peoples within Canada, far from being interesting relics of the past, are a vital part of Canada's persona, both present and future.

The other critical challenge in this edition concerns the speed at which change is coming. Recent developments such as the federal government's confirmation in November of 2015 that Canada would implement the United Nations Declaration on the Rights of Indigenous Peoples, the ongoing National Inquiry into Missing and Murdered Indigenous Women and Girls, the Supreme Court of Canada's unanimous ruling that Métis and non-status Indigenous people are "Indian" under the Constitution, and many others illustrate the dramatic changes that have come. The 94 Calls to Action in the report of the Truth and Reconciliation Commission of Canada will hopefully ensure that important changes will continue to come. The splitting of the Indigenous Affairs ministry and the addition of a cabinet minister are signs that the Trudeau government intends to keep Indigenous issues at the forefront.

All of these developments have gone hand in hand with the rise of political activism and the campaign for self-determination. "Self-determination" is a term from international law that denotes the right of peoples to freely choose how they are governed. This is the opposite of a separatist movement. What Indigenous Peoples are asking for is full and equal participation in the Canada of today and of the future, and this was the clear message of the *Report of the Royal Commission on Aboriginal Peoples*. The reaffirmation of Indigenous rights to self-determination and identity has not been a sudden development—Indigenous Peoples have always had a clear idea of who they are and what they wanted their relationships to Canada to be. The assistance and spiritual values of the Indigenous people who greeted the newcomers to this continent too often have been forgotten. The contributions made by all Indigenous people to Canada's development, and the contributions that they continue to make to our society today, have not been properly acknowledged. What is new is the demand for recognition of these things by mainstream Canadian society.

The federal government, responding as all governments must to pressures applied by the people, has taken important steps and appears to be prepared to continue on the path towards supporting the resilience and the adaptability of the Indigenous Peoples living within Canada.

Even as the federal government moves to support new initiatives aimed at supporting the resilience and adaptability of Indigenous Peoples, old wounds still need to be healed. The residential schools settlement provided some of the Indigenous survivors of designated residential schools at least some compensation for their tragic experiences of assimilation over the course of the twentieth century. Still, the pain of all of these experiences can never be taken back, and many Indigenous people, individually and collectively, will never recover what they lost. A Celebratory Walk was held in Edmonton on 30 March 2014 to symbolize the movement forward that this process has helped to create. The announcement of a payment on 5 October 2017 to the "Sixties Scoop" children is another example.[12]

While hope remains that the twenty-first century will bring positive change for all Indigenous people across Canada, many of the issues now confronting them are dramatically evident. There

© iStock/PaulMcKinnon

Candace Day Neveau addresses the crowd gathered around the controversial teepee erected by protesters as a symbol of rights due to Indigenous people at the Canada 150 celebrations in Ottawa. The teepee construction was originally resisted by security, then moved closer to the main stage in front of Parliament. Prime Minister Justin Trudeau visited the teepee as his government pursued its promise to improve the relationship between Canada and the Indigenous Peoples who live within its borders. This and other demonstrations have been ongoing throughout Trudeau's time in office to keep his government accountable to this promise.

is still a significant gap in the standard of living compared to the rest of Canada, in terms of economic development, housing, education, and health care. Unresolved land rights issues, which have always posed a tremendous strain on the relationship with the federal and provincial governments, continue to be a central issue.

In the early twenty-first century, one of many unanswered questions relating to the future of Indigenous Peoples in Canada is whether they will be accepted as partners in building a more equitable nation of nations, or if they will be forced, by governments and by the indifference of public opinion, to focus exclusively, in piecemeal fashion, on their own often desperate needs. Many questions still remain in spite of the words "We are sorry."

Glossary

Abishabis ("Small Eyes," d. 1843) Cree prophet of a millenarian religious movement that swept through northern Manitoba and Ontario during the 1840s; murdered a First Nations family near York Factory, was arrested, and was murdered during his imprisonment.

Aboriginal Action Plan A renewed partnership with Indigenous people and Indigenous organizations to recognize past mistakes and injustices, especially in regard to residential schools, announced by the federal government in January of 1998. This Plan led to an agreement on reparations in 2007 and a formal apology from the Prime Minister in June of 2008.

Aboriginal rights A legal term originally signifying the rights that Canada's Indigenous Peoples hold as a result of their ancestors' long-standing use and occupancy of land, including the right to hunt, trap, and fish, but now including the right to traditional self-government.

Aboriginal title A legal term referring specifically to the inherent Aboriginal right to land or a territory.

Alaska Highway A 1,520-mile (2,446 km) road built in 1942 from Dawson Creek, BC, to Fairbanks, Alaska, as a supply route for the Second World War.

Allied Tribes of British Columbia The first province-wide coalition of BC First Nations formed in 1916 to pursue land claims; declared illegal following 1927 amendments to the Indian Act.

Assembly of First Nations The national representative organization of the First Nations in Canada. It grew out of the National Indian Brotherhood, which changed not only its name in 1982 but also its structure to become an "Organization of First Nations Government Leaders."

assimilation The process of being absorbed into the culture or customs of another group.

Bagot Commission (1842–4) Commission headed by Sir Charles Bagot (1781–1843) that examined "Indian administration" and affirmed the government's assimilation policy.

band The definition in the Indian Register, 1997, is a "group of First Nation people for whom lands have been set apart and money is held by the Crown. Each band has its own governing band council, usually consisting of one or more chiefs and several councillors. Community members choose the chief and councillors by election, or sometimes through traditional custom. The members of a band generally share common values, traditions, and practices rooted in their ancestral heritage."

Batoche The headquarters of Louis Riel's provisional government and the site of the last battle of the Northwest Rebellion, 1885, in present-day central Saskatchewan; named after François-Xavier Letendre *dit* Batoche (*c*. 1841–1901), the founder of the community.

Battle of Beaver Dams Battle of the War of 1812–14 near Thorold, Ontario, 24 June 1813, in which Kahnawake and other Kanienkehaka warriors ambushed almost 500 American troops.

Battle of Fallen Timbers Defeat of Western Confederacy of First Nations by Americans under the command of Major-General "Mad" Anthony Wayne on 20 August 1794. The British refused to open the gates of Fort Miami to the retreating Indigenous warriors, including Shaawanwaki leader Tecumseh, which caused a breach in Indigenous–British relations.

Beothuk Indigenous inhabitants of Newfoundland at the time of the arrival of the Europeans.

Beringia The name scientists have given to the land bridge that spanned the Bering Strait between what are now Asia and North America during the Wisconsin glaciation (last ice age).

Blue Quills Opened in 1970, the first school in Canada administered by Indigenous people, near St Paul, Alberta, approximately 200 km northeast of Edmonton.

Brébeuf, Jean de (1593–1649) Jesuit missionary to the Wendat who was captured and killed by Haudenosaunee warriors during the Haudenosaunee attack on the Wendat villages in 1649.

Brock, General Isaac British general who fought alongside Tecumseh in War of 1812–14; killed in battle at Queenston Heights on 13 October 1812.

Cabot, John (Giovanni Caboto) (*c*. 1451–1498?) Italian explorer financed by England who reached the shore of North America in 1497. He set out for the New World again in 1498, but his ship disappeared.

Calder v. Attorney General (1973) Court case in which the Nisga'a of British Columbia claimed continued Aboriginal rights in their traditional territory. The Nisga'a lost on a technicality, but the case led the federal government to negotiate land claims based on outstanding Aboriginal title.

Canada First Activist group that campaigned to annex Red River to Canada in the mid-1850s.

Cartier, Jacques (1491–1557) French explorer who reached what is now eastern Canada. France used his three voyages, between 1534 and 1542, as a basis for its claim to sovereignty of North America.

Champlain, Samuel de (*c.* 1570–1635) French geographer, explorer, and founder of Quebec (1608). His writing and maps provide the only extant written information on the first 15 years of French occupation.

chiefdoms Societies where a (usually hereditary) chief is the head and where delineated class structures exist.

"code talkers" Indigenous soldiers who served as radio operators during the First World War (US, Chocktaw) and the Second World War (Canada, Cree; US, Navajo) receiving and transmitting coded messages in their Indigenous languages.

Comité National des Métis (Métis National Committee) Association formed in 1869 with John Bruce as president and Louis Riel as secretary, and actively supported by Abbé Joseph-Noël Ritchot (1825–1905) of St Norbert, for the purpose of negotiating with the federal government concerning the rights of the residents of Red River.

Compagnie des Cent Associés, La One of the societies that received a charter (1627) from France authorizing it to explore, develop, and exploit New France.

comprehensive claims Claims arising in areas where rights of traditional use and occupancy have not been extinguished by treaty or superseded by law.

compulsory enfranchisement Department of Indian Affairs policy, dating from early twentieth century to mid-century, whereby the superintendent-general had the power to enfranchise Indigenous people he considered qualified, whether they wanted it or not. This meant that the individuals concerned had the rights of other Canadian citizens, including the right to vote, but no longer had status under the Indian Act.

constitutional patriation Process of transfer of the authority to amend a country's constitution to that country, signifying independence from a colonial power. In the case of Canada, it refers to the 1982 amendment of Canada's Constitution from being a British statute to being held in Canada.

Council of Three Fires (Niswi-mishkodewin) Confederacy for joint defence against the Haudenosaunee. It was made up of the Boodwaadmii (Fire Keepers), the Odaawa (Trader Nation), and the Ojibwa (Faith Keepers).

coureurs de bois Europeans who assimilated to First Nations culture and who were particularly active in the fur trade.

Cypress Hills Indigenous sacred place, and gathering place, in southern Saskatchewan and Alberta; the site of the murders of 20–30 Nakoda people at the hands of American "wolfers" in 1873.

day schools Schools on reserves that students attended while living with their families.

Delgamuukw v. British Columbia A 1991 court case in which the Gitxsan and Wet'suwet'en claimed Aboriginal right over traditional lands in northern British Columbia.

The BC Court of Appeal rejected their claim, but in 1997 the Supreme Court of Canada overturned the earlier judgment, arguing that the lower courts had not given enough weight to oral tradition.

Deskaheh Guyohkohnyo title held by Haudenosaunee traditionalist leader Levi General (1873–1925) who sought sovereignty for his people at the League of Nations.

DEW (Distant Early Warning) Line Series of radar installations built above the Arctic Circle and extending from Alaska across northern Canada to Greenland that began operation in 1954. It was meant to serve as a warning system for over-the-pole attacks on North America by nuclear-armed bombers from the Soviet Union.

division of powers Situation in which different levels of government in a federal system have authority over different aspects of public policy.

Donnakoh–Noh (d. 1539) Chief of Stadakohna before 1536, when he and his sons Domagaya and Tayagnoagny were kidnapped by Jacques Cartier and taken to France, where he died.

Dorset Name given by scientists to a culture that thrived for more than 3,000 years in what is now northern Canada and Alaska but disappeared around 1000 ACE, replaced by the Thule. Their name derives from Cape Dorset, on Baffin Island.

Douglas, Sir James (1807–73) Governor of Vancouver Island (1851–63) and of British Columbia (1858–64), a man of mixed West Indian and Scottish heritage who earlier was Chief Trader (1835–9) and then Chief Factor at Fort Vancouver, and who was responsible for 14 treaties (1850–4) granting Aboriginal title to Coast Salish bands on southern Vancouver Island.

Douglas Creek A real estate development on lands claimed by Haudenosaunee Confederacy on the edge of Caledonia, Ontario, near Brantford and Hamilton, that led to Haudenosaunee occupation of the disputed land and bitter confrontations between Haudenosaunee activists, local residents, and outside agitators. The Ontario government purchased the land from the developer, Henco Industries, in June of 2006, but a final agreement has not been reached.

Duck Lake Town in Saskatchewan, 88 km north of Saskatoon; site of a battle on 26 March 1885 wherein Métis provisional government forces led by Gabriel Dumont routed government forces.

Dumont, Gabriel (1837–1906) Buffalo hunter, Métis chief, and military strategist. Dumont was Louis Riel's military commander during the Northwest Rebellion, 1885.

Duncan, William (1832–1918) Protestant lay missionary who, along with Tsimshian Chief Paul Legaic, founded the "model" Indigenous community of Metlakatla (1862–87). The community became increasingly totalitarian, and eventually, following a violent confrontation, Duncan led a breakaway group to form New Metlakatla on Annette Island, Alaska.

egalitarian societies Communities characterized by a lack of distinction of social ranks, in which leadership is often assumed temporarily and for a specific purpose, and where social status does not accrue to material wealth.

enfranchisement Acquisition of the right to vote.

ethnohistory The cross-disciplinary study of history that incorporates the findings and methodologies of such disciplines as anthropology, archaeology, folklore and oral history, and linguistics.

Ewing Commission Commission appointed in 1935 by the Alberta government to investigate social and economic conditions of the province's Métis population and chaired by Justice Albert Freeman Ewing. It resulted in the Métis Population Betterment Act (1938) and the creation of Métis settlements (colonies) in Alberta.

Far Northwest Term used by Euro-Canadians to describe present-day Northwest Territories, Yukon, and northern British Columbia, Alberta, and Saskatchewan.

Federation of Seven Fires A mid-eighteenth-century alliance network linking French mission Indians, led by Obwandiyag with an intent to resist European settlement, that did not survive the dislocations caused by the US War of Independence or colonial distrust of pan-Indigenism. It consisted of the Iroquois mission villages on the St Lawrence (Kahnawake, Kanesatake, Oswegatchie, and St Regis), Wabanaki (called the Abenaki at St Francois and Bécancour), and the Wendat (called the Huron of Lorette).

fee simple title The most complete form of ownership. A fee simple buyer acquires ownership of both land and buildings and has the right to possess, use, and dispose of the land as he or she wishes.

File Hills Colony Model village established on the Peepeekisis Reserve near Indian Head, Saskatchewan, and the last of such government experiments.

first meetings First communication between peoples who have no prior knowledge of each other. One historian has listed three basic types: collisions, relationships, and contacts.

First Nations Governance Act (FNGA) Legislation proposed in January of 2002 by the Department of Indian Affairs that was designed to amend, and effectively do away with, the original Indian Act. Known as Bill C-7, it created much discussion on the issue of First Nations governance but was never enacted and died when the parliamentary session ended in 2004.

Fish Creek Southern boundary of the South Branch Métis settlement, which had Batoche as its commercial centre. It was the site of an ambush, 26 April 1885, of government soldiers by Métis led by Gabriel Dumont.

fluted points Stone points with flutes (round grooves) around the edge used as spear or arrow heads.

Ghost Dance (Spirit Dance) Religious circle dance of numerous western US Indigenous groups, derived from the 1889 prophecy and subsequent teaching of the Paiute pacifist prophet Wovoka (Jack Wilson) foretelling a peaceful end to European expansion. Newcomer fears of Indigenous activism related to the Ghost Dance contributed to the 1890 massacre of Lakhóta people by the US Army at Wounded Knee in South Dakota and in the 1890s the dance appeared on Lakhóta reserves in Canada.

gift distributions Custom begun by the Indigenous Peoples and continued, briefly, by the British colonial administration of giving goods to First Nations periodically as a way of maintaining agreements and alliances.

gift exchanges Diplomatic ritual involved in the sealing of agreements between First Nations and, later, between New France and Indigenous people through the trade of goods or hostages, which resulted in blood ties.

Grant, Cuthbert (c. 1793–1854) Métis fur trader, North West Company employee, and political leader who advanced the concept of the Métis nation; killed Robert Semple, governor of the HBC-administered territories, near Seven Oaks (present-day Winnipeg) in a Métis route of HBC personnel.

Great Peace of Montreal Agreement reached in 1701 between the Haudenosaunee, the Niswi-mishkodewin, and the French to end the nearly century of conflict known as the Iroquois (Mourning) War.

guerrilla warfare Warfare characterized by irregular forces using "hit-and-run" tactics in small-scale, limited actions against European-style military forces.

gunboat diplomacy Diplomacy backed by the use or threat of military force, specifically gunboats.

Haldimand Grant Land on the Grand River in Upper Canada (Ontario) granted in 1784 to loyalist Haudenosaunee people by Frederick Haldimand, governor of Quebec. The Haudenosaunee had ceded 3 million acres (1,214,100 ha) on the Niagara Peninsula to the colonial government.

Haldimand Tract The extent of the Haldimand Grant, from the source of the Grand River north of Grand Valley in southwestern Ontario to its mouth, where it discharges into Lake Erie at Port Maitland, and including six miles (10 km) deep on each side of the river—a total of 2,842,480 acres (1,150,311 ha).

Harper, Elijah Oji-Cree chief from Red Sucker Lake and member of the Manitoba legislature (NDP, Rupertsland) who was instrumental in the failure of the Meech Lake Accord by withholding his vote for ratification.

Harrison, William Henry (1773–1841) Governor of Indiana Territory from 1800 to 1812, later ninth president of the United States. Harrison participated in the Battle of Fallen Timbers (1794) and led his troops in the 1811 Battle of

Tippecanoe, and during his governorship promoted new-comer settlement at the expense of Indigenous Peoples.

Haudenosaunee Confederacy (formerly the Five Nations and then the Six Nations League) Founded in the sixteenth century or before in the present-day Finger Lakes region of northern New York. They were, from east to west, the Kanienkehaka, Ony'ota, Onondaga, Guyohkohnyo, and Onondowaga. The league later became known as the Six Nations around 1720 when the Tuscaroras migrated north to join.

Haudenosaunee War (1609–1701) Conflict between Haudenosaunee Confederacy and French that lasted almost a century and was interspersed with attempts at peace; known as the Iroquois War in Canadian historiography and as the Mourning War to the Haudenosaunee.

Hawthorn Report (1966) Report by anthropologist Harry B. Hawthorn on Indigenous social, educational, and economic conditions. Hawthorn criticized the existing assimilation policy and presented a view of Indigenous people as "citizens plus."

Head, Sir Francis Bond (1783–1875) Soldier and colonial administrator who was lieutenant-governor of Upper Canada during the 1837 rebellion and arranged the surrender by the Ojibwa of the Saugeen ("mouth of the river") tract on the Bruce Peninsula in 1836.

Head-Smashed-In Bison jump site in present-day southern Alberta in use for more than 5,000 years. It was also a trade centre for the nations that used the site. It was declared a UNESCO World Heritage Site in 1981.

Hearne, Samuel (1745–92) HBC fur trader and explorer who, with his Indigenous guide Matonabbee, reached the Coppermine River (present-day NWT) in 1772 and later rebuilt Fort Churchill. Hearne's adoption of Indigenous methods of travel allowed him to become the first European man to reach the Arctic Ocean overland.

Heyerdahl, Thor (1914–2002) Norwegian anthropologist who developed a theory that people from South America, not Asia, had populated Polynesia. To prove his thesis, that sailors on rafts could travel the distances required for this, Heyerdahl sailed from Peru to Polynesia in the *Kon Tiki*, a replica of the balsa rafts made by South American Indigenous people. He later sailed from Morocco to the Caribbean in a replica of an ancient Egyptian papyrus boat.

Hochelaga St Lawrence Iroquoian settlement at the site of present-day Montreal.

homeguards Bands of Indigenous people who settled near French or English trading posts.

Hudson, Henry (*fl.* 1607–11) English explorer who searched for a northwest passage to China on behalf of first the English Muscovy Company and then the Dutch East India Company, for whom he also explored the Hudson River.

Hudson's Bay Company (HBC) Company that received its charter from Great Britain in 1670 to trade for furs, explore, and settle Rupert's Land, which consisted of the Hudson Bay drainage basin, all of Manitoba, most of Saskatchewan, southern Alberta, and extended north to the Arctic.

hunter–gatherer An economic strategy that involves hunting wild game and gathering wild berries, roots, and the like, as opposed to a more sedentary agriculture-based lifestyle for providing the required food for a community.

Huronia, *see* **Wendake**.

Independent Assessment Process Process set up to deal with serious cases of physical and sexual abuse as part of the residential schools reparations policy under the terms of the Indian Residential Schools Settlement Agreement.

Indian Act Canadian legislation enacted in 1876 that continues with amendments to the present day and that defines the relationship between registered status Indians and the federal government.

Indian Residential Schools Settlement Agreement A $2 billion settlement including a compensation package paid by the federal government to students who had attended Indian residential schools and funding for the Truth and Reconciliation Commission.

Indian title Seventeenth-century concept involving rights of occupancy and use, but not ownership. *See* **usufructuary right.**

Indigenous knowledge Knowledge derived from Indigenous traditions, such as living on the land in a communal sharing context within nature, and expressed through Indigenous languages.

Isapo-Muxika (Crowfoot, *c.* 1830–90) Sitsika chief in what is now southern Alberta, a chief negotiator for Treaty Seven, and adoptive father of Pītikwahanapiwīyin.

James Bay and Northern Quebec Agreement (JBNQA) Land claim agreement of 1975 between Inuit and Cree of northern Quebec and federal and provincial governments that involves a transfer of money in exchange for cession of land but fails to entrench Aboriginal rights. The JBNQA resulted from Indigenous objections to the province's James Bay hydroelectric project, begun in 1971.

Jesuits Members of the Society of Jesus, a Roman Catholic order of priests. They were principal actors in the missionary activity in New France.

Johnson, Sir William (1715–74) Military commander who was colonial Superintendent of Indian Affairs from 1755 until his death. He was married "after the custom of the country" to Koñwatsiãtsiaiéñni.

Judicial Committee of the Privy Council A board of the British Privy Council that had jurisdiction over the courts of Great Britain's colonies, including, until 1949, Canada.

Kahkewaquonaby (Rev. Peter Jones, "Sacred Feathers," 1802–56) Mississauga-Welsh Métis and Methodist minister who advocated Indigenous control of their education system.

Kelowna Accord A "national treaty" achieved by Liberal Prime Minister Paul Martin and Indigenous leaders in meetings in Kelowna, BC, that would provide $5 billion over a five-year period to improve the daily lives of Indigenous People living within Canada in terms of housing, health care, education, and economic development. The Accord, reached in late November of 2005, was never ratified by the House of Commons after the Conservatives, under Stephen Harper, gained a minority government in February of 2006.

Kiala (Quiala, *fl.* 1733–4) Mesquakie chief who sought to unify the First Nations of the eastern seaboard to oppose the French. The Mesquakie were based in the area to the west of Lake Michigan.

King Philip's War (1675–6) Last Indigenous attempt to oust Europeans from New England, led by Wampanoag chief Metacom, called King Philip by the English. It resulted in the exodus of Wabanaki to Canada.

Klondike gold rush Massive influx of southerners into the Klondike area, Yukon, following news of the discovery of gold that led to the negotiation of Treaty Eight.

Koñwatsiʔtsiaiéñni (Mary Brant, *c.* 1736–96) Highly influential Kanienkehaka leader, wife of Sir William Johnson, and sister of Thayendanegea, who together were responsible for leading the majority of the Haudenosaunee Confederacy into alliance with the British against the American revolutionaries.

League of Indians One of the first attempts at national organization by Indigenous people founded in 1919 by F.O. Loft, a Kanienkehaka leader from Brantford, Ontario, to fight treaty violations. Following Loft's death in 1934, the League split into regional organizations.

League of Six Nations Expansion of the Haudenosaunee Confederacy by the addition of the Tuscarora, who fled north from the Carolinas and sought refuge among the Five Nations around 1720.

Legaic Title for a Tsimshian chief meaning "chief of the mountain."

Little Ice Age Period between 1450 and 1850 when global temperatures fell, causing the northern sea ice to stay all year. This affected wildlife, which caused hardship for hunters. In Europe, it resulted in increased demand for furs, which spurred New World exploration.

Loft, Frederick Ogilvie (1861–1934) Kanienkehaka leader from Brantford, Ontario, and officer in the Forestry Corps who served in the First World War; founder of the League of Indians in 1919.

Longhouse religion Synthesis of traditional beliefs and ceremonies combined with the teachings of nineteenth-century Onondowaga prophet Shanyadariyoh (Handsome Lake, d. 1815) that combined elements of the Christian religion and the traditional Haudenosaunee belief system.

longhouses Communal dwellings of some First Nations, such as the Haudenosaunee, "People of the Longhouse").

Mackenzie Valley Pipeline Inquiry (1974–7) Investigation commissioned by the Canadian federal government and headed by Justice Thomas Berger to study the social, economic, and environmental impact of a proposed gas pipeline and energy corridor from the western Arctic to Alberta and further south.

Marshall, Donald, Jr (1953–2009) Mi'kmaw man released from prison in 1983 after spending 11 years in jail for a murder he did not commit; was acquitted in 1999 in a landmark court case involving Aboriginal right to fish out of season.

Mascarene's Treaty (1725) Treaty No. 239, signed between English and Wabanaki after Indigenous military defeat at Norridgewock and later ratified by other First Nations, which stated that First Nations people must behave as British subjects; named after chief negotiator, Paul Mascarene, administrator of Nova Scotia at the time of the treaty.

Matonabbee (*c.* 1737–92) Denésoliné leader who worked for HBC and guided Samuel Hearne on his third excursion in search of the Coppermine River (1772). Matonabbee ensured the success of this expedition by using the Indigenous manner of travel, which involved trekking in a family group and provisioning along the way.

Mawedopenais Ojibwa chief and leading participant in Treaty Three negotiations at Fort Francis in 1873.

"medicine chest" Phrase included in Treaty Six, negotiated between First Nations of central Saskatchewan and Alberta and the federal government in 1876, that became the legal basis for free health care for status First Nations and some Inuit.

Megumaage Mi'kmaw name for their land, in the present-day Maritime provinces.

Mesquakie War (1710–38) Called the Fox War by Euro-Canadian historians, the resistance by the Mesquakie and other Indigenous nations to French forays inland to the Upper Great Lakes. The war chief Kiala rose to prominence during this time as a proponent of pan-Indigenous solidarity.

Métis A constitutionally recognized Indigenous People created by intermarriage between Europeans and Indigenous People whose culture reflects both influences.

Metlakatla Traditional Tsimshian settlement on the coast of what is now British Columbia, and site of an Anglican mission and model village, which lasted from 1862 to 1887.

Michilimackinac From the Anishinaabe term Michi Makinong or Great Turtle, a French and then later a British fort located beside the Odaawa village at the Straits of Mackinac connecting Lakes Huron and Michigan.

Middleton, Frederick Dobson (1825–98) Army and militia officer who led Canadian forces in the Northwest Rebellion, 1885, and accepted the surrenders of Louis Riel and Pītikwahanapiwīyin.

Mikak (*c.* **1740–95**) Labrador Inuk woman who assisted the Moravians in establishing their mission among the Inuit and who was involved in the Labrador coastal trade.

Mi'kmaw War (1749–53) Mi'kmaw resistance to English settlement of Acadia (Megumaage).

millenarianism Religious belief in and anticipation of a sudden, imminent change in the social order, anticipating prosperity and happiness.

Mistahimaskwa (Big Bear, *c.* 1825–88) Cree-Ojibwa chief who refused to sign Treaty Six, working instead to unite the Cree and create an Indigenous territory. His band participated in the 1885 Northwest Rebellion, and Big Bear was convicted of treason-felony.

model villages Settlements of Indigenous people organized and administered by government officials or missionaries for the purpose of promoting Indigenous assimilation.

Moraviantown Village established in 1792 in what is now southwestern Ontario by the Moravian Brothers, a Protestant missionary group founded in 1727, for refugee Lenni Lenape people on the Canadian side of the future international border and originally called Fairfield. It was the site of a battle on 5 October 1813, part of the War of 1812–14, in which Tecumseh died.

Mourning War Haudenosaunee term for endemic, cyclical warfare; the Haudenosaunee War (1609–1701).

Muquinna Chiefly title of the Mochat band (Nuu'chah'nulth). One particular Muquinna (*fl.* 1786–1817) quarrelled in 1803 with the captain of a fur-trading ship over a defective gun, which led to the destruction of the *Boston* by a group of Nuu'chah'nulth. Muquinna was renowned for the magnificence of a potlatch he gave that same year.

National Indian Brotherhood (NIB) (1968–82) National association resulting from the split of the National Indian Council into two bodies, one representing status and treaty Indigenous groups (NIB), the other non-status Indians and Métis (Native Council of Canada).

National Inquiry into Missing and Murdered Indigenous Women and Girls Launched in response to a "Call for Action" in the report of the Truth and Reconciliation Commission, the Inquiry was established in 2015 and began its work in 2016. Prime Minister Justin Trudeau had promised to launch this Inquiry in the 2015 federal election campaign.

nativistic movements Organized and conscious efforts by members of a community to build a more satisfying culture, often by revitalizing traditional beliefs and customs.

Neolin Mid-seventeenth-century Lenni Lenape prophet who urged Indigenous people to avoid contact with newcomers and to return to their traditional values. His teachings influenced Obwandiyag. Neolin was one of two men known as the "Delaware Prophet."

Nescambiouit ("He who is so important and so highly placed because of his merit that his greatness cannot be attained, even in thought," *c.* 1660–1722) Pigwacket (Wabanaki) chief who was taken to France but returned in 1716 and attempted to form a pan-Indigenous alliance.

New England Company Non-sectarian Protestant missionary organization that founded a school for Indigenous people at Sussex Vale, New Brunswick, in 1787.

Niitsitapiikwan (Niitsitapi Confederacy) Plains coalition composed of the Siksika, Piikani, Káínawa, Tsuu T'ina, and A'ani. At its peak, it extended from the North Saskatchewan River, south to the Missouri, and from the present Alberta–Saskatchewan border to the Rocky Mountains; also known as the Blackfoot Confederacy.

Nisga'a Final Agreement Act Legislation ratified by Parliament in 2000 in which the Nisga'a gained self-governing rights to 1,900 km² of land but gave up the tax-free status they had under the Indian Act.

non-status Indian A person who has either lost status through enfranchisement or restrictions in past versions of the Indian Act, or who has been born to parents without qualifying status under the Act.

North West Company (NWC) Consortium of fur-trading firms and individuals formed in the late eighteenth century to compete with Hudson's Bay Company in the western fur trade. The HBC absorbed the NWC in 1821.

North West Mounted Police (NWMP) Police force created by 1873 legislation and sent to what is now western Canada in 1874 to maintain order, primarily by curtailing the whisky trade, and to encourage newcomer settlement. In 1904, the force was given the prefix "Royal," and in 1920 it was merged with the Dominion Police to form the Royal Canadian Mounted Police.

Northwest Passage Hoped-for and sought-after shortcut from northern Europe to China, which was the reason for the voyages of John Cabot and other early European explorers.

Northwest Rebellion Armed uprising in present-day Saskatchewan in 1885 of Métis, First Nations, and some newcomers, who were concerned about encroachment of European settlers and for their own future with the demise of the vast bison herds of the western Plains. The Rebellion, led by Louis Riel, was quelled by troops sent from eastern Canada.

numbered treaties Series of 11 treaties signed between First Nations and the Canadian government following the cession of Hudson's Bay Company land to the Canadian government. These treaties, signed between 1871 and 1921, resulted in the cession of much of present-day Ontario, Manitoba, Saskatchewan, Alberta, and the Mackenzie District of the Northwest Territories to the government.

Nunavut Land Claim Settlement (1993) Legislation that paved the way for the creation of the self-governing territory of Nunavut and the largest land claim settlement in Canadian history.

Obwandiyag (1712/1725–69) Odaawa war chief, in English known as Pontiac, who attempted to unite First Nations to resist European settlement in the Great Lakes area. Some later turned against him, and he was assassinated by an Irenweewa at Cahokia.

Odanak Present-day Saint-François-de-Sales, near Sorel, Quebec. In the 1700s, it was the largest Wabanaki settlement in New France.

ogimaa Anishinaabe word for leader. In many First Nations there are two ogimaak, one hereditary and the other elected. In others both are elected.

Oka (Kanesatake, Lake of Two Mountains) Land near Montreal granted by France in 1717 to the Seminary of St Sulpice as a mission. A long-standing dispute over ownership of the land culminated in a standoff in 1990 in which Canadian military intervened.

pass system Regulation introduced after the Northwest Rebellion that required First Nations people in the West to obtain permission from the Indian agent to leave their reserves. Although not based in any legislation, the policy was later extended to Indigenous people throughout Canada and was enforced until the mid-1940s.

pays d'en haut ("Upper Country") The region of the three Upper Great Lakes.

Peacekeepers Self-governed police force formed in Kahnawake, near Montreal, following a breakdown in relations with the Quebec provincial police. It eventually became the reserve's official law enforcement body.

pemmican Concentrated food used by Plains Métis and First Nations consisting of dried meat, pounded fine and mixed with melted fat and sometimes berries. It became a staple food of the fur trade. One kilogram of pemmican had the food value of four to eight kilograms of fresh meat or fish.

Penner Report (1983) Report of the Special Parliamentary Committee on Indian Self-Government, headed by Liberal MP Keith Penner, that recommended a distinct form of Indigenous self-government.

Pītikwahanapiwīyin (Poundmaker, c. 1842–85) Adopted son of Isapo-Muxika and a leader in Treaty Six negotiations. He was convicted of treason-felony following the 1885 Northwest Rebellion though he sought to be a peacemaker during the hostilities.

potlatch Ceremonial feast of Northwest Coast First Nations involving the host's lavish distribution of gifts. A means of redistributing wealth within communities, it was banned by the Canadian government in 1884 as being contrary to European values.

Proclamation of 1763 Proclamation by England declaring a British system of government for North American land surrendered by France but also declaring land not under European settlement as land reserved for Indigenous Peoples, which set the stage for later land surrenders by treaty.

Quebec Act of 1774 British legislation that defined the boundaries of Quebec as extending south to the Ohio Valley, recognized the Roman Catholic Church, and established French civil law as the basis for business and other day-to-day transactions.

Queenston Heights Site near Niagara Falls, Ontario, of a battle in October 1812 that saw invading American forces defeated by British and Haudenosaunee forces led by Teyoninhokarawen and the British General Sir Isaac Brock.

relocation As a policy of the Canadian federal government, it meant moving First Nations or Inuit communities to new locations.

reserve A tract of land, the legal title to which is vested in the Crown, set apart for the use and benefit of a band.

residential schools Boarding schools for Indigenous children usually run as joint government–church enterprises with the purpose of assimilating these children into the dominant society.

Riel, Louis (1844–85) Métis leader, founder of the province of Manitoba, and spiritual leader of the 1869–70 Riel Rebellion and the 1885 Northwest Rebellion; hanged for treason on 16 November 1885. His father, Louis Riel Sr, had been a leader in the Métis community.

Robinson treaties Two treaties negotiated by William Benjamin Robinson. Lake Superior chiefs signed the Robinson-Superior Treaty, 7 September 1850; chiefs from the Lake Huron region signed the Robinson-Huron Treaty, 9 September 1850.

Royal Commission on Aboriginal Peoples (RCAP, 1991–6) Commission set up in the wake of the Kanesatake standoff and chaired by Georges Erasmus, a former National Chief of the Assembly of First Nations, and René Dussault, a judge of the Quebec Appeals Court. Its final report included 440 specific recommendations.

sachem The Algonquian word for leader among the peoples of the Atlantic region.

sagamore (also sagamo, saqmaw, saqmawaq, sakimaa) In the Atlantic region, among the Mi'kmaw and Wabanaki peoples this word is used to refer to the junior of the two leaders. In the Great Lakes region it is used to denote the elders who keep and disseminate knowledge.

St Catherine's Milling v. The Queen (1885–9) Ontario court case in which the question of federal and provincial jurisdiction was central and which led to a ruling of the Judicial Committee of the Privy Council that the Proclamation of 1763, which recognized Indigenous land, was valid, but also that the British had gained title to all Indigenous lands simply by setting foot in North America.

St Laurent Oblate mission founded in 1871, and the site of a settlement on the South Saskatchewan River founded by Gabriel Dumont and other Métis in 1872; one of the cluster of Métis settlements known collectively as the South Branch.

Saint-Paul-des Métis First tract of land set aside for Métis settlement, in 1896 in Alberta.

Samson Cree Nation Central Alberta First Nation that has sought payments for oil and gas royalties through the courts since 1989. The issue concerns the Crown's management of the royalties under the Indian Act and the band's insistence that the provisions of Treaty Six give them the right to manage their own royalties.

Saugeen Tract Triangular area of 1.5 million acres (607,500 ha) on the western edge of Lake Huron adjacent to the Bruce Peninsula ceded to the federal government by the Saugeen Ojibwa Nation in August 1836 in exchange for assistance to those who moved to the Bruce Peninsula.

scrip Document used as evidence that the holder or bearer is entitled to receive something, such as cash or an allotment of land.

self-government Government controlled and directed by the inhabitants of a region rather than by an outside authority.

Sinclair, Justice Murray Ojibwa judge and the chair of the Truth and Reconciliation Commission.

"Sixties Scoop" Expression referring to the practice during the 1960s of removing Indigenous children from their communities and having them adopted into non-Indigenous families.

Sparrow v. R. Supreme Court case in 1987 in which the court ruled in favour of a Salish man of the Musqueam Band who had used a fishing net larger than allowed by law. The Court found that Aboriginal fishing, land, and hunting rights for food, social, and ceremonial purposes had priority over later restrictive legislation.

specific claims Claims concerning outstanding legal obligations on the part of the government, such as non-fulfillment of a treaty, breach of an obligation under the Indian Act, or improper actions in connection with the acquisition or disposition of land by government employees or agents.

Stadakohna Major Haudenosaunee settlement on the St Lawrence River at the time of first contact near present-day Quebec City.

status Indian A person who is recognized as a "legal" Indian according to the regulations of the Indian Act, though birth or (until 1985) marriage.

Tadoussac Innu settlement at the mouth of the Saguenay River and an important fur-trading centre in the mid-1600s.

taiga Subarctic coniferous (evergreen) forest; boreal forest.

Tamanawas rituals Religious ceremonies of western and Pacific coast First Nations people involving dancing. These and other rituals were banned from 1884 to 1951.

Tecumseh (c. 1768–1813) Shaawanwaki chief who fought American settlement in the Ohio area in the 1790s and later transformed a prophetic movement led by his brother, Tenskwatawa, into a movement aimed at retaining Indigenous land. Tecumseh sided, reluctantly, with the British in the War of 1812–14 and died at the Battle of Moraviantown in 1813.

Tenskwatawa ("Open Door," 1775?–1836) Brother of Tecumseh who, following a series of prophetic visions in 1803, promoted a revival of traditional customs and values.

Tessouat (d. 1654) Kitchesipirini of Allumette Island, also known as Le Borgne de l'Isle as he was blind in one eye, initially resisted the missionary efforts of the Jesuits but was later baptized; one of at least three ogimaak named Tessouat, he controlled travel along the Ottawa River. An earlier Tessouat (Besouat; *fl.* 1603–13) met Champlain. A third Tessouat, also known as Le Borgne de l'Isle, died in 1636.

Teyoninhokarawen (Major John Norton, Snipe, *fl.* 1784–1825) Kanienkehaka chief and army officer who worked as an interpreter and emissary for Thayendanegea in dealing with Haudenosaunee land claims and led Indigenous forces in several important battles of the War of 1812–14.

Thanadelthur (d. 1717) A Denésoliné woman, referred to as the Slave Woman in the HBC records, who was enslaved by Cree in 1713 but escaped and travelled overland to Fort York. She was instrumental in negotiating peace between the Denésoliné and the Cree.

Thayendanegea (Joseph Brant, 1742–1807) Kanienkehaka chief, spokesman for his people, Anglican missionary, and British military officer during the US War of Independence. Brantford, Ontario, is named after him.

thirst dances (sun dances) Rituals practised primarily in the Plains area involving privation and self-torture. The Canadian government banned them in the 1895 because they fuelled Indigenous resistance of assimilation. The ban was lifted in 1951.

Thompson, David (1770–1857) HBC and, later, NWC fur trader and explorer who surveyed a route to the Churchill River and the area west of Lake of the Woods along the 49th parallel, and was the first European to travel the Athabasca Pass through the Rockies to the west coast.

"three sisters" Corn, squash, and beans, the three crops central to Indigenous agriculture in the Great Lakes region. They complement each other nutritionally and agriculturally, with the beans adding nitrogen to the soil, corn providing support for the beans, and squash providing ground cover to prevent weed growth and soil erosion and to preserve soil moisture.

Thule Name given by scientists to the northern people who preceded the Inuit and whose culture spread from Alaska across what is now northern Canada to Labrador, Newfoundland, and Greenland about ACE 1000. The Inuit are the direct descendants of the Thule.

traders Individuals working for large companies who accepted furs and other goods from First Nations and Inuit in exchange for agreed-upon items such as knives, pots, beads, and guns.

Treaty of Boston (1725) Treaty signed at the end of the English–Indian War between the English and Wabanaki, Wuastukwiuk, and Mi'kmaq.

Treaty of Ghent (1814) Treaty that concluded the War of 1812–14, in which the British tried to negotiate for the establishment of an Indigenous territory but failed.

Treaty of Greenville (1795) Treaty of peace between the US government and the Wendat, Lenape, Shaawanwaki, Odaawa, Ojibwa, Boodwaadmii, Myaamiaki, Ugpi'ganjig, Wea, Kickapoo, Piankeshaw, and Kaskaskia involving huge land cessions on the part of the First Nations and opening the Ohio Valley to European settlement.

Treaty of Paris (1763) Peace treaty between Britain and France following the latter's military defeat that effectively ended the French colonial presence in North America.

Treaty of Utrecht (1713) Treaty in which France ceded Acadia to the British that ended French–British hostilities in Acadia that had begun in 1701.

trickster-transformer A common character in the tales of many Indigenous cultures, such as Old Man Coyote in Siksika tradition, who tricks others into doing his bidding, for his benefit and to the detriment of the one who has been tricked, and who also, as with Raven in the Haida tradition, is sometimes responsible for the transformation/creation of the natural world. Often, by breaking social norms or upsetting the balance of the natural world, the trickster tale reaffirms the values of the group and the need for community.

Truth and Reconciliation Commission of Canada Commission established in 2008 and chaired by Justice Murray Sinclair from 2009, which completed its community hearings and special events in 2014. The Commission mandate was to discover the truth regarding the damages done by the residential schools and, by publicizing its mission and work, to seek reconciliation between Indigenous communities and Canadian governments and the broader Canadian public, as well as within Indigenous communities. The Commission made 94 "Calls to Action" in its report.

***Tsilhqot'in* case** Also known as the William case. The Supreme Court of Canada ruled in 2014 that Aboriginal title included lands that had been used regularly and exclusively by Indigenous Peoples when the Crown asserted sovereignty.

United Nations Declaration on the Rights of Indigenous Peoples An aspirational document overwhelmingly approved by the United Nations in 2007; Canada, with the new Justin Trudeau government in 2015, has now moved to put its goals into policy and practice.

usufructuary right The legal right to use something, such as land, without ownership.

War of 1812–14 British interference in US trade during Napoleonic Wars led to conflict in North America, on both land and sea, between US and Britain, with the US seeking to annex British North America. It was the last colonial war in which First Nations people held the balance of power.

wardship The state of being under the care of another person or group of people. In the case of First Nations people, the term refers to the relationship between First Nations and the colonial or Canadian government.

Warrior movement A militant, nationalist movement among the Kanienkehaka, described as the defence arm of the Longhouse religion but not universally accepted as such. The Warrior movement was founded by Louis Hall in the early twentieth century but is opposed by some traditionalists, who point out that the teachings of Shanyadariyoh focus on peace, not warlike behaviour, and that the founder of the Haudenosaunee Confederacy, Dekanawidah ("the Peacemaker"), brought and taught peace to the Five Nations. The Warriors were principal actors during the Oka crisis and at Caledonia.

Wendake Territory in present-day south-central Ontario extending eastward from Georgian Bay that was controlled at the time of early European contact by a confederacy of Iroquoian-speaking communities whom the French called Huron but who called themselves Wendat. Known as Huronia in Euro-Canadian historiography.

"white man's burden" A phrase first used by British poet Rudyard Kipling to describe what Britain saw as its role with respect to the Indigenous people of the countries it colonized.

White Paper (1969) A white paper, or parliamentary paper, is a document in which the government presents its policy or proposed policy on a specific topic. In the *Statement of the Government of Canada on Indian Policy*, 1969, the Liberal government put forward its proposal to end Aboriginal treaty rights and special status.

Notes

Introduction

1. "Ottawa announces $800M settlement with Indigenous survivors of Sixties Scoop," *CBC News*, 5 Oct. 2017, http://www.cbc.ca/news/politics/ottawa-settle-60s-scoop-survivors-1.4342462; "Indigenous residential school records can be destroyed, Supreme Court rules," 6 Oct. 2017, http://www.cbc.ca/news/politics/indian-residential-schools-records-supreme-court-1.4343259.

2. Tŝilhqot'in National Government, "Summary of the Tsilhqot'in Aboriginal Title Case (William's Case) Decision," http://www.tsilhqotin.ca/PDFs/2014_07_03_Summary_SCC_Dejcision.pdf; Fraser Institute, "The Top Ten Uncertainties of Aboriginal Title after Tsilhqot'in," 5 Oct. 2017, https://www.fraserinstitute.org/studies/top-ten-uncertainties-of-aboriginal-title-after-tsilhqotin.

3. Where the original manuscript has survived, this can be checked, but that is rare with early imprints. See I.S. MacLaren, "Samuel Hearne's Accounts of the Massacre at Bloody Falls, 17 July 1771," *Ariel: A Review of English Literature* 22, 1 (1991): 25–51; MacLaren, "'I came to rite thare portraits': Paul Kane's Journal of His Western Travels, 1846–1848," *American Art Journal* 21, 2 (1989): 6–88.

4. Denys Delâge, "Les Iroquois chrétiens des 'réductions,' 1667–1770: i—Migration et rapports avec les Français," *Recherches amérindiennes au Québec* 20, 1–2 (1991): 64.

5. Francis Assikinack, "Social and Warlike Customs of the Odahwah Indians," *Canadian Journal of Industry, Science, and Art* New Series 3 (1858): 306; Assikinack (Assignack), Francis, *Dictionary of Canadian Biography* IX (1861–1870), http://www.biographi.ca/en/bio.php?id_nbr=4270.

6. An anonymous map of Lake Huron labels Manitoulin as Ekaentoton Isle: Lieu d'assemblée de tous les sauvages allans en traitte a Montreal. This map is part of a series of nine manuscript maps in the Bibliothèque du Service Historique de la Marine in Vincennes, France. Trigger attributes them to Claude Bernou, while Conrad Heidenreich believes that if Bernou is the author, he may have copied them from some lost maps of La Salle. See Trigger, *The Children of Aataentsic: A History of the Huron People to 1660* (Montreal and Kingston, 1976), 798; Conrad E. Heidenreich, "Mapping the Great Lakes: The Period of Exploration, 1603–1700," *Cartographica* 17 (1980): 48; Claude Bernou, "Lac Huron ou Karegnondi ou Mer Douce des Hurons," Bibliothèque du Service Historique de la Marine, Recueil 67–208 (4044b), Amérique Septentrionale, Canada, no. 48.

7. Brian D. McInnes, *Sounding Thunder: The Stories of Francis Pegahmagabow* (Winnipeg, 2016), 46.

8. Ibid., 73.

9. Spelling issues and transliteration, that is, the rendering of letters or characters of one language to another, have created a number of idiosyncratic problems. For example, the terminal sound made when pluralizing Anishinaabe, is somewhere between a "g" and a "k" in English so we see both Anishinaabeg and Anishinaabek. We also see this in the *Dictionary of Canadian Biography* profile for Francis Assikinack, whose name is also spelled Assiginack. For his people we see, among many other variations: Auxoticats (Radisson's English translator); Cheveux-relevés (Champlain); Andatahouats (as the Jesuits and Sagard recorded the Wendat name for them); Dewagunhas (recorded in the Haudenosaunee language by Cadwallader Colden in 1747); Outa8is, Outa8cs, Outaouacs, 8ta8as, Outaouais (in the official French correspondence); Ahtawwah, Uttawas, Ottawas (in the British correspondence); Tawas, (in the United States); Odahwahs (in Assikinack and others); Odawa (in the scholarly work of the 1980s and 1990s); and now, finally, with the issue of the double vowel being resolved, Odaawa people. The most interesting part of this involves the French spellings. They did not understand that the g-k sound made the word plural so they referred to the Odaawak or Odaawa people as both Outaouais and Outaouacs with a redundant terminal "s."

10. For example, to stay with the people of Francis Assikinack, the word "Odaawa" is believed to derive from the Anishinaabe word *ottauwuhnshk*, which means "bulrush." The Ojibwa scholar Basil Johnston admitted to William Newbigging that this was speculative, and based on language alone. Newbigging pointed out the French Recollect lay brother Gabriel Sagard had noted in 1623 that weaving was one of the most important Odaawa manufacturing activities: "Je vis là [in the Odaawa village] beaucoup de femmes & filles qui faisoient des nattes de joncs, grandement bien tissuës & embellies de diverses couleurs." Later Sagard added, "Quand l'hyver vient, elles [the Odaawa women] font des nattes de jonc, don't ells garnissent les portes de leurs Cabanes, & en font d'autres pour s'asseoir dessus, le tout fort proprement. Les femmes de Cheveux Relevez [Sagard's word for Odaawa] mesmes, baillent des couleurs aux joncs, & font des compartimens d'ouvrages avec telle mesure qui'il que redire." This insight that the word came from "bulrush" was important, as the previous interpretation of the word had been "trader" and this had been made to fit into a Eurocentric economic paradigm that did not accurately depict the Anishinaabe perspective. In such ways linguistic evidence and historical evidence combine to make our understanding of the past more accurate. Basil Johnston, *The Manitous: The Spiritual World of the Ojibway* (St Paul, Minn., 2001), 245; Gabriel Sagard, *Le grand voyage du pays des Hurons* (Montreal, 1998), 159, 190; Basil Johnston, personal communication, 17 Sept. 1994.

Chapter 1

1. In a general sense, "time immemorial" refers to a point that exceeds human memory. In the Indigenous sense its meaning is more finely nuanced and also refers to the fact that First Peoples see time as being cyclical. In this understanding, events from the distant past do not require a specific date as that is a linear, and Eurocentric, construct.

2. Patricia Galloway, *Practicing Ethnohistory: Mining Archives, Hearing Testimony, Constructing Narrative* (Lincoln, 2006), 8; Jennifer S.H. Brown, "Ethnohistorians: Strange Bedfellows, Kindred Spirits," *Ethnohistory* 38, 2 (Spring 1991): 120; Carolyn Podruchny, *Making the Voyageur World: Travellers and Traders*

in the North American Fur Trade (Lincoln, 2006), 7–9; Sylvia Van Kirk, Many Tender Ties: Women in Fur Trade Society, 1670–1870 (Winnipeg, 1980), 6–8.

3. Fidgi Gendron, Four Directions Medicine Wheel Booklet, 1, at: https://www.uregina.ca/science/biology/people/faculty-research/gendron-fidji/documents-fidj/Medicine-Wheel-Booklet.pdf.

4. In order to support and encourage First Peoples' languages, which is key to preserving their histories, we will use their autonyms—the names they call themselves—wherever possible. Where there are important historical reasons for doing so, other names will also be given. For example, the Mesquakie people of the Upper Great Lakes were called "Outagami" (People of the Other Shore) by the Ojibwa, "Foxes" by the English, and "Les Renards" by the French. All of these words tell us important things about Mesquakie history. Similarly, we will avoid the use of exonyms (usually English, French, or other First Peoples' terms) for place names.

5. http://www.historymuseum.ca/cmc/exhibitions/aborig/fp/fpz2f21e.shtml.

6. Please note that the terminal "k" is plural in Anishinaabe-mowin, performing the same function as terminal "s" in English. No terminal "k" indicates both the singular and adjectival modes.

7. The missionaries, who also heard this story, did not understand the word "namaybin" as the white sucker, a North American species. They substituted "sucker" with "carp," a European fish. (See Reuben Gold Thwaites, ed., The Jesuit Relations and Allied Documents, 73 vols [Cleveland, 1896–1901], 67: 155–7. The entire 73-volume Jesuit Relations is available online from Creighton University.) This story was told to the author by Doug Belanger, the Fisheries Co-ordinator of Batchewana First Nation. He also told a version of the story at the National Aboriginal Fisheries Conference in Sault Ste Marie in May of 1999. At the time of contact the Kamiga Odaawa lived at Michilimackinac with the Nassauakueton Odaawa. This group came originally from the Thunder Bay area on Lake Huron in present-day Michigan, and the French called them the Nation of the Forks in reference to the fork in the Thunder Bay River just west of present-day Alpena, Michigan. This gives considerable credence to Belanger's insistence on the particular location.

8. In addition to The Jesuit Relations, other French documentary evidence referring to the Outaouais du Sable is to be found in the works of the explorers Nicolas Perrot and Pierre-François-Xavier Charlevoix, and in the official correspondence in the Archives Nationales (AN), Colonies, C11A Canada Series.

9. "Kiskakon" may be translated literally as "cut tail" and it is the Odaawa idiom for "bear," as bears have short, stubby tails. "Sinago" is the Odaawa word for squirrel. Kaniga (sometimes written Kamiga, Kanigouet, Nigouet, or Nigouek by French officials who were struggling to understand the nuances of Odaawa pronunciation) comes from the Odaawa word for sand, "negaw." See Richard A. Rhodes, Eastern Ojibwa–Chippewa–Ottawa Dictionary (Berlin, 1993).

10. For example, in 1648 the Jesuit, Paul Raguenau, wrote of the Odaawak living to the south of Lake Huron. He mentioned the presence of five nations (he included two Ojibwa nations in his description) of Odaawak at Bkejwanong: "On the south shore of this fresh-water sea, or Lake of the Hurons, dwell the following Algonquin tribes: Ouachaskesouek, Nigouaouichirinik, Outaouasinagouek, Kichkagoneiak, and Ontaanak, who are allies of our Hurons." Although Raguenau's spellings were unique, the names may still be discerned. He was referring to the Heron and Otter nations of the Ojibwa as well as to the Sinagos, Kiskakons, and Kamigas of the Odaawak. Thwaites, ed., Jesuit Relations, 33: 151; 40: 100.

11. Chief Mack-e-te-be-nessy, History of the Ottawa and Chippewa People of Michigan (Ypsilanti, Mich., 1887), 93.

12. William W. Warren, History of the Ojibway People (St Paul, Minn., 1984), 81; Francis Assikinack, "Social and Warlike Customs of the Odahwah Indians," Canadian Journal of Industry, Science, and Art 3 (1858): 306.

13. Nin-da-waab-jig, Minishenhying Anishinaabe-aki: Walpole Island, the Soul of Indian Territory (Walpole Island, Ont., 1987).

14. Ibid., 2–4.

15. Told by Dean Jacobs, Walpole Island First Nation, to Bill Newbigging, May 1994.

16. Nin-da-waab-jig, personal interviews with Dean Jacobs and Edsel Dodge, Walpole Island First Nation, May 1994.

17. Robert Graves, The Greek Myths (London, 1955), I: 176; Ian Crofton, A Dictionary of Scottish Phrase and Fable (Edinburgh, 2012), 112.

18. http://www.historymuseum.ca/cmc/exhibitions/aborig/haida/hapmc01e.shtml.

19. Victoria Mamnguqsualuk, K.J. Butler, and Charles Moore, Keeveeok Awake! (Edmonton, 1986), 9–10.

20. The Annales School of history refers to a new direction taken by French historians in the middle of the twentieth century. These scholars moved away from the old "kings and battles" approach to history. In its place les annalistes began to study the deep currents of social change over long periods of time. This approach is well suited to the study of Indigenous history.

21. Norman Hallendy, An Intimate Wilderness: Arctic Voices in a Land of Vast Horizons (Vancouver, 2016), 287.

22. Ibid., 286. For discussion of the Tuniit, see Chapter 3, note 24.

23. The classic account of this story may be found in Basil Johnston, Ojibway Heritage: The Ceremonies, Rituals, Songs, Dances, Prayers, and Legends of the Ojibway (Toronto, 1976), 13–17.

24. Georges Sioui, Les Wendats: une civilisation méconnue (Sainte-Foy, Que., 1994), 33–4. Translated from the French by the author.

25. See, for example, Chief Mack-e-te-be-nessy, History of the Ottawa and Chippewa Indians of Michigan, 79–96.

26. For one, "The Origin of Gitxawn Group at Kitsumkalem," in Marius Barbeau and William Beynon, coll., Tsimshian Narratives 2 (Ottawa, 1987), 1–4. Others are in Marius Barbeau, Tsimshian Myths (Ottawa, 1961).

27. The Recommended Readings include references to Indigenous oral traditions, but to gain real insight readers are encouraged to listen to a story told by an Elder.

28. R. Nair, "Archeological find affirms Heiltsuk Nation's oral history," CBCNews, 30 Mar. 2017, http://www.cbc.ca/news/canada/british-columbia/archeological-find-affirms-heiltsuk-nation-s-oral-history-1.4046088.

29. L. Bourgeon, A. Burke, and T. Higham, "Earliest Human Presence in North America Dated to the Last Glacial Maximum: New Radiocarbon Dates from Bluefish Caves, Canada," PLOSone Journal, 6 Jan. 2017, http://journals.plos.org/plosone/article?id=10.1371/journal.pone.0169486#authcontrib.

30. Knut R. Fladmark, "Times and Places: Environmental Correlates of Mid-to-Late Wisconsinan Human Population Expansion in North America," in Richard Shutler Jr, ed., Early Man in the New World (Beverly Hills, Calif., 1983), 27.

See also William N. Irving, "The First Americans: New Dates for Old Bones," *Natural History* 96, 2 (1987): 8–13. Irving and paleobiologist Richard Harrington claim that a campsite at Old Crow River dates back 150,000 years. The oldest and most complete and preserved skeleton found so far (in 2007 in a deep underwater cave on Mexico's Yucatan Peninsula) has been dated to at least 12,000 years ago: Mohi Kumar, "DNA from 12,000-Year-Old Skeleton Helps Answer the Question: Who Were the First Americans?" *Smithsonian.com*, 15 May 2014, https://www.smithsonianmag.com/science-nature/dna-12000-year-old-skeleton-helps-answer-question-who-were-first-americans-180951469. For some earlier findings and discussion, see "Hemisphere's Oldest Remains Identified, Geologist Says," *Toronto Star*, 1 Nov. 1992; Joseph H. Greenberg, *Language in the Americas* (Stanford, Calif., 1987), 331–7; Greenberg, "Linguistic Origins of Native Americans," *Scientific American* (Nov. 1992): 94–9. See also Jared M. Diamond "The Talk of the Americas," *Nature* 344 (1990): 589–90.

31. Timothy Pauketat, *The Oxford Handbook of North American Archaeology* (Oxford, 2015).

32. P. Skoglund et al., "Genetic Evidence for Two Founding Populations of the Americas," *Nature*, 3 Sept. 2015, https://www.nature.com/nature/journal/v525/n7567/full/nature14895.html; N. von Cramon-Taubadel, A. Strauss, and M. Hubbe, "Evolutionary Population History of Early Paleoamerican Cranial Morphology," *Scientific Advances* 3, 2 (22 Feb. 2017), http://advances.sciencemag.org/content/3/2/e1602289.

33. Kenneth B. Harris, *Visitors Who Never Left: The Origin of the People of the Damelahamid* (Vancouver, 1974), 13–18, 22–5.

34. For an argument supporting Indigenous traditional beliefs, see Vine Deloria Jr, *Red Earth, White Lies: Native Americans and the Myth of Scientific Fact* (Golden, Colo., 1997). See also Nelson Fagundes et al., "Mitochondrial Population Genomics Supports a Single Pre-Clovis Origin with a Coastal Route for the Peopling of the Americas," *American Journal of Human Genetics* 82, 3 (2008): 583–92; http://www.cell.com/ajhg/fulltext/S0002-9297(08)00139-0.

35. Knut R. Fladmark, "The Feasibility of the Northwest Coast as a Migration Route for Early Man," in Alan Lyle Bryan, ed., *Early Man in America from a Circum-Pacific Perspective* (Edmonton, 1978), 119–28; Fladmark, "The First Americans: Getting One's Berings," *Natural History* (Nov. 1986): 8–19; Margaret Munro, "Underwater World of B.C. Could Be Missing Link in Early Man's Travels," *Edmonton Journal*, 9 Aug. 1993; Richard Shutler Jr, "The Australian Parallel to the Peopling of the New World," in Shutler, ed., *Early Man in the New World*, 43–5. See also E.F. Greenman, "Upper Paleolithic in the New World," *Current Anthropology* 3 (1962): 61; Edwin Tappen Adney and Howard I. Chapelle, *The Bark Canoes and Skin Boats of North America* (Washington, 1964), 94–8; Alice B. Kehoe, "Small Boats upon the North Atlantic," in Carrol Riley et al., eds, *Man Across the Sea: Problems of Pre-Columbian Contacts* (Austin, Texas, 1971), 275–92; Ruth Gruhn, "Linguistic Evidence in Support of the Coastal Route of Earliest Entry into the New World," *Man*, new series 23, 2 (1988): 77–100. For the view that the western corridor could have been used for migrations, see N.W. Rutter, "Late Pleistocene History of the Western Canadian Ice-Free Corridor," *Canadian Journal of Anthropology* 1, 1 (1980): 1–8. This entire issue of *CJA* is devoted to studies of the corridor. A sea route to the Americas is suggested in the oral traditions and origin stories of some Indigenous Peoples, and this "island-hopping" across the Pacific could have included many volcanic islands that, with sea rise since the last Ice Age, are now underwater. See, for example, Frank Waters, *Book of the Hopi* (New York, 1963).

Chapter 2

1. Donna Duric, "Remembering Red Hill, Display of Artifacts at GREAT," *Turtle Island News*, 9 July 2014, http://vitacollections.ca/sixnationsarchive/3237524/data.

2. Elders at Henvey Inlet First Nation, for example, have provided place names for 20 historic sites along the French River, all pertaining to features of the water course. Personal communication from Stacey Amikwabe, May 2010.

3. D. Wayne Moodie, Kerry Abel, and Alan Catchpole, "Northern Athapaskan Oral Traditions and the White River Volcanic Eruption," paper presented at Aboriginal Resource Use in Canada: Historical and Legal Aspects conference, University of Manitoba, 1988. See also Catherine McClellan, *Part of the Land, Part of the Water: A History of the Yukon Indians* (Vancouver, 1987), 54–5; Peter Schledermann, *Crossroads to Greenland: 3000 Years of Prehistory in the Eastern High Arctic* (Calgary, 1990), 314–15. Four possible ways by which the Arctic could have been peopled are presented in schematized form by Robert McGhee in *Canadian Arctic Prehistory* (Scarborough, Ont., 1978), 18–21. See also "Relics Suggest That Humans Came to New World 36,000 Years Ago," *Edmonton Journal*, 2 May 1991.

4. Alan L. Bryan, "An Overview of Paleo-American Prehistory from a Circum-Pacific Perspective," in Bryan, ed., *Early Man in America*, 306–27. The oldest stone tools known so far, crafted more than 2.5 million years ago, have been found in Ethiopia. "Oldest Known Stone Tools Found, but Makers Remain Anonymous," *Ottawa Citizen*, 23 Jan. 1997. See also Robin Ridington, "Technology, World View, and Adaptive Strategy in a Northern Hunting Society," *Canadian Review of Sociology and Anthropology* 19, 4 (1982): 469–81.

5. See Laurette Séjourné, *Un Palacio en la ciudad de los dioses, Teotihuacán, Mexico* (Mexico City, 1959), passim.

6. Although the Inca were skilled metallurgists, they used their craft largely, although not entirely, for ceremonial purposes. However, copper alloy metallurgy was more important than previously thought and was used for mundane purposes. See Izumi Shimada and John F. Merkel, "Copper Alloy Metallurgy in Ancient Peru," *Scientific American* 265, 1 (1991): 80–6. As stone and bone technology gave way to that of metals, some tribal peoples came to regard stone tools as thunderbolts. See C.J.M.R. Gullick, *Myths of a Minority* (Assen, 1985), 25; Miguel León-Portilla, *Aztec Thought and Culture* (Norman, Okla., 1963).

7. *Kenneth Wright and Alfredo Valencia Zegarra, Machu Picchu: A Civil Engineering Marvel* (Reston, Virginia, 2001), *passim*.

8. Canada's ecology, subsistence bases, and population distribution for 1500 are mapped in R. Cole Harris, ed., *Historical Atlas of Canada, Vol. 1: From the Beginning to 1800* (Toronto, 1987), plates 17, 17A, 18. Seasonal Algonquian and Iroquoian cycles are schematized in plate 34.

9. https://www.mpm.edu/wirp/ICW-141.html#maple.

10. In her study of plant uses, Francis Densmore lists over 40 informants from communities across the United States and Canada.

See Francis Densmore, "Uses of Plants by the Chippewa Indians," *The Forty-fourth Annual Report of the American Bureau of Ethnology to the Secretary of the Smithsonian Institution, 1926–1927* (Washington, 1928), 275–397.

11. Virginia Morell, "Confusion in Earliest America," *Science* 248 (1990): 439–41.

12. Brian Swarbrick, "A 9,000-year-old Housing Project," *Alberta Report* 18, 34 (1991): 50–1.

13. "Increase in Carbon Dioxide Spurred Farming, Article Says," *Globe and Mail*, 9 Oct. 1995; "Earliest Agriculture in the New World," *Archaeology* 50, 4 (July–Aug. 1997): 11.

14. The section on agriculture is partly adapted from Olive Patricia Dickason, "'For Every Plant There Is a Use': The Botanical World of Mexica and Iroquoians," in Kerry Abel and Jean Friesen, *Aboriginal Resource Use in Canada: Legal and Historical Aspects* (Winnipeg, 1991), 11–34. Thanks to Dr Walter Moser, University of Alberta, for providing the Latin names.

15. Chili peppers, first domesticated on the Gulf coast, made their way to India, where they now form part of the traditional cuisine. India is also the leading grower of peanuts, another New World crop.

16. Chrestien Le Clercq, *New Relation of Gaspesia*, ed. William F. Ganong (Toronto, 1910), 296. See also Thwaites, ed., *Jesuit Relations*, 22: 293.

17. Virgil J. Vogel, *American Indian Medicine* (Norman, Okla., 1970), 9; Daniel E. Moermon, *Medicinal Plants of Native America*, 2 vols (Ann Arbor, Mich., 1986); Charles H. Talbot, "America and the European Drug Trade," in Fredi Chiapelli, ed., *First Images of America: The Impact of the New World on the Old*, 2 vols (Berkeley, Calif., 1976), 2: 813–32. Early settlers soon learned to appreciate Indigenous medical lore and incorporated it into their own practice. See Alfred Goldsworthy Bailey, *The Conflict of European and Eastern Algonkian Cultures 1504–1700* (Toronto, 1969 [1937]), 120–1.

18. Barry Kaye and D.W. Moodie, "The Psoralea Food Resource of the Northern Plains," *Plains Anthropologist* 23, 82, pt. 1 (1978): 329–36. Use of the wild turnip as a food resource intensified with the growth of population that followed the advent of the horse. Prairie turnip flour is a good source of vitamin C.

19. Stephen Lewandowski, "Three Sisters—An Iroquoian Cultural Complex," *Northeast Indian Quarterly* 6, 1–2 (1989): 45. The story of O-na-tah, spirit of corn, tells how corn became separated from her sister plants in modern agriculture. ("O-na-tah Spirit of Corn," ibid., 40.) Archaeologist Norman Clermont has observed that in the St Lawrence Valley, early agricultural communities developed in conjunction with fishing sites. He theorizes that a series of hard winters about the year 1000 encouraged farming as a means of obtaining enough food to store for the cold months. See Clermont, "Why Did the St. Lawrence Iroquois Become Agriculturalists?" *Man in the Northeast* 40 (1990): 75–9.

20. Peter McFarlane and Wayne Haimila, *Ancient Land, Ancient Sky: Following Canada's Native Canoe Routes* (Toronto, 1999), 120.

21. Howard Webkamigad, *Ottawa Stories from the Springs/ Anishinaabe dibaadjimowinan wodi gaa binjibaamigak wodi mookodjiwong e zhinikaadek* (East Lansing, Mich., 2015), 233.

22. Only 20 per cent of Andean crops reproduce readily above 2,700 metres. On the distribution of maize as a crop, see Victor A. Shnirelman, "Origin and Early History of Maize," *European Review of Native American Studies* 3, 2 (1989): 23–8, particularly the map on page 25. On the contributions of Indigenous farmers to world agriculture, see Earl J. Hamilton, "What the New World Gave to the Economy of the Old," in Chiapelli, ed., *First Images of America*, 2: 853–84; Barrie Kavash, *Native Harvests* (New York, 1979); Jack Weatherford, *Indian Givers: How the Indians of the Americas Transformed the World* (New York, 1988). Maize is also used as raw material for a wide variety of industrial products. It has been estimated that maize as a crop is worth more each year than all the gold and silver taken out of the Americas by the conquistadors. See Arturo Warman, "Corn as Organizing Principle," *Northeast Indian Quarterly* 6, 1–2 (1989): 22. Maize, incidentally, was the staple for the transatlantic slave trade, as it prevented scurvy.

23. Corn requires 60 to 70 days to produce a crop; rice requires 120–140 days. Pierre Chaunu, *L'Amérique et les Amériques* (Paris, 1964), 19. In Europe at the time of contact, the standard yield of cereals was six units of seed collected for each unit of seed planted, a rate that under favourable circumstances could increase to 10:1. The standard for corn was 150:1; in bad years, the yield could drop to 70:1. Warman, "Corn as Organizing Principle," 21.

24. There has been spirited debate about the origin of corn as a cultigen and, consequently, an extensive list of publications. Among the articles (being shorter and perhaps more readable) are: Steve Connor, "Stone Age People Modified Crops," *The Independent*, 18 Mar. 1999, 12; Paul C. Mangelsdorf, "Mystery of Corn," *Scientific American* 183, 1 (1950): 20–4; Mangelsdorf, "Mystery of Corn: New Perspectives," *Proceedings of the American Philosophical Society* 127, 4 (1983): 215–47; Mangelsdorf, "The Origin of Corn," *Scientific American* 255, 2 (1986): 80–6; George W. Beadle, "The Ancestry of Corn," *Scientific American* 242, 2 (1980): 112–19; Walton C. Galinat, "The Origin of Maize," *Annual Review of Genetics* 5 (1971): 447–78; J.M.J. de Wet and J.R. Harlan, "Origin of Maize: The Tripartite Hypothesis," *Euphytica* 21 (1972); James H. Kempton, "Maize as a Measure of Indian Skill," *Symposium on Prehistoric Agriculture*, University of New Mexico (Millwood, NY, 1977); Louis Werner, "Caught in a Maize of Genes," *Américas* 52, 3 (May–June 2000): 6–17.

25. Henry T. Lewis and Theresa A. Ferguson, "Yards, Corridors, and Mosaics: How to Burn a Boreal Forest," *Human Ecology* 16, 1 (1988): 57–77. Fire, of course, had many more uses than those pertaining to agriculture and game management. See "Our Grandfather Fire: Fire and the American Indian," in Stephen J. Pyne, *Fire in America* (Princeton, NJ, 1982), 71–83.

26. Thwaites, ed., *Jesuit Relations*, 50: 265; the stories of Nenibozhoo also illustrate the dangers involved by ignoring resource management: "Nenibozhoo and the Ducks" and "Nenibozhoo and the Bears" in Webkamigad, *Ottawa Stories from the Springs*, 2–51.

27. The expression is borrowed from the Navajo's Blessingway ceremony.

28. Anthropologists once argued that the Great Plains could not have been inhabited to any extent before the advent of the horse and the gun. Clark Wissler wrote in 1906, "the peopling of the plains proper was a recent phenomenon due in part to the introduction of the horse and the displacement of tribes by white settlement." Wissler, "Diffusion of Culture in the Plains of North America," *International Congress of Americanists*, 15th session (Quebec, 1906), 39–52. Although Wissler later modified his position, A.L. Kroeber in 1939 was still arguing that the Plains had developed culturally "only since the taking over of the horse from Europeans." Kroeber, *Cultural and Natural Areas of Native North America* (Berkeley, 1939), 76. William Duncan Strong, "The Plains Culture Area in the Light of Archaeology," *American Anthropologist* 23, 2 (1933): 271–87, held that horse nomadism represented no more than a "thin and strikingly uniform veneer" on earlier cultural

manifestations. On the lack of specific rites among the Plains Cree for the increase of horses even though they were the symbol of wealth, see David G. Mandelbaum, *The Plains Cree* (Regina, 1979 [1940]), 63. See also John C. Lewis, *The Horse in Blackfoot Indian Culture* (Washington, 1955); Lewis, *The Blackfeet* (Norman, 1958).

29. Thomas F. Kehoe, "Corralling Life," in Mary LeCron Foster and Lucy Jane Botscharow, eds, *The Life of Symbols* (Boulder, Colo., 1990), 175–93.

30. Head-Smashed-In has been named a World Heritage Site by UNESCO. For a detailed description of the site, see Jack Brink and Bob Dawe, *Final Report of the 1985 and 1986 Field Season at Head-Smashed-In Buffalo Jump* (Edmonton, 1989), 298–303. See also: www. head-smashed-in.com.

31. Richard G. Forbis, *A Review of Alberta Archaeology to 1964* (Ottawa, 1970), 27.

32. Harris, ed., *Historical Atlas*, I: plate 15. See also Brian O.K. Reeves, *Culture Change in the Northern Plains: 1000 B.C.–A.D. 1000* (Edmonton, 1983); H.M. Wormington and Richard G. Forbis, *An Introduction to the Archaeology of Alberta, Canada* (Denver, 1965), particularly the summary and conclusion, 183–201.

33. Eleanor Verbicky-Todd, *Communal Buffalo Hunting among the Plains Amerindians: An Ethnographic and Historic Review* (Edmonton, 1984), 25–32. At a later date an offender risked being flogged or even (among the Kiowa) having his horse shot.

34. http://www.historymuseum.ca/cmc/exhibitions/aborig/haida/hapso01e.shtml.

35. See Ron Brunton, "The Cultural Instability of Egalitarian Societies," *Man* 24, 4 (1989): 673–4.

36. One exception to this rule was Onistah-Sokasin (Cal-Shirt) of the Nitayxkax Band of the Káínaa Nation of the Niitsitapi Confederacy. Another exception was Mahta Tatanka (Bull Bear) of the Oglala Band of the Lakota Confederacy. See Catherine Price, *The Oglala People 1841–1879: A Political History.* (Lincoln: University of Nebraska Press, 1996), 23-26, and "Onistah-Sokasin," *Dictionary of Canadian Biography Online*, http://www.biographi.ca/en/results.php/?ft=calf%20shirt.

37. See Thwaites, ed., *Jesuit Relations*, 6: 243; 5: 195.

38. Torture as practised in Europe was part of the judicial system rather than of warfare. At a time when nation-states were consolidating their positions, it was used as a means of control of certain elements within their own societies that for various reasons were considered undesirable. The majority of Indigenous Peoples who followed the practice (most prevalent in the East) belonged to non-state societies and used torture of outside enemies to demonstrate their community solidarity and superiority over hostile alien forces. They did not torture those within their own communities. See Olive Patricia Dickason, *The Myth of the Savage and the Beginnings of French Colonialism in the Americas* (Edmonton, 1984), xi; Dickason, "Louisbourg and the Indians: A Study in Imperial Race Relations, 1713–1760," *History and Archaeology* 6 (1976): 91–2; Nathaniel Knowles, "The Torture of Captives by the Indians of Eastern North America," *Proceedings of the American Philosophical Society* 82, 2 (Mar. 1940), reprinted in Georg Friederici, *Scalping and Torture: Warfare Practices among North American Indians* (Oshweken, Ont., 1985).

39. The Cree word for leader, of which "okima" is one form, contains the root "to give away." See Colin Scott, "Hunting Territories, Hunting Bosses and Communal Production among Coastal James Bay Cree," *Anthropologica* 28, 1–2 (1986): 171 n2. On what was expected of Montagnais chiefs, see Thwaites, ed., *Jesuit Relations*, 26: 155–63.

40. T. McHugh, *The Time of the Buffalo* (New York, 1972), 140–1.

41. Thomas Jefferys, *The Natural and Civil History of the French Dominions in North and South America, I: A Description of Canada and Louisiana* (London, 1760), 67; Thwaites, ed., *Jesuit Relations*, 6: 243.

42. Thwaites, ed., *Jesuit Relations*, 6: 243.

43. One study goes so far as to say the chief's authority was "absolute" within certain spheres but in practice was constrained by the well-being of the community. See Arthur E. Hippler and Stephen Conn, *Traditional Athabascan Law Ways and Their Relationship to Contemporary Problems of "Bush Justice"* (Fairbanks, Alaska, 1972). This would accord, at least in part, with the observation of HBC Captain Zachariah Gillam (1636 o.s.–1682) that Indigenous Peoples had "some chief persons that are above the rest, yet working with them." Cited by Toby Morantz, "Old Texts, Old Questions—Another Look at the Issue of Continuity and the Early Fur Trade Period," paper presented to the American Society for Ethnohistory, Chicago, 1989.

44. Kenneth M. Ames, "The Evolution of Social Ranking on the Northwest Coast of North America," *American Antiquity* 46, 4 (1981): 797.

45. "Moiety": half. This division of a community into two halves was for ceremonial purposes.

46. The processes by which this can occur are examined by Ames, "Evolution of Social Ranking," 789–805.

47. Ethnologist June Helm divides the Subarctic into the shield with associated Hudson Bay lowlands and Mackenzie borderlands, the cordillera, the Alaska plateau, and the region south of the Alaska range. The first division, that of the Subarctic shield and borderlands, covers approximately three-quarters of the land mass of the Arctic. June Helm, ed., *Handbook of North American Indians*, 6: *Subarctic* (Washington, 1981), 1.

48. Paroles des Tsonnontouans rapportées par Joncaire, Mai 1715, AN, Series C11A, "Canada," vol. 22, fols. 54–54v. As Jesuit Paul Le Jeune (1591–1664) observed in the St Lawrence Valley, "Besides having some kind of Laws maintained among themselves, there is also a certain order established as regards foreign nations."

49. On the importance of reciprocity, see Chrestien Le Clercq, *Nouvelle relation de la Gaspésie*, 2 vols (Paris, 1691), I: 324. Europeans, not appreciating the principle of "I give to you that you might give to me," quickly denigrated it as "Indian giving," particularly when Indigenous people, perceiving that the Europeans did not reciprocate, asked for their gifts back.

50. Chrestien Le Clercq, *First Establishment of the Faith in New France*, 2 vols, tr. John GilmaryShea (New York, 1881), I: 124.

51. Fladmark, *British Columbia Prehistory*, 50. Trade in the region is at least 10,000 years old.

52. Harris, ed., *Historical Atlas*, I: plate 14.

53. Victor P. Lytwyn, "Waterworld: The Aquatic Territory of the Great Lakes First Nations," in *Gin Das Winan: Documenting Aboriginal History in Ontario* (Toronto, 1996), 14. Gilles Havard, in *La grande paix de Montréal de 1701* (Québec, 1992), 132–5, lists 27 Great Lakes nations.

54. Harris, ed., *Historical Atlas*, I: plate 12.

55. Iroquoian languages are related to Siouan and Caddoan. The Caddo, of the US Southwest, were organized into hierarchical chiefdoms at the time of European contact; the Sioux had been connected earlier with the Mississippian Mound Builders. There is some evidence that chiefdoms had appeared among some of the Iroquois. See William C. Noble, "Tsouharissen's Chiefdom: An Early Historic 17th Century Neutral Iroquoian Ranked Society," *Canadian Journal of Archaeology* 9, 2 (1985): 131–46.

56. On the possible Basque origin of the word "Iroquois," see Peter Bakker, "A Basque Etymology for the Word Iroquois," *Man in the Northeast* 40 (1990): 89–93.

57. They called themselves Wendat, People of the Peninsula, and their land Wendaké. "Wendat" also refers to the confederacy. The name "Huron" was given them by the French because of the coiffures of the warriors, which reminded them of the bristles on the spine of a boar. Diamond Jenness, *Indians of Canada* (Ottawa, 1932), 82. Odaawa men affected a similar hairstyle. Apparently the term "huron" also referred to manner of dress, implying rusticity. See also Sioui, *Les Wendats*.

58. The French called the members of the Wendat Confederacy *les Hurons*. Although we now use their autonym "Wendat" the word "Huron" lives on in the historical documents, in the older histories, and in the geographic name Huronia, the area of southern Georgian Bay sometimes called the Penetanguishene Peninsula.

59. Gabriel Sagard, *The Long Journey to the Country of the Hurons*, tr. H.H. Langton (Toronto, 1939), 104.

60. Gabriel Sagard, *Histoire du Canada, et voyages que les frères mineurs Recollects y ont faicts pour la conversion des infidelles*, 4 vols (Paris, 1636), III: 728.

61. The 30,000 estimate for the Hurons was made by Champlain, who spent a winter in Huronia. Geographer Conrad Heidenreich believes it is probably about one-third too large; he uses the figure 20,000. Heidenreich, *Huronia: A History and Geography of the Huron Indians 1600–1650* (Toronto, 1971), 96–103.

62. The Arendarhonon, "the People of the Rock," had the second largest population among the Wendat confederates. They may have joined about 1590, long after the two founding tribes confederated, perhaps early in the fifteenth century. Their late date of joining raises the question whether the Arendarhonon came from Stadacona.

63. Bruce G. Trigger, *The Children of Aataentsic: A History of the Huron People to 1660*, 2 vols (Montreal and Kingston, 1976), I: 197.

64. Hiawatha has been identified as an Onondaga by birth and a Mohawk by adoption, and also as a Huron. Some of the versions of the origins of the league are told by Christopher Vecsey, "The Story of the Iroquois Confederacy," *Journal of the American Academy of Religion* 54, 1 (1986): 79–106. Cree-French historian Bernard Assiniwi gives his version in *Histoire des Indiens du haut et du bas Canada: moeurs et coutumes des Algonkins et des Iroquois*, 3 vols (Québec, 1973), III: 111–24.

65. Alice Beck Kehoe, *The Ghost Dance* (Toronto, 1989), 115. Hiawatha's name, "One Who Combs," was earned because he combed the snakes out of Thadodaho's hair. There are several versions of the story, one of which is recounted by Paul A.W. Wallace, *The White Roots of Peace* (Port Washington, NY, 1968), 11–17.

66. A report in the *Jesuit Relations* (21: 201) says that the Onondaga alternated men and women as head sachems.

67. "Anishinaabe" (plural, Anishinaabek) means "the people." "Ojibwa" translates as "the talk of the robin." The subsistence basis of the Odaawak is discussed in William Newbigging, "The Ottawa Settlement of Detroit," paper presented to the Canadian Historical Association, 1992. In the seventeenth century, the closely related Ojibwa, Odaawa, and Algonquin were loosely confederated into the Council of Three Fires. Today they are more or less merged as Ojibwa (Anishinaabe), a process that took off during the nineteenth century. The Nipissing, Batchewana, and Mississauga nations are among others who are included.

68. A detailed study of the exploitation of wild rice and its cultural ramifications is that of Thomas Vennum, *Wild Rice and the Ojibway People* (St Paul, Minn., 1988). See also Kathi Avery and Thomas Pawlick, "Last Stand in Wild Rice Country," *Harrowsmith* 3, 7 (May 1979): 32–47, 107.

69. Sagard, *Histoire du Canada*, IV: 846.

70. Catharine McClellan, verbal communication.

71. Marc Lescarbot, *History of New France*, eds. H.P. Biggar and W.L Grant (Toronto, 1914), 3: 195 and 250; C. Le Clercq, *New Relation of Gaspesia*, ed. W.F. Ganong (Toronto, 1910), 212.

72. For a general study of the phenomenon, see Diana Claire Tkaczuk and Brian C. Vivian, eds, *Cultures in Conflict: Current Archaeological Perspectives* (Calgary, 1989).

73. Basil Johnston, *Ojibway Ceremonies* (Toronto: McClelland & Stewart, 1982), 59.

74. Recorded by Anna Brownell Jameson, in *Winter Studies and Summer Rambles in Canada* (London, 1838), 3: 223.

75. Unidentified Tseshahts man quoted in Penny Petrone, *First Peoples, First Voices* (Toronto, 1983), 67.

76. Ernest S. Burch Jr, "War and Trade," in William W. Fitzhugh and Aron Crowell, eds, *Crossroads of Continents: Cultures of Siberia and Alaska* (Washington, 1988), 231–2.

77. By the end of the seventeenth century, a French officer would observe that Indigenous people were "never rash in declaring war; they hold frequent Councils before they resolve upon it." Louis Armand de Lom d'Arce de Lahontan, *New Voyages to North America by Baron de Lahontan*, ed. R.G. Thwaites, 2 vols (Chicago, 1905), II: 507. Le Clercq agreed: war, he wrote, was never declared except as a last resort on the advice of Old Men (Le Clercq, *New Relation*, 269.) By mid-eighteenth century Thomas Jefferys expressed a different view. Indigenous people, he wrote, rarely "refuse to engage in a war to which they have been invited by their allies: on the contrary, they seldom wait till they are called to take up arms, the least motif being sufficient to determine them to it" (Jefferys, *Natural and Civil History*, I: 53, 68). See also Daniel K. Richter, "War and Culture: The Iroquois Experience," *William and Mary Quarterly* 40, 4 (1982): 528–59.

Chapter 3

1. This section was developed from Olive Patricia Dickason, "Three Worlds, One Focus: Europeans Meet Inuit and Amerindians in the Far North," in Richard C. Davis, ed., *Rupert's Land: A Cultural Tapestry* (Calgary, 1988), 51–78.

2. The two Nordic sagas, *Eiriks saga rauda* and *Graenlendinga saga*, do not give a precise date, but archaeological work at L'Anse aux Meadows has helped scholars to date the Viking arrival to about 1000 ACE. See Tryggvi V. Oleson, *Early Voyages and Northern Approaches* (Toronto, 1963), 6; L'Anse aux Meadows National Historic Site, http://www.pc.gc.ca/en/lhn-nhs/nl/meadows.

3. William R. Morrison, *Under the Flag: Canadian Sovereignty and the Native People in Northern Canada* (Ottawa, 1984), 97. The term "Inuit," meaning "human beings" ("Inuk" in the singular), widely used among the people for themselves, was adopted by the Inuit Circumpolar Conference in 1977 for all the people formerly referred to as "Eskimo." People of the western Arctic are called Inuvialuit; other regional terms include "Inuinait" and "Inumagit." (Bishop John R. Sperry, Yellowknife, in a letter published in *Arctic* 40, 4 [1987]: 364.) "Inuit" has been officially adopted in Canada. See José Mailhot, "L'Etymologie de 'Esquimau': Revue et Corrigée," *Études/Inuit/Studies* 2, 2 (1978): 59–69; Yvon

Csonka, *Collections arctiques* (Neuchâtel, Switzerland, 1988), 11, 18. On the question of first contacts with Europeans, see Robert McGhee, *Canada Rediscovered* (Hull, Que., 1991).

4. Morrison, *Under the Flag*, 100.

5. Urs Bitterli, *Cultures in Conflict: Encounters between European and Non-European Cultures, 1492–1800*, tr. Ritchie Robertson (London, 1989).

6. Kuang-chih Chang, "Radiocarbon Dates from China: Some Initial Interpretations," *Current Anthropology* 14, 5 (1973): 525–8.

7. On the white-bone, white-meat variety, see George F. Carter, "Pre-Columbian Chickens in America," in Riley et al., eds, *Man Across the Sea*, 178–218; Carter, "Chinese Contacts with America: Fu Sang Again," *Anthropological Journal of Canada* 14, 1 (1976): 10–24. On the black-boned, dark-meated "melanotic" chicken, found in Mexico, Mesoamerica, and Guatemala, see Carl L. Johannessen, "Folk Medicine Uses of Melanotic Asiatic Chickens as Evidence of Early Diffusion to the New World," *Social Science and Medicine* 15D (1981): 427–34; Johannessen, "Melanotic Chicken Use and Chinese Traits in Guatemala," *Revista de Historia de América* 93 (1982): 73–89. Melanotic chickens were not eaten but used in magical and curing rituals by both Maya and Chinese.

8. Peter Caley, "Canada's Chinese Columbus," *The Beaver* Outfit 313, 4 (1983): 8–9. Although living in China, Hwui Shan was an Afghan and apparently spoke Chinese imperfectly, which did not help his credibility upon his return. Still, his story was officially recorded, although in condensed form. It has been inferred, from his description of people keeping herds of deer and drinking the milk, that he first arrived at the Aleutian Islands before heading south to Fu-Sang, held by some to be Mexico.

9. Japanese pottery dates from before 12,000 BCE: Fumiko Iwaka-Smith, "Late Pleistocene and Early Holocene Technologies," in Richard J. Pearson, ed., *Windows on the Japanese Past: Studies in Archaeology and Prehistory* (Ann Arbor, Mich., 1986), 199–216. Childe called pottery "the earliest conscious utilization by man of a chemical change." V.G. Childe, *Man Makes Himself* (New York, 1951), 76. Earliest pottery is associated with cooking.

10. Kehoe, "Small Boats upon the North Atlantic," 288–9; Stuart J. Fiedel, *Prehistory of the Americas* (Cambridge, 1987), 109.

11. Terry Grieder, *Art and Archaeology in Pashash* (Austin, Texas, 1979), maintains there is evidence of the potter's wheel having been used to produce Recuay ceramics, 290–360 ACE.

12. J. Blitz, "Adoption of the Bow in Prehistoric North America," *Northern American Archaeologist* 9, 2 (1988): 123–46.

13. See Gordon F. Ekholm, "A Possible Focus of Asiatic Influence in the Late Classic Cultures of Mesoamerica," in Jesse D. Jennings, ed., *Memoirs of the Society for American Archaeology*, 9, supplement to *American Antiquity* 18, 3, part 2 (1953): 72–97.

14. S.G. Stephens, "Some Problems of Interpreting Transoceanic Dispersal of the New World Cottons," in Riley et al., eds, *Man Across the Sea*, 401–5.

15. For the argument that the two species were developed in the Americas with plants that came from Africa, see Fiedel, *Prehistory of the Americas*, 161. For the case that cotton was domesticated from naturally hybridized plants growing wild in the Americas, see Joseph Needham and Lu Gwei-Djen, *Trans-Pacific Echoes and Resonances: Listening Once Again* (Philadelphia, 1985), 62. The case for the Indigenous origin of cotton in the Americas, both as a crop and in its manufacture into textiles, is presented by J.B. Hutchinson, R.A. Silow, and S.G. Stephens, *The Evolution of Gossypium and Differentiation of the Cultivated Cottons* (London, 1947), 79–80, 136–9.

16. Stephen Jett, "Trans-oceanic Contacts," in Jesse D. Jennings, ed., *Ancient Native Americans* (San Francisco, [1978]), 636; John Barber, "Oriental Enigma," *Equinox* 49 (1990): 86.

17. Thor Heyerdahl, *Early Man and the Ocean: A Search for the Beginnings of Navigation and Seaborne Civilizations* (New York, 1980), 376–7. Zoologist and amateur linguist Barry Fell has been one proponent of North African and European connections with the western hemisphere. A reasoned assessment of the strengths and failings of his arguments is David H. Kelley's "Proto-Tifinagh and Proto-Ogham in the Americas," *Review of Archaeology* 11, 1 (1990): 1–10. Kelley concludes: "We need to ask not only what Fell has done wrong in his epigraphy, but also where we have gone wrong as archaeologists."

18. Julian H. Steward advocates multilinear evolution in *Theory of Culture Change* (Urbana, Ill., 1976). Cultures have been described as symbolic structures that provide the means for human satisfaction once survival has been assured. See David Rindos, "The Evolution of the Capacity for Culture: Sociobiology, Structuralism, and Cultural Evolution," *Current Anthropology* 27, 4 (1986): 326.

19. Bob Connolly and Robin Anderson, *New Guinea Highlanders Encounter the Outside World* (London, 1988).

20. *Sweat of the Sun: Gold of Peru* (Edinburgh, 1990). This is the catalogue for the exhibition of the same name.

21. Needham and Lu, *Trans-Pacific Echoes*, 64.

22. This is the thesis of Oleson, *Early Voyages and Northern Approaches*, 9.

23. Kaj Birket-Smith, *Eskimos* (Copenhagen, 1971), 13. An account of the first meeting of Greenland Skraelings with Norsemen is reproduced, ibid., 28–9. See also L.H. Neatby, "Exploration and History of the Canadian Arctic," in David Damas, ed., *Handbook of North American Indians, 5: Arctic* (Washington, 1985), 337–90.

24. Wendell H. Oswalt, *Eskimos and Explorers* (Novato, Calif., 1979), 11. That the Skraelings of the Norse accounts were Dorset remains conjectural and hinges on the credence given to Inuit oral tradition and to the Norse sagas, and on a determination as to who the Tuniit ("original inhabitants") of Inuit tradition were. While it is widely hypothesized that the Tuniit were the Dorset people, the Tuniit, according to Inuit storytelling, were "shy" and "easily put to flight" but were "taller and stronger" than the Inuit and capable of great feats of strength; on the other hand, the Skraelings are said to have been "very little" and "small" people. In fact, the Dorset may have been considerably larger people and the Skraelings, then, would have been what are known as the Thule, the immediate predecessors of the Inuit in the Arctic. See Kate Allen, "When Science Meets Aboriginal Oral History," *Toronto Star*, 31 Aug. 2014, https://www.thestar.com/news/insight/2014/08/31/when_science_meets_aboriginal_oral_history.html.

25. By way of comparison, French cosmographer André Thevet (c. 1517–92) reported that Indigenous people at first honoured Spaniards as prophets and even as gods. Thevet, *Les singularitez de la France Antarctique*, ed. Paul Gaffarel (Paris, 1878), 139–40. See also Bruce G. Trigger, "Early Native North American Response to European Contact," *Journal of American History* 77, 4 (1991): 1195–215; Nathaniel Wachtel, *The Vision of the Vanquished: The Spanish Conquest of Peru through Indian Eyes, 1530–1570* (London, 1977).

26. Harris, ed., *Historical Atlas*, I: plate 16; Joel Berglund, "The Decline of the Norse Settlements in Greenland," *Arctic Anthropology* 23, 142 (1986): 109–35.

27. See temperature graph in Harris, ed., *Historical Atlas*, I: plate 16.

28. The argument that the Norse communities did not adapt either culturally or technologically to changing conditions is presented by Thomas H. McGovern, "The Economics of Extinction in Norse Greenland," in T.M. Wigley, M.J. Ingram, and G. Farmer, eds, *Climate and History* (Cambridge, 1981), 404–33. For example, they never adopted Inuit sea-mammal hunting technology (the most advanced in the world at that time) or skin boats, despite the unavailability of timber. Culturally, they concentrated on bigger and more elaborate churches and the latest in European fashion and dress.

29. Brian Fagan, *The Little Ice Age: How Climate Made History, 1300–1850* (New York, 2001), 11–15.

30. Alan D. McMillan, *Native Peoples and Cultures of Canada: An Anthropological Overview* (Vancouver, 1988), 246.

31. Samuel Hearne, *A Journey from Prince of Wales's Fort in Hudson's Bay to the Northern Ocean in the years 1769, 1770, 1771, and 1772*, ed. J.B. Tyrrell (Toronto, 1911), 163.

32. Fagan, *The Little Ice Age*, 31ff; Dorothy Harley Eber, *Encounters on the Passage: Inuit Meet the Explorers* (Toronto, 2008), 3–9.

33. W.A. Kenyon, *Tokens of Possession* (Toronto, 1975), 41, 121.

34. The term "Qallunaat" or "Kabloona" is thought to have origi-nated from the Inuktitut term meaning "people who pamper their eyebrows," perhaps a variation of "qallunaaraaluit," which refers to materialism, interference with nature, and greed. See Minnie Aodla Freeman, *Life among the Qalunaat* (Edmonton, 1978), after Foreword. Another translation that has been pro-posed is "people with bushy eyebrows."

35. Charles Francis Hall, *Arctic Researches and Life among the Esquimaux* (New York, 1865), 251, 290, 385.

36. Dorothy Harley Eber, *When the Whalers Were Up North: Inuit Memories from the Eastern Arctic* (Montreal and Kingston, 1989), 21–33.

37. This technology was used by the Thule of the eastern Arctic as well as the Punuk of the west, and had been adopted by the whalers of the west coast, such as the Nuu'chah'nulth (Nootka) of Vancouver Island. See Jean-Loup Rousselot, William W. Fitzhugh, and Aron Crowell, "Maritime Economics of the North Pacific Rim," in Fitzhugh and Crowell, eds, *Crossroads of Continents*, 163–72. A toggling harpoon found at L'Anse Amour Mound in Labrador, dating back to 7500 BCE, may be the oldest such weapon in the world. See James A. Tuck and Robert McGhee, "Archaic Cultures in the Strait of Belle Isle Region, Labrador," *Arctic Anthropology* 12, 2 (1975): 76–91. For a general description of Inuit whaling technology, see J. Garth Taylor, "Inuit Whaling Technology in Eastern Canada and Greenland," in Allen P. McCartney, ed., *Thule Eskimo Culture: An Anthropological Perspective* (Ottawa, 1979), 292–300.

38. Eber, *When the Whalers Were Up North*, 161–7.

39. There is no collective autonym for the Cree people. As the largest Indigenous group in Canada they have too many dialects and too many differences to be captured by a single autonym. The term "Iynu" refers to one specific group from James Bay.

40. If an "e" is substituted for the second "o," Oupeeshepow becomes Oupeeshepew, which means "always busy," according to Reg Louttit, chief of the Attawapiskat Cree north of Moose Factory (personal communication).

41. Glyndwr Williams, ed., *Andrew Graham's Observations on Hudson's Bay 1767–91* (London, 1969), 204.

42. Miller Christy, *The Voyages of Captain Luke Foxe of Hull, and Captain Thomas James of Bristol, in search of a North-West Passage, in 1631–32*, 2 vols (London, 1894), I: 137.

43. Toby Morantz, "Oral and Recorded History in James Bay," in William Cowan, ed., *Papers of the Fifteenth Algonquian Conference* (Ottawa, 1984), 181–2.

44. John S. Long, "Narratives of Early Encounters between Europeans and the Cree of Western James Bay," *Ontario History* 80, 3 (1988): 230. The earliest mention of the "Kristinaux" is in the *Jesuit Relations* of the 1640s.

45. Harris, ed., *Historical Atlas*, I: plate 23.

46. Colonial Office 194/27,263, Palliser to the Secretary of the Admiralty, 25 Aug. 1766. Cited by W.H. Whiteley, "The Establishment of the Moravian Mission in Labrador and British Policy, 1763–83," *Canadian Historical Review* 45, 1 (1964): 31, 39–40.

47. "Gaspar Corte-Real," *Dictionary of Canadian Biography Online*, http://www.biographi.ca/en/bio/corte_real_gaspar_1E.html; "The Corte Real Brothers," Library and Archives of Canada Online, https://www.bac-lac.gc.ca/eng/discover/exploration-settlement/pathfinders-passageways/Pages/new-continent.aspx.

48. For a complete account, see Nelson Foster and Linda S. Cordell, eds, *Chilies to Chocolate: Food the Americas Gave the World* (Tucson, Ariz., 1996).

49. Jean Alfonce (Jean Fonteneau), *Les Voyages avantureux du Capitaine Ian Alfonce, Sainctongeois* (Poitiers, 1559), 27v; Giovanni Battista Ramusio, *Navigations et Voyages (XVI siècle)*, tr. Général Langlois and M.J. Simon (Paris, 1933), 111.

50. J. Callum Thomson, "Cornered: Cultures in Conflict in Newfoundland and Labrador," in Tkaczuk and Vivian, eds, *Cultures in Conflict*, 199.

51. Sir Richard Whitbourne, *A Discourse and Discovery of New-found-land, with many reasons to prove how worthy and benefi-ciall a Plantation may there be made, after a far better manner than now is* (London, 1620), 2–4.

52. Leslie Upton, "The Extermination of the Beothucks of Newfoundland," *Canadian Historical Review* 58 (1977): 144–53; Ingeborg Marshall, *A History and Ethnography of the Beothuk* (Montreal and Kingston, 1996), 158–9.

53. See especially Ingeborg Marshall and Alan G. Macpherson, "William Eppes Cormack (1796–1868): The Later Years," *Newfoundland and Labrador Studies* 32, 1 (Spring 2017). Cormack, an adventurer and explorer, founded the Boeothick Institution in an effort to find and protect the remaining "Red Indians" of Newfoundland (so named because they used red ochre as body paint and on their cultural artifacts). He took Shanawdithit into his home in September 1828, where she provided him with numerous detailed drawings and other ethnohistorical details of her culture, including language. She died of tuberculosis in a St John's hospi-tal in June of 1829. Also see George W. Brown, David M. Hayne, and Frances G. Halpenny, eds, *Dictionary of Canadian Biography (DCB)* (Toronto, 1966), VI: s.v. "Demasduwit," "Shawnadithit"; Harold Horwood, "The People Who Were Murdered for Fun," *Maclean's*, 10 Oct. 1959, 27–43; Ingeborg Constanze Luise Marshall, *The Red Ochre People* (Vancouver, 1982); Marshall, *A History and Ethnography of the Beothuk*; Upton, "The Extermination of the Beothuks of Newfoundland," 133–53.

54. John Webster Grant, *Moon of Wintertime: Missionaries and the Indians of Canada in Encounter since 1534* (Toronto, 1984), 24.

55. For example, in the *Jesuit Relations* there is a chapter devoted to the differences between Europeans and Indigenous people (44: 277–309), but little, if any, mention is made of resemblances.

56. Le Clercq, *Nouvelle Relation*, 379–81.

57. Thwaites, ed., *Jesuit Relations*, 3: 91. Although Biard was speak-ing about the Mi'kmaq, this was reported for other Indigenous

societies as well. For example, see George Henry Loskiel, *History of the Missions of the United Brethren among the Indians in North America*, tr. C.I. LaTrobe (London, 1794), 132; Nicolas Perrot (1644–1718), *Mémoire sur les moeurs, coustumes et religion des sauvages de l'Amérique Septentrionale*, ed. J. Tailhan (Leipzig and Paris, 1864; Johnson Reprint, 1968), 78.

Chapter 4

1. H.P. Biggar, ed., *The Voyages of Jacques Cartier* (Ottawa, 1924), 61–2. For an Indigenous view of "an adventurer called Jacques Cartier" on the St Lawrence, see Assiniwi, *Histoire des Indiens du haut et du bas Canada*, 2: 29–81. See also Ramsay Cook, ed., *The Voyages of Jacques Cartier* (Toronto, 1993).

2. Reverend Silas Tertius Rand, "The Dream of the White Robe and the Floating Island," *Legends of the Micmacs* (New York and London, 1894). Silas Tertius Rand (1810–89) was a Nova Scotia Baptist missionary, linguist, and folklore collector who devoted his life to the Mi'kmaw. Rand collected this visionary tale from Mi'kmaw Elder Josiah Jeremy on 26 September 1869.

3. The generally accepted version of the origin of the name "Canada" is that it derived from the Iroquoian "ka-na-ta," meaning village. A good argument can be made, however, that it comes from the Innu "ka-na-dun," meaning clean land. During the sixteenth century, the term "Canadian" referred to the people of the North Shore, today's Innu, closely related to Cree and speaking a variation of the same language. These people were among the first trading partners of the French, which the Haudenosaunee people were not. Indigenous languages, besides being complex, used a wider variety of sounds and ways of making sounds than did European languages. As a result, during the early days of contact, it was simpler for an Indigenous person to learn a European language than for a European to learn an Indigenous one.

4. Olive Patricia Dickason, "Concepts of Sovereignty at the Time of First Contacts," in L.C. Green and Dickason, *The Law of Nations and the New World* (Edmonton, 1989), 223–4.

5. François de Belleforest and Sebastian Münster, *La Cosmographie universelle de tout le monde . . .*, 2 vols (Paris, 1575), 2: 2190–2.

6. Christopher Carlile's report in Richard Hakluyt, *The Principal Navigations, Voyages, Traffiques and Discoveries of the English Nation*, 12 vols (Glasgow, 1903–5), 8: 145–6; Pierre-François-Xavier de Charlevoix, *Histoire et description générale de la Nouvelle France*, 3 vols (Paris, 1744), 1: 21; Francis Assikinack, "Legends and Traditions of the Odahwah Indians," *Canadian Journal of Industry, Science, and Art* new ser. 3 (1858): 117–18; Dulhut à Frontenac, 5 avril 1679, AN, Col., C11E, 16: 2. For the restriction of movement, see Gabriel Sagard, *The Long Journey to the Country of the Hurons*, ed. and trans. G.M. Wrong (Toronto, 1939), 99.

7. Biggar, ed., *Voyages of Cartier*, 264; H.P. Biggar, ed., *A Collection of Documents Relating to Jacques Cartier and the Sieur de Roberval* (Ottawa, 1930), 463.

8. Marcel Trudel, *Histoire de la Nouvelle-France I: Les vaines tentatives, 1524–1603* (Montreal, 1963), 151–75; Antoine de Montchrestien, *Traicté de l'oeconomie politique . . .* (Paris, 1889 [1615]), S.l., s.d., 214.

9. Belleforest and Münster, *La Cosmographie*, 2: 2190–2.

10. Thwaites, ed., *Jesuit Relations*, 1: 105.

11. Bruce G. Trigger, *Natives and Newcomers: Canada's "Heroic Age" Reconsidered* (Montreal and Kingston, 1985), 146. In general, I am following Trigger, who discusses the question of the Laurentian Iroquoians in detail, 144–8.

12. Trigger, *Natives and Newcomers*, 96–100, 105–8.

13. Biggar, ed., *Voyages of Cartier*, 177–8. See also Trigger, *Natives and Newcomers*, 137, 147. Although Cartier's is a second-hand account and should therefore be treated with caution, there is archaeological evidence of large-scale warfare, as Trigger points out.

14. Roland Tremblay, "Regards sur le passé: réflexions sur l'identité des habitants de la vallée du Saint-Laurent au XVIe siècle," *Recherches amérindiennes au Québec* 29, 1 (1999): 41–52.

15. Trigger, *Natives and Newcomers*, 106–8. See also J.B. Jamieson, "Trade and Warfare: Disappearance of the St. Lawrence Iroquoians," *Man in the Northeast* 39 (1990): 79–86. Jamieson argues that the dynamics of the "St Lawrence Iroquois" disappearance had nothing to do with European trade.

16. Bailey, *The Conflict of European and Eastern Algonkian Cultures*, xviii.

17. John Witthoft, "Archaeology as a Key to the Colonial Fur Trade," in *Aspects of the Fur Trade* (St Paul, Minn., 1967), 57. John M. Cooper describes early trapping techniques in *Snares, Deadfalls, and Other Traps of the Northern Algonquians and Northern Athapaskans* (Washington, 1938).

18. Henry P. Biggar, ed., *The Works of Samuel de Champlain*, 6 vols (Toronto, 1922–36), 2: 96.

19. Biggar, ed., *Voyages of Cartier*, 76.

20. Charles A. Martijn, "Innu (Montagnais) in Newfoundland," in William Cowan, ed., *Papers of the Twenty-first Algonquian Conference* (Ottawa, 1990), 227–64.

21. Champlain was entering into an alliance according to Indigenous ritual, by which, in effect, the council was the treaty. The French had developed this practice a century earlier in Brazil. Biggar, ed., *Works of Champlain*, 1: 98–102.

22. Bruce G. Trigger, *Indians and the Heroic Age of New France* (Ottawa, 1970), 10–11.

23. See, for example, Bruce G. Trigger, "Champlain Judged by His Indian Policy: A Different View of Early Canadian History," *Anthropologica* 13 (1971): 94–100. This was a special issue devoted to essays in honour of anthropologist Diamond Jenness.

24. Thwaites, ed.,*Jesuit Relations*, 6: 7–19; Marcel Trudel, *Histoire de la Nouvelle France III: La seigneurie des Cent-Associés, 1627–1663* (Montreal, 1979), 128.

25. Le Clercq, *First Establishment of the Faith in New France*, 1: 136. See also Marc Lescarbot, *The History of New France*, ed. W.L. Grant, 3 vols (Toronto, 1907–14), 3: 25–6; Denys, *Description and Natural History*, 447–8; Thwaites, ed., *Jesuit Relations*, 3: 81.

26. Charlevoix, *Histoire et description*, 3: 87–8.

27. J.B. Tyrrell, ed., *David Thompson's Narrative of His Explorations in Western America, 1784–1812* (Toronto, 1916), 206.

28. Claude C. Le Roy dit Bacqueville de la Potherie (1663–1736), *Histoire de l'Amérique septentrionale*, 4 vols (Paris, 1722), 3: 176–7; Lahontan, *New Voyages to North America*, 1: 82. There are reports of wasteful hunting for food as well. See, for example, Glyndwr Williams, ed., *Andrew Graham's Observations on Hudson's Bay 1767–91* (London, 1969), 154, 280.

29. Charlevoix, *Histoire et description*, 1: 126. According to popular rumour, Basque whalers had been operating off the North Atlantic coast for so long that by the time French merchants arrived in the seventeenth century, they found the First Nations people and Inuit using Basque words, and Spaniards reported that Innu and Basques were able to converse with each other. Peter Bakker, "Two Basque Loanwords in Micmac," *International Journal of American*

Linguistics 55, 2 (1989): 258–60; Bakker, "The Mysterious Link between Basque and Micmac Art," *European Review of Native American Studies* 5, 1 (1991): 21–4. An early eighteenth-century observer reported that Inuktitut resembled Basque. See also Nicolas Jérémie, *Twenty Years at York Factory, 1694–1714* (Ottawa, 1926), 17; Selma Huxley, ed., *Los vascos en el marco Atlantico Norte Siglos XVI y XVII* (San Sebastian, 1988). Basque is an agglomerative language, as are those of First Nations and Inuit.

30. Johannes de Laet, *L'Histoire du Nouveau Monde, ou Description des Indes occidentales . . .* (Leyden, 1640), 36.

31. Bernard G. Hoffman, *Cabot to Cartier* (Toronto, 1961); David Sanger, "Culture Change as an Adaptative Process in the Maine–Maritimes Region," *Arctic Anthropology* 12, 2 (1975): 60–75. A Penobscot whale hunt is described in "A True Relation of the Voyage of Captaine George Waymouth, 1605, by James Rosier," in Henry Sweetser Burrage, ed., *Early English and French Voyages, Chiefly from Hakluyt, 1534–1608* (New York, 1952), 392. Abbé J.A. Maurault (1819–70) makes the point that all the Indigenous Peoples of Acadia and New England shared a similar culture and lived in much the same manner. Maurault, *Histoire des Abenakis depuis 1605 jusqu'ànos jours* (Sorel, Que., 1866), 9; see also Ruth Holmes Whitehead, *The Old Man Told Us: Excerpts from Micmac History 1500–1950* (Halifax, 1991).

32. Thwaites, ed., *Jesuit Relations*, 47: 223; Denys, *Description and Natural History*, 196; D.B. Quinn, ed., *New American World: A Documentary History of North America to 1612*, 5 vols (New York, 1979), 3: 348; Lescarbot, *History of New France*, 2: 309.

33. "Mi'kmaq" is widely accepted as meaning "allies" (Jenness, *Indians of Canada*, 267), although this is not entirely certain. The term the Mi'kmaq used for themselves was "El'nu," "true men." They were probably the Toudamans of Cartier and were certainly the Souriquois of Lescarbot; they were also called Taranteens, a reference to their trading proclivities. Wuastukwiuk (Maliseets) were known to Champlain and the early Jesuits as Etchemin or Eteminquois. The language of the Mi'kmaq shares certain characteristics with Cree, the most widespread of the Algonquian group, as well as with Arapaho of the central Plains.

34. Lescarbot, *History of New France*, 3: 312–13, 358–9.

35. Library and Archives Canada (LAC), AC, C11B 10:4–5, lettre de Joseph de Monbeton de Brouillan dit Saint-Ovide (governor of Île Royale 1718–39), le 13 sept. 1727 en délibération du conseil, le 17 fév. 1728. Similar episodes occurred in the Caribbean. See Gullick, *Myths of a Minority*, 25.

36. Ellice B. Gonzalez, *Changing Economic Role for Micmac Men and Women: An Ethnohistorical Analysis* (Ottawa, 1981), 63, 87–8.

37. For more detail, see the Olive Patricia Dickason article, on which this section is based: "Amerindians between French and English in Nova Scotia, 1713–1763," *American Indian Culture and Research Journal* 20, 4 (1986): 31–56.

38. "Les Sauvages qui seront amenés à la foi et en feront profession seront censés et réputés naturels français, quand bon leur semblera, et y acquérir, tester, succéder et accepter donations et legs, tous ainsi que les vrais régnicoles et originaires français, sans être tenus de prendre aucune lettre de déclaration ni de naturalité." *Edits, ordonnances royaux, déclarations et arrêts du Conseil d'état du roi concernant le Canada*, 3 vols (Quebec, 1854–6), 1: 10.

39. *Collection de manuscrits contenant lettres, mémoires et autres documents historiques relatifs à la Nouvelle-France*, 4 vols (Quebec, 1883–5), 1: 175, Instructions pour le Sieur de Courcelle au sujet des indiens. See also Dickason, "Louisbourg and the Indians," 38, 109–25.

40. In 1657, the French geographer Nicolas Sanson published a small atlas of North Americaen titled, *L'Amérique en plusieurs cartes et en divers traittes de geographie et d'histoire*. In his capacity of Géographe ordinaire du Roy, Sanson had access to the best sources of information, including the memoirs, correspondence, and inventories of the French marine service. In the middle of the seventeenth century, this collection included the Jesuit Relations, and the journals of Champlain and Gabriel Sagard. From these sources Sanson drew a map of northeastern North America entitled: Le Canada, ou Nouvelle France, &tc, Tirée de divers Relations des Francois, Anglois, et Hollandois &tc. See, for example, Harris, ed., *Historical Atlas*, 1: plates 34 and 35. Nicolas Sanson d'Abbeville, "Le Canada, ou Nouvelle France, &tc," Bibliothèque Nationale, Section des Cartes et Plans, Collection d'Anville, Ge. DD 2987 no. 8547; "Canada," Inventaire, Plans, Cartes, Desseins, et Descriptions, AN, Marine, 1 JJ, 2: 2; Nicolas Sanson d'Abbeville, *L'Amérique en plusieurs cartes et en divers traittes de geographie, et d'histoire* (Paris, 1657).

41. *Collection de documents inédits sur le Canada et l'Amérique publiées par le Canada Français*, 3 vols (Québec, 1888–90), 3: 196.

42. Similarly, when France was defeated in 1760, southern nations refused to recognize the British takeover, as they had never given up their lands. See Jack M. Sosin, *Whitehall and the Wilderness* (Lincoln, Neb., 1961), 66.

43. "Les sauvages sont peu de chose, étant nos alliées, mais pourraient devenir quelque chose de considérable, étant nos ennemis." (LAC, AC, C11B 4:251–6, 17 nov. 1719.)

44. The term "Acadia" has long been attributed to the explorer Giovanni da Verrazzano, who used the word "Arcadian"—Greek for utopia or idyllic place—to describe a section of the Atlantic coast of what is now Virginia and Maryland on the 1548 Gastaldo map. It seems more etymologically and geographically likely that the term comes from the Mi'kmaq "suffixe'katiq," which means place of abundance. William F.E. Morley, "Giovanni da Verrazzano," *DCB* (Toronto: University of Toronto Press, 1967), 1: 657–61.

45. LAC, AC, C11B 12:37v, Saint-Ovide à Maurepas, 25 nov. 1731. See also *Account of the Customs and Manners*, 85, "Letter from Mons. de la Varenne." A major work on French missionary activity in Acadia is Lucien Campeau's compilation of documents, *Monumenta Novae Franciae I: La première mission d'Acadie (1602–1616)* (Quebec, 1967). A second volume, *Monumenta Novae Franciae II: Etablissement à Québec (1616–1634)*, appeared in 1979.

46. Thomas Pichon, *Lettres et Mémoires pour servir à l'histoire Naturelle, Civile et Politique du Cap Breton* (La Haye and London, 1760; Johnson Reprint, 1966), 101–2.

47. Thomas B. Akins, ed., *Selections from the Public Documents of the Province of Nova Scotia* (Halifax, 1869), 178–9, Cornwallis to Captain Sylvanus Cobb, 13 Jan. 1749.

48. LAC, AC, C11B, vol. 31:63, Raymond to minister, 19 nov. 1751. On French concern that the Mi'kmaq (as well as their other allies) had no causes for complaint about gift distributions, see LAC, AC, B, vol. 45/2:260–6 [122–9]; ibid., 267–73 [129–34].

49. Dickason, "Louisbourg and the Indians," 111–14.

50. Thwaites, ed., *Jesuit Relations*, 1: 177. There were also reports of them having lived to great ages in past times. Denys told of one Mi'kmaw said to have reached the age of 160 years. He attributed such long life to the Mi'kmaq habit of drinking "only good soup, very fat." He also reported that some Mi'kmaq could recite their genealogies back for 20 generations. Denys, *Description and Natural History*, 400, 403, 410.

51. LAC, AC, C11A, vol. 122:13, 30 sept. 1705.

52. Later, they were referred to as "Canibas," wolves. "Waubun" means both "east" and "dawn" in Anishinaabe-mowin.

53. This section is a revision and extension of Olive Patricia Dickason, "The French and the Abenaki: A Study in Frontier Politics," *Vermont History* 58, 2 (1990): 82–98.

54. Dean R. Snow, *The Archaeology of New England* (New York, 1980), 38; Thwaites, ed., *Jesuit Relations*, 3: 111.

55. Marc Lescarbot, "La Deffaite des Sauvages Armouchiquois," *History of New France*, 3: 497–508.

56. In 1613, it was reported that there "has always been war . . . between the Souriquois [Mi'kmaq] and Iroquois." Thwaites, ed., *Jesuit Relations*, 1: 105.

57. Ibid., 3: 71.

58. Biggar, ed., *Works of Champlain*, 1: 103, 109; 5: 313–16; P.-André Sévigny, *Les Abénaquis habitat et migrations (17e et 18e siècles)* (Montréal, 1976), 64–5.

59. Thwaites, ed., *Jesuit Relations*, 12: 187; 34: 57; 38: 41.

60. Gordon M. Day, "Western Abenaki," in Bruce G. Trigger, ed., *Handbook of North American Indians*, 15: *Northeast* (Washington, 1978), 150. See also Thwaites, ed., *Jesuit Relations*, 24: 183–5; 36: 103.

61. Indigenous settlement patterns for 1625–1800 are mapped in Harris, ed., *Historical Atlas*, 1: plate 47.

62. The phrase is used by Gordon Day, "English–Indian Contacts in New England," *Ethnohistory* 9 (1962): 28.

63. Thomas Charland, *Histoire des Abénakis d'Odanak (1675–1937)* (Montreal, 1964), 44, 75–6; Jean Lunn, "The Illegal Fur Trade Out of New France, 1713–60," *Canadian Historical Association Annual Report* (1939): 61–76.

64. E.B. O'Callaghan and J.R. Brodhead, eds, *Documents Relative to the Colonial History of the State of New York*, 15 vols (Albany, NY, 1853–87), 9: 871, M. de Vaudreuil to the Duke of Orleans, 1716; LAC, CO 217/1:364–6, "Answer of Indians of Penobscot to the Commissioners," Apr. 1714; LAC, AC, C11B 1:340v–42, lettre de Bégon, 25 sept. 1715, dans les délibérations de Conseil; 28 mars 1716, ibid., lettre de Costebelle, 7 sept. 1715, 335–6; Pierre-François-Xavier de Charlevoix, "Mémoire sur les limites de l'Acadie," *Collection de manuscrits*, 3: 50–1.

65. *Journal of the Honorable House of Representatives of His Majesty's Province of Massachusetts-Bay in New-England* (Boston, 1744), 57, William Shirley to the General Court, 18 July 1744.

66. O'Callaghan and Brodhead, eds, *Documents*, 9: 940, "Memoir on the Present Condition of the Abenaquis, 1724."

67. "Wowurna," *Dictionary of Canadian Biography Online*, http://www.biographi.ca/en/bio/wowurna_2E.html.

68. Dickason, "Louisbourg and the Indians," 66–9. See also the warning of Jesuit Pierre de La Chasse (1670–1749) concerning the Wabanaki reaction to such a proposition in *Collection de manuscrits*, 3: 51, Memoire sur les limites de l'Acadie.

69. LAC, AC, B, vol. 47:1263–4 [279], 16 juin 1724; ibid., C11B, vol. 7, 191–193v, 10 déc. 1725.

70. This follows my "Louisbourg and the Indians," with additions and some changes.

71. O'Callaghan and Brodhead, eds, *Documents*, 4: 206–11, London Documents 10, "Mr. Nelson's Memorial about the state of the Northern Colonies in America," 24 Sept. 1696.

72. Ibid. The English quickly followed suit. One of the most famous of these episodes occurred in 1710, when four Haudenosaunee sachems were brought to London and presented to Queen Anne as kings of the League of Five Nations. See John G. Garratt, *The Four Indian Kings* (Ottawa, 1985).

73. LAC, AC, B, vol. 57/1:639 [139], Maurepas à Beauharnois, 8 avr. 1732. See also O'Callaghan and Brodhead, eds, *Documents*, 4: 206–11.

74. O'Callaghan and Brodhead, eds, *Documents*, 9: 902, Vaudreuil to Governor William Burnett, 11 July 1721.

75. Dickason, "Louisbourg and the Indians," 111–14; Victor Morin, *Les médailles décernées aux Indiens: Etude historique et numismatique des colonisations européennes en Amérique* (Ottawa, 1916).

76. O'Callaghan and Brodhead, eds, *Documents*, 9: 948–9, Abstract of M. de Vaudreuil's Despatch; ibid., 939–40, Memoir on the Present Condition of the Abenaquis, 1724.

77. An overview of Indigenous contributions to the establishment of New France is that of John H. Dickinson, "Les Amérindiens et les débuts de la Nouvelle-France," *6e Convegno Internazionale di studi canadesi* (Selva di Fasano, 1985), Sezione iii, 87–108.

78. *Massachusetts Historical Society Collections*, 2nd ser. 8 (1826): 260, Eastern Indians' letter to the Governor, 27 July 1721.

79. The town had developed as a consequence of a mission founded by Sébastian Rale at Norridgewock (today's Old Point, South Madison, Maine) in 1694. Both he and Mog were killed there in 1724; see Kenneth M. Morrison, *The Embattled Northeast: The Elusive Ideal of Alliance in Abenaki–Euramerican Relations* (Berkeley, 1984), 155–93.

80. R.O. MacFarlane, "British Policy in Nova Scotia to 1760," *Canadian Historical Review* 19, 2 (1938): 160.

81. *DCB*, 3: s.v. "Atecouando." This chief is not to be confused with the earlier one of the same name, fl. 1701–26. Chiefs were referred to by their titles rather than their personal names.

82. Ibid., 3: s.v. "Nodogawerrimet."

83. "Wampum Belts," in Onondaga Nation Online, http://www.onondaganation.org/culture/wampum.

84. *Collection de manuscrits*, 2: 54, Mémoire sur les limites de l'Acadie.

Chapter 5

1. "Wendake" is the Wendat name for the territory in southern Georgian Bay that historians had till recently referred to as Huronia. See Kathryn Magee Labelle, *Dispersed but Not Destroyed: A History of the Seventeenth-Century Wendat People* (Vancouver, 2013), 1.

2. Thwaites, ed., *Jesuit Relations*, 16: 229; 39: 49. There is a possibility that Wendat people had met French earlier, perhaps in 1600. See Trigger, *Children of Aataentsic*, 1: 246. Trigger (p. 288) refers to the Omamiwinini people as the Onontchataronon. This is a Wendat exonym for Omamiwinini.

3. Archaeological evidence suggests that the Omamiwinini absorbed some of the St Lawrence Iroquoians at some point in the sixteenth century. This helps to explain the strong bond between the Wendat Confederacy and the Omamiwinini of the Ottawa Valley. See James F. Pendergast, "The Ottawa River Algonquin Bands in a St. Lawrence Iroquoian Context," *Canadian Journal of Archaeology* 23, 1–2 (1999): 63–136.

4. Denys Delâge, *Le pays renversé: Amérindiens et européens en Amérique du nord-est, 1600-1664* (Quebec, 1985), 339–47; Carl Berger, *The Writing of Canadian History*, 2nd edn (Toronto, 1986), 101; Harold Adams Innis, *The Fur Trade in Canada: An Introduction to Canadian Economic History*, rev. edn (Toronto, 1956), 15–17; Richard White, *The Middle Ground: Indians,*

Empires, and Republics in the Great Lakes Region, 1670–1815. (Cambridge, 1991), 105.

5. Trigger, *Children of Aataentsic,* 1: 219.

6. Ibid., 1: 30; Thwaites, ed., *Jesuit Relations,* 16: 227–9.

7. Trigger, *Children of Aataentsic,* 1: 244; Thwaites, ed., *Jesuit Relations,* 16: 227–9. Wendat settlement patterns and missions are mapped in Harris, ed., *Historical Atlas,* 1: plate 34. A good, short overview of the Wendat Confederacy is Conrad E. Heidenreich, "Huron," in Trigger, ed., *Handbook of North American Indians, 15: Northeast,* 368–88.

8. Trigger, *Children of Aataentsic,* 1: 30.

9. Thwaites, ed., *Jesuit Relations,* 18: 103–7. Jesuit historian Lucien Campeau challenges this, on the grounds that the Indigenous tradition of tolerance allowed Christians and non-Christians to live in peace. Campeau, *La Mission des Jésuites chez les Hurons 1634–1650* (Montreal, 1987), 276–8.

10. Barbara Alice Mann, "'Are You Delusional?': Kandiaronk on Christianity," in B.A. Mann, *Native American Speakers of the Eastern Woodlands: Selected Speeches and Critical Analyses* (Westport, Conn., 2001).

11. Champigny au ministre, 18 août 1696, AN, C11A, 14: 183v; Relation de ce qui s'est passé de plus remarquable au Canada, 1697, AN, C11A, 15: 13v; Paroles des Outaouais adressées à Callière, 21 juin 1700, AN, C11A, 18: 78–78v; Réponse de Callière, 27 juin 1700, AN, C11A, 18: 79–80; Réponse de Callière, 27 juin 1700, AN, C11A, 18: 79–80.

12. Thwaites, ed., *Jesuit Relations,* 52: 179; Henry Warner Bowden, *American Indians and Christian Missions* (Chicago, 1981), 88; Trigger, *Natives and Newcomers,* 255.

13. Thwaites, ed., *Jesuit Relations,* 16: 33; Trigger, *Children of Aataentsic,* 2: 547, 700; Trigger, *Natives and Newcomers,* 254–5; Bowden, *American Indians and Christian Missions,* 87–8. Converts denied commercial reasons for their actions (Thwaites, ed., *Jesuit Relations,* 20: 288). Some saw Indigenous people as being capable of feigning acceptance of Christianity if they thought it was in their interest to do so. Another explanation for such behaviour would be that the Indigenous people saw nothing wrong in following the new practices when with whites, and then reverting to their own when in their own encampments. In other cases, evangelization had the effect of giving new life and new strength to Indigenous religions. John S. Long makes this point in connection with the Mushkegowuk, Inyu, and Innu of James Bay, in "Manitu, Power, Books and Wiihtikow: Some Factors in the Adoption of Christianity by Nineteenth-Century Western James Bay Cree," *Native Studies Review* 3, 1 (1987): 1–30. Even as the missionaries saw elements in Indigenous spiritual beliefs that were similar to their own, so Indigenous people identified Christian spiritual beings with those of their own beliefs. For the Innu, the Christian God resembled their Atahocan. In their view, there was plenty of room in the cosmos for both sets of spiritual beings, each with its own requirements at the appropriate times and places. Thwaites, ed., *Jesuit Relations,* 5: 153–5; Jean-Guy Goulet, "Religious Dualism among Athapaskan Catholics," *Canadian Journal of Anthropology* 3, 1 (1982): 1–18.

14. Trigger, *Children of Aataentsic,* 1: 220–1. For sixteenth-century patterns of trade and warfare in the St Lawrence Valley, see Harris, ed., *Historical Atlas,* 1: plate 33.

15. Sagard, *Histoire du Canada,* 1: 170.

16. Thwaites, ed., *Jesuit Relations,* 20: 221; 22: 179, 307, concerning the number of guns among the warriors of the Wendat Confederacy; Elizabeth Tooker, "The Iroquois Defeat of the Huron: A Review

of Causes," *Pennsylvania Archaeologist* 33, 1–2 (1963): 115–23. On the reasons why the Haudenosaunee adopted firearms despite their inefficiency at that period, see Thomas B. Abler, "European Technology and the Art of War in Iroquoia," in Tkaczuk and Vivian, eds, *Cultures in Conflict,* 173–282.

17. There were three Wendat chiefs of that name recorded during the seventeenth century. The other two were both baptized: Jean Baptiste Atironta (d. 1650) and Pierre Atironta (d. 1672). See *DCB,* vol. 1.

18. Kiche (great) and sipi (river) refers to a specific group of Anishinaabe people, under the leadership of Tessouat. They were closely related in language and culture to the Omamiwinini. Allumette Island is today's Morrison Island, near Pembroke, Ontario.

19. Of two other known chiefs with the name Tessouat, one met Champlain in 1603; his successor, also known as Le Borgne de l'Isle, died in 1636. See *DCB,* vol. 1.

20. Trigger gives a detailed account of Champlain's dealings with Tessouat in *Children of Aataentsic,* 1: 281–6.

21. Antonio de Ulloa (1716–95), *A Voyage to South America . . . ,* 2 vols, tr. John Adams (London, 1806), 2: 376–7.

22. Trigger, *Children of Aataentsic,* 1: 311. Biggar's identification of the village as Onondaga has been discounted by Trigger.

23. The Chonnonton were the most populous of the nations living in the region to the south of the Wendat Territory, between the Anishinaabe villages to the west and the Haudenosaunee villages to the east. Another non-aligned nation in this region, the Onguiaahra, gave their name to the region we now call Niagara. See William C. Noble, "The Neutral Confederacy," http://www.thecanadianencyclopedia.ca/en/article/neutral/.

24. Thwaites, ed., *Jesuit Relations,* 21: 203–5.

25. Ibid., 11: 207–9.

26. Trigger, *Children of Aataentsic,* 2: 473–6. Brûlé had apparently retained more of his French connections than previously believed. See Campeau, *Monumenta Novae Franciae II,* 808–9.

27. A description of the beaver, its living habits, how it was hunted, and how its pelts were processed for the fur trade is in Charlevoix, *Histoire et description,* 3: 94–107. See also Tyrrell, ed., *David Thompson's Narrative,* 1–4, 10–11, 198–200; Innis, *The Fur Trade in Canada.* The Wendat trade is examined in detail in Heidenreich, *Huronia,* 242–99.

28. Philippe Jacquin, *Les indiens blancs* (Paris, 1989).

29. Thwaites, ed., *Jesuit Relations,* 1: 103–7.

30. Charlevoix describes the clash in *Histoire et description,* 1: 150–2.

31. Thwaites, ed., *Jesuit Relations,* 5: 263–5.

32. Ibid., 10: 77.

33. Biggar, ed., *Works of Champlain,* 1: 283–7.

34. Ibid., 142. See also Trigger, *Children of Aataentsic,* 1: 220.

35. In Acadia there had been confrontations between Jesuits and traders. See Lescarbot, *History of New France,* 3: 48, 53.

36. The first missionary in Canada was the secular priest Jessé Fléché (d. ?1611), who spent a few weeks in Acadia in 1610, during which he baptized the paramount Mi'kmaw chief Membertou, his family, and members of his band, for a total of 21 individuals. He was followed by the Jesuits, who arrived the following year, in 1611, and were incensed to find a Mi'kmaq with eight wives who considered himself a Christian. (Thwaites, ed., *Jesuit Relations,* 1: 109–13.) The first two Jesuits to work in Canada were Pierre Biard (1567–1622) and Enemond Massé (1575–1646). The latter, trying to live Indigenous-style during the winter of 1611–12, lost so much weight that his host, Louis Membertou (son of the famous chief), feared he would die and that the French would

accuse the Mi'kmaq of having killed him. (Lescarbot, *History of New France*, 3: 56.)

37. The Recollects were naturally unhappy about this. For their views on the Jesuits, see Pierre Margry, *Découvertes et établissements dans l'ouest et dans le sud de l'Amérique septentrionale (1614–1754)*, 6 vols (Paris, 1976–86), 1: 5–15.

38. *Treizième tome du Mercure François* (Paris, 1629), 32; Thwaites, ed., *Jesuit Relations*, 6: 25; Lescarbot, *History of New France*, 1: 184. Also Dickason, *Myth of the Savage*, 251.

39. Sagard's dictionary is reproduced in Sagard, *Histoire du Canada*, vol. 4. On Le Caron, see Le Clercq, *First Establishment of the Faith in New France*, 1: 248–50. Brébeuf's translation into Wendat of Ledesma's catechism is reproduced by Margaret Vincent Tehariolina, *La nation huronne, son histoire, sa culture, son esprit* (Quebec, 1984), 436–50.

40. Thwaites, ed., *Jesuit Relations*, 11: 1472.

41. Sagard, *Histoire du Canada*, 1: 165. ". . . le sang me gelle quand je r'entre en moymesme, &considere qu'ils faisoient plus d'estat d'un castor que du salut d'un peuple . . . ." An article denying the Jesuit involvement in the fur trade is that of Patrick J. Lomasney, "The Canadian Jesuits and the Fur Trade," *Mid-America* 15 (new ser., vol. 4), 3 (1933): 139–50.

42. Thwaites, ed., *Jesuit Relations*, 5: 83; 9: 171–3; 6: 80–2.

43. Cornelius J. Jaenen, *Friend and Foe: Aspects of French–Amerindian Cultural Contact in the Sixteenth and Seventeenth Centuries* (Toronto, 1976), 75.

44. Sioui, *Les Wendats*, 55.

45. This reached such proportions that the Wuastukwiuk were called Maliseet as they were reputed to be descendants of Malouins: Jacquin, *Les Indiens blancs*, 32. This comes from Maurault, *Histoire des Abenakis*, 6 n3. Maurault claimed the Wabanaki called the mixed-bloods "Maliseets" because most of the fathers came from St Malo.

46. Thwaites, ed., *Jesuit Relations*, 5: 211; 10: 26.

47. Le Clercq, *First Establishment of the Faith in New France*, 1: 74–7, "Brief of Pope Paul V for the Canada mission, 1618."

48. Dickason, *Myth of the Savage*, 144–7; Biggar, ed., *Works of Champlain*, 2: 48. Le Jeune shared this belief: "Their natural color is like that of those French beggars who are half-roasted in the Sun, and I have no doubt the Savages would be very white if they were well covered." (Thwaites, ed., *Jesuit Relations*, 5: 23.) Some even extended this belief to Africans: "The children of this country are born white, and change their colour in two days to a perfect black." E.G. Ravenstein, ed., *The Strange Adventures of Andrew Battell of Leigh in Angola and the Adjoining Regions* (London, 1901; reprint, 1967), 49.

49. Thwaites, ed., *Jesuit Relations*, 28: 49–65.

50. Ibid., 21: 45.

51. Sagard, *Histoire du Canada*, 1: 166. See also Daniel A. Scalberg, "Seventeenth and Early Eighteenth-Century Perceptions of Coureurs-de-Bois Religious Life," *Proceedings of the Annual Meeting of the Western Society for French History* 17 (1990): 82–95.

52. Bruce G. Trigger, "Early Iroquoian Contacts with Europeans," in Trigger, ed., *Handbook of North American Indians, 15: Northeast*, 352; Karl H. Schlesier, "Epidemics and Indian Middlemen: Rethinking the Wars of the Iroquois, 1609–1653," *Ethnohistory* 23, 2 (1976): 129–45.

53. Delâge, *Le pays renversé*, 106.

54. *DCB*, 1: s.v. "Oumasasikweie."

55. Biggar, ed., *Works of Champlain*, 6: 379.

56. Thwaites, ed., *Jesuit Relations*, 27: 89–91; 28: 47.

57. See Chapter 6.

58. Guy Laflèche, *Les saints martyrs canadiens*, 2 vols (Québec, 1988), 1: 32. In an attempt to curb Haudenosaunee attacks, which were stepped up during the 1640s, French soldiers sometimes reinforced the warriors accompanying the flotillas. This was done in 1644 and again in 1645, when 60 canoes and 300 Wendat paddlers came to Trois-Rivières (Jacquin, *Les indiens blancs*, 251 n37). Such commerce brought prosperity to everyone involved; at its height, the Wendat were reported to account for 50 per cent of the French fur trade. Despite the Haudenosaunee blockade, furs valued at 200,000 to 300,000 livres were shipped to France. W.J. Eccles, *France in America* (New York, 1972).

59. Thwaites, ed., *Jesuit Relations*, 32: 99.

60. José António Brandão, *Your Fyre Shall Burn No More* (Lincoln, Neb., 1998), 98–9. See also Roland Viau, *Enfants du néant et mangeurs d'âmes: guerre, culture et sociétés en Iroquoisie ancienne* (Montreal, 1997), 40–4.

61. The two were Brébeuf and Gabriel Lalement (1610–49). They were canonized in 1930, along with six others, all Jesuits except Jean de la Lande, a donné. See Laflèche, *Les saints martyrs*, 1: 33, 299.

62. *DCB*, 3: s.v. "Orontony."

63. Delâge, "Les Iroquois chrétiens," 64.

64. See Eccles, *Canadian Frontier*, ch. 6.

65. Thwaites, ed., *Jesuit Relations*, 40: 215.

66. For a study of the factors that led to the 1701 peace, see Havard, *La grande paix*.

67. Much of the material for this section has been drawn from Dickason, "Three Worlds, One Focus," 51–78.

68. On the prehistoric trade of the Wendat Confederacy, see Trigger, *Children of Aataentsic*, 1: 176–86; on its development after the arrival of the French, ibid., 2: 608–12.

69. Thwaites, ed., *Jesuit Relations*, 1: 101.

70. Five northern routes, some of them said to be ancient, were described by the Jesuits, with the comment that they were "more difficult to travel than the high road from Paris to Orleans." The fifth route was for peoples north and west of Lake Superior. Ibid., 44: 239–45; 56: 203. See also Toby Morantz, "The Fur Trade and the Cree of James Bay," in Carol M. Judd and A.J. Ray, eds, *Old Trails and New Directions: Papers of the Third North American Fur Trade Conference* (Toronto, 1980), 23–4.

71. Kehoe, *The Ghost Dance*, 115.

72. "Zachariah Gillam," *Dictionary of Canadian Biography Online*, http://www.biographi.ca/en/bio/gillam_zachariah_1E.html.

73. Denys, *Description and Natural History*, 440–1.

74. Missionaries and traders soon noted how much the northerners prized tobacco. Thwaites, ed., *Jesuit Relations*, 56: 189.

75. Christopher L. Miller and George R. Hamell, "A New Perspective on Indian–White Contact: Cultural Symbols and Colonial Trade," *Journal of American History* 73, 3 (1986): 311–28.

76. Arthur Dobbs, *An Account of the Countries adjoining to Hudson's Bay* (London, 1744; reprint New York, 1967), 59.

77. Peter A. Cumming and Neil H. Mickenberg, eds, *Native Rights in Canada* (Toronto, 1972), 142.

78. HBC Official London Correspondence Book Outwards 1679–1741, A.6/1.6, HBC Archives; E.E. Rich, ed., *Letters Outward 1679–1694* (Toronto, 1948), 9; Cumming and Mickenberg, eds, *Native Rights in Canada*, 142 n36; Daniel Francis and Toby Morantz, *Partners in Furs: A History of the Fur Trade in Eastern James Bay 1600–1870* (Montreal, 1983), 23. These instructions were repeated to Nixon's successor, Henry Sergeant, in 1683. See A.6/1:30v, HBC Archives.

79. These were probably oral agreements along the French/Anishinaabe model. Francis and Morantz, *Partners in Furs*, 213–24; John Oldmixon, *The History of Hudson's-Bay, Containing an Account of its Discovery and Settlement, the Progress of It, and the Present State; of the Indians, Trade and Everything Else Relating to It*, in J.B. Tyrrell, ed., *Documents Relating to the Early History of Hudson Bay* (Toronto, 1931), 400–1; Edwin Thompson Denig, *Five Indian Tribes of the Upper Missouri*, ed. John C. Ewers (Norman, Okla., 1961), 112. For a discussion of gift-giving in the context of the fur trade, see Mary Black-Rogers, "Varieties of 'Starving': Semantics and Survival in the Subarctic Fur Trade, 1750–1850," *Ethnohistory* 33, 4 (1986): 368; Bruce M. White, "'Give Us a Little Milk': The Social and Cultural Significance of Gift Giving in the Lake Superior Fur Trade," in T.C. Buckley, ed., *Rendezvous: Selected Papers of the Fur Trade Conference 1981* (St Paul, Minn., 1984), 187. See also Arthur J. Ray and Donald Freeman, *"Give Us Good Measure": An Economic Analysis of Relations between the Indians and the Hudson's Bay Company before 1763* (Toronto, 1978), 60–1; E.E. Rich, "Trade Habits and Economic Motivation among the Indians of North America," *Canadian Journal of Economics and Political Science* 26 (1960): 35–53 (reprinted, with illustrations added, under the title "The Indian Traders" in *The Beaver* Outfit 301 [1970]: 5–20); A. Rotstein, "Trade and Politics: An Institutional Approach," *Western Canadian Journal of Anthropology* 3, 1 (1972): 1–28.

80. The French had earlier experienced difficulty in this regard. Galinée reported that even in his day (the second half of the seventeenth century) they had not yet mastered the techniques of fishing in the northern rivers. Margry, *Découvertes et établissements*, 1: 163–4.

81. Carol M. Judd, "Sakie, Esquawenoe, and the Foundation of a Dual-Native Tradition at Moose Factory," in Shepard Krech iii, ed., *The Subarctic Fur Trade* (Vancouver, 1984), 87.

82. Hearne, *Journey*, 185 n. For a similar reaction on the part of the Inuit at a later period, see Hall, *Arctic Researches*, 297. Jesuits reported in 1646 that when Indigenous people killed animals, "they eat the meat of these without bread, without salt, and without other sauce than the appetite." (Thwaites, ed., *Jesuit Relations*, 29: 75.)

83. HBC Archives, 1742, B.135/a/11:67, Moose Fort Journal, 1742, cited by Francis and Morantz, *Partners in Furs*, 58–9.

84. Hearne, *Journey*, 306.

85. Ibid., 85–6 n.

86. Dobbs, *An Account*, 42.

87. Apparently the people of the Wendat Confederacy had a more restrained reaction and refused to eat salted foods because they said they smelled bad. See Sagard, *Long Journey*, 118. The belief developed among Indigenous people that the reason Europeans were able to resist their witchcraft was because they ate so much salt.

88. The French had long since learned the truth of this. Gabriel Sagard said the French should never go into the woods without an experienced guide, as even such travel aids as a compass could fail. He told of Étienne Brûlé, an experienced coureur de bois, who had once lost his way and mistakenly wandered into a Haudenosaunee village, where he escaped torture and death only by a lucky happenstance. Sagard, *Histoire du Canada*, 1: 466–7; 2: 429–30. Champlain had got lost in Wendake. See Trudel, *Histoire de la Nouvelle France II*, 221. A young Indigenous lad, raised by the French and christened Bonaventure, died as a result of being lost in the woods following an accident. (Thwaites, ed., *Jesuit Relations*, 9: 221.) There has never been a study of the economic value of Indigenous contributions to European voyages of discovery in the interior of the Americas, if such would be possible. It must have been considerable.

89. John Tanner, *The Captivity and Adventures of John Tanner During Thirty Years' Residence among the Indians in the Interior* (New York, 1830). See also Jennifer S.H. Brown, *Strangers in Blood: Fur Trade Company Families in Indian Country* (Vancouver, 1980); Sylvia Van Kirk, *Many Tender Ties: Women in Fur Trade Society, 1670–1870* (Norman, Okla., 1983).

90. Sylvia Van Kirk, "Thanadelthur," *The Beaver* Outfit 304, 4 (1974): 40–5; Keith Crowe, *A History of the Original Peoples of Northern Canada* (Montreal and Kingston, 1991), 76–8. James Houston, *Running West* (Toronto, 1989), is a historical novel detailing Thanadelthur's life. Oral traditions concerning Thanadelthur are recorded in Julie Cruikshank, *Reading Voices: Dändhâts'ledenintth'é=Oral and Written Interpretations of the Yukon's Past* (Vancouver, 1991).

91. Actually, the French had encountered bison in "Florida" much earlier, as attested by an engraving of bison-hunting in André Thevet's *La Cosmographie Universelle*, 2 vols (Paris, 1575), 2: 1007v.

92. When Hearne returned from his voyage, his guides Matonabbee and Idotlyazee provided a map of the lands they had visited. June Helm's study of the chart revealed how it co-ordinates with modern maps. See Helm, "Matonabbee's Map," *Arctic Anthropology* 26, 2 (1989): 28–47. For other Indigenous maps, see Harris, ed., *Historical Atlas*, 1: plate 59. Arctic explorer Sir John Franklin (1786–1847) availed himself of First Nation and Inuit sketch maps. See Charles Mair, *Through the Mackenzie Basin* (Toronto, 1908), 96–7. About 100 Inuit maps drawn on paper for explorers have survived. Among themselves, Inuit either gave verbal instructions or drew maps on sand or snow. See David F. Pelly, "How the Inuit Find Their Way in the Trackless Arctic," *Canadian Geographic* 3, 4 (1991): 58–64.

93. Trigger, *Natives and Newcomers*, 184–94. For the varying effects of the trade on northern societies and economies, see Krech iii, ed., *Subarctic Fur Trade*.

94. HBC Archives, B.135/a/11:69, cited by Francis and Morantz, *Partners in Furs*, 59.

95. HBC Archives, B.135/a/31:27v–29v, Moose Fort Journal 1758–9.

96. HBC Archives, A.6/4:86v, cited by Francis and Morantz, *Partners in Furs*, 91.

97. Eric Ross, *Beyond the River and the Bay* (Toronto, 1970), 29–31.

98. Van Kirk, *Many Tender Ties*, 102–6.

99. Perrot, *Mémoire sur les moeurs, coustumes et relligion des sauvages*, 126–8, 292–4; Thwaites, ed., *Jesuit Relations*, 55: 105–15; Margry, *Découvertes et établissements*, 1: 96–9; William W. Warren, *History of the Ojibway People* (St Paul, 1984; 1st edn 1885).

100. "Ainsy cette nation peut connoistre qu'on prétend d'en demeurer le maistre." (Margry, *Découvertes et établissements*, 1: 89, second extrait de "l'addition au mémoire de Jean Talon au Roy," 10 nov. 1670.) Voyages of exploration were usually undertaken for the purpose of territorial expansion; for example, La Vérendrye on his western voyage left a trail of lead plaques indicating that the region was claimed by France (ibid., 6: 609), as did Galinée and Dollier de Casson, whose ostensible mission was the spreading of the faith.

101. Thwaites, ed., *Jesuit Relations*, 68: 283.

102. Donald B. Smith, "Who Are the Mississauga?" *Ontario History* 67, 4 (1975): 211–23; Leroy V. Eid, "The Ojibway–Iroquois War: The War the Five Nations Did Not Win," *Ethnohistory* 17, 4 (1979): 297–324.

103. James G.E. Smith, "The Western Woods Cree: Anthropological Myth and Historical Reality," *American Ethnologist* 14 (1987): 434–48.

104. L.J. Burpee, ed., *Journals and Letters by Pierre Gaulthier de Varennes et de La Vérendrye* (Toronto, 1927), 25.

105. John S. Milloy, *The Plains Cree: Trade, Diplomacy and War, 1790–1870* (Winnipeg, 1988), 41–66, 119–20.

Chapter 6

1. R. David Edmunds and Joseph L. Peyser, *The Fox Wars: the Mesquakie Challenge to New France.* (Norman, Okla., 1993), 158–60.

2. There is an enormous body of literature on the Haudenosaunee (known to early English history as the Iroquois) wars. Besides George T. Hunt's *The Wars of the Iroquois* (Madison, Wis., 1967), see W.J. Eccles, *Canada under Louis XIV, 1663–1701* (Toronto, 1964), especially chs 7–10; Eccles, *Frontenac the Courtier Governor* (Toronto, 1959), especially chs 8–10; Francis Jennings, *The Ambiguous Iroquois Empire* (New York, 1984). A detailed account of the war to 1646 is Leo-Paul Desrosier's *Iroquoisie* (Montreal, 1947). Bruce G. Trigger deals with aspects of Haudenosaunee–Wendat conflicts in *Natives and Newcomers*. See also Keith F. Otterbein, "Why the Iroquois Won: An Analysis of Iroquois Military Tactics," *Ethnohistory* 11 (1964): 56–63; Otterbein, "Huron vs. Iroquois: A Case Study of Intertribal Warfare," *Ethnohistory* 26, 2 (1979): 141–52.

3. Daniel K. Richter, *The Ordeal of the Longhouse: The Peoples of the Iroquois League in the Era of European Colonization.* (Chapel Hill, NC, 1992), 32–8.

4. *DCB*, 1: s.v. "Pieskaret"; Bacqueville de la Potherie, *Histoire de l'Amérique septentrionale*, I: 297–303.

5. Desrosiers, *Iroquoisie*, 304.

6. Charlevoix, *Histoire et description*, 2: 160–1.

7. François Dollier de Casson, *A History of Montreal 1640–1672*, tr. and ed. Ralph Flenley (London, 1928), 131; originally published in Montreal, 1868, from a copy of a Paris manuscript brought to Canada by Louis-Joseph Papineau, leader of the 1837–8 rebellions in Lower Canada. The manuscript does not bear Dollier de Casson's name but has been attributed to him on the strength of internal evidence.

8. Ibid., 117–18, 139.

9. LAC, MG 7, 1a, 10, Collection Moreau, vol. 841:251v, d'Endemare à François de la Vie, Fort Richelieu, 2 sept. 1644.

10. Bibliothèque Nationale, Paris, Fonds Français, vol. 10204, ff. 203–4.The French became fascinated with this style of warfare and soon were to adapt it themselves. See note 14 below.

11. Thwaites, ed., *Jesuit Relations*, 28: 57.

12. Cited by William Kip, *The Early Jesuit Missions in North America* (New York, 1846), 54. These observations would be repeated almost exactly by the British in Australia during the nineteenth century as they settled in lands the Aborigines considered theirs. See, for example, Henry Reynolds, *Frontier* (Sydney and London, 1987), 3–57.

13. Thwaites, ed., *Jesuit Relations*, 33: 229–49; Trigger, *Natives and Newcomers*, 265.

14. The French called these tactics, *la petite guerre*, and they attempted to learn from them. See Thomas Auguste Le Roy de Grandmaison, *La petite guerre, ou traité du service des troupes légères en campagne* (1756).

15. John A. Dickinson, "La guerre iroquoise et la mortalité en Nouvelle-France, 1608–1666," *Revue d'histoire de l'Amérique française* 36, 1 (1982): 31–47; Trigger, "Early Iroquoian Contacts," 352.

16. LAC, AC, C11G, vol. 6:69–70v, Mémoire sur les compagnies sauvages proposées par le Sieur de La Motte envoyé à Monseigneur en 1708; ibid., C11A, vol. 122:10–42, unsigned letter from Quebec, 30 sept. 1705. On chiefs receiving commissions, see LAC, AC, C11B, vol. 23:28v, Du Quesnel to Maurepas, 19 oct. 1741; ibid., vol. 29:63v, Des Herbiers to Rouillé, 27 nov. 1750; ibid., 68, Des Herbiers to Rouillé, 6 déc. 1750.

17. O'Callaghan and Brodhead, eds, *Documents*, 9: 363.

18. Margry, *Découvertes et établissements*, 1: 141, Récit de ce qui c'est passé de plus remarquable dans le voyage de MM. Dollier et Galinée, 1669–70.

19. O'Callaghan and Brodhead, eds, *Documents*, 9: 95, Journal of Count de Frontenac's Voyage to Lake Ontario in 1673.

20. For a detailed account of this expedition and the factors leading up to it, see Eccles, *Frontenac the Courtier Governor*, 161–72.

21. Louis Armand de Lom d'Arce de Lahontan was one French officer who saw advantages in the Indigenous style of warfare: Lahontan, *Nouveaux voyages*, 1: 238–9.

22. Bacqueville de la Potherie says that 40 Haudenosaunee men were taken. *Histoire de l'Amérique septentrionale*, 1: 332–3.

23. Observations sur l'état des affaires du Canada, 18 nov. 1689, AN, C11A, 10: 321–323; Mémoire du roi au Frontenac et Champigny, 1690, AN, C11A, 11: 141–145;Bacqueville de La Potherie, *Histoire de l'Amérique septentrionale*, 2: 231–7.

24. The Jesuit Etienne de Carheil was at the mission of St Ignace and he attended the general council meeting. There is some question as to the amount of time the Haudenosaunee warriors remained in the colony. Pierre-François-Xavier Charlevoix, *Histoire et description général de la Nouvelle-France* (Paris, 1744), 2: 429–30; Frontenac au ministre, 15 nov. 1689, AN, C11A, 10: 217–224v; Champigny au ministre, 16 nov. 1689, AN, C11A, 10: 244–250v.

25. Richter, "War and Culture," 548–53.

26. Yves F. Zoltvany, "New France and the West, 1701–1713," *Canadian Historical Review* 46, 4 (1965): 304.

27. Richter, "War and Culture," 549.

28. By the late sixteenth century when the fighting between the Haudenosaunee and the Anishinaabek and their Wendat and Tionnontaté allies broke out, the summer villages in the region were abandoned, but not forgotten. There is but one brief reference in the Odaawa oral tradition to their old establishment at Bkejwanong. Andrew Blackbird, who published his book in 1887, made specific reference to his family's ancestry and their home in the region of Detroit sometime before the arrival of the French in the Upper Great Lakes region. Blackbird's timing of the event corresponds with the outbreak of hostilities between the Odaawak and the Haudenosaunee in the late sixteenth century. See Andrew Blackbird, *History of the Ottawa and Chippewa Indians of Michigan* (Ypsilanti, Mich., 1887), 93–4. The archaeological evidence for the Anishinaabe presence, however, is abundant. James E. Fitting and Richard Zurel, "The Detroit and St. Clair River Area," in David S. Brose, ed., *The Late Prehistory of the Lake Erie Drainage Basin* (Cleveland, 1976), 246–8; David S. Brose, "An Initial Survey of the Late Prehistoric Period in Northeastern Ohio," in Brose, ed., *Late Prehistory of Lake Erie*, 47; David M. Stothers, "The Western Basin Tradition: Algonquin or Iroquois," *Michigan Archaeologist* 24 (Mar. 1978): 25–8.

29. See Leroy V. Eid, "The Ojibwa-Iroquois War: The War the Five Nations Did Not Win," *Ethnohistory* 26 (Fall 1979): 297–24;

P.S. Schmaltz, "The Role of the Ojibwa in the Conquest of Southern Ontario," *Ontario History* 76 (Dec. 1984): 326–52.

30. A terrible smallpox epidemic in the summer of 1690 badly damaged the ability of the Haudenosaunee to put warriors in the field. Monseignat, Relation de ce qui s'est passé de plus remarquable au Canada, nov. 1690, AN, C11A, 11: 38–40; Frontenac au ministre, 12 nov. 1690, AN, C11A, 11: 90; Relation de ce qui s'est passé de plus considérable au Canada, 27 nov. 1690, AN, C11A, 11: 42–42v; Richter, *Ordeal of the Longhouse*, 173.

31. Anthony F.C. Wallace, *Death and Rebirth of the Seneca* (New York, 1969), 111–14; Wallace, "Origins of Iroquois Neutrality: The Grand Settlement of 1701," *Pennsylvania History* 24 (1957): 223–35.

32. Callière et Champigny au minister, 6 nov. 1701, AN, C11A, 19: 27–28; Assemblée faite par Callière de tous les chefs de sauvages de chaque nation d'en haut, 6 aout 1701, AN, F3 Moreau de St. Méry, 8: 271.

33. Zoltvany, "New France and the West," 302–5.

34. The Haudenosaunee claimed they had conquered lands from the Appalachians to the Kentucky River and then by the Ohio River and Mississippi to the Great Lakes and the Ottawa River. This included long-past conquests being disputed rather than only territory actually occupied. Sosin, *Whitehall and the Wilderness*, 74 n58.

35. Ibid., 551.

36. Lahontan, *Nouveaux voyages*, 2: 84–9.

37. Denys Delâge, "War and French–Indian Alliance," *European Review of Native American Studies* 5 (1991): 20; Delâge, *Le pays renversé*, 339–47; Delâge, "L'alliance franco-amérindienne 1660-1701," *Récherches amérindiennes au Québec* 19 (1989): 13; Jehu Hay, Diary of the Siege of Detroit, 1 May 1763 to 6 June 1765, Manuscripts Division, William L. Clements Library; Alexander Henry, *Travels and Adventures in Canada and the Indian Territories between the Years 1760 and 1776* (New York, 1809), passim.

38. A detailed description is by Jefferys, *Natural and Civil History*, I: 62–3. The practice of adopting war captives was not unique to the Haudenosaunee.

39. Daniel K. Richter, "Iroquois versus Iroquois: Jesuit Missions and Christianity in Village Politics, 1642–1686," *Ethnohistory* 32, 1 (1985): 1–16; *DCB*, 1: s.v. "Garakontié."

40. Bacqueville de la Potherie, *Histoire de l'Amérique septentrionale*, 1: 346–64. He wrote that their Catholic faith was the only common ground between the newcomers and the French. See also Henri Béchard, *The Original Caughnawaga Indians* (Montreal, 1976).

41. Mémoire de Cadillac, 1702, AN, C11A, 20: 130–6; Ida Amanda Johnson, *The Michigan Fur Trade* (Ann Arbor, Mich., 1919), 33–4, 40–1; Louise Phelps Kellogg, *The French Régime in Wisconsin and the Northwest* (Madison, Wis., 1925), 271–2; W. Vernon Kinietz, *The Indians of the Western Great Lakes, 1615–1760* (Ann Arbor, Mich., 1940), 229; Richard White, *The Middle Ground: Indians, Empires, and Republics in the Great Lakes Region, 1650–1815* (Cambridge, 1991), 146; Richter, *Ordeal of the Longhouse*, 210.

42. Milo Milton Quaife, ed., *The Western Country in the 17th Century: The Memoirs of Antoine Lamothe Cadillac and Pierre Liette* (New York, 1962), 67–8.

43. Paroles des Folles Avoines à Vaudreuil, 23 juillet 1708, AN, C11A, 28: 211–211v; Réponse de Vaudreuil aux Outaouais de Michilimackinac, 23 juillet 1708, AN, C11A, 28: 214; Réponse de Vaudreuil aux outaouais et autres descendus avec M. d'Argenteuil, 29 juillet 1709, AN, C11A, 30: 87; White, *Middle Ground*,

154; Richard Lortie, "La guerre des Renards, 1700–1740, ou quatre décennie de résistance à l'expansionisme Français" (MA diss., Université de Laval, 1988), 17–22; R. David Edmunds and Joseph L. Peyser, *The Fox Wars: The Mesquakie Challenge to New France* (Norman, Okla., 1993), 61; Gilles Havard, *Empires et Métissages: Indiens et français dans le pays d'en haut, 1660-1715* (Paris, 2003), 441–7.

44. Mémoire de Vaudreuil pour servir d'instruction à ceux qu'il envoie chez les nations des pays d'en haut, 10 mars 1711, AN, C11A, 32: 82–93v; Vaudreuil au ministre, 25 oct. 1711, AN, C11A, 32 : 46; Ramezay au ministre, 1 nov. 1711, AN, C11A, 32: 110. Paroles de Makisabi, chef poutéouatami, 17 août 1712, AN, C11A, 33: 85–90v; Vaudreuil au ministre, 6 nov. 1712, AN, C11A, 33: 51–52v; Marest à Vaudreuil, 21 juin 1712, AN, C11A, 33: 71–2.

45. Vaudreuil au Conseil de Marine, 14 oct. 1716, AN, C11A, 36: 71–74v; Vaudreuil au Conseil de Marine, 30 oct. 1716, AN, C11A, 36: 59–60v; Louvigny au Conseil de Marine, 14 oct. 1716, AN, C11A, 36: 173–4v.

46. Assikinack, "Social and Warlike Customs," 302.

47. He was the eldest son of Nicolas-Antoine de Villiers, who led the winter raid at Grand Pré against the English in 1749.

48. Résumé des lettres de Beauharnois, 1730, AN, C11A, 52: 254–7v.

49. An account of the last phase of the so-called Fox War is by Joseph L. Peyser, "The Fate of the Fox Survivors: A Dark Chapter in the History of the French in the Upper Country, 1726–1737," *Wisconsin Magazine of History* 73, 2 (1989–90): 93.

50. Beauharnois au ministre, 10 oct. 1731, AN, C11A, 54: 417; Beauharnois au ministre, 15 oct. 1732, AN, C11A, 57: 334v; Résumé de lettres de Beauharnois, 18 fév. 1732, AN, C11A, 58: 211v; Résumé de lettres de Beauharnois et Hocquart, 1732, AN, C11A, 58: 224v; Beauharnois au ministre, 1 mai 1733, AN, C11A, 59: 4v; Beauharnois au ministre, 30 mai 1733, AN, C11A, 59: 9–9v. Beauharnois au ministre, 11 oct. 1734, AN, C11A, 61: 314v; Beauharnois au ministre, 17 oct. 1736, AN, C11A, 65: 143.

51. Louise Phelps Kellogg, *The Fox Indians during the French Regime, reprinted from Proceedings of the State Historical Society of Wisconsin 1907* (Madison, Wis., 1908), 178.

52. Akins, ed., *Public Documents of Nova Scotia*, 486, General Edward Whitmore to Lawrence, Louisbourg, 20 June 1760. See also John Stewart McLellan, *Louisbourg from Its Foundation to Its Fall, 1713–1758* (London, 1918).

53. The texts of these treaties are in Cumming and Mickenberg, eds, *Native Rights in Canada*, 300–6; William Daugherty, *Maritime Indian Treaties in Perspective* (Ottawa, 1983), 75–8; Canada, *Indian Treaties and Surrenders*, 3 vols (Toronto, 1971), 2: 199–204.

54. LAC, AC, C11B 35:125, Chevalier Augustin Boschenry de Drucour (governor of Île Royale, 1754–8), au ministre, 18 nov. 1755.

55. LAC, MG 18, E29, vol. 2, section 4, Discours fait aux sauvages du Canada par M. de Saint-Ovide, gouverneur de l'Acadie avec les Responses que les sauvages on faites.

56. There are two versions of this declaration. The earlier one is reproduced in *Report Concerning Canadian Archives*, 1905, 3 vols, 1906, 2: App. A, pt. iii, in "Acadian Geneaology and Notes" by Placide Gaudet, 239. The later one is in *Collection de documents inédits sur le Canada et l'Amérique publiées par le Canada français*, 3 vols (Quebec, 1888–90), 1: 17–19.

57. Akins, ed., *Public Documents of Nova Scotia*, 581, Council aboard the *Beaufort*, 1 Oct. 1749; ibid., 581–2, Proclamation of Governor Cornwallis, Oct. 1749.

58. LAC, Nova Scotia A 17:129–32; Nova Scotia B 1:53–5.

59. Dickason, "Louisbourg and the Indians," 99–100. "Humanity cries out against such things," a contemporary observer wrote, "which should cause a just horror." LAC, AC, C11C, vol. 8:88v, Couagne to Acaron, directeur de Bureau des Colonies, 4 nov. 1760. The proclamation authorizing the bounty still remains on Nova Scotia's books, although such bounties are prohibited by the Criminal Code. According to newspaper accounts, the government fears that revoking the law and apologizing for it would precipitate a rash of lawsuits. Richard Foot, "Colonial Bounty on Mi'kmaq Scalps Still on the Books," *National Post*, 5 Jan. 2000, A1, A2.

60. J.B. Brebner, "Subsidized Intermarriage with the Indians," *Canadian Historical Review* 6, 1 (1925): 33–6.

61. LAC, AC, C11B, vol. 31:62–3.

62. LAC, AC, C11B, vol. 32:163–6, Prevost à Antoine Louis Rouillé, Comte de Joüy (minister of the marine, 1749–54), 10 sept. 1752; ibid., vol. 33:159v, Prevost à Rouillé, 12 mai 1753; Akins, ed., *Public Documents of Nova Scotia*, 672–4, Council minutes, Halifax, 16 Sept. 1752.

63. "1752 Peace and Friendship Treaty," https://www.aadnc-aandc .gc.ca/eng/1100100029040/1100100029041.

64. A.J.B. Johnston, *Control and Order in French Colonial Louisbourg, 1713–1758.* (East Lansing, Mich., 2001), 136–7; A.J.B. Johnston, *Endgame 1758: The Promise, the Glory, and the Despair of Louisbourg's Last Decade* (Lincoln, Neb., 2007), 197–8; Fred Anderson, *Crucible of War: The Seven Years' War and the Fate of British North America* (New York, 2001), 250–6.

65. Père Pierre-Joseph-Antoine Roubaud, *Jesuit Relations*, 70: 176–82; also see Ian K. Steele, *Betrayals: Fort William Henry and the Massacre* (Oxford, 1990), 109–28; Montcalm à Bourlamaque, 15 mars 1759, H.-R. Casgrain, ed., *Collection des manuscrits du maréchal de Lévis: Lettres de M. de Bourlamaque*, 5: 291; Bougainville, "Journal," *RAPQ* (1923–4): 313.

66. LAC, CO, 217/18:277–4, Ceremonials at Concluding a Peace . . . , 25 June 1761.

67. LAC, AC, C12, vol. 1:3v, Mémoire du Roy pour servir d'instruction au Sr. Dangeac nommé au gouvernement des Iles St. Pierre et de Miquelon, 23 fév. 1763.

68. Denis A. Bartels and Olaf Uwe Janzen, "Micmac Migration to Western Newfoundland," paper presented to the Canadian Historical Association, Victoria, 1990.

Chapter 7

1. Article 40 reads: "The savages or Indian Allies of His Most Christian Majesty shall be maintained in the lands they inhabit, if they choose to reside there; they shall not be molested on any pretense whatsoever, for having carried arms and served His Most Christian Majesty; they shall have, as well as the French, liberty of religion, and shall keep their missionaries." See also Maurice Torrelli, "Les Indiens du Canada et le droit des traités dans la jurisprudence canadienne," *Annuaire Français de Droit International* 20 (1974): 227–49, 236.

2. James Sullivan, Alexander C. Flick, and Milton W. Hamilton, eds, *The Papers of Sir William Johnson*, 14 vols (Albany, NY, 1921–65), vii, 785.

3. See, for instance, the complaints of the Onondowaga: Wallace, *Death and Rebirth of the Seneca*, 114–15.

4. Johnson's Journal of Indian Affairs, 9–12 Dec. 1758, in Sullivan et al., eds, *Papers of Sir William Johnson*, 10: 69, 73. Indigenous complaints in this regard were of long standing, and they had frequently requested authorities to ban the sale of liquor. See, for example, the plea in 1722 of the Mahican to William Burnett, governor-in-chief of New York and New Jersey, 1720–8. O'Callaghan and Brodhead, eds, *Documents*, 5: 663–4.

5. The governor of Virginia reported this to the Board of Trade in 1756. See Sosin, *Whitehall and the Wilderness*, 30.

6. Peter Wraxall, *An Abridgement of Indian Affairs . . . Transacted in the Colony of New York for the Year 1678 to the Year 1751*, ed. Charles H. McIlwain (Cambridge, Mass., 1915), ix, 153 n2.

7. David A. Armour, ed., *Attack at Michilimackinac 1763* (Mackinac Island, Mich., 1988), 25. This is a reproduction of Alexander Henry's *Travels and Adventures in Canada and the Indian Territories between the years 1760 and 1764* (New York, 1809).

8. Sosin, *Whitehall and the Wilderness*, 31.

9. Gordon M. Day and Bruce G. Trigger, "Algonquin," in Trigger, ed., *Handbook of North American Indians, 15: Northeast*, 795; Robert J. Surtees, "The Iroquois in Canada," in Francis Jennings, ed., *The History and Culture of Iroquois Diplomacy* (Syracuse, NY, 1985), 70.

10. Delâge, 'Les Iroquois chrétiens.'

11. Sullivan et al., eds, *Papers of Sir William Johnson*, 3: 965.

12. The question of Obwandiyag's origins is unresolved. Howard H. Peckham discusses the evidence in *Pontiac and the Indian Uprising* (Chicago, 1947), 15–16 n2. Contemporary reports inform us that he was of better than medium height and not handsome. Ibid., 28–9.

13. Ibid., 29.

14. Robert Rogers, *Concise Account of North America . . .* (London, 1765), 240, 243. An extract is reprinted in Peckham, *Pontiac*, 59–62 n8.

15. Andrew J. Blackbird, *The History and Traditions of the Ottawa and Chippewa Tribes of Michigan* (Ypsilanti, Mich., 1887), 8.

16. Rogers, *Concise Account of North America*, 240, 243. Extract in Peckham, *Pontiac*, 59–62 n8.

17. Carl F. Klinck, ed., *Tecumseh, Fact and Fiction in Early Records* (Englewood Cliffs, NJ, 1961), 184–5. See also Colin Calloway, *Crown and Calumet: British–Indian Relations, 1783–1815* (Norman, Okla., 1987), 217.

18. *DCB*, 3: s.v., "Pontiac." The other "Delaware Prophet" had a religious message.

19. Alexander Henry, *Travels and Adventures in Canada and the Indian Territories between the years 1760 and 1776* (New York, 1809), 78–85.

20. Helen Hornbeck Tanner, ed., *Atlas of Great Lakes Indian History* (Norman, Okla., 1987), 48. For a detailed account of the uprising, see 48–53.

21. For a contrary view, see Wilbur R. Jacobs, "The Indian Frontier of 1763," *Western Pennsylvania Historical Magazine* 34, 3 (1951): 185–98.

22. Amherst did not respect the Indigenous Peoples with whom he had dealings. His correspondence makes his extreme dislike for them quite obvious. In one typical letter he made reference to the number of suspected Odaawa crimes against the British and he referred to them as "swarthy brutes whose vilest wickedness makes me shudder." His arrangements to infect people with smallpox are to be found in his correspondence with Thomas Gage, the military governor of Montreal, and with the senior British officer in the west, Colonel Henry Bouquet. In the end it was a Swiss mercenary named Simon Ecuyer who spread the infection. Amherst to Gage, 10 July 1763, Amherst Papers, William L. Clements Library, 6: 52; Amherst to Gage, 30 July 1763, ibid.,

6: 54; Amherst to Gage, 1 Aug. 1763, ibid., 6: 56; Bouquet to Amherst, 13 July 1763, Bouquet Papers, British Museum, Series 21634, fol. 325; Amherst to Bouquet, 16 July 1763, ibid., fol. 242; ibid., Series 21654: fol. 168; Blackbird, *History and Traditions of the Ottawa and Chippewa Tribes*, 9–10.

23. David Dixon, *Never Come to Peace Again: Pontiac's Uprising and the Fate of the British Empire in North America* (Norman, Okla., 2005), 228.

24. Ibid., 268.

25. Peckham, *Pontiac*, 316.

26. At the time the fort was built, the Dakota–Ojibwa War had been going on for something like a century. During a temporary peace in 1787 the combatants agreed to recognize the British King. Clayton W. McCall, "The Peace of Michilimackinack," *Michigan History Magazine* 28, 3 (1944): 367–83.

27. Koñwatsiåtsiaiéñni (Mary "Molly" Brant, consort of Sir William Johnson, superintendent of Northern Indian Affairs who had died in 1774) was a more powerful figure among the matrilineal Kanienkehaka than her famous younger brother, Thayendanegea (Joseph Brant). On her importance among her people, it was reported that "one word from her goes farther with them than a thousand from any white Man without Exception who in general must purchase their Interest at a high rate." The Haudenosaunee did not regard Thayendanegea as their leading war chief; that honour was accorded the Onondowaga leader Kaieñ'kwaahtoñ (Sayenqueraghta, d. 1786), who also fought for the British. See Barbara Graymont, *The Iroquois in the American Revolution* (Syracuse, NY, 1972), 159; Earle Thomas, *The Three Faces of Molly Brant* (Kingston, Ont., 1996).

28. Red Jacket took part in a council that removed Thayendanegea from office in 1805, but Thayendanegea managed to stay on another two years. Red Jacket, employed as a runner for the British during the American War of Independence, had been rewarded for his services with a richly embroidered red jacket. He later threw in his lot with the Americans, although he would have preferred neutrality. See Mary H. Eastman, *The American Aboriginal Portfolio* (Philadelphia, 1853), 9–13.

29. On the participation of the Six Nations in the American War of Independence, see George F.G. Stanley, "The Six Nations and the American Revolution," *Ontario History* 56, 4 (1964): 217–32.

30. George F.G. Stanley, *The War of 1812: Land Operations* (Toronto, 1983), 13–14.

31. A.L. Burt, "A New Approach to the Problem of the Western Posts," *Canadian Historical Association Report* (1931): 61–95.

32. John Leslie discusses the treaty and its background in *The Treaty of Amity, Commerce and Navigation, 1794–1796: The Jay Treaty* (Ottawa, 1979).

33. The texts of the proclamations of 1761 and 1762 and excerpts from that of 1763 are reproduced in Cumming and Mickenberg, eds, *Native Rights in Canada*, 285–92. See also Bradford W. Morse, ed., *Aboriginal Peoples and the Law: Indian, Metis, and Inuit Rights in Canada* (Ottawa, 1985), 52–4, 191–6.

34. For a detailed study of the Proclamation, see Jack Stagg, *Anglo-Indian Relations in North America to 1763 and an Analysis of the Royal Proclamation of 7 October 1763* (Ottawa, 1981).

35. Dorothy V. Jones, "British Colonial Indian Treaties," in Wilcomb Washburn, ed., *Handbook of North American Indians, 4: History of Indian–White Relations* (Washington, 1988), 189–90.

36. Robert J. Surtees, "Canadian Indian Treaties," in Washburn, ed., *Handbook of North American Indians, 4: History of Indian–White Relations*, 202.

37. Stagg, *Anglo–Indian Relations*, 386.

38. Torrelli, "Les Indiens du Canada," 237–9.

39. Jones, "British Colonial Indian Treaties," 185.

40. Torrelli, "Les Indiens du Canada," 227–49.

41. The text of the treaty is in Cumming and Mickenberg, eds, *Native Rights in Canada*, 296–8. In the Indigenous view, this guarantee was for pre-existing rights. See Federation of Saskatchewan Indians, *Indian Treaty Rights*, n.d.

42. For a Wuastukwiuk view of the two 1725 treaties, see Andrea Bear Nicholas, "Maliseet Aboriginal Rights and Mascarene's Treaty, not Dummer's Treaty," in William Cowan, ed., *Actes du dix-septième Congrès des Algonquinistes* (Ottawa, 1986), 215–29.

43. The text is in Cumming and Mickenberg, eds, *Native Rights in Canada*, 302–6.

44. David L. Ghere, "Mistranslations and Misinformation: Diplomacy on the Maine Frontier, 1725 to 1755," *American Indian Culture and Research Journal* 8, 4 (1984): 3–26.

45. Sagard, *Histoire du Canada*, 2: 444: "... Truchemens, qui souvent ne rapportent pas fidellement les choses qu'on leur dit, ou par ignorance ou par mespris, qui est une chose fort dangereuse, & de laquelle on a souvent vue arriver de grands accidents."

46. Akins, ed., *Public Documents of Nova Scotia*, 682–5; Daugherty, *Maritime Indian Treaties*, 75–8; Canada, *Indian Treaties and Surrenders*, 50–1, 84–5; Cumming and Mickenberg, eds, *Native Rights in Canada*, 307–9.

47. Akins, ed., *Public Documents of Nova Scotia*, 671, Council minutes, Halifax, 14 Sept. 1752. Indigenous resistance to land surveys had long been troubling the British. Ibid., Council minutes, Halifax, 4 Sept. 1732.

48. Max Savelle, *The Diplomatic History of the Canadian Boundary 1749–1763* (New Haven, 1940), 147.

49. Surtees, "Canadian Indian Treaties," 202; "A History of Treaty Making in Canada," Indigenous and Northern Affairs Canada Online, https://www.aadnc-aandc.gc.ca/eng/1314977704533/1314977734895.

50. Lisa Patterson, "Errant Peace Treaty," *The Archivist* 16, 6 (1989): 15.

51. Donald B. Smith, "The Dispossession of the Mississauga Indians: A Missing Chapter in the Early History of Upper Canada," *Ontario History* 73, 2 (1981): 72. Wabakinine was a signatory to several land cession treaties. See *DCB*, vol. 4.

52. Canada, *Indian Treaties and Surrenders*, 3 vols (Toronto, 1971), 1: 42ff.

53. Lillian F. Gates, *Land Policies of Upper Canada* (Toronto, 1968), 49, 51. According to historian Robert J. Surtees, the average price was four pence an acre. Surtees, "Canadian Indian Treaties," 204.

54. The importance of Indigenous Peoples in colonial policy was indicated by the wish of John Graves Simcoe, first lieutenant-governor of Upper Canada, 1791–6, to establish the capital on the site of London, to be near the Indigenous allies. See R.J. Surtees, "The Changing Image of the Canadian Indian: An Historical Approach," in D.A. Muise, ed., *Approaches to Native History in Canada: Papers of a conference held at the National Museum of Man* (Ottawa, 1977), 121.

55. The text of the grant is reproduced in Isabel Thompson Kelsay, *Joseph Brant, 1743–1807: Man of Two Worlds* (Syracuse, NY, 1984), 363. See also Gates, *Land Policies*, 14–15.

56. Charles M. Johnston, ed., *The Valley of the Six Nations: A Collection of Documents on the Indian Lands of the Grand River* (Toronto, 1964), 52. See also Kelsay, *Joseph Brant*, 370.

57. Gates, *Land Policies*, 49. On Thayendanegea's struggle with the administration, see Charles M. Johnston, "Joseph Brant, the

Grand River Lands and the Northwest Crisis," *Ontario History* 55 (1963): 267–82.

58. A later court case that involved Thayendanegea's leasing activities was *Sheldon v. Ramsay*, 1852. The issue was whether or not lands believed to belong to a certain newcomer named Mallory would be forfeited for treason. It developed that the lands in question had been leased by Thayendanegea; the court ruled that the Kanienkehaka chief had had no authority for such an action, as neither he nor the Six Nations had possessed title in fee simple. See Bruce A. Clark, *Native Liberty, Crown Sovereignty* (Montreal and Kingston, 1990), 19 and n15.

59. Surtees, "The Iroquois in Canada," 76. An outline of Thayendanegea's real estate dealings is in Johnston, ed., *Valley of Six Nations*, xlii–liv. For a study of the legal dissensions that ensued, see Sidney L. Harring, *White Man's Law* (Toronto, 1998), ch. 2.

60. Kelsay, *Joseph Brant*, 555–6. Thayendanegea had initially maintained that the purchase from the Mississauga had not been necessary, as these had been Haudenosaunee lands from time immemorial. Later he became land agent for the Mississauga, indicating a de facto acknowledgement of their title.

61. "Deserontyon," *Dictionary of Canadian Biography Online*, http://www.biographi.ca/en/bio/deserontyon_john_5E.html.

62. Surtees, "Canadian Indian Treaties," 203; Boyce Richardson, "Kind Hearts or Forked Tongues?" *The Beaver* Outfit 67, 1 (1987): 16.

63. Canada, *Indian Treaties and Surrenders*, 1: 47. Musquakie's band eventually settled in Rama Township in 1839, after several moves.

64. R.A. Humphreys, "Governor Murray's Views . . . ," *Canadian Historical Review* 16 (1935): 166–9.

Chapter 8

1. This section is an adaptation of Olive Patricia Dickason, "A Historical Reconstruction for the Northwestern Plains," *Prairie Forum* 5, 1 (1980): 19–37.

2. F.G. Roe, *The Indian and the Horse* (Norman, Okla., 1951), 54.

3. Richard Glover, ed., *David Thompson's Narrative 1784–1812* (Toronto, 1962), 241–2; Frank Raymond Secoy, *Changing Military Patterns on the Great Plains*, Monographs of the American Ethnological Society, 21 (Seattle, 1953), 33; Oscar Lewis, *The Effects of White Contact upon Blackfoot Culture* (New York, 1942), 11; George E. Hyde, *Indians of the High Plains* (Norman, Okla., 1959), 121, 133–4. See also Harris, ed., *Historical Atlas*, 1: plate 57, for a schematic diagram of the diffusion of horses.

4. James Teit, *The Salishan Tribes of the Western Plateau*, 45th Annual Report, US Bureau of Ethnology (1927–8) (Washington, 1930), 109–10; Bernard Mishkin, *Rank and Warfare among Plains Indians* (Seattle, 1940), ch. 2.

5. Glover, ed., *David Thompson's Narrative*, 240–4.

6. Roe, *Indian and Horse*, 74–5.

7. Dolores A. Gunnerson, "Man and Bison on the Plains in the Protohistoric Period," *Plains Anthropologist* 17, 55 (1972): 2. It has been theorized that the custom of burning altered the ecology of river valleys so that the subsistence base of the communities was undermined. The average life of a Plains farming village has been estimated at about 30 years.

8. George Bird Grinnell, *Blackfoot Lodge Tales: The Story of a Prairie People* (New York, 1892), 125–6. See also T. McHugh, *The Time of the Buffalo* (New York, 1972), 140–1.

9. John Price, *Indians of Canada: Cultural Dynamics* (Scarborough, Ont., 1979), 176.

10. Mishkin, *Rank and Warfare*, 10; Glover, ed., *David Thompson's Narrative*, 267–8. For other such raids, see Arthur S. Morton, ed., *The Journal of Duncan M'Gillivray of the Northwest Company at Fort George on the Saskatchewan, 1794–1795* (Toronto, 1979), 27.

11. John McDougall, *Wa-pee Moostooch or White Buffalo* (Calgary, 1908), 132–50.

12. George W. Arthur, *An Introduction to the Ecology of Early Historic Communal Bison Hunting among the Northern Plains Indians* (Ottawa, 1975), 72.

13. Philip Duke, *Points in Time: Structure and Event in a Late Northern Plains Hunting Society* (Niwot, Colo., 1991), 69–74.

14. Elliott Coues, ed., *New Light on the Early History of the Great Northwest 1799–1814*, 3 vols (New York, 1897), 2: 526.

15. John C. Ewers, "Was There a Northwestern Plains Subculture? An Ethnographic Appraisal," in Warren W. Caldwell, ed., *The Northwestern Plains: A Symposium* (Billings, Mont., 1968), 71. See also Hugh A. Dempsey, *Indian Tribes of Alberta* (Calgary, 1986).

16. Ewers, "Was There a Northwestern Plains Subculture?" 73. "Atsina" was the Blackfoot term for these people and "Gros Ventre" the French. Another name for them was "Haaninin": "chalk men" or "men of soft white stone."

17. Regina Flannery, *The Gros Ventres of Montana, Part I: Social Life*, Anthropological Series #15 (Washington, 1953), 5; Alfred L. Kroeber, *Ethnology of the Gros Ventre* (New York, 1908), 145. Another fur trader, however, found them to be lazy and "good only at stealing horses." Morton, ed., *M'Gillivray*, 26–7, 73–4.

18. Cf. James H. Howard, *The Plains-Ojibwa or Bungi, Hunters and Warriors of the Northern Prairie* (Vermillion, SD, 1965). Edwin Thompson Denig says that the Ojibwa and Cree were so intermingled as to be difficult to distinguish. See John C. Ewers, ed., *Five Indian Tribes of the Upper Missouri* (Norman, Okla., 1961), 100.

19. James G.E. Smith, "The Western Woods Cree: Anthropological Myth and Historical Reality," *American Anthropologist* 14, 3 (1987): 434–48.

20. Coues, ed., *New Light*, 2: 713–14. For a Spanish governor's ingenious argument in favour of providing guns to *indios barbaros* in order to make them less formidable, see Max L. Moorhead, *The Apache Frontier* (Norman, Okla., 1968), 127–8.

21. A Cree tradition from the Churchill River area has it that the first time they met non-Indigenous people they were presented with a gun, but without live ammunition. Once they obtained ammunition, the Cree found the gun to be "a good hunting weapon." Long, "Narratives of Early Encounters," 230, 231.

22. Secoy, *Changing Military Patterns*, 52.

23. Brian J. Smith, "How Great an Influence Was the Gun in Historic Northern Plains Ethnic Movements?" in Tkaczuk and Vivian, eds, *Cultures in Conflict*, 253–61. Diamond Jenness, for his part, had no doubts that the gun disturbed the equilibrium not only between humans and the animals they hunted, but also between human groups. Jenness, *Eskimo Administration, 2: Canada* (Montreal, 1972), 7.

24. Delegates to a Peigan–Salish (Flathead) peace council vividly described the effect that guns could have. See Glover, ed., *David Thompson's Narrative*, 390–1.

25. Ibid., 207, 240. The Shoshone were doubly unfortunate, as they were also confronted by Sioux armed with guns who pushed them westward into the mountains and sagebrush desert.

26. Hyde, *Indians of the High Plains*, 164–5.

27. Coues, ed., *New Light*, 2: 726.

28. Peter Fidler's Journal, HBC Archives, E 3/2:19, 31 Dec. 1792. See also F.W. Howay, "David Thompson's Account of His First Attempt to Cross the Rockies," *Queen's Quarterly* 40 (1933): 337. A touching account of the Niitsitapiikwan's first encounter with non-Indigenous Peoples is told by George Bird Grinnell, *The Story of the Indians* (New York, 1911), 224–40.

29. Various voyages into the interior are described by Morton, *History of the Canadian West*, 263–90.

30. Glyndwr Williams, "The Puzzle of Anthony Henday's Journal, 1754–55," *The Beaver* Outfit 309, 3 (1978): 53.

31. John C. Ewers, *The Blackfeet: Raiders on the Northern Plains* (Norman, Okla., 1989), 88.

32. Lewis, *Effects of White Contact*, 17–18.

33. Morton, ed., *M'Gillivray*, 31. That there might have been some grounds for the Niitsitapi suspicions is indicated by French practices in the Wendat trade, in which preferential treatment was accorded to converts.

34. E.E. Rich, *The Fur Trade in the Northwest to 1857* (Toronto, 1967), 158. It should be noted that Indigenous Peoples regularly used fire to control vegetation, which in turn influenced the movements of the herds.

35. Howay, "David Thompson's Account," 335; Glover, ed., *David Thompson's Narrative*, 272–9, 389.

36. Lewis, *Effects of White Contact*, 23.

37. Tyrrell, ed., *David Thompson's Narrative*, xc. For a different version, see J.E.A. Macleod, "Peigan Post and the Blackfoot Trade," *Canadian Historical Review* 24, 3 (1943): 273–9.

38. Glover, ed., *David Thompson's Narrative*, 229. Thompson, of course, was repeating hearsay.

39. Pemmican was made from dried, pounded buffalo meat mixed with buffalo fat, about five parts meat to four parts fat, to which berries were sometimes added. One kg of pemmican had the food value of four to eight kg of fresh meat or fish. The development of its manufacture, believed to have occurred about 3000 BCE, was a major factor in the emergence of the classic period of the Northern Plains Bison Hunting Culture. Brian O.K. Reeves, "Communal Bison Hunters of the Northern Plains," in Leslie B. Davis and Brian O.K. Reeves, eds, *Hunters of the Recent Past* (London, 1990), 169–70.

40. Mandelbaum, *The Plains Cree*, 246. Lewis says that among the Niitsitapiikwan, the third or fourth wife had such an inferior status that she was referred to as a "slave." Lewis, *Effects of White Contact*, 38–40.

41. Daniel Williams Harmon, *Sixteen Years in the Indian Country: The Journals of Williams Harmon*, ed. W. Kaye Lamb (Toronto, 1957), 69.

42. Glover, ed., *David Thompson's Narrative*, 177–8.

43. David G. Mandelbaum, *Anthropology and People: The World of the Plains Cree* (Saskatoon, 1967), 6.

44. Ibid.

45. Coues, ed., *New Light*, 1: 292–3; 2: 498–9; Morton, *History of the Canadian West*, 253; Alexander Mackenzie, *Voyages from Montreal on the River St. Lawrence through the Continent of America* (London, 1801), xiii–xiv. Mackenzie's work is reported to have been ghost-written. See Franz Montgomery, "Alexander Mackenzie's Literary Assistant," *Canadian Historical Review* 18, 3 (1937): 301–4.

46. Stephen Hume, "Was B.C. Discovered by Francis Drake?" *Ottawa Citizen*, 6 Aug. 2000, A5.

47. W.J. Eccles, "The Fur Trade in the Colonial Northeast," in Washburn, ed., *Handbook of North American Indians, 4: History of Indian–White Relations*, 332.

48. See Rolf Knight, *Indians at Work: An Informal History of Native Indian Labour in British Columbia 1858–1930* (Vancouver, 1978).

49. Witthoft, "Archaeology as a Key to the Colonial Fur Trade," 56–7.

50. Hearne, *Journey*, 330n. Archaeologist Clifford Hickey speculates that these beads could have been of Russian origin; Hearne thought they might be Danish from Davis Strait.

51. For a detailed account of these hostilities, see Abel, *Drum Songs*, ch. 5.

52. Trudy Nicks, "The Iroquois and the Fur Trade in Western Canada," in Judd and Ray, eds, *Old Trails and New Directions*, 86. See also Nicks, "Origins of the Alberta Métis: Land Claims Research Project 1978–1979," work paper for the Métis Association of Alberta.

53. Trudy Nicks, "Mary Anne's Dilemma: The Ethnohistory of an Ambivalent Identity," *Canadian Ethnic Studies* 17, 2 (1985): 106.

54. Rich, "Trade Habits," 35–53.

55. Glover, ed., *David Thompson's Narrative*, 273–4.

56. W.A. Sloan, "The Columbia Link—Native Trade, Warfare, and European Penetration of the Kootenays," paper presented to the Orkney-Rupert's Land Colloquium, Orkney Islands, 1990.

57. Morton, ed., *M'Gillivray*, 56.

58. Glover, ed., *David Thompson's Narrative*, 305–6; Coues, ed., *New Light*, 2: 713.

59. Kehoe, *The Ghost Dance*, 100. See, for example, Pat Moore and Angela Wheelock, eds, *Wolverine Myths and Visions: Dene Traditions from Northern Alberta* (Edmonton, 1990). Compiled by the Dene Wodih Society, this work deals with Dene prophets, particularly Nógha ("Wolverine," *fl.* 1920s) of the Dene Dháa, and recounts wolverine stories as told by the people. On northern shamanism, see Catharine McClellan, *My Old People Say: An Ethnographic Survey of Southern Yukon Territory*, 2 vols (Ottawa, 1975), 2: 529–75.

60. Leslie F.S. Upton, "Contact and Conflict on the Atlantic and Pacific Coasts of Canada," *B.C. Studies* 45 (1980): 103–15.

61. Robert T. Boyd, "Demographic History, 1774–1784," in Wayne Suttles, ed., *Handbook of North American Indians, 7: Northwest Coast* (Washington, 1990), 135.

62. F.W. Howay, "An Outline Sketch of the Maritime Fur Trade," *Canadian Historical Association Report* (1932): 5–14.

63. "Muquinna" was a chiefly title of the Mochat band and was held by several chiefs. The holder of the title referred to here not only controlled the trade of his own people, but also that of the Kwakwaka'wakw of the Nimkish River.

64. Robin Fisher, *Contact and Conflict: Indian–European Relations in British Columbia, 1774–1890* (Vancouver, 1977), 16. See also F.W. Howay, "Indian Attacks upon Maritime Traders of the Northwest Coast, 1785–1805," *Canadian Historical Review* 6, 4 (1925): 287–309.

65. *DCB*, 4: s.v. "Koyah."

66. Fisher, *Contact and Conflict*, 15. Various versions of the incident are given by F.W. Howay, "The Ballad of the Bold Northwestman: An Incident in the Life of Captain John Kendrick," *Washington Historical Quarterly* 20 (1929): 114–23.

67. One of the survivors was John Jewitt, who published his experiences in *A Journal Kept at Nootka Sound . . .* (Boston, 1807).

68. Possible motivations are discussed in Fisher, *Contact and Conflict*, 16.

69. Gabriel Franchère, *Journal of a Voyage to the Northwest Coast of North America during the Years 1811, 1812, 1813 and 1814*, ed. W. Kaye Lamb (Toronto, 1969), 124–7.

70. Fisher, *Contact and Conflict*, 35.

71. Ibid., 31, 36. Both "Legaic" and "Wiiseaks" were chiefly titles by which the incumbents were known. For example, there were five recorded Legaics, a title held by the Eagle clan. The first known holder of the title built a trade empire during the second half of the eighteenth century, which the second Legaic expanded by establishing a trading relationship with the HBC. This relationship was cemented in 1832 by the marriage of his daughter to Dr John Frederick Kennedy, an official with the Company.

72. See Michael P. Robinson, *Sea Otter Chiefs* (Vancouver, [1978]), 61–87; *DCB*, 12: s.v. "Legaic, Paul." Tsimshian stories of Legaic and Wiiseaks are in Marius Barbeau and William Beynon, coll., *Tsimshian Narratives 2* (Ottawa, 1987).

73. Fisher, *Contact and Conflict*, 32.

74. E.E. Rich, ed., *The Letters of John McLaughlin from Fort Vancouver to the Governor and Committee, First Series, 1825–38* (London, 1941), iv, app. A, Duncan Finlayson to John McLaughlin, 334–5.

75. Some estimates place the pre-contact population much lower, and the nadir at 10,000. See Thomas Berger, *Fragile Freedoms: Human Rights and Dissent in Canada* (Toronto, 1981), 229.

76. On 'Kwah, see Charles A. Bishop, "Kwah: A Carrier Chief," in Judd and Ray, eds, *Old Trails and New Directions*, 191–204. 'Kwah is remembered mainly for a confrontation with Douglas, in which he spared the latter's life.

Chapter 9

1. For purposes of administration, the English colonies were divided into two departments, the northern and the southern.

2. Reginald Horsman, *Expansion and American Indian Policy, 1783–1812* (East Lansing, Mich., 1967), 171.

3. On the intolerance of American frontiersmen to Indigenous rights, see Robert L. Fisher, "The Western Prologue to the War of 1812," *Missouri Historical Review* 30, 3 (1936): 272.

4. This was a period of profound changes in the Western world. In Europe, the French Revolution of 1789 led to the Napoleonic Wars (1803–15), another in the long series of Anglo–French conflicts, which drained human resources from such peacetime activities as the fur trade and cut off markets.

5. LAC, RG 8, series C, vol. 257:31, McGill to Prevost, Montreal, 19 Dec. 1812; George F.G. Stanley, "The Indians in the War of 1812," *Canadian Historical Review* 31, 2 (1950): 152–3.

6. Stanley, *War of 1812*, 64–5.

7. Britain, in its pursuit of the Napoleonic Wars, had insisted on its right to stop neutral vessels on the high seas in search of contraband and British deserters. In 1807, when the American *Chesapeake* refused to allow the British to take off suspected runaways, the British HMS *Leopard* fired on her, killing three of her men. The Americans retaliated with economic sanctions against Britain, though these were ineffective. See John Sugden, *Tecumseh's Last Stand* (Norman, Okla., 1985), 20.

8. Stanley, "Indians in the War of 1812"; George F.G. Stanley, "The Significance of the Six Nations' Participation in the War of 1812," *Ontario History* 55, 4 (1963): 215–31.

9. John 10:9. See R. David Edmunds, *The Shawnee Prophet* (Lincoln, Neb., 1983), 28–41.

10. For a reaction to this policy, see "Tecumseh's Claims: An American View," in Carl F. Klinck, ed., *Tecumseh: Fact, Fiction and Early Records* (Englewood Cliffs, NJ, 1961), 75.

11. Apparently the admiration was mutual. See "Brock and Tecumseh," ibid., 138.

12. Some of Tecumseh's reputation rests on the glowing accounts of imperialistic British writers of the nineteenth century, but the fact remains he was an "'uncommon genius" to use the words of the American President William Henry Harrison. See the profile in the *Dictionary of Canadian Biography Online* by Herbert Goltz: http://www.biographi.ca/en/bio/tecumseh_5E.html.

13. R. David Edmunds, *Tecumseh and the Quest for Indian Leadership* (Boston, 1984), 148–53.

14. Calloway, *Crown and Calumet*, 11.

15. *DCB*, 7: Dickson, James. The Dakota call the War of 1812 Pahinshashawacikiya, "when the Redhead begged for our help." Peter Douglas Elias, *The Dakota of the Canadian Northwest: Lessons for Survival* (Winnipeg, 1988), 8.

16. However, the Battle of Tippecanoe did prove especially useful to Governor Harrison nearly three decades later, when the catchy campaign slogan "Tippecanoe and Tyler Too" led him to the American presidency in 1840 as a war hero who defeated the "Indians." "Tyler" was his vice presidential running mate, John Tyler.

17. In the account that follows, only some battles of this war are touched on, mainly those that relate in some way to what is now Canada and the Indigenous Peoples who live within its borders.

18. Robert S. Allen, *His Majesty's Indian Allies: British Indian Policy in the Defence of Canada, 1774–1815* (Toronto, 1992), 120.

19. Stanley, *War of 1812*, 95–6.

20. A description of the battle is in Edmunds, *Tecumseh and the Quest for Indian Leadership*, 180.

21. "Tekarihogen" was the name of a chieftainship of the Haudenosaunee Confederacy (alleged by the Kanienkehaka to be the primary one), matrilineally hereditary in Ohtowa'kéhson's clan and, when she had no daughter, granted to her son. *DCB*, 6: s.v. "Tekarihogen."

22. Stanley, *War of 1812*, 65–6, 122, 128–31.

23. Edmunds, *Tecumseh and the Quest for Indian Leadership*, 192–3.

24. Calloway, *Crown and Calumet*, 202–3; Stanley, *War of 1812*, 196–9.

25. Reginald Horsman, *The Frontier in the Formative Years, 1783–1815* (New York, 1970), 179–83.

26. Carl F. Klinck, ed., *The Journal of Major John Norton* (Toronto, 1970), 291.

27. Sugden is particularly emphatic on this point: *Tecumseh's Last Stand*, 193–5. See also the list of battles in which Indigenous Peoples took part, and the percentage of their participation, in Helen Hornbeck Tanner, ed., *Atlas of Great Lakes Indian History* (Norman, Okla., 1987), 108–15. More than a third of these battles were fought after Moraviantown.

28. Many more Indigenous people than white settler-colonials fought in the war, with a number of the battles involving only Indigenous people. Apart from a few specific battles, there are no statistics available for Indigenous casualties.

29. Kerry A. Trask, "Settlement in a Half-Savage Land: Life and Loss in the Métis Community of La Baye," *Michigan Historical Review* 15 (1989): 1–27.

30. Allen, *His Majesty's Indian Allies*, 197–8; Edward S. Rogers and Donald B. Smith, eds, *Aboriginal Ontario* (Toronto, 1994), 123–4.

31. Robert J. Surtees, "Canadian Indian Treaties," in Washburn, ed., *Handbook of North American Indians, 4: History of Indian–White Relations*, 204.

32. John F. Leslie, "Buried Hatchet," *Horizon Canada* 4, 40 (1985): 944–9.

33. Delâge, *Le pays renversé*, 339–47.

Chapter 10

1. As Alexandre Taché (bishop of St Boniface, Man., 1853–71, archbishop, 1871–94) acidly observed, farming, "although so desirable, is not the sole condition in the state of civilization." Canada, Sessional Papers 1885, No. 116, "Papers . . . in connection with the extinguishment of the Indian title preferred by Half-breeds resident in the North-West Territories," 85, Taché to Col. J.S. Dennis, deputy minister of the interior, 29 Jan. 1879. Later, ranching would be advocated, as the "work suits the Indians better." Not only that, but ranching could be co-ordinated with hunting. In the view of the NWMP, "Farming is too steady and monotonous work for them, although some have fine fields." (Canada, *N.W.M.P. Report*, 1895, 5.)

2. Cited by L.F.S. Upton, "The Origins of Canadian Indian Policy," *Journal of Canadian Studies* 10, 4 (1973): 59.

3. The Sarnia, Kettle Point, and Stony Point reserves and Moore Township. William Henderson, *Canada's Indian Reserves: Pre-Confederation* (Ottawa, 1980), 10 and n56.

4. Richardson, "Kind Hearts or Forked Tongues?" 18.

5. Donald B. Smith, *Sacred Feathers: The Reverend Peter Jones (Kahkewaquonaby) and the Mississauga Indians* (Toronto, 1987), chs 6, 7. Other Indigenous clerics, all Methodists, included George Copway (Kahgegagahbowh, "He Who Stands Forever," 1818–69); Peter Jacobs (Pahtahsaga, "One Who Makes the World Brighter," *c.* 1807–94); and War of 1812 veteran John Sunday (Shah-wun-dais, "Sultry Heat," *c.* 1795–1875). Two of these, Copway and Jacobs, ran into funding difficulties that resulted in their expulsion from their ministries.

6. "170 Years Since the Move to New Credit," Mississaugas of the New Credit First Nation, http://mncfn.ca/category/culture-history.

7. This was the party that advocated for votes for freedmen (former slaves), among other civil rights. See Victor B. Howard, *Religion and the Radical Republican Movement, 1860–1870* (Lexington, Kentucky, 1990), 204.

8. John F. Leslie and Ron Maguire, *The Historical Development of the Indian Act* (Ottawa, 1978), 18–19.

9. "170 Years Since the Move to New Credit," Mississaugas of the New Credit First Nation http://mncfn.ca/category/culture-history.

10. For more on Aisance, see Smith, *Sacred Feathers*, 212–13; *DCB*, 9: s.v. "Musquakie"; 8: s.v. "Aisance."

11. Smith, *Sacred Feathers*, 349.

12. Francis Bond Head, *A Narrative*, 2nd edn (London, 1839), app. A, "Memorandum on the Aborigines of North America." This memorandum is reproduced in part in Adam Shortt and Arthur G. Doughty, eds, *Canada and Its Provinces*, 23 vols (Toronto, 1914–17), 5: 337–9. Sir Francis had been knighted in 1831, reportedly because of his demonstration of the military usefulness of the lasso.

13. The people of the Wikwemikong Unceded Indian Reserve have long been proud of their refusal to sign the McDougall Treaty in 1862. See "The making of the Manitoulin Treaty, 1862," Indigenous and Northern Affairs Canada, https://www.aadnc-aandc.gc.ca/eng/1100100028959/1100100028961#chp4; Wikwemikong Unceded Indian Reserve, "Our History," http://www.wikwemikong.ca/index.php?option=com_content&view=article&id=48&Itemid=53.

14. Peter S. Schmaltz, *The History of the Saugeen Indians* (Ottawa, 1977), 82–4. "Saugeen" is Ojibwa for "mouth of the river."

15. Donald B. Smith, *Mississauga Portraits: Ojibwe Voices from Nineteenth-Century Canada* (Toronto, 2013), 90.

16. Peggy J. Blair, "The Supreme Court of Canada's 'Historic' Decision in Nikal and Lewis: Why Crown Fishing Policy in Upper Canada Makes Bad Law," Master's thesis (University of Ottawa, 1998), 52–9. See also Victor P. Lytwyn, "Waterworld: The Aquatic Territory of the Great Lakes First Nations," in Dale Standen and David McNab, eds, *Gin Das Winan: Documenting Aboriginal History in Ontario* (Toronto, 1996), 14–28. A valuable study of the experiences of the peoples who moved to reserves around Georgian Bay after signing the Bond Head Treaty of 1836, the Robinson Huron Treaty (1850), and the Manitoulin Island Treaty (1862) is Robin Jarvis Brownlie, *A Fatherly Eye: Indian Agents, Government Power, and Aboriginal Resistance in Ontario, 1918–1939* (Toronto, 2003).

17. Smith, *Sacred Feathers*, 163–4; Schmaltz, *History of the Saugeen Indians*, 56–148.

18. B.E. Hill, "The Grand River Navigation Company and the Six Nations Indians," *Ontario History* 63, 1 (1971): 31–40; Richard C. Daniel, *A History of Native Claims Processes in Canada 1867–1979* (Ottawa, 1980), 122–30.

19. Thwaites, ed., *Jesuit Relations*, 6: 151; Lucien Campeau, "Roman Catholic Missions," in Washburn, ed., *Handbook of North American Indians, 4: History of Indian–White Relations*, 465–8.

20. J. Garth Taylor, *Labrador Eskimo Settlements of the Early Contact Period* (Ottawa, 1974); W. Gillies Ross, *Whaling and Eskimos: Hudson Bay 1860–1915* (Ottawa, 1975).

21. *DCB*, 4: s.v. "Haven, Jens." See also Jenness, *Eskimo Administration*, 9–10. The Moravian Brethren, also known as Unitas Fratrum, was a pietist Protestant missionary group founded in 1727 by Count Nikolaus Ludwig von Zinzendorf (1700–60). They already had missions in Greenland when they were invited by the British to establish in Labrador.

22. *DCB*, 4: s.v. "Mikak."

23. Barnett Richling, "Without Compromise: Hudson's Bay Company and Moravian Trade Rivalry in Nineteenth Century Labrador," in Bruce G. Trigger, Toby Morantz, and Louise Dechêne, eds, *Le Castor Fait Tout* (Montreal, 1987), 456–84.

24. An adult whale would have as much as 2,000 pounds of baleen in its jaws; in 1883, baleen brought $4.75 a pound.

25. Ross, *Whaling and Eskimos*, 138.

26. On adaptation to Euro-Canadian foods, see Morris Zaslow, *The Northward Expansion of Canada, 1914–1967* (Toronto, 1988), 153.

27. John R. Bockstoce, *Whales, Ice, and Men: The History of Whaling in the Western Arctic* (Seattle, 1986), 130, 136.

28. Ibid., 135–42.

29. Morris Zaslow, *The Opening of the Canadian North, 1870–1914* (Toronto, 1971), 258.

30. On the effects of the change of diet, see Morrison, *Under the Flag*, 74–6.

31. The name "Yukon" (Youcon, Ou-kun-ah) derives from an Indigenous word, probably Gwich'in, meaning great river or white water river. If the Bering Strait migration hypothesis is correct, then Yukon, with Alaska, would be North America's oldest inhabited region. Kenneth S. Coates and William R. Morrison, *Land of the Midnight Sun: A History of the Yukon* (Edmonton, 1988), 2, 5.

32. Ibid., 13, 25, 50.

33. McClellan, *Part of the Land*, 67–70, 75–84; Coates and Morrison, *Land of the Midnight Sun*, 23–30.

34. L.F.S. Upton, *Micmacs and Colonists: Indian–White Relations in the Maritimes, 1713–1867* (Vancouver, 1979), 82–7.

35. Ibid., 91.

36. Douglas Sanders, "Government Indian Agencies in Canada," in Washburn, ed., *Handbook of North American Indians, 4: History of Indian–White Relations*, 279.

37. Upton, *Micmacs and Colonists*, 95.

38. During the nineteenth century the porpoise was particularly valued for its oil, which was used in the manufacture and maintenance of fine watches. A bill before the Nova Scotia House of Assembly to ban the shooting of porpoises in the bay had passed two readings when Meuse made his plea that resulted in the bill's defeat.

39. "Mikak," *Dictionary of Canadian Biography Online*, http://www .biographi.ca/en/bio/mikak_4E.html; Nadine Fabbi, "Inuktitut," http://www.k12studycanada.org/files/Inuktitut.pdf. For recent research on Mikak, based on documentary and archaeological evidence, see Amelia Fay, "Big Men, Big Women, or Both? Examining the Coastal Trading System of the Eighteenth-Century Labrador Inuit," in John C. Kennedy, ed., *History and Renewal of Labrador's Inuit-Métis* (St. John's, 2014), 75–93.

40. More precisely, a reserve is "a tract of land in which the aboriginal interest is permanently preserved for a particular group of native people." Jack Woodward, *Native Law* (Toronto, 1989), 222. See also Brian Slattery, "Understanding Aboriginal Rights," *Canadian Bar Review* 66 (1987): 743–4, 769–71. A Cree term applied to reserves is "iskonikun," meaning "what is left over" or "scraps." This refers to the fact that many reserves are ill-suited for agriculture and have long since become useless for hunting and trapping. See Eleanor Brass, *I Walk in Two Worlds* (Calgary, 1987), 71.

41. Henderson, *Canada's Indian Reserves*, 4–5. See also Richard H. Bartlett, "The Establishment of Indian Reserves on the Prairies," *Canadian Native Law Reporter* 3 (1980): 3–56.

42. Upton, *Micmacs and Colonists*, 96.

43. Ibid., 99; Cumming and Mickenberg, eds, *Native Rights in Canada*, 308–9; "John Julien," *Dictionary of Canadian Biography Online*, http://www.biographi.ca/en/bio/julien_john_5E.html.

44. Upton, *Micmacs and Colonists*, 99–100.

45. Cumming and Mickenberg, eds, *Native Rights in Canada*, 102.

46. Upton, *Micmacs and Colonists*, 112.

47. *Journals of the Legislative Assembly of Prince Edward Island*, 7 Jan. 1812, 11–12; cited by Upton, *Micmacs and Colonists*, 115.

48. Ibid., 118.

49. Maurice F.V. Doll, Robert S. Kidd, and John P. Day, *The Buffalo Lake Métis Site: A Late Nineteenth Century Settlement in the Parkland of Central Alberta* (Edmonton, 1988), 13–14.

50. Paul Kane, *Wanderings of an Artist* (Edmonton, 1968 [1859]), 89.

51. Overhunting had, by this time, become a serious problem; the Nor'Westers alone regularly prepared 30 to 50 tons of pemmican each season for the company's fur brigades. A.S. Morton, *History of Prairie Settlement and Dominion Lands Policy* (Toronto, 1938), 208.

52. The Cree told Palliser that the buffalo were disappearing and that they hoped to be provided with farming implements. Irene M. Spry, *The Palliser Expedition: An Account of John Palliser's British North American Expedition, 1857–1860* (Toronto, 1963), 60; see also F.G. Roe, "Early Agriculture in Western Canada in Relation to Climatic Stability," *Agricultural History* 26, 3 (1952): 109. On pre-contact agriculture in the Red River area, see *Prehistory of the Lockport Site* (Winnipeg, 1985), 11.

53. Laura L. Peers, "Rich Man, Poor Man, Beggarman, Chief: Saulteaux in the Red River Settlement, 1812–1833," in William Cowan, ed., *Papers of the Eighteenth Algonquian Conference* (Ottawa, 1987), 265–9.

54. Both the Jurisdiction Act of 1803 and the Fur Trade Act of 1821 were concerned with extending the Canadian court system into the Northwest. The 1803 Act had been inspired by the Louisiana Purchase of the same year.

55. Morton, *History of the Canadian West*, 628.

56. Hamar Foster, "Long-Distance Justice: The Criminal Jurisdiction of Canadian Courts West of the Canadas, 1763–1859," *American Journal of Legal History* 34, 1 (1990): 6.

57. Abishabis, Dictionary of Canadian Biography, http://www .biographi.ca/en/bio/abishabis_7E.html.

58. Paul Tennant, *Aboriginal Peoples and Politics* (Vancouver, 1990), 20.

59. Knight, *Indians at Work*, 236.

60. Fisher, *Contact and Conflict*, 154–6.

61. "Wai Wei Kum History," in Wai Wei Kum Kwiakah Online, http://www.wkts.ca/history.

62. Tennant, *Aboriginal Peoples and Politics*, 21–38.

63. For example, according to Robert Cail, "So long as Douglas was governor, the Indians had only to ask to receive additional land." Cail, *Land, Man, and the Law: The Disposal of Crown Lands in British Columbia, 1871–1913* (Vancouver, 1974), 179.

64. Fisher, *Contact and Conflict*, 153–6.

65. Dennis Madill, *British Columbia Treaties in Historical Perspective* (Ottawa, 1981), 31.

66. Barry M. Gough, *Gunboat Frontier: British Maritime Authority and Northwest Coast Indians, 1846–1890* (Vancouver, 1984).

67. J.E. Michael Kew, "History of Coastal British Columbia since 1849," in Suttles, ed., *Handbook of North American Indians, 7: Northwest Coast*, 159.

68. Fisher, *Contact and Conflict*, 208.

69. Gough, *Gunboat Frontier*, 205–8.

Chapter 11

1. Crown Land Protection Act, https://www.britannica.com/topic/Crown-Lands-Protection-Act.

2. http://www.sicc.sk.ca/archive/saskindian/a78mar04.htm.

3. An Act for the Better Protection of Lands and Property of Indians in Lower Canada. http://www.thecanadianencyclopedia.ca/en/article/indian-act/; http://www.sicc.sk.ca/archive/saskindian/a78mar04.htm. Note that these Acts referred to Upper and Lower Canada although by this time they were officially Canada West and Canada East.

4. An Act to encourage the Gradual Civilization of the Indian Tribes of the Canadas, also known as the Gradual Civilization Act, http://caid.ca/GraCivAct1857.pdf.

5. Act Respecting Civilizing and Enfranchisement of certain Indians, http://caid.ca/CivEnfAct1859.pdf; http://signatoryindian.tripod .com/welcometokisikawpimootewinandgroupswebsitecopy3/id58.html.

6. An Act for the gradual enfranchisement of Indians, https://www .aadnc-aandc.gc.ca/DAM/DAM-INTER-HQ/STAGING/texte-text/a69c6_1100100010205_eng.pdf.

7. John H. Bodley, ed., *Tribal Peoples and Development Issues: A Global Overview* (Mountain View, Calif., 1988), 63–9.

8. Some of these problems are still continuing. For example, the community of Shannonville, Ontario, occupies lands that were

leased by the Haudenosaunee of Tyendinaga early in the nineteenth century to a certain Turton Penn for 999 years. Henderson, *Canada's Indian Reserves*, 38 n48.

9. Leslie and Maguire, *Historical Development of the Indian Act*, 11.

10. A clear exposition of this position is that of Herman Merivale, "Policy of Colonial Governments towards Native Tribes, as Regards Their Protection and Their Civilization," in Bodley, ed., *Tribal Peoples*, 95–104.

11. The phrase "white man's burden" owes its origin to Rudyard Kipling, who used it in reference to colonial powers and their relationship to the Indigenous Peoples whose territories they took over.

12. Dennis Madill, "Band Council Powers," in W.E. Daugherty and Madill, *Indian Government under Indian Act Legislation 1868–1951* (Ottawa, 1980).

13. John E. Hodgetts, *Pioneer Public Service: An Administrative History of the United Canadas, 1841–1867* (Toronto, 1955), 223.

14. David McNab, "The Colonial Office and the Prairies in the Mid-Nineteenth Century," *Prairie Forum* 3, 1 (1978): 21–38.

15. It was published in two parts, in *Journals of the Legislative Assembly of the Province of Canada*, 1844–5, app. EEE; and ibid., 1847, app. T.

16. Ibid., 1847, app. T.

17. Cited by Richardson, "Kind Hearts or Forked Tongues?" 23. The commissioners appear to have considered that Indigenous Peoples' loss of lands was in large part due to alienation by the First Nations themselves. Such a view would have been reinforced by the lack of Indigenous action in launching suits against trespass or for the recovery of lost lands. See the Bagot Commission Report, *Journals of the Legislative Assembly of the Province of Canada*, 1844–5, app. EEE; and 1847, app. T.

18. Thomas Anderson, for example, opposed the discontinuance, arguing that it would result in serious deprivation; see Leslie and Maguire, *Historical Development of the Indian Act*, 21.

19. Smith, *Sacred Feathers*, 184.

20. An Act for the Better Protection of Lands and Property of Indians in Lower Canada, http://www.thecanadianencyclopedia.ca/en/article/indian-act/; http://www.sicc.sk.ca/archive/saskindian/a78mar04.htm.

21. An Act for the Better Protection of Lands and Property of Indians in Lower Canada, http://www.sicc.sk.ca/archive/saskindian/a78mar04.htm.

22. Toby Morantz, "Aboriginal Land Claims in Quebec," in Ken Coates, ed., *Aboriginal Land Claims in Canada* (Toronto, 1992), 107.

23. *Schedule of Indian Bands, Reserves and Settlements* (Ottawa, 1987), 11–17. Indigenous settlements, of which there are about a dozen, are not included, as they do not have lands specifically set aside for them.

24. Some reserved the term "Indian" for those who were registered. See, for example, J. Rick Ponting and Roger Gibbins, *Out of Irrelevance* (Toronto, 1980), xv.

25. Gradual Civilization Act http://caid.ca/GraCivAct1857.pdf.

26. John L. Tobias, "Protection, Civilization, Assimilation: An Outline History of Canada's Indian Policy," *Western Canadian Journal of Anthropology* 6, 2 (1976): 16. This article was reprinted in A.L. Getty and Antoine S. Lussier, eds, *As Long As the Sun Shines and Water Flows* (Vancouver, 1983), 39–55.

27. Peter Jones, the Mississauga chief, had warned that Indigenous Peoples must feel like full partners in the new order. He pinpointed such measures as security of ownership of reserve lands and civil rights; see Smith, *Sacred Feathers*, 238–9.

28. Act Respecting Civilizing and Enfranchisement of certain Indians, http://caid.ca/CivEnfAct1859.pdf; http://signatoryindian.tripod.com/welcometokisikawpimootewinandgroupswebsitecopy3/id58.html.

29. For a study of the long Ojibwa struggle with the mining companies, see Janet E. Chute, *The Legacy of Shingwaukonse: A Century of Native Leadership* (Toronto, 1998).

30. Douglas Leighton, "The Historical Significance of the Robinson Treaties of 1850," paper presented to the Canadian Historical Association, Ottawa, 1982; Richardson, "Kind Hearts or Forked Tongues?" 24–7; George Brown and Ron Maguire, eds, *Indian Treaties in Historical Perspective* (Ottawa, 1979), 26.

31. This view is expressed in a pamphlet issued by the Federation of Saskatchewan Indians, *Indian Treaty Rights*, n.d., n.p.

32. Allen G. Harper, "Canada's Indian Administration: Basic Concepts and Objectives," *América Indígena* 5, 2 (1945): 132. See also Roger Gibbins and J. Rick Ponting, "Historical Overview and Background," in Ponting, ed., *Arduous Journey: Canadian Indians and Decolonization* (Toronto, 1986), 25.

33. Hodgetts, *Pioneer Public Service*, 209–10.

34. Robinson Huron and Robinson Superior Treaties, https://www.aadnc-aandc.gc.ca/eng/1100100028970/1100100028972.

35. A rule of thumb for determining their size was to allow 80 acres (32 ha) per family; however, there was considerable variation in practice.

36. Wikwemikong History, http://www.manitoulin-island.com/wikwemikong/communities.html.

37. Douglas Sanders, "Government Indian Agencies," in Washburn, ed., *Handbook of North American Indians, 4: History of Indian–White Relations*, 279.

38. Malcolm Montgomery, "The Six Nations Indians and the Macdonald Franchise," *Ontario History* 56 (1964): 13.

39. The price was $1.5 million, or about one penny for every three ha.

40. *Census of Canada*, 1871, 1: 332–3; 1881, 1: 300–1; 1941, 684–91.

41. Wayne Daugherty, "The Elective System," in Daugherty and Madill, *Indian Government under Indian Act Legislation*, 4.

42. Ibid., 3.

43. Tobias, "Protection, Civilization, Assimilation," 17–18.

44. An Act for the gradual enfranchisement of Indians, https://www.aadnc-aandc.gc.ca/DAM/DAM-INTER-HQ/STAGING/texte-text/a69c6_1100100010205_eng.pdf.

45. Tobias, "Protection, Civilization, Assimilation," 22–3. On legal meanings of "Indian," see Woodward, *Native Law*, 5–12.

46. Kathleen Jamieson, *Indian Women and the Law in Canada: Citizens Minus* (Ottawa, 1978), 69–73.

47. William B. Henderson, "Indian Act," in *The Canadian Encyclopedia*, http://www.thecanadianencyclopedia.ca/en/article/indian-act.

48. Dennis Madill, "Band Council Powers," in Daugherty and Madill, *Indian Government under Indian Act Legislation*, 2.

49. N.L. Barlee, "The Chilcotin War of 1864," *Canada West Magazine* 6, 4 (1976): 13–23. Another explanation of Klatsassin's behaviour has it that his people had been decimated by smallpox in 1862, and when a Euro-Canadian threatened him with death, he understood it as a return of the disease and decided that the best way to prevent that from happening was to drive out all European settlers from the area. See *DCB*, 9: s.v. "Klatsassin."

50. Robin Fisher, "Joseph Trutch and Indian Land Policy," *B.C. Studies* 12 (1971–2): 17. See also Berger, *Fragile Freedoms*, 222.

51. "Ordinance further to define the law regulating acquisition of Land in British Columbia."

52. Kew, "History of Coastal British Columbia since 1849," 159.

53. *Report of the Royal Commission on Aboriginal Peoples*, 5 vols (Ottawa, 1996), 2, part 2: 784.

54. The 1871 Census counted 9,800 Métis out of a total population of 11,400. Nathalie J. Kermoal, "Le 'Temps de Cayoge': La vie quotidienne des femmes métisses au Manitoba de 1850 à 1900," Ph.D. thesis (University of Ottawa, 1996), xliii n23, 40.

55. Pierre Falcon, "Chanson de la Grenouilliere," *Les cloches de Saint-Boniface* 13, 6 (15 mars 1914): 75–6; author's translation.

56. For the story of Grant, see Margaret MacLeod and W.L. Morton, *Cuthbert Grant of Grantown* (Toronto, 1974).

57. Barry Cooper, "Alexander Kennedy Isbister: A Respectable Victorian," *Canadian Ethnic Studies* 17, 2 (1985): 44–63; *DCB*, 11: s.v. "Isbister, Alexander Kennedy." He had gone to England at the age of 20.

58. Most of the Métis of Red River were of Cree descent and so had inherited the animosity that existed betweeen Cree and Dakota peoples.

59. For some of the colonial secretary's views, see Herman Merivale, "Policy of Colonial Governments towards Native Tribes, as Regards Their Protection and Their Civilization," in Bodley, ed., *Tribal Peoples*, 95–204; David T. McNab, "Herman Merivale and Colonial Office Indian Policy in the Mid-Nineteenth Century," in Getty and Lussier, eds, *As Long As the Sun Shines and Water Flows*, 85–103.

60. Alexander Morris, *The Treaties of Canada with the Indians* (Toronto, 1880; reprint, 1971), 169.

61. NAC, RG 6, C-1, vol. 316, file 995, William McDougall to Secretary of State for the Provinces, 5 Nov. 1869; "Copy of the Indian Agreement," *The Globe*, Toronto, 4 Sept. 1869, 3. Both references cited by Daniel, *History of Native Land Claims*, 3.

62. For details of these troubles, see Frits Pannekoek, *A Snug Little Flock: The Social Origins of the Riel Resistance of 1869–70* (Winnipeg, 1991).

63. Although the French language predominated among Red River Métis, in biological fact they were more mixed than that would indicate. Historian Diane Payment has illustrated this with names: MacGillis (Magillice), Bruce (Brousse), Sayer (Serre), McKay (Macaille), and McDougall (McDoub). Payment, *Batoche (1870–1970)* (St Boniface, Man., 1983), 1.

64. Their story is told by Elias, *Dakota of the Canadian Northwest*. See also James H. Howard, *The Canadian Sioux* (Lincoln, Neb., 1984); Roy W. Meyer, "The Canadian Sioux Refugees from Minnesota," *Minnesota History* 41, 1 (1968): 13–28; George F.G. Stanley, "Displaced Red Men: The Sioux in Canada," in Ian A.L. Getty and Donald B. Smith, eds, *One Century Later: Western Canadian Reserve Indians since Treaty 7* (Vancouver, 1978), 55–81.

65. Gerhard Ens, "Métis Lands in Manitoba," *Manitoba History* no. 5 (Spring 1983), http://www.mhs.mb.ca/docs/mb_history/05/metislands.shtml.

66. Daniel, *History of Native Land Claims*, 4, citing John Leonard Taylor, "The Development of an Indian Policy for the Canadian North-West, 1869–70," Ph.D. thesis (Queen's University, 1975), 28.

67. Riel was the grandson of Jean-Baptiste Lagimodière (1778–1855) and Marie Anne Gaboury (1780–1875), first non-Indigenous woman in the West. During the winter of 1816–17, Jean-Baptiste and a companion had travelled by foot from Red River to Montreal (17 Oct. 1816–10 Mar. 1817) to inform Lord Selkirk about the Battle of Seven Oaks. Riel's parents were farmers and did not participate in either the fur trade or the buffalo hunt.

68. On the St Paul trade, see Rhoda R. Gilman, Carolyn Gilman, and Deborah M. Stultz, *The Red River Trails: Oxcart Routes between St. Paul and the Selkirk Settlement 1820–1870* (St Paul, Minn., 1979).

69. "Declaration of the People of Rupert's Land and the North-West," 8 Dec. 1869, in E.H. Oliver, ed., *The Canadian North-West: Its Early Development and Legislative Records* (Ottawa, 1915), 904. The full Declaration is at: www.mhs.mb.ca/docs/pageant/09/rupertslanddeclaration.shtml.

70. LAC, Macdonald Papers, vol. 516, Macdonald to McDougall, 27 Nov. 1869; cited by Donald Creighton, *John A. Macdonald*, 2 vols (Toronto, 1966 [1955]), 2: 51.

71. Ontario was particularly enraged because the court martial that had condemned Scott had been made up of Métis and First Nations. See Arthur Silver, "French Quebec and the Métis Question, 1869–1885," in Carl Berger and Ramsay Cook, eds, *The West and the Nation* (Toronto, 1976), 91–113.

72. George F.G. Stanley, *The Birth of Western Canada: A History of the Riel Rebellion* (Toronto, 1960 [1936]), 129, 135–6.

73. In 1872 Macdonald sent $1,000, via Archbishop Taché, for both Riel and Ambroise-Dydime Lépine (1834–1923) to stay out of the country. Riel took advantage of the offer, but Lépine, who had headed the court martial that had condemned Scott, came back.

74. Ironically, an ultimate result of the confrontations was to split the Métis into two groups: those of Red River and Rupert's Land (the "New Nation") who had stood up for their rights, and the "others" in the rest of the country who had not made such a stand. See the *Report of the RCAP*, 4: ch. 5, "Métis Perspectives," 199–384.

Chapter 12

1. The *Report of the RCAP*, while acknowledging that Indigenous treaties were kept "alive" through periodic renegotiations to adapt them to changing circumstances (2, part 1: 11), later observed that "their central feature makes them irrevocable" (19).

2. The United States stopped making treaties with Indigenous tribes in 1871, the year that Canada signed the first of its 11 numbered treaties.

3. John S. Long, "'No Basis for Argument?' The Signing of Treaty Nine in Northern Ontario, 1905–1906," *Native Studies Review* 5, 2 (1989): 36.

4. There are 483 agreements listed in Canada, *Indian Treaties and Surrenders from 1680 to 1902*, 3 vols (Ottawa, 1891–1912; facsimile, 1971). Since then a few have been added.

5. Brown and Maguire, eds, *Indian Treaties in Historical Perspective*, 32.

6. Richard C. Daniel, "Indian Rights and Hinterland Provinces: The Case of Northern Alberta," MA thesis (University of Alberta, 1977), ch. 2.

7. Taylor, "Development of an Indian Policy," 45–6.

8. Canada, Parliament, *Sessional Papers*, 1867–8, no. 81, 18; 1869, no. 42, 20–1.

9. David J. Hall, "'A Serene Atmosphere'? Treaty 1 Revisited," *Canadian Journal of Native Studies* 4, 2 (1984), 325.

10. For an examination of the negotiations for Treaty One, see ibid.

11. Harold Cardinal, *The Unjust Society: The Tragedy of Canada's Indians* (Edmonton, 1969), 36.

12. Daniel, *History of Native Claims Processes*, 12. Canada had agreed, in 1894, that any future treaties within Ontario would require the province's concurrence. Similarly, later adhesions presented little, if any, opportunity for negotiations. The territories

involved could be considerable—in Treaty Nine, for instance, most of northern Ontario was involved in the adhesion of 1929.

13. Morris, *Treaties of Canada with the Indians*, 62.

14. Ibid.; David T. McNab, *Circles of Time: Aboriginal Land Rights and Resistance in Ontario* (Waterloo, Ont., 1999), 11.

15. The idea of train passes was not out of line, of course. The railways handed them out to privileged customers, such as persons in certain professions. In the United States, Indigenous people were allowed free rides on western railroads but were not entitled to free seats; they could ride in boxcars.

16. Morris, *Treaties of Canada with the Indians*, 69.

17. John S. Long, "Treaty No. 9 and Fur Trade Company Families: Northeastern Ontario's Halfbreeds, Indians, Petitioners and Métis," in Jacqueline Peterson and Jennifer S.H. Brown, eds, *The New Peoples: Being and Becoming Métis in North America* (Winnipeg, 1985), 145; *Report of the RCAP*, 4: 261.

18. Taylor, "Development of an Indian Policy," 29.

19. In 1904 the force was renamed the Royal North-West Mounted Police; in 1920, it became the Royal Canadian Mounted Police, which is still its designation today. On the NWMP, see R.C. Macleod, *The North-West Mounted Police and Law Enforcement, 1873–1905* (Toronto, 1976).

20. "Ta-tanka I-yotank," *Dictionary of Canadian Biography Online*, http://www.biographi.ca/en/bio/ta_tanka_i_yotank_11E.html.

21. Robert S. Allen, "A Witness to Murder: The Cypress Hills Massacre and the Conflict of Attitudes towards the Native People of the Canadian and American West during the 1870s," in Getty and Lussier, eds, *As Long as the Sun Shines and Water Flows*, 232–3; James William Daschuk, *Clearing the Plains: Disease, Politics of Starvation, and the Loss of Aboriginal Life* (Regina, Sask., 2014), 81.

22. Allen, "Witness to Murder," 234–5; Gerald R. Friesen, *The Canadian Prairies: A History* (Toronto, 1984), 134–5.

23. Philip Goldring, *Whiskey, Horses and Death: The Cypress Hills Massacre and Its Sequel*, Occasional Papers in Archaeology and History No. 21 (Ottawa, 1973).

24. Paul F. Sharp, "Massacre at Cypress Hills," *Saskatchewan History* 7 (1954): 81–99; Zaslow, *Opening of the Canadian North*, 15–17; Friesen, *The Canadian Prairies*, 133–4.

25. B.D. Fardy, *Jerry Potts, Paladin of the Plains* (Langley, BC, 1984); "Jerry Potts," *Dictionary of Canadian Biography Online*, http://www.biographi.ca/en/bio/potts_jerry_12E.html.

26. Hugh A. Dempsey has written a biography, *Crowfoot: Chief of the Blackfeet* (Edmonton, 1972). Dempsey points out (pp. 93–107) that Crowfoot was not the head chief of the Niitsitapiikwan, as generally believed by non-Indigenous people, but one of the chiefs of the Siksikawa proper. The other members of the Confederacy, the Káínawa (Blood), Tsuu T'ina (Sarcee), and Piikani (Peigan), each had their own chiefs, and they all participated in the treaty negotiations. Crowfoot, however, was particularly highly regarded by the Crown representatives, and this increased his influence among his fellow chiefs in treaty matters. Also see "Isapo-Muxika," *Dictionary of Canadian Biography Online*, http://www.biographi.ca/en/bio/isapo_muxica_11F.html.

27. Leslie and Maguire, eds, *Historical Development of the Indian Act*, 59.

28. "History and Culture of the Siksika Nation," Siksika Nation Offical Website, http://siksikanation.com/wp/history.

29. "Poundmaker," University of Saskatchewan Libraries; "Pitikwahanapiwiyin," *Dictionary of Canadian Biography Online*, http://www.biographi.ca/en/bio/pitikwahanapiwiyin_11E.html.

30. Wikaskokiseyin ("Sweetgrass") had become a chief by achieving what Maskepetoon had failed to do: he entered a Niitsitapi camp alone, killed a warrior, and captured 40 horses. By 1870 he had become principal chief of the River Cree; in the meantime, in 1865, he had adopted the name Abraham when he had been converted by Father Albert Lacombe. The HBC dubbed him "Chief of the Country." See *DCB*, 10: s.v. "Wikaskokiseyin."

31. Arthur J. Ray, *Indians in the Fur Trade: Their Role as Trappers, Hunters, and Middlemen in the Lands Southwest of Hudson Bay, 1660–1870* (Toronto, 1974), 228.

32. Hugh A. Dempsey, *Big Bear: The End of Freedom* (Vancouver, 1984), 77–8.

33. Dempsey, *Crowfoot*, 102.

34. Cited in Dempsey, *Big Bear*, 63. See also "Mistahimaskwa," *Dictionary of Canadian Biography Online*, http://www.biographi.ca/en/bio/mistahimaskwa_11E.html.

35. Dempsey, *Big Bear*, 67.

36. Leslie and Maguire, eds, *Historical Development of the Indian Act*, 100.

37. The "Indian Register" is a list maintained by the government; it consists of Band Lists and General Lists. Those who are registered and subject to the Indian Act are "status Indians."

38. "Payipwat," *Dictionary of Canadian Biography Online*, http://www.biographi.ca/en/bio/payipwat_13E.html.

39. Leslie and Maguire, eds, *Historical Development of the Indian Act*, 65.

40. *Report of the RCAP*, 2, part 2: 809.

41. Leslie and Maguire, eds, *Historical Development of the Indian Act*, 67.

42. The term "potlatch" included several different types of feasts, of which the "giveaway" was one. Jay Miller described feasts as "knots holding together the . . . social fabric." Miller, "Feasting with the Southern Tsimshian," in Margaret Seguin, ed., *The Tsimshian: Images of the Past, Views for the Present* (Vancouver, 1984), 27–39; Tina Loo, "Don Cranmer's Potlatch: Law as Coercion, Symbol and Rhetoric in British Columbia, 1884–1951," *Canadian Historical Review* 73, 2 (1992): 125–65; Stuart Piddocke, "The Potlatch System of the Southern Kwakiutl: A New Perspective," *Southwestern Journal of Anthropology* 21 (1965): 244–64.

43. For a contemporary view of the matter, see A.G. Morice, *Au pays de l'ours noir* (Paris, 1897), 146–61.

44. Alfred Scow, Royal Commission of Aboriginal Peoples (RCAP), Transcriptions of Public Hearings and Round Table Discussions, 1992–3, Ottawa, Thursday, November 26, 1992, 344-5. Available online courtesy of the University of Saskatchewan Archives: http://scaa.sk.ca/ourlegacy/permalink/30466.

45. Edward Ahenakew, *Voices of the Plains Cree* (Toronto, 1973), 182.

46. Kehoe, *The Ghost Dance*, 129–34; F.L. Barron, "The Indian Pass System in the Canadian West, 1882–1935," *Prairie Forum* 13, 1 (1988): 31. See also Katherine Pettipas, *Severing the Ties That Bind: Government Repression of Indigenous Religious Ceremonies on the Prairies* (Winnipeg, 1994).

47. George Manuel and Michael Posluns, *The Fourth World: An Indian Reality* (Don Mills, Ont., 1974), 78–9.

48. Cited by Cody Poulton, "Songs from the Gods: 'Hearing the Voice' in the Ascetic Rituals of West Coast Indians and Japanese Liturgic Drama," paper presented to the Thirty-third International Congress of Asian and North African Studies, University of Toronto, 1991.

49. Pettipas, *Severing the Ties That Bind*, 160–6.

50. On the role of the Indian Act, see John F. Leslie, *A Historical Survey of Indian–Government Relations, 1940–1970* (Ottawa, 1993), esp. 12–19.

51. Tobias, "Protection, Civilization, Assimilation," 19–20.

52. Leslie and Maguire, eds, *Historical Development of the Indian Act*, 77, 85–6.

53. Ibid., 81.

54. Ibid., 87.

55. This cry was raised by David Mills, who under Prime Minister Alexander Mackenzie had been Minister of the Interior, 1876–8. *House of Commons Debates*, 1885, vol. 2, 1580: The Franchise Bill, 4 May 1885; cited by Leslie and Maguire, eds, *Historical Development of the Indian Act*, 86.

56. Montgomery, "The Six Nations Indians and the Macdonald Franchise," 20.

Chapter 13

1. The only comparable situation concerns the overhunting of beavers in the first half of the seventeenth century when the arrival of Europeans in the Great Lakes region unsettled the rhythms of life. The reasons for the overhunting led to a famous debate over its causes. See Shepard Krech III, ed., *Indians, Animals, and the Fur Trade: A Critque of Keepers of the Game* (Athens, Ga, 1981), passim. On the bison decline, see John L. Tobias, "Indian Reserves in Western Canada: Indian Homelands or Devices for Assimilation," in D.A. Muise, ed., *Approaches to Native History in Canada* (Ottawa, 1977), 89–103.

2. Henry Youle Hind, *Narrative of the Canadian Red River Exploring Expedition of 1857 and of the Assiniboine and Saskatchewan Exploring Expedition of 1858*, 2 vols (Edmonton, 1971), 1: 360–1; Milloy, *The Plains Cree*, 107–8.

3. Morton, *History of Prairie Settlement*, 236–8.

4. P.R. Mailhot and D.M. Sprague, "Persistent Settlers: The Dispersal and Resettlement of the Red River Metis, 1870–1885," *Canadian Journal of Ethnic Studies* 17 (1985): 1–30.

5. D.W. Moodie and Arthur J. Ray make the point that hunters understood the factors that influenced bison behaviour, so they knew where to look for the herds. See Moodie and Ray, "Buffalo Migrations in the Canadian Plains," *Plains Anthropologist* 21, 71 (1976): 45–51.

6. "Gabriel Dumont," *Dictionary of Canadian Biography Online*, http://www.biographi.ca/en/bio/dumont_gabriel_13E.html; "Gabriel Dumont," in The Northwest Resistance: A Database of Materials held by the University of Saskatchewan Libraries and the University Archives, http://library.usask.ca/northwest/background/dumont. htm; Matthew Barrett, "Hero of the Half-Breed Rebellion: Gabriel Dumont and the late-Victorian Military," *Journal of Canadian Studies / Revue d'études Canadiennes* 48: 3(2014): 79–107.

7. Bob Beal and Rod Macleod, *Prairie Fire: The 1885 North-West Rebellion* (Edmonton, 1984), 41. Dumont had become buffalo-hunt captain at the age of 25.

8. Thomas Flanagan has analyzed the situation in detail in *Riel and the Rebellion: 1885 Reconsidered* (Saskatoon, 1983).

9. Some hold that Clarke was an agent provocateur for Macdonald, actively fomenting trouble as a way out of solving financial difficulties that were plaguing the construction of the Canadian Pacific Railway. See Don McLean, *Home from the Hill: A History of the Metis in Western Canada* (Regina, 1987).

10. George Woodcock, *Gabriel Dumont* (Edmonton, 1975), 81–4.

11. "Louis Riel," *Dictionary of Canadian Biography Online*, http://www.biographi.ca/en/bio/riel_louis_1844_85_11E. html; "Louis Riel," in The Northwest Resistance: A Database of Materials held by the University of Saskatchewan Libraries and the University Archives, http://library.usask.ca/northwest/background/riel.htm.

12. On Riel's return, see Geoff Read and Todd Webb, "The Catholic Mahdi of the North West: Louis Riel and Métis Resistance in Trans-Atlantic and Imperial Context," *Canadian Historical Review* 93: 2 (2012): 171–95.

13. "Mistahimaskwa," *Dictionary of Canadian Biography Online*, http://www.biographi.ca/en/bio/mistahimaskwa_11E.html; "Mistahimaskwa," in The Northwest Resistance: A Database of Materials held by the University of Saskatchewan Libraries and the University Archives, http://library.usask.ca/northwest/background/riel.htm.

14. Dempsey, *Big Bear*, 77–8; see also R.S. Allen, "Big Bear," *Saskatchewan History* 25, 1 (1972): 1–17; William B. Fraser, "Big Bear, Indian Patriot," *Alberta Historical Review* 14, 2 (1966): 1–13; *DCB*, 11: s.v. "Mistahimaskwa."

15. "Minahikosis," *Dictionary of Canadian Biography Online*, http://www.biographi.ca/en/bio/minahikosis_11E.html; "Wikaskokiseyin," *Dictionary of Canadian Biography Online*, http://www.biographi.ca/en/bio/wikaskokiseyin_abraham_10E.html.

16. Even though the Siksikawa and Cree considered each other enemies, Isapo-Muxika saw nothing anomalous in adopting Pītikwahanapiwīyin because of his striking resemblance to a son he had lost. See "Pitikwahanapiwiyin," *Dictionary of Canadian Biography Online*, http://www.biographi.ca/en/bio/pitikwahanapiwiyin_11E.html; "Pitikwahanapiwiyin," in The Northwest Resistance: A Database of Materials held by the University of Saskatchewan Libraries and the University Archives, http://library.usask.ca/northwest/background/pound.htm.

17. T.J. Brasser, *Blackfoot* (Ottawa, n.d.), 3.

18. Carter, *Lost Harvests*, 30. This carefully documented study imputes the failure of the agricultural programs to government policy rather than to the supposed inability of Indigenous people to become farmers.

19. Ibid., 112.

20. "Hayter Reed," *Dictionary of Canadian Biography Online*, http://www.biographi.ca/en/bio/reed_hayter_16E.html.

21. Long before the demise of the bison herds—in the very early days of the fur trade, in fact—some Indigenous people had already successfully taken up farming. Within a century of the establishment of the fur trade, the "three sisters," corn, beans, and squash, were being grown at their northern limit. This was in response to the needs of the posts for provisioning. See D. Wayne Moodie and Barry Kaye, "Indian Agriculture in the Fur Trade Northwest," *Prairie Forum* 11, 2 (1986): 171–84; Moodie and Kaye, "The Northern Limit of Indian Agriculture in North America," *Geographical Review* 59, 4 (1969): 513–29.

22. Cited by Beal and Macleod, *Prairie Fire*, 74.

23. Interestingly, in his travels Maskepetoon also met well-known western artists George Catlin and Paul Kane, and reportedly met US President Andrew Jackson earlier in his life. He also served as a guide for the Palliser expedition. "Maskepetoon," *Dictionary of Canadian Biography Online*, http://www.biographi.ca/en/bio/maskepetoon_9E.html.

24. "Isapo-Muxika," *Dictionary of Canadian Biography Online*, http://www.biographi.ca/en/bio/isapo_muxika_11E.html.

25. *Report of the Commissioner of the North-West Mounted Police Force*, 1884: Commissioner A.G. Irvine, 8.
26. John L. Tobias, "The Subjugation of the Plains Cree, 1879–1885," *Canadian Historical Review* 64, 4 (1983): 539; *DCB*, 11: s.v. "Kapapamahchakwew."
27. Leslie and Maguire, eds, *Historical Development of the Indian Act*, 81.
28. Beal and Macleod, *Prairie Fire*, 63, 115–16, 120; Isabel Andrews, "Indian Protest against Starvation: The Yellow Calf Incident of 1884," *Saskatchewan History* 28, 2 (1975): 41–51. Mistawasis was Pītikwahanapiwīyin's uncle and was renowned as a hunter.
29. The Métis Declaration of Rights is reproduced in full in Beal and Macleod, *Prairie Fire*, 136.
30. In the Roman Catholic Church, a novena is a series of devotions made on nine successive days for some special purpose.
31. "Kāpeyakwāskonam," *Dictionary of Canadian Biography Online*, http://www.biographi.ca/en/bio/kapeyakwaskonam_11E.html.
32. Pihew-kamihkosit ("Red Pheasant"), whose reserve was also in the region, had died just before the sortie began.
33. A Cree Anglican clergyman's view of the event is that of Dr Edward Ahenakew, "An Opinion of the Frog Lake Massacre," *Alberta Historical Review* 8, 3 (1966): 9–15. Another Cree view is that of Joseph F. Dion, *My Tribe the Crees* (Calgary, 1979). Contemporary accounts were compiled and edited by Rudy Wiebe and Bob Beal in *War in the West: Voices of the 1885 Rebellion* (Toronto, 1985). The sensationalized press accounts that contributed to public hysteria at the time are described by Sarah Carter, *Aboriginal People and Colonizers of Western Canada to 1900* (Toronto, 1999), 159ff.
34. "Frederick Dobson Middleton," *Dictionary of Canadian Biography Online*, http://www.biographi.ca/en/bio/middleton_frederick_dobson_12E.html; Friesen, *The Canadian Prairies*, 230.
35. Payment, *Batoche*, 61–2. Despite the defeat and subsequent difficulties, Batoche expanded and prospered in later years. Ibid., 136.
36. A. Blair Stonechild, "The Indian View of the 1885 Uprising," in J.R. Miller, ed., *Sweet Promises: A Reader on Indian–White Relations in Canada* (Toronto, 1991), 259–76. Gabriel Dumont's account of the rebellion was translated by George F.G. Stanley and published in the *Canadian Historical Review* 30, 3 (Sept. 1949): 249–69.
37. *Manitoba Free Press*, 7 Apr. 1885, front page.
38. This was the same statute under which eight men had been hanged in Burlington Heights, Ontario, in 1814 for high treason during the War of 1812. See William R. Riddell, *The Ancaster "Bloody Assize" of 1814* (Toronto, 1923; reprinted from *Ontario Historical Society Papers and Records* 20 [1922]: 107–25). Kapapamahchakwew ("Wandering Spirit") was one of those hanged at North Battleford.
39. See note 38. In neither case do the consequences compare with those of the Sioux uprising of 1862–3 in the United States. Of 303 Sioux who were condemned to death, 38 were executed at Fort Snelling, Minnesota, the largest mass hanging in American history.
40. Quoted in Norman Sluman, *Poundmaker* (Toronto, 1967), 270.
41. Morris, *Treaties of Canada with the Indians*, 294.
42. Flanagan, *Riel and the Rebellion*, viii. See also Flanagan's study of Riel's millennialism: *Louis "David" Riel, Prophet of the New World* (Toronto, 1979).
43. D.N. Sprague, *Canada and the Metis, 1869–1885* (Waterloo, Ont., 1988), 184.
44. John E. Foster, "The Plains Metis," in R. Bruce Morrison and C. Roderick Wilson, eds, *Native Peoples: The Canadian Experience*, 3rd edn (Toronto, 2004), 310–11.
45. http://www.canadashistory.ca/Explore/First-Nations,-Inuit-Metis/Shifting-Riel-ity-The-1885-North-West-Rebellion.

Chapter 14

1. Tobias, "Subjugation of the Plains Cree," 547–8. See also F.L. Barron and James B. Waldram, eds, *1885 and After: Native Society in Transition* (Regina, 1986).
2. Barron, "Indian Pass System," 28; Sarah A. Carter, "Controlling Indian Movement: The Pass System," *Newest Review* (May 1985): 8–9. The system lasted until 1941, but some northern reserves reported that it was still being enforced during the 1960s. Although only 28 reserves were officially designated as disloyal during the disturbances, the system was generally applied in the prairie West.
3. *Annual Report of the North-West Mounted Police*, 1895, app. B, Superintendent W.B. Steele, 45.
4. Coates and Morrison, *Land of the Midnight Sun*, 206–7.
5. Hugh A. Dempsey, *Charcoal's World* (Saskatoon, 1978). Dempsey argues that Si'k-okskitsis's behaviour was culturally appropriate. On Kahkeesaymanetoowayo, see Frank W. Anderson, *Almighty Voice* (Aldergrove, BC, 1971); Carter, *Aboriginal People and Colonizers*, 174–5.
6. Barron, "Indian Pass System," 39. In 1902, a delegation from South Africa came to study the Canadian pass system as a method of social control.
7. See Sprague, *Canada and the Metis*, 104–5, 124.
8. Payment, *Batoche*, 73–4. See also John Leonard Taylor, "An Historical Introduction to Métis Claims in Canada," *Canadian Journal of Native Studies* 3, 1 (1983): 151–81.
9. Marcel Giraud, "The Western Metis after the Insurrection," *Saskatchewan History* 9, 1 (1956): 5.
10. Joanne Overvold sees the role of women as being central to the struggle of the Métis to maintain a separate identity. She depicts the Métis of the Northwest Territories in *Our Metis Heritage . . . A Portrayal* (n.p., 1976). Her comment on the role of women is on p. 103; see also Sarah Carter, "First Nations Women of Prairie Canada in the Early Reserve Years, the 1870s to the 1920s: A Preliminary Inquiry," in Christine Miller and Patricia Chuchryk, eds., *Women of the First Nations: Power, Wisdom, and Strength* (Winnipeg, 1996). A personal statement on being Métis is by Dorothy Daniels, "Metis Identity: A Personal Perspective," *Native Studies Review* 3, 2 (1987): 7–15.
11. "The Daniels Decision, Métis Rights," Indigenous and Northern Affairs Canada, https://www.aadnc-aandc.gc.ca/eng/1100100014413/1100100014414.
12. Fumoleau, *As Long As This Land Shall Last*, 207–8; Daniel, *History of Native Claims*, 24.
13. A readable contemporary account of the two commissions is Charles Mair, *Through the Mackenzie Basin* (Toronto, 1908).
14. On Treaty Eight, see Chapter 16.
15. Zaslow, *Opening of the Canadian North*, 225–6.
16. Government control over the sale of First Nations crops was officially described as a "kindly supervision" to ensure that Indigenous people were "getting a fair deal." See Ahenakew, *Voices of the Plains Cree*, 147. This book is an eloquent depiction of Plains Cree life before and after contact.

17. Morris, *Treaties of Canada with the Indians*, 315.
18. Federation of Saskatchewan Indians, *Indian Treaty Rights*, undated pamphlet. See also Suzanne Fournier and Ernie Crey, *Stolen from Our Embrace: The Abduction of First Nations Children and the Restoration of Aboriginal Communities* (Vancouver, 1997), 54.
19. Jennifer Lorretta Pettit, "To Christianize and Civilize," Ph.D. thesis (University of Calgary, 1997), 56; "Nicholas Flood Davin," *Dictionary of Canadian Biography Online*, http://www.biographi.ca/en/bio/davin_nicholas_flood_13E.html.
20. J.R. Miller, *Shingwauk's Vision: A History of Native Residential Schools* (Toronto, 1996), 76–80.
21. Smith, *Sacred Feathers*, 160.
22. Minutes of the General Council of Indian Chiefs and Principal Men held at Orillia, Lake Simcoe Narrows, on Thursday, the 30th, and Friday, the 31st, July, 1846, on the proposed removal of the smaller gommunities [*sic*] and the establishment of manual labour schools (Orillia, Ont., 1846), 20–1. At: www.canadiana.org.
23. Thomas Gummersall Anderson, *Dictionary of Canadian Biography Online*, http://www.biographi.ca/en/bio/anderson_thomas_gummersall_10E.html.
24. Cited in Pettit, "To Christianize and Civilize," 26–7. Also see "John West," *Dictionary of Canadian Biography Online*, http://www.biographi.ca/en/bio/west_john_7E.html.
25. Pettit, "To Christianize and Civilize," 22.
26. In 1820, West used the opportunity given to him as HBC chaplain to attempt evangelizing and schooling on behalf of the Anglican Church Missionary Society. In his journal, he noted that Saulteaux chief Peguis questioned him very closely but, in the end, did not hand over his children. West, *The Substance of a Journal During a Residence at the Red River Colony, British North America* (London, 1824).
27. Federation of Saskatchewan Indians, *Indian Treaty Rights*. See also Fournier and Crey, *Stolen from Our Embrace*, 56.
28. Ganiodaio's story is told in Kehoe, *The Ghost Dance*, 116–23. The standard work on the prophet is Wallace, *Death and Rebirth of the Seneca*.
29. Pettit, "To Christianize and Civilize," 25–6.
30. Ibid., 51–2.
31. Ibid., 68.
32. Ibid., 36–40.
33. Two important studies of residential schools are Miller's *Shingwauk's Vision* and John Sheridan Milloy, *A National Crime: The Canadian Government and the Residential School System* (Winnipeg, 1999). There are many published eyewitness accounts of the industrial and residential schools. More recently, the final report of the Truth and Reconciliation Commission of Canada has provided a wealth of information and numerous "calls to action." See *Honouring the Truth, Reconciling for the Future: Summary of the Final Report of the Truth and Reconciliation Commission of Canada* (2015), http://www.trc.ca/websites/trcinstitution/File/2015/Honouring_the_Truth_Reconciling_for_the_Future_July_23_2015.pdf.
34. Davin, "Report on Industrial Schools for Indians and Halfbreeds," 10.
35. Department of Indian Affairs (DIA), *Annual Report*, 1883, CSP (No. 4) 1884, xi; cited in Miller, *Shingwauk's Vision*, 106.
36. Father Albert Lacombe complained that his Niitsitapi students were too big and too "well acquainted with the Indian fashion" to accept institutionalization. He also created controversy by hiring Jean L'Heureux, a local man rumoured to be a pedophile, as a recruiter. When he stepped down in 1885, Father Lacombe left behind a school with only three students. His successor resigned after three years as principal, claiming that only two of 25 graduates had enough education and skill to succeed. DIA, *Annual Report*, 1884, 89; cited in Pettit, "To Christianize and Civilize," 109. For more on Lacombe, see "Albert Lacombe," *Dictionary of Canadian Biography Online*, http://www.biographi.ca/en/bio/lacombe_albert_14E.html. For a description of the Dunbow School, see Raymond J.A. Huel, *Proclaiming the Gospel to the Indians and Métis* (Edmonton, 1996), 128–31. The author claims that the Oblates were aware of the allegations concerning L'Heureux.
37. Success was relative; by Father Hugonnard's statistics, about 20 per cent of students died under his care. Milloy, *National Crime*, 92.
38. Miller, *Shingwauk's Vision*, 350.
39. Huel, *Proclaiming the Gospel*, 151.
40. Cited in Arlene Roberta Greyeyes, "St. Michael's Indian Residential School, 1894–1926," MA thesis (Carleton University, 1995), 129, 138.
41. For a description of the Lytton, BC, school, see Miller, *Shingwauk's Vision*, 318–19.
42. James Gladstone, "Indian School Days," *Alberta Historical Review* 15, 1: 24; cited in Pettit, "To Christianize and Civilize," 147–8.
43. Brass, *I Walk in Two Worlds*, 45.
44. Eleanor Brass, "The File Hills Ex-Pupil Colony," *Saskatchewan History* 6, 2 (1953): 66. Mrs Brass was the daughter of Fred Dieter, one of the colony's outstanding farmers who was awarded a silver shield. Born and raised in the colony, she reminisces about her life in her autobiography, *I Walk in Two Worlds*. See also E. Brian Titley, *A Narrow Vision: Duncan Campbell Scott and the Administration of Indian Affairs in Canada* (Vancouver, 1986), 18–19; Titley, "W.M. Graham: Indian Agent Extraordinaire," *Prairie Forum* 1 (1983): 25–41; "Indian Students Forced into Marriage, Farm Life," *Globe and Mail*, 10 Dec. 1990.
45. Historian Robert Choquette, cited in Pettit, "To Christianize and Civilize," 17.
46. Greyeyes, "St. Michael's Indian Residential School," 66.
47. D.J. Hall, "Clifford Sifton and Canadian Indian Administration 1896–1905," in Getty and Lussier, eds, *As Long As the Sun Shines and Water Flows*, 126.
48. Daugherty, "The Elective System," 6.
49. The Cowessess band's election problems have been dealt with in detail by Daugherty, "The Elective System," 28–35.
50. "Governance and Administration," in Cowessess First Nation Online, https://sites.google.com/a/cowessessfn.com/cowessess-first-nation/our-people/governance-administration.
51. Tobias, "Protection, Civilization, Assimilation," 21, 24.
52. Ibid., 21.
53. Canada, Indian Affairs, *Report*, 1910–11, 196; cited by Zaslow, *Opening of the Canadian North*, 232–3. From 1909 to 1914, Laird was adviser to Indian Affairs in Ottawa.
54. Robert J. Surtees, "Indian Land Sessions in Upper Canada, 1815–1830," in Getty and Lussier, eds, *As Long As the Sun Shines and Water Flows*, 66; Peggy Martin-McGuire, *First Nation Land Surrenders on the Prairies, 1896–1911* (Ottawa, 1998), xiii. This is a detailed study of 25 surrenders, prepared for the Indian Claims Commission.
55. Richard H. Bartlett, *Indian Reserves and Aboriginal Lands in Canada: A Homeland* (Saskatoon, 1990), 26. See also Stewart Raby, "Indian Land Surrenders in Southern Saskatchewan," *Canadian Geographer* 17, 1 (Spring 1973), 36–52; Carter, *Lost Harvests*, 244–9.

56. Martin-McGuire, *First Nation Land Surrenders on the Prairies*, 461–2. See also Hall, "Clifford Sifton," 120–44.

57. Heading the Commission were Gilbert Malcolm Sproat (1876–9, for the first two years in office, as co-commissioner with Alexander C. Anderson and Archibald McKinley), Peter O'Reilly (1880–98), and A.W. Vowell (1899–1910). By 1892, the Commission was granting reserves that ranged in size from seven to 230 acres (three to 93 ha) per capita, depending on the region. Complaints from non-Indigenous settlers concerning these amounts led the province to refuse to sanction any more, leading to the dissolution of the Commission in 1910.

58. The delegation of 1906 was led by Chief Joe Capilano of the North Vancouver Squamish and other chiefs. They were listened to politely but did not get any action. See Cumming and Mickenberg, eds, *Native Rights in Canada*, 188.

59. Cumming and Mickenberg, eds, *Native Rights in Canada*, 188–9.

60. Usually called the McKenna-McBride Commission, after J.A.J. McKenna, assistant Indian commissioner for the Northwest, 1901–9, and Richard McBride, Premier of BC, 1903–15. McBride did not actually serve on the Commission.

61. Berger, *Fragile Freedoms*, 231. During this time also, commercial fishing licences were not being issued to west coast First Nations; in 1923 they were allowed to apply for them. See E.E. Laviolette, *The Struggle for Survival* (Toronto, 1973), 138.

62. These were described by Lloyd Barber as "prime development land." Barber, "The Implications of Indian Claims for Canada," address given at the Banff School of Advanced Management, Banff, Alberta, 9 Mar. 1978.

63. Reuben Ware, *The Lands We Lost: A History of Cut-Off Lands and Land Losses from Indian Reserves in British Columbia* (Vancouver, 1974), 1; Kew, "History of Coastal British Columbia since 1849," 160. The land issue became a factor in the saga of British Columbia's most famous outlaw, Peter Simon Gunanoot (*c*. 1874–1933), who eluded police for 13 years, from 1906 to 1919. Gunanoot ("Little Bear that Walks up a Tree"), a prosperous Gitxsan trapper and storekeeper of Hazelton (Gitenmaks), BC, upon being wanted for murder, took to the woods with his family. Their success in evading capture was at least partly due to the complicity of the Indigenous people of the region, who were agitating for an extension of their reserve and for payment for lands occupied by non-Indigenous people. Gunanoot eventually voluntarily surrendered, was tried, and acquitted. David R. Williams, *Simon Peter Gunanoot: Trapper Outlaw* (Victoria, 1982); Thomas P. Kelley, *Run Indian Run* (Markham, Ont., 1972).

64. The text of the Commission's report is reproduced in Ware, *Lands We Lost*, 179–98, along with the texts of the Commission's 98 interim reports proposing land alienations for a variety of reasons, pp. 114–77. A study that takes a sympathetic view of British Columbia's position on the land question is Cail, *Land, Man, and the Law*, chs 11–13.

65. The story of the political adaptation of British Columbia First Nations to non-Indigenous pressures and the development of Indigenous organizations in the province is told by Paul Tennant, "Native Political Organization in British Columbia, 1900–1960: A Response to Internal Colonialism," *B.C. Studies* 55 (1982): 3–49. The Allied Tribes lasted until 1927; its battles would be picked up by the Native Indian Brotherhood in 1931.

66. Daniel, *History of Native Claims*, 50–2. See also Wilson Duff, *The Indian History of British Columbia*, vol. 1, *The Impact of the White Man* (Victoria, 1964), 69–70; Cail, *Land, Man, and the Law*, 243.

67. James S. Frideres, *Native Peoples in Canada: Contemporary Conflicts* (Scarborough, Ont., 1983), 233–66; Leslie and Maguire, eds, *Historical Development of the Indian Act*, 120. Anthropologist Peter Kulchyski thinks that the measure may have contributed to the breakup of the Allied Tribes of BC in 1927. Kulchyski, "Headwaters: A New History," *The Press Independent* 21, 27 (12 July 1991): 5.

68. Hugh A. Dempsey, *The Gentle Persuader* (Saskatoon, 1986), 50–2.

69. Ibid., 49. Similarly, the Inuit, even those in remote communities, raised money for famine relief for Ethiopia in 1984. See "Northern Generosity Snowballs," *Globe and Mail*, 29 Nov. 1984. See also Fred Gaffen, *Forgotten Soldiers* (Penticton, BC, 1985); Terry Lusty, *Metis Social-Political Movement* (Calgary, 1973); Gaffen, *Native Soldiers, Foreign Battlefields* (Ottawa, 1993), 9–11.

70. Cited by James Dempsey, "Problems of Western Canadian Indian War Veterans," *Native Studies Review* 5, 2 (1989): 5, 6. See also James St G. Walker, "Race and Recruitment in World War I: Enlistment of Visible Minorities in the Canadian Expeditionary Force," *Canadian Historical Review* 70, 1 (1989): 5.

71. Peter S. Schmaltz, *The Ojibwa of Southern Ontario* (Toronto, 1991), 233–4; Gaffen, *Forgotten Soldiers*, 70–2; "Benefits and Land for Veterans," Canadian War Museum Online, http://www.warmuseum.ca/firstworldwar/history/after-the-war/veterans/benefits-and-land-for-veterans/.

72. Peter McFarlane, *Brotherhood to Nationhood: George Manuel and the Making of the Modern Indian Movement* (Toronto, 1993).

73. Peter Kulchyski, "'A Considerable Unrest': F.O. Loft and the League of Indians," *Native Studies Review* 4, 1–2 (1988): 95–113; Stan Cuthand, "The Native Peoples of the Prairie Provinces in the 1920's and 1930's," in Ian A.L. Getty and Donald B. Smith, eds, *One Century Later: Western Canadian Reserve Indians Since Treaty 7* (Vancouver, 1978), 31–5; Titley, *A Narrow Vision*, 102–9; Zaslow, *Northward Expansion*, 165–6.

74. Frederick Ogilvie Loft to the Chiefs of Canada, Toronto, 14 November 1919, Library and Archives Canada, RG 10, vol. 3212, File 527, 787–4.

75. "Miistatosomitai," in Virtual Museum, http://www.virtualmuseum.ca/sgc-cms/histoires_de_chez_nous-community_memories/pm_v2.php?id=story_line&lg=English&fl=0&ex=00000821&sl=9281&pos=1.

76. "Hayter Reed," *Dictionary of Canadian Biography Online*, http://www.biographi.ca/en/bio/reed_hayter_16E.html.

77. See Sarah Carter, "'We Must Farm To Enable Us To Live': The Plains Cree and Agriculture to 1900," in R. Bruce Morrison and C. Roderick Wilson, eds, *Native Peoples: The Canadian Experience*, 3rd edn (Toronto, 2004), 320–40; J.R. Miller, *Skyscrapers Hide the Heavens: A History of Indian–White Relations in Canada*, rev. edn (Toronto, 1989), 217; Kulchyski, "'A Considerable Unrest'." See also "Hayter Reed," *Dictionary of Canadian Biography Online*, http://www.biographi.ca/en/bio/reed_hayter_16E.html.

Chapter 15

1. Michael Asch, *Kinship and the Drum Dance in a Northern Dene Community* (Edmonton, 1988), 89–97.

2. These rules applied only to marriage, which meant only between men and women in those days. Since the marriage laws changed with the Civil Marriage Act in 2005, these rules now apply to anyone.

3. Six Nations of the Grand River Online, http://www.sixnations.ca/CommunityProfile.htm.

4. Titley, *A Narrow Vision*, 50.

5. Harper, "Canada's Indian Administration," 127.

6. Leslie and Maguire, eds, *Historical Development of the Indian Act*, 191.

7. A documentary novel vividly portraying the incomprehension and frustration of Euro-Canadians who very much want to help Indigenous people, but who think they can do it by telling them what to do, is Alan Fry, *How a People Die* (Toronto, 1970). The view that the administration was really concerned with non-Indigenous goals and not with those of First Nations is expressed by Shelagh D. Grant in "Indian Affairs under Duncan Campbell Scott: The Plains Cree of Saskatchewan, 1913–1931," *Journal of Canadian Studies* 18, 3 (1983): 21–39.

8. "Francis Pegahmagabow," Library and Archives of Canada Online, http://www.bac-lac.gc.ca/eng/discover/military-heritage/first-world-war/100-stories/Pages/pegahmagabow.aspx; Brian D. McInnes, *Sounding Thunder: the Stories of Francis Pegahmagabow* (Winnipeg, 2016), 143–8.

9. Brownlie, *A Fatherly Eye*, 57. Pegahmagabow's military career is described in Gaffen, *Forgotten Soldiers*.

10. Canada, *Annual Report of Indian Affairs Branch*, 1937.

11. To combat overtrapping, in the 1920s British Columbia introduced registered traplines. The program initially hurt Indigenous people, as it interfered with traditional allocations of territory, but in the long term made it possible to maintain the trapping way of life. Registration was introduced in 1940 in Manitoba, and six years later in Saskatchewan. At the end of the century, it was in general use throughout the North and in the Arctic. Oblate Archives, St Albert, Alberta, Fort Good Hope file #1, vol. 5: 28. See also Martha McCarthy, *From the Great River to the Ends of the Earth: Oblate Missions to the Dene*, 1847–1921 (Edmonton, 1995).

12. For an example of this policy, see Kenneth S. Coates, "Best Left as Indians: The Federal Government and the Indians of the Yukon, 1894–1950," *Canadian Journal of Native Studies* 4, 2 (1984): 179–204.

13. One estimate places the total number of deaths among students in all residential schools in Canada at 50,000. See the letter of Rev. Kevin D. Annett, Ganges, BC, in the *Guardian Weekly*, 6–12 July 2000, 13.

14. Titley, *A Narrow Vision*, 82–7.

15. Fournier and Crey, *Stolen from Our Embrace*, 50, 61. According to *Windspeaker* (May 1998) in a special section entitled "Classroom Edition," 4, the number of residential schools peaked at 88. Geoffrey York writes about some of these schools in *The Dispossessed: Life and Death in Native Canada* (London, 1990).

16. Titley, *A Narrow Vision*, 91, 93.

17. *Report of the RCAP*, 1: 388–9 n15.

18. "Residential School Nutrition Experiments explained to Kenora Survivors," *CBC News*, http://www.cbc.ca/news/canada/thunder-bay/residential-school-nutrition-experiments-explained-to-kenora-survivors-1.3171557; Ian Mosby, "Administering Colonial Science: Nutrition Research and Human Biomedical Experimentation in Aboriginal Communities and Residential Schools, 1942-1952," *Histoire sociale / Social History* 46, 91 (May 2013): 145–72; Noni E. MacDonald, Richard Stanwick, and Andrew Lynk, "Canada's Shameful History of Nutrition Research on Residential School Children: The Need for Strong Medical Ethics in Aboriginal Health Research," *Paediatric Child Health Online*, https://www.ncbi.nlm.nih.gov/pmc/articles/PMC3941673.

19. Truth and Reconciliation Commission of Canada, "The Erosion of Language and Culture," *Canada's Residential Schools: The Legacy*, 5: 121.

20. Norma Sluman and Jean Goodwill, *John Tootoosis* (Ottawa, 1982), 109.

21. Legacy of Hope Foundation, "We Were So Far Away: The Inuit Experience of Residential Schools," weweresofaraway.ca.

22. Cited in Jean Barman, Yvonne Hébert, and Don McCaskill, "The Legacy of the Past: An Overview," in Barman, Hébert, and McCaskill, eds, *Indian Education in Canada*, 2 vols (Vancouver, 1986), 1: 13. See also Assembly of First Nations, *Breaking the Silence: An Interpretive Study of Residential School Impact and Healing* (Ottawa, 1994).

23. Richard Foot, "Feds Responsible for Native School Abuse," *Calgary Herald*, 12 Dec. 2003, A17.

24. Cristin Schmitz, with Richard Foot, "Billions for Natives: Talks to Compensate Residential School Students Start at $4-billion," *National Post*, 31 May 2005, A1.

25. Fournier and Crey, *Stolen from Our Embrace*, 81–114; Jason Clayworth, "'Stolen' Native Wants Family, Culture Back," *Ottawa Citizen*, 10 Oct. 2000 (reprint from *Des Moines Register*); Brad Evenson, "Native Adoption Policy—A Canadian Tragedy," *Edmonton Journal*, 19 Apr. 1999; "Indian Boy Returned to Adoptive Kin in U.S.," *The Gazette*, Montreal, 21 Mar. 1999.

26. The story of the Indigenous acquisition of the school is told by Diane Persson, "The Changing Experience of Indian Residential Schooling: Blue Quills, 1931–1970," in Barman et al., eds, Indian Education in Canada, 1: 150–67.

27. Blue Quills Online, http://www.bluequills.ca/welcome/about-us.

28. Howard Adams, Prison of Grass: Canada from the Native Point of View (Toronto, 1975), 213–14.

29. "A Lesson in Misery: Canadian Indians Look Back in Anger at Residential School Days," *Globe and Mail*, 2 Dec. 1989. This is an excerpt from York's *The Dispossessed*.

30. Robert Laboucane, "Canada's Aboriginal Education Crisis," *Windspeaker* 28, 7 (2010), www.ammsa.com/publications/windspeaker/canada%E2%80%99s-aboriginal-education-crisis-column. An early example of Indigenous curriculum development was the Cree Way Project of Rupert House during the 1970s. See Richard Preston, "The Cree Way Project: An Experiment in Grassroots Curriculum Development," in William Cowan, ed., *Papers of the Tenth Algonquian Conference* (Ottawa, 1979), 92–101.

31. See, for example, "Sweet Success for Native School," *Edmonton Journal*, 1 Oct. 1990; "Bias Absent in All-Native School," ibid., 25 Nov. 1989.

32. "Bill C-33: First Nations Control of First Nations Education Act," Indigenous and Northern Affairs Canada, https://www.aadnc-aandc.gc.ca/eng/1358798070439/1358798420982.

33. *CBC News*, "Shawn Atleo Resigns as AFN National Chief," 2 May 2014, www.cbc.ca/news/politics/shawn-atleo-resigns-as-afn-national-chief-1.2630085; Jen Gerson, "The Fierce Battle for AFN Leadership Leaves Some Wondering If the Organization Can Survive," *National Post*, 16 May 2014, news.nationalpost.com/2014/05/16/the-fierce-battle-for-the-afn-leadership-leaves-some-wondering-if-the-organization-can-survive.

34. "Anishinabek Nation and Ontario Sign Historic Agreement," *Anishinabek News*, http://anishinabeknews.ca/education.

35. Leslie, *Historical Survey of Indian–Government Relations*, 3–4.

36. Years later the lot of First Nations war veterans was still giving rise to complaints and investigations. See, for example, "Indian War Veterans Mistreated: Report," *Globe and Mail*, 7 June 1984. The joint committee, during its three years of existence, heard 122 witnesses and studied 411 written briefs. Zaslow, *Northward Expansion*, 298. Particularly irritating was the practice of

awarding the traplines of Indigenous trappers to non-Indigenous veterans.

37. There were exceptions. For one, in 1920, Indigenous spokespersons had been invited to attend House of Commons hearings on amendments to the Indian Act that proposed compulsory enfranchisement. In spite of their opposition, however, the bill was passed.

38. *Indian Conditions: A Survey* (Ottawa, 1980), 84.

39. Alice B. Kehoe, "The Giveaway Ceremony of Blackfoot and Plains Cree," *Plains Anthropologist* 25, 87 (1980): 17–26.

40. E. Palmer Patterson II, *The Canadian Indian: A History since 1500* (Toronto, 1972), 171–2.

41. S. Bonesteel, *Canada's Relationship with Inuit: A History of Policy and Program Development* (Ottawa, 2006), https://www.aadnc-aandc.gc.ca/eng/1100100016900/1100100016908.

42. A detailed history of the National Indian Brotherhood and analysis of its operations is in Ponting and Gibbins, *Out of Irrelevance*, 195–279.

43. Little of this is reflected in the pamphlet, *Indians of Canada Pavilion*, given to visitors, although it presented a spectrum of Indigenous views. Its general approach is expressed in the statement: "I see an Indian, tall and strong in the pride of his heritage. He stands with your sons, a man among men." Such romanticism was more effective in literature than in politics.

44. H.B. Hawthorn, *A Survey of the Contemporary Indians of Canada: Economic, Political, Educational Needs and Policies*, 2 vols (Ottawa, 1966–7), 1: 6.

45. A seminal article on historians' approach to First Nations is James W. St G. Walker, "The Canadian Indian in Historical Writing," Canadian Historical Association, *Historical Papers* (1971): 21–51. A follow-up report, also by Walker, "The Indian in Canadian Historical Writing, 1971–1981," appeared in Getty and Lussier, eds, *As Long As the Sun Shines and Water Flows*, 340–57.

46. The social dislocations that have resulted from these shifts in values and circumstances were the subject of a special report, "A Canadian Tragedy," *Maclean's* 99, 28 (14 July 1986): 12–25.

47. Hawthorn, *A Survey of Contemporary Indians*, 1: 13.

48. R.W. Dunning, "Indian Policy—A Proposal for Autonomy," *Canadian Forum* 49 (Dec. 1969): 206–7. A detailed analysis of the birth of the White Paper is Sally Weaver, *Making Canadian Indian Policy: The Hidden Agenda 1968–1970* (Toronto, 1981).

49. *Statement of the Government of Canada on Indian Policy*, 1969, 3. See also Bradford W. Morse, "The Resolution of Land Claims," in Morse, ed., *Aboriginal Peoples and the Law*, 618–21.

50. "Statement of National Indian Brotherhood," in *Recent Statements by the Indians of Canada*, Anglican Church of Canada General Synod Action 1969, Bulletin 201, 1970, 28.

51. "Wuttunee Termed 'Traitorous,' Barred from His Home Reserve," *Globe and Mail*, 4 May 1970. William I.C. Wuttunee, Ruffled Feathers (Calgary, 1971), 136–41.

52. The text of *Citizens Plus* was reproduced in *The First Citizen* 7 (June 1970). Other Indigenous responses appear ibid. 8 (July 1970). See also Menno Boldt, *Surviving as Indians* (Toronto, 1993), 46, 66.

53. Traditionally, horns (deer antlers, buffalo horns) were considered to be instruments of power and were worn by shamans and leaders. The "Dehorners" opposed the traditional power structure.

54. This section owes a special debt to Titley, *A Narrow Vision*, 110–34; Joëlle Rostkowski, "The Redman's Appeal for Justice: Deskaheh and the League of Nations," in Christian Feest, ed., *Indians and Europe* (Aachen, 1987), 435–53; Ann Charney, "The Last Indian War," *The Idler* 29 (July–Aug. 1990): 14–22. See also

"Deskaheh," *Dictionary of Canadian Biography Online*, http://www.biographi.ca/en/bio/deskaheh_15E.html.

55. Gerald R. Alfred, *Heeding the Voices of Our Ancestors: Kahnawake Mohawk Politics and the Rise of Native Nationalism* (Toronto, 1995), 58–60.

56. Tehariolina, *La nation huronne*, 317–18.

57. The original grant to the seigneury of Sault St Louis was for 44,000 acres (17,806 ha); Kahnawake today comprises 13,000 acres (5,261 ha).

58. C.P. Stacey, "Canada and the Nile Expedition of 1884–1885," *Canadian Historical Review* 33 (1952): 319–40; Louis Jackson, *Our Caughnawagas in Egypt* (Montreal, 1885). Jackson, leader of the Caughnawaga (Kahnawake) canoemen, recounts the adventures of the Haudenosaunee as non-combatants in the expeditionary force. A brief excerpt is reproduced in Penny Petrone, ed., *First People, First Voices* (Toronto, 1983), 136–8.

59. Morantz, "Aboriginal Land Claims in Quebec," 105.

60. Charney, "The Last Indian War," 14, 17.

61. Ibid., 16. In 1996, the Peacekeepers came fully under the Quebec Police Act.

62. The Iroquoian term that translates into English as "warrior" is more nearly equivalent to "young man." The meaning of the term and the role of the Warriors in Haudenosaunee society are discussed in *Akwesasne Notes* 22, 4 (1990): 6. The Kanienkehaka *Akwesasne Notes*, which began publication in 1969, is published in the New York section of St Regis Reserve. The "ideological father" of the current Warrior movement was Louis Hall of Kahnawake (1916–93). For a fascinating analysis of Haudenosaunee tradition and spirituality and its relation to the Warrior Society, see Brian Rice, "Journeys in the Land of the Peacemaker: A Traditional Methodology to Doing Doctoral Work on Rotinonshonni Traditions and Governance," in Sandra Tomsons and Lorraine Mayer, eds, *Philosophy and Aboriginal Rights: Critical Dialogues* (Toronto, 2013), 28–41.

63. Because of an Indian Act provision that no taxes be paid on goods owned or used by Indigenous People on First Nations land, cigarettes can be sold more cheaply on reserves than elsewhere. The cigarette trade has become an important source of revenue for some reserves, particularly those near the international border. See Charney, "The Last Indian War," 17–18.

64. Ibid., 14.

65. "'Armed, Violent' Poster Stuns Fugitive Mohawks," *Edmonton Journal*, 20 Oct. 1988.

66. "Police Call Mohawks 'Terrorists' in National Ad," *Edmonton Journal*, 19 Sept. 1990. The advertisement, headed "We Oppose Terrorism," ran that same day in newspapers across Canada. The role of the Warriors in the 1990 standoff is discussed in *Akwesasne Notes* 22, 4 (1990): 8.

67. See Maria Campbell's classic *Halfbreed* (Toronto, 1973).

68. Their story is told by Murray Dobbin, *The One-and-a-Half Men* (Vancouver, 1981). Both Norris and Brady were veterans of the Second World War, Norris having served in the RCAF and Brady with the Royal Canadian Artillery. Dr Adam Cuthand, who had seen service with the Canadian army, became the founding president of the Manitoba Métis Federation in 1968.

69. Donald Purich, *The Metis* (Toronto, 1968), 144. Sources for this section are Judith Hill, "The Ewing Commission, 1935: A Case Study of Metis Government Relations," MA thesis (University of Alberta, 1977); Metis Association of Alberta et al., *Metis Land Rights in Alberta: A Political History* (Edmonton, 1981); Dan Smith, *The Seventh Fire* (Toronto, 1993).

70. *Report of the RCAP*, 4: 203.

71. http://www.metisnation.ca/index.php/who-are-the-metis/ rights; "The Daniels Decision, Métis Rights," Indigenous and Northern Affairs Canada, https://www.aadnc-aandc.gc.ca/eng/ 1100100014413/1100100014414.

72. *Report of the RCAP*, 4: 209, 258.

73. Nicks, "Mary Anne's Dilemma," 110.

74. Purich, *The Metis*, 148–9.

75. For a discussion of the Métis and Aboriginal right, see *Metisism: A Canadian Identity* (Edmonton, 1982).

76. "Pact Makes History: 'It's Our Land,' Metis Say as Getty Signs," *Edmonton Journal*, 2 July 1989, 1.

77. Marie Burke, "Métis Sign Provincial Agreement," *Alberta Sweetgrass* 6, 4 (May 1999): 3; "Deal Allows Alberta Metis to Create Justice Programs," *Edmonton Journal*, 9 Nov. 1999.

78. "Mary Two-Axe Earley," Aboriginal Multi Media Society Online, http://www.ammsa.com/content/mary-two-axe-earley-footprints.

79. The best known of the cases contesting First Nation women's loss of status when they married non-Indigenous men was that of *Attorney General of Canada v. Lavell* (1974). Jeannette Lavell, an Ojibwa, fought the issue all the way to the Supreme Court of Canada, where the decision finally went against her, as well as against Yvonne Bedard in a companion case that was heard at the same time. See Jamieson, *Indian Women and the Law*, 79–88; Janet Silman, *Enough Is Enough* (Toronto, 1994), 13–14; Pauline Comeau and Aldo Santin, *The First Canadians* (Toronto, 1990), 32–3.

80. For the criticism that Bill C-31 has substituted one form of inequality for another, see the report prepared for the Assembly of First Nations by Stewart Clatworthy and Anthony H. Smith, "Population Implications of the 1985 Amendment to the Indian Act," 1992. Incidentally, the 1999 court decision in *Corbière v. Canada* allowing off-reserve band members to vote in band elections has particularly affected reinstated Indigenous women, as many of them live off-reserve. The bands were given until 20 November 2000 to implement the decision; a request by the Assembly of First Nations and treaty chiefs across the nation that they be allowed more time was turned down by the Supreme Court. The first band council election under the new regulations was held by the Ojibwa reserve in Manitoba called "Ebb and Flow." Thomas Isaac, *Aboriginal Law Cases, Materials, and Commentary* (Saskatoon, 1995), 429–30; "Supreme Court Dismisses Delay in Off-Reserve Voting," *Ottawa Citizen*, 4 Nov. 2000.

81. Legislative Summary of Bill C-3, "Gender Equity in Indian Registration Act," https://lop.parl.ca/About/Parliament/ LegislativeSummaries/bills_ls.asp?Language=E&ls=c3&Parl= 40&Ses=3&source=library_prb#a10.

82. Bill Tremblay, "Status or Non-Status—That Is the Cultural Question," *Wawatay News* 24, 22 (6 Nov. 1997): 4.

83. *Report of the RCAP*, 4: 46–7.

Chapter 16

1. Morrison, *Under the Flag*, 32–4; Coates and Morrison, *Land of the Midnight Sun*, 43–7; Morton, *History of the Canadian West*, 708–9. Concerning whalers as traders, see Bockstoce, *Whales, Ice, and Men*, 192–4.

2. Interview with Felix Gibot recorded by Richard Lightning, Treaty and Aboriginal Rights Research of the Indian Association of Alberta, 5 Feb. 1974, in Richard Price, ed., *The Spirit of the Alberta Indian Treaties* (Edmonton, 1987), 157.

3. *Report of the North-West Mounted Police 1898*, Part 2, Patrol Report, Fort Saskatchewan to Fort Simpson, inspector W.H. Routledge, 96.

4. A fine study of the relationship between the northern Cree and the animals upon which they depend is by Robert Brightman, *Grateful Prey* (Berkeley, Calif., 1993).

5. His ships, the HMS *Erebus* and the HMS *Terror*, were found in 2014 and 2016, respectively, in the Queen Maud Gulf south of Victoria Island and in Terror Bay off King William Island, just where the Inuit oral tradition said they were. Louie Kamookak, an Inuk historian and long-time searcher, was able to point the Parks Canada expedition in the right direction. See "The Franklin Expedition: Inuit Oral Histories," Parks Canada, https://www.pc.gc.ca/en/culture/ franklin; "Louie Kamookak," https://www.louiekamookak.com.

6. "The Franklin Expedition," Parks Canada, https://www.pc.gc.ca/ en/culture/franklin; "Franklin find proves 'Inuit oral history is strong': Louis Kamookak," *CBC News*, 20 Sept. 2014, http://www .cbc.ca/news/canada/north/franklin-find-proves-inuit-oral- history-is-strong-louie-kamookak-1.2761362.

7. Department of Indian Affairs, vol. 1115, Deputy Superintendent's Letterbook, Hayter Reed to Charles Constantine, commander of the first Yukon police contingent, 29 May 1894; cited by Coates, "Best Left as Indians," 181.

8. For example, John Tetso, *Trapping Is My Life* (Toronto, 1970); Maxwell Paupanekis, "The Trapper," in Malvina Bolus, ed., *People and Pelts* (Winnipeg, 1972), 137–43. See also Hugh Brody, *The People's Land: Eskimos and Whites in the Eastern Arctic* (Harmondsworth, 1975).

9. Coates and Morrison, *Land of the Midnight Sun*, 112–13.

10. Richard Diubaldo, *The Government of Canada and the Inuit, 1900–1967* (Ottawa, 1985), 13–14.

11. Morrison, *Under the Flag*, 45–6.

12. A film, Barry Greenwald's *Between Two Worlds*, tells the story of Joseph Idlout of Pond Inlet and Resolute Bay, a leading hunter who embraced the Euro-Canadian way. He was successful enough that he and his family were the subject of a National Film Board classic, *Land of the Long Day* (1951), directed by Doug Wilkinson; the family also adorned the back of the Canadian $2 bill. Idlout ended up as a barfly, surviving on handout jobs. On 2 June 1968 he died in an accident. The happier story of another hunter who made the same transition is *I, Nuligak*, ed. and tr. Maurice Metayer (Toronto, 1966).

13. Gurston Dacks, *A Choice of Futures: Politics in the Canadian North* (Toronto, 1981), 90; David R. Morrison, *The Politics of the Yukon Territory, 1898–1909* (Toronto, 1968), ch. 3.

14. McClellan, *Part of the Land*, 43. Diamond Jenness says that by 1930 not more than a dozen—if that—could claim descent from the western Arctic's original inhabitants. (*Eskimo Administration*, 14.)

15. McMillan, *Native Peoples and Cultures of Canada*, 246.

16. Jenness, *Eskimo Administration*, 11 and n1. According to one report, four children survived. However, even after the arrival of the NWMP, self-help was still the rule in the North. In the eastern Arctic in the 1860s an Inuk shaman, Qitdlarssuaq (d. 1875), led a four-year trek to find isolated Polar Inuit in need of help. Father Guy Mary-Rousseliere, *Qitdlarssuaq: The Story of a Polar Migration* (Winnipeg, 1991).

17. Mair, *Through the Mackenzie Basin*, 60. The speech has also been attributed to Wahpeehayo ("White Partridge"), who was also in attendance.

18. Jenness was strong on this point, and highly critical of Canada's performance. *Eskimo Administration*, 17.

19. Julie Cruikshank and Jim Robb, *Their Own Yukon* (Whitehorse, 1975), 2.

20. Their sudden wealth did not make life better for Skookum Jim Mason or Dawson Charlie, Kate's brothers. The latter fell off a bridge in 1908 and was drowned; Skookum Jim retired to his home grounds at Carcross, where he died in 1916. Kate Carmack was abandoned by her husband, who went to California and re-married; Kate stayed at Carcross, where she became something of a tourist attraction. See Zaslow, *Opening of the Canadian North*, 145. The oral history related to the gold rush and its discoverers has been published in Cruikshank, *Reading Voices*.

21. H.A. Innis, "Settlement and the Mining Frontier," in W.A. Mackintosh and W.L.G. Joerg, eds, *Canadian Frontiers of Settlement* (Toronto, 1936), vol. 9, Part 2: 183.

22. *Report of the Commissioner of the North-West Mounted Police*, Northern Patrol 1897, 170. The observation was made in connection with the custom of non-Indigenous trappers to use poison bait.

23. For some recollections of what happened on the Klondike River, see Cruikshank and Robb, *Their Own Yukon*, 13–15.

24. Fumoleau, *As Long As This Land Shall Last*, 58; Richard C. Daniel, "Spirit and Terms of Treaty Eight," in Price, ed., *Spirit of the Alberta Indian Treaties*, 63. The story of the "lost patrol," 1910–11, when four policemen died, is one of the many reminders of the dangers of overconfidence in the North. The patrol, headed by Inspector F.J. Fitzgerald, was to go from Dawson to Fort McPherson; Fitzgerald not only did not take along an Indigenous guide, he had refused help when it had been offered. The story has been the subject of a CBC television drama. See Dick North, *The Lost Patrol* (Vancouver, 1995).

25. The problem as it applied in the North in general is touched upon by Ray, *Canadian Fur Trade and the Industrial Age*, 197–221.

26. Fumoleau, *As Long As This Land Shall Last*, 47. See also J.G. MacGregor, *The Klondike Rush through Edmonton 1897–1898* (Toronto, 1970).

27. Mair, *Through the Mackenzie Basin*, 23–4.

28. Daniel, "Spirit and Terms of Treaty Eight," 58.

29. Fumoleau, *As Long As This Land Shall Last*, 51.

30. Official report of Treaty Eight Commission, 1899, in Fumoleau, *As Long As This Land Shall Last*, 84. The account that follows is drawn from this report.

31. Ibid., 86.

32. Price, ed., *Spirit of Alberta Indian Treaties*, 106.

33. Daniel, "Spirit and Terms of Treaty Eight," 82.

34. Interview with Felix Gibot in Price, ed., *Spirit of Alberta Indian Treaties*, 159.

35. "Treaty Guide to Treaty Eight," Indigenous and Northern Affairs Canada, http://www.aadnc-aandc.gc.ca/eng/1100100028805/1100100028807.

36. Fumoleau, *As Long As This Land Shall Last*, 192–6.

37. John S. Long, "'No Basis for Argument'? The Signing of Treaty Nine in Northern Ontario, 1905–1906," *Native Studies Review* 5, 2 (1989): 26.

38. "Treaty Guide to Treaty 9," Indigenous and Northern Affairs Canada, https://www.aadnc-aandc.gc.ca/eng/1100100028855/1100100028857.

39. "Treaty Research Report—Treaty Ten (1906)," Indigenous and Northern Affairs Canada, https://www.aadnc-aandc.gc.ca/eng/1100100028870/1100100028872.

40. Fumoleau, *As Long As This Land Shall Last*, 142.

41. Jenness, *Eskimo Administration*, 23. See also Ray, *Canadian Fur Trade in the Industrial Age*; Zaslow, *Northward Expansion*.

42. "Treaty Guide to Treaty Number Eleven (1921)," Indigenous and Northern Affairs Canada, http://www.aadnc-aandc.gc.ca/eng/1100100028908/1100100028910.

43. Kerry Abel, "'Matters Are Growing Worse': Government and Mackenzie Missions, 1870–1921," in Kenneth S. Coates and William R. Morrison, eds, *For Purposes of Dominion* (Toronto, 1989), 82. A typescript copy, dated 5 June 1938, of Breynat's memorandum denouncing "government treatment of Indians" is in the Alberta Provincial Archives, 17.220, item 994, box 25. A marginal note says the memorandum was published in the *Toronto Star* towards the end of June and in *Le Soleil* (Quebec), 3 July 1938.

44. McClellan, *Part of the Land*, 90.

45. On some of the problems of the trapping life in more recent years, see James W. VanStone, "Changing Patterns of Indian Trapping in the Canadian Subarctic," in William C. Wonders, ed., *Canada's Changing North* (Toronto, 1976), 170–86.

46. R.G. Moyles, *British Law and Arctic Men* (Saskatoon, 1979); Gaston Carrière, *Dictionnaire biographique* (Ottawa, 1979), 8: 141.

47. For details of this and other cases about the same time, see Diubaldo, *Government of Canada and the Inuit*, 15–17. A detailed study of the first murder trial in the Arctic, in 1917, in which the two Inuit charged were found guilty but granted clemency, is Moyles, *British Law and Arctic Men*.

48. *The Inuit Way: A Guide to Inuit Culture* (Ottawa, [1990]), 6. A less idealized version, as practised by the Copper Inuit, is described by Diamond Jenness, *Report of the Canadian Arctic Expedition 1913–18, vol. 12: The Life of the Copper Eskimos* (Ottawa, 1922), 94–6. Oddly enough, the pre-gold rush mining communities in Yukon developed a system of justice that had certain resemblances to that of the Inuit. Not only was the offence itself judged, but also the character of the accused and what he was likely to do in the future. This was called "forward-looking justice." Coates and Morrison, *Land of the Midnight Sun*, 60–1; see also Penny Petrone, ed., *Northern Voices: Inuit Writing in English* (Toronto, 1988); Peter Pitseolak and Dorothy Harley Eber, *People from Our Side*, tr. Ann Hanson (Montreal and Kingston, 1993).

49. Leslie and Maguire, eds, *Historical Development of the Indian Act*, 119.

50. Jenness, *Eskimo Adminstration*, ch. 2.

51. The letters are reproduced in Diubaldo, *Government of Canada and the Inuit*, 46–7. The practice of classifying "Esquimaux" as "Indian" endured until well into the twentieth century. See, for example, the 1934 edition of *Webster's International Dictionary* (cited ibid., 45).

52. "Canada's Relationship with the Inuit: A History of Policy and Program Development," https://www.aadnc-aandc.gc.ca/eng/1100100016900/1100100016908.

53. "Indigenous and Northern Affairs Canada—2017-18 Departmental Plan," http://www.aadnc-aandc.gc.ca/eng/1483561566667/1483561606216; "What Is Indian Status?" UBC Indigenous Foundations, http://indigenousfoundations.arts.ubc.ca/indian_status.

54. Louis-Edmond Hamelin, *Canadian Nordicity: It's Your North Too*, tr. W. Barr (Montreal, 1979), ch. 6.

55. The fuss over the legal status of Inuit is examined by Frank James Tester and Peter Kulchyski, *Tammarniit (Mistakes)* (Vancouver, 1994), 13–42.

56. C.S. Mackinnon, "The 1958 Government Policy Reversal in Keewatin," in Coates and Morrison, eds, *For Purposes of Dominion*, 161.

57. Diubaldo, *Government of Canada and the Inuit*, 57. The Queen Maud Gulf Migratory Bird Sanctuary, established in 1961, is the largest protected area in present-day Canada.

58. Zaslow, *Northward Expansion*, 145.

59. Ibid., 145–6.

60. Alathea Arnaquq-Baril's 2016 film, *Angry Inuk*, is at once a powerful and a beautiful exploration of this problem. See https://www.nfb.ca/film/angry_inuk/.

61. Jenness, *Eskimo Administration*, 9.

62. Diubaldo, *Government of Canada and the Inuit*, 118.

63. Jenness, *Eskimo Administration*, 59–64; Zaslow, *Northward Expansion*, 168–73. See also E. Lyall, *An Arctic Man* (Edmonton, 1979).

64. Diubaldo, *Government of Canada and the Inuit*, 118–30; Mackinnon, "The 1958 Government Policy Reversal," 166–7. One observer likened the northern service officers who were placed in charge of these villages to the agents on First Nations reserves.

65. Robert G. Williamson, *Eskimo Underground: Socio-Cultural Change in the Canadian Central Arctic* (Uppsala, 1974), 82. See also David E. Young, ed., *Health Care Issues in the Canadian North* (Edmonton, 1988); P.G. Nixon, "Early Administrative Developments in Fighting Tuberculosis among Canadian Inuit: Bringing State Institutions Back In," *Northern Review* 2 (1988): 67. Widespread adoption of the foods, clothing, and housing of European people has been seen as injurious to Indigenous health in Canada. Zaslow, *Northward Expansion*, 153.

66. "Telling the Story of Hundreds of Inuit Sick with TB Who Were Shipped to Hamilton," *CBC News*, 9 Nov. 2016, http://www.cbc.ca/news/canada/hamilton/telling-the-story-of-hundreds-of-inuit-sick-with-tb-who-were-shipped-to-hamilton-1.3842103.

67. "Decades Later, Inuit Far from Home," *Toronto Star*, 27 Dec. 1988; "Lost Inuk's Family Found, N.W.T. Brings Him Home," *Edmonton Journal*, 5 Jan. 1989; "Families Still Search for Inuit Sent South in '40s and '50s," ibid., 23 Jan. 1989; "Inuit Unlock Mystery of 1950s Epidemic," ibid., 23 Jan. 1989.

68. The Inuit relocations of 1939–63 are studied by Tester and Kulchyski, *Tammarniit*. See also *Report of the RCAP*, 1: 411ff., and the three-volume interim report issued in 1994 under the general title, *The High Arctic Relocation*. See also, for example, Ila Bussidor and Üstün Bilgen-Reinart, *Night Spirits: The Story of the Relocation of the Sayisi Dene* (Winnipeg, 1997); "No Apology from the Federal Government to Uprooted Inuit," *Edmonton Journal*, 20 Nov. 1990.

69. Keith Watt, "Uneasy Partners," *The Globe and Mail Report on Business Magazine* (Sept. 1990): 46–7; "Inuit, Gov't Strike Land Deal" and "Inuit Dream Carries High Price Tag," *Edmonton Journal*, 17 Dec. 1991.

70. The pros and cons of the Nunavut proposal are discussed in John Merritt et al., *Nunavut Political Choices and Manifest Destiny* (Ottawa, 1989).

71. "N.W.T. Residents Narrowly Approve Nunavut," *The Gazette*, Montreal, 5 May 1992; "'Accord Signed to Create Nunavut by '99," *Edmonton Journal*, 31 Oct. 1992. See also E. Quinn Duffy, *The Road to Nunavut: The Progress of the Eastern Arctic Inuit since the Second World War* (Montreal and Kingston, 1988); John David Hamilton, *Arctic Revolution* (Toronto, 1994).

72. *Report of the RCAP*, 2, part 1: 149.

73. Relations between the Inuit and the RCMP had been strained ever since the latter's campaign in the 1950s and 1960s to kill Inuit sled dogs on the grounds that they spread diseases and were a danger to the communities. The Inuit considered the dogs an important part of their lifestyle. The RCMP later changed its tactics and apologized to the Inuit. In 1998, the dispute boiled over again when dogs killed a six-year-old girl in Iqaluit. This time a compromise was worked out, with the dogs being banned from certain areas. Janice Tibbetts, "When Mounties Shot Down Sled Dogs," *Ottawa Citizen*, 30 Mar. 1999; Adrian Humphries, "New Compromise May Save Iqaluit's Dog Sled Tradition," *National Post*, 25 Jan. 2001, A2.

74. Rob Weber, "New Government, Old Problem: Shivering in Nunavut," *Toronto Star*, 8 Apr. 2000, K4.

75. "Inuit among Groups at Higher Risk for Suicidal Thoughts," 20 Jan. 2016, *CBC News*, http://www.cbc.ca/news/canada/north/inuit-suicidal-thoughts-statscan-1.3410915.

76. Jennifer Pritchett, "Nunavut MP Faces the Future," and Nick Forster, "It Will Give Us Back Our Lives," *Ottawa Citizen*, 1 Apr. 1999.

77. John Amagoalik, *Changing the Face of Canada: The Life Story of John Amagoalik*, ed. Louis McComber (Iqaluit, Nunavut, 2007), accessed at Canadian Heritage, Listening to Our Past, www.tradition-orale.ca/english/the-creation-nunavut-s153.html. Used with the permission of John Amagoalik.

Chapter 17

1. Donald B. Smith, "Aboriginal Rights a Century Ago," *The Beaver* 67, 1 (1987): 7. See also Anthony J. Hall, "The St. Catherine's Milling and Lumber Company vs. The Queen: A Study in the Relationship of Indian Land Rights to Federal–Provincial Relations in Nineteenth-Century Canada," unpublished manuscript, 10. A survey of the Indigenous legal position in Canada is by Paul Williams, "Canada's Laws about Aboriginal Peoples: A Brief Overview," *Law and Anthropology* 1, (1986): 93–120.

2. "Treaty Three," Aboriginal and Northern Development Canada, https://www.aadnc-aandc.gc.ca/eng/1100100028671/1100100028673.

3. For the example of the Ojibwa's misunderstanding in this regard, see Smith, *Sacred Feathers*, 24–5.

4. The legal argument follows Hall, "St. Catherine's Milling," 10–15.

5. Smith, "Aboriginal Rights," 12. See also Bruce A. Clark, *Indian Title in Canada* (Toronto, 1987).

6. "A Brief Introduction of Aboriginal Law in Canada," http://www.bloorstreet.com/200block/brintro.htm.

7. Morris, *Treaties of Canada with the Indians*, 59. On Treaty Three, "The North-West Angle Treaty," see 44–76.

8. George Copway, *Life, History and Travels of Kah-ge-ga-gah-bowh* (Philadelphia, 1847), 20.

9. This account follows Daniel, *History of Native Claims*, 77–83. Donald Smith compiled the most complete bibliography on pre-1990 Oka in *Le Sauvage: The Native People in Quebec: Historical Writing on the Heroic Period (1534–1663) of New France* (Ottawa, 1974), 129–31. For a post-1990 bibliography, see Geoffrey York and Loreen Pindera, *People of the Pines* (Toronto, 1991).

10. Stanley, "The First Indian 'Reserves,'" 206–7. The 1718 deed, in English translation, as well as other documents pertaining to the case are reproduced in Beta (pseud.), *A Contribution to a Proper Understanding of the Oka Question; and a Help to Its Equitable and Speedy Settlement* (Montreal, 1879), 77–92. "Oka and Its Inhabitants," in *The Life of Rev. Amand Parent, the first French Canadian Ordained by the Methodist Church* (Toronto, 1887), 186.

11. In the words of Philippe de Vaudreuil, governor general of New France, 1703–25, the Indigenous People "ne sont point capable de conserver les choses qui leur sont les plus nécessaires." Stanley, "First Indian 'Reserves," 206.

12. Jean Lacan, *An Historical Notice on the Difficulties Arisen between the Seminary of St. Sulpice of Montreal and Certain Indians, at Oka, Lake of Two Mountains: A Mere Case of Right of Property* (Montreal, 1876), 14–17. For information on the benefactor, François Vachon de Belmont, see *DCB*, 2: s.v. "Vachon."

13. Jan Grabowski, "Mohawk Crisis at Kanesatake and Kahnawake," *European Review of Native American Studies* 5, 1 (1991): 12.

14. "Oka and Its Inhabitants," 190–1, 193; Beta (pseud.), *Contribution*, 14–15. In 1870, Parent reported 110 Indigenous Methodists at Oka.

15. Cited by Rev. William Scott, *Report Relating to the Affairs of the Oka Indians, made to the Superintendent General of Indian Affairs* (Ottawa, [1883]), 53.

16. "Joseph Onasakenrat," *Dictionary of Canadian Biography Online*, http://www.biographi.ca/en/bio/onasakenrat_joseph_11E.html.

17. In 1874, Chief Joseph became an assistant to Amand Parent. He translated the four gospels into the Haudenosaunee language. For more on the chief, see *DCB*, 11; John MacLean, *Vanguards of Canada* (Toronto, 1918), 167–79.

18. "Oka and Its Inhabitants," 205–18; Beta (pseud.), *Contribution*, 15.

19. Scott, *Report Relating to the Affairs of the Oka Indians*, 53–4.

20. Ibid., 59.

21. Michel F. Girard, "La crise d'Oka à la lumière de l'ecologie historique," *NHSG Newsletter* (Oct. 1990): 4–8.

22. Privy Council, Angus Corinthe and Others . . . Plaintiffs, and Ecclesiastics of the Seminary of St. Sulpice of Montreal, Defendants, in Canadian Indian Rights Commission Library, box 85 (1). Also, Daniel, *History of Native Claims*, 79–82.

23. Registration office, district of Two Mountains, Acte de vente entre La Compagnie de Saint-Sulpice et la Compagnie immobilière Belgo, 21 oct. 1936; cited by Michel F. Girard, *Étude historique sur la forêt du village d'Oka* (Quebec, 1990).

24. Department of Indian and Northern Affairs, Miscellaneous Correspondence, Oka, 1945–1953, vol. 1, file 0/121–1–5, Order-in-Council of 2 Apr. 1945.

25. The events leading up to the raid, and the raid itself, are described by Loreen Pindera, "The Making of a Warrior," *Saturday Night* 106, 3 (1990): 30–9. See also Craig Maclane and Michael Baxendale, *This Land Is Our Land: The Mohawk Revolt at Oka* (Montreal and Toronto, 1990); Linda Pertusati, *In Defense of Mohawk Land* (Albany, NY, 1997).

26. For an intimate portrait of one of the main figures in this drama, see the National Film Board of Canada documentary by Alanis Obomsawin, *Spudwrench—Kahnawake Man* (1997), https://www.nfb.ca/film/spudwrench_kahnawake_man.

27. Used with the permission of Ellen Gabriel, Indigenous human rights activist from Kanehsatà:ke Mohawk Territory, http://sovereignvoices1.wordpress.com.

28. http://www.rebeccabelmore.com/exhibit/Speaking-to-Their-Mother.html.

29. Rene Laurent, "Two Mohawks Get Prison Terms for Oka Violence," *The Gazette*, Montreal, 20 Feb. 1992, A1–2; Catherine Buckie, "Jury-Selection Process Ends in Trial of Mohawks," ibid., 30 Apr. 1992; Rene Laurent, "5 Mohawks Freed for Lack of Evidence," ibid., 11 June 1992, A4; Rene Laurent, "Jury Acquits All Defendants in Oka Trial," ibid., 4 July 1992, A1, A5; "Quebec Says It Won't Appeal Jury's Acquittal of Mohawks," ibid., 25 July 1992.

30. *Windspeaker* 18, 3 (July 2000): 2–3; *Calgary Herald*, 11 July 2000, A3; *Ottawa Sun*, 15 July 2000, 8; *Le Droit*, 12 juil. 2000, 28.

31. British Columbia's Hartley Bay band (near Prince Rupert), frustrated with the slow progress of settlements, has started signing its own deals with industry, environmental groups, and other First Nations. "Fed Up, B.C. Indian Band Goes It Alone in Signing Deals," *The Gazette*, Montreal, 22 July 2000, A15.

32. Mohawks Sign Historic Land Deal," *Ottawa Citizen*, 22 June 2000; "Mohawks to Get Land near Oka," *Globe and Mail*, 21 June 2000.

33. Steve Bonspeil, "The Oka Crisis Was Supposed to Be a Wakeup Call. Little Has Changed in 27 Years," *CBC News*, 11 July 2017, http://www.cbc.ca/news/opinion/oka-crisis-anniversary-1.4197880.

34. Cumming and Mickenberg, eds, *Native Rights in Canada*, 98. The case was *Rex v. Syliboy*, [1929] 1 D.L.R. 307, (1928), 50 C.C.C. 389 (NS Cty Ct).

35. Cumming and Mickenberg, eds, *Native Rights in Canada*, 99.

36. *The Mi'kmaq Treaty Handbook* (Sydney and Truro, NS, 1987), 13. Also Donald Marshall Sr, Alexander Denny, and Putus Simon Marshall, "The Covenant Chain," in Boyce Richardson, ed., *Drum Beat: Anger and Renewal in Indian Country* (Ottawa, 1989), 71–104.

37. *Simon v.The Queen*, [1985] 2 S.C.R. 387 at 404.

38. See National Indian Brotherhood, *Inquiry into the Invasion of Restigouche*, Preliminary Report, 15 July 1981.

39. Calder graduated from the Anglican Theological College of the University of British Columbia and in 1949 was elected to the BC legislature, where he served for 26 years, first for the New Democratic Party, then for Social Credit. He was Minister without Portfolio, 1972–3. In 1996, he received the National Aboriginal Achievement Award.

40. The original statement had been made by David McKay, a Greenville chief, to the Joint Reserves Allotment Commission that had been established in 1876. See David Raunet, *Without Surrender, Without Consent: A History of the Nishga Land Claims* (Vancouver, 1984), 90.

41. The case had been brought to the Supreme Court without provincial authorization.

42. See Cumming and Mickenberg, eds, *Native Rights in Canada*, 331–2; Thomas R. Berger, "Native History, Native Claims and Self-Determination," *B.C. Studies* 57 (1983): 16; David W. Elliott, "Aboriginal Title," in Morse, ed., *Aboriginal Peoples and the Law*, 74.

43. "The Bear Island Decision," *Ontario Reports* (2nd ser.), 49, part 7, 17 May 1985: 353–490. A review of the issues at stake, particularly those of forestry management, is by Bruce W. Hodgins and Jamie Benidickson, *The Temagami Experience* (Toronto, 1989). See also David T. McNab, *Circles of Time: Aboriginal Land Rights and Resistance in Ontario* (Waterloo, Ont., 1999). The Indigenous view is presented by Gary Potts, "Last-Ditch Defence of a Priceless Homeland," in Richardson, ed., *Drum Beat*, 203–28.

44. Anthony J. Hall, "The Ontario Supreme Court on Trial: Justice Donald Steele and Aboriginal Right," unpublished manuscript, 2.

45. See, for instance, Harold Cardinal's views on the subject in *The Rebirth of Canada's Indians* (Edmonton, 1977), 164–5.

46. Daniel, *History of Native Claims*, 237–8.

47. On the Constitution's adoption, see Chapter 18.

48. Woodward, *Native Law*, 66–7.

49. "R. v. George Weldon Adams (Appellant) v. Her Majesty the Queen (Respondent) and the Attorney General of Canada (Intervenor)," *Canadian Native Law Reporter* 4 (1996): 1–26. On the question of commercial fishing, however, the courts have ruled that Aboriginal right can be subjected to regulation.

50. See "Confrontation Gets Natives into Land Talks," *Edmonton Journal*, 20 Aug. 1990; also "Sioui Case," *Canadian Encyclopedia*, http://www.thecanadianencyclopedia.ca/en/article/sioui-case.

51. Clark, *Native Liberty*, 31.

52. "Supreme Court: Accept Oral History as Evidence," *Globe and Mail*, 15 Dec. 1997, A25.

53. "Nisga'a Ceremony Seals Historic Deal," *Globe and Mail*, 5 Aug. 1998. Tom Molloy, chief negotiator, and Donald Ward tell the story of the making of the treaty in *The World Is Our Witness: The Historic Journey of the Nisga'a into Canada* (Calgary, 2000).

54. Peggy Blair, "Taken for 'Granted': Aboriginal Title and Public Fishing Rights in Upper Canada," *Ontario History* 92, 1 (Spring 2000): 31–55.

55. Kevin Cox, "Native Lobster Fishery Ends but Dispute Doesn't," *Globe and Mail*, 7 Oct. 2000, A7; Graeme Hamilton, "Burnt Church Votes to End Fall Fishery Early," *National Post*, 20 Sept. 2000; "Nova Scotia Tribe to Fish for Lobster Despite Lack of Agreement with Ottawa," Associated Press state and local wire, 20 Nov. 2000. For the Mi'kmaw view of the dispute, see Paul Barnsley, "Anger Mounts," *Windspeaker* (Oct. 2000): 1, 11; for the lobster situation, see Kevin Cox, "The Real Lobster Problem," *Globe and Mail*, 2 Sept. 2000; "Ottawa, Natives Reach Compromise on Fishing," *Globe and Mail*, 23 Apr. 2001, A4.

56. This was a situation that Indigenous people across the board were keenly aware of. Rick Mofina, "Government Ignores Rights Rulings, Natives Say," *Ottawa Citizen*, 28 Feb. 2001, A3.

57. *Manitoba Métis Federation Inc. v. Canada (Attorney General)*, [2013] 1 S.C.R. 623, at: scc-csc.lexum.com/scc-csc/scc-csc/en/12888/1/document.do.

58. "Métis Celebrate Historic Supreme Court Land Ruling," *CBC News*, 8 Mar. 2013, www.cbc.ca/news/politics/métis-celebrate-historic-supreme-court-land-ruling-1.1377827; *CBC News*, "Métis Elder Won't Cut His Hair until Alberta Respects Métis Rights," *CBC News*, 7 Sept. 2017, http://www.cbc.ca/news/canada/edmonton/alberta-m%C3%A9tis-nation-rights-harvesting-consult-duty-daniels-decision-bill-loutitt-mcmurray-1.4277338.

59. The findings of the Royal Commission into the Donald Marshall Jr prosecution were reported in *Globe and Mail*, 27 Jan. 1990, A9.

60. "Justice on Trial," *Edmonton Journal*, 30 Mar. 1991, H1, H3. The commission was headed by Justice Allan Cawsey.

61. "Justice System Falls Short, Siddon Says," *Edmonton Journal*, 27 Mar. 1991. A woman's experience with the criminal justice system is described in Rudy Wiebe and Yvonne Johnson, *Stolen Life: The Journey of a Cree Woman* (Toronto, 1998).

62. Shelley Knapp, "Country's First Aboriginal Court Opens Today," *Calgary Herald*, 6 Oct. 2000, B7. See also Eric Ross, *Returning to the Teachings: Exploring Aboriginal Justice* (Toronto, 1996).

63. The Stonechild Inquiry has been published in print and electronically. Justice David H. Wright, *Report of the Commission of Inquiry into the Death of Neil Stonechild* (Saskatoon, 2004), www.stonechildinquiry.ca/.

64. "A Breakthrough in Kanesatake," *The Gazette*, Montreal, 27 Dec. 1996.

65. Harper, "Canada's Indian Administration," 313.

66. Ponting and Gibbins, *Out of Irrelevance*, 100; Dacks, *A Choice of Futures*, 199.

67. Cardinal, *The Unjust Society*, 44.

Chapter 18

1. "Trudeau Announces Review of Laws Related to Indigenous Peoples," *CBC News*, http://www.cbc.ca/news/politics/trudeau-indigenous-law-review-committee-1.3994227.

2. Douglas Sanders, "Government Agencies in Canada," in Washburn, ed., *Handbook of North American Indians, 4: History of Indian–White Relations*, 282.

3. See, for example, Heather Robertson, *Reservations Are for Indians* (Toronto, 1970).

4. The term "specific claim" came into use in 1973 following the Nisga'a decision, when Ottawa issued its policy on First Nations and Inuit land claims. Specific claims are those that concern obligations arising out of the treaties, the Indian Act, or regulations.

5. "Land Claims Office Getting No Results," *Edmonton Journal*, 26 May 1996, A3. A more positive picture is presented by the *Report of the RCAP*, 2, part 2: 547.

6. Ponting and Gibbins, *Out of Irrelevance*, 81.

7. This account is based on Darlene Abreu Ferreira, "Need Not Greed: The Lubicon Lake Cree Band Claim in Historical Perspective," MA thesis (University of Alberta, 1990). See also Boyce Richardson, "Wrestling with the Canadian System: A Decade of Lubicon Frustration," in Richardson, ed., *Drum Beat*, 231–64.

8. Amnesty International, "The Lubicon Cree: Ongoing Human Rights Violations," www.amnesty.ca/our-work/issues/indigenous-peoples/the-lubicon-cree-ongoing-human-rights-violations.

9. Dacks, *A Choice of Futures*, 148. One-third of the world's fresh water was found in Canada, half of which is in Quebec, and concern was expressed in some quarters. Paul Charest, "Les barrages hydro-électriques en territoires montagnais et leurs effets sur les communautés amérindiennes," *Recherches amérindiennes au Québec* 9, 4 (1980): 323–37. Churches also spoke out. Charles E. Hendry, *Beyond Traplines: Assessment of the Work of the Anglican Church of Canada with Canada's Native Peoples* (Toronto, 1969). See also Hugh and Karmel McCullum, *This Land Is Not for Sale* (Toronto, 1975).

10. Outstanding among these was the Committee for Original People's Entitlement (COPE), founded in 1969 by Agnes Semmler, a Gwich'in Métis who became its first president, and Nellie Cournoyea. With headquarters in Ottawa, it became the voice of the Inuvialuit.

11. Cited by Colin Scott, "Ideology of Reciprocity between the James Bay Cree and the Whiteman State," in Peter Skalník, ed., *Outwitting the State* (New Brunswick, NJ, 1989), 103.

12. The agreement was signed by the government of Quebec, three Quebec Crown corporations, the Grand Council of the Crees (of Quebec), the Northern Quebec Inuit Association, and the government of Canada. It involved 6,650 Cree living in eight communities and 4,386 Inuit in 15 communities.

13. Harvey Feit, "Legitimation and Autonomy in James Bay Cree Responses to Hydroelectric Development," in Noel Dyck, ed., *Indigenous Peoples and the Nation-State: "Fourth World" Politics*

in Canada, Australia and Norway (St John's, 1985), 28–9. For an overview of the treaty's impact, see James F. Hornig, ed., *Social and Environmental Impacts of the James Bay Hydroelectric Project* (Montreal and Kingston, 1999).

14. *James Bay and Northern Quebec Agreement Implementation Review* (Ottawa, Feb. 1982). See also Billy Diamond, "Villages of the Dammed," *Arctic Circle* 1, 3 (1990): 24–30.

15. Stanley Warner and Raymond Coppinger, "Hydroelectric Power Development at James Bay: Establishing a Frame of Reference," in Hornig, ed., *Social and Environmental Impacts*, 19–38; Philip Authier and Graeme Hamilton, "Quebec Shelves Great Whale," *The Gazette*, Montreal, 19 Nov. 1994, A1, A8.

16. www.canlii.org/en/on/onsc/doc/2006/2006canlii26171/2006canlii26171.html and www.ontariocourts.on.ca/decisions/2008/july/2008ONCA0533.pdf.

17. S. Nixon, "Mining Companies Encounter Barrier at Barriere Lake," *Intercontinental Cry*, 28 Nov. 2016, https://intercontinentalcry.org/mining-companies-encounter-barrier-barriere-lake.

18. Berger Community Hearings, Rainer Genelli, Whitehorse, vol. 23, 2374–5; cited by Robert Page, *Northern Development: The Canadian Dilemma* (Toronto, 1986), 212.

19. Thomas R. Berger, *Northern Frontier, Northern Homeland*, 2 vols (Ottawa, 1977). See also Martin O'Malley, *The Past and Future Land* (Toronto, 1976); Hugh and Karmel McCullum and John Olthuis, *Moratorium: Justice, Energy, the North, and the Native People* (Toronto, 1977).

20. Peter Foster, "Exploring Mackenzie," *National Post*, 4 Mar. 2000, D1, D8.

21. Carol Howes, "N.W.T. Gives Conditional Support to Mackenzie Valley Pipeline," *National Post*, 11 Apr. 2000; Steven Chase, "NWT Natives Push for Big Role in Mackenzie Valley Pipeline," *Globe and Mail*, 19 July 2000, B1, B4; Dan Westell, "Ownership Dispute Clogs Plans for Northern Pipeline," *Financial Times*, London, 2 Aug. 2000, 34. Two other commissions that have been influential in the development of Indigenous Peoples' claims were those of law professor Kenneth Lysyk to study a Yukon pipeline route as an alternative to the proposed Mackenzie Valley route and that of Justice Patrick Hartt to study the environment of northern Ontario. Daniel, *History of Native Claims*, 226.

22. Ponting, ed., *Arduous Journey*, 34–41. Also, David Alan Long, "Trials of the Spirit: The Native Social Movement in Canada," in Long and Olive Patricia Dickason, eds, *Visions of the Heart* (Toronto, 1996), 377–96.

23. "Status Indians Number Half a Million," *Globe and Mail*, 30 Aug. 1990, A5.

24. Michael Asch, *Home and Native Land: Aboriginal Rights and the Canadian Constitution* (Toronto, 1984), 105.

25. On possible legal implications of the constitutional provisions, see Brian Slattery, "The Constitutional Guarantee of Aboriginal and Treaty Rights," *Queen's Law Journal* 8, 1–2 (1982): 232–73.

26. J. Anthony Long, Leroy Little Bear, and Menno Boldt, "Federal Indian Policy and Indian Self-government in Canada: An Analysis of a Current Proposal," *Canadian Public Policy* 8, 2 (1982): 194.

27. Delia Opekokew, *The First Nations: Indian Government and the Canadian Confederation* (Saskatoon, 1980); see also Opekokew, *The First Nations: Indian Governments in the Community of Man* (Regina, 1982).

28. Ponting, ed., *Arduous Journey*, 321. Nungak later became president of Quebec's Makavik Corporation. With Eugene Arima, he co-authored *Eskimo stories—unikkaatuat* (Ottawa, 1969).

29. Harper, a treaty "status Indian," was the provincial Minister for Northern Affairs, 1986–8. Ovide Mercredi, a Cree of Grand Rapids, Manitoba, at that time Manitoba regional chief of the Assembly of First Nations, and Phil Fontaine, Ojibwa grand chief of the Assembly of Manitoba Chiefs, were Harper's advisers on Meech Lake. First Mercredi and then Fontaine were later elected National Chief of the Assembly of First Nations.

30. "Foes Stall Accord Again," *Edmonton Journal*, 15 June 1990. Newfoundland also failed to accept the Meech Lake Accord when Liberal Premier Clyde Wells, an opponent of the Accord who came to power after his province had initially ratified it, insisted that the agreement be put to another legislative vote or to a provincial plebiscite. As it became clear that Elijah Harper's protest in the Manitoba legislature was succeeding, Wells refused to bring the Accord to another vote in Newfoundland.

31. A study on Indigenous self-government has been prepared by the Institute for Research and Public Policy: Frank Cassidy and Robert L. Bish, *Indian Government: Its Meaning in Practice* (Halifax and Lantzville, BC, 1989). See also Frank Cassidy, ed., *Aboriginal Self-Determination: Proceedings of a conference held September 30–October 3, 1990* (Toronto, 1991).

32. Dacks, *A Choice of Futures*, 92–3; Kenneth Coates and Judith Powell, *The Modern North: People, Politics, and the Rejection of Colonialism* (Toronto, 1989); Abel, *Drum Songs*, 258–61. On the need for local control for such matters as health care, see Nancy Gibson, "Northern Medicine in Transition," in Young, ed., *Health Care Issues*, 110–21. For the early struggles for responsible government, see Lewis H. Thomas, *The Struggle for Responsible Government in the North-West Territories 1870–97* (Toronto, 1978), 234–63. For information on disease, see J.F. Marchand, "Tribal Epidemics in Yukon," *Journal of the American Medical Association* 123 (1943): 1019–20.

33. *Report of the Cree-Naskapi Commission* (Ottawa, 1988), 10.

34. Ibid.

35. The agreement was signed by the government of Canada with COPE representing the Inuvialuit.

36. "Gourmets from New York to Tokyo Feast on North's Guerin Woolly Musk-ox," *Edmonton Journal*, 21 May 1991. Muskox meat was awarded a gold medal by the Chefs of America; the wool, eight times warmer by weight than sheep's wool, competes with cashmere.

37. *Report of the RCAP*, 4: 420.

38. In this matter, the government has not followed the report of its Task Force to Review Comprehensive Claims Policy (Coolican Report), which urged that extinguishment of all Aboriginal rights be abandoned as a requirement for a claim settlement. See *Living Treaties: Lasting Agreements* (Ottawa, 1985), 43.

39. Deh Cho First Nation, *Declaration of Rights*, 1993, 1. See also *Report of the RCAP*, 4: 427.

40. Assembly of First Nations, *Self-Determination Symposium Summary Report* (Ottawa, 1990), 60. Erasmus was president of the Dene Nation, Northwest Territories, 1976–83.

41. "Innu Chief Warns Government," *Globe and Mail*, 2 Oct. 1990. A survey of various Indigenous priorities is in Richardson, ed., *Drum Beat*. See also J. Anthony Long and Menno Boldt, eds, *Governments in Conflict? Provinces and Indian Nations in Canada* (Toronto, 1988); Leroy Little Bear, Menno Boldt, and J. Anthony Long, eds, *Pathways to Self-Determination: Canadian Indians and the Canadian State* (Toronto, 1984).

42. Quoted by Rudy Platiel, "Vast Changes Sought to Aid Natives," *Globe and Mail*, 22 Nov. 1996, 1.

43. Gilles Gauthier, "Le départ d' 'un long débat,'" *La Presse*, 22 nov. 1996, B1; Dan Smith, "New Deal Urged for First Nations," *Toronto Star*, 22 Nov. 1996; "Paying the Price: How a Report Plays on Two Reserves," *Maclean's* 109, 49 (2 Dec. 1996): 16–19; Scott Feschuk, "Cost of Reforms $30-Billion, Report on Aboriginals Says," *Globe and Mail*, 22 Nov. 1996; Marty Logan, "Last Chance for Canada—Report," *Windspeaker* 14, 9 (Jan. 1997): 1.

44. *People to People, Nation to Nation: Highlights from the Report of the Royal Commission on Aboriginal Peoples* (Ottawa, 1996), ix. Also issued in French, Cree, and Inuktitut.

45. *The Gazette*, Montreal, 4 Feb. 1993. Also see "Moved Far from Their Homes, Natives Seek a Deadly Escape," *Globe and Mail*, 6 Feb. 1996.

46. Ross Howard, "A Terrible Territorial Tangle," *Globe and Mail*, 29 May 1995. The figure of 110 per cent was the apparent result of different bands laying overlapping claims.

47. For an account of the early phase of the Nisga'a claim, see Kristin Jackson, "Drawing the Line: B.C. Indians Claim a Rich Chunk of the Province," *Pacific* (*Seattle Times/Seattle Post-Intelligencer*), 2 Oct. 1988.

48. *Nisga'a Treaty Negotiations Agreement-in-Principle*, issued jointly by the Government of Canada, the Province of British Columbia, and the Nisga'a Tribal Council, 15 Feb. 1996. The agreement involved the return of almost 200 artifacts held by the Canadian Museum of Civilization. Buzz Bourdon, "Nisga'a Artifacts Heading Home," *Ottawa Citizen*, 19 Nov. 1999.

49. A detailed account of the incident, based on official documents, is Peter Edwards, "Death in the Dark: What Happened at Ipperwash," *Toronto Star*, 24 Nov. 1996, F1, F6.

50. Michael Grange, "Officer Guilty in Ipperwash Killing," *Globe and Mail*, 29 Apr. 1997. The OPP sniper, Kenneth Deane, who later resigned from the force, died in a car accident in eastern Ontario in 2006, weeks before he was scheduled to testify at the inquiry into the death of Dudley George.

51. Ross Howard, "Native Standoffs Heat Up BC Talks," *Globe and Mail*, 13 Sept. 1995; Art Wilson, "Nisga'a Sign Historic Treaty with B.C., Federal Governments," *Native Network News* (Feb. 1996): 1. For a negative view of the agreement, see Foster J.K. Griezic, "The Nisga'a Agreement: A Great Deal or a Great Steal?" *Globe and Mail*, 5 Mar. 1996.

52. The term "comprehensive claims" came into use in 1973 (see note 4, above). Comprehensive claims are those arising in areas where rights of traditional use and occupancy have not been extinguished by treaty or superseded by law. Some cases involving Aboriginal right in the English-speaking world are surveyed in Brian Slattery, *Ancestral Lands, Alien Laws: Judicial Perspectives on Aboriginal Title* (Saskatoon, 1983). The first comprehensive claim Ottawa accepted for negotiation was that of the Council for Yukon Indians, a claim that was not resolved until 1993. W.R. Morrison, *A Survey of the History and Claims of the Native Peoples of Northern Canada* (Ottawa, 1983), 44–53; "Siddon Says Yukon Land Claim Deal Won't Mean Indian Self-government," *Edmonton Journal*, 22 Oct. 1990. The tentative agreement provides for 44,440 km2 (8.6 per cent of Yukon's land mass) to be retained by the Indigenous Peoples, who also receive $257 million in compensation.

53. https://www.aadnc-aandc.gc.ca/eng/1100100030577/1100100030578.

54. *Report of the RCAP*, 5: 1.

55. *Report of the RCAP*, 5: 12. Highlights of the *Report* are available at many websites, including www.aadnc-aandc.gc.ca/eng/1100100014597/1100100014637#chp2.

56. Ibid., 2, part 1: 154–6; *People to People, Nation to Nation*, 29.

57. *Report of the RCAP*, 4: 478.

58. Quoted by John Goddard, "In from the Cold," *Canadian Geographic* 114, 4 (1994): 36–47. This account is based on his article. See also *Report of the RCAP*, 3: 396, 419.

59. J. Porter, "Ovide Mercredi Reviews Law Society of Upper Canada's Relations with Indigenous People," *CBC News*, 1 Aug. 2017, http://www.cbc.ca/news/canada/thunder-bay/ovide-mercredi-review-1.4229565.

60. F. Laurie Barron and Joseph Garcea, eds, *Urban Indian Reserves: Forging New Relationships in Saskatchewan* (Saskatoon, 1999). See also Lynda Shorten, *Without Reserve: Stories of Urban Natives* (Edmonton, 1980).

61. Rudy Platiel, "First Native Bank to Open Next Year," *Globe and Mail*, 10 Dec. 1996. See also Marybelle Mitchell, *From Talking Chiefs to Corporate Elite* (Montreal and Kingston, 1996).

62. Brian Laghi, "New Law to Reform Native Voting," *Globe and Mail*, 16 Jan. 2001, A1; Laghi, "Natives Seek Role in Nault Initiative," ibid., 17 Jan. 2001, A4.

63. Fred R. Fenwick, "First Nations Governance Act," *Law Now* 27, 3 (Dec. 2003): 3–4.

64. Paco Francoli, "Showdown on Governance Act," *Hill Times* 685 (5 May 2003): 3–4.

65. Kim Lunman, "Martin Scraps Bill to Change Indian Act," *Globe and Mail*, 9 Jan. 2004, www.theglobeandmail.com/news/national/martin-scraps-bill-to-change-indian-act/article1125291.

66. See www.fngovernance.org/about.

67. "Highlights from the Report of the Royal Commission on Aboriginal Peoples," Indigenous and Northern Affairs Canada, https://www.aadnc-aandc.gc.ca/eng/1100100014597/1100100014637.

68. Michelle Lalonde, "Aboriginals Panel Listens Only to Indians' Supporters: MP," *The Gazette*, Montreal, 8 May 1993, A4.

69. "Commission Staff Divided on Advocacy for Natives," *Edmonton Journal*, 9 Mar. 1995.

70. "A History of Indian and Northern Affairs Canada," INAC, http://www.trc.ca/websites/trcinstitution/index.php?p=890.

71. The government's position was presented by Allan MacDonald, senior policy adviser, Indian and Northern Affairs Canada, at a conference on archaeological resource management in a land claims context held by Parks Canada, Ottawa, 20–2 Jan. 1997.

72. The mixed reaction was reflected in newspaper reports. Some examples: Erin Anderssen and Edward Greenspon, "Federal Apology Fails to Mollify Native Leaders," *Globe and Mail*, 8 Jan. 1998, A4; Jack Aubry, "Native Leaders Disappointed, but Some See Reason for Hope," *Edmonton Journal*, 8 Jan. 1998, A3; Laura Eggertson, "An Apology, at Long Last," *Toronto Star*, 13 Feb. 1998, A20; Tod Mohamed, "The Politics of Saying Sorry," *Ottawa Citizen*, 1 Mar. 1998. Even the Inuit, who were not involved, had a comment, in the person of Zebedee Nungak, "Apology to Indians Soothes and Jars," *The Gazette*, Montreal, 28 Jan. 1998.

73. Lorna Dueck, "Sorry Isn't Good Enough," *Globe and Mail*, 31 Oct. 2000. See also James Brooke, "Facing Ruin from Lawsuits, Anglicans in Canada Slash Budgets," *New York Times*, 23 Aug. 2000; Rick Mofina, "Churches Have No Easy Exit from Native Lawsuits," *National Post*, 18 Sept. 2000.

74. "Truth and Reconciliation Commission Final Report," TRC Findings Online, http://www.trc.ca/websites/trcinstitution/index.php?p=890.

75. Something of the complexity of the Indigenous scene contemporary to the time period discussed here is caught in Ron F. Laliberte et al., eds, *Expressions in Canadian Native Studies* (Saskatoon,

2000). See also Ovide Mercredi and Mary Ellen Turpel, *In the Rapids: Navigating the Future of First Nations* (Toronto, 1993).

76. "Coon Come Tells Native Leaders to Sober Up," *National Post*, 28 Feb. 2001, A7; "Coon Come's Call," *Ottawa Citizen*, 1 Mar. 2001, A14; "Mr Coon Come Steps into Line of Fire," *Globe and Mail*, 2 Mar. 2001, A12; Rick Mofina, "Chiefs Aren't All Drunkards, Natives Insist," *Ottawa Citizen*, 1 Mar. 2001, A4.

77. AFN website, 28 June 2005: www.afn.ca.

78. "Policy Resolution 61," Liberal Party of Canada, https://www.liberal.ca/policy-resolutions/61-priority-resolution-aboriginal-issues.

79. "Statement by the Prime Minister on National Aboriginal Day," Office of the Prime Minister, http://pm.gc.ca/eng/news/2017/06/21/statement-prime-minister-canada-national-aboriginal-day.

80. "Trudeau Pledges to End Indian Act in Cabinet Shuffle," *Globe and Mail*, https://beta.theglobeandmail.com/news/politics/trudeau-shuffles-cabinet-and-pledges-to-end-indian-act/article36099306/?ref=http://www.theglobeandmail.com&,.

81. Media coverage of the announcements thus far paints a clear picture of the mixed reactions to the Trudeau government announcements. See: P. Bellegarde, "Why the Government's Decision to Split INAC Is a Step in the Right Direction," *Maclean's*, 1 Sept. 2017, http://www.macleans.ca/opinion/why-the-governments-decision-to-split-inac-is-a-step-in-the-right-direction/; J. Bell, "Bye, Bye INAC: Trudeau to Split Department into Two Pieces," *Nunatsiaq Online*, 28 Aug. 2017, http://www.nunatsiaqonline.ca/stories/article/65674bye_bye_inac_trudeau_to_split_department_into_two_pieces/'; M. Nielsen, "Split of INAC Into Two Ministeries Leaves Teegee Hopeful," *Prince George Citizen*, 30 Aug. 2017; V. Coburn, "The Royal Commission on Aboriginal Peoples Recommended Splitting up the Indigenous Affairs Department 20 Years Ago. The Context Today Is Much Different," *Policy Options*, 6 Sept. 2017, http://policyoptions.irpp.org/magazines/september-2017/the-dismantling-of-indigenous-and-northern-affairs-canada/.

Chapter 19

1. Parliament of Canada, 39th Parliament, 2nd Session, 11 June 2008, www.parl.gc.ca/HousePublications/Publication.aspx?DocId=3568890.

2. Heather Scoffield, "Native Patience Runs Thin Four Years after Residential-School Apology," *Globe and Mail*, 11 June 2012, www.theglobeandmail.com/news/politics/native-patience-runs-thin-four-years-after-residential-school-apology/article4248862.

3. "Supreme Court: Accept Oral History as Evidence," *Globe and Mail*, 15 Dec. 1997, A25.

4. Paul Barnsley, "Federal Court of Appeal Dismisses Samson Appeal," *Windspeaker* 24, 11 (2007): 9, www.ammsa.com/publications/windspeaker/federal-court-appeal-dismisses-samson-appeal.

5. Treaty Land Entitlement/Special Claims Unit, Department of Indian and Northern Affairs Canada, Saskatchewan Region, *A Synopsis of the Saskatchewan Treaty Land Entitlement Framework Agreement*, www.yqfn.ca/uploads/pdfs/TLE%20Framework%20Agreement%20-%20Synopsis.pdf.

6. Indigenous and Northern Affairs Canada, "Treaty Land Entitlement," https://www.aadnc-aandc.gc.ca/eng/1100100034822/1100100034823.

7. "Supreme Court: Accept Oral History as Evidence," *Globe and Mail*, 15 Dec. 1997, A25.

8. The discovery of the wrecks of Franklin's ships in 2014 and 2016 using the oral history collected by Louie Kamookak over a 30-year period is a dramatic example of the accuracy of this source. Parks Canada, "The Franklin Expedition," https://www.pc.gc.ca/en/culture/franklin.

9. Biggar, ed., *The Works of Samuel de Champlain*, 2: 283–4.

10. Francis Assikinack, "Social and Warlike Customs of the Odawah Indians," *Canadian Journal of Industry, Science, and Art* 3, 16 (1858): 297–309; Francis Assikinack, "Legends and Traditions of the Odawah Indians," *Canadian Journal of Industry, Science, and Art* 3, 14 (1858), 115–25; Andrew J. Blackbird, *History of the Ottawa and Chippewa Indians of Michigan* (Ypsilanti, Mich., 1887).

11. Blackbird, *History of the Ottawa and Chippewa Indians*, 79–80.

12. *Nisga'a Treaty Negotiations Agreement-in-Principle*, issued jointly by the Government of Canada, the Province of British Columbia, and the Nisga'a Tribal Council, 15 Feb. 1996.

13. Barbara Graymont, "Thayendanegea," *Dictionary of Canadian Biography Online*.

14. Charles M. Johnston, *The Valley of the Six Nations* (Toronto, 1964), 68–9.

15. Ibid., 50–1.

16. Isabel Thompson Kelsay, *Joseph Brant: Man of Two Worlds* (Syracuse, NY, 1984), 555.

17. Johnston, *Valley of the Six Nations*, 128.

18. S.R. Mealing, "John Graves Simcoe," *Dictionary of Canadian Biography Online*.

19. Johnston, *Valley of the Six Nations*, 128.

20. Douglas Leighton and Robert J. Burns, "Samuel Peters Jarvis," *Dictionary of Canadian Biography Online*.

21. The history of this piece of land was faithfully recorded by Canadian historian Charles Johnston in *Valley of the Six Nations*, and his painstaking work helps us to understand the issues now confronting the people of Caledonia and the members of the Six Nations who are protesting the development at Douglas Creek. Understanding is one thing, however, and resolution is another. See Johnston, *Valley of the Six Nations*, passim.

22. "Six Nations Barricades at Caledonia Continue," *Turtle Island News Online*, http://theturtleislandnews.com/index.php/2017/08/10/six-nations-barricades-caledonia-continue-people-want-ontario-talking-haudenosaunee-confederacy.

23. Linda Diebel, "Seeking Truth about Lost Children," *Toronto Star*, 29 May 2008; "Chairman Quits Troubled Residential-School Commission," *CBC News*, 20 Oct. 2008, www.cbc.ca/canada/story/2008/10/20/truth-resignation.html.

24. Truth and Reconciliation Commission of Canada, www.trc.ca/websites/trcinstitution/index.php?p=4.

25. Ibid.

26. Ibid., www.trc.ca/websites/trcinstitution/index.php?p=807.

27. Ibid.

28. Jane O'Hara with Patricia Treble, "Residential Church School Scandal," *Maclean's*, 26 June 2000.

29. Ibid.

30. Jonathon Gatehouse, "Residential Schools Cash Draws Closer," *Maclean's*, 16 Apr. 2007.

31. Miller, *Shingwauk's Vision*, 579–82.

32. Saganash: from Allan Saganash Jr, "My Brother John: Always Searching for Answers," *The Nation*, 12 Sept. 2008, 23–5, 33, www.beesum-communications.com/nation; Cameron: original essay for this volume.

33. Michael Barclay, "Gord Downie: 1964–2017. Remembering the Life and Legacy of the Tragically Hip Frontman," *Macleans.ca*, 18 Oct. 2017, http://www.macleans.ca/gord-downie-obituary/; Ben Rayner, "In Losing Gord Downie, We Lose the Tragically Hip, and So the Tragedy Is Doubled: Rayner," *Toronto Star*, 18 Oct. 2017.

34. "Truth and Reconciliation Commission of Canada: Calls to Action," http://www.trc.ca/websites/trcinstitution/File/2015/Findings/Calls_to_Action_English2.pdf.

35. Indigenous and Northern Affairs Canada, "National inquiry into Indigenous Women and Girls," https://www.aadnc-aandc.gc.ca/eng/1448633299414/1448633350146.

36. Thomas Walkom, "The Confusion behind the Inquiry into Murdered and Missing Indigenous Women," *Toronto* Star, 31 July 2017, https://www.thestar.com/opinion/commentary/2017/07/31/the-confusion-behind-inquiry-into-murdered-and-missing-indigenous-women-walkom.html.

37. "United Nations Declaration on the Rights of Indigenous Peoples," http://www.un.org/esa/socdev/unpfii/documents/DRIPS_en.pdf.

38. Indigenous and Northern Affairs Canada, "United Nations Declaration on the Rights of Indigenous Peoples," https://www.aadnc-aandc.gc.ca/eng/1309374407406/1309374458958#a1.

39. Indigenous and Northern Affairs Canada, "Speech to the United Nations General Assembly, 25 Apr. 2017, by the Honourable Carolyn Bennett," https://www.canada.ca/en/indigenous-northern-affairs/news/2017/05/speaking_notes_forthehonourablecarolynben nettministerofindigenou.html.

40. John Ivison, "First Nations Hear Hard Truth that UN Indigenous Rights Declaration Is 'Unworkable' as Law," *National Post*, 14 July 2016, http://nationalpost.com/opinion/john-ivison-first-nations-hear-hard-truth-that-un-rights-declaration-unworkable-as-law.

41. Richard Cuthbertson, "As New First Nations Chief, Atleo Calls for Unity," *National Post*, 22 July 2009, www.nationalpost.com/news/story.html?id=1819970.

42. Jorge Barrera," Confederacy of Nations Seeking Education 'Accord' with Ottawa: Document," *APTN National News*, 15 May 2014, aptn.ca/news/2014/05/15/confederacy-nations-seeking-negotiated-education-accord-ottawa-document.

43. Indigenous and Northern Affairs Canada, "Bill C-33: First Nations Control of First Nations Education Act," https://www.aadnc-aandc.gc.ca/eng/1358798070439/1358798420982.

44. Stephanie MacLellan, "Idle No More, One Year Later," *Toronto Star*, 13 Dec. 2013, www.thestar.com/news/canada/2013/12/13/idle_no_more_one_year_later.html.

45. Cultural Survival, www.culturalsurvival.org/publications/cultural-survival-quarterly/being-idle-no-more-women-behind-movement.

46. R. Deerchild, "Mandatory Learning," *CBC News*, 11 Sept. 2016, http://www.cbc.ca/radio/unreserved/exploring-the-link-between-education-and-reconciliation-1.3742630/mandatory-learning-indigenous-course-requirement-launched-at-canadian-university-1.3754056.

47. http://www.cbc.ca/player/play/777694275670/

Epilogue

1. Even Diamond Jenness subscribed to the idea of the "vanishing Indian." In his words: "Doubtless all the tribes will disappear. Some will endure only a few years longer, others, like the Eskimo, may last several centuries. Some will merge steadily with the white race, others will bequeath to future generations only an infinitesimal fraction of their blood." In any event, he added, Indigenous Peoples had already contributed everything they had that was culturally valuable to the dominant civilization. Jenness, *Indians of Canada*, 264.

2. Menno Boldt, "Social Correlates of Nationalism: A Study of Native Indian Leaders in a Canadian Internal Colony," *Comparative Political Studies* 14, 2 (1981): 205–31.

3. See the Introduction to this volume for a list of autonyms and the words they have replaced.

4. James Boswell, *The Life of Samuel Johnson* (New York, 1992), 652.

5. Note that Champlain, Sagard, and the Jesuits all used the Wendat word for this nation and as such it was not an autonym.

6. Kinietz, *Indians of the Western Great Lakes, 1615–1760*, 261, 308; R. David Edmunds, *The Potawatomis: Keepers of the Fire* (Norman, Okla., 1978), 3; Trigger, *Children of Aataentsic*, 319; Ives Goddard, "Mascouten," in Trigger, ed., *Handbook of North American Indians, 15: Northeast*, 668.

7. Richard A. Rhodes, *Eastern Ojibwa-Chippewa-Ottawa Dictionary* (Berlin, 1993), 77.

8. Ibid., 542.

9. P.F.X. de Charlevoix, *Journal d'un voyage fait par order du roi dans l'Amérique septentrionnale* (Paris, 1744), 6: 93.

10. Selwyn Dewdney, "Birth of a Cree–Ojibway Style of Contemporary Art," in Getty and Smith, eds, *One Century Later*, 117–25.

11. National Gallery of Canada, "Our Masterpieces, Our Stories" (2017), https://www.gallery.ca/2017.

12. "Agreement-in-Principle Reached to Resolve Sixties Scoop Litigation," https://www.canada.ca/en/indigenous-northern-affairs/news/2017/10/agreement-in-principlereachedtoresolvethe sixtiesscooplitigation.html.

Index